American Language Hub

LEVEL 4
Teacher's Book

CHARLOTTE RANCE

macmillan education

Macmillan Education Limited
4 Crinan Street
London N1 9XW

Companies and representatives throughout the world

American Language Hub Level 4 Teacher's Book ISBN 978-0-230-49737-5
American Language Hub Level 4 Teacher's Book with Teacher's App
ISBN 978-0-230-49738-2

Written by Charlotte Rance

First published 2020

Teacher's Edition credits:
Original design by emc design ltd
Page make-up by SPi Global
Cover design based on original design by Restless
Cover photograph by plainpicture/Westend61/Uwe Umstätter
Picture research by SPi Global.

Author's acknowledgements
Charlotte Rance would like to thank the whole team for their hard work and invaluable support. Also, a special thank you to Stacey Hughes for all her advice and guidance. Finally, to her partner Matt Conway for his constant support.

The authors and publishers would like to thank the following for permission to reproduce their photographs:

Getty Images/Alexander Spatari/Moment W24, Getty Images/Antenna W46, Getty Images/Caiaimage/Chris Ryan W20, Getty Images/Caiaimage/Paul Bradbury W49, Getty Images/Caiaimage/Tom Merton W28, Getty Images/Caiaimage/Sam Edwards W27, Getty Images/Carol Yepes/Moment W7, Getty Images/DigitalVision/Flashpop W1, Getty Images/DigitalVision/Flashpop W31, Getty Images/DigitalVision/Jose Luis Pelaez Inc W12(tr), Getty Images/DigitalVision/Reza Estakhrian W23, Getty Images/DigitalVision/Tom Werner W9, Getty Images/Ezra Bailey/Iconica W5, Getty Images/E+/Georgijevic W8, Getty Images/E+/izusek W17(c), Getty Images/E+/peeterv W32, Getty Images/E+/pidjoe W16, Getty Images/E+/SolStock W26, Getty Images/E+/SolStock W29, Getty Images/France/Westend61 W15, Getty Images/Frontdoor Images/Getty Images Plus/Stone W38, Getty Images/Getty Images Plus/Jeff Hunter/Photographer's Choice W21, Getty Images/Hero Images W40, Getty Images/Jeff Rotman/The Image Bank W11, Getty Images/Moment/R.Tsubin W41, Getty Images/MStudioImages TBXIII(tl), Getty Images/Vietnam/Westend61 W13; **Guardian News & Media Limited** pTBXIII(bl); **Macmillan Education Limited**/Alamy Stock Photo/Anton Lebedev W30, Macmillan Education Limited/Alamy Stock Photo/imageBROKER W3, Macmillan Education Limited/Alamy Stock Photo/Lebrecht Music & Arts W37, Macmillan Education Limited/Alamy Stock Photo/Pat Canova W39, Macmillan Education Limited/Alamy Stock Photo/Victor Paul Borg W45, Macmillan Education Limited/Blend Images- KidStock/Getty Images W35, Macmillan Education Limited/Brian Jackson/Getty Images/iStockphoto Thinkstock Images W47, Macmillan Education Limited/BRAND X PICTURES W44, Macmillan Education Limited/Busakorn Pongparnit, Krunja/Getty Images W12(c), Macmillan Education Limited/Caiaimage/Getty Images/Paul Bradbury W4, Macmillan Education Limited/Caiaimage/Getty Images/Paul Bradbury W34, Macmillan Education Limited/Coberschneider/Getty Images/RooM RF W43, Macmillan Education Limited/Digital Vision/Uwe Krejci W17(tl1), Macmillan Education Limited/Digital Vision/Uwe Krejci W17(bl1), Macmillan Education Limited/Flickr RF/Lijuan Guo Photography W12(cr), Macmillan Education Limited/Geber86/Getty Images W14, Macmillan Education Limited/Getty Images/iStockphoto/Sorayut W12(cl), Macmillan Education Limited/Getty Images/Marin Tomas W19, Macmillan Education Limited/Getty Images/valentinrussanov, ValentinRusanov W17(bl2), Macmillan Education Limited/Getty Images/Westend61 W12(tc), Macmillan Education Limited/Getty Images/Westend61 W49, Macmillan Education Limited/Getty Images/Xavier Arnau W36, Macmillan Education Limited/PHOTODISC W12(tl), Macmillan Education Limited/UWE_UMSTAETTER,Westend61 W17(tl2), Macmillan Education Limited/Westend61 W6, Macmillan Education Limited/www.imagesource.com W48.

Commissioned photograph by **Sharp Focus** TBXIII(br)

The author and publishers are grateful for permission to reprint the following copyright material:

Extracts from: *700 Classroom Activities New Edition* © David Seymour and Maria Popova, 2005 Published by Macmillan Education Limited. Used by Permission. All Rights Reserved;

Extracts from: *Learning Teaching 3rd Edition Student's Book* © Jim Scrivener 2011, Published by Macmillan Education Limited. Used by Permission. All Rights Reserved;

Extracts from: *Sound Foundations: Learning and Teaching Pronunciation 2nd Edition: English Pronunciation* © Adrian Underhill, 2005, Published by Macmillan Education Limited. Used by Permission. All Rights Reserved;

Extracts from: *Beyond the Sentence: Introducing Discourse Analysis* © Scott Thornbury, 2005, Published by Macmillan Education Limited. Used by Permission. All Rights Reserved;

Extracts from: *Teaching English Grammar: What to Teach and How to Teach it* © Jim Scrivener, 2010, Published by Macmillan Education Limited. Used by Permission. All Rights Reserved;

Extracts from: *Teaching Reading Skills in a Foreign Language* © Christine Nuttall, 2009, Published by Macmillan Education Limited. Used by Permission. All Rights Reserved.

Additional sources: Ministry of Justice, Proven reoffending statistics: January to March 2017, gov.uk, TB96; Wilson, R. 2017, Census: More Americans have college degrees than ever before, The Hill, W28

Student's Book credits:

Written by Louis Rogers

Designed by emc design ltd
Picture research by Emily Taylor

Full acknowledgements for illustrations and photographs in the facsimile pages can be found in the Student's Book ISBN 978-0-230-49731-3.

The author and publishers are grateful for permission to reprint the following copyright material: Extract from 'How Wolves Change Rivers – video' by GrrlScientist. Originally published in The Guardian, 03/04/2014. © 2018 Guardian News and Media Limited or its affiliated companies. All rights reserved. Reprinted with permission of The Guardian, pp50–51; Extract from '2 Most Viral Social Media Campaigns of this Decade so far!' by Salman Aslam. © 2009–2019 Omnicore Agency. All rights reserved. Reprinted with permission of Omnicore Agency, pp116–117

Printed and bound in Brazil.

2024
24

Contents

Student's Book Introduction

American Language Hub is a new six-level general English course for adult learners, which takes the complexity out of teaching English. It is designed to promote effective communication and helps to build learners' confidence with regular opportunities for meaningful practice. With its firm pedagogic foundation and syllabus aligned to the revised CEFR, American Language Hub has clear learning outcomes which make it easy to use in a variety of teaching situations.

8 MYSTERY

The true mystery of the world is the visible, not the invisible.
Oscar Wilde

An ancient sequoia forest in Mendocino County, California

OBJECTIVES

- speculate about past events
- summarize a cultural story
- write and perform a short scene
- speculate about the causes and consequences of a crime
- discuss how to test an idea
- write a complex essay

Work with a partner. Discuss the questions.

1 Read the quote. What do you think Wilde means? Do you agree with him? Why/Why not?
2 What crime novels or TV shows do you enjoy watching? Tell your partner about one of them.
3 What crimes are the biggest problem in your society? What do you think can be done to deal with them?

MYSTERY 85

The engaging photograph and famous quotation help teachers to focus students and familiarize themselves with the ideas in the unit. Teachers can also encourage students to label the picture.

Student's Book unit opener
The first page of every American Language Hub unit is the unit opener. It is an exciting visual opportunity for students to engage with the theme of the unit and see at a glance the CEFR learning objectives for each lesson.

There is a quick warm-up speaking activity. Teachers can use this time to prepare the class for their lesson and delay the main start for five minutes until all the students arrive.

Student's Book Lessons 1 and 2 first spread

Reading and Listening

Reading and listening sections allow students to practice their receptive skills. All sections have tasks that move from global to detailed understanding so students can achieve a good overall comprehension. The key skills focus is clearly marked in the activity titles. The texts and scripts also present target vocabulary, grammar or pronunciation.

Skills labels

By focusing students' attention on the skills labels next to each exercise number, teachers can highlight which skills are being practiced and recycled.

Grammar

The American Language Hub approach to grammar is inductive. Students are exposed to new language in context. Each grammar section prompts the student to notice the feature in context and to discover its form and use. Students then have further opportunities for controlled practice before using their new language in more authentic spoken or written output.

8.1 Myths and legends

- Speculate about past events
- Summarize a cultural story

S – decoding: similes and metaphors
V – word families
G – past modals of deduction
P – thought groups

READING

A Do you believe that ghosts, aliens or monsters exist? How certain are you on a scale of 1–5 (1 = I'm sure they don't exist, 5 = I'm sure they do exist)? Write notes.

B SPEAK Work in groups. Compare your answers from Exercise A. Explain your ideas, giving examples where appropriate.

HOW DO YOU EXPLAIN THAT?

There is nothing like an unexplained mystery to capture the public imagination. We seem drawn to violent or supernatural causes, yet the real explanation is usually far less dramatic. Here we explore two unusual incidents with obvious explanations.

THE FLANNAN ISLES LIGHTHOUSE

On December 15,1900, a passing ship noticed that the lighthouse on Flannan Island, off the coast of Scotland, wasn't working. Bad weather made it impossible for a ship to reach the island before December 26th, when the Eilean Mòr docked to deliver supplies to the three men that were living there – Thomas Marshall, James Ducat and Donald MacArthur. Strangely, the lighthouse was like a ghost town, with no one in sight and an uneaten meal on the table. Stranger still, despite the bad weather, one of the men had left his waterproof clothing behind, a chair had been knocked over and all of the clocks had stopped. An extensive search of the island was conducted but none of the men were ever found.

Once the unusual events had been reported, the public immediately began to speculate about what had happened. [1]Many believed that the men must have been murdered. [2]Others suggested they might have been eaten by a sea monster or could even have been carried away by a ghost ship in the night.

Although the speculation continued for years, the most likely explanation is the terrible weather. Since their bodies have never been found, [3]the three men must have been blown into the sea and drowned. [4]Two of them may have been working outside when the other noticed a huge wave approaching. As quick as a flash, he must have rushed outside to warn his friends, leaving his waterproof clothing behind and knocking over the chair. Some of the more unusual clues, such as the untouched meal, are thought to have been made up because they certainly weren't included in the original report.

THE DYATLOV PASS INCIDENT

On February 2, 1959, nine hikers set out to climb Kholat Syakhl ('Mountain of the Dead') in Russia but never returned. Three weeks later, a search party found the group's badly damaged tent abandoned and half covered in snow. Footprints left by people who were either barefoot or wearing little on their feet led rescuers to the edge of a forest where they found five bodies, each with missing or ripped clothing. Although the hikers had sustained few external injuries, their skin had turned a strange shade of orange and investigators found high levels of radiation on their clothing. The other four bodies were found on May 4th, almost 100 meters away. Although better dressed than the first group, they had major injuries, including broken ribs and a fractured skull. Rescuers must have turned white as a sheet when they discovered that one of the female hikers was missing her tongue.

Theories of what had happened soon began to circulate. [5]Some thought the group might have been murdered by the indigenous Mansi people. Others suggested they had been attacked by wild animals or even a yeti. [6]However, the hikers can't have been murdered or attacked by animals because there were no signs of a fight. It is far more likely that the destruction of the tent and the second group's physical injuries were caused by an avalanche, while the missing tongue was probably eaten by a wild animal. The first group's lack of clothing can be explained by something called 'paradoxical undressing' – a phenomenon in which people in the final stages of hypothermia start to feel incredibly hot and take off their clothes in an attempt to cool down. Their orange skin and the radiation levels on their clothing are thought to have been caused by overexposure to the sun.

Glossary

avalanche (n) a large amount of snow and ice that suddenly falls down a mountain

86 MYSTERY

C SCAN Scan *How do you explain that?* What explanations were originally given for each mystery?

D READ FOR DETAIL Read the stories again and answer the questions.

1 What had been left in the lighthouse?
2 What does the writer say happened to the men?
3 What does the writer think caused the chair to fall over?
4 Where were the two groups of bodies found?
5 What physical injuries had the hikers sustained?
6 What explanation is given for the missing tongue?

E DECODE: SIMILES AND METAPHORS Read the stories again. Answer the questions by identifying similes and metaphors in the text. Use the information in the box to help you.

Decoding: similes and metaphors

In articles describing dramatic events, writers frequently use descriptive language to make the story more engaging. Two common techniques used are:

a **Similes** – comparing one thing to another using *as* or *like*. *He may look small, but he's* ***as brave as a lion.***

b **Metaphors** – describing something as if it were something else. *The snow* ***was a white blanket.*** *(= It wasn't actually a blanket; it just looked like one.)*

1 What was the lighthouse like when the ship arrived?
a like a small town b empty
2 How does the writer think the third man left the kitchen?
a slowly b quickly
3 How does the writer think the rescuers felt when they discovered the female hiker?
a frightened b angry

F SPEAK Work in groups. Why do you think people look for unusual explanations to mysteries, when there are frequently more obvious solutions?

8.1

GRAMMAR

Past modals of deduction

A Work in pairs. Look at the highlighted sentences in the article. Which sentence(s) mean …

1 it's almost certain that something happened or is true.
2 it's possible that something happened or is true.
3 it's impossible that something happened or is true.

B WORK IT OUT Complete the structures in the box.

Past modals of deduction

We use modals of deduction to make guesses about what happened in the past.

a We use ______ + *have* + past participle to say we're sure something happened because there's strong evidence.
b We use ______ / ______ / ______ + *have* + past participle to say we think something is possible, but we aren't sure.
c We use ______ + *have* + past participle to say we're sure something didn't happen because there's strong evidence.

C Work in pairs. Go to the Grammar Hub on page 136.

D SPEAK Work in pairs. Read the situations (1–3) and discuss what you think happened using past modals of deduction.

1 Hundreds of children got sick at a school in New York. Children who brought in their own lunch were unaffected.
2 Tasmin took the train to work as normal and went to buy coffee from a café nearby. However, when she went to pay, she discovered her wallet was missing.
3 A math teacher was amazed when one of his students finished their exam in 20 minutes. The exam has 100 questions and usually takes an hour and a half.

SPEAKING

A DISCUSS Work in groups. Read *The Hopkinsville goblin case* and discuss what you think happened.

The Hopkinsville Goblin Case

In 1955, the Sutton family and their friend Billy Ray Taylor were relaxing on their porch. Suddenly, Billy Ray saw lights in the sky and shouted for everyone to come and take a look. They saw what they thought was an alien with glowing eyes, a large head, pointed ears and claws. The family and their friend grabbed their guns and started shooting. They heard their bullets hitting something metal, which they thought must have been the alien's spaceship.

B Go to the Communication Hub on page 151 and compare your ideas from Exercise A with the likely solution.

MYSTERY 87

Topics

American Language Hub topics contextualize the language input for the lesson. They have been selected to allow opportunities for personalization.

Speaking

Each lesson starts with a CEFR unit objective which the lesson is designed to address. Students will often use the grammar, vocabulary and pronunciation from the lesson to complete a speaking activity linked to the unit objective. American Language Hub allows students to safely practice speaking in pairs after most sections. This ensures that they feel confident to take an active role in the final speaking task.

Student's Book Lessons 1 and 2 second spread

Reading and Listening Skill

Every unit includes a task designed to practice a key reading or listening skill. This ensures students are given the tools they need to effectively process a wide variety of texts and scripts. By the end of each book, students will have been exposed to 12 different key skills for reading or listening.

Pronunciation

In American Language Hub, lessons focus on both word-level and sentence-level pronunciation. This not only allows students to improve their accuracy but also their fluency through sentence-level intonation, which helps students understand how to add meaning through pronunciation.

8.1

LISTENING

A SPEAK Work in pairs. Look at the illustrations of three famous myths from around the world. What do you think happens in each story? Where do you think these stories are from?

8.1 **B LISTEN FOR GIST** Listen to an interview with an expert on myths and legends. Check your ideas from Exercise A.

8.1 **C LISTEN FOR DETAIL** Listen again. Choose the correct options (a, b or c) to complete the sentences.

1 According to Phillip Norris, myths and legends …
   a usually have the same origin.
   b are similar in neighboring countries.
   c have similar themes across cultures.
2 The tales of Sinbad the Sailor are given as an example of …
   a a hero myth.
   b a monster myth.
   c an urban legend.
3 Sinbad and his crew go to the castle on the island …
   a to look for food.
   b to escape from their attackers.
   c to shelter from the storm.
4 Anyone who looks directly at Medusa …
   a is bitten by the snakes in her hair.
   b is turned to stone.
   c is killed by Perseus.
5 The Yeti and Bigfoot are given as examples of …
   a stories inspired by wild animals.
   b ancient legends.
   c modern monster myths.
6 To call Hanako-San, you have to …
   a knock on the bathroom mirror three times.
   b say her name three times.
   c knock on the bathroom door three times and say her name.
7 According to Phillip Norris, myths like Hanako-San are …
   a unique to Japan.
   b surprisingly different across cultures.
   c popular with young children.

D SPEAK Work in groups. Why do you think myths and legends are still told today? Why do you think new ones are still created? Explain your reasoning.

VOCABULARY

Word families

A Complete the word families in the table. Use the information in the box to help you.

Word families

A word family is a group of words with the same root. Learning the associated words (e.g. the verb, noun, adjective and adverb) can help you to understand texts more easily and improve your accuracy when writing.

Verb	Noun	Adjective	Adverb
–	1	mythical	–
2	belief	3	believably
–	4	heroic	heroically
5	representation	representative	representatively
–	6	traditional	7
transform	8	transformational	–

B Complete the sentences with the correct form of the words in parentheses.

1 The minotaur is a ____________ (*myth*) creature with the head of a bull and the body of a man.
2 The main character usually ____________ (*hero*) saves a princess or someone else in distress.
3 Snakes are frequently used to ____________ (*represent*) danger.
4 ____________ (*tradition*), stories were told and not written down so there are frequently variations of a legend.
5 Many stories frequently include the ____________ (*transform*) of a person into some kind of monster.

PRONUNCIATION

Thought groups

8.2 **A** Listen to the first part of a story from the interview. Mark any pauses with (/). Why do you think the speaker pauses at these points?

As in many of the stories, Sinbad's ship is caught in a terrible storm and driven off course. They sail toward a small island but are attacked by a tribe of monkeys carrying spears. Fearing for their lives, Sinbad and his crew swim to the island and rush to a castle they see at the top of a hill.

8.3 **B** Read the next part of the story. Mark where you think the speaker will pause with (/). Then listen and check.

Tired and hungry from their escape, the crew falls asleep on the floor of the castle but is awoken to find the ground shaking. In the doorway to their room stands a giant over 20 meters tall. His eyes burn like fire, his teeth are long and sharp, and his huge mouth has the lips of a camel. Sinbad and his crew try to run away but one of them is caught and eaten by the giant.

C SPEAK Work in pairs. Practice telling the story from Exercise B. Remember to use pauses to make the story easier to follow.

8.1

SPEAKING HUB

A PREPARE Work in pairs. Look at the pictures and use the words in the box to discuss what you think each myth might be about.

Greeks hidden horse war

fake lake monster Scotland

accident coat forest hitchhiker

B PLAN Work in groups of three. Student A – Go to the Communication Hub on page 147. Student B – Go to the Communication Hub on page 149. Student C – Go to the Communication Hub on page 152.

C PRESENT Summarize the myth you have just read about to your group. Use your notes to help you.

D DISCUSS Work in pairs. Think about myths and legends in your own country. Tell your partner:

- who the myth was about
- what the origins of the myth were
- what happened in the myth

Specul[illegible] about past events
Summar[illegible] a cultural story

Vocabulary

American Language Hub teaches vocabulary in topic-related sets to help students categorize the new words they learn. Key vocabulary sets are built on and reviewed in the back of the book.

Speaking Hub

At the end of each lesson, students perform a longer speaking turn which is staged to allow planning and ideas creation. Students should apply their learning from the whole unit in the performance of their long speaking turn.

Student's Book Lesson 3

Topic Video
The first video in the lesson is a real-life news report or documentary clip. This video provides the context and input for the topic of the lesson. All the videos focus on current, real-world issues.

Café Hub
The second video is an episode from Café Hub, an amusing 'situation comedy' series. Meet Sam, Malcolm, Amanda, Harry and Emily as they discuss and face issues related to the topic in the first video.

Café Hub

10.3 Watch on demand

A – from … to   S – circumlocution

103

The rise of streaming

COMPREHENSION

A Work in groups. Discuss the questions.

1. Do you prefer streaming movies on platforms like Netflix and Amazon Prime or going to the movie theater?
2. Overall, do you think streaming services have had a positive or negative effect on the movie industry?
3. How do you think movie theaters could adapt to survive the rise of 'on demand' content?

Glossary

influx (n) the arrival of a large amount of people or things at the same time
metric (n) a system or standard for measuring things

B Watch a news report about the rise of video streaming services. Choose the best summary (1 or 2).

1. Streaming services like Netflix have provided a platform for films that might not otherwise have been made.
2. Streaming services like Netflix are now forcing people in the film and TV industry to rethink their approach.

C Watch the report again and answer the questions.

1. According to the presenter, what is usually essential to the success of large film franchises?
2. According to the first interviewee, what won't audiences be able to stream online?
3. Which two examples does the presenter give of cinemas diversifying their business?
4. According to the independent producer, why are many people leaving the film industry to work in TV?

D Work in pairs. Read the extract from the report. What do you think might explain lower ticket sales but higher overall attendance?

Box office sales are no longer the sole metric of success. In fact, so far this year, box office receipts are down, whilst cinema admissions are up.

Glossary

cinema **(n) (British)** = movie theater **(n) (American)**
mum **(n) (British)** = mom **(n) (American)**

AUTHENTIC ENGLISH

A Work in pairs. Read the extract from the report. Why do you think the speaker uses *from … to*? What does this emphasize?

As a result of this revolution, cinemas are changing. They're diversifying to become hubs for community events, **from** live conversation **to** meeting places for new mums.

B Read the information in the box and check your answer to Exercise A.

from … to

In natural spoken English, *from … to* is generally used when talking about the highest and lowest points in a range:

Subscription packages cost anywhere **from** *$22* **to** *$65 a month.*

However, it can also be used to make arguments sound more persuasive by giving two very different examples that show how big the range of something is.

These days, we can stream everything **from** *the latest blockbuster movies* **to** *children's cartoons.*

Although this structure usually follows the main claim or argument, it can also be used to introduce it:

From *the atmosphere* **to** *the size of the screen, a movie theater offers a great deal that streaming services simply cannot match.*

C Work in pairs. Take turns completing the sentence prompts with *from … to* and your own ideas.

1. My hometown has a lot to offer, …
2. …, there are many clear benefits of social media.
3. There are a lot of people who could play me in a movie, …
4. There's a lot we can do to tackle climate change, …
5. …, there are a lot of advantages to being self-employed.
6. There are multiple reasons to go vegetarian, …

My hometown has a lot to offer, from world-class theater to excellent burgers and fries.

118 MEDIA

Some big news

SAM   MALCOLM   AMANDA   HARRY   EMILY

A Work in pairs. To what extent would the following factors affect your decision to take a new job?

- length of the commute
- salary
- working hours
- vacation time, benefits and perks

B Watch the video and answer the questions.

1. What are the advantages of Amanda's new job?
2. Why do you think she is reluctant to take it?

SPEAKING SKILL

A Match the extracts (1–3) to their meanings (a–c).

1. Well, that's certainly not near here.
2. And I know that I certainly wouldn't be disappointed if you decided not to go.
3. I guess I just need to be given a good reason to stay by someone, really.

a. I don't want you to go.
b. Give me a reason to stay.
c. It's really far away.

B Work in pairs. Are Harry and Amanda being vague or direct? Why?

C Read the information in the box and check your answers to Exercise A.

Circumlocution

Using more words than is necessary when fewer would do is called circumlocution. This is something we do to be vague or evasive, usually because we are embarrassed, uncomfortable or simply want to avoid saying something. Circumlocution is typically signaled by phrases such as: *I guess what I'm trying to say is …, I just kind of want you to know that …, I suppose what I mean is …*

C Work in pairs. Take turns breaking the bad news below to each other using circumlocution.

- All the money has been stolen out of their bank account.
- You have spilled coffee on their brand-new white carpet.
- You had said that they could have the day off tomorrow, but now you need them to come in to work.
- You have forgotten to send the important letter that they asked you to mail.
- They are going on vacation tomorrow, but the airline they are flying with has gone out of business.

SPEAKING HUB

A PREPARE Work in pairs. Brainstorm the advantages and disadvantages of video streaming services.

B PLAN Work in two groups. You are going to debate the following:

Video streaming services have had a negative impact on the movie and television industry.

Group A – You agree with the idea above.
Group B – You disagree with the idea above.

Plan your arguments. Think about how to support your position, as well as what the other group might say.

C SPEAK Hold your debate.

Give your opinion on streaming services

➤ Turn to page 163 to learn how to write a persuasive essay.

MEDIA 119

Variety of English
The glossary boxes on these pages point out differences between American English and British English.

Authentic English
The first video also provides an opportunity to learn a variety of phrases that students can use to bring authenticity to their language output.

Speaking Skill
The second video provides a model for a speaking skill. Each skill helps students develop fluency and manage discussions successfully.

Student's Book Hubs

Writing Hub

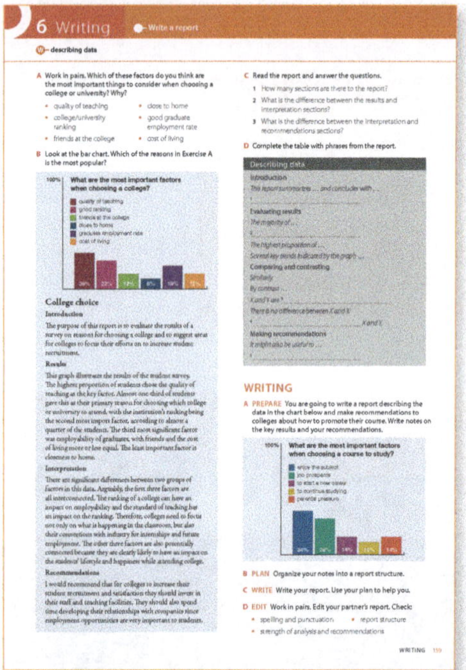

The Student's Book has an individual writing page at the back of the book for each unit. Each writing lesson is aligned to the unit topic and teaches a different writing genre and writing skill. Students can see completed writing models to analyze before they begin to write their own work.

Grammar Hub

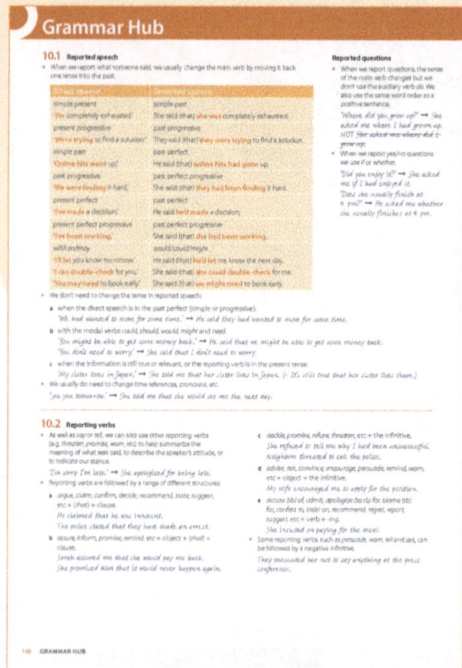

Clear explanations and further practice activities for each grammar point in the syllabus are provided at the back of the book. These can be used in class or set for homework to free up classroom time for communication.

Vocabulary Hub

The Vocabulary Hub provides extra practice of key vocabulary presented in each unit. As with the Grammar Hub sections, these can either consolidate work done in class or be used for further self-study.

Communication Hub

The Communication Hub is used to set up longer communicative activities, such as information exchanges, quizzes and role plays.

Workbook

A Workbook is sold separately for American Language Hub. This includes 360 print activities practicing the language from the Student's Book. For each lesson there are corresponding practice exercises of grammar, vocabulary and pronunciation. There is further practice of the reading and listening skills from Lessons 1 and 2. There is also a page dedicated to the unit's writing genre and skill. All of these pages develop learning from the main lessons of the Student's Book.

Vocabulary and Grammar

The Workbook practices vocabulary and grammar that students have attended to in the Student's Book. By reminding themselves of the words and skills they have recently seen, students are better able to imbed learning and have it ready for recall during speaking practice.

Listening and Reading

The Workbook provides additional listening and reading texts that explore the topics in the Student's Book. These give students the opportunity to develop the key receptive skills from the unit.

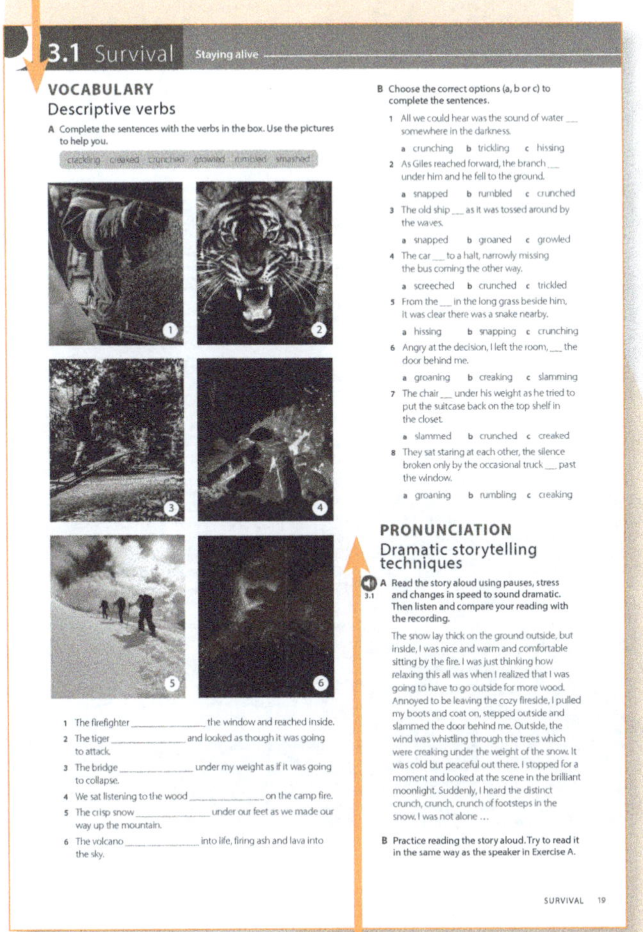

3.1 Survival Staying alive

VOCABULARY

Descriptive verbs

A Complete the sentences with the verbs in the box. Use the pictures to help you.

crackling creaked crunched growled rumbled smashed

1 The firefighter ________ the window and reached inside.
2 The tiger ________ and looked as though it was going to attack.
3 The bridge ________ under my weight as if it was going to collapse.
4 We sat listening to the wood ________ on the camp fire.
5 The crisp snow ________ under our feet as we made our way up the mountain.
6 The volcano ________ into life, firing ash and lava into the sky.

B Choose the correct options (a, b or c) to complete the sentences.

1 All we could hear was the sound of water ___ somewhere in the darkness.
a crunching b trickling c hissing
2 As Giles reached forward, the branch ___ under him and he fell to the ground.
a snapped b rumbled c crunched
3 The old ship ___ as it was tossed around by the waves.
a snapped b groaned c growled
4 The car ___ to a halt, narrowly missing the bus coming the other way.
a screeched b crunched c trickled
5 From the ___ in the long grass beside him, it was clear there was a snake nearby.
a hissing b snapping c crunching
6 Angry at the decision, I left the room, ___ the door behind me.
a groaning b creaking c slamming
7 The chair ___ under his weight as he tried to put the suitcase back on the top shelf in the closet.
a slammed b crunched c creaked
8 They sat staring at each other, the silence broken only by the occasional truck ___ past the window.
a groaning b rumbling c creaking

PRONUNCIATION

Dramatic storytelling techniques

3.1 A Read the story aloud using pauses, stress and changes in speed to sound dramatic. Then listen and compare your reading with the recording.

The snow lay thick on the ground outside, but inside, I was nice and warm and comfortable sitting by the fire. I was just thinking how relaxing this all was when I realized that I was going to have to go outside for more wood. Annoyed to be leaving the cozy fireside, I pulled my boots and coat on, stepped outside and slammed the door behind me. Outside, the wind was whistling through the trees which were creaking under the weight of the snow. It was cold but peaceful out there. I stopped for a moment and looked at the scene in the brilliant moonlight. Suddenly, I heard the distinct crunch, crunch, crunch of footsteps in the snow. I was not alone …

B Practice reading the story aloud. Try to read it in the same way as the speaker in Exercise A.

SURVIVAL 19

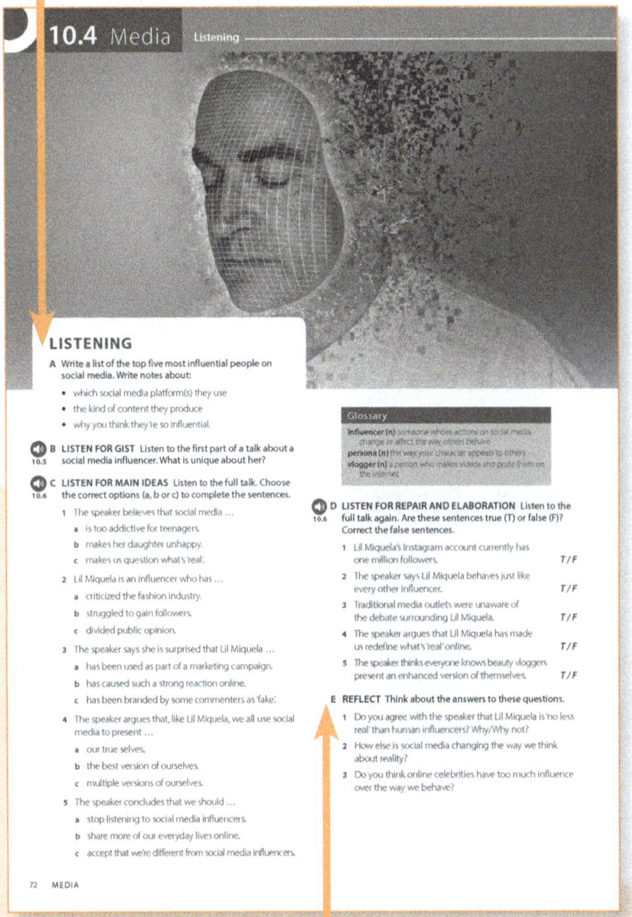

10.4 Media Listening

LISTENING

A Write a list of the top five most influential people on social media. Write notes about:

- which social media platform(s) they use
- the kind of content they produce
- why you think they're so influential.

10.5 B LISTEN FOR GIST Listen to the first part of a talk about a social media influencer. What is unique about her?

10.6 C LISTEN FOR MAIN IDEAS Listen to the full talk. Choose the correct options (a, b or c) to complete the sentences.

1 The speaker believes that social media …
a is too addictive for teenagers.
b makes her daughter unhappy.
c makes us question what's 'real'.
2 Lil Miquela is an influencer who has …
a criticized the fashion industry.
b struggled to gain followers.
c divided public opinion.
3 The speaker says she is surprised that Lil Miquela …
a has been used as part of a marketing campaign.
b has caused such a strong reaction online.
c has been branded by some commenters as 'fake'.
4 The speaker argues that, like Lil Miquela, we all use social media to present …
a our true selves.
b the best version of ourselves.
c multiple versions of ourselves.
5 The speaker concludes that we should …
a stop listening to social media influencers.
b share more of our everyday lives online.
c accept that we're different from social media influencers.

Glossary

influencer (n) someone whose actions on social media change or affect the way others behave
persona (n) the way your character appears to others
vlogger (n) a person who makes videos and posts them on the internet

10.6 D LISTEN FOR REPAIR AND ELABORATION Listen to the full talk again. Are these sentences true (T) or false (F)? Correct the false sentences.

1 Lil Miquela's Instagram account currently has one million followers. T / F
2 The speaker says Lil Miquela behaves just like every other influencer. T / F
3 Traditional media outlets were unaware of the debate surrounding Lil Miquela. T / F
4 The speaker argues that Lil Miquela has made us redefine what's 'real' online. T / F
5 The speaker thinks everyone knows beauty vloggers present an enhanced version of themselves. T / F

E REFLECT Think about the answers to these questions.

1 Do you agree with the speaker that Lil Miquela is 'no less real' than human influencers? Why/Why not?
2 How else is social media changing the way we think about reality?
3 Do you think online celebrities have too much influence over the way we behave?

72 MEDIA

Pronunciation

The Workbook also consolidates the pronunciation topics from the Student's Book through further controlled practice.

Reflect

Each reading and listening page has a Reflect section so that students can use their Workbooks in class if they wish to reflect on their learning with their peers.

American Language Hub for Teachers

Teacher's Book

Procedural notes
The lessons include procedural notes for teachers. These offer support to teachers on how to deliver the lesson rather than telling them how to teach. The notes are designed to be brief and easy to read.

Worksheets
The bank of communicative worksheets at the back of the Teacher's Book provides additional controlled and freer practice of every vocabulary and grammar section.

Interleaved pages
Every level of American Language Hub has a Teacher's Book interleaved with pages of the Student's Book. The answers to all of the Student's Book activities are annotated on the page so there is no need for teachers to flip back and forth to find information.

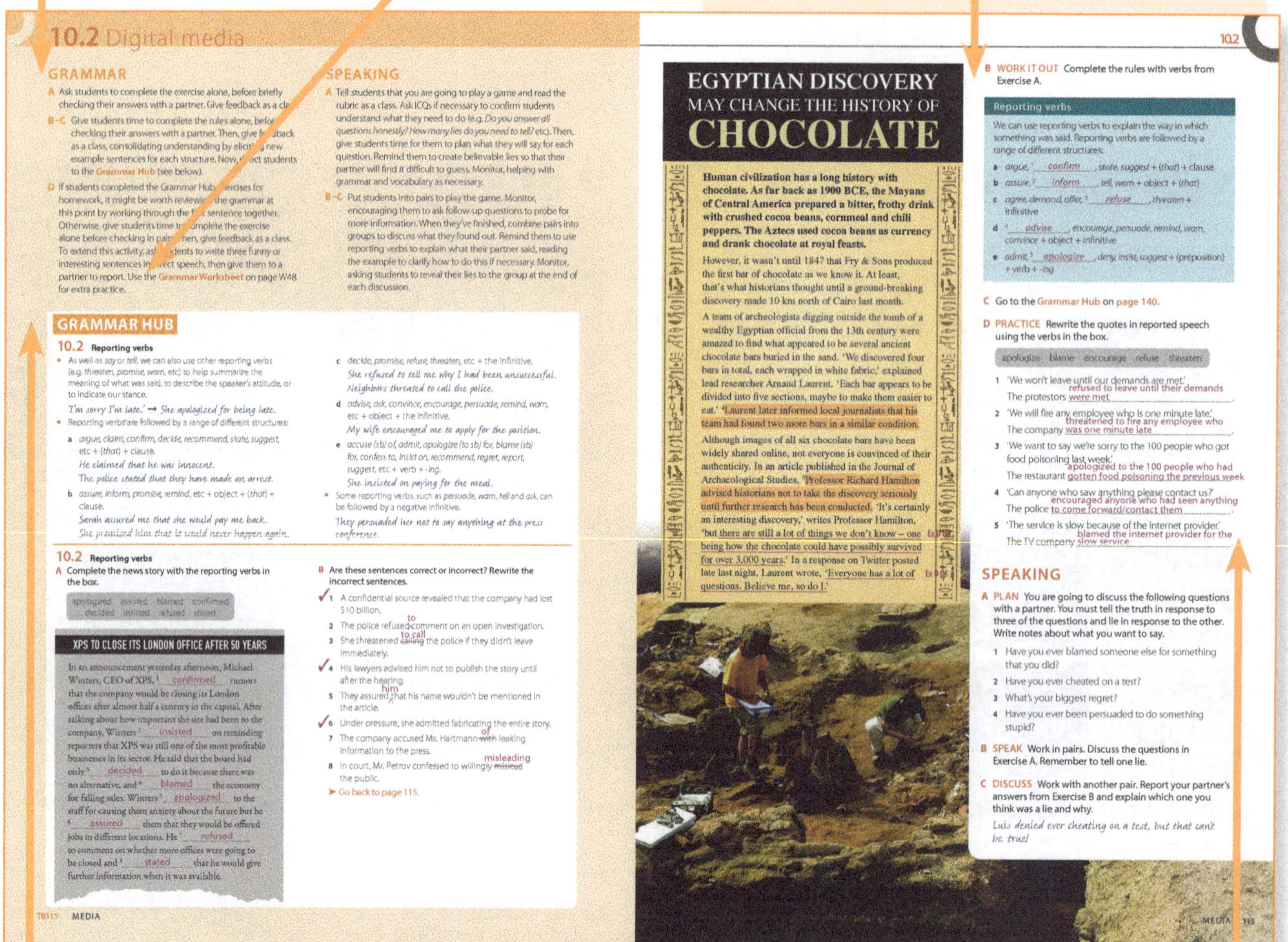

Grammar explanations
Where the Student's Book asks the students to look at the Grammar Hub, the teacher can find this already annotated on the Teacher's Book page. For ease of use, the Grammar Hub reference activities at the end of the Student's Book have been added to the Teacher's Book pages at the location they will be used in the course. This makes it easier for teachers to mark homework in class or refer to succinct grammar explanations.

Annotated answers
The answers are annotated on the interleaved pages of the Student's Book. These provide a quick reference tool for teachers.

Teacher's Book: Macmillan Books for Teachers

Lead-in

Suggested lead-ins can be used to activate prior knowledge, generate interest in the lesson topic or focus on useful lexis.

Extra activities

Extra activity boxes help teachers extend the content of the lesson, both in and out of the classroom.

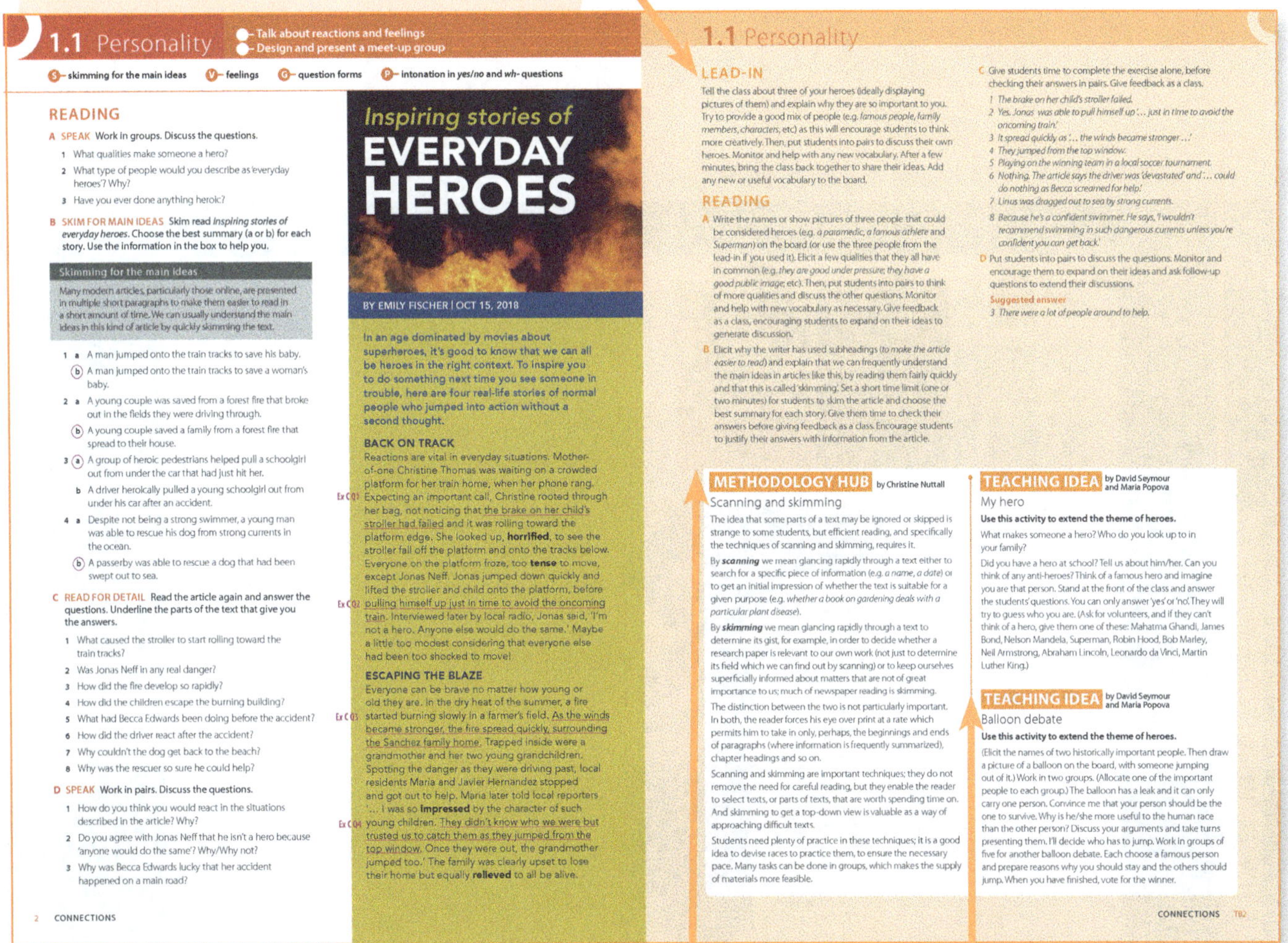

1.1 Personality

- Talk about reactions and feelings
- Design and present a meet-up group

S – skimming for the main ideas V – feelings G – question forms P – intonation in *yes/no* and *wh*- questions

READING

A SPEAK **Work in groups. Discuss the questions.**

1. What qualities make someone a hero?
2. What type of people would you describe as 'everyday heroes'? Why?
3. Have you ever done anything heroic?

B SKIM FOR MAIN IDEAS **Skim read *Inspiring stories of everyday heroes*. Choose the best summary (a or b) for each story. Use the information in the box to help you.**

Skimming for the main ideas

Many modern articles, particularly those online, are presented in multiple short paragraphs to make them easier to read in a short amount of time. We can usually understand the main ideas in this kind of article by quickly skimming the text.

1. a A man jumped onto the train tracks to save his baby.
   (b) A man jumped onto the train tracks to save a woman's baby.
2. a A young couple was saved from a forest fire that broke out in the fields they were driving through.
   (b) A young couple saved a family from a forest fire that spread to their house.
3. (a) A group of heroic pedestrians helped pull a schoolgirl out from under the car that had just hit her.
   b A driver heroically pulled a young schoolgirl out from under his car after an accident.
4. a Despite not being a strong swimmer, a young man was able to rescue his dog from strong currents in the ocean.
   (b) A passerby was able to rescue a dog that had been swept out to sea.

C READ FOR DETAIL **Read the article again and answer the questions. Underline the parts of the text that give you the answers.**

1. What caused the stroller to start rolling toward the train tracks?
2. Was Jonas Neff in any real danger?
3. How did the fire develop so rapidly?
4. How did the children escape the burning building?
5. What had Becca Edwards been doing before the accident?
6. How did the driver react after the accident?
7. Why couldn't the dog get back to the beach?
8. Why was the rescuer so sure he could help?

D SPEAK **Work in pairs. Discuss the questions.**

1. How do you think you would react in the situations described in the article? Why?
2. Do you agree with Jonas Neff that he isn't a hero because 'anyone would do the same'? Why/Why not?
3. Why was Becca Edwards lucky that her accident happened on a main road?

2 CONNECTIONS

Inspiring stories of
EVERYDAY HEROES

BY EMILY FISCHER | OCT 15, 2018

In an age dominated by movies about superheroes, it's good to know that we can all be heroes in the right context. To inspire you to do something next time you see someone in trouble, here are four real-life stories of normal people who jumped into action without a second thought.

BACK ON TRACK

Reactions are vital in everyday situations. Mother-of-one Christine Thomas was waiting on a crowded platform for her train home, when her phone rang. Ex C Q1 Expecting an important call, Christine rooted through her bag, not noticing that the brake on her child's stroller had failed and it was rolling toward the platform edge. She looked up, **horrified**, to see the stroller fall off the platform and onto the tracks below. Everyone on the platform froze, too **tense** to move, except Jonas Neff. Jonas jumped down quickly and lifted the stroller and child onto the platform, before Ex C Q2 pulling himself up just in time to avoid the oncoming train. Interviewed later by local radio, Jonas said, 'I'm not a hero. Anyone else would do the same.' Maybe a little too modest considering that everyone else had been too shocked to move!

ESCAPING THE BLAZE

Everyone can be brave no matter how young or old they are. In the dry heat of the summer, a fire Ex C Q3 started burning slowly in a farmer's field. As the winds became stronger, the fire spread quickly, surrounding the Sanchez family home. Trapped inside were a grandmother and her two young grandchildren. Spotting the danger as they were driving past, local residents Maria and Javier Hernandez stopped and got out to help. Maria later told local reporters '... I was so **impressed** by the character of such Ex C Q4 young children. They didn't know who we were but trusted us to catch them as they jumped from the top window. Once they were out, the grandmother jumped too.' The family was clearly upset to lose their home but equally **relieved** to all be alive.

1.1 Personality

LEAD-IN

Tell the class about three of your heroes (ideally displaying pictures of them) and explain why they are so important to you. Try to provide a good mix of people (e.g. *famous people, family members, characters*, etc) as this will encourage students to think more creatively. Then, put students into pairs to discuss their own heroes. Monitor and help with any new vocabulary. After a few minutes, bring the class back together to share their ideas. Add any new or useful vocabulary to the board.

READING

A Write the names or show pictures of three people that could be considered heroes (e.g. *a paramedic, a famous athlete* and *Superman*) on the board (or use the three people from the lead-in if you used it). Elicit a few qualities that they all have in common (e.g. *they are good under pressure; they have a good public image*; etc). Then, put students into pairs to think of more qualities and discuss the other questions. Monitor and help with new vocabulary as necessary. Give feedback as a class, encouraging students to expand on their ideas to generate discussion.

B Elicit why the writer has used subheadings (*to make the article easier to read*) and explain that we can frequently understand the main ideas in articles like this, by reading them fairly quickly and that this is called 'skimming'. Set a short time limit (one or two minutes) for students to skim the article and choose the best summary for each story. Give them time to check their answers before giving feedback as a class. Encourage students to justify their answers with information from the article.

C Give students time to complete the exercise alone, before checking their answers in pairs. Give feedback as a class.

1. *The brake on her child's stroller failed.*
2. *Yes. Jonas 'was able to pull himself up '... just in time to avoid the oncoming train.'*
3. *It spread quickly as '... the winds became stronger ...'*
4. *They jumped from the top window.*
5. *Playing on the winning team in a local soccer tournament.*
6. *Nothing. The article says the driver was 'devastated' and '... could do nothing as Becca screamed for help.'*
7. *Linus was dragged out to sea by strong currents.*
8. *Because he's a confident swimmer. He says, 'I wouldn't recommend swimming in such dangerous currents unless you're confident you can get back.'*

D Put students into pairs to discuss the questions. Monitor and encourage them to expand on their ideas and ask follow-up questions to extend their discussions.

Suggested answer

3 *There were a lot of people around to help.*

METHODOLOGY HUB by Christine Nuttall

Scanning and skimming

The idea that some parts of a text may be ignored or skipped is strange to some students, but efficient reading, and specifically the techniques of scanning and skimming, requires it.

By ***scanning*** we mean glancing rapidly through a text either to search for a specific piece of information (e.g. *a name, a date*) or to get an initial impression of whether the text is suitable for a given purpose (e.g. *whether a book on gardening deals with a particular plant disease*).

By ***skimming*** we mean glancing rapidly through a text to determine its gist, for example, in order to decide whether a research paper is relevant to our own work (not just to determine its field which we can find out by scanning) or to keep ourselves superficially informed about matters that are not of great importance to us; much of newspaper reading is skimming.

The distinction between the two is not particularly important. In both, the reader forces his eye over print at a rate which permits him to take in only, perhaps, the beginnings and ends of paragraphs (where information is frequently summarized), chapter headings and so on.

Scanning and skimming are important techniques; they do not remove the need for careful reading, but they enable the reader to select texts, or parts of texts, that are worth spending time on. And skimming to get a top-down view is valuable as a way of approaching difficult texts.

Students need plenty of practice in these techniques; it is a good idea to devise races to practice them, to ensure the necessary pace. Many tasks can be done in groups, which makes the supply of materials more feasible.

TEACHING IDEA by David Seymour and Maria Popova

My hero

Use this activity to extend the theme of heroes.

What makes someone a hero? Who do you look up to in your family?

Did you have a hero at school? Tell us about him/her. Can you think of any anti-heroes? Think of a famous hero and imagine you are that person. Stand at the front of the class and answer the students' questions. You can only answer 'yes' or 'no'. They will try to guess who you are. (Ask for volunteers, and if they can't think of a hero, give them one of these: Mahatma Ghandi, James Bond, Nelson Mandela, Superman, Robin Hood, Bob Marley, Neil Armstrong, Abraham Lincoln, Leonardo da Vinci, Martin Luther King.)

TEACHING IDEA by David Seymour and Maria Popova

Balloon debate

Use this activity to extend the theme of heroes.

(Elicit the names of two historically important people. Then draw a picture of a balloon on the board, with someone jumping out of it.) Work in two groups. (Allocate one of the important people to each group.) The balloon has a leak and it can only carry one person. Convince me that your person should be the one to survive. Why is he/she more useful to the human race than the other person? Discuss your arguments and take turns presenting them. I'll decide who has to jump. Work in groups of five for another balloon debate. Each choose a famous person and prepare reasons why you should stay and the others should jump. When you have finished, vote for the winner.

CONNECTIONS TB2

Methodology Hub

Ideas for professional development from Jim Scrivener's *Learning Teaching Third Edition*, Adrian Underhill's *Sound Foundations*, Christine Nuttall's *Teaching Reading Skills in a Foreign Language*, Scott Thornbury's *Beyond the Sentence* and *The New A–Z of ELT* are presented in every unit to help new teachers pick up helpful tips to add to their repertoire or just reflect on a new way to use American Language Hub with their class.

Teaching Idea

Tips and ideas from the *Macmillan Books for Teachers* series are included in the teacher's notes to give some new ideas for instant communicative activities in the lesson. These can usually be used without paper preparation as warm-ups to get the class moving or as a flexible stage where there is time to fill.

Teacher's App

The American Language Hub Teacher's Book comes with a Teacher's App, which gives access to the Resource Center, Test Generator and Classroom Presentation Kit.

The Classroom Presentation Kit is designed to be displayed on an interactive whiteboard (IWB) or using a projector, and it enables teachers to play video and audio or show interactive activities in class. It is not only user-friendly for the teacher but also for the student, with activities being clearly visible for the whole class. Answer-by-answer reveal enables teachers to elicit student responses and check answers one by one.

Tools

Embedded tools make it possible to highlight and annotate texts to prompt noticing or self-correction. Teachers have the option to turn on an audio script, which is timed to sync with the conversation, when listening to audio.

Teachers can zoom into each activity with one click. Then, they can either move smoothly through the activities or zoom out to see the whole page. They can also create a whiteboard area for additional notes.

Video

Teachers can also access the video and audio for the course, including the authentic video from *The Guardian*.

Homework

The app allows teachers to assign homework directly to their students' devices and alert them when they have activities to complete.

Preparation and Practice

Teachers can also configure student preparation and practice using the Teacher's App. Using the practice activities available, teachers can select and publish content to their students which they will receive through a push notification when they access their app. This enables teachers to personalize the amount and type of practice students do every week and to track their progress. Students can practice the grammar or vocabulary for the week before they go to class, allowing more time in the class for communication.

Test Generator

The Teacher's App also gives access to the Test Generator. In the Test Generator, teachers can create tests or use the pre-built tests for each level of the course and print these to assign to students. There are unit tests, mid- and end-of-course tests for each level, testing vocabulary, grammar and the four skills.

Student's App

Each Student's Book includes a code for the Student's App, to engage and encourage your students to practice their English on the move. Students can access grammar, vocabulary and pronunciation activities to prepare them for the lesson. Students are able to complete activities with varying levels of challenge and earn points.

Preparation
Allows more time for communicative activities in the class by providing pre-lesson exposure to the language covered in the Student's Book.

Practice
Provides additional practice to consolidate, review and extend areas covered in the Student's Book.

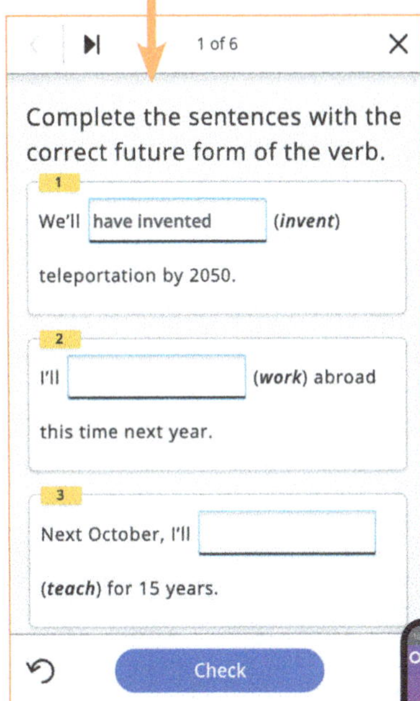

Rewards
A reward system helps to maintain student motivation.

Video

Three types of video are available with the course. Café Hub contains a real-life news or documentary clip and a situation comedy which models speaking skills. Video Hub uses content from *The Guardian* as a resource for authentic English. All the videos from the course relate to the unit topics and offer listening practice and scaffolding for speaking output.

Video Hub

Café Hub

Student's Book Contents

	LESSON • OBJECTIVES	GRAMMAR	VOCABULARY	PRONUNCIATION
U6	**COMING OF AGE**			
6.1	**The right method?** (p62) Discuss rules in education Talk about changes to education in your country	**obligation, prohibition and permission**	education	intonation to show interest
6.2	**Traditions of youth** (p66) Discuss age milestones in your country Debate the best time to start college	**articles**	compound adjectives phrases with *make* and *do*	intrusive /j/ sounds
6.3	Café Hub **A new perspective** (p70) give your opinion on an aspect of education		emphatic structures	
	UNIT REVIEW (p72)	**WRITING** (p159) Write a report | KEY SKILL Describing data		
U7	**COMMUNITY**			
7.1	**Open spaces** (p74) Discuss community development projects Discuss responses to hypothetical situations	**first conditional with different future forms** **unreal conditionals**	verbs to describe change	connected speech in conditionals
7.2	**Make a change** (p78) Talk about wishes and regrets Design and present a community project	***wish* and *if only***	three-part phrasal verbs compound nouns	two-stress phrasal verbs
7.3	Café Hub **A shared vision** (p82) give your opinion on a social initiative		*you know*	
	UNIT REVIEW (p84)	**WRITING** (p160) Write a formal letter of complaint | KEY SKILL Hedging		
U8	**MYSTERY**			
8.1	**Myths and legends** (p86) Speculate about past events Summarize a cultural story	**past modals of deduction**	word families	thought groups
8.2	**Who did it?** (p90) Write and perform a short scene Speculate about the causes and consequences of a crime	**order of adjectives**	easily confused verbs crime	adding information
8.3	Café Hub **Fact or fiction?** (p94) discuss how to test an idea		understatement	
	UNIT REVIEW (p96)	**WRITING** (p161) Write a complex essay | KEY SKILL Writing conclusions		
U9	**BUSINESS**			
9.1	**Customers** (p98) Talk about the risks and benefits of apps Make an effective complaint about a product or service	**adjective clauses**	dependent prepositions: verbs	pitch on non-essential adjective clauses
9.2	**Products** (p102) Conduct a survey about what influences our purchases Design and present an ad campaign	**determiners and quantifiers**	science advertising	connected speech: determiners and quantifiers
9.3	Café Hub **Raising capital** (p106) discuss investment opportunities		illustrating your argument	
	UNIT REVIEW (p108)	**WRITING** (p162) Write a proposal | KEY SKILL Using discourse markers in formal writing		
U10	**MEDIA**			
10.1	**Reporting the news** (p110) Give opinions on recent news stories Intervene appropriately in a discussion	**reported speech**	traditional media	avoiding interruption
10.2	**Digital media** (p114) Report a conversation Plan and create a viral marketing ad	**reporting verbs**	social media adjective + noun collocations	using intonation to attract and keep interest
10.3	Café Hub **Watch on demand** (p118) give your opinion on streaming services		*from … to*	
	UNIT REVIEW (p120)	**WRITING** (p163) Write a persuasive essay | KEY SKILL Concession		

Welcome

GRAMMAR

The passive voice

A Complete the sentences with the passive voice form of the verbs in the box.

arrest cancel destroy kill release take

1 Apparently, over 700,000 people ___are killed___ by mosquitos every year.
2 A decision ___will be taken___ by the management board later in the week.
3 Three men ___have been arrested___ in connection with an attempted robbery in Soho last week.
4 The band's debut album ___was released___ on August 27, 1991.
5 'We regret to inform passengers that the 7:36 flight to San Diego, California ___has been canceled___.'
6 Over 600 homes ___were destroyed___ in the forest fires that hit the area last month.

Zero, first and second conditionals

B Choose the correct options (a, b or c) to complete the conditional sentences.

1 If you don't hurry up, ___ the beginning of the movie.
(a) we'll miss b we'd miss c we'd have missed
2 Let me know if ___ any help with anything.
a you'll need (b) you need c you'd need
3 If ___ the fire alarm, leave the building by the nearest exit.
a you'll hear b you'd heard (c) you hear
4 I can't help you unless ___ me what's wrong.
a you'd tell (b) you tell c you'd have told
5 If I had the money, ___ all my food there.
a I'll buy (b) I'd buy c I'd have bought
6 If ___ Emily, I'll tell her to give you a call.
(a) I see b I'll see c I'd see

VOCABULARY

Word formation

A Complete the sentences with the correct form of the words in parentheses.

1 I thought that was a really ___productive___ (*product*) meeting actually.
2 Just relax. Try not to ___overthink___ (*think*) it.
3 That reminds me, I need to ___renew___ (*new*) my passport.
4 Sorry, but I think you may have ___misunderstood___ (*understand*) the question.
5 There's simply no ___scientific___ (*science*) evidence to support that.

Collocations

B Choose the correct options to complete the collocations.

1 We're sorry to announce that there are ***serious*** / ***severe*** delays on the central line.
2 Many new business owners find it difficult to ***make*** / ***create*** a profit in their first year.
3 I'm finding it really difficult to ***stay*** / ***remain*** motivated right now.
4 LeBron James has ***made*** / ***given*** the decision not to renew his contract with the Cleveland Cavaliers.
5 Scott seems pretty confident that his team will ***reach*** / ***make*** their target by June.
6 My brother-in-law actually ***does*** / ***runs*** a small business from home.
7 The government has ***launched*** / ***released*** a new campaign focusing on mental health.
8 Annoyingly, we got stuck in ***serious*** / ***heavy*** traffic on our way back.

C SPEAK Work in pairs. Discuss the questions.

1 What can you do to help stay motivated at work and in your studies?
2 Do you know anyone that runs a successful business? What do they do?
3 What's the most difficult decision you've ever made?

PRONUNCIATION

Intonation

0.1 **A Draw arrows in the parentheses to show whether the intonation rises (↗) or falls (↘) at each point in the sentences. Then listen and check.**

1 Oh, really? (↗) Wow! That sounds great! (↗)
2 It's a formal dinner, (↗) so it's important that you look nice. (↘)
3 You've been to New York before, (↘) haven't you? (↗)
4 Hmm … I'm not sure really. (↘) Maybe tomorrow afternoon? (↗)
5 OK. (↘) I'll speak to Alicia and get back to you. (↘)

Silent consonants

0.2 **B Underline the silent consonants in each word. Then listen and check.**

1 dishonest
2 listen
3 designer
4 climbing
5 muscle
6 knowledge

Women in a minimalist photo shoot in Copenhagen, Denmark

Connection (n) a relationship between people, groups of people, things or events
Synonyms: partnership (n), tie (n), relationship (n)
Collocations and idioms: *close* connection, *establish a* connection, *in* connection *with*

Euripides is suggesting that anyone who is around to offer support when you're going through a difficult experience is a true friend; those that fade away at this point are not.

Euripides (480 BCE–406 BCE) was one of the most famous playwrights in ancient Greece. He wrote over 90 plays, at least 18 of which have survived, and his innovative ideas have heavily influenced European theater.

OBJECTIVES

- talk about reactions and feelings
- design and present a meet-up group
- compare, contrast and summarize short biographies
- talk about people that have influenced you
- give your opinion on the role of inherited ability in success
- write a formal letter asking for information

Work with a partner. Discuss the questions.

1 Read the quote. Do you agree with Euripides? Why/Why not?

2 Can online relationships ever be as close as face-to-face relationships? Why/Why not?

3 What are the most important relationships in your life? Why?

CONNECTIONS 1

OBJECTIVES

Read the unit objectives to the class.

UNIT OPENER QUESTIONS

1 Read the quote as a class and elicit its meaning (see above). Then, put students into pairs to discuss whether or not they agree with it. Give feedback as a class and encourage students to listen and respond to each other with their own ideas.

2 Elicit the difference between *online* and *face-to-face* relationships (*online relationships are those formed and/or maintained via social media, email, etc and face-to-face refers to people you have a relationship with in real life*). Then, elicit one or two benefits of each, adding any useful emergent language to the board. Next, put students back into pairs to think of more ideas. Monitor and help with any new vocabulary before bringing the class back together to continue the discussion.

3 Elicit a few examples of different types of relationships (e.g. *friends*, *family*, *colleagues*, etc), then explain an important relationship in your life to demonstrate the task. Next, put students into pairs again to discuss their own relationships. Monitor, taking notes of any useful emergent language to cover later on.

WORKSHEETS

Lesson 1.1 Personality

Vocabulary: Feelings (W1)

Grammar: Question forms (W2)

Lesson 1.2 Who we are

Grammar: Tense review (W3)

Vocabulary: Personality adjectives (W4)

Vocabulary: Noun suffixes (W5)

1.1 Personality

- Talk about reactions and feelings
- Design and present a meet-up group

S – skimming for the main ideas V – feelings G – question forms P – intonation in *yes/no* and *wh-* questions

READING

A SPEAK Work in groups. Discuss the questions.

1 What qualities make someone a hero?
2 What type of people would you describe as 'everyday heroes'? Why?
3 Have you ever done anything heroic?

B SKIM FOR MAIN IDEAS Skim read *Inspiring stories of everyday heroes*. Choose the best summary (a or b) for each story. Use the information in the box to help you.

Skimming for the main ideas

Many modern articles, particularly those online, are presented in multiple short paragraphs to make them easier to read in a short amount of time. We can usually understand the main ideas in this kind of article by quickly skimming the text.

1 a A man jumped onto the train tracks to save his baby.
(b) A man jumped onto the train tracks to save a woman's baby.

2 a A young couple was saved from a forest fire that broke out in the fields they were driving through.
(b) A young couple saved a family from a forest fire that spread to their house.

3 (a) A group of heroic pedestrians helped pull a schoolgirl out from under the car that had just hit her.
b A driver heroically pulled a young schoolgirl out from under his car after an accident.

4 a Despite not being a strong swimmer, a young man was able to rescue his dog from strong currents in the ocean.
(b) A passerby was able to rescue a dog that had been swept out to sea.

C READ FOR DETAIL Read the article again and answer the questions. Underline the parts of the text that give you the answers.

1 What caused the stroller to start rolling toward the train tracks?
2 Was Jonas Neff in any real danger?
3 How did the fire develop so rapidly?
4 How did the children escape the burning building?
5 What had Becca Edwards been doing before the accident?
6 How did the driver react after the accident?
7 Why couldn't the dog get back to the beach?
8 Why was the rescuer so sure he could help?

D SPEAK Work in pairs. Discuss the questions.

1 How do you think you would react in the situations described in the article? Why?
2 Do you agree with Jonas Neff that he isn't a hero because 'anyone would do the same'? Why/Why not?
3 Why was Becca Edwards lucky that her accident happened on a main road?

Inspiring stories of

EVERYDAY HEROES

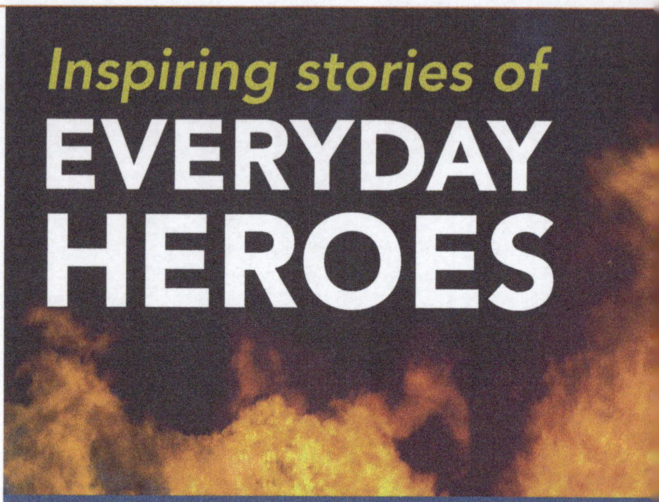

BY EMILY FISCHER | OCT 15, 2018

In an age dominated by movies about superheroes, it's good to know that we can all be heroes in the right context. To inspire you to do something next time you see someone in trouble, here are four real-life stories of normal people who jumped into action without a second thought.

BACK ON TRACK

Reactions are vital in everyday situations. Mother-of-one Christine Thomas was waiting on a crowded platform for her train home, when her phone rang.
Ex C Q1 Expecting an important call, Christine rooted through her bag, not noticing that the brake on her child's stroller had failed and it was rolling toward the platform edge. She looked up, **horrified**, to see the stroller fall off the platform and onto the tracks below. Everyone on the platform froze, too **tense** to move, except Jonas Neff. Jonas jumped down quickly and lifted the stroller and child onto the platform, before
Ex C Q2 pulling himself up just in time to avoid the oncoming train. Interviewed later by local radio, Jonas said, 'I'm not a hero. Anyone else would do the same.' Maybe a little too modest considering that everyone else had been too shocked to move!

ESCAPING THE BLAZE

Everyone can be brave no matter how young or old they are. In the dry heat of the summer, a fire
Ex C Q3 started burning slowly in a farmer's field. As the winds became stronger, the fire spread quickly, surrounding the Sanchez family home. Trapped inside were a grandmother and her two young grandchildren. Spotting the danger as they were driving past, local residents Maria and Javier Hernandez stopped and got out to help. Maria later told local reporters '… I was so **impressed** by the character of such
Ex C Q4 young children. They didn't know who we were but trusted us to catch them as they jumped from the top window. Once they were out, the grandmother jumped too.' The family was clearly upset to lose their home but equally **relieved** to all be alive.

LEAD-IN

Tell the class about three of your heroes (ideally displaying pictures of them) and explain why they are so important to you. Try to provide a good mix of people (e.g. *famous people, family members, characters*, etc) as this will encourage students to think more creatively. Then, put students into pairs to discuss their own heroes. Monitor and help with any new vocabulary. After a few minutes, bring the class back together to share their ideas. Add any new or useful vocabulary to the board.

READING

A Write the names or show pictures of three people that could be considered heroes (e.g. *a paramedic, a famous athlete* and *Superman*) on the board (or use the three people from the lead-in if you used it). Elicit a few qualities that they all have in common (e.g. *they are good under pressure; they have a good public image*; etc). Then, put students into pairs to think of more qualities and discuss the other questions. Monitor and help with new vocabulary as necessary. Give feedback as a class, encouraging students to expand on their ideas to generate discussion.

B Elicit why the writer has used subheadings (*to make the article easier to read*) and explain that we can frequently understand the main ideas in articles like this, by reading them fairly quickly and that this is called 'skimming'. Set a short time limit (one or two minutes) for students to skim the article and choose the best summary for each story. Give them time to check their answers before giving feedback as a class. Encourage students to justify their answers with information from the article.

C Give students time to complete the exercise alone, before checking their answers in pairs. Give feedback as a class.

1 *The brake on her child's stroller failed.*
2 *Yes. Jonas was able to pull himself up '... just in time to avoid the oncoming train.'*
3 *It spread quickly as '... the winds became stronger ...'*
4 *They jumped from the top window.*
5 *Playing on the winning team in a local soccer tournament.*
6 *Nothing. The article says the driver was 'devastated' and '... could do nothing as Becca screamed for help.'*
7 *Linus was dragged out to sea by strong currents.*
8 *Because he's a confident swimmer. He says, 'I wouldn't recommend swimming in such dangerous currents unless you're confident you can get back.'*

D Put students into pairs to discuss the questions. Monitor and encourage them to expand on their ideas and ask follow-up questions to extend their discussions.

Suggested answer

3 *There were a lot of people around to help.*

METHODOLOGY HUB by Christine Nuttall

Scanning and skimming

The idea that some parts of a text may be ignored or skipped is strange to some students, but efficient reading, and specifically the techniques of scanning and skimming, requires it.

By ***scanning*** we mean glancing rapidly through a text either to search for a specific piece of information (e.g. *a name, a date*) or to get an initial impression of whether the text is suitable for a given purpose (e.g. *whether a book on gardening deals with a particular plant disease*).

By ***skimming*** we mean glancing rapidly through a text to determine its gist, for example, in order to decide whether a research paper is relevant to our own work (not just to determine its field which we can find out by scanning) or to keep ourselves superficially informed about matters that are not of great importance to us; much of newspaper reading is skimming.

The distinction between the two is not particularly important. In both, the reader forces his eye over print at a rate which permits him to take in only, perhaps, the beginnings and ends of paragraphs (where information is frequently summarized), chapter headings and so on.

Scanning and skimming are important techniques; they do not remove the need for careful reading, but they enable the reader to select texts, or parts of texts, that are worth spending time on. And skimming to get a top-down view is valuable as a way of approaching difficult texts.

Students need plenty of practice in these techniques; it is a good idea to devise races to practice them, to ensure the necessary pace. Many tasks can be done in groups, which makes the supply of materials more feasible.

TEACHING IDEA by David Seymour and Maria Popova

My hero

Use this activity to extend the theme of heroes.

What makes someone a hero? Who do you look up to in your family?

Did you have a hero at school? Tell us about him/her. Can you think of any anti-heroes? Think of a famous hero and imagine you are that person. Stand at the front of the class and answer the students' questions. You can only answer 'yes' or 'no'. They will try to guess who you are. (Ask for volunteers, and if they can't think of a hero, give them one of these: Mahatma Ghandi, James Bond, Nelson Mandela, Superman, Robin Hood, Bob Marley, Neil Armstrong, Abraham Lincoln, Leonardo da Vinci, Martin Luther King.)

TEACHING IDEA by David Seymour and Maria Popova

Balloon debate

Use this activity to extend the theme of heroes.

(Elicit the names of two historically important people. Then draw a picture of a balloon on the board, with someone jumping out of it.) Work in two groups. (Allocate one of the important people to each group.) The balloon has a leak and it can only carry one person. Convince me that your person should be the one to survive. Why is he/she more useful to the human race than the other person? Discuss your arguments and take turns presenting them. I'll decide who has to jump. Work in groups of five for another balloon debate. Each choose a famous person and prepare reasons why you should stay and the others should jump. When you have finished, vote for the winner.

VOCABULARY

A Read the following sentence from the text as a class – *She looked up,* ***horrified****, to see the stroller fall off the platform and onto the tracks below* – and elicit synonyms of horrified (e.g. *terrified, shocked, frightened*, etc). Then, elicit the matching definition in the exercise (5). Next, ask students to complete the rest of the definitions alone before checking their answers with a partner. Give feedback as a class, providing further explanations or examples for each word as necessary. Have students practice pronunciation for the new vocabulary, focusing on anything they may find difficult (e.g. *awkward*).

B Give students time to complete the exercise alone, eliciting the answer to the first question if necessary. Ask them to compare answers with a partner before giving feedback as a class.

C Direct students to the Vocabulary Hub (see TB121). Use the Vocabulary Worksheet on page W1 for extra practice.

D Choose one of the adjectives from this section, and tell the class about the last time you felt this way. Then, put students into pairs to do the same for all of the adjectives in the section. Monitor and encourage students to ask follow-up questions to extend their discussions. Make a note of the most interesting stories and call upon students to share these with the class if you have time.

SPEAKING

Put students into groups to discuss what to do in each of the situations. If necessary, give students time to read each scenario alone and write notes before starting their discussions. Monitor and help with grammar and vocabulary as necessary. Give feedback as a class, encouraging further discussion.

Extra activity

Play a game of *Back to the Board* with the class. Ask one student to volunteer to sit in a chair at the front of the classroom with their back to the board. Write one of the emotion words from the lesson on the board behind them. Ask the class to give the student clues about the word without saying it, miming or translating the word. Allow 30 seconds for the student to guess the word. Repeat the activity with a new volunteer, and allow the first student to take on the role of teacher and choose the word on the board. As a variation, you could put students into teams and award one point for every correctly guessed word. You could also offer bonus points if the team is able to use the word in a grammatically correct sentence.

METHODOLOGY HUB by Jim Scrivener

Post-activity

It is usually important to have some kind of feedback session on the activity. This stage is vital and is typically under-planned by teachers! The students have worked hard on the task, and it has probably raised a number of ideas, comments and questions about the topic and about language. Many teachers rely on an 'ask the class if there were any problems and field the answers on the spot' approach. While this will often get you through, it can also lead you down dark alleys of confusing explanations and long-winded spontaneous teaching. It can also be rather dull simply to go over things that have already been done thoroughly in small groups. So, for a number of reasons, it is worth careful planning of this stage in advance – especially to think up alternatives to putting yourself in the spotlight answering a long list of questions.

- Groups meet up with other groups and compare answers/opinions.
- Students check answers with the printed answers in the Teacher's Book (which you pass around / leave at the front of the room / photocopy and hand out, etc).
- Before class, you anticipate what the main language problems will be and prepare a mini-presentation on these areas.
- During the last few minutes of a long task, go around the groups and warn them that each group will be asked to 'report back' to the whole class. Ask them to appoint a spokesperson and to agree on the main message they want to say. You could ask them to choose just one point from their discussion that they think is worth sharing.
- When checking answers, ask for groups to exchange and compare their answers across the room themselves …
- … or get a student to come up front and manage the answer-checking, rather than doing it all yourself (you could give this student the answer sheet!).
- Collect all answer sheets, then redistribute them for 'correcting' by other students. When everything has been checked, students pair up with those who marked their paper and listen/explain/justify/argue, etc.
- Correct one student's answers; that student then goes on to correct other answers, etc.
- Divide the board up into spaces for answers and throw markers to different students who fill the board up with their answers (each answer written by a different student). The whole group looks at the finished board and comments/ corrects.

THE STRENGTH OF MANY

Sometimes what you need is a whole group of heroes. **Thrilled** at having just won a local soccer tournament, 10-year-old Becca Edwards was riding her bike home from school one evening when she was hit by a car that had driven through a red light. The car stopped, trapping Becca underneath. **Devastated** by what had happened, the driver could do nothing as Becca screamed for help. Luckily for her, the accident took place on a busy main road. Nine pedestrians ran to help, working together to lift the car up just enough for a tenth hero to pull the schoolgirl out from underneath. Mark Benson, the first paramedic at the scene, said Becca was lucky to be alive and praised the quick response of the passers-by.

Ex C Q5

Ex C Q6

DANGER AT THE BEACH

Michael was happily throwing sticks into the ocean for his dog, Linus, when suddenly it all went wrong. Strong currents dragged poor Linus out to sea and he wasn't able to swim back to shore. Terrified that Linus might die, but not a particularly strong swimmer, Michael stood helpless and **frustrated** on the beach. All of a sudden, a man came running past and dived into the water. After a brief struggle, he managed to pull Linus back to the shore where he was met with a huge round of applause from the crowd of onlookers that had gathered. 'Initially, I felt kind of **awkward** on the beach because I didn't know what to do' said the young hero. 'But I'm pretty confident in the water, so I just jumped in. I'm glad I could help out, but I wouldn't recommend swimming in such dangerous currents unless you're confident you can get back. A person's life is much more important than a dog's!'

Ex C Q7

Ex C Q8

VOCABULARY

Feelings

A Scan the article again. Complete the definitions with the adjectives in bold.

1 ___relieved___ feeling happy because something bad has stopped or hasn't happened

2 ___tense___ feeling nervous, worried and not able to relax because of what might happen

3 ___awkward___ feeling embarrassed and not relaxed

4 ___devastated___ feeling very shocked and upset

5 ___horrified___ feeling very shocked or frightened

6 ___thrilled___ feeling very happy and excited

7 ___impressed___ feeling admiration for someone because of an unusually good achievement, quality or skill

8 ___frustrated___ feeling annoyed or impatient because you can't do or achieve what you want

B Complete the sentences with adjectives from Exercise A.

1 I felt a little ___awkward___ at first because I wasn't wearing a suit like everybody else.

2 I was just really ___frustrated___ because the police wouldn't let me help.

3 It'd been a horrible flight and I was pretty ___relieved___ when the plane finally landed.

4 Firefighter Mark Cox was ___thrilled___ to receive an award for bravery after the incident.

5 You couldn't help but be ___impressed___ by how quickly he reacted to the danger.

6 The crowd grew ___tense___ as they waited to see if firefighters would reach the child in time.

7 I was ___devastated___ to hear that my grandmother had died because we were very close.

8 We were all ___horrified___ as the elevator fell 15 floors toward the ground.

C Go to the Vocabulary Hub on page 142.

D SPEAK Work in pairs. When was the last time you felt any of these emotions? What happened?

SPEAKING

SPEAK Work in groups. Read the scenarios (1–3) and discuss what you would do in each and why.

1 You're on a busy train when the woman in front of you suddenly falls over. Her eyes are closed and she doesn't appear to be breathing.

2 You're walking home late at night when you see a group of men shouting at a terrified businessman. You think they might attack him.

3 A fire breaks out in the house across the street. The elderly woman that lives there has difficulty walking and has poor hearing.

a

b

LISTENING

A SPEAK **Work in pairs. Read the information about Get Together and discuss the questions.**

1 What is the purpose of Get Together?

2 What kind of groups are available?

3 Do you think this is a good idea? Why/Why not?

Get Together

Home About us Contact Login Sign up

Get Together helps connect millions of people with similar interests around the world. Ex A Q1 The basic idea is simple – find people in your local area that share your passion and form a group. Meet regularly to play together, learn new skills or just make new friends.

Our members have rediscovered their passion for reading, trained for triathlons, even changed their careers – the possibilities are endless. Ex A Q2 Whatever you're interested in, you're sure to find a group that suits you.

Members	Groups	Countries
25 million	185,967	148

1.1 **B LISTEN FOR MAIN IDEAS** **Listen and match the conversations (1–3) to the pictures (a–c).**

Conversation 1 b Conversation 2 c Conversation 3 a

1.1 **C LISTEN FOR DETAIL** **Listen again. Are these sentences true (T) or false (F)? Correct the false sentences.**

1 a Both speakers at the ukulele group regularly go to meet-ups. This is the woman's first Get Together. T / (F)

b They have played the ukulele for the same amount of time. The woman has been playing for a year and the man has been playing for two and a half years. T / (F)

2 a The man's apartment is in a convenient location. He says the apartment is a really long way from the station. T / (F)

b The man has done a 10K race before. (T) / F

3 a Martin needs to return the registration form as soon as possible. There's no rush to return it. T / (F)

b Martin and Yumi both enjoyed the Haruki Murakami novel *Norwegian Wood*. (T) / F

D SPEAK **Work in groups. Discuss the questions.**

1 What are the benefits of joining a group like this?

2 Do you think this is the best way to meet new people in your area? Why/Why not?

3 What Get Together groups would you like to join in your area? Why?

GRAMMAR

Question forms

1.2 **A** **Listen to extracts from the conversations again. Complete the questions.**

1 **Sarah:** Yeah, same really. It just seemed like a fun thing to do. Anyway, who's leading the group tonight?

Mark: Uh, Lucy, I think. She's actually a professional musician, so we're in good hands.

2 **Fyodor:** Well, I like Rochester, but my apartment is a really long way from the train station and I don't really get along with my roommates.

Alana: Fair enough. Why don't you like them?

Fyodor: Well, one of them works night shifts so he always comes home really late and the other just spends all his time in his room.

3 **Fyodor:** I suppose so. Who do you live with?

Alana: A couple of friends I've known since college. They can definitely be annoying sometimes, but I wouldn't want to live with anyone else.

4 **Martin:** Excuse me, could you tell me where I sign in for the book club Get Together?

Yumi: Uh, yeah, right here actually. I'm running the group tonight. Can I take your name, please?

LISTENING

1.1 **A–D** Work through the exercises. Allow time for peer correction and encourage students to justify their answers with examples from the conversations.

1 To connect people around the world with similar interests.
2 reading, triathlons, clubs for people changing careers, etc.

GRAMMAR

1.2 **A** Play the audio for students to complete the extracts, then give them time to compare their answers with a partner. Give feedback as a class, but don't go into the grammar of each question at this point.

B Give students time to complete the rules alone, using the examples in Exercise A to help them. Then, ask them to check their answers in pairs before giving feedback as a class. Consolidate understanding with further explanations and examples of each of the points in the box as necessary.

C Direct students to the **Grammar Hub** (see TB5).

D–E Work through the first question as a class, adding the correct answer to the board. Then, give students time to complete the remaining questions alone before checking their answers with a partner. Give feedback as a class. Next, put students into pairs to discuss the questions. Monitor and encourage students to ask follow-up questions to extend their discussions. Use the **Grammar Worksheet** on page W2 for extra practice.

AUDIO SCRIPT

1.1

Listening, Exercise B
Mk = Mark S = Sarah F = Fyodor A = Alana
Mn = Martin Y = Yumi

Conversation 1

Mk: Hello. I haven't seen you here before.
Ex C Q1a **S:** Uh, no, I've just joined actually. This is my first Get Together.
Mk: Oh, well, you chose a good group. Everyone here's pretty friendly and we all have a similar level of ability, which helps.
Ex C Q1b **S:** That's a relief. I've been learning for about a year or so now. How about you? Have you been playing long?
Mk: Uh, yeah a little bit longer … for about two and a half years. I think I'm alright but I'm no expert.
S: Yeah, me neither. Do you ever perform at all?
Mk: Me? Ha ha! No, no. I'm definitely not good enough for that. I'm just doing this for fun really. How about you?
S: Yeah, same really. It just seemed like a fun thing to do. Anyway, who's leading the group tonight?
Mk: Uh, Lucy, I think. She's actually a professional musician, so we're in good hands.
S: Well I certainly need all the help I can get!

Conversation 2

F: Excuse me, could you tell me where the changing rooms are?
A: Sure. I'm going there now if you want to come with me. I'm Alana by the way. You're new to the Get Together, aren't you?
F: Uh, yeah I am. I've just moved to the area. I was a member of the running Get Together before I moved here.
A: Where were you living before?
F: I was living in Chicago but I got a new job, so I moved to New York. I'm living in Rochester right now, but I might actually move.
A: Oh, really? How come?
Ex C Q2a **F:** Well I like Rochester but my apartment is a really long way from the train station and I don't really get along with my roommates.
A: Fair enough. Why don't you like them?
F: Well, one of them works night shifts so he always comes home really late and the other just spends all his time in his room. Maybe I should just look for a place on my own.
A: Maybe, although roommates can be pretty fun if you can find the right people.
F: I suppose so. Who do you live with?
A: A couple of friends I've known since college. They can definitely be annoying sometimes, but I wouldn't want to live with anyone else.
F: Sounds fun. Anyway, have you been running long?
A: Uh, no, not long really. I just wanted to, you know, get more into sports and I loved running in college, so I thought I'd give it a try.
F: I see. Are you planning to enter any races this summer or is it a little too soon?
A: Well, I was actually thinking of signing up for the 10K at the end of September.
Ex C Q2b **F:** The one in Richmond, Virginia? You definitely should. Ten kilometers sounds like a long way, but it's actually not too bad. I just put in a lot of training and was completely fine on the day.
A: OK, good to know. Maybe we could do it together?
F: Ha ha! Maybe. I'm doing a half marathon the week before though, so I might not have the energy for another race!

Conversation 3

Mn: Excuse me, could you tell me where I sign in for the book club Get Together?
Y: Uh, yeah, right here actually. I'm running the group tonight. Can I take your name, please?
Mn: It's Martin Pajak.
Y: Oh, yes. I remember your name from your emails.
Ex C Q3a Could I ask you to fill out this form when you get a chance? No rush to return it. Have you had time to finish the book yet?
Mn: Uh, just about! I really like Haruki Murakami.
Y: Oh, really? Me too. Which is your favorite Murakami novel?
Mn: Um, probably *Norwegian Wood*, but I also loved *After Dark*.
Ex C Q3b **Y:** *Norwegian Wood* was the first Murakami book that I ever read. I thought it was amazing.
Mn: Oh, well if you like Murakami, you'd probably like Banana Yoshimoto. Especially her first novel, *Kitchen*.

PRONUNCIATION

1.3; 1.4

A–B Work through the exercises, allowing time for peer correction as appropriate.

SPEAKING HUB

A–D Put students into groups to work through the exercises. Monitor and support as necessary.

GRAMMAR HUB

1.1 Question forms

Questions with *be*, *have* and *do*

- We usually use the auxiliary verbs *be*, *have* and *do* to form questions. These come before the main verb.

Question word	Auxiliary	Subject	Main verb	
	Is	he	coming	this weekend?
	Have	you	seen	her?
When	did	they	move	in?

Subject questions

- When the question word (*who*, *what*, etc) is the subject, we don't use an auxiliary.

Question word	Main verb	
What	happened	to you?
How	are	you?

Indirect questions

- Indirect questions begin with phrases such as *Can you tell me …?* After the phrase, we use the same word order as a sentence, not a question.

Do you think it will rain? NOT ~~Do you think will it rain?~~

Can you tell me where you live? NOT ~~Can you tell me where do you live?~~

Questions ending in a preposition

- When a question word is the object of a preposition, the preposition usually comes at the end of the sentence.

Who did you brother live with?

What did you use it for?

Questions with negative auxiliaries

- When we ask negative *wh-* questions, we use the auxiliary verb, even in subject questions. Negative *wh-* questions can be used to confirm something you believe to be true, to express an opinion in a more formal manner or to focus on a smaller number of answers.

*OK, who **doesn't** want pizza? (= I think most people **will** want pizza)*

1.1 Question forms

A Correct the mistakes in each question.

1 Does he ~~lives~~ live near here?
2 What ~~she has~~ has she done to her hair?
3 Where do you work?
4 Which ~~is team~~ team is winning?
5 Haven't you already ~~be~~ been on vacation?
6 Who ~~with~~ do you live? with?
7 When ~~he told~~ did he tell you that?
8 What ~~was~~ happened next?

B Rewrite the direct questions as indirect questions.

1 Where did you get your information?
Can you tell me where you got your information?
2 Is it going to snow later, do you think?
Do you think it's / it is going to snow later?
3 What do you think of the new recycling laws?
Can I ask you what you think of the new recycling laws?
4 Where does Alejandro come from?
Do you know where Alejandro comes from?
5 Has the mail arrived yet?
Could you see if the mail has arrived yet?

C Complete the questions in the interview.

Interviewer: Where [1] are you from?
Mia: I'm from Seattle, Washington.
Interviewer: How long [2] have you been / lived here (for)?
Mia: I've been here for about five years now.
Interviewer: Who [3] do you live with?
Mia: With friends, but I'm looking to find an apartment of my own.
Interviewer: So when [4] did you decide to become an actor?
Mia: I guess I decided to become an actor when I was about five!
Interviewer: What [5] do you like doing / to do / do you do in your free time?
Mia: I don't have much free time, but when I am free, I like spending time with friends and family.
Interviewer: Do you think [6] you'll / you will always be an actor?
Mia: Oh yes. I think I'll always be an actor. I can't imagine doing anything else!

➤ Go back to page 5.

PRONUNCIATION

Intonation in *yes/no* and *wh-* questions

A (1.3) Listen to the questions from the conversations. Draw arrows to show whether the intonation rises (↗) or falls (↘) at the end of each question.

1. Have you been playing long? ↗
2. Where were you living before? ↘
3. Who do you live with? ↘
4. Have you had time to finish the book yet? ↗

B (1.4) Circle the arrows to predict which intonation will be used in each question. Then listen and check.

1. Is there an application fee? [↗] / [↘] — (↗ circled)
2. What kind of event could we run? [↗] / [↘] — (↘ circled)
3. How often does the group meet? [↗] / [↘] — (↘ circled)
4. Do you need any special equipment? [↗] / [↘] — (↗ circled)
5. Is everyone happy with that? [↗] / [↘] — (↗ circled)

B WORK IT OUT Choose the correct options to complete the rules.

Question forms

Indirect questions

We use indirect questions when we want to be more polite. They usually start with phrases like *Could you tell me …?*, *Do you know …?* and *Would you mind …?* In indirect questions, we use the same word order as a statement (i.e. [1]*verb + subject* / *subject + verb*) and we don't use the auxiliary *do*.

Questions with prepositions

If a verb is followed by a preposition, the preposition comes at the [2]*beginning* / *end* of the sentence.

Subject questions

When we ask about the subject of a sentence, we use the same word order as a statement, and the question word (e.g. *when, who, what, which*, etc) replaces the [3]*subject* / *object*.

Negative questions

When we ask negative *wh-* questions, we [4]*use* / *don't use* the auxiliary verb, even in subject questions.

C Go to the Grammar Hub on page 122.

D PRACTICE Reorder the words to make questions.

1. would / most like to meet / which / you / famous person
   Which famous person would you most like to meet ?
2. is / can / ask / your earliest memory / I / what
   Can I ask what your earliest memory is ?
3. think / you / is more important / diet or exercise / do
   Do you think diet or exercise is more important ?
4. English / you / why / are / studying
   Why are you studying English ?
5. your job / what / like about / you / don't
   What don't you like about your job ?

E SPEAK Work in pairs. Discuss the questions in Exercise D.

SPEAKING HUB

A PLAN Work in groups. Brainstorm a list of things you like doing or are interested in.

B PREPARE Choose one of your ideas from Exercise A to use as the focus of a new meet-up group. Write notes about:

- what you'll actually do at the meet-ups
- where / how often you'll meet
- what special events you might organize
- how much members will need to pay and why

C PRESENT Present your ideas to the class. Ask other groups follow-up questions to get more information.

D DISCUSS As a class, discuss which meet-up groups would work best in your area and why.

- Talk about reactions and feelings
- Design and present a meet-up group

- Compare, contrast and summarize short biographies
- Talk about people that have influenced you

G – tense review
V – personality adjectives; noun suffixes
L – listening for the main ideas
P – connected speech: final consonant and initial vowel

READING

A SPEAK Work in groups. What do you know about the people in the article below?

B READ FOR GIST Read *The long road to success* and choose the sentence (1–3) that best describes the connection between the two people.

1 famous people that had difficult childhoods
2 famous people that overcame challenges to succeed
3 famous people that failed in college

C SCAN Scan the article again and check (✓) the person that each sentence is about.

Which person …	Stephen Hawking	Vera Wang
1 had an unusual childhood?	✓	
2 didn't meet their academic potential?	✓	
3 had a significant change in their career?		✓
4 was inspired to start a new business?		✓
5 lived much longer than people expected?	✓	
6 is very rich and successful today?		✓

The long road to success

It's easy to think that the rich and famous have always lived a privileged life, but many have overcome great adversity to get to where they are today. When life presents us with challenges, how we react can determine how successful we become.

Stephen Hawking

What was his early life like?
Keeping bees in the basement of their crumbling St. Albans home, making fireworks in the greenhouse and driving around in a former London taxi, the Hawking family was certainly a little eccentric. In fact, they frequently ate dinner in silence [1]while each of them was reading a book.

Was he always a gifted academic?
At school, Hawking was thought of as bright but not brilliant. In his first year of high school, [2]he was the third worst student in the class. He also admitted to being a lazy student at Oxford University, only spending about an hour a day studying.

When did his condition develop?
Hawking first recognized something was wrong when he started to occasionally trip and fall while studying for a PhD at Cambridge University. At 21 years old, he was diagnosed with amyotrophic lateral sclerosis (ALS), and given just two years to live.

How did this affect him?
Hawking said that before he was diagnosed with ALS, he had been bored with life. Being told that he would not live to complete his PhD encouraged the young physicist to focus on his studies.

What made him famous?
Hawking is most famous for his research into black holes. By his early thirties, he had won many awards and went on to publish numerous papers and books, including *A brief history of time*. He was still proposing groundbreaking ideas about space and time until his death 50 years later.

Glossary

ALS (n) amyotrophic lateral sclerosis is a serious disease that affects nerve cells and causes muscles to become smaller and weaker

Vera Wang

Did she always want to work in fashion?
From the age of eight years old, Wang wanted to become a professional figure skater. After years of training and competing, she realized that no matter how hard she trained, she would never make the Olympic team. She gave up figure skating and moved to Paris to study Art History. It was there in the French capital that Wang realized she wanted to pursue a career in the fashion industry. After [3]she had completed her year in another country, Wang moved back to the US where she worked as a sales person at Yves Saint Laurent. It was at this point she met *Vogue* fashion director Frances Stein, who told Wang to give her a call when she graduated. A year and a half later she did, and spent the next 17 years working as an editor at the magazine.

How did she get into fashion design?
Wang left *Vogue* in 1982 and lived in Paris for several years before taking a position as design director at Ralph Lauren in New York. When planning her wedding in 1989, she was so disappointed by the lack of fashionable wedding dresses that she decided to design her own. A year later, she opened her own bridal shop, from which [4]she has built a fashion empire worth millions. [5]Today, she is worth over $600 million and is considered one of America's most successful self-made millionaires. Her clothes are worn by everyone from Michelle Obama to Kim Kardashian. She remains heavily involved in her company and is known for working long hours and holding frequent meetings to ensure she knows [6]exactly what's happening.

1.2 Who we are

LEAD-IN

With books closed, tell students about a turning point in your life. This could be real or made-up, but make sure to include information about what you changed and why. Arrange students in pairs and ask them to discuss a turning point from their own lives.

READING

A Direct students' attention to the pictures in the article and put them into groups to discuss what they know about the two celebrities. Remind them not to read the text at this stage. Give feedback as a class, eliciting a brief summary for each person (*Stephen Hawking was a famous British physicist, renowned for his theories on black holes. Vera Wang is a famous fashion designer, who is best known for her line of wedding dresses*).

B Elicit the meaning of *overcome* (*to succeed in dealing with or controlling a problem*), then give students time to read the text and complete the exercise. Ask them to check their answers in pairs before giving feedback as class. Take this opportunity to clarify any new or unfamiliar vocabulary in the article at this stage (drawing attention to the glossary box).

C Elicit the meaning of *scan* (*to look over a text to find specific information*), then give students time to read the article again to complete the exercise. Ask them to check their answers in pairs before giving feedback as class. Encourage them to justify their answers with examples from the text.

METHODOLOGY HUB by Scott Thornbury

Reading

Reading is a receptive skill. But the fact that it is receptive does not mean that it is passive: reading is an active – even interactive – process. Readers bring their own questions to the text – based on their own background knowledge – and they use these to interrogate the text, modifying their questions and coming up with new ones according to the answers they get. In order to do this, they draw on a range of knowledge bases. They need to be able to decode the letters, words and grammatical structures of the individual sentences – what is called **bottom-up processing**. But they also enlist **top-down processes**, such as drawing on discourse and schematic knowledge, as well as on immediate contextual information. Discourse knowledge is knowing how different text types – such as news reports, recipes or academic papers – are organized. Schematic knowledge is the reader's existing knowledge of the topic. Reading involves an interaction between these different levels of knowledge, where knowledge at one level can compensate for lack of knowledge at another. Research suggests, though, that relying on top-down knowledge is unreliable and that fluent reading requires rapid and automatic decoding skills above all. But possibly the most important predictor of fluent reading ability, both in the first and second language, is having an extensive vocabulary: the more words you know, the easier it is to read.

GRAMMAR HUB

1.2 Tense review

Simple present	**He enjoys** parties.
Present progressive	**I'm watching** the news.
Simple past	**He got up** early this morning.
Past progressive	**I was walking** the dog.
Present perfect	**I've lived** here for 12 years.
Past perfect	**I'd seen** the movie several times.

- We use the simple present to talk about general truths or actions that always/usually/never happen as part of our daily routines.
- We use the present progressive for things that are happening now or around now.
- We use the simple past to talk about past states or completed actions in the past.
- We use the past progressive to describe the background to a story or something that was in progress at a particular time in the past. We also use it with the simple past to describe an action that was interrupted.

  We were driving home when we had an unexpected phone call.

- We use the present perfect to talk about a state or action that started in the past and is still happening now. We also use it to announce news.
- We use the past perfect to talk about a past action that occurred before another past action. This tense is frequently used with the simple past.
- With the negative and question forms of these tenses, we use an auxiliary verb (*be*, *do* or *have*, depending on the tense).

  She doesn't feel well.
  It didn't cost a lot.
  I haven't finished yet.
  Had they been there before?

Be careful!

- Certain time words and expressions, such as *now*, *just*, *already*, *recently*, *every day*, etc, help us to identify which tense we need to use.

  *I was traveling across the country **at the time**.*
  *I have **just** finished the last series on Netflix.*
  *Actually, I saw him at the gym **yesterday**.*

D Since this is a common activity type (both in the book and in various exams), take time to clarify that students must complete each sentence with a maximum of two words and that these must come from the article itself; they cannot use synonyms or change the form. If necessary, complete the first sentence as an example, then give students time to complete the exercise alone, before checking their answers with a partner. Give feedback as a class.

E Put students into pairs to discuss the question, explaining that they don't have to choose someone famous – they can also talk about people they know. Monitor and encourage students to extend their discussions with follow-up questions.

GRAMMAR

A Draw students' attention to the first highlighted sentence and elicit the name of the tense (*simple past*). Then, give students time to complete the exercise alone before briefly checking their answers in pairs. Give feedback as a class, eliciting new examples of each tense and their structure and adding these to the board.

B Give students time to complete the rules alone, before checking their answers with a partner. Remind them to use the examples in the text and those on the board to help them. Give feedback as a class, giving further explanation and examples for each point as necessary.

C Direct students to the **Grammar Hub** (see TB6 and below).

D Direct students' attention to the picture of Saroo Brierley, and ask students what they know about him. Explain that he was the inspiration for the movie *Lion*, before giving students time to complete the text alone. Ask them to check their answers in pairs before giving feedback as a class.

E Model the exercise by giving some examples from your own life. Encourage students to ask you questions, adding any useful emergent language to the board. Then, put students into pairs to discuss their own experiences. Monitor, focusing on the accuracy of the tenses covered in this section. Use the **Grammar Worksheet** on page W3 for extra practice.

SPEAKING

A–C Put students into A/B pairs. Direct students to the **Communication Hub** (see TB121) and ask them to follow the instructions. Next, give pairs time to share what they have learned. Monitor and help with new vocabulary as necessary. Finally, combine pairs into groups of four to discuss the questions. Monitor and encourage students to justify their opinions with examples. If you have time, open the discussion up to the class.

GRAMMAR HUB

1.2 Tense review

A Choose the correct options to complete the sentences.

1 I *am* / *was* watching television when I started to feel sick.
2 Joanna was ashamed because she *has* / *had* done something wrong.
3 I *am never feeling* / *have never felt* relaxed around him – I don't know why.
4 We *were taking* / *had taken* the wrong turn and were now completely lost.
5 I'm pretty sure I *met* / *have met* you at Jenna's party last year.
6 While I *was walking* / *had walked* home, I slipped on some ice and broke my ankle.
7 I *live* / *have lived* here for about a year and a half now.
8 James *studies* / *is studying* French at Harvard next year.

B Complete the sentences with the correct form of the verb in parentheses.

1 Jochen is an anxious person who doesn't / does not like (*not like*) doing new things.
2 It wasn't awkward at the party because I 'd/had already met (*already meet*) everyone there.
3 The question is: why was Tom there – who was he waiting (*wait*) for?
4 I have some really exciting news – I 've/have started (*start*) a new job!
5 We 're/are working (*work*) on a secret project these days.
6 Tell me about yourself. How long have you worked / have you been working (*work*) for this company?

C Complete the sentences with the correct form of the verbs in the box. Use contractions where possible.

forget have know meet snow think walk work

1 It was snowing heavily and I wasn't wearing a winter coat.
2 She 's been working / 's worked for the company for almost five years now.
3 It's difficult because he doesn't know many people in the area.
4 We didn't have much money back then, but we were happy.
5 I knew I 'd met her before, but I couldn't figure out where.
6 I 'm thinking about starting my own company.
7 I was walking down the road in the sunshine when out of nowhere, it suddenly started pouring rain.
8 She only realized she 'd forgotten her passport when she got to the airport.

➤ Go back to page 7.

D READ FOR DETAIL Read again. Complete the sentences with no more than two words from the article.

1 Stephen Hawking was considered a ___lazy___ student at Cambridge University.
2 Before finding out about his illness, he only studied for ___an hour___ each day.
3 He was told he would live for just ___two___ more years.
4 He was given a lot of ___awards___ for his early work.
5 Vera Wang gave up her dream of becoming a professional ___figure skater___ after realizing she would never make the Olympic team.
6 She worked as a ___sales person___ before joining Vogue shortly after graduation.
7 She left Vogue in 1982, after ___17 years___ working as an editor.
8 Her personal fortune is thought to be more than ___$600 million___.

E SPEAK Work in pairs. Can you think of anyone else that has overcome huge challenges in order to succeed?

GRAMMAR
Tense review

A Scan the article again. Match the highlighted sentences (1–6) to the tenses below.

_5_ simple present
_2_ simple past
_3_ past perfect
_1_ past progressive
_6_ present progressive
_4_ present perfect

B WORK IT OUT Complete the rules with the tenses in Exercise A.

Tense review

We use the [1] ___simple past___ to talk about past states or completed actions in the past.

We use the [2] ___present progressive___ to talk about things happening now or around now.

We use the [3] ___present perfect___ to talk about a state or action that started in the past and is still happening now.

We use the [4] ___simple present___ to talk about something that is generally true.

We use the [5] ___past progressive___ to talk about an action in the past that was in progress when something else happened.

We use the [6] ___past perfect___ to talk about a past action that occurred before another past action.

C Go to the **Grammar Hub** on **page 122**.

D PRACTICE Complete the text with the correct form of the verbs in parentheses.

Saroo Brierley

Saroo Brierley [1] ___was___ (*be*) born in Ganesh Talai, a suburb in Khandwa, India. His family was poor and regularly had to beg for food and money. When he was five, Saroo [2] ___took___ (*take*) a train with his older brother, Ghuddu, from Khandwa to the city of Burhanpur, where Ghuddu had a job cleaning trains at night. By the time they arrived, Saroo was so tired he fell asleep on the platform. Ghuddu told him to wait there but when he [3] ___didn't return___ (*not return*), Saroo grew impatient and got on a train that [4] ___was waiting___ (*wait*) at the platform. He fell asleep and when he woke up, he realized that he [5] ___had traveled___ (*travel*) to Kolkata by mistake – 1,500 km away from home.

After living on the streets for three weeks, he was placed in a local orphanage. An Australian family adopted him and he [6] ___spent___ (*spend*) the next 25 years living in Australia. Saroo wanted to find his family. Using his memories and Google Earth, Saroo eventually [7] ___found___ (*find*) his hometown in India.

Before his story was turned into an internationally successful book and movie, Saroo [8] ___was helping / helped___ (*help*) his dad run a business. Now he [9] ___is working___ (*work*) as a motivational speaker until he decides what to do next. Since living in Australia, Saroo [10] ___has had___ (*have*) a happy life and always feels lucky.

E SPEAK Work in pairs. Discuss the questions.

1 What challenges do you have in your life right now?
2 What is the biggest challenge you have ever faced? How did you deal with it?

SPEAKING

A PREPARE Student A – Go to the **Communication Hub** on **page 149**.
Student B – Go to the **Communication Hub** on **page 152**.

B SPEAK Tell your partner about the person you read about.

C DISCUSS Work in groups. Discuss the questions.

1 What are the similarities between the two people you read about?
2 Who do you think had bigger challenges to overcome? Why?

LISTENING

A SPEAK Work in pairs. Tell your partner about your closest friends. How are they similar/different? Is it important to have different types of friends? Why/Why not?

1.5 **B LISTEN FOR MAIN IDEAS** Listen to an interview about friendship, personality and success. Put the following topics in the order they are discussed. Use the information in the box to help you.

> **Listening for the main ideas**
>
> Talks, speeches and interviews usually contain multiple main ideas, based around one central theme. Speakers frequently introduce each new idea or point with phrases such as *the next is*, *another one is*, *the last is*, etc. Identifying these phrases can help you focus on the key information that follows.

_6_ a work colleague who makes you laugh
_4_ a complete opposite of you
_1_ a best friend you can rely on
_3_ a very honest friend who tells you the truth
_5_ a neighbor in your community
_2_ a friend who is not afraid

1.5 **C LISTEN FOR DETAIL** Listen to the interview again. Choose the correct options (a, b or c) to complete the sentences.

1 According to research, we can only maintain a friendship group of …
   a several hundred people.
   (b) no more than 50 people.
   c no more than 20 people.

2 Open-minded adventurers are people who …
   a are always making new friends.
   (b) don't find new situations stressful.
   c like habit and routine.

3 It's important to have a friend who …
   a will constantly praise you.
   b is very flexible.
   (c) will be brutally honest with you.

4 Moving a lot affects our relationships with …
   (a) our neighbors.
   b our colleagues.
   c our relatives.

5 Successful people …
   a prioritize work over everything else.
   b work longer hours than their colleagues.
   (c) feel part of a group.

D SPEAK Work in groups. Discuss the questions.

1 What positive and negative effects does social media have on our relationships?
2 How well do you know your neighbors/colleagues/classmates? Do you consider any of them friends?

VOCABULARY

Personality adjectives

1.6 **A** Complete the extracts with the personality adjectives in the box. Then listen and check.

arrogant	down-to-earth	easy-going	loyal
open-minded	self-centered	stubborn	witty

1 We all need a _loyal_ best friend. Someone who will support us no matter what happens.
2 This person is an _open-minded_ adventurer. They always force us into new and different situations.
3 They are _easy-going_ and open to new ideas, cultures and activities. None of these things stress them out.
4 No, these people aren't _arrogant_. They just have a lot of self-belief.
5 They'll tell you when you're being _self-centered_ and should think about others more.
6 Or they'll tell you you are being _stubborn_ and need to be more flexible.
7 She's very _down-to-earth_. She just does everything in this very sensible, practical way. I guess she is a helpful person to have around!
8 Having no _witty_ people to have a laugh with would make work very boring.

LISTENING

A Describe a close friend to the class, explaining how you know them and how you are similar or different. Then, put students into pairs to talk about their own friends. Monitor, helping with any new or unfamiliar vocabulary as necessary. Bring the class back together and nominate one or two pairs to share the main points from their discussion. Add any useful emergent language to the board.

1.5 **B** Talk through the skills box as a class, clarifying anything students don't understand. Next, play the audio for students to complete the exercise, then give them time to check their answers in pairs. Give feedback as a class.

1.5 **C** Give students time to read the questions and answer options before playing the audio again for them to complete the exercise. Ask them to compare answers with a partner before giving feedback as a class. Encourage students to justify their answers with examples from the interview, referring to the audio script below if necessary.

D Put students into groups to discuss the questions.

VOCABULARY

1.6 **A** Give students time to complete the sentences alone, before playing the audio for them to check their answers. Give feedback as a class, giving further examples of each adjective if necessary and practicing good pronunciation.

AUDIO SCRIPT

1.5

Listening, Exercise B
P = Presenter R = Richard Bonnel

P: Now, we all know that friends are important, but according to our next guest, the type of friends we choose can have a dramatic impact on how successful we are. Here to explain why, is the psychologist Richard Bonnel. Richard, welcome to the show.

R: Thanks for having me.

P: So Richard, we all have hundreds of friends these days …

R: Well, we all know hundreds of people on Facebook, Twitter and other social media sites but how many are actually our friends is debatable. [Ex C Q1] Realistically, research tells us that we can't maintain a friendship group of more than 50 people and, you know, in fact it's probably much smaller if we consider just the people we regularly communicate with.

P: So what type of friends are important to have in your life?

R: Well, our research shows that very successful people surround themselves with six different types of friends. Not six friends but six types. [Ex B] We all need a loyal best friend. Someone who will support us no matter what happens. Someone who knows everything about you. They know all of your secrets but they still love you anyway.

P: I definitely have one of those. There's no way I'd ever let them on this show. They have far too many stories about me!

R: You probably don't need to worry. You can trust them to keep any embarrassing secrets private! Well, they might let one or two things out just for fun … [Ex B] The next type is really important to make your life more interesting. This person is an open-minded adventurer. They always force us into new and different situations. They challenge us. They push us to try new things. They are easy-going and open to new ideas, cultures and activities. [Ex C Q2] None of these things stress them out. Basically, they break us out of our normal routine.

P: I actually think I'm that friend to a lot of people. I'm always taking people to new places and making them do new things.

R: I don't doubt it. These people, they're usually great with people, self-confident and like the attention of others.

P: Are you saying I'm arrogant?

R: No, these people aren't arrogant. They just have a lot of self-belief. Other people probably love it because they are much more cautious than you. You add a little spice to their life! [Ex B] Another type of friend that people need, is one they probably don't always like or want. That's someone who is really honest even when it upsets you.

P: How is that useful?

R: [Ex C Q3] Well, this person will tell you when your hair looks awful or your clothes look terrible. They'll tell you when you're being self-centered and should think about others more. Or they'll tell you you are being stubborn and need to be more flexible. It's tough to hear, but it's usually true.

P: I do have a friend like that. She's very down-to-earth. She just does everything in this very sensible, practical way. I guess she is a helpful person to have around!

R: Right, exactly. Equally, it's important to not just surround ourselves with like-minded people. [Ex B] We should have some friends who are the complete opposite of us.

P: Why would you want to do that? Surely, you'd just argue?

R: Maybe, but it opens your mind to different ways of seeing the world. It makes you a more accepting person.

P: True. So, are there any other types of people we should surround ourselves with?

R: Well, the last two are not really types of people but friends we should try to make because of our circumstances. [Ex C Q4] We all move around much more these days and typically have no idea who our neighbors are, but they are important to know. [Ex B] Dependable neighbors can help in difficult situations and make you feel happier about where you live.

P: That is so true. I'm really happy where I live now and it's mainly because of the people living near me.

R: How about work? Are you happy at work?

P: Well, I think I'm pretty lucky. I actually love my job.

R: [Ex C Q5] It's vital that you do. Successful people always work with people they like. Most people spend at least 50% of their waking hours at work. On top of that, people commute to work, work overtime, and think about work. It can take over your life. Imagine feeling isolated at work. No one to talk to. [Ex B] Having no witty people to have a laugh with would make work very boring. A depressing thought, isn't it?

P: When you put it like that, I think I might need to find a new job!

B Give students time to complete the sentences alone before checking their answers with a partner. Remind them to use the examples in Exercise A to help. Give feedback as a class.

C Direct students to the **Vocabulary Hub** (see TB121). Use the **Vocabulary Worksheet** on page W4 for extra practice.

D–E Give students time to complete the quiz alone, then put them into pairs to describe each other's personalities. Model the activity with a stronger student if necessary. If you have time, bring the class back together and nominate pairs to explain their reaction to their partner's description.

PRONUNCIATION

1.7 A Explain that in natural, spoken English, words can frequently sound like they are joined together. If necessary, give an example of a sentence said in a slow, deliberate manner and the same sentence said more naturally as an example. Then, play the audio for students to complete the exercise. Give feedback as a class, but don't explain why the sounds are linked at this stage.

B Put students into pairs to discuss the questions, then give feedback as a class. Practice natural pronunciation of the example in Exercise A and provide other examples to practice if necessary.

1.8 C Give students time to make predictions before playing the audio for them to check. Play the recording again for students to repeat the sentences.

VOCABULARY

Write the following sentence on the board, setting *ambitious* in a different color – *To be successful in business, you need to be really ambitious.* Next, elicit what part of speech *ambitious* is (*an adjective*) and how to change it into a noun (adding *-ion*). Then, elicit an example sentence that has the same meaning as the first, using a noun (e.g. *You need to have a lot of ambition to succeed in business*), setting the suffix in a different color. Explain that *-ion* is an example of a suffix and that being able to manipulate words in this way will help improve your vocabulary. Now, give students time to complete the sentences alone, before checking their answers in pairs. Give feedback as a class, eliciting further examples of nouns that take each suffix. Use the **Vocabulary Worksheet** on page W5 for extra practice.

SPEAKING HUB

A–D Give some examples of people that have had a big influence on your life, briefly explaining why they are important to you. Then, give students time to make their own lists. Next, ask students to focus on one of the people on their lists and to use the questions to help them write notes. Monitor and help with new vocabulary as necessary. Now put students into pairs to discuss their ideas. Finally, bring the class back together to discuss similarities between the people that have influenced them, adding any useful emergent language to the board.

TEACHING IDEA by David Seymour and Maria Popova

Someone who …

Use this activity to review and build on personality adjectives.

Listen to this list of 20 descriptions of people. For each one, yell out an adjective that describes the person, then write down the number and name of someone you know who is like that. Don't write the adjective.

Someone who …

1 keeps losing things (careless, forgetful, absent-minded)
2 always drops/breaks things (clumsy)
3 thinks bad things will happen (pessimistic, negative)
4 goes to a lot of parties (outgoing, sociable, gregarious)
5 keeps to himself (introverted, unsociable, withdrawn, closed)
6 never smiles (moody, grumpy, bad-tempered, miserable)
7 makes you yawn (boring, uninteresting, dull)
8 likes making things (creative, artistic)
9 keeps things clean (neat, organized, efficient)
10 never thinks about others' feelings (uncaring, insensitive, selfish)
11 always arrives late for meetings, etc (unpunctual, unreliable)
12 makes you laugh all the time (funny, humorous, silly)
13 thinks good things will happen (optimistic, positive)
14 hurts people or animals (cruel, sadistic, mean)
15 doesn't like talking about her achievements (modest, unassuming)
16 is easy to get along with (friendly, affable, easy-going)
17 brags about himself a lot (conceited, arrogant, big-headed)
18 never changes her mind even when she knows she's wrong (stubborn, obstinate)
19 never gives presents (mean, tight-fisted)
20 always cries at weddings, in the movie theater, etc (emotional, sentimental, hysterical)

METHODOLOGY HUB by Adrian Underhill

Liaison

Liaison refers to the smooth linking or joining together of words in connected speech. Of course two words can have a silence between them, but liaison is concerned with the way sounds are fused together at word boundaries.

Say each of the following phrases and notice how you join the words together:

in English   my uncle   far away   go away

Now say each one without joining two words together. Notice the difference.

Fully liaised speech is characterized by a seamless, continuous quality, where final consonants are linked to following initial vowel sounds and initial consonants to preceding final vowel sounds. It is also an essential ingredient of both rhythm and intonation.

Poorly linked speech is typically rather jerky, perhaps staccato, and the resulting lack of flow makes it more difficult for the speaker to take advantage of the stress system and so for the listener to focus on the content of the message.

METHODOLOGY HUB by Scott Thornbury

Affixation

In English, there are two main word-formation processes: affixation and compounding. Affixation is the process of adding affixes (either prefixes or suffixes) to the root word. It is an extremely productive way of forming new words. Affixes may be grammatical, as are *-ing*, *-ed*, *-s* in *caring*, *cared* and *cares*, in which case they are known as inflections. Inflections belong to the same word class. Or affixes may be lexical, as in *careful*, *uncaring*, *carefree*, *carelessness*. Such words – usually belonging to a different word class – are called derivations. The following relatively recent words were formed by affixation (the affixes are underlined): *<u>cyber</u>crime*, *<u>auto</u>correct*, *<u>super</u>bug* and *share<u>ware</u>*.

B Choose the correct adjectives to complete the sentences.

1 My neighbor is really *easy-going* / *open-minded*. He's always willing to consider new ideas or opinions.

2 In a difficult situation, she stays calm. She's so *loyal* / *down-to-earth* and knows exactly what to do.

3 She never gets stressed. She's so *easy-going* / *witty*.

4 I find her really *arrogant* / *self-centered*. It's like she thinks she is better than everyone.

5 Even when I've done stupid things, she has always been *loyal* / *down-to-earth* and supported me.

6 There's no point arguing with him. He's just so *stubborn* / *arrogant* and won't change his mind.

7 I think she's really *easy-going* / *witty* actually. She's always making relevant jokes.

8 Stop being so *self-centered* / *stubborn*. Try to think about other people for once!

C Go to the Vocabulary Hub on page 143.

D Complete the personality quiz.

What kind of person are you?

Rate yourself on a scale of 1–5.
1 = Strongly disagree 5 = Strongly agree

You find it easy to stay focused even when you are under pressure.	1 2 3 4 5
You usually start conversations.	1 2 3 4 5
You rarely do something just out of curiosity.	1 2 3 4 5
You feel more important than other people.	1 2 3 4 5
Getting what you want is more important than keeping others happy.	1 2 3 4 5
Making other people laugh is important to you.	1 2 3 4 5
You try to win arguments even when you might be wrong.	1 2 3 4 5
You don't believe in hiding your feelings to keep people happy.	1 2 3 4 5

E SPEAK Work in pairs. Describe your partner's personality using their answers to the quiz in Exercise D. Do you agree with their description of you?

PRONUNCIATION

Connected speech: final consonant and initial vowel

1.7 **A** Listen to the sentence and draw (‿) between any words that link together.

Most people spend‿at least 50 percent‿of their waking hours‿at work.

B Work in pairs. Look at the example in Exercise A and discuss the questions.

1 Does the first word end in a consonant or a vowel sound?
a consonant sound

2 What sound does the next word begin with?
a vowel sound

1.8 **C** Read the sentences. Draw (‿) to predict which words are connected. Then listen and check.

1 They‿are open-minded‿and friendly.

2 She achieved‿a lot despite having‿a difficult childhood.

3 He built‿a successful business‿at‿a young‿age.

4 We spent‿a lot‿of‿our time together going for walks‿in the country.

5 We hung‿out‿at the beach, went‿out‿at night‿and played games‿online together.

VOCABULARY

Noun suffixes

We use the following suffixes to change adjectives to nouns:
-ion (e.g. *ambitious* > *ambition*)
-ity/-ty (e.g. *flexible* > *flexibility*)
-ence (e.g. *different* > *difference*)
-ness (e.g. *stubborn* > *stubbornness*)
-ism (e.g. *pessimistic* > *pessimism*)

Complete the sentences with the noun form of the adjectives in parentheses. Use the information in the box to help you.

1 I think what I value most in a friend is ___loyalty___ (*loyal*).

2 ___Optimism___ (*optimistic*) is a great quality for a close friend to have.

3 Her ___determination___ (*determined*) to succeed had a great influence on me.

4 Frankly, I was amazed by his ___arrogance___ (*arrogant*).

5 She took ___responsibility___ (*responsible*) for her actions.

6 He always gave me the ___confidence___ (*confident*) to try new things.

SPEAKING HUB

A PREPARE Make a list of people that have had a big influence on you (e.g. a teacher, your best friend, a grandparent, etc).

B PLAN Choose one of the people in Exercise A to tell your partner about. Use the following questions to write notes:

1 What was their personality like?

2 Why did they have such an influence on you?

3 What things did you do together?

C SPEAK Work in pairs. Use your notes from Exercise B to talk about the person you chose. Ask follow-up questions to find out more about them.

D DISCUSS As a class, discuss the types of people that influenced you. What personality traits do they share?

- Compare, contrast and summarize short biographies
- Talk about people that have influenced you

Café Hub

1.3 Keeping it in the family

A– idioms: family S– developing and introducing new topics

The Special Olympics

COMPREHENSION

A Work in pairs. Successful athletes are usually not the only person in their family to compete at the highest level. Why do you think this is?

B Watch a news report about a competitor at the Special Olympics. The report focuses on this person because …

1 he is competing at the highest level in his sport.
(2) his great grandfather was also a successful athlete.
3 he is competing in multiple events.

C Watch again. Complete the sentences with no more than three words from the report.

1 Daniel Wolff won the ___four hundred / 400 meters___ event at the Special Olympics in 2015.
2 His great grandfather won a ___gold medal___ at the Berlin Olympics in 1936.
3 Daniel's grandfather describes his achievement as '___something really special / special___
4 This year's Special Olympics has drawn crowds of ___half a million / 500,000___ people.
5 ___Thirteen / 13___ people in Daniel's family have come to watch him compete.

D Are these sentences true (T) or false (F)? Correct the false sentences. Then watch the report again to check.

1 Daniel's grandfather believes that sporting ability is genetic. (T) / F
2 Daniel was confident before the event that he would win. He said he was feeling amazed and a bit surprised that he had won. T / (F)
3 The reporter believes Daniel had a good level of support at the event. (T) / F
4 His father didn't think it was fair to leave his children at home. (T) / F
5 The 400 meters is the only event Daniel is taking part in. The reporter says Daniel is going 'for more gold later in the week'. T / (F)

AUTHENTIC ENGLISH

A Work in pairs. Read the extract from the report. What do you think the expression in bold means?

Daniel Wolff crosses the line to win the 400 meters and shows that athletic success really can **run in the family**.
If an ability, quality, disease, etc runs in the family, many family members have it.

B Read the information in the box and check your answer to Exercise A. Why is this idiom appropriate for the report? This expression is appropriate as the report focuses on sporting ability that runs in the Wolff family.

Idioms: family

Idioms are a group of words whose meaning is different from the meaning of the individual words. Since this can make them difficult to remember, one way to record new idioms is to group them by topic. Some common idioms in English are connected to the topic of family:

*You have to choose your brother. Remember – **blood is thicker than water**!* (= used to say that family relationships are always more important than any others)

*Athletic ability **runs in the family** – both he and his father played for their country.* (= if an ability, quality, disease, etc runs in the family, many family members have it)

C Read the sentences (1–3) and try to guess the meaning of the idioms in bold.

1 His grandfather was also a famous author – writing must **be in the blood**. If an ability, skill, quality, etc is in your blood, it is natural for you because it already exists in your family.
2 She **followed in her** mother's **footsteps** and trained to become a doctor. To do the same thing as someone else did in the past (especially someone in your family).
3 He **is the spitting image of** his father at that age. To look extremely similar to someone.

D Work in pairs. Discuss the questions.

1 Do you think any of your skills, abilities, etc are in your blood?
2 Have you followed in the footsteps of anyone in your family?
3 Have you ever been told you are the spitting image of someone?

Family matters

SAM MALCOLM AMANDA HARRY EMILY

A Work in pairs. What job do you have now or want to have in the future? What makes you particularly suitable for it?

B Watch the video. What runs in Harry's family? What runs in Sam's family? Untidiness/messiness runs in Harry's family; working in catering runs in Sam's family.

SPEAKING SKILL

A Watch the video again and complete the extracts from the conversation.

Sam: And I must remember to get the paper towels for the toilets. [1] Speaking of which, did the hand soap arrive in the delivery?

Sam: I'm just so excited about getting this new café off the ground – I don't want to forget anything. Anyway, how are you getting on?

Sam: Oh really? You're not going to blame your upbringing are you?

Harry: [2] Strange you should mention that because untidiness really does run in my family. I mean, you should have seen the state of our house when I was growing up!

Sam: [3] Talking of things that run in the family, I actually saw this really heartwarming story on the news …

B Work in pairs. Discuss the questions. Then read the information in the box to check your answers.

1 What is the function of the phrases you wrote in Exercise A? The phrases are used to introduce an idea related or relevant to what's just been said.

2 What is different about *anyway*? It introduces a completely new and unrelated topic.

Developing and introducing new topics

Developing topics

During a conversation, a speaker may say something that reminds us of relevant information or a related topic. To introduce our idea, we can use the following expressions:

Speaking/Talking of which …, Talking of [topic] …, Actually, that reminds me of …, Strange you should mention that (because) …

Introducing new topics

We use *anyway* to introduce a completely unrelated topic.

Anyway, I think we should …

C Work in pairs. Student A – Talk about one of the topics below. Student B – Listen and either develop or change the topic. Then swap roles.

- a movie that you saw recently
- a news item you read recently
- a restaurant you went to recently
- an interesting thing that happened to you recently
- a trip you went on recently
- an athletic event you saw recently

SPEAKING HUB

A PREPARE Work in pairs. Brainstorm a list of factors that affect our abilities and skills.

B PLAN Work in two groups. You are going to debate the following:

Practice has no effect on ability – we inherit our abilities from our parents.

Group A – You agree with the idea above.

Group B – You disagree with the idea above.

Plan your arguments. Think about how to support your position, as well as what the other group might say.

C SPEAK Hold your debate.

D REFLECT Which group put forth the more persuasive argument? Which side do you agree with?

Give your opinion on the role of inherited ability in success

➤ Turn to page 154 to learn how to write a formal letter asking for information.

The Special Olympics

LEAD-IN

With books closed, tell the class about a member of your family that you are similar to. Then, put students into pairs to do the same. Monitor, helping with new vocabulary as necessary. Give feedback as a class, nominating individual students to share one or two things they have learned about their partner.

COMPREHENSION

A Ask students if they can think of any famous sporting/athletic families (e.g. *the Andretti family*, *the Williams sisters*, etc). Next, put students into pairs to discuss the question. Monitor and assist as necessary, then open the discussion up to the class.

B ▶ Tell students they are going to watch a news report about the Special Olympics and elicit what it is (*a multi-sport event for athletes with intellectual disabilities*, e.g. *autism*, *Down's syndrome*, etc). Then, play the video for students to complete the exercise. Ask them to briefly check their answers in pairs before giving feedback as a class.

C ▶ Review the instructions for this type of exercise (e.g. students can only use a maximum of three words, these must come from the video itself, etc), before playing the video again for students to complete the sentences. Give them time to check their answers with a partner before giving feedback as a class.

D ▶ Play the video one last time, giving students time to correct the false sentences once it's finished. Ask them to check their answers in pairs, then give feedback as a class.

AUTHENTIC ENGLISH

A–B Put students into pairs to discuss the question before reading the box to check their answers. In feedback, clarify any misunderstanding and encourage students to share similar idioms from their own languages.

C Give students time to guess the meanings of the idioms alone before discussing their ideas with a partner. Give feedback as a class, giving further explanations and examples as necessary.

D Put students into pairs to discuss the questions. Monitor and encourage them to extend their discussions by asking follow-up questions. If you have time, nominate individual students to explain what they found out about their partners to the class.

Family matters

A Explain to the class why you chose to go into teaching and what makes you suitable for the job. Then, put students into pairs to do the same for their jobs (or those they would like to have). Monitor and help with new vocabulary as necessary.

B ▶ Tell students they are going to watch the first episode of a video series about the characters at the top of the page. Then, play the video for students to answer the questions. Give feedback as a class, encouraging students to give examples from the conversation to justify their answers. You can find the video script for *Family matters* on the Teacher's Resource Center.

SPEAKING SKILL

A ▶ Play the video again for students to complete the extracts. Give them time to check their answers with a partner, before giving feedback as a class. Don't explain the function of the phrases at this point.

B Put students into pairs to discuss the question, then read the box to check their answers. Give feedback as a class.

C Model the activity with a strong student. Then, put students into pairs to do the same. Monitor, focusing on how accurately students use the phrases. Give feedback, highlighting any common errors.

SPEAKING HUB

A Write the following question as the title of a spider diagram on the board – *What affects our abilities and skills?* Then, elicit one or two ideas and add them to the spider diagram. Next, give students time to note down other factors.

B Tell the class that they are going to have a debate and read the statement. Then put students into A/B groups. Tell the As to write notes about why they agree with the statement and Bs to write notes about why they disagree.

C Set a time limit for students to discuss their arguments for and against the statement. Monitor, encouraging debate by asking students to explain why they agree or disagree with each other.

D As a class, discuss which group they thought was the most persuasive and why. Encourage students to share their own opinions on the subject as they discuss the debate. Finish the activity with a class vote on which side won the argument.

▶ VIDEO SCRIPT

The Special Olympics
P = Presenter Dg = Daniel's grandfather
Df = Daniel's father D = Daniel
PAA = PA Announcement

Ex C Q1 **P:** Daniel Wolff crosses the line to win the 400 meters and shows that athletic success really can 'run in the family'.

Ex C Q2 **Dg:** My father won a gold medal in Berlin and, I've seen his race many times on film, and this was, just, you know, er, altogether very thrilling.
Ex D Q1 / Ex C Q3 It's obviously the genes have come through. And with his autism it's great that he can achieve something really special, you know?

PAA: [*Daniel John Wolff!*]

Df: How are you feeling, Daniel?

Ex D Q2 **D:** Amazed. And a bit surprised for winning.

Ex C Q4 **P:** Half a million spectators are attending events at the Special Olympics venues like here, where the
Ex D Q3 athletics is being held, and Daniel hasn't been
Ex C Q5 short of support either. No fewer than 13 family members were cheering him on.

Df: It was only going to be me and my wife originally,
Ex D Q4 er, but, er, we thought, 'We can't leave the kids at home and … and then two of the aunties and one of the uncles and my mum and dad, a cousin and his wife and kids from Seattle came down as well.

Dg: Well done, Daniel! I nearly had a heart attack; it was so exciting.

P: They're the best family you could … you could ask for?

D: Yeah. The most helpful and supportive.

Ex D Q5 **P:** And Daniel will have all that support behind him when he goes for more gold later in the week. Stuart Pollitt, BBC London News, Los Angeles.

1 Writing

Write a formal letter asking for information

W structuring formal letters

A Read the letter and answer the questions.

1. What is the purpose of the letter? To find out more information about a French language club.
2. Who will read it? The organizer of the club.
3. Why does the writer use a formal register? Because they are writing to someone they don't know.

B Match the parts of the letter (1–5) with their function (a–e).

- **a** expected response 4
- **b** reason for writing 2
- **c** sign-off 5
- **d** salutation or greeting 1
- **e** information required 3

To: French language club
From: John

[1]Dear Sir / Madam,

[2]I am writing to inquire about the French language club you organize to find out whether the club is suitable for me or not.

[3]First, I was wondering if you could tell me how many members there are. Also, could you tell me when you meet and how often? I want to make sure it's possible for me to attend regularly. Could you also tell me how much it costs? Is there a fee to join and then a weekly fee to pay? Lastly, would it be possible to tell me the approximate level of the group members and whether we have any formal lessons as well?

[4]I would be grateful if you could let me know by email before the next meeting. Hopefully, I will be able to join before then. Thanks in advance for your help.

[5]Kind regards,
John

C Complete the box with sentences from the letter.

Structuring formal letters

Saying why you're writing
I am writing to apply for … *I am writing to inquire about joining*
[1] *the French language club you organize.*

Organizing information
Could you let me know …?
[2] *I was wondering whether you could tell me …*

Asking for a response
If you could …
[3] *I would be grateful if you could …*

Sign-off
Yours truly …
[4] *Kind regards*

WRITING

A PREPARE Read the task below and write notes about who you are writing to, what you need to know and what action you expect them to take.

> You are interested in joining the hiking club in your area. Write a letter of inquiry and find out:
> - how many members there are in the club
> - how often they organize walks and where they go
> - ask whether there are any fees involved in joining
> - what specialist equipment you need.

B PLAN Organize your notes into an appropriate structure for a letter of inquiry.

C WRITE Write your letter of inquiry. Use your plan to help you.

D EDIT Work in pairs. Edit your partner's essay. Check:

- spelling and punctuation
- all information in the task has been covered
- an appropriate structure/tone has been used

154 WRITING

Refer students to this letter as a model for the writing task.

Refer students to this checklist when editing their partner's work.

LEAD-IN

With books closed, write *kind regards, bye, best wishes, see ya, catch you later, I hope to hear from you soon* on the board and elicit what they have in common (*ways of saying goodbye*) and how they are different (*level of formality*). Ask students to work with a partner to put the phrases into two groups: formal or informal writing, then try to add three more phrases to each list. Give feedback as a class.

WRITING

A Give students time to read the letter and answer the questions. Give feedback as a class.

B Ask students to complete the exercise alone, before checking with a partner. Give feedback as a class.

C Read the skills box as a class, giving further explanation and examples as necessary. Then, give students time to complete the exercise alone before giving feedback as a class.

WRITING TASK

A Read the task as a class and give students time to write notes about what they will include in their letters.

B Give students time to organize their notes into a plan. Monitor and help with structure as necessary.

C Tell students to write their letters. Monitor, providing support with structure and vocabulary as necessary.

D Put students into pairs to edit each other's work. Encourage students to give each other feedback by sharing one aspect of the letter they were particularly impressed by and one element that could be improved. Students can then edit and rewrite their letters in class or for homework.

Unit 1 Review

VOCABULARY

A Choose the correct options (a, b or c) to complete the sentences.

1 They were ___ to arrive at the airport just in time for their flight.
   (a) relieved   b devastated   c furious
2 I was completely ___ when we lost the World Cup final on penalties.
   a thrilled   b relieved   (c) devastated
3 Louis was ___ to find out his daughter had been offered a place at Yale University.
   a disgusted   (b) thrilled   c horrified
4 I'm pretty ___ by your lack of enthusiasm.
   (a) frustrated   b impressed   c relieved
5 Everyone sat in ___ silence as I broke the bad news.
   a relieved   b disgusted   (c) stunned

B Complete the sentences with the adjectives in the box.

easy-going   loyal   optimistic   sensitive   stubborn   witty

1 Why does he have to be so ___optimistic___ all the time? Not everything in life is good!
2 This girl I met at the party was so ___witty___. I was laughing all night!
3 I don't think I've ever seen him get stressed or upset. He's so ___easy-going___.
4 The team has a lot of ___loyal___ fans. They're still buying tickets – even at $120 a game!
5 Stop being so ___stubborn___ and just admit that you're wrong!
6 How can we break the news to her? She's such a ___sensitive___ person.

C Complete the text with the correct form of the words in parentheses.

Perfectionism

Do you find it hard to live up to your own [1] ___expectations___ (*expect*)? Do you experience [2] ___frustration___ (*frustrate*) when you work with lazy people? If so, you might be a perfectionist. The positive thing about working with a perfectionist is their [3] ___reliability___ (*reliable*), [4] ___dedication___ (*dedicate*) and [5] ___professionalism___ (*professional*). However, if you are a perfectionist, don't assume everyone will want to work with you because of these characteristics. Your constant criticism of other people can affect their [6] ___confidence___ (*confident*). Your [7] ___stubbornness___ (*stubborn*) and inability to admit you might be wrong are not attractive either. You probably won't be worried about that, though, because you're likely to be convinced of your own [8] ___superiority___ (*superior*).

GRAMMAR

A Choose the correct options to complete the sentences.

1 Could you tell me *where is the reception desk* / *where the reception desk is*, please?
2 So why *didn't you* / *you didn't* like the movie?
3 Really? So, *what was happening* / *what happened* then?
4 Who *Javier is meeting* / *is Javier meeting*?
5 Which candidate *are you going to vote for* / *are you going to vote*?
6 Why *you don't come* / *don't you come* out this evening?
7 *You haven't* / *Haven't you* finished the homework yet?
8 Do you mind telling me *how old you are* / *how old are you*?
9 Can I ask what you think *you are doing* / *are you doing?*
10 Why *you are so* / *are you so* worried about it?

B Complete the conversations with the correct form of the words in parentheses.

1 **A:** ___Have you ever been___ (*you / ever / be*) to Japan?
B: Yes, I actually ___taught___ (*teach*) English in Tokyo for three years after college.

2 **A:** ___Do you know___ (*you / know*) Yara?
B: Yes, I ___'ve/have known___ (*know*) her since college.

3 **A:** Why ___aren't/weren't you___ (*be / you*) at work today? I thought you had an important meeting.
B: I ___'ve/have had___ (have) a tough week, so I decided to take a day off.

4 **A:** What ___were you doing___ (*you / do*) when you heard the news?
B: I ___was just putting___ (*just / put*) Mia to bed when my brother called.

5 **A:** ___Have you found___ (*you / find*) a new job yet?
B: Maybe. I actually ___had___ (*have*) an interview last week.

6 **A:** Where ___were you going___ (*you / go*) when you had the accident?
B: I ___was driving___ (*drive*) to work.

7 **A:** Oh no! My yoga class ___starts___ (*start*) in five minutes and I can't find my mat!
B: Calm down. Try to think. Where ___did you last see___ (*you / last / see*) it?

8 **A:** I kept getting lost when I ___went___ (go) to Berlin last week.
B: It's difficult to learn your way around a place you ___'ve/have never been___ (*never / go*) to before.

Underwater view of a boy jumping into a swimming pool.

Lifestyle (n) the way in which a person or group of people lives and works (e.g. the type of food you eat, what you like doing in your free time, etc)
Other key words: plunge (v) to fall or move down very quickly; seize (v) to take something with force
Collocations and idioms: *(un)healthy* lifestyle, *a* lifestyle *choice*, *a change in* lifestyle

Goethe is suggesting that the most interesting way to live your life is to embrace new experiences, not be afraid to try new things.

Johann Wolfgang von Goethe (1749–1832) was a German writer and statesman. His works included novels, poetry, memoirs and scientific essays. His early success led him to become a notable person in the court of the Duke of Saxe-Weimar, where his work contributed to many reforms.

OBJECTIVES

- talk about health and lifestyle choices
- plan and conduct a lifestyle survey
- conduct an interview about lifestyle changes
- debate the impact of smartphones
- give your opinion on food choices
- write an article giving advice

Work with a partner. Discuss the questions.

1 Read the quote. What do you think Goethe means? Do you agree with him? Why/Why not?
2 Do you dive into the unknown or do you play it safe?
3 What is most important to you in life?

LIFESTYLES 13

OBJECTIVES

Read the unit objectives to the class.

UNIT OPENER QUESTIONS

1 Read the quote as a class, clarifying the meaning of *plunge* and *seize* if necessary. Then, put students into pairs to discuss the question. Monitor, encouraging students to explain their reasoning. Open the discussion up to the class, writing any useful emergent vocabulary on the board.

2 Elicit the meaning of *dive into the unknown* (*willingly do something you have no experience or understanding of*) and *play it safe* (*not take any risks*). Then, put students into pairs to discuss the question. Monitor and help with any new or unfamiliar vocabulary. Bring the class back together, nominating one or two students to share the main points from their discussions.

3 Give one or two examples of things that are important to you and why. Then, put students back into pairs to do the same. Monitor and help with grammar and vocabulary as necessary. Open up the discussion to the class, encouraging students to comment on each other's ideas.

WORKSHEETS

Lesson 2.1 A full life

Vocabulary: Health and fitness (W6)

Grammar: Present perfect and present perfect progressive (W7)

Lesson 2.2 Change

Grammar: *used to, would, get used to, be used to* (W8)

Vocabulary: Adverbs of stance (W9)

Vocabulary: Adverb + adjective collocations (W10)

2.1 A full life

- Talk about health and lifestyle choices
- Plan and conduct a lifestyle survey

V – health and fitness
G – present perfect and present perfect progressive
L – listening for reasons
P – connected speech: present perfect progressive

VOCABULARY
Health and fitness

A SPEAK Work in pairs. Brainstorm a list of things that have positive or negative effects on our health.

B Complete the definitions (a–f) with the words in bold.

1 A lack of healthy lunch options has led to worrying levels of childhood **obesity**.
2 Drinking a lot of coffee can cause **anxiety** and negatively affect sleep.
3 Fatty foods like butter and cheese can increase levels of **cholesterol**.
4 She suffered from **depression** after losing her job.
5 There are around 500 **calories** in an average slice of chocolate cake.
6 My husband's been under a lot of **stress** at work recently.

a ___calorie___ (n) a unit for measuring how much energy you get from food
b ___cholesterol___ (n) a type of fat in the blood that can cause heart disease if you have too much
c ___obesity___ (n) a condition in which someone is too fat in a way that is dangerous for their health
d ___depression___ (n) a medical condition in which a person is so unhappy they cannot live a normal life
e ___stress___ (n) pressure or worry caused by problems in everyday life
f ___anxiety___ (n) the feeling of being very worried that something bad is going to happen

C Complete the sentences with words from Exercise B.

1 I suffer a lot from ___depression___ in the winter. I'm much more positive in the summer months.
2 Keeping your diet low in fatty foods can help lower ___cholesterol___.
3 Nuts have more ___calories___ in them than you might think.
4 ___Obesity___ is a huge problem in my country. Almost a quarter of the population is dangerously overweight.
5 ___Anxiety___ is one of my biggest issues. I worry so much about everything.
6 I worry about my ___stress___ levels. I'm under too much pressure at work.

D Go to the **Vocabulary Hub** on **page 143**.

E SPEAK Work in pairs. What effects do the following have on our health?

- junk food
- smoking
- lack of exercise
- poor work–life balance

READING

A PREDICT Work in pairs. Look at the pictures (1–6) and the corresponding sub-headings in the article. Discuss how you think each of these things might help people to live longer.

B SCAN Read *Six ways to live longer* and check your predictions from Exercise A.

C READ FOR DETAIL Read the article again and answer the questions. Underline the parts of the text that give you the answers.

1 Why might owning a pet be good for your physical health?
2 What is different about the Japanese diet?
3 Why do people who think about details tend to live longer?
4 What charitable activity can help you live longer?
5 What does singing reduce?
6 What don't negative people pay attention to?

D SPEAK Work in pairs. Discuss the questions.

1 Why do you think owning a dog might reduce the risk of heart disease?
2 Why do you think 'smaller plates' have a positive effect on Japanese health?
3 Which of the suggested lifestyle changes in the text would you be happy to make? Why?
4 What other changes could you make to improve your overall health?

1

LEAD-IN

Explain to students what you do to stay healthy (e.g. *go to the gym*, *eat a balanced diet*, etc) and what more you think could do. Then, put students into groups to do the same. Monitor, helping with any new or useful vocabulary. Give feedback as a class, asking each group to explain which of them they think is the healthiest and which is the most unhealthy and why. Add any useful emergent vocabulary to the board.

VOCABULARY

A Elicit the word *smoking* (possibly by miming or showing the class a picture) and whether it is good or bad for your health (*bad*). Write the word *healthy* as the title of one spider diagram on the board, *unhealthy* as the title of another and add *smoking* to the unhealthy side. Elicit one or two more ideas for each spider diagram, before putting students into pairs to discuss more ideas. Monitor, helping with any new or unfamiliar vocabulary. Give feedback as a class, building up the spider diagrams on the board.

B Read the first sentence together and elicit the meaning of *obesity* using the clues like *a lack of healthy lunch options* and *worrying* to help. Then, elicit the matching definition (*c*). Next, give students time to complete the remaining definitions alone before checking their answers with a partner. Give feedback as a class, practicing good pronunciation (especially for words like *anxiety* that students may struggle with). You could also take this opportunity to elicit any collocations the students know (e.g. *cause stress, suffer from depression/anxiety*, etc).

C Give students time to complete the sentences alone before checking their answers with a partner. Remind weaker groups to use the definitions to help them. Give feedback as a class.

D Direct students to the **Vocabulary Hub** (see TB121).

E Put students into pairs to discuss the question. Monitor, reminding them to use the vocabulary from this section to help them explain their ideas. Bring the class back together to share their ideas and encourage students to explain their reasoning with examples. Use the **Vocabulary Worksheet** on page W6 for extra practice.

READING

A Direct students' attention to the title of the text, subheadings and pictures. Then, put them into pairs to discuss how each activity might increase their *life expectancy* (*the average time a person can expect to live*). Monitor, helping with any new or unfamiliar vocabulary, but don't confirm anything at this stage.

B Give students two to three minutes to scan the article to check their predictions. Then, put them into pairs to summarize what they have read. Once they have finished, take a few minutes to clarify the meaning of any new or unfamiliar vocabulary in the text (e.g. *optimist, pessimist*, etc), giving a definition and example for each and adding them to the board.

C Give students time to read through the questions before completing the exercise. Remind them to underline the sentences or passages in the text that give them the answers. Give them time to check their answers in pairs before giving feedback as a class. Encourage students to justify their answers with information from the text.

D Put students into pairs to discuss the questions. Monitor, asking follow-up questions to extend their discussions. Bring the class back together to discuss their ideas, adding any new or useful emergent vocabulary to the board.

Suggested answers

1 *Since they have to regularly walk dogs, dog owners get a lot of exercise and are therefore less at risk of heart disease.*

2 *This means they consume fewer calories overall.*

SPEAKING

A Put students into groups to discuss the questions. Monitor, helping with any new or unfamiliar vocabulary as necessary. Write a note about any interesting points that might help extend the class discussion in the next exercise.

B Give each group time to share their conclusions with the class. Encourage other groups to respond to each other's ideas and ask follow-up questions. Help keep the discussion going, by bringing up anything you noted down during the group discussions. Add any new or useful emergent vocabulary to the board.

METHODOLOGY HUB by Jim Scrivener

Dealing with lexis during reading or listening work

While students are mainly working on reading or listening skills, you are less likely to spend time on lexis, since this might clash with the reading, listening or other objectives. During such stages, you are likely only to:

- deal with an item when a student specifically asks about it
- give brief, to-the-point explanations or translations, rather than detailed presentations
- offer help quietly to the one or two students who ask, rather than to the whole class
- sometimes refuse help and tell students to do their best without knowing some items.

After the first phase of listening or reading work

Once the learners have become comfortable with the text, you can focus attention on lexical items in the text and how they are used. Here are some things that you could ask:

- Can you guess the meaning of this word from the meaning of the text around it?
- Find some words in the text that mean …
- Find some words in the text connected with the subject of …
- In line X, what does … mean?
- Find words and sort them into three separate groups under these headings: …
- Why does the writer use the word … here?
- Find words in the text that match this list of synonyms.
- What words come before/after the word … What other words collocate with this word?
- Can you remember any other phrases you know with this word in them?
- Can you find any multiword items (i.e. groups of words that go together / chunks)?
- What's the opposite of this word?
- How many different words does the writer use to describe the …?

AUDIO SCRIPT

2.1

Listening, Exercise C
P = Presenter

P: OK, let's move onto our next topic. Now, according to a recent survey conducted by The Institute for Social Research, the public, in general, is terrible at sticking to their New Year's resolutions. Apparently, 43% of people surveyed broke their resolution within the first month and 86% lasted less than a year. (Ex C) To test the accuracy of these results, we sent reporter Emily Hussan out onto the city streets to see just how many of you have managed to successfully give something up for the New Year.

2.2

Listening, Exercise D
P = Presenter S1 = Speaker 1 S2 = Speaker 2
S3 = Speaker 3 S4 = Speaker 4 S5 = Speaker 5

Speaker 1

P: Sorry, excuse me. We're interviewing people about whether they've managed to stick to their New Year's resolutions. Did you make any this year?

S1: Yeah, I did actually. Well, the whole family did really. (Ex E) My family and I felt that, well, we really didn't spend enough time together. You know, I found we hardly ever spoke to each other. We, uh, just sat around using our various devices in our own little worlds. (Ex D Q1) We've been living without smartphones and tablets for a couple of months now. I bought everyone really old-fashioned phones that you could only call and text on.

P: How did your children feel about that?

S1: Oh, well, the children went crazy! They were really mad at us!

P: Was it worth it?

S1: Definitely! It was really hard to cope with at first, but since then our lives have, well, changed for the better. We've been spending more time together as a family. And, um, I think we have a better relationship. And you know what? We are all sleeping better as a result of giving up technology.

Speaker 2

P: So, did you try to give anything up for the New Year?

Ex D Q2 **S2:** Yeah, I've actually given up coffee.

P: Oh, really? Why?

S2: Well, at the end of last year, I was really stressed at work and it had started to affect my sleep. I was only getting about two or three hours every night and this put me in a bad mood the next day. I thought about exercising more, but I've never really been a gym kind of person. Then I thought, 'Maybe I drink too much coffee'. I used to drink, like, four or five cups a day, but I cut this down to two, (Ex E) then stopped entirely to try and help me sleep better.

P: Good job! And did it work?

S2: Absolutely! I've been living without coffee for months now and get at least seven hours sleep every night. You should try it!

Speaker 3

P: Did you make any resolutions back in January?

S3: Well, I always knew that I didn't have a great diet but didn't realize just how bad sugar is for you. (Ex E) Obviously it can affect your weight, but it can also lead to heart disease, diabetes … even some forms of cancer. Anyway, I read this article that said you should only have a maximum of six teaspoons a day, and I was having way more than that.

P: What, like cakes and chocolate and stuff?

S3: Well yeah, but there's also a lot of sugar in things you wouldn't expect like yogurt, bread …

P: Bread?

Ex D Q3 **S3:** Yep! Most processed foods have added sugar. Anyway, I've managed to lose a little weight since cutting down and it's really made me think about my diet in general. I've only had three chocolate bars this month!

Speaker 4

P: So have you made any changes since the New Year?

S4: Not by choice! My car's in the garage right now, so I've been riding my bike to work for the past two weeks.

P: No … sorry, I meant resolutions.

Ex D Q4 **S4:** Oh, I see. Yes, well this is going to sound weird, but I've stopped using shampoo.

P: Um, really?

S4: Ha ha! Yep. I've only washed my hair twice this month. Pretty disgusting, huh?

P: It doesn't sound great to be honest.

S4: Well, my hair was pretty greasy at first and I'm sure I didn't smell too great either, but after a few weeks my body seemed to adjust.

P: So why did you decide to give it up? To help the environment?

S4: Uh, no. A lot of people say shampoo contains harmful chemicals, but I don't really think that's true. (Ex E) I actually gave it up because of a friend. She said that my hair was in really bad condition and suggested I try washing it less. I haven't used shampoo since December and my hair feels great. And I've saved a lot of money!

Speaker 5

P: Did you try to give anything up for the New Year?

S5: No, not really. I haven't given anything up for a long time.

P: When did you last give something up?

Ex D Q5; Ex E **S5:** Um, I'm not sure really. Well actually, I've been vegan for five years now. I wanted to reduce my carbon footprint, which I've managed to do.

P: Oh, really? How's that possible?

S5: Well, it takes so much more water to produce meat.

P: Really? Why?

S5: Well, obviously the animals we eat need to drink water and a surprisingly large amount of water is used to grow their food.

P: Oh, right. How do you feel personally?

S5: I feel healthier. I've lost weight and have more energy.

SIX WAYS TO LIVE LONGER

For the first time, people are expected to live a shorter life than their parents. Higher levels of obesity, a reliance on processed foods and more sedentary lifestyles are all taking their toll. If we want to live longer and healthier lives, there are many things we can do to slow the aging process and it doesn't just involve eating more healthily and going to the gym.

1 GET A PET

If exercise isn't your thing, then maybe you should consider getting a pet. Scientists in Sweden found that people who owned a dog had a much lower risk of various heart diseases and other illnesses. Dogs obviously need walking but having a pet is also good for many mental health issues such as lowering stress, fear and anxiety.

2 MOVE TO JAPAN

A dramatic solution would be to move to a new country. The Japanese lifestyle is arguably much healthier than in many other countries. First, they eat a lot less fat and lower their cholesterol by eating less dairy and swapping red meat for fish. They also make healthier food choices by eating seaweed, a lot of vegetables and by eating fewer **processed foods**. They use smaller plates and have a lower **calorie** intake than most other countries. Therefore, Japan has a very low obesity rate, with just under 4% of the population considered obese.

3 THINK OF THE DETAILS

People who think carefully about everything and pay a lot of attention to detail tend to live longer. Those who are careful with money, put everything in its right place and focus on details don't comfort eat as much as other people, and sleep better. People who carefully think things through deal better with stress and generally see the positives in most situations. They also have less risky lifestyles.

4 HELP OTHERS

In general, having strong social ties is a good predictor for living a longer and healthier life. People who take care of others are much more likely to make and keep friends throughout their life. Not only will you feel better if you help others but you will also live longer. A study in the US found that people who volunteer regularly in their lifetime live significantly longer than those who don't.

5 SING

People who regularly sing, especially in groups, tend to have a longer life expectancy. Researchers at Harvard and Yale universities in the US found that singing in a choir makes you happier and healthier than others. Singing can reduce stress levels and also helps to improve your immune system so that you are better able to fight illnesses.

6 DON'T COMPLAIN

Positive people live longer. If you're an optimist, then you are likely to live 12 years longer than a pessimist. Researchers at the US Mayo Clinic found that pessimists are more likely to get viral illnesses and they are much less likely to check their own physical health. Positive people also have a lower risk of suffering from heart disease and are better able to cope with stress.

SPEAKING

A DISCUSS Work in groups. Discuss the questions.

1 Why do you think so many people continue to do things that are widely known to be harmful to their health?

2 Do you think it is more important to focus on your physical or mental health? Why?

3 What can be done to reduce the risk of obesity, heart disease and other illnesses that are all associated with modern lifestyles?

4 What could be done to increase life expectancy in your country?

B PRESENT Present the main conclusions of your discussion to the rest of the class. Explain your reasoning.

LISTENING

A SPEAK Work in pairs. Look at the pictures (a–f) and discuss the questions.

1 Which of these things would you find difficult to give up? Why?
2 What are some of the potential benefits of giving these things up?
3 What other things do people typically try to give up?
4 Have you ever tried to give anything up? How successful were you?

B PREDICT People frequently decide to give things up at the start of a new year. How successful do you think they are? What percentage of people do you think break their New Year's resolution after:

a a month? b a year?

2.1 **C LISTEN FOR GIST** Listen to the first part of a radio show about lifestyle changes and check your predictions from Exercise B. a 43% b 86%

2.2 **D LISTEN FOR MAIN IDEAS** Listen to the next part of the radio show. Match the speakers (1–5) to the things that they have given up from Exercise A. There is one more option than you need.

Speaker 1 smartphones
Speaker 2 coffee
Speaker 3 sugar
Speaker 4 shampoo
Speaker 5 meat

2.2 **E LISTEN FOR REASONS** Listen to the interviews again. What reason(s) does each speaker give for their lifestyle change? Write notes. Use the information in the box to help you.

Listening for reasons

In interviews, speakers are frequently asked to explain their reasons for a particular action or belief. Reasons are usually signaled with:

- **Fixed words and expressions** (e.g. *because (of), since, that's why, due to the fact that, in order to, etc*). ***Since** my family still lives in the area, we decided to move back there.*
- **Infinitives of purpose**
I stopped eating red meat ***to help*** *reduce my blood pressure.*

However, speakers don't always explicitly state their reasons for something. Sometimes we need to guess the implied meaning from context:

I just remember reading a lot of articles about the impact smoking can have, not only on your health, but on the health of everyone around you. I quit last summer, and I feel much, much healthier.

(= We can guess from the context that the speaker stopped smoking because of the articles they read.)

1 To spend more time with her family.
2 To help him sleep better.
3 Because it can lead to negative health effects like heart disease, diabetes and some forms of cancer.
4 To improve the condition of his hair.
5 To reduce his carbon footprint and improve his health.

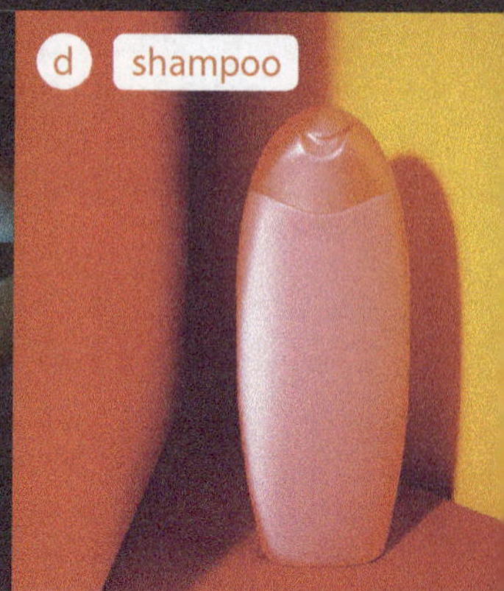

GRAMMAR

Present perfect and present perfect progressive

A **Work in pairs. Read the extracts from the radio show and answer the questions.**

1 Which sentence describes a finished action? Which describes an unfinished action?
  a Yeah, I've actually given up coffee. finished action
  b We've been spending more time together as a family. unfinished action
2 Which sentence focuses on the present effect and which focuses on the action itself?
  a I've managed to lose a little weight. present effect
  b We've been living without smartphones and tablets for six months now. action
3 Which sentence is a temporary action and which is permanent?
  a My car's in the garage right now, so I've been riding my bike to work for the past two weeks. temporary action
  b Well, this is going to sound weird, but I stopped using shampoo. permanent action
4 Which sentence focuses on frequency? Which focuses on duration?
  a I've only had three chocolate bars this month! frequency
  b I've been living without coffee for months now. duration

LISTENING

A Tell students about something you have given up in your lifetime and why you did it. Then, direct students' attention to the pictures and put them into pairs to discuss the questions. Monitor, helping with new vocabulary as necessary. Bring the class back together to share their ideas. Add any useful emergent vocabulary to the board.

2.1 **B–C** Elicit when people frequently decide to make changes in their lives (*at the start of a New Year*) and what this is called (*a New Year's resolution*), adding the latter to the board. Ask the class if they ever make New Year's resolutions and call on one or two students to share their examples. Then, ask whether people always keep their resolutions (*they don't*) and give students time to make predictions about the percentages of people that don't. Then, play the audio for students to check their answers. See the **Audio script** on TB15.

2.2 **D** Play the next part of the show for students to match the speakers to the things they have given up. Clarify there is one option that they don't need. Give them time to check their answers before giving feedback as a class.

2.2 **E** Write the following sentence stem on the board, adding a timeframe if relevant/interesting – *I gave up* …, and ask students to remember what you talked about at the start of the lesson. Next, add *because* … in a different color and elicit the reason you gave earlier. Put a bracket above this clause and elicit what it is (*a reason*). Next, elicit other ways to rewrite your sentence using other fixed expressions and an infinitive of purpose. Now, tell students that they are going to listen to the show again and ask them to write notes about the reasons each speaker gives. Then, give them time to check their answers in pairs before giving feedback as a class.

GRAMMAR

A Work through the first question as a class, then put students into pairs to discuss the rest. Give feedback, giving further explanations and examples as necessary.

B Give students time to complete the rules and briefly check their answers in pairs. Give feedback as a class, encouraging students to match each rule to an example in Exercise A.

C Direct students to the **Grammar Hub** (see below and TB17).

D Give students time to complete the sentences alone before checking their answers with a partner. Then, give feedback as a class. For each sentence, encourage students to explain why the tense they used is appropriate.

E Elicit how to form the first question (*How many times have you checked social media today?*) and model how you would answer it (try to give detail here, using present perfect, rather than a short answer). Then, put students into pairs to discuss the questions. Monitor, focusing on the accuracy of their grammar and encouraging them to ask follow-up questions for more information. Use the **Grammar Worksheet** on page W7 for extra practice.

Extra activity

Before class, prepare a set of (x10) sentence stems that can be completed with the present perfect or present perfect progressive (e.g. *My hands are dirty because … [I've been cleaning the kitchen all morning.], My legs hurt because … [I've been to the gym three times this week!]*, etc). In class, once you've worked through the grammar section, put students into groups. Ask each group to nominate one person to write and call out answers. Then, read out the stems, awarding one point to the first group to give a grammatically correct sentence.

GRAMMAR HUB

2.1 Present perfect and present perfect progressive

	Positive	Negative	Question
Present perfect	**He's improved** his fitness level.	**They haven't finished** their meeting yet.	**Have you lost** weight?
Present perfect progressive	**I've been trying** to give up sugar.	**She hasn't been sleeping** very well.	**Have you been avoiding** me?

- We use the present perfect for finished actions with a present effect, and the present perfect progressive for unfinished actions.

  I've read that book before, actually.
  (= I finished the book.)
  I've been reading a great book recently.
  (= I started it and I'm still reading it.)

- We use the present perfect to emphasize the result of an action, and the present perfect progressive to emphasize the action itself.

  I've cleaned the bathroom.
  (emphasizing the result: the bathroom's now clean)
  I've been cleaning the bathroom all morning.
  (emphasizing the action: the cleaning)

- We use the present perfect to suggest that something is permanent and the present perfect progressive to suggest that something is temporary.

  I've lived here my whole life. (= long-term/permanent)
  I've been living here while I look for a new apartment.
  (= short-term/temporary)

- We use the present perfect to say how often something has happened and the present perfect progressive to say how long something has been happening.

  I've been to the gym every day this week. (= number of times)
  I've been going to the gym for the past two months.
  (= length of time)

Be careful!

- We don't usually use state verbs such as *be*, *have*, *know* and *seem* in the present perfect progressive.

  She's had short hair for several months now.
  NOT ~~She's been having short hair for several months now.~~

PRONUNCIATION

2.3 **A** Remind students that you looked at one form of connected speech in the last unit and elicit the point you covered (that words ending with a consonant sound usually link to the next word if it begins a vowel sound). Explain that you are going to focus on another form of connected speech and play the audio so they can answer the question. Give them time to briefly check their answers in pairs, before giving feedback as a class. Next, play the recording again and encourage students to copy the pronunciation of each sentence.

2.4 **B** Explain that learning about connected speech not only improves your speaking but also your listening. Then, play the audio so students can complete the sentences and give them time to check their answers with a partner. Give feedback as a class.

2.4 **C** Play the audio again, pausing between each sentence so students can copy the pronunciation.

SPEAKING HUB

A Give students examples from your own life of things that you are doing too much or too little of in the four topic areas. Then, give students time to write their own notes.

B Ask students to remember the examples you gave in the previous exercise and elicit how to use the subject of one to form a question (e.g. *How often have you been to the gym this month?*). Then, put students into pairs to write six of their own questions. Monitor, helping with grammar and vocabulary as necessary.

C Ask students to stand up, walk around the class and ask each other their questions. Monitor, helping them to give each other advice (like the examples in the Student's Book) and be prepared to answer questions yourself.

GRAMMAR HUB

2.1 Present perfect and present perfect progressive

A Choose the correct options to complete the conversations.

1 **A:** How long have you ***known*** / ***been knowing*** Emily?
B: Uh, about five years now, I think.

2 **A:** Did you tell everyone about the change of venue?
B: I think so. Oh no! I've just ***realized*** / ***been realizing*** that I forgot to tell Piotr!

3 **A:** How's your essay going?
B: I've ***planned*** / ***been planning*** it for the past three hours so I'm almost ready to start writing.

4 **A:** Who'll be there this evening?
B: Just me and my sister. She's ***stayed*** / ***been staying*** with me while her apartment is being redecorated.

5 **A:** I saw Toby in town today.
B: Yes, his boss has ***given*** / ***been giving*** him a week off from work.

6 **A:** So, what have you been up to?
B: I've been ***working*** / ***worked*** on a new book. I should finish it by the end of the year.

B Complete the sentences with the present perfect or present perfect progressive form of the verbs in the box. Add pronouns if necessary.

avoid	be	decide	do	find	know
leave	notice	only go out	think	use	wait

1 They 've/have been thinking about moving now that their son has left home.

2 Ren 's/has been using the new shampoo for six months and she 's/has noticed a big improvement in her hair.

3 Lucia 's/has decided to quit her job because she 's/has been finding / 's/has found it more and more stressful over the last few months.

4 Why have you been avoiding me? Have I done something to upset you?

5 I 've/have known Farid for years, but we 've/have only been going out for a few weeks!

6 I 've/have been waiting for you for hours! Where have you been all this time?

C Use the prompts to write sentences in the present perfect or present perfect progressive.

1 Kim / not work / here for long, so she / not met / all of her colleagues yet Kim hasn't worked / hasn't been working here for long, so she has not met all of her colleagues yet.

2 I think Jamila and Kalid / already / send out / the invitations
I think Jamila and Kalid have already sent out the invitations.

3 I'm afraid I / not clean / the living room yet because I just / not have / time
I'm afraid I haven't cleaned the living room yet because I just haven't had time.

4 Jimmy / drive / for hours, so he must / be / exhausted
Jimmy has been driving for hours so he must be exhausted.

5 I / know / about this for a long time
I've known about this for a long time.

6 How long / it / be / since you / quit / your job
How long has it been since you quit your job?

7 You / visit / this museum before
Have you visited this museum before?

8 We / eat / vegan food for two months now
We've eaten / been eating vegan food for two months now.

➤ Go back to page 17.

B WORK IT OUT Choose the correct options to complete the rules.

Present perfect and present perfect progressive

a finished vs unfinished
We use the present [1]*perfect* / *perfect progressive* for finished actions with a present effect, and the present [2]*perfect* / *perfect progressive* for unfinished actions.

b result vs action
We use the present [3]*perfect* / *perfect progressive* to emphasize the result of an action, and the present [4]*perfect* / *perfect progressive* to highlight the action itself.

c temporary vs permanent
We use the present [5]*perfect* / *perfect progressive* to suggest that something is permanent, and the present [6]*perfect* / *perfect progressive* to suggest something is temporary.

d frequency vs duration
We use the present [7]*perfect* / *perfect progressive* to say how much / many times something has happened, and the present [8]*perfect* / *perfect progressive* to say how long something has continued to happen for.

C Go to the **Grammar Hub** on **page 124**.

D PRACTICE Complete the sentences with the present perfect or present perfect progressive of the verbs in parentheses. If both are possible, use the present perfect progressive form.

1 I 've/have stopped (*stop*) working 12 hours a day.
2 She 's/has been trying (*try*) to spend less time on social media but she's finding it hard.
3 I 've/have been working (*work*) at a restaurant to pay my college fees.
4 I 've/have been (*be*) to the gym five times this week.
5 I 've/have been exercising (*exercise*) all morning. I can't wait for lunch.
6 I 've/have given up (*give up*) junk food and now I feel great!

E SPEAK Work in pairs. Use the prompts to ask and answer questions in the present perfect or present perfect progressive.

1 How many times / you / check / social media today?
2 What / you / give up / in the last ten years? Why?
3 What / you / do / recently in order to be healthier?

PRONUNCIATION

Connected speech: present perfect progressive

2.3 **A** Listen to three extracts from the radio show. Is there a pause between the words in bold? Is the strong or weak form of *been* used? No; weak

1 We**'ve been spending** more time together as a family.
2 Absolutely! I**'ve been living** without coffee for months now.
3 I**'ve been riding my bike** to work for the past two weeks.

2.4 **B** Listen and complete the sentences.

1 She's been working really hard recently.
2 I've been using my phone too much lately.
3 He's been eating less junk food.
4 They've been spending more time together.
5 We've been going to the gym a lot lately.

2.4 **C** Listen again and repeat the sentences.

SPEAKING HUB

A PREPARE What have you been doing too much of recently? What have you not been doing enough of recently? Write notes about:

- use of technology
- diet
- exercise
- family

B PLAN Work in pairs. Write six questions you could ask other students about their habits. Use your notes from Exercise A to help you.

1 *What unhealthy foods have you been eating too much of?*
2 *How often have you seen your family this month?*

C SPEAK Ask other students in the class your questions. Try to give each other advice on changes you could make.

A: *How often have you seen your family this month?*
B: *I haven't seen them at all! I'm just so busy all the time.*
A: *Well maybe you could try calling them once a week? You don't need to talk for long, but it's important to stay in touch.*

- Talk about health and lifestyle choices
- Plan and conduct a lifestyle survey

2.2 Change

- Conduct an interview about lifestyle changes
- Debate the impact of smartphones

G – *used to, would, get used to, be used to*
P – catenation: *used to*
S – identifying assumptions
V – adverbs of stance; adverb + adjective collocations

LISTENING

A SPEAK Work in pairs. You're going to listen to an interview with a family that has moved from the city to a remote island. What do you think would be the advantages and disadvantages of such a move?

2.5 **B LISTEN FOR GIST** Listen to the interview. Which members of the family are happy with the move? Which aren't? Frank and his son are happy with the move. His daughter, Katie, isn't. It isn't clear if his wife is happy or not.

2.5 **C LISTEN FOR DETAIL** Listen to the interview again. Choose the correct options (a, b or c) to complete the sentences.

1 Frank made the decision to leave New York because …
 (a) he found his job too demanding.
 b he found his lifestyle uneventful.
 c he couldn't afford to live there.

2 Since moving to the island, the family …
 (a) largely eats food that is home-grown or caught.
 b has to spend a lot of money at the local store.
 c generally has a much better diet than before.

3 Frank says that the family's new lifestyle …
 a was surprisingly easy to adapt to.
 b is less physically demanding.
 (c) has tested them financially.

4 Katie cannot stream media on the island because …
 a the mountains affect her phone signal.
 (b) the internet connection is terrible.
 c the family cannot afford the internet.

5 Katie is homeschooled by her mother because …
 a there isn't a good school on the island.
 (b) she is planning to take US exams.
 c it gives her more time to gather food.

6 Frank thinks his son enjoys life on the island because …
 a there are lots of young children to play with.
 (b) he's allowed to play outside all day.
 c he hated growing up in New York.

D SPEAK Work in pairs. Imagine moving to a small island far away from where you live. What would you miss? What would you be happy to leave behind?

GRAMMAR

used to, would, get used to, be used to

A Work in pairs. Match the extracts from the interview (1–4) to their meaning (a–d).

1 I **used to work** long hours and it was stressful. c
2 I'**m used to getting up** at 6 o'clock every day … d
3 Financially, it has also been much harder but **we're getting used to** it. a
4 Back in New York **he'd complain** about his job constantly. b

a This situation is still strange, but it's becoming more familiar.
b This habit was true in the past but isn't true now.
c This situation was true in the past but isn't true now.
d This was strange at first but is normal for me now.

B WORK IT OUT Complete the rules with the words in the box.

be used to get used to used to / didn't use to would

used to, would, get used to, be used to

We use [1] ___used to / didn't use to___ + base form to talk about finished habits and states: things that were true in the past but aren't true now.

We can also use [2] ___would___ + base form to talk about finished habits and routines, but not to talk about states.

We use [3] ___be used to___ to talk about something that was unfamiliar but is not unfamiliar now.

We use [4] ___get used to___ to talk about something that is still unfamiliar and not a current habit.

C Go to the Grammar Hub on page 124.

2.2 Change

LEAD-IN

Tell students about a big move you have made in your life (e.g. *going to college, moving to another city*, etc). Then, put students into pairs to brainstorm other reasons people move. Add any useful language to the board.

LISTENING

A Put students into pairs to discuss the question, then bring the class back together to share their ideas.

2.5 **B** Play the audio and encourage students to write notes. Give feedback as a class.

2.5 **C** Play the audio again. Give students time to check their answers in pairs, then give feedback as a class.

D Put students into pairs to discuss the questions.

GRAMMAR

A Put students into pairs to match the extracts to their meanings. Give feedback as a class.

B Give students time to complete the rules alone, before checking their answers with a partner. Give feedback as a class.

C Direct students to the **Grammar Hub** (see TB19).

D Ask students to complete the sentences alone, using the skills box for reference if necessary. Give feedback as a class. Use the **Grammar Worksheet** on page W8 for extra practice.

E Give students time to rewrite the sentences alone, helping with grammar and vocabulary as necessary.

F Put students into pairs to discuss their sentences.

AUDIO SCRIPT

2.5

Listening, Exercise B

I = Interviewer F = Frank K = Katie

I: Many of us have dreamed of escaping the rat race and getting away from our stressful lives, but few of us have ever actually taken the plunge. Well, on today's show we have one family who has done just that. Joining us from their beachfront home is Frank Gerrard and his daughter Katie. Thanks for joining us today. It looks beautiful there! Can you hear me OK?

F: Yes, I can hear you.

I: Now, you've made a dramatic change to your life. What were you doing before?

Ex C Q1 **F:** I had a terrible job! I used to work long hours and it was stressful. I was exhausted and overworked. I used to dream of living a quieter and more peaceful life … You know, getting back to nature and that sort of thing. So, I quit my job, sold the family home and we moved here.

I: Wow! That's really a dramatic change! How's it all been going?

Ex B **F:** It's been amazing! We have a small plot of land next to our house and we grow a lot of our own food. I go fishing and hunting every day.

I: Is there a local store?

Ex C Q2 **F:** There is, but we hardly ever go. I want to grow or catch everything.

I: So was the change easy for you?

F: Actually, it was a lot harder getting used to the new lifestyle than I thought it would be. When I worked in an office, I was so physically tired all the time because I just sat at my desk all day writing emails. I never really got up and walked around until it was time to go home, and even then I just walked to the station and sat on a train for half an hour. Now I have so many more physical tasks to do to produce the food we need. I'm used to getting up at six o'clock every day now and working hard until it
Ex C Q3 gets dark. Financially, it has also been much harder but we're getting used to it.

I: Would you make the same decision again?

F: For me, definitely! I wouldn't change a thing. As for my family, well I'm not so sure. They miss New York a lot and actually, I'm so busy all the time that we don't really spend that much more time together. We also have way less money now – not that there's much to spend it on!

I: Well this seems like a good point to bring in your daughter. Katie, how did you feel about the decision?

K: I understand why Dad did it. Back in New York, he'd complain about his job constantly. He hated it.
Ex B Mom just wanted him to be happier. But, well I think it was a stupid idea. He's just having a midlife crisis! Why would anyone want to move here?

I: So, you're not happy there then?

K: No. I used to see my friends all the time in New York. We'd go shopping or hang out in the park. What is there to do here? Walk up another mountain? The internet is terrible too. When I was bored in
Ex C Q4 New York, I used to watch Netflix on my phone or listen to something on Spotify. That kind of thing is just out of the question now because our internet connection is so bad. We also don't seem to have any money now, which is weird – shouldn't we be better off?

I: OK, and what's school like there?

K: It's the worst thing ever! I'm homeschooled now.
Ex C Q5 There's a small school on the island, but my parents want me to take US exams, so Mom is teaching us. I never ever leave the house!

I: Do you think you'll grow to love it?

K: No! I'm really stressed actually. What job can I do here? Where will I go to college? I'm getting used to being isolated from everyone, but I need to think about my future. In New York, I would always think about the exciting jobs and opportunities I could have in the future. I don't want a life like this – all day gathering food. It's boring!

I: Are there any positives about the move?

K: Seriously? No. Well, to be fair, I do enjoy swimming and sunbathing every day, but generally no, I'm bored a lot of the time. I guess I'm not used to it yet.

Ex B
Ex C Q6 **F:** Well, our youngest loves it here. New York isn't great for young children. I was always too worried to let him play outside alone. Now he's out there all day! He would hate to move back to New York. It isn't great for teenagers though, so it might change as he gets older.

K: It definitely will. He's going to be so bored!

I: Well, thank you both for joining us.

2.2 Change

PRONUNCIATION

2.6 **A** Play the audio so students can answer the questions. Give feedback as a class, explaining that *used to* sounds like **/juːstə/** when said in natural, rapid speech. Model and practice the sentences with the class.

2.7 **B** Play the audio, pausing after each sentence so students can copy the pronunciation. If you have time, you could provide further practice with the students' own sentences in Exercise E of the Grammar section.

SPEAKING

A–C Give a few examples of how your life has changed in one or two areas on the list. Then, give students time to make a brief list of their own. Next, ask them to focus on the three biggest changes and to use the questions to help them write detailed notes. Finally, put them into groups to discuss their ideas. Monitor, encouraging students to ask follow-up questions to keep the discussions going.

GRAMMAR HUB

2.2 *used to / would / be used to / get used to*

	Positive	Negative	Question
used to	**I used to work** in a hotel.	**He didn't use to get** so stressed.	**Did she use to have** long hair?
would	**They would take** the bus to work.	**She wouldn't have** anything for breakfast.	**Would he usually come** home late?
be used to	**He's used to getting** up early.	**I'm not used to eating** such spicy food.	**Are you used to driving** on the right now?
get used to	**He** soon **got used to wearing** glasses.	**I haven't gotten used to** the cold weather.	**Are you getting used to living** in the country?

- We use *used to* + base form to talk about past habits, repeated actions and states or situations that have changed.

  I used to get up really early on the weekend.
  He didn't use to have a beard.

- We also use *would* + base form to talk about past habits and repeated actions.

  The children would spend hours playing in the yard.

- We use *be used to* + verb + *-ing*/noun to talk about a situation which is now normal or familiar. We use the negative form to talk about a situation which is new or strange.

  I'm used to living on my own.
  I'm not used to the cold weather.

- We use *get used to* + verb + *-ing*/noun to talk about a situation which is becoming more familiar.

  I'm getting used to working in an office.
  I haven't gotten used to the food yet.

Be careful!

- We cannot use *would* to talk about past states.

  They used to live in Panama. NOT ~~*They would live in Panama.*~~

2.2 *used to / would / be used to / get used to*

A Choose the correct options to complete the sentences.

1 People *didn't use to* / *wouldn't* be able to look everything up on Google.
2 Sofia is slowly *used* / *getting used* to living back home with her parents.
3 *Did you use to* / *Would you* have a smartphone when you were younger?
4 *I'm still not used* / *I didn't use* to having short hair!
5 The children always *got used* / *used* to spend their allowance on candy.
6 Jakob *got* / *was* used to wearing glasses fairly quickly.
7 *Were you* / *Have you gotten* used to the new software yet?
8 As a child, Milo *would* / *was used to* become demotivated very easily.

B Complete the text messages with the correct form of *used to*, *be used to* and *get used to*.

How's the new job going? Have you [1] gotten used to the commute yet?

Not really. It [2] used to take about 20 minutes to get to work. Now it takes over an hour!

I know the feeling! I [3] am used to having a long drive to work – I've been doing it for a while now – but I still [4] haven't gotten used to getting up so early!

It's horrible, isn't it? I [5] used to get up at seven thirty. These days, that's when I have to leave the house. And I'm still [6] not used to getting home so late, either.

➤ Go back to page 19.

D PRACTICE Complete the sentences with *used to*, *would*, *be used to* or *get used to* and the verbs in parentheses.

1. I ___used to look___ (*look*) very different when I was younger.
2. I ___didn't use to like___ (*not / like*) mornings but now I enjoy getting up early.
3. When I was a teenager, I ___used to eat / 'd/would eat___ (*eat*) a lot of junk food.
4. I ___'m/am used to working___ (*work*) long hours now. I've done it for years.
5. I am ___getting used to cooking___ (*cook*) for myself but I'm still not great at it.
6. When I was younger, I ___used to / 'd/would play___ (*play*) video games for hours.
7. I ___'m/am not used to driving___ (*not / drive*). I only passed my test recently.
8. I've decided to cut down on sugar. I ___'m/am getting used to eating___ (*eat*) less but it's a little boring!

E PRACTICE Rewrite the sentences in Exercise D so they are true for you.

F SPEAK Work in pairs. Discuss your sentences from Exercise E. Ask follow-up questions for more information.

PRONUNCIATION

Catenation: *used to*

2.6 **A** Listen to these extracts from the interview. Do we pronounce the final /d/ in *used to*? Do we use the strong or weak form of *to*? No; weak

1. I used to dream of living a quieter and more peaceful life.
2. I'm getting used to being isolated from everyone.
3. I guess I'm not used to it yet.

2.7 **B** Listen and repeat the sentences.

1. She used to have long hair.
2. Have you gotten used to living on your own?
3. I'm used to getting up early every day.
4. I actually used to drink a lot of coffee.
5. Don't worry, he's used to it by now.

SPEAKING

A PREPARE Think about how your life has changed in the last ten years. Make a list of positive changes in these areas:

- where you live
- family
- work
- education
- free time
- health

B PLAN Write notes about the three biggest changes in Exercise A. Use these questions to help you:

- What prompted the change?
- How has the change affected your life?
- Are you used to the change yet?

C SPEAK Work in groups. Take turns explaining your changes. Ask follow-up questions for more information.

READING

A SPEAK Work in groups. What are some of the positive and negative effects of social media?

B SCAN Read *The big debate* quickly. Which of your ideas from Exercise A are discussed?

C READ FOR GIST Read the article again. Choose the most appropriate debate question (1–4) for the article.

1 Should social media be banned?

2 Have relationships in society gotten worse?

3 Has social media made us less social?

4 Should we reconnect with the people around us?

THE BIG DEBATE

PETE LOMAS, PSYCHOLOGIST

Admittedly, the internet is pretty much the greatest invention of all time. However, I'd argue that social media is the worst invention to appear in this internet era. It seems to me that despite being 'in contact' with more and more people, we are in fact losing contact – meaningful contact – with most people in our lives.

[a]Beyond question, we're less comfortable in social settings than we once were. **Sadly**, we have all sat around a table where no one is really talking as they skim through their social media. Research by Ofcom has found that 51% of adults and 65% of teenagers have used their smartphone while socializing. **Frankly**, this is going to have a negative impact on our relationships. In fact, in some countries, groups of friends now have a rule – if you check your phone during dinner in a restaurant, then you have to pay for everyone. Are we really in a position where we need to fine people to get them to pay attention to us?

[b]Unfortunately, it's not just affecting how we interact but it is also making us feel worse, not better. **Naturally**, constant communication transforms how you feel, especially if you monitor emails, text messages and status updates. There is even an acronym for this phenomenon: FOMO – 'fear of missing out'. [c]As I see it, anything social should make us feel involved but social media is clearly making some people feel left out rather than part of something.

Social media should be renamed anti-social media. [d]In an already isolated world, social media is cutting us off from the world around us even further.

AMY DAY, APP DEVELOPER

From my perspective, social media has **undoubtedly** enhanced our relationships with others. It is true that not all of our online relationships are as close as our face-to-face connections but, on the other hand, it has allowed us to reconnect with lost friends, maintain connections and build new ones.

[e]From my point of view, modern life had already made us all fairly isolated individuals. We work long hours. We commute long distances. We move to cities where we know nobody, just for work. Our families all move around, not just in the country we live in, but also to different countries. I'm sure that social media has **simply** emerged from the pressures of modern life and our desire to connect with others despite these obstacles.

Apparently, we are giving up face-to-face relationships with people in favor of less personal social media ones. In all honesty, I don't think this could be further from the truth. According to research by Marketing Charts using data from Nielsen, in the space of five years, TV viewing by 18–24 year olds has fallen from 25 hours a week to **merely** 12. Those aged over 50 still watch over 40 hours a week and this figure isn't declining. Young people are clearly giving up anti-social activities in favor of other ways of interacting.

People who argue that social media has made us less interactive with the world around us clearly have the image in their mind of people on a train with their heads down looking at their phones. These people aren't choosing to be antisocial. [f]Far from it – they are choosing to interact with the people they deem important in their own lives.

READING

A Ask students how they keep in touch with their friends and add any examples of social media platforms (e.g. *Facebook*, *Instagram*, etc) to a list on the board. Next, draw brackets around the list and elicit what they are examples of (*social media platforms*), adding the title to the board. On either side of this, write the headings *positive effects* and *negative effects* and elicit one or two examples for each. Now, put students into pairs to discuss more ideas. Give feedback as a class, encouraging students to justify their ideas with examples, and build up two bulleted lists on the board.

B Give students two to three minutes to scan the text to see if any of their ideas are mentioned. Bring the class back together to clarify anything in the text that they don't understand. This might also be a good opportunity to do some vocabulary building by highlighting any useful collocations in the text (e.g. *negative impact*) and how they might be manipulated (e.g. *negative attitude/effect*, etc).

C Ask students to read the text again and choose the best debate title. Give them time to check their answers in pairs, before giving feedback as a class. Encourage students to explain why they ruled out the three incorrect options.

METHODOLOGY HUB by Christine Nuttall

Doing what the reader must for himself

The reader's most basic task is to associate the printed marks on the page with the spoken language they know. A teacher who reads the text aloud before starting work on it has already done this for the students.

The reader next has to make sense of the text. So if the teacher begins by explaining or summarizing it, they are defeating the object of the lesson: they are telling the student something a reader should find out for themself. If, as the lesson proceeds, the student encounters problems and the teacher at once explains or translates, again this is the wrong kind of help: the student has to understand only the teacher, not the text.

All these activities are valid in some circumstances, but they do not promote the independent skills of silent reading. They lead students to see the reader's role as a passive one, for most of the work has been done for them. The teacher's well-meant help has undermined the purpose for which they are teaching.

Help of this kind also devalues the text itself. When the meaning is obtained largely through the intervention of the teacher (especially if they translate it into the mother tongue), the printed text becomes almost redundant.

You may argue that without help of this kind, your students could not possibly understand the assigned texts. However, research shows that we commonly underestimate students. They may be capable of understanding far more than they at present have a chance to attempt. You can only find out by trying.

TEACHING IDEA by David Seymour and Maria Popova

Information technology

Use this to develop the theme of the impact technology has on society.

What are the greatest changes brought about by computers? Do you think there will ever be intelligent computers, i.e. computers that can learn?

In groups, list the advantages and disadvantages of modern technologies, e.g. *International telephone calls are very cheap. Working on computers all day is bad for your health.*

In groups, imagine a world without computers. How would this affect your day-to-day life? Make a list of five inconveniences, e.g. *I'd have to go to the library to get information rather than look on the internet.*

METHODOLOGY HUB by Jim Scrivener

Guided discovery

An alternative to giving explanations about language points is to create activities that allow learners to generate their own discoveries and explanations. Tasks at just the right level will draw attention to interesting language issues. Teacher questions (and use of other techniques) will 'nudge' the learners toward key points. In this way, long explanations can be avoided and learners can take a more active role in their own progress.

Your role in guided discovery is to (a) select appropriate tasks; (b) offer appropriate instructions, help, feedback and explanations; (c) manage and structure the lesson so that all learners are involved and engaged and draw the most possible from the activity.

The key technique is to ask good questions, ones that encourage the learners to notice language and think about it. These questions may be oral (i.e. asked live in class) or they might be on a worksheet that leads learners in a structured way to make conclusions. This kind of guidance is sometimes referred to as 'Socratic questioning', i.e. leading people to discover things that they didn't know they knew via a process of structured questions.

You can:

- ask questions that focus on the meaning (concept questions)
- ask questions that focus on the context (context questions)
- ask questions that focus on the form
- offer appropriate examples for analysis and discussion
- ask learners to analyze sentences from texts
- ask learners to reflect on language they have used
- ask learners to analyze errors
- ask learners to hypothesize rules
- set problems and puzzles concerning the language item
- help them to stay focused if they get sidetracked
- raise their awareness as to what they have learned.

Guided discovery is demanding on both you and the learner, and although it may look artless to a casual observer, it isn't enough to throw a task at the learners; let them do it and then move on. Guided discovery requires imagination and flexibility. Your job here is not simply to pass over a body of information but rather to create the conditions in which that information can be learned. This seems to be a particularly fruitful way to work in the language classroom.

D Write the following sentence on the board – *As we all know, social media has made people unsociable.* Ask students whether they think this is true or not. Then, ask whether some people were unsociable before social media (*they were*) and whether there's any evidence to support the statement (*there isn't*). Explain that when we make statements like this that you think are true, but you don't have any evidence or proof for it, this is called an assumption. Tell students that other phrases we use to introduce assumptions are *Without a doubt …* and *Beyond question …*, and elicit some examples of other assumptions. Next, write the example from the skills box on the board and explain that it contains a hidden or implied assumption. Elicit the assumption (*that online contact isn't meaningful*). Now, ask students to read the article again in detail and match the underlined sentences to the assumptions. Give them plenty of time to do this as it's fairly challenging. Ask them to check their answers in pairs, before giving feedback as a class.

E Put students into groups to discuss the questions. Monitor, encouraging students to keep their discussions going by asking follow-up questions. If you have time, open the discussion up to the class.

VOCABULARY

A Write the first sentence from the text on the board, setting *Admittedly* in a different color – *Admittedly, the internet is pretty much the greatest invention of all time.* Elicit what type of word *Admittedly* is (*an adverb*), then ask whether it tells us about how the writer does something, how often the writer does something or what the writer thinks about something (*what the writer thinks about something*). Tell students this kind of adverb is called an adverb of stance and elicit which definition it matches (*1*). Then, give students time to complete the exercise alone before checking their answers with a partner. Give feedback as a class, providing further explanation and examples as necessary.

B Give students time to complete the sentences alone before checking their answers in pairs. Give feedback as a class. Use the **Vocabulary Worksheet** on page W9 for extra practice.

VOCABULARY

Write the following sentence on the board – ______ *effective people get up really early in the morning.* Elicit what type of word you need to fill in the blank (*an adverb*) and what it could be (*highly*, *really*, *very*, etc), adding the students' ideas to the board. If the students have suggested an adverb that doesn't collocate very well, cross it out and explain that the remaining combinations are example of collocations (words frequently used together) and elicit the type (*adverb + adjective*). Now, give students time to complete the exercise alone before checking their answers in pairs. Give feedback as a class, eliciting other possible collocations for each sentence. Use the **Vocabulary Worksheet** on page W10 for extra practice.

SPEAKING HUB

A Give the class one or two examples of how you use technology to help maintain relationships (e.g. *email*, *Facebook*, etc). Then, put students into pairs to discuss their own ideas.

B Tell students that you are going to hold a debate, and write the following statement on the board – *Smartphones have had a negative impact on our personal relationships.* Next, divide the class into two groups and tell Group A to write notes in favor of the statement and Group B to write notes against it. Remind them to use their ideas from Exercise A to help them. Monitor, encouraging students to think of evidence or examples to support their ideas.

C Arrange the classroom so that the two groups are facing each other. To begin the debate, ask each group to present a summary of their position. Encourage students to write notes during the opposition's summary as this will help them to argue their point. With a weaker class, you may want to allow extra time for the groups to work to come up with counter-arguments based on their notes from the opening summaries. Once each group has presented their argument, let the debate begin. While the students are debating, ensure that everyone has a chance to participate. Allow time at the end for each group to summarize their key points again, then take a class vote to decide which side of the argument they agree with.

TEACHING IDEA by David Seymour and Maria Popova

Throw and catch

Use this activity to review adverbs.

Stand in a circle. Throw a ball (a ball of paper will do) from one person to another in the circle. As you throw it, yell out an adverb. When you catch it, you have five seconds to use the adverb in a sentence. The class decides if your sentence is correct. If it isn't, you are out of the game. The last student left standing is the winner. For example –

A (throwing) – *Fluently!*

B (after catching) – *He speaks fluently.*

A (throwing) – *Greedily!*

B (after catching) – *He ate his dinner greedily.*

TEACHING IDEA by David Seymour and Maria Popova

Prompts

Use this activity to review *be used to*.

In pairs, listen to these prompts and agree on an explanation using *be (not) used to*. Write it down, e.g. *I'm so tired. – I'm not used to working shifts. / I can't get used to working shifts.*

- I don't think I'll ever get used to working shifts.
- Don't touch my dog!
- It was so embarrassing.
- Elephants don't like zoos.
- I find him difficult to live with.
- I can't drink this tea.
- They don't like New York.
- This country is too cold for me.

Compare your explanations with another pair. Which do you like better?

D IDENTIFY ASSUMPTIONS Read the article again. Match the sentences in the text (a–f) with the assumptions (1–6). Use the information in the box to help you.

Identifying assumptions

Writers frequently make assumptions about what groups of people think or the opinions of others. These are signaled with phrases such as *As we all know …*, *Without a doubt …* and *Beyond question …*, which are used to try to convince the reader of a certain point of view.

The assumption can also be implied rather than stated directly. For example:

It seems to me that despite being 'in contact' with more and more people, we are in fact losing contact, meaningful contact, with most people in our lives.

(= assumes that online contact is not meaningful.)

1 Previous generations were all good at socializing. a
2 Nobody that uses social media feels like they're part of a group. c
3 Social media makes nobody feel positive. b
4 The world was disconnected before social media. e
5 Everyone on their phone is using social media. f
6 Everyone in the modern world felt disconnected anyway. d

E SPEAK Work in groups. Which of the assumptions in the text do you agree with? Which do you disagree with? Why?

VOCABULARY

Adverbs of stance

A Scan the article again. Complete the definitions with the adverbs in bold.

1 admittedly used to say that something is true even though it may weaken your argument
2 apparently based only on what you have heard, not on what you are certain is true
3 frankly used to emphasize that you are about to give your honest opinion, even though the person you are talking to might not like it
4 merely used to emphasize that something is small or unimportant
5 naturally in the way that you would expect
6 undoubtedly used to say that something is certainly true or is accepted by everyone
7 sadly used to show that you think something is bad or wrong
8 simply used to emphasize that you are saying something in a plain and straightforward way

B Choose the correct options to complete the sentences.

1 *Naturally / Sadly*, all new developments come with both advantages and disadvantages.
2 *Merely / Admittedly*, I see less of my friends in person now.
3 *Frankly / Apparently*, we have a weaker sense of community than we used to, but I'm not sure I agree.
4 Social media is *merely / apparently* another method of communication.
5 *Simply / Frankly*, I think social media enhances relationships.
6 The internet has *undoubtedly / apparently* enhanced many aspects of our lives. I don't think anyone could question that.
7 I think many people regret the breakdown of communities. *Sadly / Naturally*, many communities are not as close as they once were.
8 It's very *simply / merely* the best solution to the problem.

VOCABULARY

Adverb + adjective collocations

Some adverbs and adjectives are commonly used together. For example, we say *strongly opposed* NOT ~~*deeply opposed*~~ or ~~*utterly opposed*~~. Learning these collocations will help make your language sound more natural.

Complete the sentences with the adverbs in the box.

absolutely bitterly deeply highly ridiculously

1 It is highly likely that more and more of our relationships will be conducted using phones.
2 It is absolutely ridiculous to say that smartphones have been negative for relationships.
3 I think society should be deeply concerned about the negative impact of smartphones.
4 Smartphones make it ridiculously easy to stay in touch with people.
5 I was bitterly disappointed when my friend started checking her phone during dinner.

SPEAKING HUB

A PLAN Work in pairs. How do you use technology to support your relationships?

B PREPARE Work in two groups. You are going to debate the following:

Smartphones have had a negative impact on our personal relationships.

Group A – You agree with the statement above.

Group B – You disagree with the statement above.

Plan your arguments. Think about how to support your position, as well as what the other group might say.

C SPEAK Hold a class debate.

Conduct an interview about lifestyle changes
Debate the impact of smartphones

Café Hub

2.3 Clean eating

A– adding emphasis S– backchanneling and lexical repetition

Ella's story

COMPREHENSION

A **Work in groups. Look at the picture and discuss the questions.** 'Clean eating' refers to eating only foods that are regarded as healthy; nothing processed or refined.

1. You are going to watch a video about clean eating. What do you think this term means? Why?
2. Do you pay close attention to your diet? Why/Why not?
3. Who or what influences the food you eat?

Glossary

gluten (n) a natural, sticky substance found in some foods (e.g. wheat)
vegan (n) someone who doesn't eat anything made from animals or fish, including eggs, milk and cheese

B **Watch the interview with Ella Mills and answer the questions.**

1. Why is Dr. Yeo interviewing Ella Mills for the program?
2. What do all of Ella's recipes have in common?
3. What made Ella decide to change her diet?
4. What did Ella give up as part of her change in diet?

C **Watch the interview again. Are these sentences true (T) or false (F)? Correct the false sentences.**

1. Ella's first cookbook wasn't very successful when it was originally published. It was 'the fastest-selling ever in the UK.' T / (F)
2. Ella decided to become a vegetarian more than ten years ago. She says that 'even ten years ago' she was 'the least vegetarian person you would have ever met'. T / (F)
3. Ella felt that her original medical treatment wasn't working effectively. (T) / F
4. Ella was initially doubtful that a change in diet could improve her condition. (T) / F
5. The fact that many others could identify with her experience encouraged Ella to continue sharing her story online. (T) / F

D **Work in groups. Discuss the questions.**

1. Because Dr. Yeo refers to 'Professor Google' in the video, what do you think his attitude is toward seeking medical advice online?
2. Do you think it's a good idea to search for medical advice online? Why/Why not?

Suggested answer: We can infer from this comment (and the way in which it is said) that Dr. Yeo doesn't think seeking medical advice online is the best approach to healthcare.

AUTHENTIC ENGLISH

A **Work in pairs. Read the extracts from the interview (1–4). Underline the words and phrases used to make the sentences more emphatic.**

1. … and her debut cookbook was the fastest-selling ever in the UK.
2. I was the least vegetarian person you would have ever met in your life.
3. … and I came across lots of stories of people who'd used a change in diet and lifestyle to help manage all kinds of conditions, which I was, to be honest, incredibly skeptical of …
4. Her story of how she changed her diet to change her health has proved hugely influential.

B **Read the information in the box and check your answers to Exercise A. How else can you make what you say more emphatic?**

Adding emphasis

In informal spoken English, speakers frequently use superlatives, adverbs of degree, *ever/never* and expressions like *in your life* to exaggerate or make their sentences more emphatic. Doing so helps maintain the interest of the listener or highlight the importance of what's being said.

C **Work in pairs. Take turns talking about the following topics. Use the techniques in Exercise B to make your descriptions more emphatic.**

1. a terrible meal you once had
2. an amazing movie you've seen
3. a terrifying experience

The worst meal I've ever had was when I was on vacation in Thailand. I was with my …

You are what you eat

SAM MALCOLM AMANDA HARRY EMILY

A Work in pairs. Discuss what you had for breakfast and what you think your partner's choices say about them.

B Watch the video. What are the differences between Emily and Malcolm's attitudes toward food?

SPEAKING SKILL

A Watch the video again. Complete the box with examples from the conversation.

> **Backchanneling and lexical repetition**
>
> **Backchanneling**
>
> Giving signals to show we are interested in what the other speaker is saying is called backchanneling.
>
> To show interest, we say things like *I see* or just make noises like [1] Mm-hmm, Uh-huh.
>
> To show surprise, we say single words like [2] Really?, Amazing!, Wow!.
>
> **Lexical repetition**
>
> Another way to show we're engaged is lexical repetition. Sometimes this means using the same words as someone else. For example, when Emily first talks about clean eating, Malcolm starts his next turn by saying *clean eating* to show that he is following the topic. Another form of lexical repetition is to rephrase what has been said.
>
> ***Emily:*** *For me, it's about eating mindfully – I mean, really thinking about what you're putting into your body and how your body uses the energy.*
>
> ***Malcolm:*** *I see. So it's just about trying to eat* [3] a healthy balanced diet?
>
> ***Emily:*** *Yeah, making sure your body is getting* [4] a range of good nourishing food.

B Work in pairs. Student A – Make a comment about one of the topics below. Student B – Rephrase your partner's comment to show you're engaged. Then swap roles.

- the weather today
- a type of food you like
- a movie you like
- a country you've been to
- a city you know
- what you are wearing
- a singer or band

A: It's nice and sunny today.
B: Oh, it's beautiful, isn't it?

SPEAKING HUB

A PREPARE Brainstorm a list of the advantages and disadvantages of becoming a vegan.

B PLAN Do you think you could become a vegan? Why/ Why not? Use your ideas from Exercise A to write notes.

C DISCUSS Work in pairs. Discuss whether or not you would be prepared to become a vegan. Explain your reasoning.

A: I don't think I could ever be a vegan. I enjoy eating meat too much.
B: But what about the health benefits? A lot of people believe that vegans have a much longer, healthier life.

Give your opinion on food choices

➤ Turn to page 155 to learn how to write an article giving advice.

2.3 Clean eating

Ella's story

LEAD-IN

Ask the class if anyone has a special diet (e.g. *vegetarian*, *vegan*, etc) and encourage them to explain why. Add any useful emergent language to the board and encourage class discussion.

COMPREHENSION

A Put students into groups to discuss the questions.

B ▶ Play the interview for students to answer the questions.

1 *To find out how the clean movement has become so popular; she's one of the most influential figures in the movement, with over a million followers on Instagram.*
2 *They are vegan.*
3 *She developed a rare medical condition (postural [orthostatic] tachycardia syndrome, or 'POTS').*
4 *Meat, dairy, refined sugar, gluten and processed foods.*

C ▶ Play the interview again for students to complete the exercise.

D Put students into groups to discuss the questions.

AUTHENTIC ENGLISH

A–B Put students into pairs to discuss the extracts, then give feedback as a class.

Other ways to add emphasis include changing the sentence stress and intonation; using cleft sentences (e.g. The thing I like about [X] is …); fronting/inversion (e.g. Beautiful it was ..., Never have I seen …'); using a dummy auxiliary *(e.g. I **do** like it, I really do).*

C Put students into pairs to practice adding emphasis.

You are what you eat

A Put students into pairs to discuss their breakfast choices. Monitor, helping with any new or unfamiliar vocabulary.

B ▶ Tell students they are now going to watch the next episode of the Café Hub series. Play the episode, then give feedback as a class. You can find the **video script** for *You are what you eat* on the Teacher's Resource Center.

Emily believes that it is important that we eat food that is good for us. She likes food that makes her feel good and gives her energy. Malcolm thinks that we shouldn't spend all our time worrying about how fattening food is. For him, what is more important is that the food tastes good.

SPEAKING SKILL

A ▶ Read through the skills box as a class, giving further examples as necessary. Then, play the video again. Give feedback as a class.

B Put students into pairs to practice the skill. Monitor, helping with grammar as necessary.

SPEAKING HUB

A Ask students to think back to the interview with Ella Mills and elicit the type of diet she followed (*vegan*) and a brief definition (*someone who doesn't eat anything made from animals or fish, including eggs, milk and cheese*). Next, elicit one or two advantages and disadvantages of this diet and add them as bullets in a table on the board. Then, put students into pairs to discuss more ideas.

B–C Give students time to write notes, before putting them into pairs to discuss their ideas.

▶ VIDEO SCRIPT

Ella's story
D = Dr. Yeo E= Ella

Ex B Q1 **D:** To find out how the clean movement has become so popular, I'm going to cook for someone who's become one of its most influential figures. Ella Mills is 'Deliciously Ella'. She has nearly a million
Ex C Q1 followers on Instagram and her debut cookbook was the fastest-selling ever in the UK.

E: Hello!

D: Oh, hi! Ella.

E: Pleased to meet you.

D: Thank you very much for … I've been nervous. I've been nervous because I've never cooked for you. And … and I normally …

E: OK. No, it's going to be amazing!

D: And I normally cook for … for … for … carnivores. It's a terrible … terrible thing to say.

E: OK, don't worry.

D: Umm, but obviously I'm cooking for you, and so I'm … I'm going down the route of your philosophy using … using plants. I'm going to
Ex B Q2 cook Ella's spiced sweet potato stew. Like all her food, it is vegan.

Ex C Q2 **E:** I was the least vegetarian person you would have ever met in your life. Even ten years ago. Hated vegetables. Hated fruit.

D: No sweet potatoes?

E: Not even a sweet potato!

Ex B Q3 **D:** Ella decided to change her diet when she developed a rare condition called postural tachycardia syndrome.

E: I had the, kind of, classic issue of POTS, which is you can't control your heart rate properly, umm,
Ex C Q3 so I spent about six months or so in bed just taking all these drugs and they just didn't have enough of an effect.

D: As the medical options ran out, Ella did what many of us would.

E: Obviously, I went to Google, because that's what you do these days, right?

D: Professor Google. Pro … Professor Google.

E: Umm, which obviously can be a dangerous game, but, umm, and I started researching like, kind of, alternative things I could look at, and I came across lots of stories of people who'd used a change in diet and lifestyle to help manage
Ex C Q4 all kinds of conditions, which I was, to be honest, incredibly sceptical of, it seemed quite bizarre to me that you could … that could be an effective thing, umm, but at this point kind of, you know, anything's worth a try really.

Ex B Q4 **D:** Overnight, Ella gave up meat, dairy, refined sugar, gluten and processed foods. Her story of how she changed her diet to change her health has proved hugely influential.

E: It was quite cathartic for me the first time I shared
Ex C Q5 it, but it was also amazing the number of people that would get in touch and say, you know, that they could relate to it for some reason or another, and I think that was also another reason to keep talking about it, because it … it made sense of what I was doing.

2 Writing

Write an article giving advice

Using different structures to give advice

A Work in pairs. You are going to read an article titled *Clear the mess and clear your mind*. What advice do you think the author might give?

B Read the article quickly. Which of your ideas from Exercise A does the author mention?

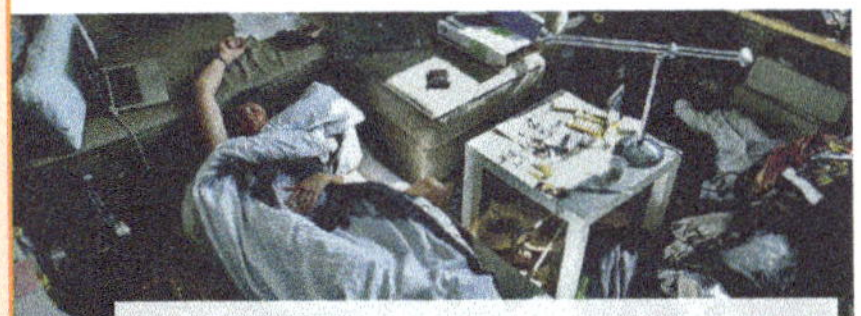

Clear the mess and clear your mind

What better way to start the new year than getting rid of some clutter? Doing so will not only make your house feel more organized, but could also lower your stress levels. Hopefully, the following tips should help you get started!

Throw things away

We keep far more things than we really need to and many of these can be thrown away or given to someone else to use.

- Do you really need or like all of your clothes? Why not go through your closet and see if there's anything you can donate to charity?
- If you don't watch it, listen to it or read it, sell it on eBay. You'll make a little bit of money and have more space!
- Don't forget to look in the garage. Most people use these areas to store things they just don't need or want.
- Don't keep broken things that you know you'll never fix.

Stay motivated

Decluttering can be hugely satisfying, but only if you can stay motivated. Use these basic rules to help you:

- Make sure you don't spend too long decluttering. If you are tired, take a break. It's much harder to make good decisions when you can't think properly!
- Don't leave a task incomplete. If you don't finish what you started, you're likely to become demotivated.

Good habits

Clutter can quickly build up again, so it's important to develop good habits for the future. Use these basic rules to help you:

- Avoid putting things into a pile. Putting them back where they belong will help keep things neat.
- Remember to never buy something on impulse. You can always buy it later if you really want it.

C Read the article again. Complete the table with examples from the text.

Using different structures to give advice
If + simple present + imperative
1 *If you don't watch it, listen to it or read it, sell it on eBay.*
2 *If you're tired, take a break.*
negative imperative
3 *Don't forget to look in the garage.*
4 *Don't keep broken things that you know you will never fix.*
5 *Don't leave a task incomplete.*
positive imperative
6 *Avoid putting things into a pile.*
7 *Remember never to buy something on impulse.*

D Rewrite the sentences using the words in bold.

1. Drinking coffee after 9 pm is not a good idea.
   Avoid drinking coffee after 9 pm.
2. Why not try putting $20 into a savings account every week?
   Try to put $20 into a savings account every week.
3. If you don't use your gym membership, cancel it.
   It's a good idea to cancel your gym membership if you don't use it.
4. Maybe you could turn your phone off in the evenings.
   Try turning your phone off in the evenings.
5. Try to exercise at least three times a week.
   Don't forget to exercise at least three times a week.
6. Recording the food you eat every day is a good idea.
   Remember to record the food you eat every day.

WRITING

A PREPARE Work in pairs. Brainstorm advice you could give about one of these topics:

- reducing stress
- improving your diet
- getting in shape

B PLAN Organize your notes from Exercise A into a plan for an article. Think about the clearest way to present your ideas, using headings where appropriate.

C WRITE Write your advice article. Use your plan to help you.

D EDIT Work in pairs. Edit your partner's essay. Check:

- spelling and punctuation
- use of expressions to give advice
- appropriacy of the ideas (e.g. Is the advice clear? Is it good advice?)

WRITING 155

Refer students to this article as a model for the writing task.

Refer students to this checklist when editing their partner's work.

LEAD-IN

Elicit a list of everyday life problems and ask students to discuss what advice they would give to someone in each situation. Then, as a class, try to agree on the best solution for each problem.

WRITING

A–B Put students into pairs to discuss the question. Next, give students time to read the article quickly to see if any of their ideas are mentioned. Give feedback as a class, encouraging students to share any ideas they thought of that weren't covered in the text.

C Read the skills box as a class, eliciting examples for each structure. Then, give students time to complete the exercise alone before giving feedback as a class.

D Go through the first sentence on the board, then students complete the rest alone before checking their answers in pairs.

WRITING TASK

A–B Put students into pairs to think of more advice you could give. Monitor, helping with grammar and vocabulary as necessary. Next, give students time to organize their notes into a plan and remind them to use the article about decluttering as a model. Monitor and help them with structure if necessary.

C Students should now write their articles. Monitor and provide support with structure and vocabulary when necessary.

D Put students into pairs to edit each other's articles. Encourage students to give each other positive feedback. Students can then rewrite their articles either in class or for homework.

Unit 2 Review

VOCABULARY

A Match the causes (1–6) to their effects (a–f) to form full sentences.

1 High-**calorie** diets … d
2 Regular **physical** exercise … a
3 Strong friendship groups can **reduce the risk of** … b
4 A low-calorie diet may **slow the aging process** … f
5 Eating heavily **processed foods** may result in … c
6 Maintaining a good **level of fitness** could be positive … e

a can result in reduced levels of **stress**.
b **depression** occurring.
c a person's **cholesterol** levels rising.
d could lead to higher levels of **obesity**.
e for a person's **mental health**.
f and lead to a longer **life expectancy**.

B Replace the words in italics with adverbs from the box.

admittedly apparently frankly merely naturally sadly simply undoubtedly

1 I didn't say you had to do it, I ~~*only*~~ merely suggested you might want to.
2 Have you heard about Mark and Emily? ~~*I'm not sure, but I was told*~~ Apparently, they're having a baby!
3 That's ~~*just*~~ simply not true! We sent them multiple emails asking for more time.
4 Tom didn't get the job. ~~*As you'd expect*~~ Naturally, he's pretty disappointed, but I'm sure he'll get over it.
5 ~~*It's obvious that*~~ Undoubtedly, stress has played a large part in her decision.
6 ~~*To be honest*~~ Frankly, I think you need to spend more time with your family.
7 ~~*It's true that*~~ Admittedly, I don't exercise enough.
8 ~~*I'm disappointed that*~~ Sadly, we can't go on vacation this summer.

C Choose the best adverbs to complete the collocations.

1 I'm *bitterly* / *deeply* concerned about his mental health right now.
2 You should try the 'couch to 5K' running plan. It's *highly* / *ridiculously* easy.
3 This diet is *absolutely* / *deeply* terrible. I don't see how anyone can stick to it.
4 I was *bitterly* / *absolutely* disappointed when I heard I didn't get the job.
5 It's *ridiculously* / *highly* likely that she'll pass the exam and get into the university.
6 It was *bitterly* / *deeply* cold outside and I'd forgotten my winter coat.
7 Have you ever seen *The Shining*? It's *highly* / *absolutely* terrifying!
8 The actor admitted he was *deeply* / *ridiculously* ashamed of his behavior.

GRAMMAR

A Complete the conversations with the present perfect or present perfect progressive form of the verbs in the box.

decorate have live reply send travel

1 A: We must be almost there by now – we 've/have been traveling for hours!
B: Don't worry, not long to go!
2 A: Have you managed to get in touch with Andy yet?
B: No! I 've/have sent him half a dozen emails, but he still hasn't replied.
3 A: Where are you staying right now?
B: I 've/have been living with my parents while I look for a new apartment.
4 A: What are you working on?
B: The same thing! I 've/have been decorating the same house for weeks now!
5 A: Do you want to go out for coffee?
B: No, I'd better not. I 've/have had three already this morning.

B Complete the letter with *used to, would, be used to* or *get used to* and the correct form of the verbs in the box.

arrive be (x2) drive go know live run

Before the internet

In the past, if someone 'followed' you, then you [1] would run / used to run quickly in the opposite direction. 'Going viral' [2] used to be a bad thing and 'trolls' were only toys and not unpleasant people. Arguments [3] used to go / would go on for a long time because no one could quickly find the answer on their phone. People [4] used to know everyone's phone numbers by heart. If you wanted to meet your friends, they [5] used to arrive / would arrive on time, otherwise it was impossible to find them later. Today, people [6] are used to driving without a map and never having to plan their trips. We all seem to have [7] gotten used to living in a world where people speak to their devices as if they're human! I have to say that of all these changes – one thing I'll never [8] get used to is these devices spying on me!

Richard Solomon

Cleveland, Ohio

C Work in pairs. Discuss the questions.

1 What did you used to look like when you were younger?
2 What's something that you used to hate, but now love?
3 Do you think you're used to speaking in English yet?
4 What would someone have to get used to if they lived in your country?

Nearing the summit of the Totem Pole in Tasmania, Australia.

Survival (n) the fact or state of continuing to live or exist, especially in difficult conditions.
Synonyms: preservation (n), continuity (n)
Collocations and idioms: *fight for* survival, survival *skills*, survival *instincts*

The quote from Plato suggests that fear is natural and that courage just means overcoming those fears when you need to.

Plato (428 BCE–348 BCE) was an ancient Greek philosopher who was the student of Socrates, teacher of Aristotle and the founder of the Academy in Athens, the first university to be opened in the West. The majority of his writing has survived to the present day and his ideas are still hugely influential on Western thought.

OBJECTIVES

- create a collaborative story
- tell a personal anecdote
- discuss priorities in a survival situation
- talk about fears and offer advice
- describe a trip or journey
- write a short story

Work with a partner. Discuss the questions.

1 Read the quote. What do you think Plato means?
2 Look at the picture. What would you be afraid of if you were alone in this place?
3 What skills and strengths do you have to survive a challenging situation?

SURVIVAL 25

OBJECTIVES

Read the unit objectives to the class.

UNIT OPENER QUESTIONS

1 Draw students' attention to the image and elicit what sport is shown (*rock climbing*) and whether anyone in the class has tried or would like to try something like this. Then, read the quote as a class and elicit the meaning of *courage* (*the ability to deal with dangerous/difficult situations without being frightened*) and how it relates to the image (*the woman is showing great courage in what is a very dangerous situation*). Next, put students into pairs to discuss the question. Monitor, encouraging students to explain their reasoning. Open the discussion up to the class, writing any useful emergent vocabulary on the board.

2 Put students back into pairs to discuss the picture. Monitor and ask follow-up questions to extend the discussions. Bring the class back together to share their ideas, again adding any useful emergent vocabulary to the board.

3 Read the question as a class and elicit one or two skills or strengths the woman in the picture needs to survive in that situation. Next, elicit another type of challenging situation (ideally something very different from the picture, e.g. *being in a large amount of debt*) and elicit the kind of characteristics you would need to survive it. Now, put students into pairs a final time to discuss new situations. Monitor and support with new or unfamiliar vocabulary as necessary. Bring the class back together to discuss their ideas.

WORKSHEETS

Lesson 3.1 Staying alive

Grammar: Narrative tenses (W11)

Vocabulary: Descriptive verbs (W12)

Lesson 3.2 Fear and danger

Grammar: Alternatives to *if* in conditionals (W13)

Vocabulary: Phrasal verbs to describe problems (W14)

Vocabulary: Dependent prepositions: adjectives (W15)

3.1 Staying alive

- Create a collaborative story
- Tell a personal anecdote

S – following the sequence of a narrative
G – narrative tenses
V – descriptive verbs
P – dramatic storytelling techniques

READING

A SPEAK Work in pairs. Discuss how you might survive in the following situations.

1. Your plane crashes in the jungle and you're lost without a phone.
2. On a climb in the Alps, you trip and break your ankle.
3. Your boat sinks, but you manage to swim to a desert island.
4. While driving through the Sahara, your jeep breaks down, miles from any towns.
5. There's a fire in your office building and you're on the top floor.

B READ FOR GIST Read *Nigerian cook survives for three days in an underwater air bubble* and answer the questions. Write notes.

1. Who is the main focus of the story?
2. What happened to the Jascon-4?
3. How did the ship's cook survive for three days?
4. What happened to the other crew members?
5. How was the cook eventually rescued?

C FOLLOW THE SEQUENCE OF A NARRATIVE Read the article again. Put the events in the order they happened. Use the information in the box to help you.

Following the sequence of a narrative

Articles describing the sequence of past events don't always present the information in chronological order. To help you identify the order in which things happened, look for:

Time expressions

Writers use a combination of specific time expressions (e.g. *at 5 am, on May 26th*, etc) and phrases (e.g. *24 hours later, over the next three days*, etc) to highlight key points in the narrative.

Tenses

Identifying which tense has been used and why (e.g. past perfect to show that one action happened before another) will also help you to understand when events happened in relation to each other.

__1__ He woke up and went to the bathroom.
__4__ He found some equipment.
__8__ He gave the divers a huge shock.
__6__ He thought he heard sharks outside.
__5__ He stopped the water coming in.
__2__ The boat was turned over by a powerful wave.
__3__ He opened the door and went into the passageway.
__7__ He knocked on the wall with a hammer.
__9__ He spent two days recovering.

Nigerian cook **SURVIVES** *for* **THREE DAYS** *in* **UNDERWATER AIR BUBBLE**

Ex B Q1 **Harrison Okene was trapped 30 meters below the surface in freezing waters.**

Harrison Okene was a happy young man who was about to get married in a few days. At the time, he was working as a cook on a boat and before getting married, he had to go on one last trip. Unfortunately, it quickly turned into a nightmare.

The events started to unfold at 5:00 am on May 26th. The crew of the Jacson-4 had been sleeping while the boat was resting 20 miles off the Nigerian coast. While a violent storm was raging, Okene got up to go to the
Ex B Q2 bathroom. As he was standing in the bathroom, a huge wave hit the boat. It turned over and plunged 30 meters below the surface, with Okene and the rest of the crew still inside. Water quickly began to fill the cabin, blocking the bathroom door as the boat sank into the ocean. Using all his strength, Okene forced open the door and headed out into the passageway. Wearing nothing but pajamas, he waded through the passageway in total darkness toward the only light he could see. Quickly he grabbed a drink and a few tools and made it to the light.

Stuck in a small pocket of air, he blocked the sides with furniture to keep the water out. Ex B Q3
Unknown to Okene, all of his crewmates had already drowned. Ex B Q4 With hardly any air to breathe, time was running out. Hungry, cold and tired, Okene thought he could hear sharks circling the boat and started to lose hope. However, his luck was about to change.

When a rescue crew arrived, they assumed everyone had died since the boat had been resting on the seabed for 60 hours. Realizing the sounds he had heard were human, Okene started banging on the wall with a hammer. Thinking he wouldn't be discovered, he jumped into the water and began swimming through the ship. Ex B Q5 Seeing a rescue diver swim past him, Okene reached out to touch the man on the shoulder. Although initially terrified, the diver realized he'd found a survivor and called for support. Shortly afterward, Okene was strapped to diving equipment and taken back to the surface where he spent two days in a decompression chamber.

3.1 Staying alive

LEAD-IN

Tell students an anecdote (real or made-up) of a time you survived a dangerous situation. Encourage students to ask questions during the story, adding any useful emergent language to the board. Next, put students into groups to share their own stories (or stories about someone they know or have read about if this is easier). Monitor, encouraging students to ask follow-up questions for more information. Write notes about two or three of the most interesting stories and bring the class back together to discuss them. Add any new or useful emergent vocabulary to the board.

READING

A Read the first situation as a class. Elicit any possible dangers (e.g. *running out of food*, *getting lost*, etc) and try to agree on a solution as a class. Next, put students into pairs to discuss what they would do in the remaining situations. Monitor, encouraging students to explain their reasoning and helping with any new vocabulary. Give feedback as a class and try to agree on one solution for each situation. Add any useful emergent vocabulary to the board.

B Tell students that they will now read a real-life survival story. Give them time to complete the exercise alone before checking their answers with a partner. Give feedback as a class, encouraging students to justify their answers with information from the text. Take this opportunity to clarify any new or unfamiliar vocabulary in the article before moving on.

1 *Harrison Okene, the boat's cook.*
2 *It was hit by a huge wave during a storm, turned over and sank.*
3 *He found a small pocket of air, used furniture to block out the water and waited.*
4 *They all drowned.*
5 *A rescue diver heard him banging on the side of the boat and found him swimming past. Okene was then strapped to diving equipment and taken back to the surface.*

C Explain that articles that focus on a narrative don't always present the events in chronological order and elicit why this might be (*possibly to make the article more dynamic, exciting or easier to read*). Elicit what can help you follow the narrative (e.g. *time expressions*, *tenses*, etc) and add examples of each to the board. Then, give students time to complete the exercise alone before checking their answers with a partner. Give feedback as a class, encouraging students to use examples from the text to support their ideas. Focus in particular on the use of narrative tenses at this point as students will review these in the next section, so any groundwork that can be done now will help.

GRAMMAR HUB

3.1 Narrative tenses

	Positive	Negative	Question
Simple past	**The rescue team found** Jose and **carried** him to safety.	Unfortunately, **the rescue team didn't see** the survivors.	So what **did you do** next?
Past progressive	At the time, **most of us were trying** to get some sleep.	**I wasn't looking forward to** the trip.	What **were you doing** when the storm hit?
Past perfect	They returned to find that **the tornado had destroyed** their house.	They suddenly realized that **the helicopter hadn't seen** their signal.	**Had you been** in that kind of situation before?
Past perfect progressive	**She'd been swimming** for hours by the time she was rescued.	Although **they hadn't been driving** long, everyone was exhausted.	How long **had you been climbing** for?

- We use the simple past for completed actions that are the main events in a story.
  After some hours alone in the woods, Wei ate his last chocolate bar.
- We use the past progressive (*was/were* + verb + *-ing*) to describe:
  - **a** actions in progress at a particular point in a story.
    He was charging his phone at the time.
  - **b** longer actions or situations that are interrupted by a shorter action.
    They weren't wearing life jackets when the boat capsized. NOT ~~*They didn't wear life jackets when the boat capsized.*~~
  - **c** the general background of a story.
    The skies were getting dark, the winds were picking up and the passengers were beginning to worry.
- We use the past perfect (*had* + past participle) to describe past actions or situations that happened before one of the main events in the story, or before the story began.
  A lot of insects had bitten Francesco before he decided to use the insect repellent.
- We use the past perfect progressive (*had* + *been* + verb + *-ing*) to describe longer actions or situations that started before one of the main events and have continued up to that point.
  We'd been waiting for hours before we were rescued.

Be careful!

- We usually use the past progressive after *while* and *as*.
  While she was standing by the side of the road, a car with dark windows pulled up.
- We can usually use either the simple past or past perfect after *as soon as* and *by the time*.
  By the time I'd realized what was happening, Jilly had left.

GRAMMAR

A Write the first sentence on the board and work through it together as a class. Elicit which contextual clues in the sentence indicate the required tense (e.g. *at the time* is usually used with past progressive tense), before highlighting the answer in the article. Then, ask students to complete the sentences alone before finding the correct answers in the text. Give feedback as a class.

B Give students time to complete the rules alone before checking their answers with a partner. Give feedback as a class, providing further explanations and examples as necessary.

C Direct students to the **Grammar Hub** (see below and TB26).

D Give students time to complete the real-life survival story before checking their answers in pairs. Give feedback as a class, eliciting which contextual clues help them decide which tenses to use. Use the **Grammar Worksheet** on page W11 for extra practice.

E Write the first sentence of a dramatic survival story on the board (e.g. *unable to get any further without fuel, the pilot was forced to crash land the plane into the ocean*). Elicit a sentence telling the next part of the story using a narrative tense and add it to the board. Next, put students into groups and ask them to continue the story by each adding a sentence to a piece of paper, then passing it on. Monitor and help with their grammar as necessary. Set a time limit for the task and toward the end, encourage students to finish their stories. If you have time, put students into new pairs and ask them to share their stories.

SPEAKING

A Direct students to the **Communication Hub** (see TB121).

B Call on one group to tell their story to the class, encouraging other students to share any different ideas or extra details they came up with.

GRAMMAR HUB

3.1 Narrative tenses

A Choose the correct options (a, b or c) to complete the sentences.

1 Nozomi ___ her bike when it started raining.
(a) was riding b rode c had ridden

2 We ___ down the side of the mountain when our rope snapped.
a had climbed (b) were climbing c climbed

3 The ship ___ into a rock, but no one was hurt.
a had crashed b was crashing (c) crashed

4 I ___ my tent when suddenly I heard a strange noise in the forest behind me.
a packed away b had packed away (c) was packing away

5 The next day, they saw that the hurricane ___ the house off the ground!
a was lifting (b) had lifted c lifted

6 When the wave hit the ship, everyone ___ to panic.
a had started (b) started c was starting

7 The sun ___ and the conditions were perfect for hiking.
(a) was shining b had shone c shone

8 We ___ for eight hours when the captain told us to prepare for an emergency landing.
a were flying (b) had been flying c flew

B Complete the story with the correct form of the verbs in the box.

approach carry faint fall fly happen serve take off

Something strange [1] happened the last time I was on a plane. I [2] was flying to Moscow on a business trip. We [3] 'd/had taken off from Frankfurt about an hour before, and the cabin crew [4] was serving drinks. Suddenly, one of the cabin crew near me just [5] fell to the floor. We didn't know if he [6] 'd/had fainted or had had a heart attack. Other members of the crew rushed to help him, and [7] carried him to the back of the plane. Just as we [8] approached / were approaching Moscow, the captain made an announcement, telling us that the crew member was fine. I was very relieved.

➤ Go back to page 27.

METHODOLOGY HUB by Scott Thornbury

Narrating

The ability to tell a story in a second language, whether a simple joke or the account of a weekend outing, is extremely satisfying. It can also be very important, as when reporting an accident, for example, or filing an insurance claim. It is a good idea, therefore, to introduce learners to narrating language – and to provide opportunities to practice it – at an early stage in their learning. This in turn assumes that learners are able to use past tense forms, so the sooner these are taught, the better. Many teachers customarily start their lessons with some chat about recent activities; this is a good opportunity to support (through scaffolding) the learners' emerging storytelling skills. Other narrative-telling techniques are the use of *picture stories* (a sequence of pictures that tell a story) or *short video clips; chain stories* (where each learner writes the continuation to an introductory sentence, such as *It was a dark and stormy night …*; they then pass their sheet of paper to the learner sitting on their right, and each student continues the story in their own way, and so on, until each sheet of paper has returned to its owner); and *mini-sagas,* where learners have to write a story that is exactly 50 words long.

GRAMMAR

Narrative tenses

A Complete the sentences with the correct form of the verbs in parentheses. Then scan the article again to check your answers.

1. At the time, he ___was working___ (*work*) as a cook on a boat.
2. While a violent storm ___was raging___ (*rage*) outside, Okene got up to go to the bathroom.
3. It ___turned___ (*turn*) over and plunged 30 meters below the surface, with Okene and the rest of the crew still inside.
4. Unknown to Okene, all of his shipmates ___had already drowned___ (*already / drown*).
5. When a rescue crew arrived, they assumed everyone had died, as the boat ___had been resting___ (*rest*) on the seabed for 60 hours.

B WORK IT OUT Choose the correct tenses to complete the rules in the box.

Narrative tenses

We use the [1]*simple past / past perfect* for completed actions that are the main events in a story.

We use the [2]*past progressive / simple past*:

- for actions in progress at a particular point in time.
- when a longer action is interrupted by a shorter action.
- to set the scene of a story.

We use the [3]*past perfect / past perfect progressive* for completed actions that happened before the main event.

We use the [4]*past perfect / past perfect progressive* for longer actions that started before other events and continued up to these events.

C Go to the **Grammar Hub** on **page 126**.

D PRACTICE Complete the text with the correct form of the verbs in parentheses.

NEWS SPORT CULTURE LIFESTYLE SEARCH

7-YEAR-OLD JAPANESE BOY SURVIVES FOR OVER A WEEK ALONE IN THE WOODS

FAMILY DAY OUT TURNS TO DISASTER

A family day out looking for wild vegetables quickly turned to disaster when a boy's parents decided to punish his bad behavior. Yamato Tanooka [1] ___was throwing___ (*throw*) stones at cars as he waited for his parents. Spotting his behavior, his father quickly [2] ___became___ (*become*) very angry and [3] ___yelled___ (*yell*) at him. To punish their son, Mr. and Mrs. Tanooka [4] ___left___ (*leave*) him on the side of the road and [5] ___drove___ (*drive*) a few hundred meters away. By the time they [6] ___'d/had driven___ (*drive*) back to the spot, Yamato [7] ___had already left___ (*already / leave*). His father [8] ___called___ (*call*) the police and [9] ___said___ (*say*) he [10] ___'d/had become___ (*become*) separated from his son while they [11] ___were picking___ (*pick*) wild vegetables. In the meantime, Yamato [12] ___had walked___ (*walk*) off into the woods, upset that his father [13] ___had told___ him ___off___ (*tell off*). When the army finally [14] ___found___ (*find*) Yamato, he [15] ___'d/had been living___ (*live*) for six days on his own in woods that are home to brown bears. Yamato told reporters that he [16] ___'d/had been walking / had walked___ (*walk*) for five hours through the woods when he found an old army cabin. Afraid of the dark, he decided to hide there and wait for his parents to find him.

E PRACTICE Work in groups. Write the first sentence of a dramatic story. Pass your sentence to the student on your right. Add another sentence to the story you have just received. Keep doing this until your story is complete.

SPEAKING

A PREPARE Go to the **Communication Hub** on **page 150**.

B PRESENT Choose one person to tell your story to the class. Listen to the other stories and ask questions about the details.

LISTENING

A Label the pictures (1–6) with the activities in the box.

bungee jumping | free running | free climbing | potholing | skydiving | whitewater rafting

B SPEAK Work in pairs. Discuss the questions.

1 Which of these sports do you think is the most dangerous? Why?

2 Why do you think some people enjoy doing dangerous sports like these?

3 Have you ever done any of these sports? Would you like to? Why/Why not?

3.1 **C LISTEN FOR GIST** Listen to a radio talk show about extreme sports and answer the questions. Write notes.

1 Which of the sports from Exercise A do the speakers talk about? free climbing, potholing and free running

2 How many of the speakers have been injured while doing their sport? one (Lee broke his ankle while free running)

1 bungee jumping

2 skydiving

3.1 **D LISTEN FOR DETAIL** Listen again and choose the correct options (a, b or c) to complete the sentences.

1 Paul started free climbing when he was …
  a 10 years old. b 17 years old. (c) 27 years old.

2 Paul thinks climbing without safety equipment …
  a is a terrible idea.
  (b) is a good challenge.
  c allows him to go higher.

3 Paul was most scared when …
  a he was caught in strong winds during a climb.
  b the bridge he was crossing on broke.
  (c) a snake shot out of a crack in a rock.

4 Hayley thinks that …
  (a) potholing is more challenging than rock climbing.
  b rock climbing is too challenging.
  c potholing is more like walking than climbing.

5 Hayley was lost underground for …
  a a few minutes. (b) a few hours. c a few days.

6 Lee started free running …
  a because his friends were doing it.
  (b) because he saw a video of people doing it.
  c because he wanted something more challenging than gymnastics.

7 Lee most enjoys …
  a the physical challenge of free running.
  (b) the way free running makes you look at a city.
  c the risks involved in free running.

8 Lee says that …
  a you should push yourself beyond your limits.
  b you need to be very competitive to be good at free running.
  (c) you should only do what you know you are capable of.

E SPEAK Work in groups. Discuss the questions.

1 Who do you think had the most frightening experience. Why?

2 Which of the sports would you like to try? Why?

4 potholing

3 free climbing

LISTENING

A Draw students' attention to the first picture and elicit which sport it shows (*bungee jumping*). Add this to the board with the phonemes and practice the pronunciation. Give students time to label the remaining pictures before checking their answers in pairs. Give feedback as a class, adding each sport to the board with the phonemes and practicing the pronunciation.

B Put students into pairs to discuss the questions. Monitor and encourage them to justify their ideas with examples.

3.1 **C** Tell students they are going to listen to a radio talk show about extreme sports, then play the audio for them to answer the questions. Give students time to compare their answers in pairs before giving feedback as a class. See the **Audio script** below and TB29.

3.1 **D** Give students time to read the questions before playing the audio again. Ask them to check their answers in pairs before giving feedback as a class.

E Put students into groups to discuss the questions. Monitor and encourage them to ask follow-up questions to keep the discussions going.

Extra activity
As a class, build up a list of extreme sports on the board (e.g. *bungee jumping*, *skateboarding*, *mountain biking*, etc). Now, write the following question – *Which sport is more dangerous?* Finally, nominate students to come to the front of the class to take part in quickfire debates, arguing for and against two of the sports on the board.

AUDIO SCRIPT

3.1

Listening, Exercise C
I = Interviewer P = Paul H = Hayley L = Lee

I: OK, welcome back to the show. Tonight we're talking about extreme sports. Why do so many people take part in such dangerous activities? Where's the fun in putting yourself at such risk? Maybe our next caller can help answer some of these burning questions. Paul, what dangerous sport do you do and why?

Ex C **P:** I'm into climbing. Especially free climbing.

I: When did you first get into climbing?

P: When I was four years old, my dad took me walking in the foothills of the Alps. I can still remember the snow crunching under our feet as we walked together. We always had a lot of fun, but I didn't really get into climbing until I was 17. I remember standing in front of a really steep rock face and thinking, 'Can I do this?'.

Ex D Q1 **I:** When did you move onto free climbing?

P: Probably about ten years later. By that point I'd become a pretty good climber and wanted a new challenge. I love the excitement, fear and challenge of it. My father thought it was a great idea because he'd been a good climber too, but my mother was terrified.

Ex D Q2

I: Have you ever had any accidents?

P: Well, I've had a lot of terrifying moments. Once, I was high up the side of a mountain in Argentina, when the wind started to pick up. It was too dangerous to climb down, so I just had to hold on and wait. In some places, there are also these tiny wooden bridges attached to the side of the mountain to help you get from one ledge to another. Sometimes the wood groans under your weight, which can be a little scary, but so far none have ever actually broken!

I: OK, so what's the most dangerous thing that's ever happened to you?

P: Well, a few years ago I was in South Africa with a few of my friends and we'd almost finished the first part of an all-day climb. I was just pulling myself up when I saw a huge snake right in front of me. I am terrified of snakes, so I just froze as it started to hiss and arch backwards. I waited for another few minutes, not moving, and then it just seemed to get bored and slithered back into a crack in the rock. It was the most terrifying moment ever and it had nothing to do with climbing!

Ex D Q3

I: Thanks for calling in, Paul. Hope you don't meet any more snakes on your climbs.

I: We have our second caller, Hayley, with us now. Hayley, what dangerous sport are you into?

Ex C **H:** Potholing!

I: What, climbing through caves and things?

H: Yeah, that's right. It's a lot of fun, actually.

I: Hmm …, not sure I'd enjoy it. Anyway, how long have you been potholing for?

H: I first got into potholing in college. There was a climbing and caving society that I joined. I had done a lot of climbing but I'd never done any potholing before. It was amazing!

I: How does it compare to climbing?

H: With climbing, you can see a lot of the route in front of you. Potholing is so dark, and the spaces can be really small, so it's difficult to plan your next move. Usually, you start at the entrance to a cave and simply walk in, but within a few hundred meters you have crawled on your belly, swum underwater, and squeezed your body through tiny gaps. The challenges are just so much more varied.

Ex D Q4

I: And is it a dangerous sport?

H: It's more dangerous than it sounds. You can suffer from a lack of oxygen or too much carbon dioxide. You can get trapped. You can drown when there's a sudden storm. You can even fall to your death climbing. There are literally hundreds of ways you can die!

I: Sounds scary! What was your most terrifying experience?

H: Once, I got lost when I was deep underground in Mexico. It can be silent for just a few minutes and all you can hear is water trickling around you. It's actually very worrying because you have no maps and no way of communicating with people outside and getting help. Luckily, we managed to get back out the way we had come. By then we had been lost underground for several hours. It was terrifying and took me weeks to get over it!

Ex D Q5

I: Thank you, Hayley. I have to say, potholing sounds terrifying! So now on to our last caller, Lee. Good evening, Lee.

L: Good evening!

3.1 Staying alive

VOCABULARY

A Explain that some verbs in English describe a sound and use an example in the classroom (e.g. *slamming the door*, *miming biting into an apple*, etc) to elicit an example. Add the verb you elicit to the board in a contextualized sentence (e.g. *Furious, the teacher slammed the door as he left the classroom.*) and elicit other examples of actions that would cause a similar noise. Then, put students into pairs to work through the questions. Give feedback, consolidating understanding by eliciting more examples for each verb.

B–C Give students time to complete the sentence alone before checking their answers with a partner. Then, give feedback as a class before directing students to the **Vocabulary Hub** (see TB121).

D Put students into pairs to rework the story using descriptive verbs. With weaker classes, work through the first sentence as a group. Bring the class back together to build up one story together on the board. Use the **Vocabulary Worksheet** on page W12 for extra practice.

PRONUNCIATION

3.2 **A** Elicit ideas on what techniques make someone a good storyteller (e.g. *pausing for emphasis*, *speed of delivery*, etc) and build up a spider diagram on the board. Then, play the audio for them to complete the exercise, then give them time to compare their answers with a partner. Give feedback as a class, ideally presenting the story on the board, marking the pauses and stress together.

3.2 **B** Play the audio again for students to focus on how the speaker changes the speed of their delivery to sound more dramatic. Give students time to discuss their ideas in pairs before giving feedback as a class.

He slows down to build tension and speeds up for excitement or to quickly get through the less interesting parts.

3.3 **C–D** Ask students to annotate the story alone before playing the audio for them to check their answers. Then, put them into pairs to practice telling the story as dramatically as possible. Monitor and encourage them to perfect each part of the story using the techniques covered in this section.

He rushes through the first sentence to get to the more dramatic part of the story; slows down when describing the fire to build tension; speeds up when the glass smashes to add excitement.

SPEAKING HUB

A–C Tell students an amazing, terrifying or embarrassing story (real or made-up) about yourself. Try to make the story as dramatic as possible and ensure you cover where it happened, who it involved and the key details of what happened. Encourage students to be active listeners by asking questions as you tell your story. Next, tell students that they are going to tell their stories and give them time to write notes alone. Now, put them into pairs to practice telling their stories. Monitor and encourage them to use techniques from the Pronunciation section to make their stories as dramatic as possible. Finally, put students into groups to share their stories. Encourage students to be active listeners by asking follow-up questions.

3.1 (continued)

Ex C **I:** So, Lee, what extreme sport are you into?
L: I'm a free runner.
I: OK, so when did you first get into it?
L: It started from when I was a child. I used to do gymnastics when I was young, so I was always
Ex D Q6 into climbing and jumping. Then a friend at school showed me a video of a group of people free running and I thought, 'Why not give it a try?'
I: What do you enjoy most about free running?
Ex D Q7 **L:** Well, it makes you look at cities in different ways compared to other people. People usually don't even look up when they walk around a city. They focus on everything at eye level – stores, people, cars. You actually really appreciate the architecture more from up high. Every city is a new physical challenge. I get excited and my adrenalin starts pumping!
I: How dangerous is free running?
Ex D Q8 **L:** It can be very dangerous. You need to be very aware of your own ability and try not to push yourself too hard. Unfortunately, because it is competitive, people are always pushing themselves to do more and more dangerous things. I have broken a lot of bones. Once, when I jumped between two buildings, I slipped and
Ex C Q2 fell 20 meters. Luckily, I didn't break anything. This other time though, I fell just a couple of meters and I broke my ankle. I can still hear my ankle snap as I landed. It was so painful!
I: Oh, wow! That sounds horrible. Anyway, thanks for joining us, Lee. OK, listeners – we're just going to a short commercial break before we take our next caller.

TEACHING IDEA by David Seymour and Maria Popova

Story words

Use this activity to review recently studied vocabulary and narrative tenses.

In groups, select 20 recently learned items of vocabulary and write them on a large piece of paper. Swap your paper with another group. Put the one you receive in the middle of your group and take turns using the words in a story, adding one line each.

TEACHING IDEA by David Seymour and Maria Popova

Onomatopoeia

Use this activity to review and build on onomatopoeic verbs.

In pairs, listen to these descriptions. Discuss how you write the sounds in your language and in English, e.g. *the sound two cars make as they collide – Crash!*

- the noise a car horn makes (*beep*)
- what a cat does when it's happy (*purr*)
- the noise of a saucepan falling on the floor (*clang*)
- the sound of frying meat (*sizzle*)
- what a snake does (*hiss*)
- the sound you hear when you stick a pin into a balloon (*pop*)

In pairs, look at these words and say them. Guess what makes each sound. Compare your ideas with another pair.

buzz, tinkle, squeak, growl, hum, squelch, rustle, crunch, thud

What are some of the 'sound words' in your language?

VOCABULARY
Descriptive verbs

A **Work in pairs. For each extract, choose the option that makes the same sound as the verb in bold.**

1 I can still remember the snow **crunching** under our feet as we walked together.
   (a) old leaves under your feet
   b your feet in an empty hospital hallway
2 Sometimes the wood **groans** under your weight, which can be a little scary, but so far none have ever actually broken!
   a grass under your feet
   (b) floorboards under your feet
3 I am terrified of snakes, so I just froze as it started to **hiss** and arch backwards.
   a the wind closing a door
   (b) air slowly escaping from a tire
4 It can be silent for just a few minutes and all you can hear is water **trickling** around you.
   (a) a slow-running tap
   b a large, powerful river
5 I can still hear my ankle **snap** as I landed.
   (a) a branch breaking
   b a window breaking

B **Complete the sentences with the correct form of the verbs in Exercise A.**

1 The snake ___hissed___ and slithered back into the undergrowth.
2 The leaves were ___crunching___ under our feet as we crept slowly through the forest.
3 I could hear the branch of the tree ___groaning___ under my weight before it ___snapped___ and I fell to the ground.
4 Every time it rained, I could hear water ___trickling___ down the wall behind my bed.

C **Go to the Vocabulary Hub on page 144.**

D **SPEAK Work in pairs. Use descriptive verbs to make this story more interesting.**

I was walking through the forest with fallen leaves under my feet. The trees were blowing in the wind. Suddenly, I heard a branch break behind me. I turned to see a huge dog running toward me.

PRONUNCIATION
Dramatic storytelling techniques

3.2 **A** **Listen to this extract from the talk show. Mark the pauses with (/) and underline any words that are emphasized.**

Well,/a few years ago I was in South Africa with a few of my friends and we'd almost finished the first part of an all-day climb./I was just pulling myself up when I saw a huge snake right in front of me./I am terrified of snakes, so I just froze as it started to hiss and arch backwards./I waited for another few minutes, not moving,/and then it just seemed to get bored and slithered back into a crack in the rock./It was the most terrifying moment ever and it had nothing to do with climbing!

3.2 **B** **Listen to the story again. When does the speaker speed up and slow down? Why do you think he does this?**

C **Read the story extract. Predict where you think the pauses will be, which words the speaker will stress and when they will speed up.**

So a few months ago I was staying at my parents' house when this strange thing happened./We were all enjoying the warmth of the crackling fire/as the trees creaked in the wind outside./Suddenly,/we heard glass smashing upstairs/ and something heavy banged on the floor./We rushed upstairs to find that a huge branch had crashed through the roof of the house.

3.3 **D** **Listen and check your answers to Exercise C. Then, practice telling the story with a partner.**

SPEAKING HUB

A **PLAN** **Think of the most amazing, terrifying or embarrassing moment in your life. Write notes about:**

- where you were
- who you were with
- what happened

B **PREPARE** **Work in pairs. Tell your stories and work together to make them more dramatic or exciting.**

C **PRESENT** **Work in small groups. Tell your stories as dramatically as you can. Ask questions to get more information.**

- Create a collaborative story
- Tell a personal anecdote

3.2 Fear and danger

- Discuss priorities in a survival situation
- Talk about fears and offer advice

G – alternatives to *if* in conditionals
S – listening for definitions, examples and explanations
P – intonation in conditional sentences
V – phrasal verbs to describe problems; dependent prepositions: adjectives

READING

A SPEAK Work in groups. Discuss what you would do in the following situations.

1 You're caught in some quicksand in the desert. As you're sinking you see a large stick nearby.

2 You're attacked by a swarm of killer bees in the woods. There's a house in the distance and a lake a few meters away.

3 You're doing parachute jump, but your parachute fails. If you stretch out, you could probably reach your friend.

B READ FOR GIST Complete the interview with the questions (a–d).

a Is that in your show this time?

b Can we expect any dangerous animals this year?

c Are you feeling excited about your new series starting next week?

d What can viewers expect from this series?

C READ FOR DETAIL Read again. Choose the correct options (a or b) to complete the sentences.

1 Chuck advises carrying a stick in the desert …

a to move quicksand away from your body.

(b) to stop yourself sinking into quicksand.

2 When you are in quicksand, Chuck suggests …

a moving quickly to escape.

(b) getting out carefully.

3 Chuck says that hitting killer bees …

a is the first form of defence against them.

(b) is likely to make the situation worse.

4 If you follow his advice, Chuck says you may break your arm when …

(a) your friend's parachute opens.

b your parachute opens.

D SPEAK Work in groups. Has anyone you know ever been in a life-threatening situation? How did they survive?

CHUCK ADAMS:

SURVIVE THE WILD

In the office of *Live, Play, Work Magazine*, we're all very excited to see the return to TV of Chuck Adams and his series *Survive the Wild*. Tom Wood caught up with Chuck to ask him about surviving in the desert, killer bees and why breaking your arm is sometimes the best thing to do …

Tom: It's great to see you again, Chuck! 1 c

Chuck: I am. The first series was incredibly popular and we're taking viewers into some even more exciting situations in the new series.

Tom: 2 d

Chuck: Well, we look at how to survive dangerous situations in different locations. From mountains to deserts to the Arctic. For example, in the desert or along the coast, always carry a stick in case you need it. Quicksand is really dangerous! As soon as you start to sink, put the stick on the surface of the sand and lie on it. If you do this, it will stop you from sinking. Once you stop sinking, you need to crawl, climb and almost swim out. You'll be OK as long as you move slowly out of the sand. If you move too quickly, you'll sink. Ex C Q1 Ex C Q2

Tom: Sounds like hard work! Last series you looked at surviving crocodile attacks and shark attacks. 3 b

Chuck: Definitely! We have all sorts, including killer bees! People sometimes freeze when they see a bee, but this won't stop it from stinging you. And definitely don't try to hit them – this just makes them angrier. If bees fly around you, try to find shelter as quickly as possible. Provided you can get into a building, or shelter in long grass, you'll be fine. A lot of people jump into water to get away. Don't do this. The bees will just be waiting for you when you come up! Ex C Q3

Tom: That sounds horrible! What about surviving accidents? 4 a

Chuck: Of course! People usually do parachute jumps with other people. If your parachute doesn't open, grab the person near you, lock your arms together and hold onto each other. When your friend opens their parachute you will survive, but you will also probably break your arm – so be prepared for some pain! Ex C Q4

Tom: I feel a little sick at the thought of breaking my arm!

Chuck: Maybe, but unless you lock arms, you won't survive!

Tom: Well we can't wait for the show to return next week! Thanks for speaking to us today.

3.2 Fear and danger

LEAD-IN

Tell students that you are planning an extreme adventure next year (e.g. *climbing a mountain in the Alps, hiking through the Amazon*, etc) and can only take one large backpack. Elicit a few ideas about what you should take with you and why, adding them to the board. Then, put students into groups to make their own lists, explaining that they must agree on ten items. Bring everyone back together to share their ideas and try to agree on a list as a class.

READING

A Give students time to read each scenario, clarifying the meaning of any key vocabulary (e.g. *quicksand, swarm, parachute*, etc). Then, put students into groups to discuss each situation. Monitor, helping with grammar and vocabulary as necessary. Bring the class back together to share their ideas. Try to agree on one solution for each scenario, but don't confirm any answers at this stage.

B Ask students to read the title and introduction to the article and elicit what Chuck Adams does (*he is a survival expert*). Then, give students time to complete the interview alone before checking their answers with a partner. Give feedback as a class, encouraging students to explain which information in the text gave them the answers.

C Read the questions as a class and encourage students to underline the key words in each. Then, give them time to complete the sentences alone before checking their answers in pairs. Give feedback as a class, encouraging students to justify their answers with information from the text.

D Put students into groups to discuss the questions. Monitor, encouraging them to ask follow-up questions to keep the discussions going. Choose one or two of the most interesting stories for groups to share with the class. Add any new or useful emergent language to the board.

GRAMMAR HUB

3.2 Alternatives to *if* in conditionals

- We use *unless* to mean *if … not*.

  Generally, bears won't attack you unless they think you're a threat. (= They won't attack you if they don't think you're a threat.)

  Unless this weather improves, we'll be stuck in the camp all day. (= If the weather doesn't improve, we'll be stuck in the camp all day.)

- We use *provided (that)* and *as long as* to mean *only if*.

  They should be back soon provided (that) they don't take a wrong turn. (= They should be back soon, but only if they don't take a wrong turn.)

  As long as you stay on the path, you won't get lost. (= You won't get lost, but only if you stay on the path.)

- We use *in case* to talk about doing something now to prepare for a possible future situation.

  I'll take a waterproof jacket in case it starts raining. (= because it's possible it will start raining)

  She's going to stay in a safe spot in case she encounters a bear. (= because it's possible that she will encounter a bear)

- We use *as soon as* to mean *in the shortest possible time / immediately*.

  I'll call you as soon as I hear anything. (= I'll call you immediately after I hear something.)

Be careful!

- Even though we're talking about the future, we use a present tense after future time clauses.

  We'll leave as soon as the storm clears. NOT ~~*We'll leave as soon as the storm will clear.*~~

  Elephants won't attack you unless you run toward them. NOT ~~*Elephants won't attack you unless you will run toward them.*~~

TEACHING IDEA by Jim Scrivener

In case

Use these activities to practice using *in case*:

But Mom … I'm grown up now!

Make pairs. A is an 18-year-old, getting ready to leave home and go to college. B is an over-protective parent who is suggesting a lot of possible problems, what to take, what not to do (*Take a dictionary in case you can't buy one there. Get insurance for your iPad© in case you lose it. Don't go out after 9 pm in case you get mugged.*) Elicit or model one or two examples and then get students to think of more and then role-play the scene.

The expedition

Prepare a list of items that might be useful on an expedition to the South Pole (or Sahara, Amazon). Pairs discuss which five items are most important (*We have to take the snake serum in case we get bitten.*) Collect ideas from the whole class and reach a compromise solution.

Why do we need them?

Write the names of jobs/professions (*doctor, soldier, teacher, cleaner*) at the top of separate pieces of paper. Give one to each group. Ask students to think of a reason why we need their profession in our society (*We need doctors in case we get sick.*). When they have finished, they pass the paper to another group and get a new one. They should add a new 'in case' i.e. *not* the same idea as the last one (*We need doctors in case there is a disaster.*) and pass it on one more time (to make three ideas in total on each sheet). When ready, groups read out the three sentences but knocking on the table instead of saying the job name (*We need <knock> in case we get sick*). The other students should guess the missing jobs.

3.2 Fear and danger

GRAMMAR

A Write the first sentence on the board and elicit what kind of structure this is (*conditional*). Ask why it might be useful to carry a stick (*you could use it to help you walk, to defend yourself with*, etc) and if you will definitely need to use one or if it's just a good idea to carry one because it might be useful (*the latter*). Next, elicit which answer option is correct for the first sentence (*b*) and which word or phrase in the example is used instead of *if* to highlight this meaning (*in case*). Consolidate understanding of *in case* by eliciting appropriate ways to finish other contextual sentences (e.g. *I always take an umbrella to work in case …*). Now, put students into pairs to work through the remaining extracts together. Give feedback as a class, giving further examples or explanations of each alternative to *if* to consolidate understanding.

B–C Give students time to complete the rules alone before checking their answers with a partner. Give feedback, further clarifying the meaning of structure as necessary. Then, direct students to the **Grammar Hub** (see below and TB30).

D Read the first situation as a class, eliciting a few pieces of advice using conditional structures. Prompt students if necessary (e.g. *You should try to find cover in case …, As long as it doesn't …*, etc). Then, put students into pairs to discuss their own ideas. Monitor, helping with new vocabulary as necessary. Give feedback as a class, eliciting one or two pieces of good advice for each situation. Use the **Grammar Worksheet** on page W13 for extra practice.

PRONUNCIATION

A–B (3.4) Tell students they are now going to focus on intonation in conditional sentences. Play the audio for students to analyze the intonation patterns. During class feedback, ask what the similarity between the intonation patterns is (*it generally rises on the if clause and falls on the main clause*), then play the audio again, pausing between each sentence for students to listen and repeat.

SPEAKING

A Tell students that they are going to discuss how to survive a dangerous situation and elicit the meaning of *survival priorities* (*the order of things we need to do in order to survive*). Then, give students time to read the scenario and write notes. Monitor and help with any new or unfamiliar vocabulary.

B Draw students' attention to the pictures and give them time to write notes about how each might help them with the survival priorities they listed in Exercise A. With a weaker class, work through an example together using one of the items and the example priority (*Make a shelter*).

C Put students into groups to discuss survival priorities. Monitor, encouraging them to use conditional structures to explain their ideas. In feedback, call on groups one by one to share their discussions and encourage other students to respond to each other's ideas.

GRAMMAR HUB

3.2 Alternatives to *if* in conditionals

A Choose the correct options to complete the sentences.

1 They'll survive in the woods ***provided*** / ***unless*** they have enough food.
2 ***Unless*** / ***Provided*** we leave right now, we'll never make it back to the camp before dark.
3 I'll let you start the fire ***as soon as*** / ***as long as*** you know what you're doing!
4 Do Yoon is bringing extra water ***as long as*** / ***in case*** we run out.
5 Let's give Margie a call ***as soon as*** / ***as long as*** we reach the cabin.
6 ***As long as*** / ***Unless*** you have a better suggestion, let's have pizza tonight.
7 I wrote their number on a piece of paper ***in case*** / ***unless*** my phone battery dies.
8 We'll go fishing at the river tomorrow ***as long as*** / ***in case*** it doesn't rain.

B Are these sentences correct or incorrect? Rewrite the incorrect sentences.

1 We'll call the police as soon as we will get to safety.
2 I'll cancel the trip unless Tara will decide to go with me.
3 You can go to the party provided you're back home by 11 o'clock.
4 Unless the taxi doesn't come soon, we're going to be late.
5 Take some seasickness pills with you in case the ocean will be rough.
6 Will you call me as soon as you arrive at the airport?
7 He'll sleep on the ship as long as the weather won't be too bad.
8 I'll take the risk provided you think it's worth it.

C Match the numbers (1–10) with the letters (a–j) to make conditional sentences.

1 Provided you don't make any sudden movements, i
2 She won't use her credit card g
3 You won't get into trouble a
4 Astrid should give David the money now c
5 As long as you promise to pay him back, f
6 I'll come with you as j
7 Unless we stay late, e
8 I'm going to take a map with me d
9 Provided that we stay somewhere cheap, b
10 I'll buy the tickets h

a provided you tell the truth.
b I'd love to come with you to Paris.
c in case she doesn't see him later.
d in case we get lost.
e we'll never get all this work done on time.
f he said that he would get the food for the party.
g unless it's an emergency.
h as soon as they're available online.
i you should be perfectly safe.
j long as we make sure we're back home by five.

➤ Go back to page 31.

GRAMMAR

Alternatives to *if* in conditionals

A **Work in pairs. Read the extracts from the interview and choose the correct meaning.**

1 … in the desert or along the coast, always carry a stick in case you need it.
   a Take a stick because you will definitely need it.
   (b) Take a stick because you might need it.

2 As soon as you start to sink, put the stick on the surface of the sand and lie on it.
   (a) When you start sinking, use the stick immediately.
   b When you start sinking, use the stick when you can.

3 You'll be OK as long as you move slowly out of the sand.
   (a) It's the only way to get out of the sand.
   b It's one way to get out of the sand.

4 Provided you can get into a building, or shelter in long grass, you'll be fine.
   (a) You will only be fine if you get into a building or shelter in long grass.
   b You will be fine whatever happens.

5 Maybe, but unless you lock arms, you won't survive!
   a Don't do this and you might survive.
   (b) Do this or you won't survive.

B **WORK IT OUT Complete the rules with words and phrases in the box.**

as long as   as soon as   in case   provided (that)   unless

Alternatives to *if* in conditionals

We use [1] *unless* to mean *if … not*.
We use [2] *provided (that)* and [3] *as long as* to mean *only if*.
We use [4] *in case* to talk about doing something now to prepare for a possible situation.
We use [5] *as soon as* to mean in the shortest time possible.

C **Go to the Grammar Hub on page 126.**

D **SPEAK Work in pairs. Give advice about the following situations using conditional conjunctions.**

1 You're in the middle of a field when a thunderstorm begins.
2 You're swimming in the ocean when you see a shark swim by.
3 You're lost in the country when your phone battery dies.
4 You're driving along when your car runs out of gas.

As long as you can walk to a gas station, you'll be able to buy gas.

PRONUNCIATION

Intonation in conditional sentences

3.4 **A** **Listen to the conditional sentences. Draw arrows to mark rising (↗) or falling (↘) intonation.**

1 Provided you don't run (↗), the bull won't chase you (↘).
2 Take a flashlight (↗) in case it gets dark (↘).
3 Unless you find a water source (↗), you won't survive (↘).

3.4 **B** **Listen again and repeat the sentences.**

SPEAKING

A **PREPARE Read the scenario. Make a list of survival priorities.**

You are on a small plane that has crashed on a river in a jungle. You can swim to the side of the river, but you can only take a few things with you before the plane sinks. As far as you know, you're a long way from the nearest town and may have to spend a few nights in the jungle.

1 Make a shelter
2 …

B **PLAN You have found the items below in the plane. Write notes on how you could use each item to help you achieve your priorities from Exercise A.**

C **DISCUSS Work in groups. Together you must decide on three survival priorities and how you will use the items from Exercise B.**

A: I think we should use the rope to make a shelter.
B: That's fine by me, as long as we can save some of the rope for fishing.

LISTENING

A SPEAK Work in pairs. Look at the pictures and discuss the questions.

1 What fears are shown in the pictures?
2 Do you think these fears are rational (i.e. based on facts, not emotion) or irrational? Why?
3 What other common fears can you think of?

3.5 **B LISTEN FOR GIST** Listen to an extract from an audiobook about fear. Put the topics in the order they are discussed.

4 the influence of memory
5 potential dangers of the modern world
1 the physical effects of fear
3 how we assess a perceived threat
2 the brain's initial response

3.5 **C LISTEN FOR DEFINITIONS, EXAMPLES AND EXPLANATIONS** Listen to the extract again. Complete the notes below with no more than three words or a number. Use the information in the box to help you.

Listening for definitions, examples and explanations

Speakers usually use the following to make their ideas clearer:

Definitions

To explain topic-specific language, speakers usually provide definitions. These are usually clearly signaled by phrases such as *This is defined as …*, *This means …*, but can also be given mid-sentence (e.g. *Claustrophobia – a fear of being in a small or crowded place – is frequently …*).

Examples

To help clarify an idea, speakers use examples. These are signaled by phrases such as *For instance …*, *Such as …*, *An example of this is …*

Explanations

To make something easier to understand, speakers may also give explanations. These can be signaled by phrases such as *In other words …*, *That's to say …*, *Let me explain …*

Natural reactions

The amygdala is the section 1 of the brain *associated with our emotional responses.*

2 Fight or flight *is the body's natural response to a perceived threat.*

The hippocampus and the prefrontal cortex help us to distinguish between a 3 real *and a perceived threat.*

Our 4 memories and experience *influence this decision.*

We usually focus on dramatic or emotional events (e.g. although skin cancer causes over 5 2,500 *deaths a year, people worry more about plane crashes).*

Increased stress and anxiety can have a 6 negative impact *on our immune system > could lead to physical and mental health issues. Issue of the modern world?*

D SPEAK Work in pairs. Discuss the questions.

1 Do you think the 'fight or flight' response is useful in the modern world? Why/Why not?
2 Why do you think people frequently refuse to change their mind about something even when shown evidence against it?
3 What kinds of things do people fear now that they didn't fear 20 years ago?

VOCABULARY

Phrasal verbs to describe problems

A Match the phrasal verbs (1–7) to their definitions (a–g).

1 go through d
2 sort out a
3 put up with b
4 talk over f
5 deal with c
6 work out e
7 weigh out g

a do what is necessary to solve a problem
b accept someone or something unpleasant in a patient way
c accept and control a difficult emotional situation so that you can start to live a normal life again despite it
d experience something difficult or unpleasant
e solve a problem by considering the facts
f discuss a problem or a plan
g consider the good and bad aspects of something in order to reach a decision about it

fear of public speaking (glossophobia)

fear of spiders (arachnophobia)

3.2 Fear and danger

LISTENING

A Elicit the name for extreme fears (*phobias*) by sharing any that you have with the class. Ask if any students have phobias. Then, put students into pairs to discuss the questions.

3.5 **B** Tell students they are going to listen to part of an audiobook about fear. Give them time to read the topics, then play the audio for students to put the topics into the correct order. Have students discuss their answers with a partner before giving feedback as a class.

3.5 **C** Explain that in more academic texts like this, speakers usually use terms and ideas that students are unfamiliar with, then go through the techniques in the box. Next, give students time to read the notes and predict which type of word fits in each blank and what that word might be. Play the audio again, clarifying that they must only use a maximum of three words or a number in each blank and that these must come from the text itself.

D Put students into pairs to discuss the questions. Monitor and encourage them to ask follow-up questions to extend their discussions. If you have time, open up the questions for class-wide discussion.

VOCABULARY

A Tell students about a couple you know (real or made-up) that is facing a difficult situation right now. Encourage them to ask questions to show that they are engaged. Finish by adding the following sentence to the board: *I really can't imagine what they're going through*, setting *going through* in a different color. Elicit what part of speech *go through* is (*a phrasal verb*) and ask students to find an appropriate definition from the list (a–g). Next, work through the remaining phrasal verbs before checking their answers with a partner. Give feedback as a class, eliciting an example sentence for each phrasal verb, practicing the pronunciation for anything students are struggling with (e.g. *weigh up*).

AUDIO SCRIPT

3.5

Listening, Exercise B

Chapter 2 – Phobias and rational fears

Suddenly, you see something in the corner of your
Ex B eye. Your palms start sweating, your heart beats faster and your muscles become tense. A tiny spider is crawling across the bathroom wall …

Why is it that many of us fear things that are, relatively speaking, completely harmless, yet don't think twice about real, everyday risks such as driving to work or heart disease?

The ability to calculate risk is essential to the survival of any species. Indeed, one of the most primitive human instincts is to assess our environment for potential threats. This heightened awareness of our surroundings is controlled by a section of the brain
Ex C Q1 called the amygdala. It is responsible for our fear, anger, sadness and our levels of aggression. It determines how we should react to the things we see before us. Is that a tiger waiting in the bushes or just a trick of the light? Should we run away or stay
Ex C Q2 and fight? This response – commonly referred to as 'fight or flight' – is what makes our heart beat faster and our palms start to sweat. This is actually an essential human instinct, but it's worth noting that for some, the response seems to be overly sensitive. They perceive threats where most people wouldn't and are generally far more anxious as a result. A little like an overly sensitive car alarm that goes off every time somebody walks by.

Ex B So it is the amygdala that triggers our initial reaction
Ex B; to a perceived threat. But how do we determine
Ex C Q3 + 4 whether the threat is real or not? For this, we rely on the hippocampus and the prefrontal cortex. They compare contextual information with our memories and experience, and decide whether we should be afraid or not. This is useful, because it allows us to decide, for example, to run away when we see a snake in the jungle but remain calm when we see one in a zoo. Essentially, the decision-making part of our brain can tell the emotional part to relax when there is no real threat.

Ex B The fact that we rely on our knowledge and experience to determine our emotional response is key to understanding our fears. If, for example, you had a terrifying experience with a dog when you were younger, this is highly likely to influence your reaction to them now. Similarly, if your only knowledge of an airline company is that one of their planes crashed recently, you might well be too afraid to fly with them, even if their overall safety record is very good. Although we are capable of remembering facts or statistics, humans tend to focus on the
Ex C Q5 emotional and the dramatic. For example, according to a cancer research study, skin cancer leads to around two and a half thousand deaths every year. Statistically, this is definitely something worth worrying about. In comparison, there are very few plane crashes every year. Yet when we go on vacation, many of us worry more about the plane crashing than whether or not we remembered to pack our sunscreen. While our brains are constructed to help us identify, assess and react to potential
Ex C Q6 threats, the heighted levels of anxiety this may cause can actually have a hugely negative effect on our bodies. For example, high levels of stress have a negative impact on the immune system, potentially leading to an increased risk of depression, heart
Ex B disease and diabetes. And unfortunately, it seems that modern society is designed to increase stress and anxiety. We've become accustomed to 24-hour news coverage, instant access to information and a constant flow of messages, yet it could well be that instead of improving our lives, these all have a negative impact on our physical and mental health. If this is true, how we adapt to our increasingly connected world will be fundamental to our continued survival as a species.

B–C Give students time to complete the sentences alone before checking their answers with a partner. Give feedback as a class, then put students into pairs to discuss the questions. Monitor, encouraging students to use examples to help explain their ideas. Bring the class back together and nominate one person from each pair to share the most interesting things they discussed. Use the **Vocabulary Worksheet** on page W14 for extra practice.

VOCABULARY

Write the following sentence on the board – *I'm absolutely terrified _ flying!* Elicit which type of word is missing (*a preposition*) and what that word is (*of*). Highlight that no other preposition can be used in this sentence (ask about specific examples, e.g. *with*, *about*, to reiterate the point) and elicit what we call words that are commonly used together (*collocations*). Tell students that collocations like these are called dependent prepositions and that you are going to focus on adjectives. Next, add a vertical line dissecting the sentence between *terrified* and *of* and elicit more examples from the class. Add an interesting or unusual example using a noun and elicit the possible structures used after a dependent preposition (*noun* or *-ing*). Now, give students time to complete the sentences alone before checking their answers with a partner. Give feedback as a class, eliciting further examples for each dependent preposition to consolidate understanding. Use the **Vocabulary Worksheet** on page W15 for extra practice.

SPEAKING HUB

A Tell students they are going to discuss people's phobias and how to deal with them. Then, give them time to read the scenarios and write notes. Monitor, helping with any new or unfamiliar vocabulary.

B Put students into groups to discuss the questions, using their notes to help them. Suggest that each group choose one person to write notes during the discussion to help them present their ideas later on. Monitor, asking follow-up questions to keep the discussions going, and encouraging students to justify their opinions.

C Ask each group to nominate one person to present the main ideas of their discussion to the class. Alternatively, work through each scenario as a class, discussing the questions in Exercise B and trying to agree on the best solution for each.

Extra activity

If you feel comfortable doing so, share a fear that you have, how it affects your life and how you cope with it. Then, put students into pairs to discuss their own fears. If they don't feel comfortable talking about their own fears (or don't have any), suggest that they talk about someone they know. Bring the class back together to share the main points of their discussion, adding any useful emergent language to the board.

TEACHING IDEA by Jim Scrivener

Phrasal verbs

Use these activities to practice using *in case.*

Call my bluff

Make small groups. Hand out four or five sentences with a phrasal verb (*The milk has gone bad, Can you put me up tonight?*, etc) to each group and ask them to keep them secret from the other groups. For each phrasal verb, the groups should prepare three definitions – two of which are untrue and one of which is true (*'gone bad' – (1) been spilled (2) become sour (3) been stolen by someone*). When students are ready, groups read out their sentence and each of their definitions. Students vote for which one they think is the correct definition. The group wins one point for every student who votes for one of the wrong definitions.

Finding interesting collocations

Choose an interesting set of phrasal verbs (*give up, get over, look up, blow up*). Ask students to think of a funny or unexpected collocation for each one (*give up mountain climbing*) and then use it in an amusing sentence (*My 80-year-old grandma finally gave up mountain climbing last summer.*).

Tic-tac-toe

Select nine phrasal verbs that all have the same particle (*give up, look up, take up, clean up*). Divide the class in two – X and O. Draw a large 3 x 3 grid on the board and write a phrasal verb in each of the nine squares. Teams take turns trying to make a good sentence using one of the phrasal verbs. If you agree that it is a good, grammatically accurate sentence, they 'win' the square and write their symbol. The winning team is the one that makes a line of three symbols.

Literal and idiomatic use

Make a list with pairs of sentences where Sentence A has a literal meaning and Sentence B has a harder-to-guess idiomatic meaning *(a) He took off his dirty shoes before going into the house (b) The plane took off.* Leave the first two sentences as examples, but after that, delete one sentence in each pair. Pairs see if they can think of sentences to replace the missing ones. At the end, compare with your original list.

B Choose the correct verbs to complete the questions.

1. Do you think you are good at *working out* / *dealing with* how to solve problems?
2. Do you *talk over* / *deal with* your plans with the people around you?
3. What could you *put up with* / *sort out* more easily – a room full of spiders or snakes?
4. When was the last time you *weighed out* / *put up with* the risks and benefits before making a decision?
5. What scary situation have you recently had to *go through* / *weigh out*? What happened?
6. How would you *sort out* / *weigh out* a situation where everyone was panicking?
7. In general, how well do you *deal with* / *go through* risky situations?

C SPEAK Work in pairs. Discuss the questions in Exercise B.

VOCABULARY

Dependent prepositions: adjectives

Dependent prepositions: adjectives

Some adjectives are usually followed by specific prepositions. These are called 'dependent prepositions' and they are followed by either a noun or *-ing*. For example:

My mother has always been terrified of spiders. NOT ~~*My mother has always been terrified about spiders.*~~

Choose the correct prepositions to complete the sentences.

1. I'm really anxious *about* / *to* speaking in public.
2. I feel a little ashamed *of* / *for* my fear of flying. I know it's not rational.
3. I'm sick *about* / *of* feeling this way – I really need to get some help.
4. I'm envious *for* / *of* people who can stay calm in dangerous situations.
5. They became suddenly aware *of* / *from* the danger around them.
6. I'm not really scared of anything, but I try to be sensitive *toward* / *for* people with a lot of phobias.

SPEAKING HUB

A PREPARE Read the scenarios (1–3). Write notes about what each person is afraid of and how it affects their life.

1. Emily Ronson is a 26-year-old graphic designer working in Seattle, Washington. She takes the subway to work every day but hates every minute of the 40-minute trip. Being in tight spaces with a lot of people makes her feel incredibly anxious. Sometimes, she feels so overwhelmed that she gets off the train and waits until it's less busy. Sometimes, this makes her late for work. She's ashamed of her fear so she hasn't told anyone about it.
2. Helen Masters is a retired police officer from Brazil. Several times over the past decade, she has had to cancel her vacation because she had a panic attack shortly after boarding the plane and demanded to get off. She knows this is an issue but has decided to live with it. Now she rarely travels out of the country and cannot see her grandchildren because they live in the UK.
3. Tom Hawksby is a 43-year-old accountant at a large computer software company in New York. Recently, the company hasn't been doing well and hundreds of people have lost their jobs. Tom is worried that he'll lose his job, too, and finds it difficult to sleep at night. This is making him tired and angry at work.

B DISCUSS Work in groups. Use your notes from Exercise A to discuss the questions.

1. Which of the fears do you think are irrational? Which are rational? Why?
2. How well do you think each person copes with their fear?
3. Do you think their fear is a big issue? Why/Why not?
4. What would you do in their position?

C PRESENT Choose one person from your group to present the main points of your discussion to the rest of the class.

fear of flying (aviophobia)

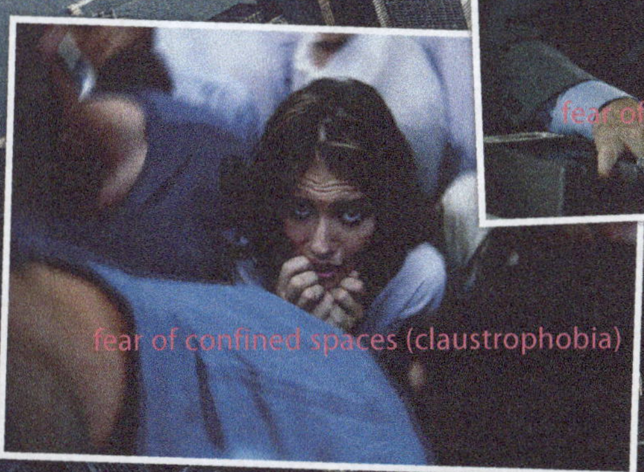
fear of confined spaces (claustrophobia)

fear of heights (acrophobia)

- Discuss priorities in a survival situation
- Talk about fears and offer advice

The great Tepui challenge

COMPREHENSION

A Work in groups. You are going to watch a video of people climbing Amaurai Tepui, a mountain in Venezuela. What do you think are the biggest challenges they will face?

B Watch the video. What makes the climbers think about giving up?

C Watch the video again. Are these sentences true (T) or false (F)? Correct the false sentences.

1 The team starts day five of the climb ~~near the summit of~~ halfway up the mountain. T / **F**
2 Presenter, Steve Backshall, hopes the improved weather indicates ~~the end of the storm season~~ a change in their luck. T / **F**
3 The team is attempting to become the first to climb this part of the mountain. **T** / F
4 One indication of the coming storm is the mass movement of birds. **T** / F
5 The team survives the storm by ~~climbing back down the mountain~~. holding onto the side of the mountain T / **F**
6 Steve thinks it would be a shame to give up having come so far. **T** / F

D Work in pairs. Read the extracts from the video. What do the words in bold refer to? Watch the video again to check your answers.

1 **It** would be nice after yesterday, wouldn't it? a change in their luck
2 There's a big storm coming and **they** know it. the birds
3 **It** left us clinging to the cliff. the storm
4 We've got to get off **this thing**; someone's going die. the rock face / the mountain
5 … nothing is worth risking **this** for. their lives

E Work in groups. Discuss the questions.

1 What do you think Steve means when he says, 'You could taste the fear'? **Suggested answer:** That the fear was so intense it was like you could taste it.
2 Would you like to take part in such an extreme challenge? Why/Why not?

AUTHENTIC ENGLISH

A Work in pairs. Read the extract from the video. What do you think *fingers crossed* means? to hope something will happen in the way you want it to

Steve: What do you reckon? Do you think our luck's changing?
Cameraman: Fingers crossed. It would be nice after yesterday, wouldn't it?

B *Fingers crossed* is actually part of a longer idiom. Which of the following do you think completes it?

a Have your … **b** Keep your … c Make your …

C Work in groups. Read the information in the box and guess the meaning of the shortened idioms in bold.

Shortened idioms

Some idioms are so common in informal spoken English that speakers don't need to say them in full for listeners to understand them.

*I've always been unhappy there but having my pay cut was **the last straw** [that broke the camel's back].*

*He called you a liar? Well, **if the shoe fits** [wear it].*

*I'm not surprised Max had a party while we were away. You know what they say – **when the cat's away** [the mice will play].*

*I was just thinking that, too. **Great minds** [think alike].*

D Work in pairs. Take turns reading the sentences and responding with an appropriate shortened idiom.

1 Why does my boss keep saying I'm lazy?
2 Nobody was doing any work when I got back.
3 Apparently we both bought him the same leaving gift.
4 Well, I worked pretty hard so hopefully I'll pass.
5 So, what made you fire her in the end?

Snake Mountain

SAM MALCOLM AMANDA HARRY EMILY

A Work in pairs. Why do you think people take part in extreme challenges (e.g. climbing mountains, sailing great distances, etc)?

B Watch the video. Write notes about Malcolm's story (e.g. where it happened, who he was with, etc).

C Work in pairs. Summarize Malcolm's story. Use your notes from Exercise B to help you.

SPEAKING SKILL

A Watch the video again and complete the extracts.

Sam: And I bet having all those snakes around doesn't make it any easier.
Malcolm: Eh? Snakes?
Sam: 1 ___What I mean is___, if it's called 'Snake Mountain', I assume there are a lot of snakes.

Malcolm: ... we needed an adventure before we started trying to make our way in the world. Well, 2 ___what I should say is___, we were looking for an excuse to postpone looking for a job.

Malcolm: None of us knew what we were doing! Well, 3 ___that's not quite true___, Peter was a pretty good climber, but the rest of us, well ...

Malcolm: We couldn't see a thing. Well, 4 ___that's not entirely true___, but visibility was down to about a meter.

Malcolm: So we just carried on all the way to the summit. Though, 5 ___to be honest___, I wasn't really thinking straight at the time!

B Work in pairs. What is the function of the phrases you wrote in Exercise A? To correct a mistake in something you've said.

C Read the information in the box to check your answers to Exercise B.

Backtracking

Sometimes in conversation we need to correct a mistake in something we've said. This is called backtracking. To do this, we use phrases such as:

What I mean is ... / What I meant was ..., That is to say ..., What I should say is ... / What I should have said was ..., That's not entirely true ..., When I say ... I really mean ...

D Work in pairs. Student A – Talk about your trip to work or school today in great detail. When necessary, rephrase what you said to make your description clearer. Student B – Listen and ask questions, forcing Student A to backtrack. Then swap roles.

SPEAKING HUB

A **PREPARE** Brainstorm a list of interesting, dangerous or exciting trips or journeys you have been on.

B **PLAN** Choose a trip or journey from your list in Exercise A. Write notes about the following:

- Where were you and why?
- When did this happen?
- Who were you with?
- What were the key events?
- How did you feel before, during and after?

C **SPEAK** Work in groups. Take turns telling your stories. Listen and ask questions where appropriate. Reformulate and backtrack if you need to.

A: So I was all alone on the boat and I could see a storm coming. I kept saying to myself, 'Fingers crossed that I don't sink.'
B: Weren't you scared?
A: Well yeah, to be honest, I was terrified. But it was still an amazing moment.

D **REFLECT** Whose story was the most exciting? Was it the story itself or the way it was told that made it so exciting?

Describe a trip or journey

➤ Turn to page 156 to learn how to write a short story.

The great Tepui challenge

LEAD-IN

Elicit the name of a famous mountain, the range it's a part of and which continent it's on (e.g. *Everest, the Himalayas, Asia*). Then, put students into groups to think of more. Bring the class back together and build a list on the board.

COMPREHENSION

A Put students into groups to discuss the questions. Monitor and help with any new or unfamiliar vocabulary.

B ▶ Play the video for students to answer the question. Give them time to check their answer in pairs before giving feedback as a class.

They are caught in a huge storm and have to cling to the side of the cliff as rocks fall from above. This incident made them fear for their lives and ultimately question whether they should turn back.

C ▶ Play the video again for students to complete the exercise. Give feedback as a class.

D ▶ Put students into pairs to discuss the extracts. Then, play the video again for them to check their answers before giving feedback as a class.

E Put students into groups to discuss the questions.

AUTHENTIC ENGLISH

A–B Put students into pairs to discuss the extract, then check their answers. Give further examples as necessary.

C Put students into groups to discuss the idioms in the box, then give feedback as a class.

the last straw *is used to say that something was the last of a series of events that finally makes you stop accepting a bad situation*

if the shoe fits *is used to tell someone that a criticism of them is probably accurate*

when the cat's away *is used to say that people will behave badly if the person in charge isn't there*

great minds *is said to someone just after you've discovered that they have had the same idea as you*

D Read the first sentence as a class and how you could respond to it using a shortened idiom (*Well,* **if the shoe fits**!). Then, put students into pairs to do the same for the remaining sentences.

Snake Mountain

LEAD-IN

As a class, build up a spider diagram of extreme challenges on the board (e.g. *climbing a mountain, running a marathon*, etc). Then, put students into groups to discuss which they would like to do and why.

A Put students into pairs to discuss the question. Monitor and help with grammar and vocabulary as necessary.

B–C ▶ Tell students they are now going to watch the next episode of the Café Hub series. Then, play the video for students to write notes. Give feedback as a class. You can find the **video script** for *Snake Mountain* on the Teacher's Resource Center.

Malcolm and some friends climbed 'Mont du Serpent' – Snake Mountain – in 1986, just after finishing university/college. The weather was fine at first, but then it got so foggy they couldn't see farther than a meter. They kept on walking, but he slipped and nearly fell over the edge of the cliff. Luckily, he managed to grab on to a rock as he fell and his friends pulled him back to safety. They were about to climb back down, but the weather improved so they continued to the summit instead.

SPEAKING SKILL

A–C ▶ Play the video again so students can complete the extracts. Give them time to check their answers in pairs before giving feedback. Next, put them back into pairs to discuss the meaning of the phrases in the previous exercise. Then, ask them to read the skills box to check their answers.

D Demonstrate the activity with a stronger student. Then, put students into pairs to do the same.

SPEAKING HUB

A–B Give students time to make a list of all of the interesting, dangerous or exciting trips or journeys they have been on. When they've finished, ask them to choose one from their list to share and give them time to write notes.

C–D Put students into groups to tell their stories. Monitor, encouraging them to ask follow-up questions for more information and to backtrack to make their stories clearer or more accurate as necessary.

▶ VIDEO SCRIPT

The great Tepui challenge
S = Steve Backshall C = Cameraman
Sm = Sound man

Ex C Q1 **S:** Day five of the climb, and we wake on a precarious ledge, halfway up the mountain.
C: What a difference a day makes.
S: It's the first time we've woken up we've not been inside a cloud. I can actually see the mountains.
Ex C Q2 And blue sky. What do you reckon? Do you think our luck's changing?
Ex D Q1 **C:** Fingers crossed. It would be nice after yesterday, wouldn't it?
Ex C Q3 **S:** The previous day, our attempt to become the first people to climb this vertical rock face almost ended
Ex C Q4; Ex D Q2 in disaster. The birds are all coming in to roost. There's a big storm coming and they know it. What a
Ex C Q5; Ex D Q3 storm! It left us clinging to the cliff. And then came the rock fall.
C: No, no, no, no! Head! Head!
Ex D Q4 **S:** We've got to get off this thing; someone's gonna die. You could taste the fear.
Sm: It's just really dangerous, isn't it up here.
Ex D Q5 **S:** It's only a matter of, you know, we … we … nothing is worth risking this for. Now I kind of feel we should keep going. What about you?
C: Yeah.
S: You do?
C: Yeah. Give it a bash.
Ex C Q6 **S:** Well, we've come an awful long way – it'd be a shame to give up so easy.

3 Writing

Write a short story

W– using adverbs to add detail to a story

A Work in pairs. What is the worst vacation experience you have ever had?

B Read the story and answer the questions. Underline the parts of the text that gives you the answers.

1 What did they regret? Not getting off the boat.
2 Did anyone fall into the sea? No
3 Where did they have to sleep? On the beach.

Vacation from HELL

Two years ago, my wife and I took a summer vacation in Sicily, Italy. The town we were staying in was beautiful, but there wasn't a lot to do. So, a few days into our stay, we decided to book a boat trip to the volcanic Aeolian islands. I'd just bought a new camera, so I was really looking forward to trying it out in such an amazing place. However, the night before we were due to leave, a terrible storm hit the south coast of Italy, so we assumed our trip would be canceled. The next morning, as we were strolling down to the harbor, the sea looked incredibly rough as the waves smashed against the rocks. Surprisingly, the trip went ahead anyway. We boarded the boat and waited nervously for it to leave. The waves were

Ex B Q1 getting pretty violent and I thought about getting off several times but decided to wait and see if things would be better at sea. It was a decision that I was soon to regret as the boat rumbled out of the harbor.

At first, everything was strangely calm, and we wondered why we had been so nervous in the first place. But then the wind started to howl all around us. We rocked backward and forward as huge waves slammed violently against the boat, soaking us to the skin. Terrifyingly, benches were thrown from one side of the boat to the other and people all around us were

Ex B Q2 sliding across the deck. Fortunately, no one fell over the side.

Finally, we reached the islands. We rapidly left the boat and sat shaking on the harbor wall. The staff assured us that the boat would return in three hours, but we were too terrified to go through that again. Strolling around the island, we tried desperately to find a hotel for the night so that we could return the next morning on the larger and safer car ferry. However, it was the peak of the summer and all of the hotels were booked up so we had no choice but to

Ex B Q3 spend the night on the beach. An exciting day out had swiftly turned into the trip from hell!

C Read the story again and put the events in the order they happened.

1 arranged a boat trip
4 nervously boarded the boat
7 searched desperately for a hotel
2 a terrible storm erupted
5 waves smashed across the boat
8 slept on the sandy beach
3 walked to the harbor expecting the trip to be canceled
6 benches were thrown side to side and people slid across the deck

D SCAN Complete the box with the highlighted adverbs in the text.

Using adverbs to give detail to a story

We use adverbs of manner (e.g. *slowly*, nervously, violently, desperately, rapidly) to talk about how something happens.

We use adverbs of stance (e.g. *strangely*, incredibly, surprisingly, strangely, fortunately) to describe how we feel about something.

E Rewrite the sentences using the adverbs in bold.

1 It was incredible how dangerous the roads were on the island. **incredibly**
The roads on the island were incredibly dangerous.
2 We were nervous as we waited for the rescue team to come. **nervously**
We waited nervously for the rescue team to come.
3 I was surprised the rescue team took such a long time to arrive. **surprisingly**
The rescue team took a surprisingly long time to arrive.
4 It didn't take long for the fire to spread through the building. **rapidly**
The fire spread rapidly through the building.

WRITING

A PREPARE You are going to write a short story about a nightmare trip or vacation. Write notes about:

- the location
- the people involved
- how you felt
- the key events
- contextual details (e.g. the weather, landscape, etc)

B PLAN Organize your notes from Exercise A into a plan for a short story.

C WRITE Write your short story. Use your plan to help you.

D EDIT Work in pairs. Edit your partner's story. Check:

- spelling and punctuation
- use of adverbs
- use of narrative tenses

Refer students to this story as a model for the writing task.

Refer students to this checklist when editing their partner's work.

LEAD-IN

Elicit one or two ideas about what makes a good vacation (e.g. *the location*, *food*, etc), then put students into pairs to discuss their own ideas.

WRITING

A Tell students about a terrible vacation you have had, using plenty of adverbs throughout. Then, put students into pairs share their own stories.

B Give students time to read the story and answer the questions alone. Allow time for peer correction before giving feedback as a class.

C Ask students to complete the exercise alone, then give feedback as a class.

D Read the skills box as a class, giving further examples and explanation as necessary. Then, give students time to complete the exercise alone, before giving feedback as a class.

E Work through the first sentence as a class, then give students time to complete the others alone. Allow time for peer correction, before giving feedback as a class.

WRITING TASK

A–B Give students time to write notes using the bulleted list, before arranging them into a plan.

C Tell students to write their stories. Monitor, encouraging them to use adverbs to make their stories more engaging. Monitor and help with grammar and vocabulary as necessary.

D Put students into pairs to edit each other's articles. Encourage students to give each other positive feedback. Students can then rewrite their stories either in class or for homework.

Unit 3 Review

VOCABULARY

A Choose the correct options (a, b or c) to complete sentences.

1 All I could hear was water _____ down the rock face.

a crunching **(b)** trickling c hissing

2 As he leaned forward, the branch _____, sending him falling toward the ground.

(a) snapped b rumbled c crunched

3 The old wooden bridge _____ under the weight of all of the cars.

a snapped **(b)** groaned c growled

4 Suddenly, a young child walked into the road. Slamming on the brakes, the car _____ to a halt.

(a) screeched b crunched c slammed

5 The gravel _____ under the car's tires as it slowly pulled away.

a hissed b snapped **(c)** crunched

6 In a rage, she stormed out of the room and _____ the door.

a smashed b creaked **(c)** slammed

B Complete the second sentence so it has a similar meaning to the first, using the words in bold.

1 It was a terrible experience for them to endure.

go through

They had to go through a terrible experience.

2 Someone needs to organize the details of the party.

sort out

They need to sort out the details of the party.

3 Try not to get so stressed at work.

stay calm

Try to stay calm at work.

4 I can't quit my job until I find a new one.

put up with

I'll have to put up with my job until I find a new one.

5 The management team is discussing the issues together before they make a decision.

talk over

Before making a decision, the management team is talking over the issues.

6 The government must do something about the high level of unemployment.

deal with

The government must deal with the high level of unemployment.

7 What's wrong with my computer?

work out

Can you work out what's wrong with my computer?

8 Let's look at the options and decide which one is best.

weigh out

To decide which one is best, we need to weigh out the options.

C Complete the collocations with the adjectives in the box.

anxious ashamed aware envious sensitive sick

1 You should be ashamed of your behavior! It's embarrassing!

2 I'm sick of having to clean up after you all the time.

3 I'm feeling a little anxious about the job interview next week.

4 I think she's envious of your results – you're always at the top of the class.

5 Maybe you just need to be more sensitive toward other people's feelings.

6 You need to be more aware of how your actions affect the people around you.

GRAMMAR

A Choose the correct options to complete the sentences.

1 They ***left*** / *were leaving* the house and ***walked*** / *were walking* to the station.

2 I *felt* / ***was feeling*** pretty nervous until we ***scored*** / *were scoring* the second goal.

3 I ***hadn't taken*** / *hadn't been taking* my cell phone, so I ***had*** / *was having* no way of contacting them.

4 By the time I ***had gotten*** / *got* to the movie theater the movie *started* / ***had already started***.

5 ***I'd been waiting*** / *I'd waited* in line for 40 minutes before someone *had served* / ***served*** me.

6 I *packed* / ***was packing*** my suitcase when the phone ***rang*** / *had rung*.

7 I ***was working*** / *worked* at my desk when a bird ***flew*** / *was flying* into the window.

8 He was exhausted because he *had worked* / ***had been working*** all night. He ***hadn't slept*** / *hadn't been sleeping* for 24 hours.

B Complete the sentences with *as long as, as soon as, in case, provided (that)* or *unless*. Sometimes more than one option is possible.

1 Call me as soon as you hear from him!

2 Don't disturb me unless it's really urgent.

3 You should bring a snack in case you get hungry.

4 As long as / Provided (that) you work hard, you'll get a pay raise this year.

5 I'm going to buy extra food in case more people come to the party.

6 As soon as you finish the swimming portion, you need to get right onto your bike.

7 I won't accept a contact request on LinkedIn unless I know them already.

8 It looks like we should get there on time as long as / provided (that) the traffic isn't too bad.

A father and daughter programming a VR simulator.

Future (n) the time that follows the present time
Collocations and idioms: *the immediate* future (*within the next few days or weeks*), *for the foreseeable* future (*ongoing, without a plan to end*), *in the not too distant* future (*very soon*)

Roosevelt is suggesting that you can find future success and happiness by following your dreams.

Eleanor Roosevelt (1884–1962) was an American political activist and humanitarian and one of the most influential women of her time. She was outspoken on the issues of women's rights and equal treatment for African and Asian Americans. Roosevelt was the First Lady of the United States for 12 years during her husband Franklin D. Roosevelt's four terms as President (1933–1945) and later became the American delegate to the United Nation's General Assembly.

OBJECTIVES

- talk about future plans and goals
- make predictions about the future of work
- evaluate future predictions
- debate a range of transportation proposals
- give your opinion on automation in the workplace
- write a for and against blog post

Work with a partner. Discuss the questions.

1 Read the quote. What do you think Roosevelt means? Do you agree with her? Why/Why not?
2 What technological developments do you think will change the world in the future?
3 Are you generally optimistic or pessimistic about the future of the world? Why?

THE FUTURE 37

OBJECTIVES

Read the unit objectives to the class.

UNIT OPENER QUESTIONS

1 Read the quote as a class, then put students into pairs to discuss the questions. Monitor, encouraging students to explain their reasoning. Open the discussion up to the class, writing any useful emergent vocabulary on the board.

2 Draw students' attention to the image and read the caption as a class. Encourage students to share their experiences with VR and elicit one or two ideas of how it might change the world in the future. Next, put students into pairs to discuss the question. Monitor, suggesting topics (e.g. *medicine*, *transportation*, *wearable technology*, etc) if students get stuck. Bring the class back together to share their ideas, again adding any useful emergent vocabulary to the board.

3 Elicit the meaning of *optimistic* (*always believing good things will happen*) and *pessimistic* (*always believing that bad things will happen*), what part of speech they are (*adjectives*) and the noun form of both words (*optimist* and *pessimist*). Next, share one or two of your ideas about the future and elicit whether you are an optimist or a pessimist to consolidate understanding of the terms. Now, put students into pairs to discuss their own ideas. Monitor, encouraging students to explain their reasoning with clear examples. Bring the class back together to share their ideas and encourage further discussion as appropriate.

WORKSHEETS

Lesson 4.1 My future

Grammar: Future forms (W16)

Vocabulary: Noun + preposition collocations (W17)

Vocabulary: Nouns and verbs with the same spelling (W18)

Lesson 4.2 What will life be like?

Grammar: Future perfect, future progressive and future perfect progressive (W19)

Vocabulary: Intensifiers (W20)

4.1 My future

- Talk about future plans and goals
- Make predictions about the future of work

G future forms
S identifying evidence
V noun + preposition collocations; nouns and verbs with the same spelling
P nouns and verbs with the same spelling

LISTENING

A Look at the pictures (a–e). Rank these life decisions from most to least important.

B SPEAK Work in pairs. Compare your ideas from Exercise A. Explain your reasoning. What do you agree about? What do you disagree about?

4.1 **C LISTEN FOR GIST** Listen to a podcast about turning points in people's lives. Match the speakers to the change they talk about.

1 Lucy
2 Hadiyah
3 Frank

a planning how to spend their retirement
b packing in preparation for a year of traveling
c getting organized for a new arrival

4.1 **D LISTEN FOR DETAIL** Listen to the podcast again. Choose the correct option (a, b or c) to complete the sentences.

1 Lucy is planning to …
 a take a course in Spain
 b drive across Russia
 c work in the UK

2 Which country isn't Lucy going to?
 a Russia
 b China
 c Brazil

3 Hadiyah's husband …
 a thinks they are having a boy.
 b thinks they are having a girl.
 c is happy with a boy or a girl.

4 Who in Hadiyah's family are they thinking of naming the baby after?
 a one of the grandmothers
 b one of the aunts
 c one of her sisters

5 Frank has just bought …
 a a new car.
 b a new RV.
 c a fishing rod.

6 Frank is planning to …
 a go on a cruise.
 b retire in Florida.
 c take a road trip.

c where to live

4.1 **E LISTEN FOR KEY INFORMATION** Listen again. Use the table to write notes about each speaker

	Lucy	Hadiyah	Frank
What is each speaker excited about?	traveling on the trans-Siberian railroad	for everyone to meet our new baby	seeing famous landmarks like the Statue of Liberty
What hasn't each speaker decided?	whether to go to the United Kingdom	the baby's name	where to go apart from New York and Florida
What new skill does each speaker talk about?	learning Spanish	learning to manage her time a little better	fishing

F IDENTIFY ASSUMPTIONS Work in groups. Read the extracts (1–2). Do you agree with the assumptions each speaker makes? Why/Why not?

1 Everyone there speaks some English, anyway.
2 Everyone wants to retire, don't they?

a whether to have a family

b what to wear

d what job to do

4.1 My future

LEAD-IN

Tell students about a big decision (real or made-up) that you are trying to make. Elicit ideas about what you should do and try to agree on one course of action as a class. Next, put students into groups to discuss decisions they or someone they know has to make and encourage them to agree on one clear solution for each. If they can't think of anything current, encourage them to talk about decisions they had to make in the past.

LISTENING

4.1 **A–E** Students complete the exercises, checking their answers in pairs.

F Put students into groups to discuss the assumptions. Monitor, encouraging students to give examples to support their answers. Bring the class back together to share their ideas.

AUDIO SCRIPT

4.1

Listening, Exercise C

P = Presenter L = Lucy H = Hadiyah F = Frank

P: Lenox is a small town in Massachusetts, in the US. Like many other towns in this area, not a lot has changed here over the years, but for these three residents, life is about to change forever.
Ex C Lucy Warner has just graduated from high school and is going to start studying for a law degree at Harvard in the fall of next year. However, since she's never left Lenox, she wants to take a year off to go traveling. When I spoke to her, she was busy packing her bags.

L: Can you pass me that bag? The red one behind you …

P: Sure. First of all, congratulations on graduating!

L: Thanks!

P: So, when do you leave?

L: Next Sunday!

P: Wow! So soon.

L: I know! Scary!

P: So, anything specific planned?

L: Well, um, I'm flying to Paris because I have a friend there. Then I'm taking the train to Spain, where I'm staying for a couple of months.

P: Oh right. Why so long in Spain?

Ex D Q1; Ex E **L:** I want to improve my Spanish. I speak a little, but it's well, just tourist Spanish really. I'm starting a month-long course in Spanish in September. The classes are three days a week from nine to four.

P: That sounds great.

L: Yeah, I don't know. It's just a little fun really. I don't really need another language – everyone there speaks some English anyway!

P: Sounds cool though. Any other exciting plans?

Ex D Q2; Ex E **L:** I'm really excited about taking the Trans-Siberian Express across Russia into Asia. I think it'll be amazing, a once in a lifetime experience. After that, I'll probably spend a lot of time in China. Then, I'm going to visit as many countries as I can.

P: All without flying?

L: Well I'm definitely flying to Australia! I want to work there for a few months and Ex E then I might go to the United Kingdom. I don't know if I'll have enough money, though.

P: Another person from Lenox about to have a massive life change is Ex C Hadiyah Khan. Hadiyah is expecting her first baby. When I spoke to her, she was busy decorating the nursery. So, big changes ahead for you.

H: Yeah, I'm a little worried about it all actually!

P: Yeah, I think that's only natural. When's the baby due?

H: At the end of May, although apparently first babies are always late! A lot of our time is going to be spent getting things ready for the baby.

P: Do you know if it's a boy or a girl?

Ex D Q3 **H:** We don't – we wanted to keep it a surprise. My husband thinks it's going to be a girl, though.

P: Oh really? Why?

H: Everyone in our family has had girls!

P: Have you chosen any names yet?

Ex E; Ex D Q4 **H:** No, we can't decide. There's the possibility of naming her Farrah after my grandma or Nabila after my husband's grandma. If it's a boy, who knows?

P: So, how do you feel?

H: I'm so excited! I've always dreamed of having children. Ex E I can't wait for everyone to meet our new baby. I know it's going to be exhausting, though. My sister has two children and I can see it isn't easy. But, you know, it'll be a lot of fun too. I'm honestly just really excited! One thing I am worried about though is getting everything done. Parents are always really busy, so Ex E I'm definitely going to have to get better at managing my time.

P: At another stage of their life is Frank Schmitt. Having worked in the local bank for the last 30 years, Ex C Frank is now finally retiring. When I caught up with Frank, he was busy buying fishing equipment.

F: What do you think of this fishing rod?

Ex E **P:** Um, I have no idea – I don't know much about fishing to be honest!

F: Me neither. It's just something I finally have time to do.

P: That's right, you're retiring soon.

F: I am, I am, and I can't wait!

P: Do you think you'll miss work?

F: I suppose there's the risk of getting bored, but I doubt it. Everyone wants to retire, don't they? I'll probably just spend the first few months at home relaxing but then we're planning a big vacation.

P: A cruise?

Ex D Q5 + 6 **F:** No, but another typical senior citizen trip! We bought a huge RV and we're going to travel to different places in the US for a year.

P: Great! Where are you going to go?

Ex E **F:** We haven't planned it exactly. I'm excited to see some of the famous landmarks – the Statue of Liberty, for example. I've been to New York several times, but I've never seen the Statue of Liberty! Ex E We're going to start in New York and head down to Florida. After that I'm not sure. I'm looking forward to being more spontaneous!

P: I loved Seattle. You should go there.

F: Really? That's a good idea. I'll add it to the list!

4.1 My future

GRAMMAR

4.2 **A** Play the recording for students to complete the sentences.

B–C Give students time to complete the rules alone, before giving feedback as a class. Clarify anything they don't understand with further examples as necessary, then direct them to the **Grammar Hub** (see below). Use the **Grammar Worksheet** on page W16 for extra practice.

D Ask students to complete the exercise alone, before giving feedback as a class.

VOCABULARY

Give students time to read the skills box alone and complete the exercise. Give feedback as a class. Use the **Vocabulary Worksheet** on page W17 for extra practice.

SPEAKING

A Draw students' attention to the bulleted list and the example questions. Then, give them time to think of more questions.

B Put students into pairs to conduct their interviews. Monitor, encouraging them to ask follow-up questions to extend their discussions.

GRAMMAR HUB

4.1 Future forms

- We use *will* + base form:
  - **a** for decisions made at the moment of speaking (including promises, offers, plans and requests).
    That's a good idea – I'll call him now.
    That looks heavy – I'll carry it for you.
  - **b** to make predictions based on personal opinions or feelings (usually with adverbs like *definitely, certainly, possibly*, etc to show how sure we are).
    Tom will definitely be late – he always is!
    Mom won't like that movie. It's not her sort of thing.
- We use *be going to* + base form:
  - **a** to talk about general intentions and plans made before the moment of speaking.
    I'm going to look for a new job.
  - **b** to make predictions based on present evidence.
    The traffic's not moving – we're going to be late!
- We use the simple present to talk about a timetabled or scheduled event.
  Our flight leaves at 8:30 am on Monday.
  My job interview is tomorrow morning.
- We use the present progressive to talk about future arrangements and fixed plans.
  We're staying in a hostel for the first three nights.
  (= We've already booked the hostel.)
  I'm meeting Sarah at 7:30 pm outside the restaurant.
  (= We've already arranged to meet at that time and place.)

4.1 Future forms

A Choose the correct options to complete the sentences.

1 I ***have*** / *am having* French class every Monday night at seven o'clock.
2 ***I'm meeting*** / *I will meet* friends for lunch on Sunday.
3 ***We'll probably*** / *We're going to* move this year but I'm not certain.
4 It looks like they *will* / ***are going to*** win. They're 4–0 up with only a minute left to play.
5 I think the plane *arrives* / ***will arrive*** late.
6 I've had enough of this job! I'm *looking for* / ***going to look for*** a new one.

B Complete the post with the correct future form of the verbs in parentheses. Use contractions where possible.

Emily | 20 mins ago

So, big news! I have a place at NYU to study Performing Arts, so [1] I'm moving (*I / move*) to New York in September! Apparently, I can stay in the residence halls near the main campus, but I've decided [2] I'm going to look for (*I / look for*) my own apartment. Wouldn't that be amazing? [3] I'll definitely have to (*I / definitely / have to*) get a job to pay the rent, but it would be nice to have my own space. I've never lived in another country before, so [4] it's going to be (*it / be*) difficult to be so far away from my family. But everyone's been so supportive! Anyway, my [5] flight leaves (*flight / leave*) early on August 28th so if any of you want to meet up before then, just send me a message and [6] I'll get back (*I / get back*) to you.

C Are these sentences correct or incorrect? Rewrite the incorrect sentences.

1 Having my young nephews to stay in the house next week ~~is being~~ exhausting! is going to be / will be
✓2 The lecture starts at seven tomorrow evening, not eight.
✓3 I'm afraid that we aren't going on a cruise this year.
4 I'm feeling really tired, so I think I ~~go~~ to bed soon. 'll/will go / 'm/am going to go
5 Are you ~~starting~~ going to start looking for a job anytime soon?
6 ~~We meet~~ We're/We are meeting / We're/We are going to meet Andy and Karim for lunch on May 12th.
✓7 I probably won't get there until at least ten thirty.
8 I~~'m helping~~ 'll/will help you do the dishes, if you like.

➤ Go back to page 39.

GRAMMAR
Future forms

4.2 **A Listen and complete the extracts with the correct future form of the verbs in parentheses.**

1. I __'m flying__ (*fly*) to Paris because I have a friend there.
2. The classes __are__ (*be*) three days a week from nine to four.
3. Then, I __'m going to visit__ (*visit*) as many countries as I can.
4. Parents are always really busy, so I __'m definitely going to have__ (*definitely / have*) to get better at managing my time.
5. Do you think you __'ll miss__ (*miss*) work?
6. That's a good idea. I __'ll add__ (*add*) it to the list!

B WORK IT OUT Choose the correct tenses to complete the rules.

Future forms

We use the [1]*simple present / present progressive* for definite future arrangements.

We use [2]*going to / will* + base form to talk about general intentions.

We use [3] *going to / will* + base form for decisions made at the moment of speaking.

We use [4]*simple present / present progressive* for timetabled events.

We use [5]*will + base form / present progressive* for making predictions.

We use [6]*will / going to* + base form for predictions based on something we know.

C Go to the **Grammar Hub** on **page 128**.

D PRACTICE Complete the sentences with the correct form of the verbs in the box.

break come fly go leave miss see text

1. There's no milk left? OK, I __'ll/will text__ Bea and ask her to pick some up.
2. That chair doesn't look very strong – I think it __'s/is going to break__!
3. We __'re/are flying__ with JetBlue on the way out, but haven't booked the return flight yet.
4. The next train to Cambridge __leaves__ at 5:12 pm.
5. She probably __won't come__ – she doesn't really like parties.
6. After college, I __'m/am going to go__ traveling for a year. Not sure where though.
7. We're still miles away from the airport – we __'re/are going to miss__ our flight!
8. I __'m/am seeing__ her on Friday, actually. We have a meeting at 2 pm.

VOCABULARY
Noun + preposition collocations

Noun + preposition collocations

Some nouns and prepositions are commonly used together. For example, we can say *the reason for* but not ~~*the reason of*~~.

Correct the prepositions in each sentence.

1. Congratulations ~~for~~ on passing the exam!
2. I'm hoping to take a course ~~for~~ in accounting.
3. I need to make more time ~~of~~ for my family.
4. We're planning to visit a lot of places ~~of~~ in Europe.
5. There's the possibility ~~to~~ of changing jobs next summer.
6. I'm a little worried. There's the risk ~~for~~ of not getting into college.

SPEAKING

A PREPARE You are going to interview your partner about their plans and goals for the future. Write questions about:

- home
- study
- work
- family
- travel
- achievements

1 *What are you going to do after your course finishes?*
2 *Would you like to go traveling?*

B SPEAK Interview your partner. Ask follow-up questions to find out more information.

A: *When does your course finish?*
B: *At the end of July.*
A: *So, what are you going to do afterward?*
B: *Hmm ... I'm not sure. I'll probably try and find a job in a café or something.*

READING

A SPEAK Work in groups. Which jobs do you think will be most affected by robots in the future? Why?

B SCAN Read *The future of work* quickly. Which of your ideas from Exercise A are mentioned?

THE FUTURE OF WORK

Few people would argue that society hasn't [1]**benefited** enormously from technological advancements. However, the future of many jobs may be hanging in the [2]**balance** due to the increased use of robotics in the workplace.
Ex C Q1 According to Osbourne and Frey from Oxford University, almost 50% of jobs worldwide are at risk of being automated over the next 20 years. Taxi drivers could be replaced by driverless cars. In some warehouses, robots already move [3]**produce** around more efficiently than workers. Even the role of teachers could be dramatically affected as more and more of the learning process moves online. There's also a greater risk of change in certain countries where there are a high number of people employed in manufacturing. For example, the World Bank
Ex C Q2 estimates that some countries risk up to 60% of jobs possibly being replaced by robots and automation, simply because technology is usually able to [4]**produce** more than human workers, with better accuracy and attention to detail. Yet many economists argue that despite the risks of increased automation, there are still many opportunities and [5]**benefits** ahead.

Although to many this may feel like a new problem, in reality it is a [6]**challenge** that has existed for years.
Ex C Q3 Since the invention of the printing press, machines have continued to replace humans in the workplace. In fact, people have always worried about technology taking their jobs. During the Industrial Revolution in England, the Luddites – a group of clothes and textile makers – protested against new technology in factories by destroying machinery. They weren't against the technology, but they didn't like the [7]**control** and power it gave to factory owners to make working conditions worse. In the late 1950s, there were also widespread protests across the US in response to the [8]**influence** of automation on the shipping industry.

Although technological advances frequently [9]**challenge** society, overall levels of unemployment have never risen consistently. Periods of increased unemployment are usually temporary and associated with a recession. We don't run out of work – work simply changes and new
Ex C Q4 jobs are created. People were once employed to open doors on trains and take people's tickets. Farmers, factory workers and elevator operators have all lost their jobs due to technological changes. People have simply moved on and found new types of employment.

Automation will no doubt [10]**influence** society greatly as it starts to [11]**control** more and more aspects of our lives. However, arguably, it won't change the total number of jobs in the economy. Studies into the impact of automation on employment focus only on which existing jobs could be replaced. They do not address the subject of which new jobs might be created. While planes and boats may not Ex C Q5
have a crew on board, they will still need to be operated by someone remotely. As more and more of life moves online, we may find we need fewer traditional police officers and that experts in preventing online crime will become increasingly important. Jobs that we cannot even imagine right now will become vital.

While many of our jobs are no doubt under threat, it is a dramatic exaggeration to present the idea that huge numbers of people will find themselves unemployed because of automation. Humans will always be vital in the workforce, just not necessarily in ways we are used to. Technology may even free up humans to work less and allow them more free time to [12]**balance** the pressures of work, family and other interests.

Glossary

recession (n) period when trade and industry are not successful and there is a lot of unemployment

4.1 My future

READING

A Draw students' attention to the black and white image in the text and elicit what it shows (*workers assembling cars in a factory*). Now, focus on the color image at the bottom of the page and elicit the difference (*robots have replaced the human workers*). Now, put students into groups to discuss jobs that they think may be affected like this in the future. Monitor, encouraging students to explain their reasoning. Bring the class back together to discuss their ideas and write notes on the board.

B Give students time to scan the article to see if any of their ideas are discussed. Then, give brief feedback as a class, taking time to clarify any new or unfamiliar vocabulary in the article before moving on. This could also be a good point to do some vocabulary building as there is a lot of useful language in the text that will test students' ability to manipulate words (e.g. *robot* > *robotic* > *robotics* > *roboticist*, etc). One way to do this is to draw a table on the board with parts of speech as the headings (e.g. *verb*, *noun*, *adjective*, etc) and elicit the various forms of a word from the class, highlighting any useful affixes.

TEACHING IDEA by David Seymour and Maria Popova

Discoveries and inventions

Use this to extend the topic of technology.

What technological developments and scientific discoveries have there been in the last hundred years? In small groups, make a list of discoveries/inventions and the advances that have resulted from them. Agree on a list of the top ten most significant discoveries and inventions. Here are some suggestions.

the wheel, electricity, the light bulb, vaccinations, nuclear fission, the silicon chip, the internal combustion engine, printing, the alphabet

What would happen if there was suddenly no electricity in the world?

TEACHING IDEA by David Seymour and Maria Popova

Science fact or fiction?

Use this activity to extend the theme of science fiction influencing real life.

Has anybody in the class read a good science-fiction book, e.g. *Brave New World* or *Fahrenheit 451*? Tell us about the kind of future society depicted in the book you read. Has any of it already come true? In small groups, discuss the ways technology can help society in the future and the ways it can also threaten society.

TEACHING IDEA by David Seymour and Maria Popova

One day …

Use this activity to extend the theme of predictions.

I'm going to dictate one prediction about the future to each person. Mingle and collect the other students' opinions on your prediction. Write down their answers. (Dictate each sentence quickly, but go through them two or three times so that students get another chance to take down their prediction. After the survey, elicit the results and write them on the board.)

Computers will take over the world.
Time travel will be possible.
We will find life in other solar systems.
Unintelligent clones will do all the hard work.
Disease will be eliminated.
People will live on Mars.
A comet will wipe out life on Earth.
We will learn how to travel at the speed of light.
English will be the only language in the world.

METHODOLOGY HUB by Christine Nuttall

Learning when to ignore difficult words

One mark of a skilled reader is the ability to decide what may safely be ignored. This is something many students have never contemplated: it may seem wrong, because it is not done in class. Therefore it needs to be done in class to make it more respectable. It may also seem dangerous, and it is, which is why it needs to be practiced under your guidance.

When tackling a difficult text, readers should have these questions in mind:

Before reading: Why am I going to read this? What do I want to get from it?

While reading: Do I need to stop and look up the meaning of this word, or can I get the gist without it?

After reading: Do I have what I wanted? If not, where in the text is it hidden? Can I get at it by looking up any words? If so, which?

This procedure is of course not so simple to put into practice. It takes a competent reader to be aware that they are not understanding and it sometimes takes a very skilled one to be aware *why* they are not. So our responsibility includes helping students to:

- recognize that they do not understand
- locate the sources of difficulty
- develop strategies for coping with difficulty (including strategies for not wasting time on words they don't need to know).

Here are some suggested activities to help students practice when to ignore difficult words.

1 To show that it is possible to get the gist without understanding every word, supply a fill-in-the-blank text (lexical items omitted here and there, with omissions indicated). Ask some simple top-down questions that can be answered from the incomplete text.
2 The same sort of exercise as in **1**, but using complete texts with difficult words which are not essential to the gist.
3 To help students identify the words they really need to look up, supply a short text containing a few new words and simple questions requiring understanding of some of them. The task is to see how many questions can be answered without looking up any words and to make students think very carefully before choosing which to look up. This can be done competitively, the winner having correct answers and fewest words looked up.

C Write the following sentence on the board – *It's clear that the Earth's climate is changing.* Elicit why this isn't a good argument by itself (*no supporting evidence is given*) and what kind of evidence could be used to support it (e.g. *statistics, scientific research, news and weather reports about natural disasters,* etc). Next, elicit what structures could be used to present the evidence (e.g. *According to ..., ... states/estimates/reports that ...,* etc). Now, give students time to read the article again to find evidence to support the list of arguments. Ask them to check their answers in pairs before giving feedback as a class.

D Put students into pairs to discuss the questions. Monitor, helping with any new or unfamiliar vocabulary. Bring the class back together to share their ideas, encouraging students to give examples or evidence to support their arguments. Add any useful emergent language to the board.

VOCABULARY

A Read the first sentence in the text as a class and elicit what part of speech *benefited* is (*a verb*). Next, give students time to categorize the other words in bold before briefly checking their answers with a partner. Give feedback as a class.

Nouns: 2, 3, 5, 6, 7, 8
Verbs: 1, 4, 9, 10, 11, 12

B Write the first sentence on the board and elicit what part of speech is needed to fill in the blank (*a noun*) and what form it needs to be (*plural because it will complete the fixed expression, 'one of the ...'*). Next, elicit which of the words in bold from Exercise A best fits the blank (*benefit*) and how to change the form (*adding an 's' to make it plural*), before adding it to the fill-in-the-blank sentence on the board. Now, give students time to complete the remaining exercises alone before checking their answers with a partner. Give feedback as a class, eliciting which clues in the sentences helped them find the answers. Use the **Vocabulary Worksheet** on page W18 for extra practice.

PRONUNCIATION

4.3 A Play the pairs of sentences and for students to answer the question. Give feedback as a class, highlighting that although the spelling is the same, the stress isn't always.

No. The stress is the same in sentences 1a and b (the first syllable is stressed), but different in 2a and b (on the second syllable in 2a and the first in 2b).

4.4 B Play the audio for students to identify the stress in each pair. Ask them to check their answers with a partner, before giving feedback as a class. If you have time, play the audio again, pausing after each sentence for student to copy the pronunciation of each form.

SPEAKING HUB

A Tell students that you recently read an article about the possibility of robot dentists being used in private healthcare (or show them a picture to represent the concept). Elicit a few pros and cons of this idea, possibly building up a list of each on the board (*Suggested answers: pros – they wouldn't get tired, they are probably cheaper in the long run, etc; cons – they cannot feel or understand pain, they would be really expensive up front*, etc). Next, give students time to follow this process for the bulleted lists of jobs.

B Put students into groups to discuss their ideas. Monitor, helping with any new or unfamiliar vocabulary and encouraging students to justify their opinions with evidence and examples.

C Bring the class back together to share the key points of their discussion. Encourage other students to ask follow-up questions to stimulate class-wide discussion. Add any useful emergent vocabulary to the board.

METHODOLOGY HUB by Jim Scrivener

A few keys to getting a good discussion going

- **Frame the discussion well** Don't just jump in the deep end. It usually helps to find ways to lead in at the beginning and ways to close at the end. A lead-in may be no more than a brief focus on a picture; it could be a text that everyone reads and which naturally flows into the topic. It could be a personal recollection from you.
- **Preparation time** Your students may need some quiet time before the speaking activity, not to write out speeches (this is to be a speaking activity, not a reading aloud one), but maybe to look up vocabulary in their dictionaries, think through their thoughts, write a note or two, etc.
- **Don't interrupt the flow** If at all possible, avoid classroom management techniques that interfere with the natural flow of conversation. I'm thinking particularly about learners having to put their hands up before they speak. Try alternatives such as keeping a watchful eye on the class and noticing those small movements and looks that suggest someone wants to speak, and then invite them to speak with a gesture or by a natural comment such as *Dasha, what do you think?*
- **Role cards** Giving students brief role cards sometimes helps, e.g. 'You are a motorist who uses Reddo gasoline. Explain how you want to support green issues but also need to drive your car'. It can sometimes be easier to speak in someone else's character than in your own.
- **Buzz groups** If a whole-class discussion seems to be dying on its feet, try splitting the class up into 'buzz groups', i.e. quickly divide the class into small sets of four or five students. Ask them to summarize the discussion so far, particularly considering if they agree with what different people have said. After a few minutes (with students still in groups), ask them to think of three comments or questions that would be interesting to share with the whole class. Then, bring the whole class back together and continue the discussion. The entire buzz-group stage may take only about three or four minutes but can help inject a lot more energy into a discussion.
- **Break the rules** Don't feel that you can never bend the above rules; sometimes, it may make sense to go straight into the discussion (possibly because you want them to get some practice at unprepared speaking or because the subject is burning so strongly that it just demands to be started immediately).

C IDENTIFY EVIDENCE Read the article again. Underline the evidence used to support the arguments below. Use the information in the box to help you.

> **Identifying evidence**
>
> Good writers use evidence to support the argument or point they're trying to make. This can include references to specific studies, examples and statistics.

1. A large proportion of jobs are at risk from technological developments.
2. Some countries may suffer more than others due to automation.
3. Jobs have always been at risk from technological developments.
4. Many old jobs now no longer exist.
5. New jobs will be created that do not currently exist.

D SPEAK Work in pairs. Discuss the questions.

1. Do you think society needs to worry about automation affecting people's jobs? Why/Why not?
2. How might the increased use of robots and automation benefit society?
3. What skills do you think people need to develop to protect themselves from automation?

VOCABULARY

Nouns and verbs with the same spelling

A Scan the article again. Which of the words in bold (1–12) are nouns? Which are verbs? Nouns: 2, 3, 5, 6, 7, 8 Verbs: 1, 4, 9, 10, 11, 12

B Complete the sentences with the correct form of the words in Exercise A.

1. One of the ___benefits___ of robotics could be more free time for individuals.
2. We need to ___balance___ the convenience of automation with the need for employment.
3. We should constantly ___challenge___ companies that get away with paying lower taxes.
4. There's no doubt that technology ___has influenced___ the way in which all industries work.
5. Some people think that automation gives companies more ___control___ over workers.
6. Robots make it quicker and easier for companies ___to produce___ their products.

PRONUNCIATION

Nouns and verbs with the same spelling

4.3 **A** Listen to the pairs of sentences. Are both forms of the words in bold pronounced the same way? No – sometimes the word stress changes.

1. a The key **benefit** of increased automation is greater efficiency.
   b Technology should be used to **benefit** humans, not replace them.
2. a I think we'll all need to **upgrade** our skills.
   b This system is an **upgrade** to the previous one.

4.4 **B** Listen to the pairs of sentences. Underline the stressed syllable in each of the words in bold.

1. a An **increase** in automation will have a negative impact on jobs.
   b We need to **increase** the number of automated jobs in education.
2. a Robots are increasingly used to **produce** more and more products.
   b A lot of people are eating local **produce** to reduce their environmental impact.
3. a Many people would **reject** the idea of a machine being a doctor.
   b Products produced by machines usually lead to fewer **rejects** being made.

SPEAKING HUB

A PREPARE Would you be happy for a robot to do any of these jobs? Why/Why not? Write notes.

- a doctor
- a bus driver
- a waiter
- a sales clerk
- a teacher
- an accountant

B DISCUSS Work in groups. Discuss your ideas from Exercise A. Are there any other jobs that you think could be automated?

C PRESENT Explain the main points of your discussion to the class. Which jobs do you think could be automated? Which couldn't? Why?

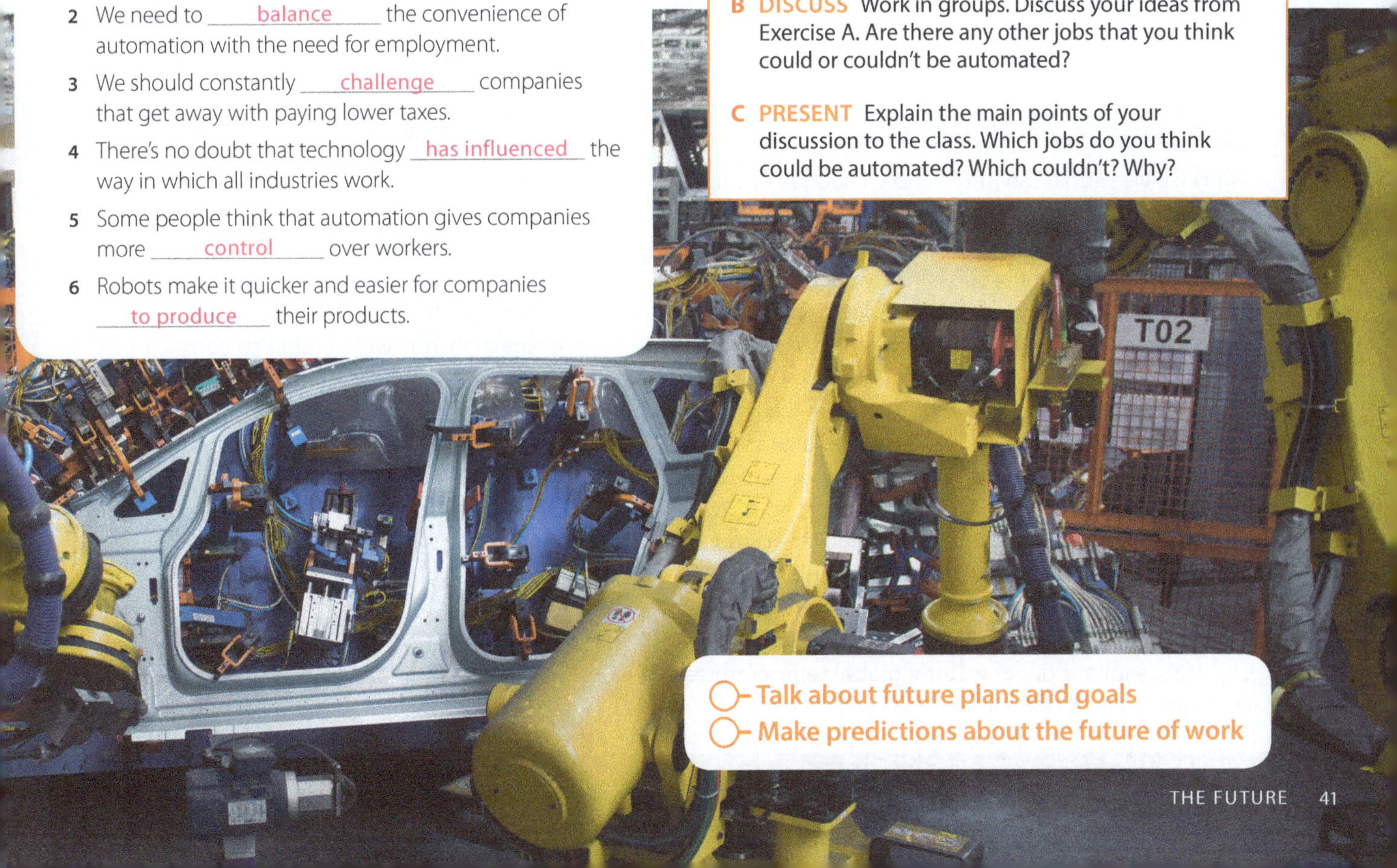

- Talk about future plans and goals
- Make predictions about the future of work

4.2 What will life be like?

- Evaluate future predictions
- Debate a range of transportation proposals

G– future perfect, future progressive and future perfect progressive
S– identifying agreement and disagreement V– intensifiers P– intonation with intensifiers

READING

A SPEAK Work in groups. Discuss which of the following will become common within the next decade.

- driverless cars
- virtual reality in the classroom
- space tourism
- 3D printing in the home

B PREDICT Work in pairs. Look at the subheadings in *When science fiction becomes science fact*. What predictions do you think each section will make about the future?

C READ FOR GIST Read the article quickly. Which of your ideas from Exercise B are mentioned?

D IDENITFY OPINION Read the article again. Write Y (Yes) if the statement agrees with the writer's opinion. Write N (No) if it contradicts the writer's opinion. Write NG (Not Given) if it is impossible to say what the writer thinks.

1 The author thinks pollution is the main threat to cities. N
2 AI and robotics will dominate both our home and work lives. NG
3 Humans and robots will work side by side. Y
4 Social media will affect people's real-life status. N
5 People will have little contact with each other. NG
6 We need laws to restrict the influence of social media. NG

WHEN SCIENCE FICTION BECOMES SCIENCE FACT

In 1989, the movie *Back to the Future 2* predicted that 26 years into the future, people would make video calls, use wearable technology and tablet computers, and play video games hands-free. While these predictions probably seemed pretty unrealistic at the time, all have come true in some form or another. Even the famous hoverboard could soon become a reality, as car giant Lexus has recently developed a working prototype. So, are predictions made in movies and TV always this accurate? Here we take a look at some of the key predictions made in science fiction over the past 30 years and assess which, if any, are likely to come true.

ENVIRONMENT

Many movies set in the future show changes to our environment. *Blade Runner* is set in the year 2049 and shows a dark future in which pollution levels in the city are shockingly high, and the sun is rarely seen. The natural environment has been almost completely destroyed and industrial cities dominate the landscape. While this movie focuses on the pollution and poor air quality in major cities, in reality the biggest environmental threat to cities is arguably rising sea levels. Recent estimates suggest that if we are unable to dramatically reduce the amount of carbon dioxide released into the atmosphere over the next few decades, [1]sea levels will have risen so much by 2050 that hundreds of millions of people will lose their homes. At present, the city most affected would be Shanghai. Projections show that the majority of the city will disappear under water if global temperatures increase by just three degrees.

Ex D Q1

TECHNOLOGY

Perhaps the most common types of predictions made in movies center around technology. According to Alex Proyas's movie *I, Robot*, by 2035 robots will have evolved to such a point that they will be able to carry out most human tasks.
[2]By 2035, we will have been living with computers for around 100 years, and while many predictions estimate that robots will be doing almost 50% of jobs worldwide within the next 20 years, a world like Proyas's is still a long way from reality. [3]It is much more likely robots will be working alongside humans, rather than replacing them. Ex D Q3

4.2 What will life be like?

LEAD-IN

Before class, make a list of five predictions for the future that you think might get your students talking (e.g. *People will no longer use Facebook*). Try to avoid any overlap with the bulleted list in Exercise A of the Reading section. In class, write the following sentence on the board – *My top five predictions for 20XX* (adding a date that is at least ten years in the future). Add your predictions one by one underneath, explaining them if necessary. Don't get drawn into a discussion at this point. Now, put students into pairs to discuss whether they agree with the predictions or not. Monitor and help with grammar and vocabulary as necessary. Bring the class back together to share their ideas. Next, put students into groups to make a list of their own predictions. Again, monitor to help with language as required. Bring the class back together again to share their ideas. Encourage other students to comment, explaining whether or not they agree and why.

READING

A Show students a picture of a driverless car and elicit what it is. Next, ask students whether they think driverless cars will become popular by the year 2029. Encourage students to explain their reasoning and stimulate class discussion as appropriate. Now, put students into groups to discuss the remaining bulleted topics. Monitor and help with any new or unfamiliar vocabulary. Open the discussion up to the class, writing any useful emergent vocabulary on the board.

B–C Draw students' attention to the subheadings in the text and elicit one or two predictions for the first category. Next, put them into pairs to discuss more ideas. Monitor and support with new or unfamiliar vocabulary as necessary. Bring the class back together to briefly share their ideas, before giving students time to read the article. Take this opportunity to discuss any parts of the text that students found surprising or confusing.

D Read the instructions as a class, clarifying that they should write Y if they can find information in the article that matches the sentence, N if they find information that contradicts it and NG if nothing is written about the topic at all. Highlight that although all of the options might sound like something the writer would say or agree with, this doesn't mean they should write Y – they must find supporting information in the text. Next, give students time to complete the exercise and encourage them to underline sentences that support Y or N answers. Then, ask them to check their ideas in pairs before giving feedback as a class. Encourage students to justify their answers with sentences from the text.

E Put students into groups to discuss the questions. Monitor and encourage them to explain their reasoning. Give feedback as a class, encouraging other students to ask follow-up questions to stimulate class-wide discussion. Add any useful emergent language to the board.

GRAMMAR HUB

4.2 Future perfect, future progressive and future perfect progressive

	Positive	Negative	Question
Future perfect	**The movie will have started** by the time we get there!	**I won't have finished** the report by tomorrow morning.	**Will you have left** by then?
Future progressive	**I'll be seeing** her on Monday, so I could ask her then.	**We won't be using** driverless cars for at least another 50 years.	So, what **will you be doing** this time tomorrow?
Future perfect progressive	In 2041, **we'll have been using** the internet for 50 years.	**I won't have been running** long enough to try a half-marathon in July.	How long **will you have been traveling** by then?

- We use the future perfect (*will* + *have* + past participle) to talk about something that will be finished before a specific time in the future.

  By 2050, we will have greatly improved the air quality in our cities.
- We use the future progressive (*will* + *be* + verb + *-ing*) to talk about an action that will be in progress at a specific time in the future.

  Hopefully, I'll be working in New York by then.
- We use the future perfect progressive (*will* + *have* + *been* + verb + *-ing*) to talk about an action or situation that will continue up to a specific time in the future.

  On July 9th, I'll have been working here for seven years.
- Certain time words and expressions are used with these tenses.

  In 50 years, we'll have stopped using gas-powered vehicles.
  This time next year, we'll be studying in France.
  By 2020, we will have been living together for 20 years.

Be careful!

- Do not confuse these three tenses. The future perfect is used for *completed* actions in the future, while the future progressive is used for actions *in progress* at a certain point in the future. The future perfect progressive refers to how long something will be in progress before a certain point in the future.

  I will have paid for my house by 2025. NOT ~~*I will be paying for my house by 2025.*~~
  I will be living in the US in five years. NOT ~~*I will have lived in the US in five years.*~~
  I will have been living here for 15 years in 2025. NOT ~~*I will be living here for 15 years in 2025.*~~

4.2 What will life be like?

GRAMMAR

A Focus students on the three highlighted sentences in the article, then give them time to complete the exercise alone. Allow time for students to compare their answers in pairs before giving feedback as a class.

B–C Add the highlighted sentences from Exercise A to the board one at a time, eliciting what tense they are (*1 future perfect, 2 future perfect progressive, 3 future progressive*) and the structure for each (*1 will + have + past participle, 2 will + have + been + -ing, 3 will + be + -ing*). Then, give students time to scan the article again for additional examples. Give feedback as a class, adding the examples to your lists on the board. Give additional explanations or examples for each tense as necessary, then direct students to the **Grammar Hub** (see below and TB42).

D–E Give students time to complete the sentences alone, before checking their answers in pairs. Give feedback as a class, encouraging students to explain which clues in each sentence gave them the answer. Next, put students into pairs to discuss the predictions in Exercise D. Monitor, focusing on how accurately students use the future forms covered in this section. Bring the class back together, nominating students to share the most interesting things they discussed. Use the **Grammar Worksheet** on page W19 for extra practice.

SPEAKING

A Tell students they are going to discuss the movie and TV predictions. Give them time to write notes about their opinions to prepare for the discussion. Monitor and help with grammar and vocabulary as necessary.

B Put students into pairs to discuss their ideas from Exercise A. Monitor, encouraging students to extend their discussions by explaining their reasoning and asking follow-up questions as appropriate. Bring the class back together to discuss each movie prediction one by one.

Extra activity

Write a set of future predictions on different slips of paper and put them into a hat. Try to ensure that they are interesting and can be argued both for and against (e.g. *By 2025, grocery stores will have stopped using plastic entirely; In 20 years, everybody will be driving electric cars; By the end of the decade, humans will have walked on the surface of Mars*; etc). Now hold a series of quickfire debates by calling out pairs of students to come to the front of the class, choose a sentence and argue for/against it. Alternatively, you could set up a more traditional debate, giving groups times to prepare their arguments.

GRAMMAR HUB

4.2 Future perfect, future progressive and future perfect progressive

A Choose the correct options (a, b or c) to complete the sentences.

1 It's a nine-hour flight. My plane leaves at 9 am, so at 11 am, I ___.
  (**a**) 'll be flying over the Atlantic **b** 'll have landed in New York
2 Do you really think you'll ___ at the same company in ten years?
  a have worked (**b**) be working
3 This time next year, he ___ for Real Madrid for ten years.
  (**a**) 'll have been playing **b** 'll be playing
4 Do you think you ___ English in five years?
  a 'll have studied (**b**) 'll still be studying
5 Is it possible that they ___ the use of fossil fuels by the time our children grow up?
  a 'll be banning (**b**) 'll have banned
6 What will you ___ at three tomorrow? If you're free, let's meet up for coffee.
  a have done (**b**) be doing
7 Next Sunday, I ___ here for two years.
  (**a**) 'll have been living **b** 'll be living

B Complete the sentences with the future perfect, future progressive or future perfect progressive form of the verb in parentheses.

1 ___Will you have finished___ (*you / finish*) your studies by the end of the year?
2 I started learning English over four years ago, so in December, I will ___have been studying___ (*study*) it for exactly five years.
3 Within the next ten years, robots ___will have taken___ (*take*) over a lot of tasks.
4 What kind of world do you think we ___'ll/will be living___ (*live*) in 50 years from now?
5 If the sea level rises, these cities ___will have completely disappeared___ (*completely / disappear*) in 100 years.
6 In June of next year, you ___'ll/will have been working___ (*work*) here for five years.

➤ Go back to page 43.

E SPEAK Work in groups. Discuss the questions.

1 Which of the predictions in the article do you think will come true? Why?

2 What else do you think might happen in each of the categories over the next twenty years?

GRAMMAR

Future perfect, future progressive and future perfect progressive

A **Scan the article again. Match the highlighted sentences (1–3) to the things they describe (a–c).**

a an action or situation that will be finished before a specific time in the future 1

b an action or situation that will continue up to a specific time in the future 2

c an action or situation that will be in progress at a specific time in the future 3

COMMUNICATION

Movies are also full of predictions about the future of communication. The communicators in *Star Trek* are incredibly similar to modern cell phones, and the 1927 classic *Metropolis* showed video calls long before the creation of Skype. Our increased reliance on smartphones is taken a step further in the movie *Her*, where the main character has a relationship with a computer operating system that has a female voice.

If it's still popular in 2025, we will have been using Facebook for just over twenty years.

The Netflix series *Black Mirror* shows a future where the 'like' feature of Facebook impacts on people's actual lives. The more likes someone gets, the higher their social status is in real life. As a result they can get better cars, houses and jobs. Although this is unlikely to happen, it does Ex D Q4 draw our attention to the worrying impact of social media on society.

B WORK IT OUT Scan the text again and complete the box with one more example of each tense.

Future perfect, future progressive and future perfect progressive

We use the **future perfect** to talk about something that will finish before a specific point of time in the future.
1 ... by 2035, robots will have evolved to the point that they will be able to carry out most human tasks.

We use the **future progressive** to talk about an action or situation that will be in progress at a specific time in the future.
2 ... robots will be doing almost 50% of jobs worldwide within the next 20 years.

We use the **future perfect progressive** to talk about an action or situation that will continue up to a specific time in the future.
3 If it's still popular in 2025, we will have been using Facebook for just over 20 years.

C **Go to the Grammar Hub on page 128.**

D PRACTICE Complete the predictions with the future perfect, future progressive or future perfect progressive form of the verbs in parentheses.

1 I 'll/will have changed (*change*) jobs by the end of the year.

2 I 'll/will be living (*live*) in the same place in thirty years.

3 I 'll/will have visited (*visit*) five new countries by the end of the decade.

4 By the end of the month, I 'll/will have bought (*buy*) a new phone.

5 By the end of the decade, I 'll/will have been working (*work*) for the same company for over twenty years.

6 In five years, I 'll/will still be studying (*still / study*) English.

E SPEAK Work in pairs. Which predictions in Exercise D do you think will become true for you? Why?

SPEAKING

A PREPARE **Read the following predictions from different science fiction movies. Which do you think will become true? Write notes.**

Police will be able to predict the future, preventing serious crimes before they happen. *Minority Report* (2002)

You will be able to pay to have your memory of a relationship that went wrong permanently erased. *Eternal Sunshine of a Spotless Mind* (2004)

Humans will learn how to communicate with aliens. *Arrival* (2016)

The Earth will be so damaged that humans will look for a new planet to call home. *Interstellar* (2014)

The rich will control cities from high-rise towers, while the poor will work machines underground. *Metropolis* (1927).

B SPEAK **Work in pairs. Compare your ideas from Exercise A. Explain your reasoning.**

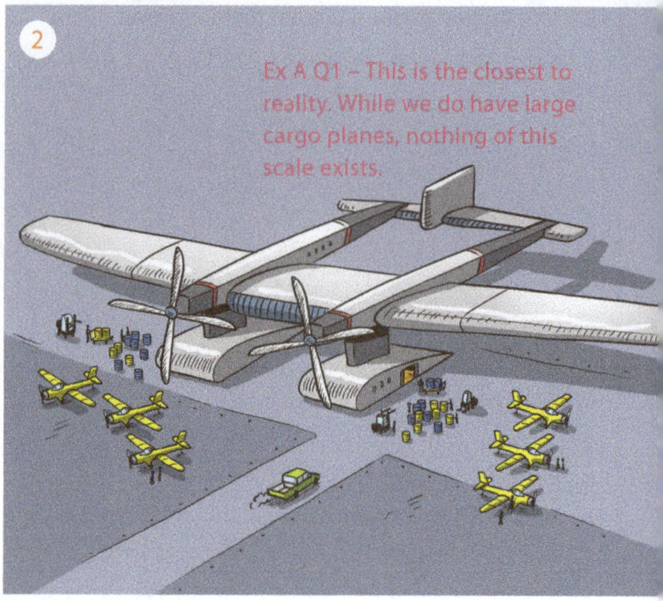

LISTENING

A SPEAK **Work in pairs. Look at the pictures (1–3) and discuss the questions.**

1 Which of the predictions about future transportation came true?

2 Which didn't come true and why do you think they failed? None of the predictions came true.

3 How do you think transportation will change over the next ten years?

4.5 **B LISTEN FOR GIST** **Listen to a public debate about the future of transportation. Put the modes of transportation in the order they are discussed.**

4 hypersonic jets — 1 driverless cars

2 hyperloop trains — 3 flying bikes

4.5 **C IDENTIFY AGREEMENT AND DISAGREEMENT** **Listen again. Who makes the following points – Mark or Sarah? To what extent to they agree with each other? Use the information in the box to help you.**

Identifying agreement and disagreement

When arguing about a topic, speakers use expressions such as *I completely agree*, *I can't see …*, *Yes, but …*, etc to signal agreement or disagreement. These are typically followed by reasons and examples to counter or support the original point.

Speakers also highlight agreement or disagreement by responding with a single adverb (e.g. *Seriously?*, *Definitely!*, etc).

1 Driverless cars will soon become a common sight on our roads.

2 Driverless cars have better reactions than human drivers.

3 Hyperloops are safer than existing train systems.

4 Hyperloop train systems are unlikely to get the funding they need.

5 We're unlikely to develop flying cars within the next two decades.

6 There may be a market for space tourism in the future.

D SPEAK **Work in pairs. Read the driverless car scenario Sarah describes in the discussion. What do you think the car should do? Explain your reasoning.**

How can a car make a decision about what to do in a dangerous situation? Should it protect the driver at all costs? What if doing so might mean injuring somebody else? What does it do then? I just think it would be incredibly dangerous to have driverless cars on the road.

VOCABULARY

Intensifiers

A **Read the extracts from the discussion. Complete the definitions below with the words in bold.**

1 The way we get around is going to be **entirely** transformed.

2 I **firmly** believe there is no chance driverless cars will become popular.

3 It's **undoubtedly** true that driverless cars will have more consistent and quicker reactions than most drivers.

4 But it would **greatly** improve our lives!

5 Hyperloop train systems are **widely** expected to happen.

6 … **especially** things that save significant time, like the Hyperloop train…

7 … it will become **significantly** cheaper over time.

8 You seem **incredibly** focused on speed!

a entirely completely, or in every way

b significantly in a way that is relevant or that has an important effect on something

c undoubtedly used for saying that something is certainly true or is accepted by everyone

d greatly very much

e incredibly extremely

f widely by a lot of people, or in a lot of places

g firmly strongly

h especially used when mentioning conditions that make something more relevant, important or true

LISTENING

A Draw students' attention to the illustrations and put them into pairs to discuss the questions. Monitor, helping with new or unfamiliar vocabulary as necessary. Bring the class back together to share their ideas, encouraging further discussion as appropriate.

4.5 **B** Play the audio for students to order the modes of transportation. Ask them to briefly check their answers in pairs before giving feedback as a class. If necessary, ask CCQs at this point to check student understanding of *hypersonic jets* (e.g. *How are hypersonic jets different to regular planes?*) and *hyperloop trains* (e.g. *What do hyperloop trains travel through?*). See the **Audio script** below and TB45.

4.5 **C** Write the following sentence on the board – *By the year 20XX* (add a date at least ten years in the future), *everyone will be using driverless cars.* Ask students whether they agree or disagree, building up a list of the signaling phrases they use on the board (e.g. *I completely disagree because …, I agree with you up to a point, but …,* etc). Ask how people can show agreement or disagreement with only one word (e.g. *Absolutely! Nonsense!* etc) and add examples to your lists on the board. Tell students they are going to listen to the debate again and highlight that they need to do two things – identify which speaker makes each statement and write notes about whether the other speaker agrees with them or not. Now, play the audio again for students to complete the exercise. Put students into pairs to compare their answers before giving feedback as a class.

1 *Mark. Sarah disagrees, saying, '… it is absolutely ridiculous' and that she firmly believes '… there is no chance driverless cars will become popular.'*

2 *Mark. Sarah partially agrees but says '… it's still slightly concerning.'*

3 *Mark. Sarah agrees, saying, 'Yes, they are very safe.'*

4 *Sarah. Mark disagrees, saying, 'Hyperloop train systems are widely expected to happen. Countries around the world are investing time and money into their own Hyperloop systems.'*

5 *Sarah. Mark disagrees, saying, 'I don't think (we're 25 years away from anything like a flying car)' and gives the example of flying bikes in the Dubai police force.*

6 *Mark. Sarah partially agrees, saying, 'There may be a small market for it, but only among the super-rich.' There may be a small market (for space tourism) …, but goes on to say only rich people will be able to afford it.*

D Talk students through the scenario Sarah describes, using a diagram to support students' understanding. Next, put students into pairs to discuss the dilemma. Monitor, encouraging students to explain their reasoning with examples. Bring the class back together to share their ideas, exploring any differences of opinion.

VOCABULARY

A Write the following sentence on the board – *I disagree with you.* Now, elicit what you could add to the sentence to make it sound more emphatic, adding an intensifier (e.g. *totally, completely,* etc) to the sentence in a different color when/if one is mentioned. Tell students that adverbs used like this are often referred to as intensifiers, and give them time to complete the definitions for the intensifiers in bold. Ask them to check their answers in pairs before giving feedback as a class.

AUDIO SCRIPT

4.5

Listening, Exercise B
P = Presenter M = Mark S = Sarah

P: Good morning, everyone. Welcome to today's debate. Transportation is changing rapidly around the world. More and more cars are becoming electric. Drones are being used for deliveries. So, of all the future predictions about transportation and travel, which are most likely to come true? Here to discuss this with me today are Sarah Atkinson, technology blogger and editor at *The Neo Futurist*, and Mark Edwards, transport correspondent for *The Evening Express*. So, first, let's talk about driverless cars – do you think we will see these on our roads any time soon? (Ex B)

M: Definitely! The way we get around is going to be entirely transformed. It's not a matter of *if*, but *when* this happens. These are incredibly exciting times! (Ex C Q1)

P: Sarah, what do you think?

S: Sorry, but that is absolutely ridiculous. I firmly believe there is no chance driverless cars will become popular. How can a car make a decision about what to do in a dangerous situation? Should it protect the driver at all costs? What if doing so might mean injuring somebody else? What does it do then? I just think it would be incredibly dangerous to have driverless cars on the road.

M: People's reactions and decision-making are absolutely terrible! It's undoubtedly true that driverless cars will have more consistent and quicker reactions than most drivers. (Ex C Q2)

S: Maybe, but it's still slightly concerning. Driverless cars frequently crash during testing. A driverless bus crashed in its first *hour* of tests in Las Vegas! It's a dangerous development and we simply don't need it.

M: But it would greatly improve our lives! We could work in the car on the way to work. We could have a second car that took the kids to school. You could jump in and out of driverless taxis just paying with your card.

S: The level of associated risk is crazy! Imagine if the car taking your kids to school had an accident. It's a terrifying idea, but fortunately I think it's highly unlikely to happen any time soon.

P: OK, so what about the Hyperloop? Elon Musk's vision of future trains? A pod travels through a tunnel with no friction or air resistance, making it a very fast and efficient way of travelling. (Ex B)

M: Well, I for one think they're an incredibly safe alternative to our current train systems. They could also cut trip times down by 80 to 90%. Imagine that. A four-hour train ride could be completed in less than an hour! (Ex C Q3)

S: Yes, they are very safe, but it won't happen. A Hyperloop train has to be in a fixed tunnel using air pressure and magnets to move the train. The big problem is that they are likely to run just between a few points that are miles apart and go past all of the other big places in between. They will literally go straight past millions of passengers. Governments simply won't spend the money and companies won't either because it will be hard to make a profit. (Ex C Q4)

B–C Give students time to complete the sentences alone before checking their answers with a partner. Give feedback as a class, before directing students to the **Vocabulary Hub** (see TB121).

D Read the bulleted list of topics as a class, then give your opinion on one of them using an intensifier to demonstrate the activity. Next, put students into pairs to practice themselves. Monitor, encouraging students to ask follow-up questions to keep the discussions going. Bring the class back together for further discussion if you have time. Use the **Vocabulary Worksheet** on page W20 for extra practice.

PRONUNCIATION

4.6 **A** Explain that we not only use intensifiers to make sentences grammatically more emphatic, we also use intonation to highlight them. Then, play the extract for students to answer the questions.

A rise-fall intonation is used to emphasize the adverb.

4.7 **B** Play the audio, pausing after each sentence for students to copy the intonation used on the intensifiers. Provide further individual and choral practicing as necessary. If you want to, you could extend this section by putting students into pairs to write their own sentences with intensifiers and practice saying them with emphatic intonation.

SPEAKING HUB

A Tell students that a new form of transportation is going to be built in your city and ask them to briefly read through the three options. Encourage them to write down at least two advantages and two disadvantages for each transportation option.

B Divide the class into three groups (A, B and C) and allocate each a mode of transportation from Exercise A. Explain that you are going to debate which is the best form of transportation for your city and that each group will be given time to present their arguments. Give groups time to discuss ideas and encourage them to write notes about the weaknesses of the other forms of transportation to help them in the debate (e.g. *The Eco Bus will only cost $300 million to build unlike the others which are much more expensive.*).

C To begin the debate, ask each group to present a summary of why their mode of transportation is the best. Encourage students to write notes during the oppositions' summaries because this will help them to argue their point. With a weaker class, you may want to allow extra time for the groups to work to come up with counter-arguments based on their notes from the opening summaries. Once each group has presented their argument, let the debate begin. During the debate, ensure that all students have an equal chance to participate by nominating individuals to share opinions and respond to points. Allow time at the end for each group to summarize their key points again, then take a class vote to decide which group's argument was most convincing.

4.5 (continued)

Ex C Q4 **M:** Nonsense! Hyperloop train systems are widely expected to happen. Countries all around the world are investing time and money into their own Hyperloop systems. They're undoubtedly cheaper than building a normal high-speed train and travel times will be greatly reduced. Dubai to Abu Dhabi, normally a two-hour drive, would take just 12 minutes on a Hyperloop train! Why wouldn't cities invest in it?

P: I can imagine some of these developments happening – especially things that save significant time, like the Hyperloop train, and things that free up personal time, like driverless cars. I can imagine companies investing in and developing these ideas because they could make a lot of money, but what about something more futuristic, like the flying cars we see in movies?

M: This always seems like something purely from
Ex C Q5 science fiction, but I don't think flying cars are actually that unrealistic. The technology isn't that far off …

S: Oh, come on. I think you're exaggerating there! We're at least 25 years away from anything like a flying car.

M: Hmm, I don't think so. Dubai police already have
Ex B self-driving cars and robot police officers. Now they're adding a flying bike to their force. It will greatly improve response times in cities with serious traffic problems.

S: The laws and the health and safety issues here would be frightening!

M: Yes, but society has dealt with major changes before. Imagine what it was like on the early passenger planes taking people on vacation.. That must have been surprising to society and a lot of rules and laws must have been needed, but society coped and moved on.

P: Actually, that brings me to my next point. What about the travel industry? How do you see that changing?

Ex B; Ex C Q6 **M:** Well, I think we're likely to see hypersonic jets and space tourism in the not too distant future.

S: Space tourism? I can't see that really taking off – if you'll excuse the pun! There may be a small market for it, but only amongst the super rich.

M: Well, we'll see about that. But when it comes to hypersonic jets, I have no doubt that the technology is improving all the time and it's very likely it will become significantly cheaper over time. That means it would be affordable for most people. The Sabre jet developed in the UK could get you from Britain to Australia in four hours. That's almost 20 hours quicker!

S: You seem incredibly focused on speed! I'd be much more interested in a solar plane that was better for the environment. Even if it took me an extra day to get somewhere! In general people think more about the environment today. It's a bigger concern than speed.

M: That could happen as well. I absolutely love the idea of getting places quicker, though. Who wants to sit on a plane for two days? I somewhat agree with your opinion on space travel, though. It's an experience rather than a vacation.

P: Thank you both. Now let's move on to the Q&A section of the debate. Does anyone have any questions on driverless …

B Choose the correct intensifiers to complete the sentences.

1 Many of these inventions seem *undoubtedly* / *incredibly* unlikely to happen.
2 It's *entirely* / *greatly* possible that all cars will be driverless in the future.
3 There are *significantly* / *firmly* more passengers using the system than it was designed for originally.
4 Travel times would be *greatly* / *entirely* improved.
5 You are *undoubtedly* / *especially* right.
6 I *firmly* / *widely* believe that safety is more important than convenience.
7 That is *especially* / *widely* true when it comes to a company making a profit.
8 It is *significantly* / *widely* believed that commercial flights will eventually be powered by solar energy.

C Go to the Vocabulary Hub on page 145.

D SPEAK Work in pairs. Use intensifiers to give your opinions on the topics below.

- the likelihood of space tourism
- police traveling by hover bikes
- the widespread use of hyperloop trains

Space tourism in our lifetime seems incredibly unlikely.

PRONUNCIATION
Intonation with intensifiers

4.6 **A** Listen to the extract from the debate. What intonation does the speaker use on the intensifiers: rising (↗), falling (↘) or rise-fall (↗↘)? What effect does this have?

rise-fall; it emphasizes the adverb

They're undoubtedly cheaper than building a normal high-speed train and travel times will be greatly reduced.

4.7 **B** Listen and repeat the sentences.

1 The city is incredibly congested!
2 The idea is entirely unrealistic. It will never happen.
3 Considering the environmental impact has become increasingly important.
4 Travel times will be greatly reduced.

SPEAKING HUB

A PLAN Read the information cards and write notes about the advantages and disadvantages of each form of transportation.

CITY TRAIN

Completion:	2030
Design:	Spacious and modern. Built-in wi-fi. First-class meeting tables
Cost:	$5 billion
Ticket cost:	$10 day ticket
Speed:	Much faster than road vehicles. Delays less likely

ECO BUS

Completion:	2022
Design:	Eco-friendly using renewable energy
Cost:	$300 million
Ticket cost:	$3 day ticket
Speed:	Faster than cars because it uses a designated bus lane. Delays possible

TROLLEY SYSTEM

Completion:	2025
Design:	A simple subway train. Many roads will need to be redesigned to fit trolleys
Cost:	$2 billion
Ticket cost:	$5 day ticket
Speed:	Relatively slow-moving. Delays possible

B PREPARE Work in three groups. You are going to propose a new transportation system for your city. Group A – City Train, Group B – Eco Bus, Group C – Trolley System. Prepare you arguments.

C DISCUSS Debate the best method as a class. Remember to question the weaknesses in the other methods.

- Evaluate future predictions
- Debate a range of transportation proposals

Flippy the robot

COMPREHENSION

A Work in pairs. You are going to watch a news report about a burger-flipping robot. What do you think the advantages and disadvantages of this kind of technology are?

B Watch the report. Which of your ideas from Exercise A are mentioned?

C Watch again. Complete the sentences with no more than three words from the report.

1 A combination of image recognition and heat-sensing technology tells Flippy which burgers need turning over.

2 The introduction of Flippy may lead to fewer human employees in the future.

3 CaliBurger will spend an estimated twelve thousand dollars / $12,000 a year on maintenance.

4 Human employees frequently find the working conditions difficult and many leave after a few weeks.

5 Flippy isn't fully autonomous yet and regularly made mistakes that a human employee wouldn't.

6 David Zito, the CEO of Miso Robotics, is confident that Flippy will get smarter with time.

7 The presenter believes it won't be long before Flippy can both prepare (the) food and serve customers.

8 Roboticists predict that new jobs will emerge to replace those lost.

D Work in groups. Do you agree with the following predictions made in the report? Why/Why not?

1 It won't be long before the majority of unskilled jobs are automated.

2 In the future, it will be odd to go to a restaurant that isn't almost fully automated.

AUTHENTIC ENGLISH

A Read the extract from the report. Why do you think the speaker says *right*?

It's not a very fun job, **right**? Er, it's hot, it's greasy, it's dirty, erm, it hurts your wrist, **right**?

B Read the information in the box and check your answers to Exercise A. *Right* is used instead of a question tag to check information or to ask if the listener agrees.

> ***right***
>
> In informal spoken English, speakers frequently use *right* in place of a question tag to check information or to ask if someone agrees with them.
>
> *You have tomorrow off,* ***right?***
> (= You have tomorrow off, don't you?)
>
> *You know where you're going,* ***right?***
> (= You know where you're going, don't you?)

C Read the extract in Exercise A again. Which regular question tags could be used instead of *right*?

It's not a very fun job, **is it?** It hurts your wrist, **doesn't it?**

D Work in pairs. Take turns using prompts (1–6) to make sentences with *right*.

1 You want to check that the movie starts at 9 pm.

2 You think your friend has met Yuki before.

3 You're not sure if a friend can speak Japanese.

4 You think a colleague is going to Seville next week.

5 You think a friend finishes early on Fridays.

6 You want to check if your friend knows how to get to the station.

So, the movie starts at 9 pm, right?

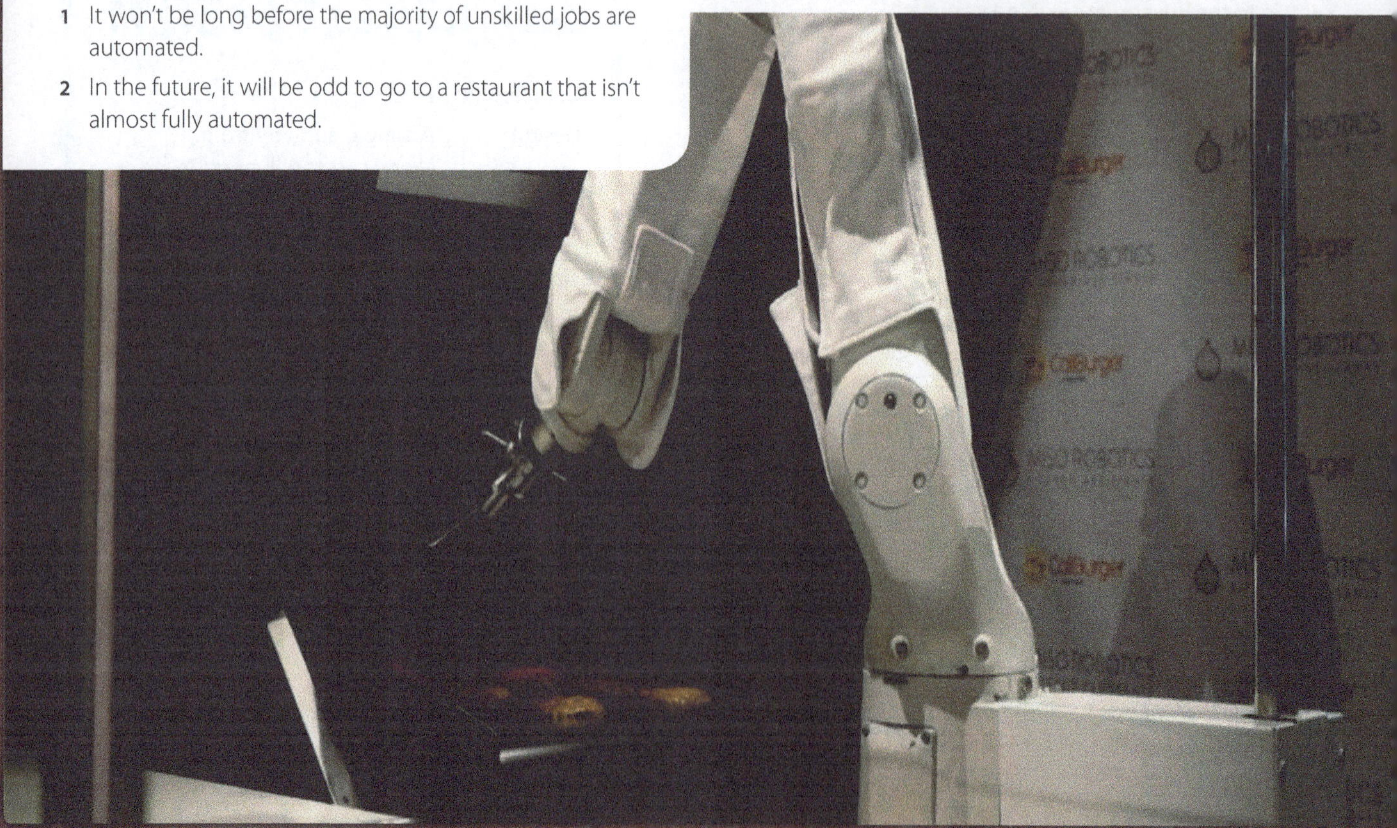

The perfect coffee

A Work in pairs. What's your favorite café? Why do you like it so much?

B Watch the video. Choose the best summary (1–3) of what Sam thinks customers want from an independent café.

1 They want to be served quickly and efficiently.
2 They want to make use of the latest technology.
3 They want to feel like a valued part of a community.

SPEAKING SKILL

A Watch the video again. Complete the box with examples from the conversation.

Asking for clarification

In conversation, we frequently need to check that we have understood something correctly. A common way to do this is to use a signaling phrase followed by an explanation of what we think the speaker meant.

Sam: *I want the people who come to our café to feel that it is their space. So I often allow local clubs to hold meetings here or we host events like book signings or talks.*

Amanda: So you mean that *the café can be a hub for the local community?*

We use a number of other phrases for asking for clarification, some of which are more formal than others:

More formal

1 *Correct me if I'm wrong ...*
2 *... just so I understand correctly ...*

Less formal

3 *Is that right?*
4 *How do you mean?*

B Work in pairs. Tell your partner about your job or a job you would like to have. Listen to your partner and ask for clarification of what they tell you. Then swap roles.

Talk about:

- what skills and knowledge you need
- who you work with
- what you like/dislike about the job
- what your responsibilities are
- what equipment you use

SPEAKING HUB

A **PREPARE** Work in pairs. You are going to conduct an interview about increased automation in the restaurant industry.

Student A – You are a journalist. Choose which questions to ask from the list below and add some of your own.

Student B – You are the interviewee. Write notes about your responses to the questions below.

- How might the industry benefit from increased automation?
- Which jobs do you think are most at risk from this trend?
- How do you think the public would react?

B **SPEAK** Conduct the interview. Ask each other for clarification if you need to.

Correct me if I'm wrong, but you seem to be saying that you'd be happy for robots to help prepare, but not serve your food. Is that right?

C **DISCUSS** As a class, discuss whether increased automation in the workplace is mainly positive or negative.

Give your opinion on automation in the workplace

➤ Turn to page 157 to learn how to write a for and against blog post.

Flippy the robot

LEAD-IN

Elicit five tasks that a chef has to do every day (e.g. *chop vegetables, boil pasta*, etc). Then, discuss whether each could be automated or not. Now, put students into groups and give each a different job to discuss (e.g. *lawyer, taxi driver*, etc) in the same way. Bring the class back together to share their ideas.

COMPREHENSION

A–B ▶ Elicit one or two advantages and disadvantages of technology like Flippy. Then, put students into pairs to discuss more. Bring the class back together to share their ideas, then play the video to see which are mentioned.

Advantages: saves the company money in the long term, safer, more consistent results, removes the need for monotonous jobs

Disadvantages: makes regular mistakes, robot not totally autonomous, can't actually hand the burger over to the customer

C ▶ Play the video again for students to complete the exercise. Give feedback as a class.

D Put students into groups to discuss the predictions. Monitor, encouraging students to justify their answers.

AUTHENTIC ENGLISH

A–B Put students into pairs to discuss the extract. Then, give students time to read the skills box to check their answers.

C Give students time to complete the exercise and briefly check in pairs before giving feedback as a class.

D Read the first sentence and the example at the bottom to demonstrate the exercise. Then, put students into pairs to practice using *right*.

The perfect coffee

LEAD-IN

Elicit one or two ideas from the class about what makes a good café, then put students into groups to discuss more. Bring the class back together to share their ideas.

A Tell students about your favorite café in the area, explaining how often you go there and why you keep going back. Next, put students into pairs to discuss their own favorite cafés.

B ▶ Tell students they are now going to watch the next episode of the Café Hub series. Give students time to read three potential summaries, before playing the video for them to choose the best one. Give feedback as a class. You can find the **video script** for *The perfect coffee* on the Teacher's Resource Center.

SPEAKING SKILL

A ▶ Read through the example in the skills box before playing the video again for students to write down more examples. Give students time to briefly check their answers in pairs before giving feedback as a class.

B Give students time to write notes about each bullet point, then put them into pairs to discuss their jobs.

SPEAKING HUB

A–B Put students into pairs, assigning each a role to play and giving them time to write notes. Monitor, helping with grammar and vocabulary as necessary. Then, ask them to conduct their interviews.

C Ask one or two pairs to share the ideas they discussed in their interview as a way to open up class discussion.

▶ VIDEO SCRIPT

Flippy the robot

P = Presenter C = CaliBurger rep D = David Zito

P: This is Flippy, a robot that can replace one of life's most basic unskilled jobs. Ex C Q1 It uses image recognition and heat-sensing technology to know which burgers need flipping. It can handle at least 12 burgers at once. But like so many instances of robotics appearing in the workplace, there's little doubt over what the eventual impact will be.

C: There will be changes in the way workers are hired and the types of jobs available, but …

Ex C Q2 **P:** What does that mean? Does that mean a typical restaurant in the future might have fewer human employees than it does now?

C: I … I … I think … I think that is … is very possible.

P: Flippy is being installed in 50 locations run by California-based chain, CaliBurger. Ex C Q3 Each robot costs the company $60,000, plus $12,000 a year to run. The first robot will be found here, in Pasadena, just north of Los Angeles.

C: It's not a very fun job, right? Er, it's hot, it's greasy, it's dirty, erm, it hurts your wrist, right? So people come in and we train them, which is a significant expense, Ex C Q4 they work for a few weeks and then they leave, so the robotic systems make a perfectly consistent burger across all of our restaurants, everywhere in the world.

Ex C Q5 **P:** It still does need a bit of a helping hand, however, and it made regular mistakes that no human ever would.

D: If I threw anybody in behind a grill tomorrow, right? And asked them to start cooking. Would you make a mistake? Would you accidentally forget to flip a burger? That's why there's a human at the end of this process, right? And so it's an assistant. Ex C Q6 This will get smarter and smarter over time. We're really just getting started with what this technology can do.

P: So this is …

D: Here we go!

P: … the robot-made burger. I've had a few burgers in my time – that's pretty good. Flippy is obviously pretty sophisticated and it does replace some of the monotonous tasks in a typical fast-food kitchen. Ex C Q7 What it can't do yet, of course, is actually prepare the food and hand it over to a customer, but you've got to think – it's surely only a matter of time.

C: A day will come where it will be odd to go into a restaurant where you don't have all the benefits of robotic systems, right? Where you're not, you know, confident in the safety and security of the food because there's humans touching the food.

Ex C Q8 **P:** Robot makers say jobs will eventually emerge to replace what's lost, though nobody yet seems to know what those jobs might be. Dave Lee, BBC News in Pasadena.

4 Writing

Write a for and against blog post

W structuring a for and against blog post

A Read the introduction to the blog post. What issue is the writer going to discuss? *Whether or not to ban cars from city centers to address congestion.*

B Work in pairs. Brainstorm ideas for and against the issue.

C Scan the blog post. Which of your ideas from Exercise B are mentioned?

About Blog Contact Search

In order to deal with congestion in cities, some people think that private vehicles should be banned from city centers. Others, however, feel that this is an unrealistic solution and that alternatives would work more effectively. This post will consider both perspectives.

[1]One of the arguments in favor of banning cars is that they are simply unnecessary if public transportation is effective. The needs of individuals can arguably be met by heavy investment in public transportation and the replacement of roads with bike paths. A good example of a city that has taken this idea to heart is Oslo, which plans to ban all cars from the city center by 2019 – approximately six years before a nationwide city ban comes into effect. Oslo is planning to replace almost 50 kilometers of road with bike lanes by the time the city goes car-free.

[2]On the one hand, banning cars seems like a simple way to address congestion in city centers. Yet, on the other hand, serious investment is required to make this feasible. One issue is that extensive public transportation networks would be required to replace cars in city centers. Many networks are seriously outdated or limited in their coverage. Furthermore, many countries simply do not have the financial means to build and extend their networks on such a scale.

[3]I believe that banning cars from city centers is only feasible in cities that already have an effective public transportation system. For everywhere else, cars are simply the most efficient way to get around.

[4]To conclude, while many cities are making steps toward banning cars from city centers, doing so requires heavy investment which many countries may not be able to afford. Realistically, we are a long way from car-free city centers.

Refer students to this blog post as a model for the writing task.

D Match the paragraphs (1–4) to their functions (a–d).

a Arguments for *1*
b Personal opinion *3*
c Conclusion *4*
d Arguments against *2*

E Complete the box with phrases from the blog.

Structuring a for and against blog post

Introduction
Many people think that …
1 *… some people think that …*

To give arguments for and against
Some people argue that …
Others think …
2 *One of the arguments in favor …*
3 *On the one hand …*
4 *Yet, on the other hand, …*

To give examples / more information
For example …
5 *A good example of this …*

To give your opinion
I am convinced that …
6 *I believe that …*

Conclusion
In conclusion, …
7 *To conclude …*

WRITING

A PREPARE Read the blog topic and write notes of arguments for and against.

Building more bicycle lanes is the best way to address pollution in city centers.

B PLAN Organize your notes from Exercise A into a plan for a for and against blog post.

C WRITE Write your blog post. Use your notes to help you.

D EDIT Work in pairs. Edit your partner's blog. Check:

- spelling and punctuation
- use of phrases to structure their argument
- strength of ideas

Refer students to this checklist when editing their partner's work.

WRITING 157

LEAD-IN

Ask students to make a list of the top three problems in their town or city. Then, put them into groups to discuss each issue and possible solutions. Monitor, encouraging students to use examples to help explain their ideas.

WRITING

A Give students time to read the introduction and answer the question. Give feedback as a class.

B Write the headings *For* and *Against* on the board, then elicit one or two arguments for each. Then, put students into pairs to think of more arguments. Give feedback as a class, building up the lists on the board.

C Give students time to read the full blog post to see if any of their ideas were mentioned.

D Read through the functions as a class, then give students time to match them to the paragraphs. Give feedback as a class.

E Give students time to scan the blog post again to find more examples for this section. Give feedback as a class.

WRITING TASK

A–B Add the blog topic to the board and elicit one or two arguments for and against it, mirroring the process you followed at the start of the lesson. Then, give students time to think of more arguments alone. Next, ask students to organize their notes into the following structure – introduction, arguments for, arguments against, conclusion.

C Tell students to write their blogs. Monitor and provide support with structure and vocabulary when necessary.

D Put students into pairs to edit each other's articles. Encourage students to give each other positive feedback. Students can then rewrite their articles either in class or for homework.

VOCABULARY

A Choose the correct prepositions to complete the sentences.

1 I want to take a course *in / on / for* accounting next year.
2 There's a risk *with / of / for* the company going out of business before the end of the year.
3 Do you have any knowledge *of / in / on* spreadsheets?
4 Congratulations *about / for / on* the birth of your new baby daughter!
5 There are a lot of historic places of interest *at / in / on* the northern part of the country.
6 Is there any possibility *for / of / about* getting a refund?

B Complete the sentences with words from the box.

balance	benefit	challenge
control	influence	produce

1 We are being expected ___to produce___ far more than is humanly possible!
2 I'm so exhausted all the time. I think I just need a better work–life ___balance___.
3 Always ___challenging___ yourself to try something new is extremely important.
4 The trend toward digital ___has influenced___ the new direction of the company.
5 If this deal goes through, XKOM ___will control___ 65% of the market.
6 One of the ___benefits___ of exercise is that it lowers your stress levels.

C Choose the correct options (a, b or c) to complete the sentences.

1 He usually exaggerates so I'm not ___ sure I believe him.
a entirely b firmly c widely
2 They've ___ improved the new model.
a entirely b incredibly c significantly
3 ___, everyone survived the plane crash.
a Undoubtedly b Incredibly c Widely
4 The price of tickets may vary ___ between distributors.
a firmly b greatly c especially
5 I ___ believe that closing the company was the right decision to make.
a firmly b widely c significantly
6 New England is usually pretty cold, ___ in the winter.
a greatly b incredibly c especially
7 The population will ___ continue to rise as more people move there for work.
a incredibly b undoubtedly c firmly
8 It is ___ believed that AI will place many jobs at risk.
a widely b especially c entirely

GRAMMAR

A Complete the article with *will*, *going to* or the present progressive form of the verbs in parentheses. Sometimes more than one answer is possible.

Four changes to make to your life

At the start of every year, we all make promises to change certain aspects of our life. 'I [1] ___'m/am going to exercise___ (*exercise*) more and 'I [2] ___'m/am going to eat___ (*eat*) more healthily' we say. But we typically fail to keep our promises. So what simple changes can we make that will make a big difference and be easy to achieve?

❶ Get up and go to sleep at the same time. You [3] ___'ll/will feel___ (*feel*) a lot more refreshed.

❷ Be punctual. It reduces stress. If you start arriving early for things, you [4] ___'ll/will find___ (*find*) that life starts to feel less frantic.

❸ Routine is good, but you should also be spontaneous occasionally. When a friend says, 'I [5] ___'m/am going to___ (*go*) the beach this weekend, do you want to come?' Say, 'Great! I [6] ___'ll/will come___ (*come*).'

❹ Try to be optimistic. For example, if your company is struggling, don't think 'I [7] ___'m/am going to lose___ (*lose*) my job.' Be positive and think about the new good job you might get.

Make these simple changes in your life and I am sure you [8] ___'ll/will be___ (*be*) happier in the long run.

B Choose the correct options to complete the sentences.

1 Can we meet later? I *'ll be watching / 'll have watched* the World Cup final then.
2 At the end of this month, I *'ll be working / 'll have been working* at this company for 20 years!
3 Just think – this time next week, we *'ll be lying / 'll have been lying* on a beach in Hawaii.
4 I can't believe she's changing jobs again. She *'ll have had / 'll be having* three different jobs this year!
5 I *won't be finishing / won't have finished* this work by the deadline. I just don't have enough time.
6 *Will you be going / Will you have gone* to Sarah's party on Saturday?
7 In three years, I *'ll have completed / 'll be completing* college and I'll be starting to look for work.
8 This is ridiculous! In ten minutes time I *'ll have been waiting / 'll be waiting* for almost two hours!

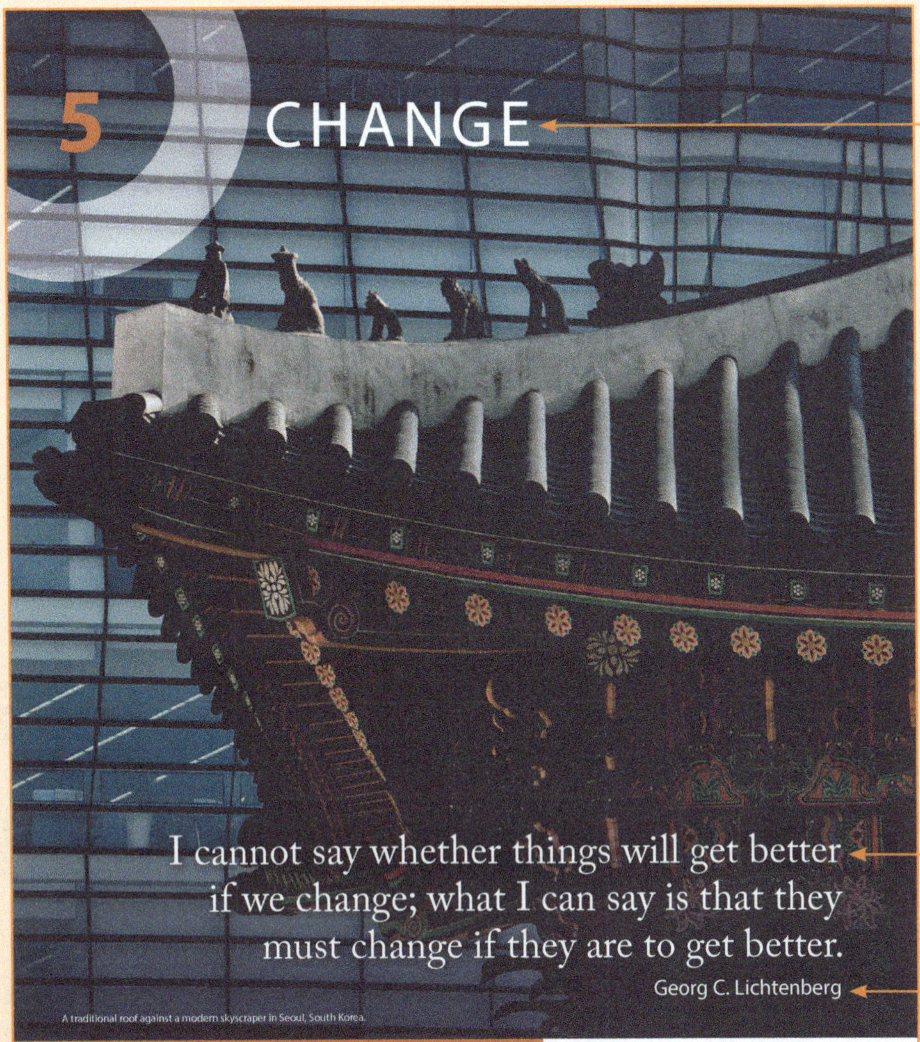

A traditional roof against a modern skyscraper in Seoul, South Korea.

Change (n) the process by which things become different
Synonyms: transformation (n), conversion (n)
Collocations and idioms: *fundamental* change, *dramatic* change, *a* change *for the worse/better*, *have a* change *of heart* (*change your mind about something*)

Lichtenberg is suggesting that although we cannot guarantee that anything will improve with change, he believes it is essential that things do change if they are to improve at all.

Georg Christoph Lichtenberg (1742–1799) was a German experimental physicist, remembered for his research into electricity. Lichtenberg was a popular figure in European intellectual circles and counted Goethe and Kant among his acquaintances. He has a crater on the moon named after him and also proposed the standard paper size system used across the world.

OBJECTIVES

- summarize a sequence of past events
- evaluate a range of proposals
- talk about changes in your town or city
- evaluate candidates and put together a team
- discuss ways to help the environment
- write a problem solution article

Work with a partner. Discuss the questions.

1 Read the quote. What do you think Lichtenberg means? Do you agree with him? Why/Why not?

2 What are the biggest changes in the world that have happened in your lifetime?

3 What is the most positive change you have ever made?

CHANGE 49

OBJECTIVES

Read the unit objectives to the class.

UNIT OPENER QUESTIONS

1 Read the quote as a class, then put students into pairs to discuss the questions. Monitor, encouraging students to explain their reasoning. Open the discussion up to the class, adding any useful emergent vocabulary on the board.

2 Share an example of a big, global change that has happened in your lifetime (e.g. *the invention of cell phones / the internet*, *the fall of the Berlin Wall*, etc) and how it affected you or those around you. Now, put students into pairs to discuss their own ideas. Monitor, helping with new or unfamiliar vocabulary as necessary. Bring the class back together to share their ideas, again adding any useful emergent vocabulary to the board.

3 Tell students about a positive change (real or made-up) that you have made in your life. Explain what motivated the change and how it has improved your life. Next, put students into pairs to discuss their own experience. Bring the class back together to share their ideas and encourage further discussion as appropriate.

WORKSHEETS

Lesson 5.1 Changing environment

Grammar: The passive voice (W21)

Vocabulary: Green vocabulary (W22)

Grammar: Causative *have* and *get* (W23)

Lesson 5.2 Changing places

Vocabulary: Describing areas of a city (W24)

Vocabulary: Prefixes (W25)

Grammar: *-ing* and infinitive forms (W25)

5.1 Changing environment

- Summarize a sequence of past events
- Evaluate a range of proposals

S – identifying cause and effect
G – the passive voice; causative *have* and *get*
V – green vocabulary
P – glottal stops

READING

A SPEAK Work in pairs. Look at the food chain diagram and discuss the questions.

1 What does the diagram show?
2 In this diagram, the wolf is the top predator. What do you think that means?
3 What would happen if you removed the wolf from this food chain? Why?

B SCAN Read *How wolves change rivers* quickly and check your answers to Exercise A.

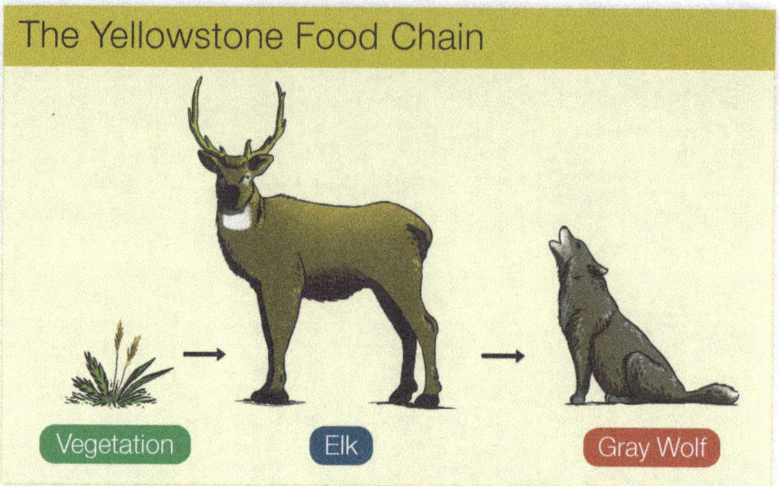

HOW WOLVES CHANGE RIVERS

Wolves are top predators and their beneficial effects on entire ecosystems are gradually being understood.

Wolves are crucial for maintaining a healthy ecosystem – a fact that many people overlooked when they were being hunted and killed in vast numbers across the United States at the start of the 20th century.

Meanwhile, the populations of other animals exploded. The entire ecosystem of the American countryside changed as a result of rapidly expanding populations of elk.

After years of political discussion, conservation biologists finally got their way and the gray wolf, *Canis lupus*, was reintroduced to several areas in the northern Rocky Mountains of the United States. One of those areas was Yellowstone National Park.

Although researchers only reintroduced a total of 41 wolves to the park, their beneficial influences soon became clear, and continue to be seen to this day. Since wolves are top predators that mainly hunt sick or aging elk, their reintroduction had two main effects. First, it slowed the expansion of the elk population, which had exploded without natural predators. Second, it actually improved the overall health of the elk population since only the strongest and fittest survived.

The presence of wolves even changed elk behaviors. For example, they stopped eating in valleys where they could easily be attacked by wolves. Because of this, native plants were able to regrow, increasing biodiversity by providing food and shelter to a growing variety of plants and animals.

Amazingly, the presence of wolves also changed many rivers in the park. After the reintroduction of the wolves, researchers noticed that riverbanks became stronger, the rivers became deeper and small pools formed. Why? Again, the plants that had been eaten by the elk had time to recover, strengthening the riverbanks and in turn, changing the geography of the park itself.

Basically, humans conducted a huge real-life experiment by removing and then reintroducing a top predator from a large area of land. Initially, the changes caused by the lack of wolves were too small to be noticed. But the results of their reintroduction clearly indicate that wolves are essential to restoring and maintaining the ecosystem of the entire region.

This type of relationship is known as a 'trophic cascade'. In Yellowstone National Park, researchers observed the effect when the removal of the top predator started a chain of effects that affected the entire web of life. Similar effects have been identified throughout the natural world, from the Amazon rainforest to the eastern Pacific Ocean.

As more species are reintroduced around the world, no doubt more will be learned about the impact each has not just on ecosystems, but also on the surrounding landscapes.

Glossary

biodiversity (n) the variety of different types of plant and animal life in a particular region
ecosystem (n) all the living things in an area and how they affect each other and the environment
predator (n) an animal that kills and eats other animals

LEAD-IN

Draw or display a picture of a predator (e.g. *a crocodile or a shark*) on the board and elicit what it hunts (e.g. *small birds*, *fish*, etc). Add the prey to the board and connect them with an arrow. Ask students to suggest whether they can think of anything that eats the crocodile/shark (*jaguars and leopards are known to eat crocodiles, while sharks are eaten by larger sharks or orcas*) and add these to the food chain. Then, elicit the words *predator* (*an animal that kills and eats other animals*) and *prey* (*an animal that is hunted and killed by another animal*), adding these as labels to the board. Next, tell students that the entire diagram is called a *food chain*, adding this as a title to the board. Now, elicit the names of other large predators, adding them in a big pool to the board and choose one to focus on as a class. Finally, put students into groups, challenging them to write the longest food chain they can think of. Monitor, helping with new or unfamiliar vocabulary as necessary. Bring the class back together to share their ideas. Nominate the group with the longest food chain to explain each step and encourage other students to add to or edit it. Add any useful emergent language to the board.

READING

A–B If you haven't used the lead-in above, you could work through the first two discussion questions as a class, adding any useful emergent language to the board. Next, put students into pairs or small groups to discuss the final question. Monitor, encourage students to use examples to justify their ideas and write a note about any useful emergent language. Bring the class back together to briefly share their ideas, but don't confirm anything at this stage. Now, give students time to read the article to confirm their ideas. Give feedback as a class, going through each of the discussion questions in Exercise A. Encourage students to give examples from the article. This is a fairly challenging text, so take this opportunity to clarify any new or unfamiliar concepts or vocabulary. In particular, ensure students have a good understanding of the terms in the glossary box before moving on.

1 *The diagram shows the relationship between vegetation, elk and the Gray Wolf in Yellowstone park; the wolf preys on the elk, which in turn feeds on vegetation.*
2 *This means that the wolf is not hunted by any other animal in this ecosystem.*
3 *A reduction in wolf numbers at the start of the 20th century caused the populations of other animals to explode. The entire ecosystem of the American countryside changed as a result of rapidly expanding populations of elk.*

C Write the following sentence on the right-hand side of the board – *The Elk population grew.* Elicit what caused this in Yellowstone and write the following on the left-hand side of the board – *Wolves were hunted to extinction.* Draw an arrow between the two sentences and elicit what we call this kind of relationship (*cause and effect*). If students aren't sure, add the title *cause* above the sentence *Wolves were hunted to extinction* and elicit what a cause leads to. Add the title *effect* above the sentence *The Elk population grew*. Now, go back to your diagram and elicit a full sentence that describes the cause and effect relationship between the two sentences (e.g. *The extinction of the wolves led to an increase in the elk population*), adding any correct answers to the board. Ensure all signaling phrases are set in a different color for reference. Now, give students time to read the article again and complete the exercise. Ask students to check their answers in pairs before giving feedback as a class.

D Write the word *dodo* on the board, or show students a picture, and elicit what is special about this bird (*it no longer exists on our planet*) and what this is called (*extinction*). Elicit a sentence to describe the dodo, manipulating the form of *extinction* as necessary (e.g. *The dodo became extinct in 1681.*) and add this to the board. Now, put students into groups to discuss the questions. Monitor, encouraging students to support their ideas with examples and evidence. Write a note about any important collocations (*to become extinct*, *to be driven to extinction*, etc) that come up. Bring the class back together to share their ideas, adding any useful emergent language that you wrote down to the board.

GRAMMAR

A Write the following sentence on the board – *The reintroduction of wolves changed the rivers.* Ask whether this is active or passive (*active*) and how to change it to the passive voice (*The rivers were changed by the reintroduction of wolves*). Add the passive voice sentence to the board. Next, draw students' attention to the first underlined sentence in the text and ask whether it is active or passive (*passive*). Now, give students time to underline the remaining nine examples of the passive voice in the text before briefly checking their answers in pairs. Give feedback as a class.

B Draw students' attention to the first underlined sentence in the text and elicit what tense it is (*present progressive*). Next, put students into pairs to analyze the other sentences that they underlined. Monitor, asking questions if necessary to help students identify the tense (e.g. *Does it refer to the past, present or future? Is the action finished or unfinished?* etc). Give feedback as a class.

C Give students time to complete the rules alone, using the sentences they underlined in Exercise A to help them. Ask them to briefly check their answers in pairs before giving feedback. Give further explanations or examples of each rule as necessary to consolidate understanding.

D–E Write the first fill-in-the-blank sentence on the board and elicit how to complete it with the correct passive voice form of the verb. Next, give students time to work through the remaining sentences on their own before comparing answers with a partner. Give feedback as a class. Direct students to the **Grammar Hub** (see TB51). Use the **Grammar Worksheet** on page W21 for extra practice.

Extra activity

A classic way to practice the passive voice is with a quiz (e.g. *Who was Harry Potter written by? Where was the last soccer World Cup held?* etc). The class can be divided into groups and awarded one point for each correct answer.

One way to extend and personalize this type of activity is to have the students generate the questions themselves. Put them into small groups and give them time to research and write five questions.

Monitor, encouraging them to use multiple sources to verify their information. It might also be worth recommending that they avoid questions about inventions (e.g. *Who was soccer invented by?*) since usually there isn't a clear answer and this may lead to arguments. You should also encourage them to use a range of tenses (e.g. *How many people have been killed by sharks so far this year?*) to make sure they're reviewing everything covered in this lesson.

SPEAKING

A Direct students to the **Communication Hub** (see TB121) and read through the instructions as a class. Bring the class back together to share their ideas.

Suggested answers

1 *Malaria spread throughout Borneo.*
2 *A chemical (DDT) was sprayed to kill the mosquitoes.*
3 *The mosquitoes were all killed.*
4 *Lizards ate insects and were affected by the DDT.*
5 *The lizards were caught by cats.*
6 *Cats were killed from eating the lizards.*
7 *Rat numbers started increasing.*
8 *New diseases started to affect people.*
9 *More cats were parachuted in.*
10 *Balance was restored.*

B Put students into new pairs to discuss the question. Monitor, helping with grammar and vocabulary as necessary. Bring the class back together to share their ideas.

GRAMMAR HUB

5.1 The passive voice; causative *have* and *get*

The passive voice

Simple present	**Most of the children are taken** to school by bus.
Present progressive	**We aren't being told** the truth about the extent of the damage.
Present perfect	**Has the amount of waste been reduced**?
Simple past	**The deer was killed** by a hunter.
Past progressive	**The forest was being cut down** by construction companies.
Past perfect	**The law hadn't been changed** for years.
will	How **will the park be affected** by the road?
Modals	**The plans can't be changed** now.
The infinitive	**This area** is too polluted **to be used**.

- We use the passive voice (*be* + past participle) when:
  - **a** we don't know who or what caused something to happen, or when this is not important.
    A fire was started in a small area of forest near the park entrance. (= We don't know who started the fire.)
  - **b** we want to focus on the action, not what caused it.
    Huge amounts of CO_2 are being added to the atmosphere every year. (= The focus here is the CO_2 – we aren't really interested in who or what is adding it.)
  - **c** it's obvious from the context who or what caused the action.
    The law has already been changed in many countries. (= It's obvious that it was the government of these countries that changed the law.)

Be careful!

- When we say who performed an action, we use *by*.
  The research is being carried out by the US National Park Service.

5.1 The passive voice

A Rewrite the sentences in the passive voice, omitting the agent where appropriate.

1 Millions of people watch the World Cup final.
The World Cup final __is watched by millions of people__.
2 High CO_2 levels are causing global warming.
Global warming __is being caused by high CO_2 levels__.
3 We've recently fitted our attic with insulation.
Our attic __has recently been fitted with insulation__.
4 When did they announce the winners of the competition?
When __were the winners of the competition announced__?
5 The council is going to cut down the tree.
The tree __is going to be cut down (by the council)__.
6 A plumber needs to install this kind of shower.
This kind of shower needs __to be installed by a plumber.__.

B Complete the paragraph with the correct passive form of the verbs in the box.

pick up confirm deliver inform pack print send take

ONLINE SHOPPING
behind the scenes

Someone has just ordered some new clothes online. But what happens behind the scenes before the items can [1] __be delivered__ to their door? Once the credit card payment [2] __has been / is confirmed__, an order confirmation email [3] __is sent__ automatically to the customer, and the people on the packing team [4] __are informed__ of the order. One of them then picks up the items from the warehouse in order for them to [5] __be packed__. Next the shipping label [6] __is printed__, and either the package [7] __is picked up__ by a courier or it [8] __is taken__ to the post office for its trip to the customer.

C IDENTIFY CAUSE AND EFFECT Read the article again. Are the sentences true (T) or false (F)? Correct the false sentences. Use the information in the box to help you.

Identifying cause and effect

Texts frequently indicate a cause and effect relationship between different events. These relationships are usually signaled by fixed phrases such as *cause, bring about, lead to, as a result of, the main consequence was*, etc.

1. Wolves started to die out because ~~there were not enough elk to eat~~. they were being hunted and killed T / (F)
2. Growing elk numbers affected all the other plants and animals. (T) / F
3. Reintroducing wolves meant elk populations ~~grew~~. fell T / (F)
4. Reintroducing wolves made elk populations healthier. (T) / F
5. A wider range of plants started to grow again as wolf numbers grew. (T) / F
6. The regrowth of plants meant that rivers became deeper. (T) / F

D SPEAK Work in groups. What animals are in danger of extinction in your country? What is being done about it?

GRAMMAR

The passive voice

A Scan the article again and underline ten examples of the passive voice. The first has been underlined for you.

B SPEAK Work in pairs. Discuss the questions.

1. What tenses are the examples in Exercise A?
2. Which include a modal verb? could easily be attacked
3. Which are in the infinitive form? to be seen; to be noticed

C WORK IT OUT Choose the correct options to complete the rules.

The passive voice

We form the passive voice with *be* + [1]*simple past* / *past participle*.

The passive voice can be formed with [2]*all* / *some* tenses – only the form of *be* changes.

We use the passive voice when:

- we [3]*know* / *don't know* who or what caused an action
- it's [4]*important* / *not important* who or what caused an action
- we want to focus on the person or thing that [5]*did the action* / *received the action*.

D PRACTICE Complete the sentences with the correct form of the verbs in parentheses.

1. As the population continues to grow, more and more land ___is used___ (*use*) for farming.
2. Very few fossil fuels ___were burned___ (*burn*) before the Industrial Revolution.
3. Thousands of trees ___were being cut down___ (*cut down*) every year before the government changed the law.
4. The future of humans ___could be threatened___ (*could / threaten*) by further increases in temperature.
5. Many species ___will be affected___ (*affect*) by climate change over the decade.
6. Plastic bags ___have been banned___ (*ban*) recently in many countries.
7. Global temperatures ___have been rising___ (*rise*) for over a century.
8. Some people feel that the use of packaging needs ___to be controlled___ (*control*).

E Go to the **Grammar Hub** on **page 130**.

SPEAKING

A PREPARE Go to the **Communication Hub** on **page 151**.

B DISCUSS Work in pairs. What are the main predators in your country? What other animals would be affected if they became extinct?

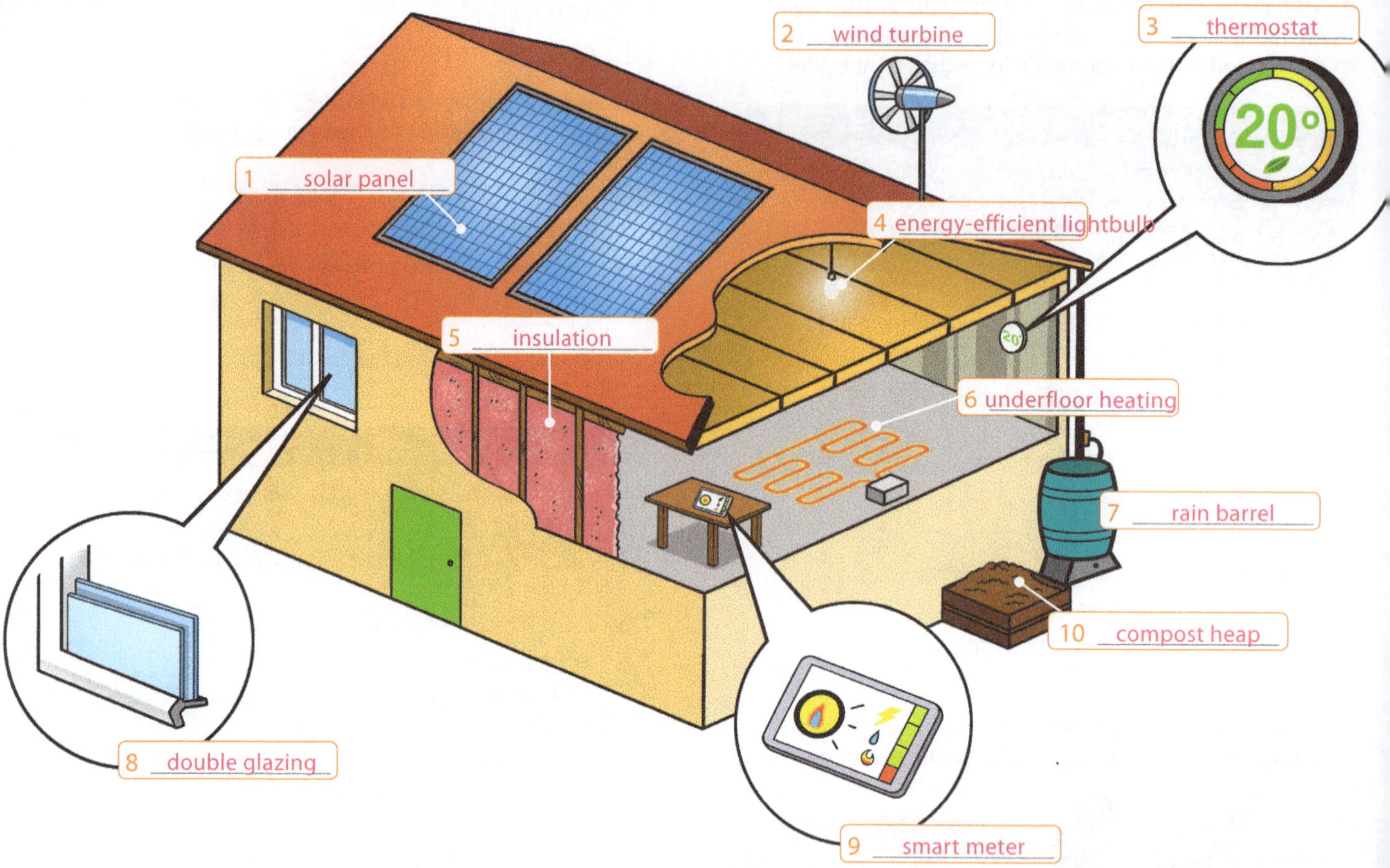

VOCABULARY

Green vocabulary

A Label the picture with words in the box.

compost heap double glazing energy-efficient lightbulb insulation smart meter solar panels thermostat underfloor heating rain barrel wind turbine

B Complete the sentences with words from Exercise A.

1 Turning down your thermostat by just one degree can save money and energy.

2 Using solar panels to produce energy from the sun can save you money.

3 Underfloor heating can be used to extract heat stored in the ground through the floor of the house.

4 Energy-efficient lightbulbs last much longer and use less energy than traditional ones.

5 Use a rain barrel to capture rain which can then be used in the garden and the toilet system.

6 Families frequently throw away a lot of food that could instead have been put in a compost heap.

7 Using a wind turbine can produce clean energy on windy days.

8 Installing a smart meter helps keep track of energy use and may even save money.

9 Since warm air rises, it is important that you have insulation to keep the heat in.

10 Double glazing is much better at keeping heat in than traditional windows are.

C SPEAK Work in pairs. Which of these do you have in your home? Which would you install if you had the money?

LISTENING

5.1 **A LISTEN FOR KEY WORDS** Listen to a radio interview about an eco-friendly home. Which of the features in the vocabulary section are not mentioned?

wind turbine, compost heap, thermostat

5.1 **B LISTEN FOR DETAIL** Listen again. Complete the sentences with no more than four words from the interview.

1 Harry is making changes because he was surprised by his first energy bill.

2 He made simple changes himself, such as putting energy-efficient lightbulbs in each room and fitting attic insulation.

3 The solar panels make 50% / fifty percent of the energy he needs.

4 The beehive means the roof is a source of food as well as energy.

5 The rain barrel now means the toilet uses rainwater.

6 The underfloor heating helps lower Harry's energy bills.

7 The smart fridge means they waste less food.

8 The new shower turns off automatically to save water and energy.

5.1 Changing environment

VOCABULARY

A Focus students on the illustration and elicit what it shows (*an eco-friendly house*) and what that means (*it's a house that has been designed to do as little harm as possible to the environment*). Give students time to label the illustration alone, before checking their answers with a partner. Give feedback as a class, clarifying understanding if necessary and practicing pronunciation (focusing particularly on some of the words students may struggle with such as *thermostat*, *rain barrel*, *wind turbine*, etc).

B Work through the first sentence as a class, encouraging students to explain which clues gave them the answers (e.g. it has to be something you can turn down and that doing so will *'save money and energy'*). Then, give students time to complete the remaining sentences before checking their answers with a partner. Give feedback as a class, calling on pairs one by one to share their answers with the class.

C Put students into pairs to discuss the questions. Use the **Vocabulary Worksheet** on page W22 for extra practice.

LISTENING

5.1 **A** Tell students they are going to listen to a radio interview with a man that is trying to make his house more eco-friendly. Then, play the interview for them to identify the vocabulary items that aren't discussed. Give brief feedback, clarifying anything students don't understand at this point.

5.1 **B** Read the first sentence as a class, eliciting what kind of word(s) fill in the blank (*a noun*) and why (*it completes the structure – surprised by + something*). Next, ask questions to elicit which noun might fill in the blank (e.g. *What kind of surprise might encourage you to make eco-friendly changes to your house?*). Now, remind students that they can only use words from the interview itself and that they cannot change the form. Then, play the audio again and give students time to check their answers in pairs before giving feedback as a class.

AUDIO SCRIPT

5.1

Listening, Exercise A
P = Presenter E = Emily H = Harry

P: We continue this month's focus on going green with a look at eco-friendly homes. Emily Montague reports from a green housing renovation project in Los Angeles.

E: So, Harry, you've decided to make your home much more eco-friendly. What prompted the change? (Ex B Q1)

H: Well, I used to live in a small apartment and I moved into this house a year ago. I was shocked when I got my first energy bill. Three months here cost almost as much as I spent in a whole year in my apartment! I realize that it's a much bigger place, but I just couldn't believe how much more the bill was.

E: So how did you get started?

Ex B Q2 **H:** Well, I did some of the easy things myself first. I put energy-efficient lightbulbs in every room and put new attic insulation in, but I wanted to make a lot more changes. If you come out into the backyard, I'll show you what we're working on now.

E: Ah, I can see you're having solar panels installed.

Ex B Q3 **H:** We are. By having these, we can produce about 50% of our own energy every year. In the summer, we'll produce more than we need and then we can sell it back to the energy companies. There's something else that's interesting about this roof though …

E: Oh, really? What's that?

H: The company also transformed the roof into a small garden. They put in wild flowers that attract bees. We've had a bee hive put in at the end of the garden and now we produce our own honey. This will make our roof an energy source and a food source! (Ex B Q4)

E: Amazing! Oh, and what's that over there?

Ex B Q5 **H:** That's a rain barrel, but it's not just for the garden. We've had our toilet system changed. Our toilet now flushes with rainwater. Any extra water comes down here to this rain barrel for the garden. We save a lot of water this way. These windows are new as well.

E: Aren't they just double glazing?

H: They are, but they are much more modern and energy efficient. They have a type of glass fitted that reflects energy back into the house. They also have a different type of gas in between instead of air. This helps to further reduce heat loss.

E: I can hear a lot of work going on as well. What else are you having done?

H: You see this box here? It takes heat from the ground into the house. Come into the living room … We're getting underfloor heating fitted. It reduces our energy bills and it looks a lot better than radiators! And, here's the kitchen. (Ex B Q6)

E: Wow! That is one modern-looking fridge!

H: I was fed up with throwing out so much food, so I bought this fridge. We order our food online and the fridge knows what we have in it. It then recommends food to cook! It's amazing really and we waste less food. (Ex B Q7)

E: I can hear people working upstairs. What are you having done up there?

H: Come up. We're having a new energy-efficient shower installed. It limits how long you can shower for and how much water is used. It obviously saves energy and stops water wastage but it also saves time. (Ex B Q8)

E: How so?

H: It turns off automatically once you've used a certain amount of water. It means some people can't spend all morning in the shower!

E: Not sure I'm too fond of that idea! Any other plans?

H: Yes, we need to get the walls better insulated. I want to use a natural product though, so we're just waiting for it to be delivered. We're also getting a smart meter installed. Hopefully, it'll help us keep an eye on how much – or how little – energy we're using!

E: Thank you, Harry, for showing us around your home. I have to say, it looks amazing!

5.1 Changing environment

GRAMMAR

5.2 **A** Focus students on the extracts from the interview and ask if anyone can remember what the missing words are. Elicit one or two ideas but do not confirm or correct them at this time. Play the audio for students to complete the sentences. Allow time for peer checking before nominating individual students to share their answers.

B Write the following sentence on the board – *Camille is installing solar panels on her roof.* Elicit who is doing the work, Camille or someone else (*Camille*). Elicit that this is fairly unusual – we normally get someone else to do this kind of work for us. Now, add the causative version of the sentence to the board – *Camille is having solar panels installed.* Again, ask if this means Camille is doing the work or someone else (*someone else*). Explain that in English grammar, this is called a causative structure and we can use *have* or *get* fairly interchangeably. Next, elicit the structure (*have/get* + object + past participle), then elicit one or two more examples that students can relate to (e.g. *Having your hair cut*, *Getting your phone repaired*, *Having your teeth whitened*, etc), and add these to the board. Finally, give students time to complete the sentences alone before checking their answers in pairs. Give feedback as a class.

C Direct students to the **Grammar Hub** (see below). Use the **Grammar Worksheet** on page W23 for extra practice.

PRONUNCIATION

5.3 **A** Play the audio for students to answer the question, then give them time to briefly check their answers in pairs. Give feedback as a class, explaining that not pronouncing the /t/ in this way is called a glottal stop and is fairly common in natural, spoken English.

5.4 **B** Play the audio, pausing between each sentence for students to copy the pronunciation. Practice each sentence individually and chorally if necessary to consolidate the pronunciation point.

Note
Glottalization differs depending on regional accents. In American English, a glottal flap is more common than a glottal stop. The glottal flap results in the articulation of /d/ instead of /t/ instead of the omission of a letter that occurs in a glottal stop.

SPEAKING HUB

A Explain to the class that your school has been awarded $30,000 to spend on environmentally friendly improvements and they must decide which of the listed options to spend the money on. Then, give students time to write a note about one or two advantages and disadvantages of each idea in preparation for the discussion to come.

B Put students into groups to discuss the best way to spend the $30,000. Explain that they will present their ideas to the class so they should have clear reasons for their choices.

C Ask each group to explain to the class how they would spend the money and why. You may want to encourage each student to take a specific role (e.g. each talking about a different improvement) so that everyone has a chance to speak. Close the activity with a class vote on which plan was the best.

GRAMMAR HUB

Causative *have* and *get*

Positive	Negative	Question
I'm having solar panels **installed**.	**We haven't had** the windows **replaced** yet.	**Are you getting** a smart meter **fitted**?

- We use causative *have* and *get (have/get* + object + past participle) to say that someone does something for us – typically for tasks we can't or don't know how to do ourselves.

  My parents are having a new garage built.

- We can also use causative *have* to describe something unwelcome or negative happening to us.

  I've had my bike stolen twice this month!

Causative *have* and *get*
Put the words in the correct order to make sentences with causative *have* and *get*.

1 getting / I'm / the / locally. / posters / printed
I'm getting the posters printed locally

2 to / bike / going / get / repaired? / your / When / you / are
When are you going to get your bike repaired

3 the heating system / at / an electrician. / by / need / get / looked / I / to
I need to get the heating system looked at by an electrician

4 has / her / hair / wife / six weeks. / My / every / cut
My wife has her hair cut every six weeks

5 teeth / tomorrow. / having / checked / are / their / The dogs
The dogs are having their teeth checked tomorrow

6 new / expensive? / Will / very / having / installed / a / kitchen / be
Will having a new kitchen installed be very expensive?

7 having / After / better. / painted, / house / it / much / so / looked / our
After having our house painted, it looked so much better

8 had / their / neighbors / house / night. / into / Our / last / broken
Our neighbors had their house broken into last night

➤ Go back to page 53.

GRAMMAR
Causative *have* and *get*

5.2 **A** Listen and complete the extracts from the interview.

1 Ah, I can see you're ___having___ solar panels ___installed___.

2 We're ___getting___ underfloor heating ___fitted___.

3 We need ___to get___ the walls better ___insulated___.

B PRACTICE Complete the sentences using the prompts in parentheses. Use the information in the box to help you.

> **Causative *have* and *get***
>
> We use the causative *have* and *get* (*have / get* + object + past participle) to say that someone does something for us – usually for tasks we can't or don't know how to do ourselves. Compare these sentences:
>
> *Camille is installing solar panels on her roof.*
> (= she is doing it herself.)
>
> *Camille is having solar panels installed on her roof.*
> (= someone is installing them for her.)

1 I ___had the car repaired___ (*have / the car / repair*) at the garage last weekend.

2 We're ___getting the house painted___ (*get / the house / paint*) right now.

3 We're also ___having a smart energy meter fitted___ (*have / a smart energy meter / fit*) to check how much energy we're using.

4 We ___had a roof garden created___ (*have / a roof garden / create*) last year to help keep heat in.

5 I'd like ___to get new flooring installed___ (*get / new flooring / install*) in the living room.

C Go to the **Grammar Hub** on **page 130**.

PRONUNCIATION
Glottal stops

5.3 **A** Listen to the extract from the interview. Is the /t/ in the highlighted words pronounced or not pronounced? Not pronounced

We're also getting a **smart** meter installed. Hopefully, **it'll** help us keep an eye on how much – or how little – energy we're using!

5.4 **B** Listen and repeat the sentences.

1 It's a great way to save money on your bills.

2 We'd like to start growing our own food.

3 We should save about $100 a year.

4 We need to get quotes for the underfloor heating.

SPEAKING HUB

A PLAN A local school has $30,000 to spend to make the school more environmentally friendly. Write notes about the advantages and disadvantages of each idea.

ORGANIC GARDEN
Cost $500. The food grown could be served in the school cafeteria and save the school $300 a year. It would mean less playground space for the children.

DOUBLE GLAZING
Cost $25,000. This would save the school $2,000 a year in heating bills. The installation would take a long time and some classrooms couldn't be used for a while.

WIND TURBINES
Cost $10,000. There is the potential to save $1,000 per year but the school is not in a very windy location.

SOLAR PANELS
Cost $16,000. There is the potential to save $1,400 per year and the school is in a sunny location.

WATER SAVING TOILETS
Cost $3,000. This solution won't save the school any money, but it will reduce waste water a lot.

ENERGY SAVING BULBS
Cost $300. Saving the school $60 per year. This solution is quick and easy to implement.

B DISCUSS Work in groups. Discuss how to spend the $30,000. Explain your reasoning.

C PRESENT Explain which options you chose in Exercise B and why.

- Summarize a sequence of past events
- Evaluate a range of proposals

5.2 Changing places

- Talk about changes in your town or city
- Evaluate candidates and put together a team

V – describing areas of a city; prefixes
P – words that lose a syllable
S – listening for rhetorical questions
G – *-ing* and infinitive forms

READING

A PREDICT Work in pairs. Look at the pictures of Dubai. What do you think causes a city to grow so quickly? What do you think the effects of such quick growth are?

B SCAN Scan *Rise of the megacities* and check your predictions from Exercise A.
Causes - work, better facilities and living standards; Effects - possibility of slums

C READ FOR ORGANIZATION Read the article again. Fill in the blanks (1–6) with the sentences (a–f).

- **a** Gyeonggi, on the southern outskirts of the city, has gained more than five million residents in the last 30 years.
- **b** Today, it is a city of over a million but 60 years ago, its population was under 20,000.
- **c** However, in recent years, rapid urbanization has been happening at a rate never seen before.
- **d** Unfortunately, for many people, especially in poorer countries, this has not always been the case.
- **e** At the heart of this rapid expansion in urban populations are the same factors that have been there for centuries.
- **f** So, where and why is this happening at such an astounding rate?

D SPEAK Work in pairs. What are the main advantages and disadvantages of living in a major city?

Rise of the MEGACITIES

Large cities are not a new phenomenon. Attracted by work, better facilities and living standards, there have been cities with a population of over a million people for around 2,000 years. [1] c This is particularly evident in the Middle East and across Asia, where many cities have swelled to populations in excess of ten million. Places that even just a few decades ago were nothing more than small farming towns or fishing villages now have millions of people living in them. [2] f

Seoul, in South Korea, is a prosperous **urban** area today, but in the 1950s it was a much poorer and smaller place. Once Seoul began to expand, much of the population growth was in the central **commercial** area. This has changed in the last 20 or 30 years, since much of the growth has been in the **suburbs**, where huge **residential** areas have been built on the edge of the city. [3] a Overpopulation has meant redeveloping traditional **industrial** areas of the city, where vast **housing** projects have expanded the population greatly. Although the growth of Seoul has been extraordinary, it has been a large city for decades. Abu Dhabi, on the other hand, was once not much more than a small village, and has grown immensely in recent times. [4] b It is not the only city to grow at this rapid rate, so what has led to this rapid expansion?

Population growth in general has come about due to falling death rates and improved life expectancy, but city populations are growing for numerous reasons. [5] e High levels of unemployment and a lack of resources have always pushed people away from **rural** areas. There is a perception that life will be better in a city, as the future residents are attracted to the prospect of well-paid jobs, greater opportunities to find work, better health care and education. [6] d All too many cities have illegal **slums** with poor living conditions, little or no electricity and limited access to clean drinking water. Yet this does not seem to deter new residents as both the central area and suburban populations continue to expand.

The trend of urbanization is unlikely to slow down any time soon, with millions of people expected to move to urban areas in the future, no doubt creating more megacities in the process. From Bogota to Chengdu, the march of the megacities shows no signs of stopping across the world.

LEAD-IN

With books closed, write *The top five most populated cities in the world* on the board. Put students into pairs and give them three minutes to discuss which five cities they think will be on the list. In feedback, nominate students to share their answers and build up the complete list on the board.

1 *Tokyo, Japan (38,001,000)*
2 *Delhi, India (25,703,168)*
3 *Shanghai, China (23,740,778)*
4 *Sao Paulo, Brazil (21,066,245)*
5 *Mumbai, India (21,042,538)*

READING

A–B Draw students' attention to the color photo in the text and elicit which city it shows (*Dubai*). Next, tell students that the black and white photo also shows Dubai over 50 years ago and elicit the main differences (e.g. *no high-rise buildings, fewer roads, cars*, etc). Now, put students into pairs to discuss the question. Monitor and write a note about any interesting or useful vocabulary. Next, give students time to read the article to confirm their ideas. Give feedback as a class, clarifying anything students didn't understand and adding any useful emergent vocabulary to the board.

C Explain that six sentences have been removed from the article and students will need to decide which best fit each blank. Elicit a few ideas about the best way to approach this task (e.g. *read the sentence before and after the blank, look for key words in the removed sentences and synonyms around the blank*, etc), then give students time to complete the exercise alone. Ask them to check their answers with a partner, before nominating individuals to share their answers with the class. See the **Methodology Hub** below for more background on this type of activity and how to approach it.

D Put students into pairs to discuss the question. Monitor, encouraging them to use examples to justify their ideas. Bring the class back together to share their ideas, stimulating further discussion as appropriate.

Extra activity

Put students into groups and tell them that they're going to give a presentation on a megacity. Assign each group a city (e.g. *Tokyo, Jakarta, São Paulo*, etc) and give them time to research facts that highlight how rapidly the city has developed (e.g. *how the population has grown over the past century*) and any other interesting information they can find that shows just how big the city is (e.g. *how many people use the main stations every day*). Finally, bring the class back together to share what they've learned.

TEACHING IDEA by David Seymour and Maria Popova

Modernization

Use this activity to review past passives and extend the theme of urban development.

Imagine you arrive back in your hometown after some time away and you discover that the local government has made a lot of changes. Work in small groups and write passive voice sentences to describe these changes, e.g. *A brand new shopping and movie theater complex has been built on the site of the old skating rink. All the factories have been demolished and the river is being cleaned up to encourage tourists.*

(This activity is also good for the past perfect, if the return home was in the past, e.g. *The last time I went back to my city, a lot of changes had been made …*) In groups, discuss some of the changes that should be made to the area you live in, e.g. *The main road should be made into a pedestrian zone. That old building on the corner should be knocked down.*

In your groups, discuss some changes you think should be made to this school and/or classroom.

TEACHING IDEA by David Seymour and Maria Popova

Public transportation

Use this activity to extend the theme of overpopulation.

How does the public transportation system here compare with the system in another city you know well? How do you travel to class?

In small groups, discuss the advantages and disadvantages of bike riding and driving to work.

Agree on a list of ten transportation policies for a smoggy, congested, over-populated city. You will need to find a way of encouraging people out of their cars and onto public transportation.

METHODOLOGY HUB by Scott Thornbury

Sentence insertion

Insertion exercises require (and therefore test) the ability to recognize how coherence works and are now popular in some public ELT examinations. To do this kind of task requires students to insert sentences into a text and relying on more than simply recognizing cohesive ties (such as *however, but*, etc), although this is of course very important. It also involves the ability to understand and follow the thread of the argument, sentence by sentence, including recognizing what is 'new information' in each sentence. This in turn involves more than simply understanding the words and the grammar.

To prepare learners for this kind of task requires, therefore, that attention be given to formal ties between sentences, including the use of reference and conjuncts. It also means encouraging learners to read for meaning – stepping back, as it were, from the text in order to get its overall gist. For example, learners would be advised to read the whole text first, before attempting to re-insert the missing sentences. Since paragraphs (in academic writing) typically start out by presenting the writer's case, going on to elaborate it or give examples, before finally summarizing it, it's generally a good idea to pay special attention to the beginnings and endings of paragraphs.

VOCABULARY

A Give students time to complete the exercise alone before checking their answers with a partner. During class feedback, try to give real-life examples from your city if possible.

B Give students time to complete the sentences alone, before checking their answers with a partner. Give feedback as a class.

C Briefly demonstrate the exercise by describing your city (or another that you know well), using two or three of the words from this section. Then, put students into pairs to do the same. Monitor, encouraging students to ask follow-up questions to keep their discussions going. In feedback, nominate students to share the most interesting things they discussed. Use the **Vocabulary Worksheet** on page W24 for extra practice.

PRONUNCIATION

5.5 A Give students time to read the sentences and predict the number of syllables in each word. Then, play the audio for them to check their ideas. Give feedback as a class, eliciting which syllables are not pronounced in each word (*reas~~o~~nable, consid~~e~~rable, tradition~~a~~lly*). Explain that pronouncing words like this can help students sound more natural, and try to elicit one or two more examples (e.g. *veg~~e~~table, comf~~or~~table*, etc).

5.6 B Give students time to predict which syllables will not be pronounced in each sentence, before playing the audio for them to check. Then, play the recording again, pausing after each sentence for students to copy the pronunciation. Practice as necessary.

VOCABULARY

A Write the following sentence on the board – *Many old structures had to be built after the disaster.* Elicit whether this is correct or not (*it isn't*), why (*if the structures were old, they can't be built, only repaired*) and how to correct it without changing the main verb entirely (*add the prefix re-*) and add the prefix in a different color. Tell students that letters added to the start of words like this are called prefixes and elicit one or two other examples that they are familiar with. Now, give students time to complete the exercise alone, before checking their answers in pairs. Give feedback as a class, eliciting new examples for each prefix to consolidate understanding.

B Direct students to the **Vocabulary Hub** (see page TB121). Use the **Vocabulary Worksheet** on page W25 for extra practice.

SPEAKING

A Tell students they are going to discuss the main changes to their towns and cities over the past decade and give them time to write notes about each of the bulleted topics. Monitor, helping with grammar and vocabulary as necessary.

B–C Put students into pairs to discuss their towns and cities. Monitor, encouraging them to give examples or evidence to support their ideas and ask follow-up questions to keep the discussions going. Then, put students back into pairs to discuss the questions. Monitor, writing a note of any useful emergent language to add to teach when the discussions have finished.

METHODOLOGY HUB by Jim Scrivener

Topic webs

Word webs can be extended into topic webs. Learners write a topic in the center box and then add some useful subheadings in the other boxes. Then they collect and group words under these subheadings, connecting each new word by a line to the appropriate box.

This way of recording lexical items may reflect more accurately the way that we store lexical item networks in our brains – and may therefore be more useful for students than the traditional lists.

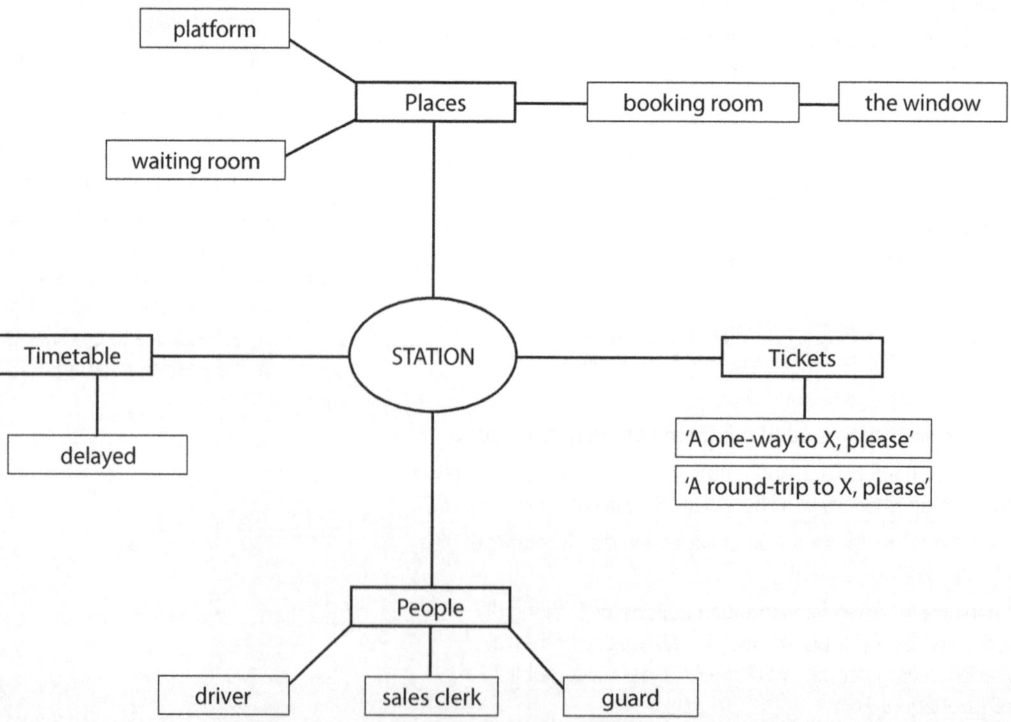

FIGURE 8.8 Topic web

VOCABULARY
Describing areas of a city

A Scan the article again. Complete the definitions with the words in bold.

1 ___suburbs___ (n) an area where people live that is outside the city
2 ___industrial___ (adj) relating to industry
3 ___urban___ (adj) relating to towns and cities, or happening there
4 ___slums___ (n) a poor area of a town where the houses are in very bad condition
5 ___residential___ (adj) relating to where people live rather than work
6 ___housing___ (n) buildings for people to live in
7 ___commercial___ (adj) relating to business
8 ___rural___ (adj) relating to or in the country

B Choose the correct options (a, b or c) to complete the sentences.

1 Over half of the world's population live in ___ areas and this is expected to grow.
(a) urban b commercial c slums
2 Depopulation in ___ areas has led to even less work and fewer facilities.
a commercial b suburb (c) rural
3 The ___ area is home to some of the largest banks and financial companies in the world.
a industrial (b) commercial c residential
4 When people have families, they frequently move to the ___ to have more space.
(a) suburbs b housing c residential
5 ___ areas with good transportation connections are usually more expensive to live in.
a Slum b Industrial (c) Residential
6 A lack of affordable ___ can lead to people living in poor conditions.
a suburbs (b) housing c slums
7 When traditionally ___ areas are in decline, many of the old factories are frequently converted to apartments.
(a) industrial b commercial c rural
8 The biggest ___ in the world has over half a million people living in poor quality housing.
a suburb (b) slum c urban

C SPEAK Work in pairs. Use the words in Exercise A to describe your city or a city you know well.

PRONUNCIATION
Words that lose a syllable

5.5 **A** How many syllables are there in the underlined words? Write the number next to each sentence. Then listen and check.

1 There are reasonable transportation connections in the area. ___3___
2 There has been a considerable rise in the cost of living. ___4___
3 Traditionally, industrial areas have been converted into housing. ___4___

5.6 **B** Cross out the syllables that are not pronounced in the sentences below. Then listen and check.

1 It's preferable to live in a central area since the shopping is better.
2 Much has changed, especially in terms of the transportation system.
3 My personal preference is to live near the transportation network.

VOCABULARY
Prefixes

Prefixes

Prefixes are added to the beginning of a word to change the meaning. For example, *mega-* is added to the beginning of a word to mean *very big or important* (e.g. *megacity*).

A Complete the words in bold with a prefix from the box.

extra- il- over- re- sub- un-

1 The cost of housing has led to some ___il___**legal** housing areas being built.
2 There have been some ___extra___**ordinary** new buildings constructed in the center of the city.
3 ___Over___**population** has become a problem in my city.
4 They have ___re___**developed** the old industrial area of the city.
5 The ___sub___**urban** areas around the city have expanded rapidly.
6 Many were ___un___**happy** about the construction of a large grocery store on the site.

B Go to the Vocabulary Hub on page 145.

SPEAKING

A PREPARE Write notes about important changes in your town or city over the past ten years. Think about:

- transportation
- the cost of living
- shopping
- housing

B SPEAK Work in pairs. Tell your partner about how your town or city has changed.

C DISCUSS Work in pairs. Discuss the questions.

1 Do you think the changes in your city have been mostly positive or negative? Why?
2 What changes would you like to see in the future?

LISTENING

A SPEAK Work in pairs. Read the FAQs page and discuss the questions.

1 What is Mars One? A project with the goal of starting a human settlement on Mars.
2 Would you qualify to be a Mars One astronaut?
3 Would you like to apply? Why/Why not?
4 What do you think you would find most difficult about being a Mars One astronaut?

5.7 **B LISTEN FOR MAIN IDEA** Listen to three radio interviews with Mars One candidates. Answer the questions with A (Agatha), T (Tim) or B (Bernie).

Who …

1 is confident about their physical ability? T
2 would miss the city atmosphere? B
3 thinks their attitude and work experience are important? A
4 is going to have little contact with others to prepare for the mission? B
5 would miss having a normal life? T
6 is worried about losing part of their morning routine? A

5.7 **C LISTEN FOR RHETORICAL QUESTIONS** Listen again. Check (✓) the questions that are used rhetorically. Use the information in the box to help you.

Listening for rhetorical questions

A rhetorical question is a question asked for effect, not because the speaker expects an answer. They are usually used to emphasize when the speaker thinks something is obvious, or to express surprise, doubt or agreement.

☐ Isn't that scary?
☐ Surely, being a scientist is the most important thing you bring to the team?
☑ Can you prepare yourself?
☑ Can anyone live without coffee?
☐ Can you take a short break?
☑ Who doesn't enjoy a challenge?
☑ Why would I be scared?

D INFER MEANING Work in groups. Tim says that 'everyone wants to leave their mark behind'. What do you think he means by this? How do you want to make your mark?

E SPEAK Work in small groups. Discuss which candidate you would choose for the mission and why.

HOME | NEWS | FAQS | MESSAGE BOARD

MISSION TO MARS

FAQS

What is the Mars One project?

The Mars One project was founded in 2011 with the goal of starting a human settlement on Mars.

How will candidates be selected?

Candidates will be selected through online applications, interviews, group challenges and simulations.

How old must candidates be?

The selection process is open to anyone over the age of 18.

What physical requirements are there?

Candidates must be healthy and have a good level of fitness. They must be between 157 and 190 cm tall.

What language(s) must you speak?

The official language of the project is English. However, you do not need to have a good level of English to take part in the selection process. You can apply in English, Spanish, Portuguese, French, German, Russian, Arabic, Mandarin Chinese, Korean, Indonesian or Japanese.

When will it happen and how long will it take?

Six teams of four will be chosen for training. They will train together until the launch in 2024. It takes seven months to get to Mars in an extremely challenging environment.

LISTENING

A Elicit what students know about Mars. Then, put them in pairs to answer the questions.

5.7 **B** Play the audio for students to complete the activity, then give them time to compare their answers in pairs. Give feedback as a class. This is a fairly long listening text, so you might want to stop after each interview to go through the answers. See the **Audio script** below and TB57.

5.7 **C–D** Students complete the exercises, checking their answers in pairs.

E Put students into new groups to discuss which, if any, of the candidates they would choose. Monitor, encouraging groups to reach a unanimous decision. Bring the class back together to share their ideas.

AUDIO SCRIPT

5.7

Listening, Exercise B
I = Interviewer A = Agatha T = Tim B = Bernie

I: For centuries, man has been obsessed with the idea of going to Mars. Indeed, for a long time, our little red neighbor was the focus of almost all science fiction, but now, for some it might become a reality. We spoke to three of the Mars One candidates hoping to take part in the first manned mission to Mars. I caught up with one of the candidates, Agatha Nowak, in the library of her university. Agatha, nice to meet you. Why do you want to sign up?
A: Well, partly this will be a break, you know, a break from the usual day-to-day stuff. Like cleaning, shopping, studying … Also though, I'm a PhD student and I think it's important to advance science whenever the opportunity presents itself. To me, the Mars One project is exactly this kind of opportunity. The technological advancements made after the moon landings were amazing and I think this project could have the same effect.
I: But this is a one-way ticket. You'll never come back to Earth! Isn't that scary?
A: It is, but I'm also really excited.
I: So, why do you think you would be a good candidate?
Ex B Q3 **A:** I'm a really positive person with a lot of energy. I work really well as part of a team and get along with everyone. That's going to be key.
I: Surely, being a scientist is the most important thing you bring to the team?
A: I don't know. Maybe. Being a scientist isn't enough; you need to be able to live in a small space with other people for a very long time! We can't, you know, just pack up and leave if we're not happy.
I: True! How are you preparing yourself for it?
A: Can you prepare yourself? I don't know. One guy I know is eating just dried and canned food to get used to the lack of fresh things. I'm not sure that's a great idea. We need as many nutrients as possible before we go!
I: What are you expecting when you first land on Mars?
A: A lot of hard work! We'll have limited food. We'll have to eat dried and rehydrated food at first. Once we establish a community, I think we'll have to attempt to grow our own food, which is going to be challenging. And we also need to build somewhere to live. I've watched people try to build a shelter in the wild on TV and they really struggle. Imagine trying to do it in a spacesuit!
Ex B Q6 **I:** What are you going to miss most?
A: I really appreciate drinking a good cup of coffee every morning. Can anyone live without coffee? I read about the coffee machine on the International Space Station, so I'm hoping we get one!
I: Another candidate hoping to join the mission is Tim Davis. Tim loves to challenge himself and is hoping this will prove the ultimate challenge. Can we take a short break?
T: Sure.
I: How far will you run later?
T: Just a short 30K run. Nothing too hard.
I: That sounds pretty far to me!
Ex B Q1 **T:** Not really. I've run a lot of marathons and a few ultramarathons. I'll never forget running across the Sahara Desert for seven days. I've always tried to challenge myself physically. I've climbed the tallest mountains in three continents of the world.
I: You like a challenge then?
T: Who doesn't enjoy a challenge? There aren't many left for me on this planet, so why not go to another one?
I: Are you worried or scared at all?
T: Why would I be scared? There's risk in everything we do, and people are just bad at assessing it. Some people worry about flying but you're much more likely to die driving to the airport.
I: True. So, you seem very driven.
T: I am. Everyone wants to leave their mark behind, don't they? Most people choose to have children as their legacy. This will be mine. I'm going to Mars to be a part of history. I'm excited, not scared.
I: What are you going to miss?
Ex B Q5 **T:** Well, probably just the simple things in everyday life. I'll miss my friends and family a lot. I'll definitely miss fresh food and just being able to pop into the stores to buy something whenever I want.
I: Are you ready?
T: As ready as I'll ever be. I'm not worried about the physical aspect, but emotionally I think it's going to be tough.
I: The last candidate I spoke to is 50-year-old Bernie Johnson. Bernie is an environmentalist from the south. When I caught up with him, Bernie was doing a little last-minute shopping.
B: … yeah, maybe. Can you pass me a bag?
I: Sure, here you go. So, why do you want to sign up anyway? It's such a long way.
B: It's vital for the future of humans! We have to learn to live independently of planet Earth. The world is not going to end anytime soon, but we have made a real mess of things.
I: Why do you think we've been so terrible?
B: Well, you know, we've made a mess of Earth! We've used a lot of natural resources, driven species to extinction and chopped down most of the forests of the world!
I: So, what are you doing to prepare yourself for the mission?

GRAMMAR

5.8 **A** Give students time to complete the extracts alone, before playing the audio so they can check their answers.

B–D Give students time to work through the exercises alone and check in pairs, before giving feedback as a class. Then, direct them to the **Grammar Hub** (see below).

E–F Give students time to complete the sentences alone before checking in pairs. Give feedback as a class, before putting students back into pairs to discuss the sentences. Use the **Grammar Worksheet** on page W25 for extra practice.

SPEAKING HUB

A–B Direct students to the **Communication Hub** (see TB121). Students work in groups to decide which person to send on *Mars One*. Allow time for each group to present their discussion to the class.

5.7 (continued)

Ex B Q4 **B:** I'm trying to live a more isolated life. Some people get really stressed when they forget to take their phone with them. I'm turning off my phone and permanently disconnecting the internet. For my vacation this year, I'm not going away anywhere … I'm staying at home for a month.

I: Is that why you're buying a lot of canned and dried foods?

B: That's right. I'm going to spend a month not talking to anyone except my wife. I'm buying enough food to last for four weeks and we aren't going to leave the living room.

I: Is your wife happy with that?

B: Well, she'd rather be going to Greece or somewhere nice, but, you know, she supports me. It's going to be difficult to live just inside one room, but I think it will be great preparation. I have promised her an amazing vacation next year to make up for it!

I: And how does she feel about you going to Mars?

B: Actually, she seems pretty happy about it …

I: Fair enough. So if you did get selected, what would you miss about Earth?

B: Well, my wife, obviously. But in general, I think I'll miss being connected to other people. Our world is so small now, really. When you feel lonely, you can pick up your phone to connect with a lot of people in seconds.

I: True. Anything else? Like food or something else?

Ex B Q2 **B:** Um, I don't know. Actually, yes. Strangely, I think I'll miss everyday noises. I'm used to living in a big city and there are so many sights and sounds to keep you stimulated. In space, all you can hear is endless silence. That could be very disturbing!

GRAMMAR HUB

5.2 *-ing* and the infinitive

- We use verb + *-ing*:
  - **a** after prepositions.
    *I'm thinking **about moving** to another company.*
  - **b** as the subject or object of a sentence.
    ***Traveling** around South Korea was amazing.*
  - **c** after certain verbs (e.g. *admit, avoid, finish, mind*, etc).
    *I **don't mind living** in the suburbs.*
- We use the infinitive:
  - **a** after adjectives.
    *It can be **difficult to find** your dream job.*
  - **b** to talk about purpose (i.e. what someone wants to achieve).
    I came to New York to improve my level of English.
    (= This explains why I came here.)
  - **c** after certain verbs (e.g. *agree, attempt, decide, hope, manage, promise*, etc).
- The base form is always used after modal verbs (e.g. *may, might, would*, etc) and after the verbs *let* and *make*.
  *I think I **would make** an excellent candidate for the Mars One program.*

Be careful!

- Some verbs can be followed by either verb + *-ing* or the infinitive, but with a change of meaning (e.g. *forget, go on, regret, remember, stop, try*, etc)
  *I'll never **forget waking up** in Tokyo for the first time. (= I have a memory of this.)*
  *My daughter never **forgets to call** me on my birthday. (= She doesn't forget to do this.)*

5.2 *-ing* and infinitive forms

A Choose the correct options to complete the sentences.

1. We agreed ***to do*** / ***doing*** our project on the topic of megacities.
2. He really appreciates ***to be*** / ***being*** able to travel so much.
3. The council has passed a law ***protect*** / ***to protect*** old buildings.
4. They let us ***walk*** / ***to walk*** around the museum at night.
5. Did you manage ***to book*** / ***booking*** the tickets for the tour?
6. They made her ***completing*** / ***complete*** an online application form.
7. I'm really looking forward to ***having*** / ***have*** a few days off from work.
8. ***Invite*** / ***Inviting*** so many people to dinner really wasn't a good idea.

B Are these sentences correct or incorrect? Rewrite the incorrect sentences.

1. After a poor start, he went on ~~winning~~ to win the game in the end.
2. I fondly remember ~~to visit~~ visiting Abu Dhabi when I was about your age.
3. ✓ I forgot to tell you that I entered that photography competition.
4. We regret ~~informing~~ to inform passengers that the flight to Seoul has been delayed.
5. Stop ~~to talk~~ talking about your vacations all the time – it's making me jealous!
6. ✓ We tried to book tickets for the Coffee Museum in Dubai but it was closed.

➤ Go back to page 57.

GRAMMAR

-ing and infinitive forms

5.8

A Complete the extracts with the correct form of the verbs in parentheses. Then listen and check.

1 For centuries, man has been obsessed with the idea of ____going____ (*go*) to Mars.

2 I think it's important ____to advance____ (*advance*) science whenever the opportunity presents itself.

3 ____Being____ (*be*) a scientist isn't enough.

4 I really appreciate ____drinking____ (*drink*) a good cup of coffee every morning.

5 I'll never forget ____running____ (*run*) across the Sahara Desert for seven days.

6 I'm going to Mars ____to be____ (*be*) a part of history.

7 We have to learn ____to live____ (*live*) independently of planet Earth.

8 Some people get really stressed when they forget ____to take____ (*take*) their phone with them.

9 In space, all you can ____hear____ (*hear*) is endless silence.

B SPEAK Work in pairs. Look at sentences 5 and 8 in Exercise A. What's the difference in meaning of the word *forget* in each of these sentences?

Sentence 5 refers to a past memory, sentence 8 refers to something to remember for the future.

C WORK IT OUT Match the examples in Exercise A to the rules in the box.

-*ing* and infinitive forms

We use verb + *-ing*:

a after prepositions __1__

b as the subject of a sentence __3__

c after some verbs (e.g. *admit, appreciate, avoid, finish, give up, mind, suggest*, etc) __4__

We use the infinitive:

d after adjectives __2__

e to talk about purpose __6__

f after some verbs (e.g. *attempt, decide, expect, learn, manage, need, promise*, etc) __7__

We use the base form:

g after modal verbs __9__

Some verbs can be followed by either verb + *-ing* or the infinitive, but with a change of meaning (e.g. *forget, remember, try, go on*, etc)

h __5__ / __8__

D Go to the Grammar Hub on page 130.

E PRACTICE Complete the sentences with the correct form of the verbs in the box.

be do get have like plan produce work

1 ____Having____ a positive attitude is the key to being a good team player.

2 It's important ____to like____ everyone you work with.

3 One way of ____being____ more effective on a team is to become an active listener.

4 Never promise ____to do____ more work than you can manage. You will let your team down.

5 Only teams with strong leaders can ____produce____ good results.

6 Always remember ____to plan____ what you need to discuss in a team meeting, so you don't waste any time.

7 I'm worried about not ____getting____ along with the other people on the team.

8 We need ____to work____ together if we want to succeed.

F SPEAK Work in pairs. Do you agree with the sentences in Exercise E? Why/Why not?

SPEAKING HUB

A Go to the Communication Hub on page 147.

B PRESENT Tell the class which candidates you chose, which you rejected and why.

- Talk about changes in your town or city
- Evaluate candidates and put together a team

5.3 Getting into the habit

A– conditional counterarguments S– taking the floor

Reward or penalty?

COMPREHENSION

A **Work in pairs. Look at the picture. Do you think cups like these are environmentally friendly? Why/Why not?**

These kinds of cups aren't environmentally friendly because they usually cannot be recycled.

Glossary

disposable (adj) designed to be used once, then thrown away

B **Watch a news report about an environmentally friendly scheme at a university. Choose the best summary (1 or 2).**

(1) The university found that a reward scheme had no meaningful effect on student behavior. By adopting a penalty scheme instead, they were able to reduce the number of disposable cups sold every year.

2 The university found that a penalty scheme had no meaningful effect on student behavior. By adopting a reward scheme instead, they were able to reduce the number of disposable cups sold every year.

C **Watch the news report again and answer the questions.**

1 How did the university originally try to encourage students to start using reusable cups?
2 What was the issue with the original scheme?
3 How did the university address this issue?
4 What else did the university do to encourage use of non-disposable cups?
5 Was the penalty scheme a success? Why/Why not?
6 How has the penalty scheme affected sales of hot drinks?

D **Work in groups. Do you agree that you have to use penalties to meaningfully change behavior? Why/Why not?**

Glossary

high street (n) (British) = **main street (n) (American)**
a scheme (n) (British) = **a plan or system (n) (American)**

AUTHENTIC ENGLISH

A 01:33–01:41 **Watch the last part of the report again and complete the extract.**

Presenter: So this might work on a campus. That doesn't mean it's going to work on the high street, where people have a lot more choice.

Interviewee: ___Although I think it would if___ government were to legislate for it.

B **Work in pairs. Read the extract again. Why does the speaker use a conditional? Which word does she stress? Why?**

C **Read the information in the box to check your answers to Exercise B.** she uses a conditional to counter the presenter's argument; she stresses 'would' to emphasize her disagreement

Conditional counterarguments

In discussions, speakers sometimes use conditional structures to make a counterargument. These usually begin with conjunctions and use words, phrases or ideas from the original argument. The stress is usually put on the modal verb to emphasize the contrast between the two ideas.

A: It's a nice idea, but just doesn't work in practice. Nobody wants to carry around a reusable cup everywhere they go.

B: But they might if coffee shops offered bigger discounts.

D **Work in pairs. Take turns reading the arguments (1–3) and responding with a conditional.**

1 Sadly, most people like the convenience of disposable water bottles. This isn't going to change anytime soon.
2 Social media isn't dangerous. It's just a fun way to stay in touch with old friends.
3 Electric cars are a great idea, but will never replace gasoline-powered vehicles on our roads.

A green suggestion

A Work in groups. Do you think where you work or study does enough to protect the environment? Why/Why not?

B Watch the video and answer the questions.

1 What eco-friendly change does Harry suggest?
2 Why does Amanda support this idea?
3 What is Sam's criticism of the idea?

SPEAKING SKILL

A Read the extract from the conversation. Why do you think Amanda finishes Harry's sentence?

Harry: People respond better to a penalty than a …

Amanda: … reward. It's what we do at my office.

Amanda finishes Harry's sentence to take the opportunity to speak (i.e. take the floor) and to show that she agrees with and understands what he is saying.

B Read the information in the box and check your answers to Exercise A.

Taking the floor

In discussions, one speaker will regularly interrupt another so they can start speaking. This is called taking the floor. In the video, Sam interrupts Harry by saying [1] *Can I just say that …* and Malcolm interrupts Sam by saying [2] *Sorry to interrupt …*.

To keep the floor, we need to avoid interruption. In the video, Harry stops Sam from interrupting him by saying [3] *Hang on! I haven't finished*.

We can also take the floor by agreeing or disagreeing with what someone has said.

Sam: Yes, well, I think we already do a fair bit to help the environment.

Harry: [4] *But don't you think* *we could do more?*

Amanda: And it does seem to have changed how people behave.

Harry: [5] *I know what you mean*. *People begin to feel that it's normal to have their own cup. It's not something that deserves a special reward.*

Sam: [6] *But surely people will get annoyed if* *we start penalizing them.*

We can also show agreement or understanding by finishing someone's sentence, like Amanda does to Harry.

C Watch the video again. Complete the box with examples from the conversation.

D Work in groups. Discuss one of the following topics using strategies from the box to take or keep the floor.

- recycling
- wind farms
- solar panels
- electric cars
- plastic packaging
- food waste

SPEAKING HUB

A PREPARE Work in groups. Write a list of five ways you could be more environmentally friendly in the following areas:

- travel and transportation
- recycling
- saving water
- eating smart
- reducing and reusing
- clothing

B PLAN Rank the points in Exercise A in order of importance. Try to reach an agreement in the group.

A: *I really think recycling plastics is a top priority. We should all carry refillable water bottles with us.*

B: *Really? But surely people wouldn't want to carry a water bottle everywhere.*

A: *But they might if governments made plastic bottles expensive and provided a lot of places where we can refill our bottles.*

C PRESENT Present your list to the class. Explain your reasoning.

Discuss ways to help the environment

➤ Turn to page 158 to learn how to write a problem solution article.

Reward or penalty?

LEAD-IN

With books closed, write three sentences (two true and one false) on the board about your recycling/reusing habits. Try to make this interesting but believable to keep students engaged (e.g. *My roommate and I share shoes; I always try to fix clothes before buying new ones; I drive a hybrid car*; etc). Next, tell students they have to guess which sentence is false by asking you questions.

COMPREHENSION

A Put students into pairs to discuss the question. Then, bring the class back together to share their ideas.

Cups like these can be difficult to recycle since they're usually covered in a thin layer of plastic that is difficult to separate.

B ▶ Give them time to read the summaries before playing the video. Give feedback as a class, taking the time to clarify how the scheme in the video works because this is key to overall comprehension.

C ▶ Play the video again and ask students to write notes to answer the questions. Give them time to discuss their answers in pairs before giving feedback as a class.

1. *They offered a 25p discount [on purchases of hot drinks] for anyone that brought a reusable cup.*
2. *Not enough students took advantage of it (i.e. few students started bringing in their own cups).*
3. *Instead of offering a 25p discount, they lowered the price of hot drinks by 25p and started charging students that needed a disposable cup 25p extra.*
4. *They started giving out free reusable cups to first year students.*
5. *Yes – they've saved a large number of disposable cups; more students are using reusable cups; the scheme is growing in popularity.*
6. *It hasn't – sales of hot drinks have remained the same.*

D Put students into groups to discuss the question.

AUTHENTIC ENGLISH

A–B ▶ 01:33–01:41 Play the last part of the video again for students to complete the extract. Briefly check the answer as a class, before putting students into pairs to discuss the questions.

C–D Give students time to read the skills box to check their answers to Exercise B. Then, put them into pairs to practice making conditional counterarguments.

A green suggestion

LEAD-IN

Elicit one or two things people can do to be green and add them to a spider diagram on the board. Then, put students into groups to discuss more ideas. Bring the class back together to share their ideas.

A Elicit ways in which your school tries to protect the environment (e.g. *recycling bins, using energy-efficient lightbulbs*, etc). Then, put students into groups to discuss the school in more detail or where they work.

B ▶ Tell students they are now going to watch the next episode of the Café Hub series. Then, play the video for students to answer the questions. Give feedback as a class. You can find the **video script** for *A green suggestion* on the Teacher's Resource Center.

1. *Dropping the price of all coffee and charging customers extra for using a disposable cup.*
2. *The same scheme, or system, seems '… to have changed how people behave …' at her office.*
3. *He's worried that customers will get annoyed by the introduction of the scheme/system.*

SPEAKING SKILL

A–B Read through the extract as a class and elicit ideas in response to the question. Now, give students time to read the box to check their answers and briefly confirm as a class.

C ▶ Consolidate understanding by giving further explanations and examples as necessary. Now play the video again for students to complete the box. Note, the answers are not presented in the same order as they appear in the video, so if students are struggling to keep up, you could put them into groups to focus on the three categories.

D Demonstrate the activity with one of the stronger students, then put them into groups to practice themselves.

SPEAKING HUB

A Put students into groups to make their lists. Monitor, helping with new or unfamiliar vocabulary as necessary.

B Give groups time to rank their points from Exercise A, explaining that they must come to an agreement. Monitor, encouraging them to use phrases from the skills box to help them keep or take the floor.

C Ask groups to share their top five recommendations, encouraging them to explain their choices with examples.

▶ VIDEO SCRIPT

Reward or penalty?

P = Presenter Sm = Staff member S = Student

P: University of Winchester campus used to get through 191,000 disposable cups every year – typically made from a mixture of paper and plastic; these
Ex C Q1 hardly ever get recycled – this was despite a 25p discount for those who brought a reusable cup.

Sm: We offered the discount for a number of years – 25p
Ex C Q2 off – it was great, but not enough people took it up.

P: So the campus decided to make a subtle change
Ex C Q3 to its prices. Instead of offering that 25p discount for bringing a reusable cup, they cut the price of hot drinks by 25p and introduced a 25p penalty if you needed a disposable cup. The prices hadn't really changed, but the new expectation was that you would bring a reusable cup. Is it then about penalty rather than reward when it comes to changing people's behavior?

Sm: Yeah, absolutely. You have to have the penalty to get the meaningful behavior change.

Ex C Q4 **P:** To help the scheme, they also gave out free reusable cups to first year students.

S: Normally I always have my Costa cup with me, like, the reusable one.

Ex C Q5 **P:** In its first year, the campus saved 34,000 cups. And
Ex C Q6 the scheme is growing in popularity. Overall, hot drink sales have not declined. Reusable cups are now used in about a third of hot drinks sales on campus. So this might work on a campus; that doesn't mean it's going to work on the high street where people have a lot more choice.

Sm: Although I think it would if government were to legislate for it. I think we've shown that if you commit to the scheme, you can have the success that … that we've had.

5 Writing

Write a problem solution article

W describing problems and solutions

A Read the introduction to the problem/solution article. What is the main focus of the article?

Overcrowding in cities is among the principal dangers facing society today. This article will first look at some of the problems this causes and then suggest a number of possible solutions.

B Work in pairs. Brainstorm possible problems and solutions for this topic.

C Scan the blog post. Which of your ideas from Exercise B are mentioned?

The main issue facing cities today is overcrowding, and the result is added pressure on public facilities. Schools, hospitals and roads are pushed to the breaking point as the city struggles to keep up with the rapid population increase. A good example of this is the pressure placed on hospitals and doctors, who are expected to deal with growing numbers of patients despite no increase in staff. One way to tackle the increased pressure on public facilities is to regulate building. When building new housing, rules should be put in place to ensure that enough new facilities are constructed at the same time. For instance, for every 1,000 new apartments, an elementary school and a doctor's office should be built by the construction firm.

One of the other foremost problems that occurs as a consequence of overcrowding is the increased levels of traffic. As a result, air pollution increases and traffic slows down. For example, in Mexico City, traffic has slowed to an average of around 10 kmph. One solution might be to build more bike lanes around city centers. This will allow commuters to navigate the city more quickly and will lower the CO_2 emissions. One example where this has been done successfully is Copenhagen in Denmark, where hundreds of meters of bike paths have been built.

In order to tackle the problems of overcrowding, cities should focus not only on building more housing but also on providing the infrastructure needed to support the growing population.

D Read the first paragraph again. Put the following in order to show the paragraph structure.

4 state the solution
1 state the problem
5 explain how this will solve the problem
2 show the results of the problem
6 give an example of the solution
3 give an example of the problem

E Complete the skills box with phrases from the article.

Describing problems and solutions

Introduction

X is one of the biggest issues we face …

1 *… is among the principle dangers facing society …*

Problems and results

The biggest threat to …

The foremost problem …

2 *The main issue facing …*

3 *… of the other foremost problems …*

Examples and results

The result is …

4 *… a result …*

A good example of this is …

Solutions and explanations

One way to tackle the issue of X is to …

5 *One solution might be …*

This will allow …

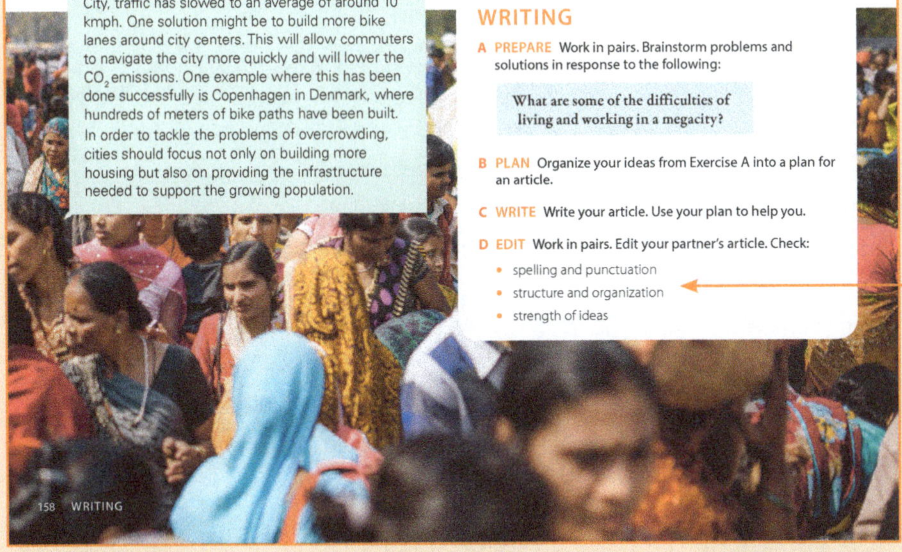

WRITING

A PREPARE Work in pairs. Brainstorm problems and solutions in response to the following:

What are some of the difficulties of living and working in a megacity?

B PLAN Organize your ideas from Exercise A into a plan for an article.

C WRITE Write your article. Use your plan to help you.

D EDIT Work in pairs. Edit your partner's article. Check:

- spelling and punctuation
- structure and organization
- strength of ideas

158 WRITING

Answer
The focus of the article is the issues caused by overcrowding in cities and how to address them.

Refer students to this article post as a model for the writing task.

Refer students to this checklist when editing their partner's work.

LEAD-IN

Write the following on the board: *lack of green spaces, overcrowding, pollution, crime, outdated infrastructures*. Then, put students into groups to rank the problems from most (1) to least important (5). Bring the class back together to share their ideas.

WRITING

A Give students time to quickly read the introduction and answer the question. Give feedback as a class.

The focus of the article is the issues caused by overcrowding in cities and how to address them.

B–C Elicit one or two problems that overcrowding causes and possible solutions, adding students' ideas to the board. Now, put students into pairs to discuss more ideas. Bring the class back together to share their ideas, building up the table on the board together. Then, give students time to read the article to see if it covers any of their ideas.

D Ask students to read the first paragraph of the main text again to analyze its structure. Give them time to check their answers in pairs before giving feedback as a class.

E Read through the skills box as a class, clarifying meaning if necessary. Then, give students time to complete the box with examples from the article before checking their answers in pairs. Give feedback as a class.

WRITING TASK

A–B Read the question as a class and explain that students will now write a problem and solution article. Follow the same process as Exercise B to build up a list of one or two problems and solutions on the board, before putting students into pairs to discuss more ideas. Next, ask students to organize their ideas into a plan, using the model text as a guide. Monitor, helping with structure as necessary.

C Tell students to write their articles. Monitor, reminding them to follow the paragraph structure covered in Exercise D and phrases in the skills box to help them.

D Put students into pairs to edit each other's articles. Encourage students to give each other positive feedback. Students can then rewrite their articles either in class or for homework.

Unit 5 Review

VOCABULARY

A Complete the definitions with the words in the box.

insulation smart meter solar panel thermostat rain barrel wind turbine

1 __rain barrel__ a large container used to collect rain for watering plants
2 __wind turbine__ a large machine like a windmill used for producing electricity using the wind
3 __insulation__ material used to prevent heat, cold, noise, etc from passing through something
4 __smart meter__ an electronic device used to record how much electricity is used
5 __solar panel__ a piece of equipment that uses energy from the sun to create electricity
6 __thermostat__ a piece of equipment that controls the temperature in a building

B Complete the sentences with the words in the box.

housing residential rural slums suburbs urban

1 They are building a new __residential__ area near me with over 2,000 new homes.
2 The cost of __housing__ has increased by almost 20% in the last year.
3 I don't really like living in the __suburbs__. It's too far from the city and there isn't much to do.
4 In countries such as Germany and England, almost 80% of the population lives in __urban__ areas.
5 Because of high unemployment, many people leave __rural__ areas and move to cities to look for work.
6 In many __slums__, many thousands of people have to share just one toilet.

C Complete the article with the correct form on the words in parentheses.

Simple ways to be more environmentally friendly

Climate change is a threat to all of us. You can help tackle this issue by making some of the following changes:

1 **Buy a reusable bottle**

Many plastics are used just once and can't be [1] __recycled__ (*recycle*). Many people believe single-use plastics are [2] __unnecessary__ (*necessary*) and should be banned. To help prevent plastic pollution, take a reusable water bottle with you instead of buying a plastic one.

2 **Bike to work**

Air pollution is also a major problem, particularly in [3] __overcrowded__ (*crowded*) cities. Campaigners would like heavily polluting vehicles to be made [4] __illegal__ (*legal*). In the past, a lot of bike paths were [5] __substandard__ (*standard*) but there has been a lot of recent investment in building new bike paths. Riding your bike to work is a great way to help reduce pollution while also getting some exercise!

GRAMMAR

A Complete the sentences with the correct passive form of the verbs in the box.

build film finish hold inform left

1 Parts of *Star Wars: The Last Jedi* __were filmed__ in the salt plains of Bolivia.
2 An emergency meeting __is being held__ to discuss possible responses.
3 The public __has been informed__ about the potential risk and is advised to avoid the area.
4 The house, which was the family home of the Harrogates, __was built__ in 1858.
5 As they pulled into their drive, they noticed that the window __had been left__ open.
6 The new shopping mall was scheduled to be completed by now but it __won't be finished__ until next May.

B Complete the sentences with the correct form of the words in parentheses.

1 **A:** Can you give me a ride tonight?
B: No, sorry. I __m/am having my car serviced__ (*my car / service*) right now.
2 **A:** __Have you had your shower fixed? / Have you fixed your shower?__ (*you / your shower / fix*)?
B: Not yet. Someone's coming to look at it tomorrow.
3 **A:** Have you seen Emily?
B: Yes, she's __having her nails painted__ (*nails / paint*).
4 **A:** Why are they eating out so much?
B: They are __having a/their kitchen installed__ (*kitchen / installed*) this week.
5 **A:** Everyone on TV has such white teeth!
B: I know. Actually, I'm thinking about __having my teeth whitened__ (*teeth / whiten*).

C Choose the correct options (a or b) to complete the sentences.

1 Chris has offered ___ me with the project I'm doing about homelessness.
(a) to help b helping
2 Mark has been in touch. Did you remember ___ him an email?
(a) to send b sending
3 I don't want ___ to work today, but I have so much to do.
(a) to go b going
4 Lucy texted. They're trying ___ to the party by eight.
(a) to get b getting
5 Our kids miss ___ in Madrid and wish we could move back.
a to live (b) living
6 These videos on YouTube are great to help you learn how ___ the guitar.
(a) to play b playing

6 COMING OF AGE

Anyone who stops learning is old, whether at 20 or 80. Anyone who keeps learning stays young.
Henry Ford

It's widely believed that our ability to learn new things declines with age.

OBJECTIVES

- discuss rules in education
- talk about changes to education in your country
- discuss age milestones in your country
- debate the best time to start college
- give your opinion on an aspect of education
- write a report

Work with a partner. Discuss the questions.

1 Read the quote. Do you agree with Ford? Why/Why not?

2 What are the most important birthdays in your country (e.g. 18, 21, 50, etc)? How are they celebrated?

3 If you could give your younger self one piece of advice, what would it be and why?

COMING OF AGE 61

Coming of age (n) the age at which someone matures emotionally or is legally considered an adult
Synonyms: adult (n), maturity (n)

Ford is suggesting that if we keep learning and trying new things in life, then we will stay 'young' regardless of our actual age.

Henry Ford (1863–1947) was a very successful American businessman who founded the Ford Motor Company. He is famous for developing the first mass-produced automobile, transforming from a luxury item to one that was affordable for ordinary people. He also introduced many key business innovations including the assembly line in factories.

OBJECTIVES

Read the unit objectives to the class.

UNIT OPENER QUESTIONS

1 Focus students on the picture and ask whether or not they agree with the caption. Next, read the quote as a class and put students into pairs to discuss it. Monitor, helping students to articulate their ideas as necessary. Bring the class back together, nominating one or two pairs to share the main points of their discussions. Encourage other students to question or comment on each other's ideas. Add any useful emergent vocabulary on the board.

2 Elicit what people can legally do at the age of 18 in your country and build up a bulleted list on the board. Next, put students into pairs to discuss what other birthdays are significant in their country and why. Monitor, helping with new or unfamiliar vocabulary as necessary. Bring the class back together to share their ideas, again adding any useful emergent vocabulary to the board.

3 Share a piece of advice you would give your younger self and why. Then, put students into pairs to do the same. Bring the class back together to share their advice and encourage further discussion as appropriate.

WORKSHEETS

Lesson 6.1 The right method?

Grammar: Obligation, prohibition and permission (W26)

Vocabulary: Education (W27)

Lesson 6.2 Traditions of youth

Grammar: Articles (W28)

Vocabulary: Compound adjectives (W29)

Vocabulary: Phrases with *make* and *do* (W30)

6.1 The right method?

- Discuss rules in education
- Talk about changes to education in your country

G – obligation, prohibition and permission
V – education
P – intonation to show interest
S – pronoun referencing

LISTENING

A SPEAK Work in groups. Look at the school rules (1–6). Which do you think are reasonable? Which do you think are unreasonable? Why?

6.1 **B LISTEN FOR GIST** Listen to a radio interview about different school systems. Choose the best summary (1–3).

1 Both guests had a similar school experience but disagree about which system to use today.
(2) Both guests enjoyed their school experience but disagree about the best system to use today.
3 Both guests agree that students need rules, and that current systems should be stricter.

6.1 **C LISTEN FOR DETAIL** Listen again. Complete the sentences with no more than two words from the interview.

1 In Jessica's school, students and teachers could ___vote___ on the rules.
2 Jessica thinks students behave better when they have the ___power___ to make decisions.
3 Jessica thinks teenagers want more ___control___ of their environment as they're becoming adults.
4 In Jessica's school, students got excellent ___(exam) results___ and went on to further education and to have good jobs.
5 In Andrew's school, everyone had to have the ___same___ hair, bags and clothes.
6 Children who broke the rules in Andrew's school had to wear ___a tag___ around their necks.
7 Andrew thinks more ___rules___ make things fairer because all teachers behave the same.
8 Jessica felt her experience at school made her more ___mature___ when she left.

D SPEAK Work in pairs. Which school would you prefer to study at? Why?

SCHOOL RULES

1 Bathroom breaks during class limited to three times a week.
2 Students must not dye their hair.
3 Any student arriving more than five minutes late will be given cleaning duties.
4 Male students are strictly forbidden from having facial hair.
5 Shorts may not be worn between September 15th and May 15th.
6 No groups larger than five anywhere on school grounds.

6.1 The right method?

LEAD-IN

Write the following sentences on the board – *1 _____ are limited to three times a week; 2 Students must not _____ their hair; 3 Any students arriving more than five minutes late will be given _____; 4 Male students are strictly forbidden from having _____*. Elicit that these are school rules, and put students into pairs to guess the missing words. Bring the class back together to share their ideas, before asking students to check their answers in the book. Take this opportunity to pre-teach any vocabulary that is new to the students (e.g. *dye*, *facial hair*, etc) before moving on.

LISTENING

A Put students into groups to discuss the questions. Monitor, encouraging students to explain their reasoning. Bring the class back together to share their ideas, discussing each rule in turn. Add any useful emergent language to the board.

6.1 **B** Give students time to read the summaries carefully, before playing the audio. Ask them to check their answers with a partner before giving feedback. See the **Audio script** below and TB63.

6.1 **C** Clarify that students must use no more than two words to complete each sentence and that whatever they write must come from the interview itself – they cannot change the form. Play the audio again, and allow time for peer correction before giving feedback as a class.

D Put students into pairs to discuss the question. Monitor, encouraging them to ask follow-up questions to keep their discussions going and to justify their opinions with examples. You could end this activity with a class vote to decide which one is more popular.

AUDIO SCRIPT

6.1

Listening, Exercise B
P = Presenter J = Jessica A = Andrew

P: Hello, and welcome to another edition of *Society Today*. I'm your host Rachel Baxter. So the global school rankings are out again, and they seem to indicate that stricter schooling systems get better results. Here to discuss whether it's time we moved toward a stricter schooling system in the US are Andrew Jones, head of the Lighthouse Academy in Michigan, a school well-known for its 'no nonsense' approach, and mother-of-two, Jessica Wilding. Jessica recently removed her children from a school in Grand Rapids, Michigan because she thought the rules there were simply too strict. Good morning, both of you.

J and A: Good morning.

P: So Jessica, you went to a very open and relaxed school where children were allowed to pretty much do whatever they wanted.

J: Uh, yes, that's right. We weren't forced to do anything we didn't want to. Teachers and students were treated as equals. [Ex C Q1] Every semester, a vote was held so we could decide on rules together. I loved this system and was disappointed to find my children didn't have this level of freedom.

P: So you put them in another school?

J: I did, and I think it was the right decision. The school they're at now is great. Amazing, in fact. The only rule they have is that their actions must not harm anyone else. Every week they have a school meeting and vote on all sorts of issues together. I thrived under this kind of system and I think my children will, too.

A: I'm sorry, but it sounds ridiculous to me. Students that get to decide their own rules will use it as an excuse to behave badly.

J: I'm sorry, but that simply isn't true. Students don't need to follow old-fashioned rules to understand what they should or shouldn't do. [Ex C Q2] Students behave well when they are given power to decide what they can't do. I think this is really important, especially for teenagers.

A: Well, I couldn't work in such a system! Rules are important.

J: I completely agree, but I think students should have a say in exactly what those rules are. I genuinely feel that most problems with teenagers come because we make them follow rules, but [Ex C Q3] they're growing into adults and simply want more control of their environment. They can make very sensible decisions when given trust.

P: But surely students given this much freedom will just choose not to go to classes?

A: Exactly!

J: I'm not sure. In my school, students weren't obliged to attend classes. We could also move up a year group earlier than normal or stay back a little longer if we felt like we needed more time. We could choose our subjects and didn't have to take ones we didn't like. We could even repeat things if we wanted. People weren't left behind.

A: That's very interesting actually. How did they decide when you took exams?

J: Well, in many cases people took subjects and exams earlier than they were supposed to. If you enjoy a subject, you want to do well in it. I don't think students should be required to go to classes or to study certain subjects. If you struggle in physics and you're not ever really going to use it in the future, why study it?

A: Now that I can't agree with. People end up …

[Ex C Q4] **J:** Why on earth not? The exam results in our school were excellent. Many students managed to get into excellent colleges and go on to have very good careers.

A: Yes, but people end up working in all sorts of jobs they never thought they would have. If you don't get a well-rounded education, it could massively affect your future.

P: Interesting! Now Andrew, you're head of one of the strictest schools in the US, and you also had a similar experience as a child yourself. Why do you think it works?

A: I believe that young students need structure. They simply need to know what the rules are.

P: Could you give us some examples of the types of strict rules you had as a child?

A: Sure. We weren't allowed to have dirty shoes. [Ex C Q5] Basically, everyone had to look the same – no unusual haircuts, the same bag, the same hairbands and even the same coats. We weren't allowed to talk to each other or look at the clock. We also had to focus on our work and we weren't allowed to misbehave and distract others.

6.1 The right method?

GRAMMAR

6.2 **A–C** Give students time to complete the exercises alone, before giving feedback as a class. Then, direct them to the **Grammar Hub** (see below and TB64).

D–E Ask students to complete the exercise alone, then give feedback as a class. Then, give them to time to rewrite the sentences before discussing them in pairs. Use the **Grammar Worksheet** on page W26 for extra practice.

PRONUNCIATION

6.3; 6.4 **A–B** Play the recording for students to complete the exercises. Give feedback as a class.

C–D Give students time to write three interesting facts about themselves. Then, put them into pairs to share their ideas. If you have time, bring the class back together to share the funniest or most unusual things they found out about each other.

SPEAKING

A–B Tell the class about one or two rules at your school that you didn't like and explain why. Then, put students into pairs to discuss their own schools. Next, model the next stage by explaining how you would change one of the rules at your school. Then, put students into pairs to do the same.

C–D Allow time for each pair to present their rules, encouraging the class to question or comment on each other's ideas.

6.1 (continued)

J: Not distracting people and talking – fine. But does it really matter what color your hair is or what bag you have? That seems ridiculous.

A: I've put many of the same rules in place in my school.

Ex C Q6 **P:** What happened if you broke the rules?

A: We had to wear a tag around our neck with a message such as 'I have 24 hours to straighten up my uniform' if we looked sloppy. If we behaved badly in class, we had to study on our own. We were forced to do this for five classes. Hundreds of children had to do this. I have similar rules in my school.

J: You're joking! How embarrassing!

A: The students are better behaved.

J: Oh, come on! I don't think the punishment fits the crime there. I agree children are supposed to learn right from wrong but being forced to study on their own for wearing the wrong color hairband! That's clearly unreasonable. The punishment should fit the crime.

P: That seems sensible to me. So, Andrew did you enjoy your experience at school?

A: I did. You quickly learned what you needed to do. You got to know what the rules were and how you were expected to behave. It actually made it really fair having more rules. We didn't have the 'strict' teacher because they were all strict. I was really happy there. We had a lot of fun. We went on some amazing school trips. We had all the usual sports teams and parties. It was great! (Ex C Q7)

J: Just don't break the rules! I suppose I just loved my school. I felt like an equal and included. I think it actually made me more mature when I went to college. A lot of people see that moment as 'freedom', but we had had that for years. That time at school was the happiest time of my life, actually. (Ex C Q8)

A: Me too!

P: Interesting that such different systems made you both happy. Thank you for coming in today.

J: Thanks for inviting us!

A: Great to be here.

P: Next on the show, we have several students from …

GRAMMAR HUB

6.1 Obligation, prohibition and permission

Strong obligation

- We use *have to, must, need to, be obliged to* and *be required to* to talk about things that we are obligated to do / are necessary.

The meeting starts at 9:00 am, so you must be here before then.
(= It's necessary for you to be here before 9:00 am.)
You need to buy a ticket before boarding.
(= It's necessary to buy a ticket.)

Lack of obligation

- We use *don't have to, don't need to, be not obliged to* and *be not required to* to talk about things that we aren't obligated to do / aren't necessary.

The dress code is semi-formal, but staff members aren't required to wear ties. (= They can wear ties if they want to, but it's not necessary.)

Be careful!

- We cannot use *must not* in this way.

They don't have to study music if they don't want to. NOT ~~*They must not study music if they don't want to.*~~

Weak obligation

- We use *should* to talk about things that are advised, recommended or suggested, but aren't necessary.

You should read the report before our meeting with Alex tomorrow. (= It isn't necessary to read the report, but it's a good idea.)

- We use *be supposed to* to talk about things we're expected to do according to a rule or arrangement.

I'm supposed to go to that meeting at 2:00 pm, but I really don't want to!

Prohibition

- We use *must not, can't* and *be not allowed to* to talk about things that are prohibited / not permitted.

You can't smoke anywhere inside the building. (= You're not permitted to smoke.)

GRAMMAR

Obligation, prohibition and permission

6.2 **A** Complete the extracts with the words in the box. Then listen and check your answers.

allowed needed obliged should required supposed

1 I'm not sure. In my school, students weren't ___obliged___ to attend classes.
2 I don't think students should be ___required___ to go to classes or to study certain subjects.
3 Well, in many cases people took subjects and exams earlier than they were ___supposed___ to.
4 We weren't ___allowed___ to have dirty shoes.
5 That's clearly unreasonable. The punishment ___should___ fit the crime.
6 You quickly learned what you ___needed___ to do.

B WORK IT OUT Choose the correct options to complete the rules.

obligation, prohibition and permission

Strong obligation

We use *have to, must, need to, be obliged to, be required to* to talk about things that [1]*are necessary* / *aren't necessary*.

Lack of obligation

We use *don't have to, don't need to, be not obliged to, be not required to* to talk about things that [2]*are necessary* / *aren't necessary*.

Weak obligation

We use *should, be supposed to* to talk about things that [3]*are recommended* / *aren't recommended*.

Prohibition

We use *must not, can't, be not allowed to* to talk about things that [4]*are permitted* / *aren't permitted*.

Permission

We use *can, let* or *be allowed to* to talk about things that [5]*are permitted* / *aren't permitted*.

C Go to the Grammar Hub on page 132.

D PRACTICE Choose the correct options (a, b or c) to complete the sentences.

1 My parents didn't ___ me go out alone until I was 18.
   a require b need (c) let
2 I'm going to ___ my children have a lot more freedom than I had.
   (a) let b allow c need
3 I was ___ do a lot of housework, but usually I didn't bother.
   a allowed to b need to (c) supposed to
4 I ___ practice the piano for an hour every day. I hated it!
   a didn't have to b could (c) had to
5 I think people ___ be allowed to drive at 16. You can work then, so having a car would help.
   (a) should b have to c must
6 We ___ study a foreign language. I think it was a mistake, because languages are important.
   a had to (b) didn't have to c must not

E SPEAK Work in pairs. Change the sentences in Exercise D so they are true for you.

PRONUNCIATION

Intonation to show interest

6.3 **A** Listen to this exchange from the radio show. What kind of intonation does Jessica use to show interest: rise (↗), fall (↘) or rise-fall (↗↘)?

rise-fall

Andrew: We had to wear a tag around our neck with a message such as 'I have 24 hours to straighten up my uniform' if we looked sloppy. If we behaved badly in class, we had to study on our own. We were forced to do this for five classes. Hundreds of children had to do this. I have similar rules in my school.

Jessica: You're joking! How embarrassing!

6.4 **B** Listen to the same exclamations said in two different ways. For each exclamation, choose the speaker (a or b) that shows the most interest.

1 How embarrassing! a / (b)
2 Interesting! (a) / b
3 That's ridiculous! a / (b)
4 That's amazing! a / (b)
5 What a nightmare! a / (b)

C Write down three interesting facts about yourself.

D SPEAK Work in pairs. Take turns telling each other your facts from Exercise C. Use intonation to express interest. Then ask follow-up questions for more information.

SPEAKING

A PREPARE Work in pairs. Think about all of your previous schools. Discuss rules that you didn't like and why.

A: At my elementary school, anyone that forgot their uniform had to do the whole class in their underwear!

B: Really? How embarrassing!

B PLAN Work in pairs. Make a list of five rules for the perfect school, for both students and teachers. Use your ideas from Exercise A to help you.

C PRESENT Present your rules to the class. Explain your reasons for each.

Our first rule is simple – students must be given a say in the topics and subjects they cover. We think that …

D DISCUSS As a class, discuss how to improve your language school. Would any of the rules from Exercise C improve your school experience?

VOCABULARY

Education

A Look at the infographic. Complete the definitions with the words in bold.

1 ___state school___ (n) a school that is free because it is funded by the government

2 ___private school___ (n) a school that you pay money to attend

3 ___boarding school___ (n) a school where students also live full-time

4 ___compulsory___ (adj) something that must be done because of rules or laws

5 ___higher education___ (n) education at a university or at a college of a similar level

6 ___curriculum___ (n) the subjects studied in a school, college, etc.

EDUCATION AROUND THE GLOBE

With fees of about $133,000 a year, *Le Rosey* in Switzerland is the world's most expensive **private school**.

Wearing a school uniform isn't **compulsory** in most high schools in the US, although there is usually a fairly strict dress code.

State schools in France have one of the shortest school years with nearly 4 months of vacation, but the longest school day in the world with up to 40 hours a week in the final years.

A lot of the **curriculum** in Canadian schools is taught in both English and French.

England is home to the world's oldest **boarding school**. Students have lived and studied in The King's School since 597 CE.

According to the Organization for Economic Co-operation and Development, 66% of students in Finland go into **higher education** to get a degree. This is the highest rate in Europe.

B Go the Vocabulary Hub on page 145.

C SPEAK Work in groups. Discuss the questions.

1 At what age do people start elementary school in your country? Do you think this is the right age? Why/Why not?

2 Would you send your children to private school if you could afford it? Why/Why not?

3 Which subjects are compulsory in your country?

4 Do you think higher education should be provided for free? Why/Why not?

5 Do you think lectures are an effective way to learn? Why/Why not?

READING

A Listen to an interview about a new movie. When is it set? Who does the actress play in the movie? 6.5

the beginning of the 19th century; Agnes Grey – governess

B Listen again. Complete the summary of school life in the period with no more than three words from the interview. 6.5

Most children used to [1] ___work___ and didn't go to school. Some [2] ___poor___ boys could get scholarships but not girls. Girls from rich families sometimes went to boarding school, but most were taught at [3] ___home___ by a governess. A governess was a little like a [4] ___well-educated babysitter___

C PREDICT Work in pairs. You're going to read an adapted extract from Anne Brontë's novel *Agnes Grey*. What do you think might be hard for her as the governess of two young rich children?

D SCAN Read the extract and check your predictions from Exercise B.

Agnes Grey

Ex E Q1 Teaching and looking after the children became harder, rather than easier, as I got to know them. Master Tom not only refused to be controlled but tried to control me and his sister. He often refused to do his lessons. Ex E Q2 Sometimes I had to sit with my chair against the door in order to keep him in the schoolroom. At last, after trying to push me out of the way, and making faces at me, he would finally do his work.

Ex E Q3 Tom, however, was not as bad a pupil as Mary Ann. If I asked her to read a book or do some writing, she Ex E Q4 would drop to the floor and yell loudly. She was too heavy for me to pick her up and she would lie there until the lunch bell meant she could escape. Then she would jump up with a big smile on her face. She knew she had won.

Ex E Q5 In desperation, I decided that I should focus on two very important things in order to change their behaviour. I had to be patient and I had to be strict. Ex E Q6 So, I focused on doing this with all my strength over the coming weeks. However, it did not matter how hard I tried. Their behaviour did not get any better.

I will never forget one cold snowy January afternoon. The children had come into the schoolroom, shouting that they planned 'to be naughty,' and they had done Ex E Q7 exactly that. Mary Ann took my bag and started to Ex E Q8 look at what was inside it. When she saw that it only contained my work papers and books, she threw it on the fire! I ran to the other side of the room and pulled the bag out of the fire. Then Tom jumped up from his chair and yelled, 'Let's throw her desk out of the window!' He grabbed my desk, which contained my letters and what little money I owned. I quickly went to rescue it. Both children then ran away from me, out of the house and into the snow, where they rolled about shouting with happiness.

6.1 The right method?

VOCABULARY

A–B Give students time to complete the definitions alone, before checking their answers in pairs. Give feedback as a class, then direct students to the **Vocabulary Hub** (see TB121).

C Put students into groups to discuss the questions. Monitor and assist with any new or unfamiliar vocabulary as necessary. Use the **Vocabulary Worksheet** on page W27 for extra practice.

READING

6.5 **A** Play the interview for students to answer the questions. Allow them to briefly compare answers before giving feedback as a class.

6.5 **B** Play the interview again for students to complete the summary. Then, put them into pairs to compare answers, before giving feedback as a class.

C–D Put students into pairs to discuss the question. Monitor, helping with new or unfamiliar vocabulary as necessary. Bring the class back together to share their ideas, adding any useful emergent vocabulary to the board. Then, give students time to scan the article to check their predictions. Take this opportunity to clarify the meaning of any new vocabulary or passages that students are struggling with.

GRAMMAR HUB

6.1 Obligation, prohibition and permission

A Complete the conversations with the correct form of the words and phrases in the box.

be required to | be supposed to | have to | must not | not need to

1 **A:** You ___must not___ tell anyone that I'm here. I want it to be a surprise!
B: OK, I promise!

2 **A:** ___Are___ visitors legally ___required to___ wear helmets?
B: Absolutely! It's far too dangerous not to.

3 **A:** What do you ___have to___ get in town today?
B: A new suit for my job interview next week.

4 **A:** Do you want to play tennis tomorrow?
B: No, I can't. I ___'m/am___ not ___supposed to___ put pressure on my wrist until it heals properly.

5 **A:** Should we plan to get to the airport at two?
B: We ___don't/do not need to___ get there so early. Three should be fine.

B Complete the second sentence so it has a similar meaning to the first using the words in bold.

1 Booking our flights soon is probably a good idea. **should**
I think ___we should book___ our flights soon.

2 A high level of English is essential for all applicants. **obliged**
All applicants ___are obliged to have___ a high level of English.

3 My parents said I could stay up to watch the final. **let**
My parents ___let me___ stay up to watch the final.

4 I don't know why they didn't let us take our bikes on the train. **allowed**
I don't know why we ___weren't allowed to___ take our bikes on the train.

5 Taking food and drink into the library isn't permitted. **can't**
You ___can't take___ food and drink into the library.

6 It's your choice whether you come with us. **have**
If you don't want to, you ___don't have to___ come with us.

➤ Go back to page 63.

AUDIO SCRIPT

6.5

Reading, Exercise A
P = Presenter J = Jane

P: Welcome back. Joining me now to talk about her new movie is the actress Jane Nash. So Jane, you've just finished work on your latest movie, an adaptation of the book *Agnes Grey*. When is the book set?

Ex A / Ex B Q1 / Ex B Q2 **J:** It's set at the beginning of the 19th century, when very few people in England went to school. Children generally had to work to earn money for their family. Only rich families could afford to send their children to school. I mean there were some scholarships for boys from poor backgrounds, but not for girls.

P: Shocking to think that so recently not everyone got an education!

Ex B Q3 **J:** I know. And it's not like it was easy to get a scholarship. Only the brightest could pass the entrance exam. If a family was rich, a girl might attend a boarding school but more likely she had a governess who taught her at home.

P: A governess? Sounds like a pretty serious person! And that's who you play, isn't it?

Ex A / Ex B Q4 **J:** Yes, I play Agnes Grey, a governess. A governess was usually a well-educated woman who needed to earn money to support her family. They were pretty much a well-educated babysitter, though.

P: Doesn't sound like a fun job.

J: No, it was tough. You could have some terribly behaved children and no support or help. Life could be terrible for a governess! It was supposed to be homeschooling but it was part parenting, part discipline and a tiny bit of education.

P: Interesting! OK, so now we have a short clip from the movie to show people …

E Write the following sentences on the board, setting *they* in a different color – *At first, Agnes Grey found it difficult to control Master Tom and Mary Ann. In fact, they often refused to study at all.* Elicit what *they* refers to (*Master Tom and Mary Ann*), and draw a box around *Master Tom and Mary Ann* and an arrow connecting *they* to it. Elicit what part of speech *they* is (*a pronoun*) and whether it refers to an idea before or after it (*before*). Elicit why a writer might do this (e.g. *to avoid repetition, to help better organize the text*, etc). If you think it's useful/appropriate, tell students that this is called *cataphoric* referencing. Next, write the following sentence on the board, setting *she* in a different color – *Before she became a governess, Agnes Grey lived with her mother and her sister, Mary.* Elicit what *she* refers to (*Agnes Grey*) and follow the same process as above to connect it to *Agnes Grey*. Elicit whether it refers to an idea before or after it (*after*) and, if appropriate, tell them that this is called *anaphoric* referencing. Now, give students time to complete the exercise alone before comparing their answers with a partner. Give feedback as a class, encouraging peer correction as necessary.

F Put students into groups to discuss the questions. Monitor, helping with vocabulary as necessary. Bring the class back together and discuss each question in turn, nominating groups to share their ideas and encouraging other students to respond.

1 *'make faces' means to use facial expressions to show how you feel or make someone laugh. In this context, it's likely that Tom was showing that he wasn't happy about being made to study.*

SPEAKING HUB

A Show students a picture that represents an old-fashioned school punishment in your country and ask whether they think it still exists or not. Explain that physical punishments (e.g. students being hit with a hand or stick) are called *corporal punishment*. Add this term to the board and ask students whether it is still common in their countries and how they feel about this. Elicit one or two other ideas of how education has changed in general, before giving students time to write notes about their own countries. Monitor, helping with new or unfamiliar vocabulary as necessary.

B Put students into pairs to discuss the questions. Monitor, encouraging students to highlight any similarities and differences between their countries. If your students are all from the same country, encourage them to talk about differences between their schools. Bring the class back together, nominating pairs to share the most interesting things they found out. Add any useful emergent language to the board.

C Put students into groups to discuss the questions. Monitor, encouraging students to keep their discussions going by asking follow-up questions. Bring the class back together to share their ideas, asking each group to give a summary of their discussions. Add any useful emergent language to the board and stimulate further class-wide discussion as appropriate.

TEACHING IDEA by David Seymour and Maria Popova

Discipline

Use this activity to extend the theme of school discipline.

How do you think disobedient and disruptive schoolchildren should be disciplined? In groups, decide on the best methods.

corporal punishment, lines, discussion, expulsion, detention, parents, young offender institutions / reform schools, privileges, child psychologist

In groups, tell each other about something bad that you, or somebody you know, did at school. What was the punishment? Was there anybody at your school who was particularly disruptive or delinquent? Do you know what happened to him/her in later life?

TEACHING IDEA by David Seymour and Maria Popova

Past obligation

Use this activity to review modals of obligation, prohibition and permission.

Imagine you arrive late for an important appointment. In pairs, think of some excuses based on other obligations, e.g. *I'm sorry I'm late. The car broke down and I had to take it to the garage.* (Elicit some of the excuses to find the most creative.) In small groups, ask and answer questions about the rules at school and at home when you were a child. Here are some questions to help you.

Did you have to …? Could you …? Were you allowed to …?

Think about these subjects.

punctuality, politeness, eating, studying, sport, uniform, phone, going out, homework, boyfriends and girlfriends

METHODOLOGY HUB by Jim Scrivener

Chunk and collocation spotting

Teachers sometimes ask 'Are there any words you don't understand?' after students have read a text. But this may be a problematic question, as students could read a text and believe that they understand all the lexical items, but miss the fact that they have not registered that familiar words may be being used in new ways and combinations.

This leads us to a variation on the third idea: collecting items from a text but with a focus on longer pieces of text. For example, you could ask students to:

- find pairs of words that seem to go together: e.g. in the sentence *He had very good communication skills*, students may not know that *communication skills* is a common collocation (or that *good communication skills* is also very common)
- find phrases of three or more words long that seem to be a frequently used 'fixed' chunk: e.g. *It's well worth avoiding City Creek Center if you possibly can* contains *It's well worth avoiding* and *if you possibly can* (and probably City Creek Center is also a chunk, but one in which you can substitute different town names in the first position)
- underline ten nouns (or words used as nouns) and then search out which verb is used in connection with each one: e.g. in the sentence *Although the potatoes were rather old, we boiled them along with the carrots*, the noun *potatoes* is connected to the verb *boiled*.

'Chunk spotting' is a great classroom (or homework) learning activity. It usually astonishes students and teachers to realize how much of authentic texts are made out of these 'pre-fabricated' pieces of language.

E PRONOUN REFERENCING Read the extract again. Match the pronouns (1–8) to the people or things they refer to. Use the information in the box to help you.

Pronoun referencing

Writers frequently use pronouns to refer backward and forward to different ideas in a text. These help to make the text more organized and the language more varied for the reader. Identifying what ideas these pronouns refer to will help you to understand a text better.

1 them (line 2) the children
2 him (line 6) Master Tom
3 her (line 10) Mary Ann
4 she (line 10) Mary Ann
5 their (line 17) the children's (behavior)
6 this (line 19) being patient and strict
7 that (line 25) to be naughty
8 it (line 26) Agnes's bag

F SPEAK Work in groups. Discuss the questions.

1 In the first paragraph, Tom is described as 'making faces' at Agnes. What do you think this means?
2 What do you think Agnes could have done differently to control Tom and Mary Ann's behavior?
3 In the novel *Agnes Grey*, the children are allowed to choose when they study. Do you think this is a good idea? Why/Why not?

SPEAKING HUB

A PLAN Think about how education has changed in your country over the past 50 years. Write notes about:

- discipline
- subjects
- age of starting/leaving education
- college

B SPEAK Work in pairs. Use your notes to discuss changes in your country. What are the main differences between 50 years ago and now?

C DISCUSS Work in groups. Discuss the questions.

1 Has education in your country improved over the past 50 years? Why/Why not?
2 What would you change about the current education system in your country?
3 Is there anything from 50 years ago that you'd like to reintroduce to the current system?

- Discuss rules in education
- Talk about changes to education in your country

6.2 Traditions of youth

- Discuss age milestones in your country
- Debate the best time to start college

G – articles
V – compound adjectives; phrases with *make* and *do*
P – intrusive /j/ sounds
S – decoding: idioms

READING

A SPEAK Work in pairs. Discuss the questions.

1 At what age do you think someone becomes an adult? Why?
2 What events or celebrations happen in your country to show that someone is becoming an adult?

B SCAN Read *Coming of age* quickly. Match the ages (1–3) to the things they represent (a–c).

1 7 or 8 — b
2 20 — c
3 16 — a

a When you can learn to drive and leave school in the US.
b When childhood is over in Vanuatu.
c When someone becomes an adult in Japan.

C READ FOR DETAIL Read the article again and answer the questions. Underline the parts of the text that give you the answers.

1 In Vanuatu, what do mothers hold when their children complete their first jump? What happens to the item?
2 Which official venue do participants visit during the *Seijin-no-Hi* celebrations?
3 What traditions are associated with Sweet 16 celebrations?
4 What does giving a car to someone on their 16th birthday represent in the US and Canada?

D SPEAK Work in groups. What other coming-of-age ceremonies do you know of? What happens in them?

GRAMMAR

Articles

A Complete the extracts with *a, an, the* or – (no article). Then scan the article again to check your answers.

1 They traditionally signify a point in someone's life when __–__ childhood is over.
2 In __–__ Vanuatu, __a__ small island in __the__ Pacific Ocean, young boys jump from __a__ 30-meter-high tower…
3 The vine is cut to a length that will just stop them from hitting __the__ ground…
4 It is __an__ ancient tradition that started almost 1,300 years ago.
5 In recent years, __the__ popularity of __the__ festival has declined…
6 Sweet 16 is the term given to __the__ coming-of-age party to celebrate __a__ teenager's 16th birthday.

COMING OF AGE

Coming-of-age events are important in many cultures. They traditionally signify a point in someone's life when childhood is over. Immediately afterward, the person is considered to have a different role within society. However, from shows of strength and bravery to simply having a big party, these life-changing events vary greatly throughout the world.

VANUATU LAND DIVE

Thrillseekers will love this high-risk ceremony! In Vanuatu, a small island in the Pacific Ocean, young boys jump from a 30-meter-high tower, with a bungee-like vine tied to their ankles. The vine is cut to a length that will just stop them from hitting the ground, but, unlike a bungee rope, it isn't elastic!

From the age of seven or eight boys are allowed to jump from a smaller tower. (Ex B Q1) During their first few dives, their mothers hold an item which represents their childhood. (Ex C Q1) Once they have completed the jump, the item is thrown away to symbolize that their childhood has ended. As they grow older, boys jump from taller towers to show their manliness to their community.

SWEET 16

Sweet 16 is the name given to the coming-of-age party to celebrate a teenager's 16th birthday. It doesn't have a long history and there are no specific traditions to follow. (Ex C Q3) However, it has grown in popularity in the US and Canada in recent years. The concept became well-known when MTV launched a show called *My Super Sweet Sixteen*, in which cameras followed parents spending hundreds of thousands of dollars on elaborate parties for their children, who wanted the biggest and best party in town.

In most states, 16 is also the age when people can leave school and when they can start to drive. (Ex B Q3) As a result, one tradition that has developed is the gift of a car. This symbolizes the person's increased freedom and responsibility as they become older. (Ex C Q4)

SEIJIN-NO-HI

The coming-of-age festival called *Seijin-no-Hi* is held in Japan on the second Monday of January. It is an ancient tradition that started almost 1,300 years ago. The festival symbolizes the point at which the Japanese believe people become mature members of society – 20 years old. (Ex B Q2) It is also the age at which they are permitted to vote.

During the day, 20-year-olds taking part dress up in their finest traditional clothes and attend a ceremony in local city offices. (Ex C Q2) Government officials give speeches and small gifts are handed out. These young adults then go on to celebrate at parties in the evening. In recent years, the popularity of the festival has declined and many have stayed away from the celebrations.

6.2 Traditions of youth

LEAD-IN

Think about how old you were when something significant happened to you that you'd be happy to talk about with the class. Write this age on the board and get students to try and guess what happened to you (e.g. if you wrote *30*, students might ask *Did you start studying for a master's degree? Did you get married?* etc). Next, ask students to draw five circles of different sizes in their notebooks. In each circle, they should write an age that is significant to them (e.g. *when they graduated*, *when they got married*, etc). Now, ask students to mingle around the classroom, trying to guess what happened to each other at the ages they've written down. Monitor, writing down any useful emergent vocabulary. Bring the class back together and nominate students to share the most interesting thing they found out about a classmate. Add any useful new language to the board.

READING

A Put students into pairs to discuss the questions. Monitor, helping with new vocabulary as necessary. Bring the class back together to share their ideas, stimulating further discussion as necessary. Note, the *Macmillan dictionary* defines an adult as 'someone who is no longer a child and is legally responsible for their actions'.

B Give students time to scan the article and complete the exercise alone before checking their answers in pairs. Give feedback as a class, encouraging students to explain which parts of the text gave them the answers.

C Ask students to read the article again in more detail, encouraging them to underline the parts of the text where they find the answers. Allow time for them to compare their answers in pairs before giving feedback as a class. Encourage students to justify their answers with sentences from the article.

1 *An item that represents the boy's childhood, which is thrown away after the jump to '… symbolize that their childhood has ended.'*
2 *Local city offices*
3 *According to the writer, there are '… no specific traditions to follow.'*
4 *Increased freedom and responsibility*

D Put students into groups to discuss other coming of age ceremonies. Monitor, encouraging students to ask follow-up questions to extend their discussions. Write down two or three of the most interesting/different festivals and nominate pairs to explain them to the class. Add any useful emergent language to the board.

GRAMMAR

A Ask students to complete the sentences from *Coming of age* with the correct article without looking at the text. Then, give them time to scan the article again to check their answers before giving feedback as a class. Avoid clarifying or explaining any of the rules at this point.

GRAMMAR HUB

6.2 Articles

- We use the indefinite article (*a/an*):
  - **a** when we talk about something for the first time.
    *My sister-in-law just bought **a** new car.*
  - **b** when it's not clear or important which exact thing is being talked about (e.g. when something is one of many).
    *I'm going to **a study group** later with **a friend**.*
    *I actually read **a really interesting book** about entrepreneurs.*
- We use the definite article (*the*):
  - **a** when there's only one of something.
    *Sorry, could you close **the door**? (= There's only one door in the room.)*
  - **b** when it's clear to both speaker and listener which specific thing is being talked about.
    *What do you think of **the new science teacher**?*
  - **c** with superlatives.
    *Jupiter is **the biggest** planet in the solar system.*
  - **d** with rivers, some mountains, oceans, seas, plural country names, groups of islands and deserts.
    *Amazingly, he managed to land on **the Hudson River**.*
- We use no article:
  - **a** to talk about things in general.
    More money needs to be spent on education in this country.
  - **b** with most towns, cities, countries, continents, states, lakes and mountains.
    *Yale is an American university in **New Haven, Connecticut**.*

B–C Ask students to complete the rules alone before checking their answers in pairs. Give feedback as a class, providing further explanation and examples for each rule as necessary. Then, direct students to the **Grammar Hub** (see below and TB66).

D Put students into A/B pairs. Direct students to the **Communication Hub** (see TB121).

E Put students back into pairs to share what they've learned. Monitor, focusing on how accurately they use articles, not the fluency of their explanation. To extend this activity, you could ask students to research other coming-of-age festivals from around the world and report their findings back to the class. Use the **Grammar Worksheet** on page W28 for extra practice.

PRONUNCIATION

6.6 **A** Tell students that you are going to focus on another aspect of connected speech and play the audio. Highlight that although none of the connected words begin or end with a 'y', they sound like they are connected by a /j/ sound when said at a natural speed. Explain that speaking like this will make them sound more natural and that recognizing when it happens may also help with their listening skills. Then, play the recording again for students to copy the pronunciation.

6.7 **B** Give students time to predict which words they think will be linked with a /j/ sound, then play the audio again for them to check. Now, play the recording again, pausing between each sentence for students to copy the pronunciation.

VOCABULARY

Write the following sentence on the board – *My brother's commute lasts two hours*. Then write the following stem below – *My brother has ...* – and elicit how to finish it so that it has the same meaning as the first sentence (*My brother has a two-hour commute.*), writing *two-hour* in a different color. Next, elicit what part of speech *two-hour* is (*an adjective*) and explain that when two or more words are joined together like this to form an adjective, it's called a 'compound adjective'. Elicit other examples that students may know (e.g. *old-fashioned*, *well-known*, etc) and add them to the board in contextual sentences. Now, ask students to complete the sentences alone, using the information in the box to help them. Give them time to compare their answers in pairs before giving feedback as a class. Use the **Vocabulary Worksheet** on page W29 for extra practice.

SPEAKING

A Tell students what age people are allowed to leave school in your country (e.g. *in the US, school is compulsory until 16 years old in most states, but many students choose to stay in school until they graduate at 18, or later if they go to college*). Ask students whether they think this is the right age to leave school, and encourage them to share their reasons. Next, ask students to write notes about their own countries using the bulleted lists. Monitor, encouraging students write down reasons or examples to support their ideas.

B–C Put students into groups to discuss the question, explaining that they must agree on one age for each milestone. Then, bring the class back together, nominating each group in turn to present their ideas. Stimulate further class discussion as appropriate and add any useful emergent language to the board.

GRAMMAR HUB

6.2 Articles

A Choose the correct articles to complete the sentences.

1 How long have you lived in *a* / *the* / – US, Misha?
2 I saw *an* / *the* / – amazing documentary on Netflix last night.
3 For their wedding anniversary this year, my parents are going to *a* / *the* / – Paris.
4 What do you think of *a* / *the* / – new sound equipment in the lecture hall?
5 My roommate Idris is a nurse at *an* / *the* / – hospital on Jones Street.
6 It's not a bad idea to do away with *a* / *the* / – meat in your diet.
7 This is by far *a* / *the* / – worst food I've ever eaten!
8 My dad's school wasn't in New York City; it was in *a* / *the* / – small town out in the country.

B Complete the sentences with *a*, *an*, *the* or – (no article).

1 Seeing kids in school uniforms is an unusual sight around here.
2 Lizzie, just do your best on the exam tomorrow – that's all you can do.
3 Imagine riding a camel in the burning heat of the Sahara Desert.
4 I've never been to a job interview before.
5 One thing I could never do without is – books.
6 How cold does it get in – Antarctica in the winter?
7 I was really excited to see that the book Sean gave me for my birthday is signed by the author.
8 How old were you when you first went to – college?

C Are these sentences correct or incorrect? Rewrite the incorrect sentences.

1 Lina will be waiting for us once we get off ~~a~~ the bus.
2 Aisha got accepted by ~~the~~ a university in the US – in California, I believe.
✓ 3 It was a successful meeting despite all the interruptions.
✓ 4 The Houses of Parliament in London are right next to the River Thames.
5 ~~An exercise~~ Exercise is always hard, but it's worth it if you value your health.
6 Most people these days have ~~the~~ a smartphone, don't they?
7 Fran is very good at finding ~~the~~ bargains.
8 I'm simply too scared to try ~~a~~ bungee jumping.

➤ Go back to page 67.

B WORK IT OUT Complete the rules with the titles in the box.

definite article (*the*) indefinite article (*a/an*) zero article (-)

Articles

[1]We use the indefinite article (*a/an*):
- when we talk about something for the first time
- when it's not clear or important which one of a group is being talked about

[2]We use the definite article (*the*):
- when there's only one of something
- when it's clear which thing we're talking about (usually because we've mentioned it before)
- with superlatives
- with rivers, some mountains, oceans, seas, plural country names, groups of islands and deserts

[3]We use the zero article (-):
- to talk about things in general
- with most towns, cities, countries, continents, states, lakes and mountains

C Go to the Grammar Hub on page 132.

D PRACTICE Work in pairs. Student A – Go to the Communication Hub on page 151. Student B – Go to the Communication Hub on page 152.

E SPEAK Work in pairs. Tell your partner about the coming-of-age ceremony you have just read about.

PRONUNCIATION
Intrusive /j/ sounds

6.6 **A** Listen to the sentence below. Notice the /j/ sound that appears between the words connected with a (‿).

The‿American legal system is complex, and laws vary from state to state. Depending on the state, the‿age you can get a full drivers licence is anywhere between 16 and 18 years old.

6.7 **B** Read the sentences below. Draw a (‿) between any words that you think are connected by a /j/ sound. Then listen and check.

1 The‿average age to drive a car in most countries is 18.
2 In Bangladesh, many children leave the‿education system at ten years old.
3 You can vote in Scotland from the‿age of 16.
4 In the UK, the‿older generation could leave school at 14.

VOCABULARY
Compound adjectives

Compound adjectives

Compound adjectives are single adjectives formed from two (or more) words. Many are joined with a hyphen (-), especially when they come before a noun.

Compound adjectives can:
- include numbers, e.g. *30-meter-high*
- use participles, e.g. *old-fashioned, well-known*
- have multiple parts, e.g. *coming-of-age*
- combine adjectives and nouns, e.g. *high-risk*

Do not add an *s* to compound adjectives with numbers, (e.g. *30-meter-high* not ~~*30-meters-high*~~).

Complete the sentences with the compound adjectives in the box.

coming-of-age last-minute old-fashioned seven-bedroom up-to-date well-known

1 For the most up-to-date information on flights, please visit our website.
2 My parents have some pretty old-fashioned ideas about raising children.
3 Apparently, he just bought a huge seven-bedroom house outside Houston.
4 It's a coming-of-age movie about three young friends growing up together.
5 I'm going to be late because there was a last-minute change to the schedule.
6 We've booked a well-known author to speak at next month's event.

SPEAKING

A PLAN Write notes on the age people can do these things in your country. Do you think these are the right ages? Why/Why not?

- leave school
- drive a car
- start work
- retire

B DISCUSS Work in groups. What do you think is the best age for each of the things in Exercise A? Try to agree on one age for each.

C PRESENT Tell the class the ages you chose for each event and explain your reasons.

AGE AND ACHIEVEMENT

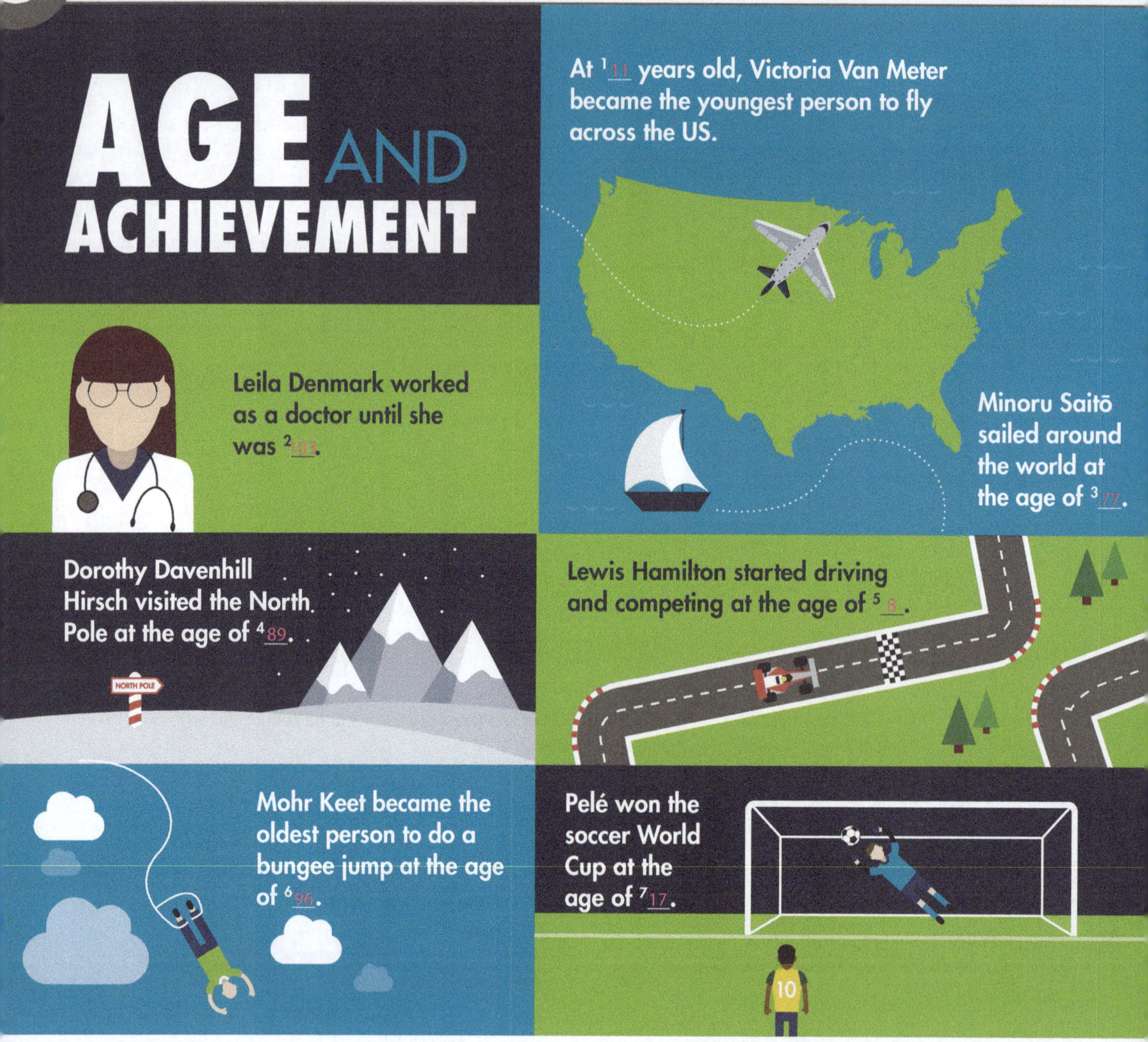

LISTENING

A PREDICT Predict when the achievements in the infographic were accomplished, using the ages in the box.

8	11	17	77	89	96	103

B COMPARE Work in pairs. Compare your predictions from Exercise A. Explain your reasoning.

C SPEAK Work in pairs. Discuss the questions.

1 What do you think motivated each person?
2 What difficulties do you think they might have faced?
3 What were you doing / What do you think you'll be doing at each age?

D DISCUSS Work in groups. Discuss the questions.

1 You are going to listen to three interviews from a TV show called *Age is just a number*. What do you think the title means? Do you agree with this idea?
2 The interviewees talk about achievements at the ages of 14, 28 and 70. What key events usually happen at these ages?

6.8 **E LISTEN FOR GIST** Listen and match the speakers (1–3) to an achievement (a–d). One achievement is not mentioned.

Speaker 1	a getting into college
Speaker 2	b winning a competition
Speaker 3	c starting their own company
	d getting over a fear

LISTENING

A–B Read the first sentence in the infographic as a class and try to agree together which age in the box best fits the blank. Then, give students time to predict the other ages in the infographic before discussing their ideas in pairs. Monitor, encouraging students to justify their answers with examples. Bring the class back together to confirm the answers.

C Put students back into pairs to discuss the questions. Monitor, helping with new or unfamiliar vocabulary as necessary. Bring the class back together to share their ideas, adding any useful emergent language to the board.

D Put students into groups to discuss the questions. Monitor, encouraging students to explain their reasoning. Bring the class back together to continue the discussion, again adding any useful emergent vocabulary to the board.

Suggested answer

1 *The expression is generally used to mean that age is a meaningless concept – people can achieve anything at any age.*

6.8 **E** Tell students that you are going to listen to three interviews with people that have achieved things at unusual ages. Then, play the audio for them to complete the exercise. Ask them to briefly check their answers in pairs, before giving feedback as a class.

AUDIO SCRIPT

6.8

Listening, Exercise E

I = Interviewer J = Janice Ka = Kayley R = Robbie

1

Ex E **I:** So Janice, you started your own business when you were 70.

J: Yes, it all started soon after I had grandchildren. They're amazing, but exhausting! I live around the corner from my daughter and so I used to do her a favor and take care of the grandchildren a couple of mornings a week. Every time they came over, I would, uh, make up games or do activities and that kind of thing, you know. They absolutely loved doing arts and crafts! Well, to be honest, I enjoyed it as well. If I tried to do anything else, they were just really hard to control. They weren't doing any harm, they were just full of energy – running around and shouting constantly. It was just noise! But with arts and crafts, they would sit there and focus on what they were doing. Taking care of the kids turned out to be a blessing in disguise because it led to me starting my business.

I: How did that happen?

J: Well, I'd kind of always wanted my own business, but never been brave enough. One year, I organized my granddaughter's birthday party around arts and crafts and they all loved it. Ex F Q1 I was worried about setting up my own business, but I decided to bite the bullet and set up a pottery café in my seventies. The parents love it. They can get involved with the kids or just sit and have a cup of coffee.

I: And how well has the business done?

J: Well, you know, it's hard, but I'm doing my best. Like any business, really, we had a loss in the first year. Now we're making a profit. Ex F Q2 I'm not rolling in money but I make enough. But really I'm so happy I've made a success out of this. It's the first job I've ever loved! I wish I'd done it sooner.

2

I: Hi Kayley, how old are you?

Ka: I'm 14.

Ex E **I:** And you're about to start college?

Ka: Yeah, I know. Weird or what? I'm off to study English Literature in September. I took my school exams four years early and achieved A grades in all of them.

I: That's amazing! Why do you think you are so successful academically?

Ka: I don't know. I think, well, I think most people could do the same if they got their act together. Ex F Q3 I didn't find school that difficult to be honest. It's not exactly rocket science, is it? Anyway, age is just a number. I think schools should do away with age restrictions for taking exams. Some people are ready much earlier than others.

I: Are you worried about going to college at such a young age? Most people go when they are 18 or 19.

Ka: Definitely! What are the other kids gonna make of me? It's going to be difficult to have a good social life, but that only makes up a small part of the college experience. People are generally nice, and I think they'll make allowances for my age. I hope I make a good impression, but I am a little worried.

I: And what do you hope to do when you graduate?

Ka: I love making up my own stories and really hope to be a children's book author. I write and illustrate stories for my younger cousins and they love them.

3

Ex E **I:** So Robbie, you've always had a terrible fear of heights and flying. You were 28 when you first went on a plane. So, how did you get over your fear?

R: Well, I was getting married about five years ago and my wife really wanted to go to the Maldives for our honeymoon, but she knew that wasn't an Ex F Q4 option. She cut me a lot of slack and didn't push for a trip because she knew I was terrified! She did start looking for vacation spots in the US, but I could tell she wasn't happy. She was trying to make the best of the situation by doing without the exciting honeymoon, but I felt so guilty. I decided to try hypnotherapy to see if that would get rid of my fear. Amazingly, it worked!

I: But since then you have really embraced not being afraid of heights and flying, right?

R: Yes, I've taken up flying and I'm now a certified pilot. I've done ten parachute jumps from a plane as well, and tried bungee jumping and base jumping.

I: That's amazing. A whole new world opened up to you!

R: Totally! My wife now gets slightly annoyed with how much time I spend doing these things, but we do have a lot more fun and exciting vacations!

6.8 **F** Write the following sentence on the board, setting *a blessing in disguise* in a different color – *Failing my driving test was a blessing in disguise, because it made me a much better driver in the end.* Ask students whether they think *a blessing in disguise* has a positive or negative meaning and why (*positive; 'blessing' is a positive word, the speaker ultimately improved*) and what type of expression it is (*an idiom*). Elicit any other idioms students can remember from the Café Hub lessons in Unit 1 or 3 (e.g. *runs in the family, fingers crossed*, etc) and add these to the board in contextual sentences. Explain that idioms are usually used in informal, spoken English and that identifying them can help you understand meaning. Tell them that you are going to listen to the interviews again and that they should listen for idioms to help them answer the questions. Play the audio for students to answer the questions, then put them into pairs to compare their answers. Don't confirm answers at this stage.

G Put students into pairs and direct them to the **Audio script** (see page TB68) to check their answers and identify the idioms. Give feedback as a class, consolidating understanding of the new idioms by eliciting new contextual examples for each and adding them to the board. Then, ask them to share other idioms in their own countries. Bring the class back together to share their idioms, adding any new English idioms that emerge during the discussion to the board.

VOCABULARY

6.9 **A–B** Play the audio so students can complete the sentences with phrases with *make* or *do*. Ask them to briefly discuss the phrases in pairs before giving feedback as a class. Don't confirm the meaning of the phrases at this stage; just check the answers to each blank. Now, discuss the first sentence as a class and match it to a definition (*c*). Next, give students time to complete the rest of the exercise alone, highlighting that sentence 7 has two phrases (*7a* and *7b*). Ask students to check their answers in pairs before giving feedback as a class. Consolidate understanding of each phrase by eliciting new contextual sentences and adding them to the board.

C–D Work through the first sentence as a class, then give students time to complete the others alone. Allow time for peer correction before going through the answers as a class. Next, put them back into pairs to discuss the questions. Monitor and support as necessary. Bring the class back together, opening up some of the more interesting questions for class-wide discussion. Add any useful emergent language to the board. Use the **Vocabulary Worksheet** on page W30 for extra practice.

SPEAKING HUB

A Tell students how old you were when you started college, and elicit from them what the normal age to start college is in their country. Ask whether people typically go to college straight after school and encourage students to say whether they feel this is a good thing. Elicit one or two ideas from the students, then put them into pairs to discuss more.

B–C Tell students that they are going to have a debate and read the statement as a class. Encourage one or two students to share their initial ideas, then split them into two groups, A and B. Allocate time for the students to prepare for the debate. Remind them that that they should also spend time thinking about the arguments the opposing team might make and how they could counter them. Monitor, helping with grammar and vocabulary as necessary. When the preparation time is over, allow each team to make an opening statement before beginning the debate. At the end of the debate, take a class vote to decide which opinion is the most widely shared.

METHODOLOGY HUB by Scott Thornbury

Idiom

An idiom is a word sequence (usually a phrase or a clause) whose meaning is not literal, i.e. it cannot easily be worked out from its individual words. Thus, when somebody calls your argument *a red herring*, they do not mean that your argument is *a fish of the genus Clupea that is colored red*, but that it is irrelevant and distracting. Idioms are also formulaic in that they are used and understood as if they were a single unit. You do not normally say *Your argument is a herring which is red*, or *Your argument is a reddish herring* or *The red herring of your argument is …* It is always *a red herring*. The degree of transparency of idioms can vary on a scale from the almost literal, as in the expression *to feel like a fish out of water* (meaning *to feel awkward in unfamiliar surroundings*), to the semi-literal, as in *to fish something out* (meaning *to retrieve something*), to the totally obscure, as in the case of *a red herring* or *a different kettle of fish.*

There are a number of ways of classifying idioms, according to both their form and their function. The following are some more common types:

- metaphorical compounds/phrases: *a hot potato; a king's ransom; the tip of the iceberg; a lone wolf*
- restricted collocations (i.e. collocations that are relatively fixed): *pitch black; breakneck speed; the bitter end; fat chance*
- phrasal verbs: *pick up* (e.g. a language); *get along* (with somebody)
- frozen similes: *as old as the hills; as easy as pie*
- binomials and trinomials: *safe and sound; spick and span; hook, line and sinker; lock, stock and barrel*
- proverbs and catchphrases: *waste not, want not; get a life!*
- euphemisms: *spend a penny; pass away*
- 'true' idioms (i.e. fixed and non-literal 'turns of phrase'): *spill the beans; fly off the handle; let the cat out of the bag*

6.8 **F LISTEN FOR DETAIL** Listen to the interviews again and answer the questions. Use the information in the box to help you.

Decoding: idioms

Idioms (e.g. *a blessing in disguise, blood is thicker than water,* etc) are frequently used in informal spoken English. They can be difficult to understand because their meaning is different from the meaning of the individual words. To help with this, listen for contextual clues before and after the idiom.

1 How did Janice feel about starting her business?
  a She felt very confident.
  (b) She was worried but pushed herself to do it.
  c She started it without really thinking.
2 How successful is Janice's business?
  a She's making a lot of money.
  (b) She's making a reasonable amount of money.
  c She's losing money.
3 What does Kayley say about school?
  a It was challenging.
  b It was boring.
  (c) It was easy.
4 How did Robbie's wife feel about their honeymoon plans?
  (a) She was fine because she understood his fears.
  b She was angry because she thought his fear was irrational.
  c She was fine because she wanted to stay in the US.

G SPEAK Work in pairs. Look at the audio script on page 171 to find the idioms that gave you the answers in Exercise F. Do you have any similar idioms in your country?

VOCABULARY

Phrases with *make* and *do*

6.9 **A** Listen and complete the extracts from the interview. What do you think each phrase means?

1 I used to ___do her a favor___ and take care of the grandchildren a couple of mornings a week.
2 They ___weren't doing any harm___, they were just full of energy.
3 Well, you know… it's hard but I'm ___doing my best___.
4 I think schools should ___do away with___ age restrictions for taking exams.
5 People are generally nice, and I think they'll ___make allowances___ for my age.
6 I hope I ___make a good impression___, but I am a little worried.
7 She was trying to [a] ___make the best of___ the situation by [b] ___doing without___ the exciting honeymoon…

B Match the phrases in Exercise A (1–7) to their definitions (a–h).

a to be positive about a situation you don't like but can't change ___7a___
b to succeed in living or working without someone or something ___7b___
c something that you do for someone in order to help them ___1___
d to get rid of something ___4___
e try to make something work ___3___
f causing no serious damage or injury ___2___
g to consider the reasons for somebody's behavior and not judge them too severely ___5___
h to make other people notice you in a positive way ___6___

C Complete the questions with the correct form of the phrases in Exercise A.

1 Do you ignore people's age, or do you think you ___make allowances___ for people because of their age?
2 When you ___do a favor___ for someone, do you expect them to do something in return?
3 Does eating junk food occasionally ___do any harm___?
4 Is there a time in your life when you had to ___make the best of___ a difficult situation?
5 Since my business is failing in its first year, should I keep ___doing my best___ to make it work or close it?
6 Should governments ___do away with___ unemployment pay and benefits?
7 What's the best way to ___make a good impression___ on others?
8 What would be the hardest thing to ___do without___ for a year?

D SPEAK Work in pairs. Discuss the questions in Exercise C.

SPEAKING HUB

A PLAN Work in pairs. What are the advantages and disadvantages of going to college right after you leave high school?

B PREPARE Work in two groups. You are going to debate the following:

Most teenagers don't know what career they want when they finish high school. Instead of making such a big decision at 18, they should work or travel for at least a year before going to college.

Group A – You agree with the idea above.

Group B – You disagree with the idea above.

Plan your arguments. Think about how to support your position, as well as what the other group might say.

C SPEAK Hold your debate.

- Discuss age milestones in your country
- Debate the best time to start college

Café Hub

6.3 A new perspective

A– emphatic structures S– using correct register

A floating school

COMPREHENSION

A Work in pairs. Look at the picture and discuss the questions.

1. What kind of building do you think it is? Why?
2. Do you think it's temporary or permanent? Why?
3. Where do you think it is?

B Watch a news report about the building in Exercise A and check your answers.

C Watch the news report again. Choose the correct options (a, b or c) to answer the questions.

1. What does the reporter mean when he says that 'water is in the blood' of these children?
   - (a) They are used to living and working on the water.
   - b They parents expect them to become fishermen.
   - c They never travel to the mainland.
2. What does the reporter mean when he says the school is 'widening horizons' for the children?
   - a It provides them with the chance to travel.
   - b It provides them with a unique view of their community.
   - (c) It provides them with more opportunities in life.
3. Which of the following doesn't the reporter describe on his tour of the school?
   - (a) the number of students
   - b the conditions in the classroom
   - c the view from the classroom
4. Which sentence best describes the school's founder?
   - a His father was the oldest of 22 children and the first to get an education.
   - (b) He is the youngest of 22 children and the first to get an education.
   - c He is the father of 22 children and the first to get an education.

D Work in groups. Discuss the questions.

1. What do you think the reporter means when he says, 'What the community lacks in glamour, it makes up for in grit'?
2. What do you think the reporter means when he says, 'the school has given students the opportunity to think big'?

AUTHENTIC ENGLISH

A Work in pairs. Read the extract from the video. What type of clause is used at the beginning of the sentence? How does this affect the emphasis?

What's unique about this classroom is that it's open air.

B Read the information in the box and check your answers to Exercise A.

Emphatic structures

Speakers frequently emphasize a specific part of a sentence by building up to it with an essential adjective clause. Beginning the clause with *What* puts the emphasis on the information after *be*.

What's really interesting about the school is the location.
(= the emphasis is on *the location*)

We can also use *the thing that*, *the* + adj + *thing* and *all I* + verb to achieve the same effect.

The most impressive thing at my school was the main hall.

All I wanted to do was play soccer, not study!

C Work in pairs. Take turns completing the sentences (1–5) with your own ideas.

1. What's unique about my hometown is …
2. What I don't miss about school is …
3. The thing that I worry about most is …
4. The interesting thing about my country is …
5. All I want for my birthday this year is …

Who are you talking to?

SAM MALCOLM AMANDA HARRY EMILY

A Work in pairs. Discuss what you think makes a good presentation. Explain your reasoning.

B Watch the video and answer the questions.

1 What has Malcolm agreed to help Harry with?
2 Why is he qualified to do this?
3 Does Harry improve with Malcolm's help?

SPEAKING SKILL

A Watch the video again. What does Malcolm think is the main issue with Harry's presentation?

B Look at the two different versions of Harry's introduction. Identify the informal and formal features. Use the information in the box to help you.

1 Hey guys! How's things? So glad you were able to drop by for my little chat today. I'm gonna be talking 'bout some of the cool ideas that people have come up with for teaching kids in developing countries. I'll be letting you know if I think they're any good and …

2 Thank you for coming to my presentation today. I am going to be talking about some of the educational innovations that governments and individuals have devised for teaching children in developing countries. I will be assessing these on their effectiveness and …

Using correct register

Informal register

We generally use an informal register when we are talking to our friends and family. Some common features of an informal register are:

- Shortened sentences – *~~(I'm)~~ so glad you were able to …*
- Phrasal verbs – *OK if we quickly run through this presentation now?*
- Slang – *Cheers, dude.*
- Idioms – *… he'll give me a hand …, OK if I take five?*
- Abbreviations – *… I've seen it on TV.*

Formal register

In addition to avoiding the features listed above, we frequently use less direct language when we are being formal, such as *I would be grateful if you could …, I was wondering if I might …, I'm sorry, but I'm afraid …*

C Work in pairs. Why is it important to adapt your register to your audience?

D Work in pairs. Student A – Do one of the following in an informal register. Student B – Say the same thing in a formal register. Then swap.

- Ask your partner if you can do something.
- Offer something to your partner.
- Refuse an invitation from your partner.
- Apologize to your partner for something.

A: Shut the window, will you?
B: Excuse me, I was just wondering if I could ask you to close the window?

SPEAKING HUB

A PREPARE Work in pairs. Choose one of the topics to give a presentation about. Write notes.

- the right time to go to college
- school rules and discipline
- different school systems

B PLAN Organize your notes from Exercise A into a plan for a formal presentation.

C PRESENT Work in groups. Give your presentation and answer any questions.

D DISCUSS Work in new pairs. Tell your partner what you learned in the presentations using an informal register.

Give your opinion on an aspect of education

➤ Turn to page 159 to learn how to write a report.

A floating school

LEAD-IN

Tell students to imagine that you are going to form a new city or town and elicit what buildings it should contain. Add all suggestions to the board, no matter how ridiculous. Now, put students into groups and ask them to decide which five buildings are most important for building a community and why. Monitor, encouraging students to give reasons for their choices. Bring the class back together to share their ideas. Try to agree together on a top five list.

COMPREHENSION

A–B ▶ Put students into pairs to discuss the questions. Monitor, helping with any new or unfamiliar vocabulary, but do not correct or confirm answers at this point. Then, play the video for students to check their answers.

1 *It's a floating school.*

2 *Although not explicitly stated in the video, we can infer that the building is permanent because of the nature of the construction.*

3 *It's in the Makoko slum, in Lagos, Nigeria.*

C ▶ Give students time to read through the questions, before playing the report again. Ask them to check their answers with a partner, then give feedback as a class.

D Put students into groups to discuss the questions. Monitor, helping with grammar and vocabulary as necessary. Bring the class back together to share their ideas.

Suggested answers

1 *The people may come from humble backgrounds but are strong and determined.*

2 *It encourages them to be ambitious and think about opportunities outside the village.*

AUTHENTIC ENGLISH

A–B Put students into pairs to discuss the extract, then give them time to read the skills box to check their answers. Give feedback as a class, eliciting further examples of both structures.

An essential adjective clause; it puts the emphasis on the clause after 'be'.

C Put students into pairs to practice using emphatic structures. Monitor, helping students to structure their sentences if necessary.

Who are you talking to?

LEAD-IN

Put students into pairs to discuss a time when they had to speak in front of a group of people. Encourage them to share when it was, who they spoke to and the topic of the speech. Bring the class back together, nominating students to share their anecdotes.

A Elicit one or two ideas about what makes a good presentation, then put students into pairs to continue the discussion. Bring the class back together to share their ideas.

B ▶ Tell students they are now going to watch the next episode of the Café Hub series. Play the video so they can answer the questions, then give feedback as a class. You can find the **video script** for *Who are you talking to?* on the Teacher's Resource Center.

1 *Malcolm has agreed to help Harry a presentation for his sociology course.*

2 *Because he used to teach sociology.*

3 *Yes. Malcolm says, 'I think you've got it, my boy.'*

SPEAKING SKILL

A ▶ Play the video again for students to answer the question.

Malcolm thinks that Harry's style is too informal for an assessed presentation for university/college.

B Read through the skills box as a class, giving further examples as necessary. Next, give students time to complete the exercise alone, before giving feedback as a class.

Informal features

Slang – 'Hey, guys, How are things?', … *some of the* cool *ideas* …; … *teaching* kids …

Shortened sentences – '~~(I'm)~~ so glad …'

Phrasal verbs – '… you were able to drop by *for …'; '… people have* come up *with …'*

Abbreviations – 'I'm gonna *be talking* 'bout …'

Formal features

Harry doesn't use slang, shortened sentences, phrasal verbs or abbreviations. He uses more formal terms, like 'presentation' instead of 'little chat', 'innovations' instead of 'ideas', etc.

C Put students into pairs to discuss the question. Monitor, helping as necessary. Bring the class back together to share their ideas.

D Put students into pairs to practice the skill.

SPEAKING HUB

A–D Work through the stages, supporting as necessary.

▶ VIDEO SCRIPT

A floating school
P = Presenter N= Noah

P: They call it 'Little Venice' and the school run is under way. Ex C Q1 These children are the sons and daughters of fishermen – water is in the blood. What their community lacks in glamour, it makes up for in grit. Ex C Q2 But change has come to Makoko. An extraordinary floating school, widening horizons and giving the children a leg-up in life. This classroom is on the first floor of the floating school, but what's remarkable about this structure is that if you walk upstairs, you will find my favorite feature of this boat, follow me in here, and this is it – a second classroom. Ex C Q3 And what's unique about this classroom is that it's open-air and there's a cool breeze blowing through as the children learn. But there's one more thing you should know about this classroom, take a look at this – it's a unique view of the community from which all the children come from. The school has given the children an opportunity to think big.

N: So the kind of community that I …

P: The school was founded by Noah – the first in his family to get an education.

N: I feel very, very lucky when I went to school. Because I know the challenges. Ex C Q4 Because out of 22 children of my dad, I'm the last one of the family. And I'm the lucky guy that goes to school.

P: Lunchtime and the meals arrive. It's all part of a community pulling together to give their kids a chance. Martin Patience, BBC News, Lagos.

6 Writing

Write a report

W describing data

A Work in pairs. Which of these factors do you think are the most important things to consider when choosing a college or university? Why?

- quality of teaching
- college/university ranking
- friends at the college
- close to home
- good graduate employment rate
- cost of living

B Look at the bar chart. Which of the reasons in Exercise A is the most popular? *quality of teaching*

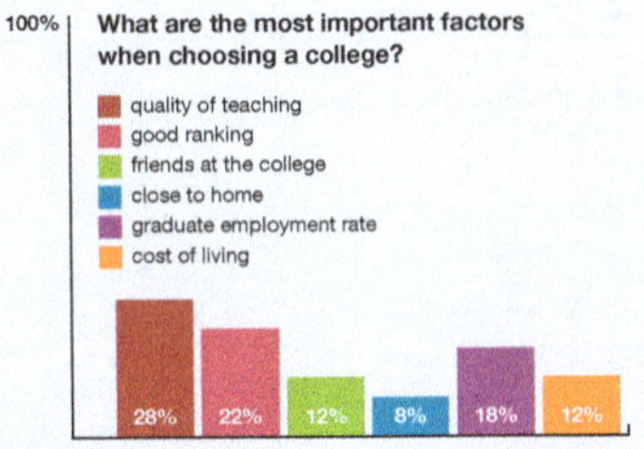

College choice

Introduction

The purpose of this report is to evaluate the results of a survey on reasons for choosing a college and to suggest areas for colleges to focus their efforts on to increase student recruitment.

Results

This graph illustrates the results of the student survey. The highest proportion of students chose the quality of teaching as the key factor. Almost one-third of students gave this as their primary reason for choosing which college or university to attend, with the institution's ranking being the second most import factor, according to almost a quarter of the students. The third most significant factor was employability of graduates, with friends and the cost of living more or less equal. The least important factor is closeness to home.

Interpretation

There are significant differences between two groups of factors in this data. Arguably, the first three factors are all interconnected. The ranking of a college can have an impact on employability and the standard of teaching has an impact on the ranking. Therefore, colleges need to focus not only on what is happening in the classroom, but also their connections with industry for internships and future employment. The other three factors are also potentially connected because they are clearly likely to have an impact on the students' lifestyle and happiness while attending college.

Recommendations

I would recommend that for colleges to increase their student recruitment and satisfaction they should invest in their staff and teaching facilities. They should also spend time developing their relationships with companies since employment opportunities are very important to students.

C Read the report and answer the questions.

1 How many sections are there to the report?
2 What is the difference between the results and interpretation sections?
3 What is the difference between the interpretation and recommendations sections?

D Complete the table with phrases from the report.

Describing data

Introduction

This report summarizes … and concludes with …

1 *The purpose of this report is to …*

Evaluating results

The majority of …

2 *This graph illustrates …*

The highest proportion of …

Several key trends indicated by the graph …

Comparing and contrasting

Similarly,

By contrast …

X and Y are 3 *more or less equal*

There is no difference between X and Y.

4 *There are significant differences between X and Y.*

Making recommendations

It might also be useful to …

5 *I would recommend that …*

WRITING

A PREPARE You are going to write a report describing the data in the chart below and make recommendations to colleges about how to promote their course. Write notes on the key results and your recommendations.

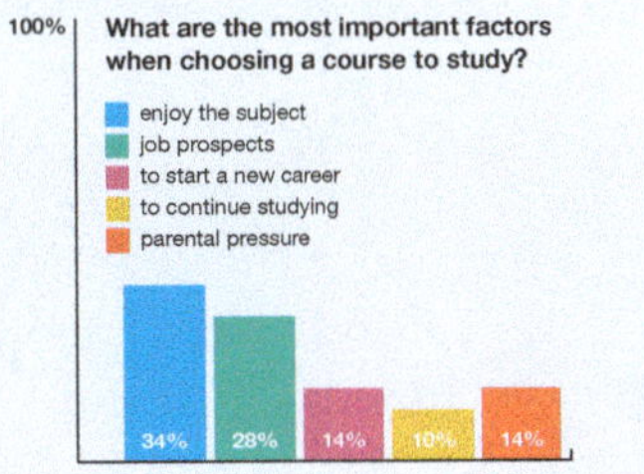

B PLAN Organize your notes into a report structure.

C WRITE Write your report. Use your plan to help you.

D EDIT Work in pairs. Edit your partner's report. Check:

- spelling and punctuation
- report structure
- strength of analysis and recommendations

WRITING 159

Answers

1 Four
2 The results just describe the graph, while the interpretation section talks about what the results mean.
3 The recommendations section talks about what should be done based on the interpretation of the results.

Refer students to this report writing task.

Refer students to this checklist when editing their partner's work.

LEAD-IN

Tell students about what college or university you went to, giving a list of reasons you chose it (e.g. *it had a good reputation, it was the best in the country for my subject*, etc). Then, put students into pairs to do the same. Bring the class back together to share their ideas.

WRITING

A–B Put students into pairs to rank the factors, before bringing the class back together to share their ideas. Next, give students time to compare their rankings to the bar chart.

C Give students time to read the report and answer the questions. Encourage them to underline the parts of the text that give them the answers. Allow time for students to compare their answers with a partner before giving feedback as a class.

D Read through the skills box as a class, clarifying the usage of each stem as necessary. Then, give students time to complete the box before giving feedback as a class.

WRITING TASK

A Read the question as a class, then give students time to write notes alone.

B Give students time to organize their notes from Exercise A into a report structure, using the model text to help them. Monitor, encouraging students to focus on only one or two ideas in each paragraph.

C Tell students to write their reports. Monitor, helping with structure and vocabulary as necessary. Remind them to use the model answer and the skills box to help them.

D Put students into pairs to edit each other's reports. Encourage students to give each other positive feedback. Students can then rewrite their reports either in class or for homework.

VOCABULARY

A Choose the correct options (a, b or c) to complete the sentences.

1 The fees for my ___ are $20,000 a year.
   a state school
   (b) private school
   c higher education
2 More and more people are staying in ___ until they complete a master's degree.
   (a) higher education
   b graduate
   c campus
3 There were over 500 students in my ___ on International Management today because we had an exam.
   a curriculum
   b seminar
   (c) lecture
4 The university has its own ___ that you need to pass to get in.
   (a) entrance exam
   b scholarship
   c seminar
5 My sister has won a ___ to a top college.
   (a) scholarship
   b seminar
   c graduate
6 I'd like to do a ___ course in something like electronics.
   a compulsory
   b curriculum
   (c) vocational

B Work in groups. Discuss the questions.

1 Would you rather stay on campus while in college or commute from home? Why?
2 Which subjects do you think should be added/removed from the school curriculum in your country? Why?

C Complete the second sentence so it has a similar meaning to the first, using the words in bold.

1 They've just moved into a house with three bedrooms.
   three-bedroom
   They've just moved __into a three-bedroom house__.
2 The décor in this restaurant isn't very modern.
   old-fashioned
   The décor __in this restaurant is old-fashioned__.
3 The author Haruki Murakami is well known in Japan.
   well-known
   Haruki Murakami is a __well-known author in Japan__.
4 Isaac's commute takes two hours!
   two-hour
   Isaac has __a two-hour commute__.

D Match the numbers (1–8) to the letters (a–h) to form full sentences.

1 I'm not happy with my apartment but I'm trying to … c
2 We've been trying … g
3 Can you … a
4 I think you need to make … f
5 Just one soda a day isn't going to … b
6 What do you think of this suit? I want to … e
7 It's hard living in a new city but I'm … d
8 This new system will allow us … h

a do me a favor?
b do any harm.
c make the best of it.
d doing my best.
e make a good impression.
f allowances for his lack of experience.
g to do without a car for the last month.
h to do away with a lot of paperwork.

GRAMMAR

A Choose the correct options to complete the sentences.

1 I was ***supposed to*** / ***required to*** finish it by five but I can't be bothered.
2 You ***don't need to*** / ***must not*** bring anything to the party but you can if you want to.
3 I think you ***'re required to*** / ***should*** complain to the manager. You might get a refund.
4 We ***must not*** / ***needn't*** leave any garbage or we'll get fined.
5 You ***are required to*** / ***should*** show ID or they won't let you in.
6 We ***aren't allowed to*** / ***should*** accept gifts from our clients or we could get in trouble.
7 You really ***are required to*** / ***need to*** drink more water when it's this hot!
8 You ***aren't supposed to*** / ***can't*** smoke in public buildings. It's against the law.

B Work in pairs. Discuss any rules or obligations in your school or work that you'd like to change and why.

C Complete the sentences with *a, an, the* or – (no article).

1 __–__ education should be free for everyone.
2 Did you go to __the__ movies last night?
3 He ran seven marathons through __the__ Sahara Desert.
4 I'll meet you on __–__ Main Street at seven.
5 Do you have __an/the__ address for the apartment?
6 Do you have __–__ signal on your phone?
7 We're having __a__ party to celebrate his 21st birthday.
8 __–__ Germany went out of the World Cup in the group stages.

A group of young community farmers displaying the produce of their shared allotment.

Community (n) a group of people in a larger society who are the same in some way
Synonyms: group (n), association (n)
Collocations and idioms: *a sense of* community, community *spirit*, *pillar of the* community (*someone who is well-respected or important to the area*)

Ibsen is suggesting that communities function through shared responsibility and that everyone should be ready and willing to lead.

Henrik Ibsen (1828–1906) was a Norwegian playwright, director and poet who was one of the founders of modernism in the theater. He is frequently referred to as 'the father of realism' and his major works include *Peer Gynt*, *A Doll's House* and *Hedda Gabler*. He is considered one of the most influential playwrights of all time.

OBJECTIVES

- discuss community development projects
- discuss responses to hypothetical situations
- talk about wishes and regrets
- design and present a community project
- give your opinion on a social initiative
- write a formal letter of complaint

Work with a partner. Discuss these questions.

1 Read the quote. What do you think Ibsen means? Do you agree with him? Why/Why not?
2 What do you do to help people in your local community?
3 What do you like most about where you live?

COMMUNITY 73

OBJECTIVES

Read the unit objectives to the class.

UNIT OPENER QUESTIONS

1 Read the quote as a class, then put students into pairs to discuss it. Monitor, helping with new or unfamiliar vocabulary as necessary. Bring the class back together to share their ideas, adding any useful emergent language to the board.

2 Tell students about something that you or someone you know does to help your local community. Explain what they do, how often and how it helps the community. Then, put students into pairs to discuss their own experiences. Write a note about any interesting projects that students are involved in and ask them to share their experience with the class.

3 Tell students about where you live, explaining what you like about it. Now, put students into pairs to discuss their own areas. Bring the class back together, and nominate two or three students to share their ideas.

WORKSHEETS

Lesson 7.1 Open spaces

Grammar: First conditional with different future forms (W31)

Vocabulary: Verbs to describe change (W32)

Grammar: Unreal conditionals (W33)

Lesson 7.2 Make a change

Grammar: *Wish* and *if only* (W33)

Vocabulary: Three-part phrasal verbs (W34)

Vocabulary: Compound nouns (W35)

7.1 Open spaces

- Discuss community development projects
- Discuss responses to hypothetical situations

G – first conditional with different future forms; unreal conditionals
S – identifying speculation
V – verbs to describe change
P – connected speech in conditionals

LISTENING

A SPEAK Work in groups. Look at the picture and discuss the questions.

1 Are there any buildings like this in your town or city?
2 What were they originally used for? What are they used for now?
3 What do you think would be a better use of the space?
4 Is it better to repurpose them or knock them down? Why?

7.1 **B LISTEN FOR MAIN IDEA** Listen to the talk. Match the original spaces to what they are used for now and the main reason for the change.

	Original space	New use	Main reason for the change
1	industrial estate	art gallery	to inspire local children
2	warehouse	community garden	to educate local children
3	wasteland	community park	to tackle obesity

C SPEAK Work in pairs. Summarize what you remember about each of the projects. Use the information in Exercise B to help you.

7.1 **D LISTEN FOR DETAIL** Listen to the talk again. Are these sentences true (T) or false (F)? Correct the false sentences.

1 Originally, the industrial estate was going to be used for offices. T / F
2 The park gives many urban children their first taste of nature. T / F
3 The gallery exhibits artwork inspired by the city. T / F
4 Local schools can exhibit work ~~twice~~ for two weeks a year. T / F
5 Many people don't eat fresh produce because of the expense. T / F
6 All the ~~food from the garden~~ leftover food from the café is given to homeless people. T / F

E SPEAK Work in groups. Would any of the regeneration projects described in the talk work well in your town or city? Why/Why not?

GRAMMAR

First conditional with different future forms

7.2 **A** Listen and complete the extracts with the correct form of the verbs in parentheses.

1 In fact, if we ___maintain___ (*maintain*) our current numbers, we ___will have had___ (*have*) 15,000 visitors in our first year.
2 If we ___give___ (*give*) kids opportunities like this, what ___are they going to achieve___ (*they / achieve*) in the future?
3 If you ___are thinking___ (*think*) about starting a garden, ___speak___ (*speak*) to me later.
4 If we ___don't come___ (*not come*) together as a community, neighborhoods like mine ___will fall___ (*fall*) apart.
5 If you ___care___ (*care*) about your community, ___do___ (*do*) something to improve it.

B WORK IT OUT Choose the correct options to complete the rules.

First conditional with different future forms

We use the first conditional to talk about something that is possible in the [1]*past / future*.

We can use any [2]*present / future* tense in the *if*-clause and any [3]*present / future* tense or an imperative in the main clause.

C Go to the **Grammar Hub** on **page 134**.

LEAD-IN

Tell students about a famous building that has been repurposed (e.g. *the Tate Modern in London used to be a power station but is now a modern art gallery*). Then, put students into groups to talk about similar buildings they know.

LISTENING

A Put students into groups to discuss the questions. Monitor, helping with any new or unfamiliar vocabulary.

7.1 **B–C** Play the audio for students to complete the exercise. Then, put them into pairs to summarize what they remember. Give feedback as a class.

7.1 **D** Play the talk again for students to complete the exercise. Give feedback as a class.

E Put students into groups to discuss the question. Monitor, helping with grammar and vocabulary as necessary.

GRAMMAR

7.2 **A** Play the audio for students to complete the sentences, before checking their answers with a partner. Give feedback as a class.

B–C Give students time to complete the rules alone before checking their answers with a partner. Now, direct students to the **Grammar Hub** (see TB75).

AUDIO SCRIPT

7.1

Listening, Exercise B
P = Presenter

P: I grew up in a poor, inner-city neighborhood in Greater Manchester in the UK. This is what my neighborhood looked like when I was a kid – abandoned factories, empty blocks of apartments and playgrounds covered in broken glass and graffiti. I couldn't wait to leave, so I worked hard and got into King's College in London. Life in the south was great, but I couldn't stop thinking about my hometown and what it could have been. So, when I graduated, I moved back to Manchester and started the Open Spaces project. The goal of the project was simple – find buildings and spaces that have been abandoned and turn them into something that would better serve the community.

Ex B Our first project was an old industrial estate by the river. It hadn't been used for years and nature had

Ex D Q1 naturally taken over. There was a plan to knock down the old buildings and construct new offices, but we thought it would be better as a space for the local community. We had to fight against developers to keep the land. So, how did we manage to get the

Ex B; Ex D Q2 local council to give us the land? Well, we approached it from an educational perspective. Many kids in large cities like this never have any experience of the countryside or wildlife, so we campaigned to develop an education center for schools across the city. Now, we have an area of local plants and wildlife for children to explore. We've also built a space for teaching the children about the local wildlife and the importance of protecting the environment in general. There are also bike paths for local people to use. So, was it a success? Absolutely. In fact, if we maintain our current numbers, we will have had 15,000 visitors in our first year. For many of the kids, this is their only experience of having been shown nature.

Ex B The council was so inspired by the success of the community park that they asked us to look for

Ex B similar opportunities around the city. When we found this old warehouse north of the river, we decided to turn it into a gallery. We wanted to use it

Ex D Q3 to inspire young people to get into art. We got local artists to produce original pieces for the opening and to contribute any other work they had that reflected the city. We have both indoor and outdoor spaces for people to exhibit their work. To involve the local community more, we also have a section dedicated to art produced by local school

Ex D Q4 children. For two weeks every year, a different school gets to exhibit their students' work. The children are so inspired by this. Their work is alongside real artists' work. They come down with their families and friends and they're amazed to see their work on display. If we give kids opportunities like this, what are they going to achieve in the future? That's what I find really inspiring!

So, by this point we'd created a community park

Ex B; Ex D Q5 and a public art gallery. So what next? Well, in a lot of poor areas, there are really high levels of obesity. Families eat takeout and microwave meals. They don't eat fresh produce because they find that it's too expensive. So, when we found a small space of wasteland that wasn't used and was largely full of garbage, we decided to build a large community garden. People are free to take the produce we grow in the garden. They can leave a donation if they want but they don't have to. We built an organic café by he entrance and use the profit to maintain the garden. Everyone who works

Ex D Q6 there is a volunteer. Any leftover food from the café is given away at the end of the day to homeless people. This has been by far the most inspiring project. People are starting to use public land all across the city to start small food gardens. Now, there are nearly 20 such gardens across the city. If you're thinking about starting a garden, speak to me later. A few years ago, I'd never grown anything; now I'm somewhat of an expert – especially in zucchini!

If we don't come together as a community, neighborhoods like mine will fall apart. We need people to help us take this forward. To take back our city and transform people's lives. Whether you want to start a skate park, an outdoor music venue or simply another organic garden. If you care about your community, do something to improve it. People like you can help bring back the community spirit we've lost. All it takes is a good idea and a little hard work. Thank you.

7.1 Open spaces

D If students completed the Grammar Hub exercises for homework, it might be worth reviewing the grammar at this point by working through the first sentence together. Otherwise, give students time to complete the exercise alone before checking in pairs. Then, give feedback as a class. Use the **Grammar Worksheet** on page W31 for extra practice.

VOCABULARY

A Ask students to read *Transforming Main Street* on their own, then briefly summarize the project with a partner. Then, give students time to complete the definitions alone before getting back into pairs to check their answers. Give feedback as a class, consolidating understanding of each new word by eliciting new example sentences and adding them to the board.

B Take the time to review prefixes and suffixes by eliciting ways to manipulate the forms of the words in Exercise A where possible (e.g. *transform*, *transformation*; *construction*, *reconstruction*; etc). Then, work through the first sentence as a class, before giving students time to complete the remaining sentences alone. Ask them to check their answers with a partner before giving feedback as a class.

C Put students into pairs to discuss the questions. Monitor, focusing on fluency, rather than accuracy, of grammar. If appropriate, open up one or two questions for class-wide discussion. Use the **Vocabulary Worksheet** on page W32 for extra practice.

SPEAKING

A Focus students' attention on one of the labels on the map and ask why this would be a problem for the area (e.g. *a disused factory might have a lot of dangerous equipment left inside; the badly damaged road prevents access to the area*; etc). Then, put them into pairs to discuss the remaining problems. Monitor, helping with grammar and vocabulary as necessary. Bring the class back together, ensuring students have a good understanding of each issue and building a bulleted list on the board.

B Read the first issue in your bulleted list as a class and elicit one or two ideas about how it could be addressed. Then, put students into groups to discuss and agree on three changes to make in the area, ranked in order of importance. Monitor, encouraging students to justify their ideas with conditional arguments (e.g. *If we convert the factory into a skate park, teenagers will have somewhere to go after school.*).

C Ask each group to present their ideas to the class, encouraging them to explain their reasoning for each change. Stimulate class discussion, by encouraging other students to question and comment on each other's ideas. Add any useful emergent language to the board. To close this activity, take a class vote on the best three ideas.

GRAMMAR HUB

7.1 First conditional with different future forms; Unreal conditionals

First conditional

- We use the first conditional (*if* + present + future) to talk about something that will probably happen in the future.
- We can use any present tense in the *if* clause (e.g. simple present, present progressive, present perfect, etc) and any future form in the main clause (e.g. *will*, *be going to*, future progressive, etc).

  If the weather improves, we're going to hold the event outside.
  If you're staying in tonight, I'll order us a pizza.
  They're going to let us know if their train is delayed.
  I'll be amazed if we've finished the meeting by three o'clock.
- We can also use an imperative in the main clause.

  Come and meet us later if you finish early.

Be careful!

- We can put the *if* clause or the result clause first. The only difference is we do not use a comma if we begin with the result clause.

  If the weather's nice tomorrow, we'll go to the beach.
  We'll go to the beach tomorrow if the weather's nice.

7.1 First conditional with different future forms

Correct the mistakes in the sentences.

1 Let me know if ~~you'll~~ you need any help with anything.
2 We're going to miss the beginning if we ~~won't~~ don't leave soon.
3 If everything goes well, we'll have ~~been finishing~~ finished by Friday.
4 Could I borrow that book if you ~~won't be~~ aren't using it?
5 Don't go to work if you ~~won't be~~ aren't feeling well.
6 If ~~I'll~~ I get a bonus this year, I'm going to go to Hawaii.
7 I'll ~~have~~ let you know if I think I'm going to be late.
8 If ~~you'll~~ you have been there before, you'll know how busy it gets.

➤ Go back to page 75.

D PRACTICE Choose the correct options to complete the sentences.

1 If everything goes according to plan, ***we'll have opened*** / *we'll open* a total of 20 community gardens in the city by 2020.
2 We're going to convert this old factory into a skate park if ***we get*** / *we'll get* the funding.
3 If they don't hurry up, the project *isn't* / ***won't be*** finished on time.
4 ***We'll be looking*** / *We'll have looked* at the plans tomorrow if you want to come along.
5 If you go to the meeting, ***ask*** / *to ask* the residents how they feel.
6 If ***they're growing*** / *they'll be growing* their own vegetables, they should sell them, too.

VOCABULARY

Verbs to describe change

A Read *Transforming Main Street*. Complete the definitions with the words in bold.

1 ___extend___ to make longer or bigger
2 ___relocate___ to move to another place
3 ___convert___ to change the use of something
4 ___demolish___ to knock down or destroy
5 ___restore___ to repair something so that it looks the same as it did originally
6 ___construct___ to build or make something like a building, road or machine
7 ___transform___ to change something completely

Home News Contact

Transforming Main Street

Our main priority is to **transform** the public spaces in the city center.
We need to encourage large chains to **relocate** to the city center to make Main Street a thriving shopping area again.
The next most important thing is to deal with the former industrial area. There is the potential to **convert** this into residential properties, stores, cafés and restaurants.
We should **demolish** some of the worst buildings but **restore** any of historical interest.
To make this development a success, we will need to **extend** the blue subway line into the area and **construct** new schools for the residents' children.

B Complete the questions with the correct form of the verbs in Exercise A.

1 Do you think it's better to ___restore___ old buildings or ___demolish___ them to make way for new ones? Why?
2 What is one change that would completely ___transform___ your hometown for the better?
3 Your hometown wants to ___construct___ a new road through a local park. How would you feel?
4 What could old unused Main Street stores be ___converted___ into now that most people shop online?
5 Why do you think so many stores ___relocate___ from the main street to out-of-town shopping malls?
6 Do you think it is better to ___extend___ public transportation to all parts of a city or to encourage more bike riding? Why?

C Work in pairs. Discuss the questions in Exercise B.

SPEAKING

A PREPARE Work in pairs. Look at the map of an abandoned area and discuss the main issues.

B PLAN Work in groups. Discuss how the area could be improved for the local community. Agree on three changes to make and rank them in order of importance.

I think the easiest area to address is the park. If we clean up the garbage, children will have somewhere to play soccer.

C PRESENT Present your ideas to the class. Explain your reasoning.

READING

A SPEAK Work in pairs. Discuss the questions.

1. What are the most important elements of a successful restaurant?
2. Why do you think so many restaurants close within their first year?

B SCAN Scan *It could have been so much better …* quickly. What is it about?

1. The rise and fall of China Garden.
2. Why you shouldn't start a business.
3. (circled) Why China Garden is failing.

C IDENTIFY SPECULATION Read the article again and answer the questions. Underline the parts of the text that gives you the answers. Use the information in the box to help you.

Identifying speculation

Speculation is when someone guesses reasons behind something without necessarily having all the facts, e.g. *I don't know … maybe it's the right restaurant, but just the wrong location.*

1. Why does Mei Lù think the business is failing?
2. What does Mario Coniglio believe makes the chefs' standard of cooking lower?
3. What does he feel creates a bad atmosphere for the customers?
4. What would encourage Nicki Wright to eat at China Garden more frequently?
5. What does Alex Mullins feel would have attracted more customers when the restaurant first opened?
6. What does he think the problem is with the restaurant's ingredients?

D SPEAK Work in pairs. What are the top three issues you think the owner needs to address?

GRAMMAR

Unreal conditionals

A Work in pairs. Read the following sentences from the article. Do they describe things that actually happened or imaginary situations? Do they describe possible results in the past, present or future?

1. If I hadn't set up China Garden, I would have continued working in an office job that I hated for the rest of my life. imaginary; past
2. If there was less competition in the area, I think the business would be much more successful. imaginary; present
3. If they'd spent more money on promotion in the area, more people would know about the restaurant. imaginary; present

B WORK IT OUT Match the sentences (1–3) in Exercise A to the rules (a–c).

Unreal conditionals

a **Second conditional** 2

We use *if* + simple past + *would/might/could* + base form to talk about the consequences of an imagined present or future.

b **Third conditional** 1

We use *if* + past perfect and *would/might/could* + *have* + past participle to talk about the past consequences of a hypothetical, different past.

c **Mixed conditionals** 3

We can use a mixture of the second and third conditional by using *if* + past perfect + *would/might/could* + base form. This is used to imagine the present consequences of a hypothetical, different past.

C Go to the **Grammar Hub** on **page 134**.

IT COULD HAVE BEEN SO MUCH BETTER …

In New York, there are hundreds of good Chinese restaurants already in existence, so establishing a new one is always going to be extremely challenging. China Garden is a family-run restaurant selling Chinese and Asian fusion food in New York's Chinatown. However, the restaurant is in trouble. Last year it lost almost $300,000. If things continue in the same way, the restaurant won't be there in six months.

When we met with the owner, Mei Lù, she was understandably not in a very positive mood. 'I always wanted to run my own restaurant. If I hadn't set up China Garden, I would have continued working in an office job that I hated for the rest of my life. But now I'm really starting to regret the decision. If there was less competition in the area, I think the business would be much more successful. I don't know … Maybe it's the right restaurant, but just the wrong location.' So, is Mei right? Did she just set up business in the wrong part of the city or are there other reasons behind the restaurant's poor performance? We spoke to the staff, locals and critics to dig a little deeper. (Ex C Q1)

Mario Coniglio has been the head waiter at China Garden since it opened last July. Despite the competition, he thinks the location is fine, but the number of items on the menu is having a negative effect on the business. 'The menu is enormous, and a lot of customers seem to find it difficult to know where to start. If we had fewer options, customers could choose more easily. Also, our chefs could probably (Ex C Q2)

READING

A Put students into pairs to discuss the questions. Monitor, helping with any new or unfamiliar vocabulary. Bring the class back together to share their ideas.

B Give students time to scan the article and choose the most appropriate summary. Ask them to briefly compare their answers with a partner before giving feedback as a class.

C Write the following sentence on the board – *The most expensive burger in the world costs $5000.* Encourage students to speculate about why the burger costs so much, adding all of their ideas to the board, no matter how ridiculous. Now, ask whether they know why the burger is so expensive or if they are just guessing. Tell them that guessing the reasons for something without knowing any or all of the facts is called *speculation*, and add this word to the board. Before moving on, explain why the burger is so expensive (*it contains expensive ingredients like wagyu beef, foie gras and black truffles and is served with a very expensive bottle of wine*). Now, ask students to read the article again and answer the questions. Give feedback as a class.

1 the location; 2 the size of the menu; 3 the angry manager; 4 more competitive prices; 5 spending more money on promotion; 6 they aren't fresh

D Put students into pairs to discuss the question. Monitor, encouraging students to justify their choices. Bring the class back together to share their ideas and try to agree on a top three list of issues to address.

GRAMMAR

A Put students into pairs to discuss the questions. Monitor, asking plenty of CCQs to lead students to the correct answers (e.g. *Did she set up China Garden or continue working in an office? Is she describing something that actually happened or just imagining? Did they spend a lot of money on promotion?* etc). Give feedback as a class, encouraging students to explain their reasoning.

B–C Give students time to complete the box alone, before checking their answers with a partner. Give feedback as a class, eliciting new examples of each conditional structure to consolidate understanding. Elicit how to rewrite one or two of the examples with the main clause coming first to show how to manipulate the structures. Then, direct students to the **Grammar Hub** (see below).

GRAMMAR HUB

Unreal conditionals

Second conditional

- We use the second conditional (*if* + simple past + *would/might/could* + base form) to talk about imaginary or hypothetical situations in the present or future and their consequences.

  If I had enough money, I'd open a restaurant. (= I don't have enough money; I'm just imagining.)

  We couldn't order things online if credit and debit cards didn't exist. (= This is hypothetical, because credit and debit cards do exist.)

Third conditional

- We use the third conditional (*if* + past perfect + *would/could/might have* + past participle) to talk about a hypothetical situation in the past and its consequences.

  If I had known about the event, I'd definitely have gone to it. (= I didn't know about the event so I didn't go to it.)

Mixed conditionals

- We can also use a mixture of second and third conditionals (*if* + past perfect + *would/might/could* + base form) to talk about a hypothetical past situation with a present result.

  If you'd spent more time studying, you wouldn't be so nervous now.

A Choose the correct options to complete the conditional sentences.

1. If you found a better job, you ***can*** / ***could*** start saving some money.
2. Ellie would prefer it if she ***didn't have*** / ***hadn't had*** to share a room.
3. ***We'll*** / ***We'd*** have been waiting for hours if you hadn't stopped to give us a ride.
4. If the car had gone over the cliff, we wouldn't ***get*** / ***have gotten*** out alive.
5. I'd join a gym if I ***wasn't*** / ***hadn't been*** so lazy!
6. If she ***saw*** / ***'d seen*** me, she'd have waved.
7. You ***won't*** / ***wouldn't*** be standing here talking to me now if you'd actually won the lottery.
8. If I'd entered the competition, I'm sure ***I'd*** / ***I'll*** have done better than Mo did.

B Complete the profile with the correct form of the verbs in the box. Add modal verbs where appropriate.

attract be can do still have succeed turn out

Business profile: Sean Taylor / the restaurant *Pie*

Sean no longer has *Pie*, the restaurant in Orlando, Florida he opened two years ago, but says that if he [1] 'd/had done things differently in the past, maybe he [2] 'd/would still have it today. The first mistake Sean made was to prepare the food himself. If he'd employed a chef, maybe it [3] 'd/would/could/might have turned out better for the business. Sean says that if he [4] could, he would go back in time and spend more time running the restaurant. He strongly believes the business [5] would/could have succeeded if he'd spent more time with his customers. Second, he didn't promote and market it effectively. If he had done that, he [6] 'd/would/could/might have attracted more diners. Third, if he had tried to sell the restaurant rather than just closing it, he [7] wouldn't/might not be in the poor financial situation he's in now.

➤ Go back to page 77.

D If students completed the Grammar Hub exercises for homework, it might be worth reviewing the grammar at this point by working through the first sentence together. Otherwise, give students time to complete the exercise alone before checking in pairs. Then, give feedback as a class.

E Demonstrate the activity by rewriting the first sentences in Exercise D so it's true for you. Encourage students to ask you follow-up questions for more information. Then, give students time to do the same for the full set of sentences. Monitor, helping with grammar as necessary. Now, put students into pairs to discuss their ideas. Monitor, encouraging them to ask follow-up questions to keep their discussions going. Use the **Grammar Worksheet** on page W33 for extra practice.

PRONUNCIATION

7.3 **A** Tell students that you are going to focus on another aspect of connected speech, then play the recording so they can answer the questions. Ask them to briefly check their answers with a partner, before giving feedback as a class. If appropriate, you could elicit why it is important to recognize features like this in natural spoken English (*it helps us not only to produce more natural-sounding English but should also improve their listening skills*).

7.4 **B** Give students time to predict which words are connected before playing the audio for them to check their answers. Play the recording again, pausing between each sentence for students to copy the pronunciation. Focus on natural pronunciation of the linked words and use of the weak *have*.

SPEAKING HUB

A Read the first situation as a class and elicit one of two possible solutions. Then, give students time to think of ideas for the remaining situations alone. Monitor, helping with new or unfamiliar vocabulary as necessary.

B Put students into pairs to discuss possible solutions. Monitor, encouraging students to use conditional structures to express their ideas. Remind them that they have to agree on one clear solution for each situation.

C Put students into new pairs to explain their solutions from Exercise B. Monitor, encouraging pairs to highlight the main similarities and differences between their approaches. Again, encourage the pairs to settle on one clear solution to each situation. Bring the class back together, working through each situation in turn and calling on groups to share their ideas.

METHODOLOGY HUB by Jim Scrivener

Eliciting

Eliciting means drawing out information, language, ideas, etc from the students. It is a technique based on the principles that:

- students probably know a lot more than we may give them credit for
- starting with what they know is a productive way to begin new work
- involving people in a question-and-answer movement toward new discoveries is usually more effective than simply giving 'lectures'.

Eliciting enables me to start from where the learners are and then to work forward from there. The learners have a real effect on the outcomes of the lesson in terms of ideas, language and pace. With constant learner involvement, I can work more at their speed rather than my own. I can find out where the real difficulties and problems are.

There are three steps to eliciting:

1 I convey a clear idea to the students, maybe by using pictures, gestures or questions, etc.
2 They then supply the appropriate language, information or ideas.
3 I give them feedback.

Advice when eliciting

Here is some advice for elicitors. Two pieces in the list are spurious: which ones?

1 Give sufficient information. Eliciting doesn't mean 'Guess what's in my head'. Don't try to elicit your grandmother's maiden name.
2 Use hand gestures to indicate who is being asked to speak, either a gesture for 'anyone' or to a specific individual. If everyone speaks at once, it can be hard for students to know which answer was OK and which was not.
3 Give very clear feedback on each student utterance. They want to know if what they said was acceptable. You could use simple gestures or facial expressions to register 'OK' or 'Not OK' to students.
4 If someone gives an incorrect answer, get them to repeat it two or three times and then say the correct answer yourself.
5 If they can't provide an answer, don't stretch the eliciting out too long. Silence or wrong answers are evidence that they need your input.
6 When you have an appropriate answer, make sure it is clearly established as a good answer, maybe by getting it repeated by a variety of individuals.
7 Don't use eliciting with monolingual classes.
8 Use eliciting regularly as a basic technique in most lessons for keeping your class active and involved.

D PRACTICE Complete the sentences with the correct form of the verbs in parentheses. Use contractions where possible.

1 If I started a business, it 'd/would be (*be*) in IT because I have a lot of ideas in that area.

2 If I saw someone committing a crime, I wouldn't stop (*stop*) it myself because it's too dangerous. I'd/would call (*call*) the police.

3 If I had a lot of money, I'd/would buy (*buy*) a sports car.

4 I'd/would be (*be*) a lot happier now if I hadn't dropped out of college.

5 I'd/would work (*work*) much harder if I was paid more.

6 If I hadn't taken my current job, I wouldn't have met (*meet*) my husband.

E SPEAK Work in pairs. Change the sentences in Exercise D so they are true for you. Ask follow-up questions for more information.

A: I'd be a lot happier if I hadn't failed my exams.
B: Which exams did you fail?

cook to a much higher standard. How can three chefs cook from a menu that has 500 dishes on it? It's crazy!' So, is this the only problem? 'No, I wish it was! Mei gets angry really quickly. It's embarrassing for both the staff and the customers. If she were able to stay a little calmer, the whole atmosphere would be much better.' Ex C Q3

It's not only the staff that is unhappy. Customers just don't come back for a second visit. Local food-lover Nicki Wright went to China Garden when it first opened but hasn't been back since. To her, the restaurant simply doesn't offer good value for money. 'The food actually isn't that bad. It's just so much more expensive than other restaurants in the area. If the prices were more competitive, I'd probably eat there more frequently.' Ex C Q4 The critics also aren't impressed. Alex Mullins, author of the popular food magazine *The Bite*, told us: 'It's a great location. They just didn't do a good job of advertising when they first opened. It's simple. If they'd spent more money on promotion in the area, more people would know about the restaurant. Ex C Q5 They do need to improve the food as well. It would taste so much better if they used fresh, locally sourced ingredients. Ex C Q6 The supply is here in New York; they just need to manage the restaurant better.'

While owner Mei Lù blames the location for her restaurant's failure, it's clear that there are many other issues that need to be resolved. While Mei is accepting of some of the criticisms, she strongly disagrees with others, especially the size of the menu. 'We offer customers a wide range of dishes from all over China and beyond. I don't see why that's a problem.'

Whether Mei manages to make a success of her lifelong dream remains to be seen, but one thing is clear – she has a lot more to learn.

PRONUNCIATION

Connected speech in conditionals

7.3 **A** Listen and repeat the clauses. Is there a pause between the words in bold? Is the pronunciation of *have* strong or weak? No; weak

1 Customers **would have** paid more if ...
2 Customers **might have** preferred it if ...
3 The staff **couldn't have** been friendlier if ...

7.4 **B** Draw a (‿) to show connected speech in the following sentences. Then listen, check and repeat.

1 I wouldn't‿have spent the money if I'd known it was such a risk.
2 If the restaurant had been busier, it would‿have survived longer.
3 If the menu had been simpler, it might‿have been easier to choose.
4 I think it could‿have worked if they'd focused more on advertising.

SPEAKING HUB

A PREPARE Read the situations (1–4) and write notes about what you would do in each.

1 Your dream business is failing. You spent too much money, employed too many friends and borrowed too much from the bank. In order to continue, you need to sell the family home and move into a rented apartment.

2 When you chose your degree in architecture there were a lot of construction jobs in the country. Now the property market has crashed. You have been offered a job as a math teacher.

3 $50,000 was transferred into your bank account by accident. You spent half of the money and the police have arrested you.

4 You left your passwords written in a book in a drawer. Your roommates found it and started posting on your social media for fun. Some of your friends have now unfriended you.

B PLAN Work in pairs. Discuss your ideas from Exercise A. Try to agree on the best solution for each situation.

A: If someone posted things through any of my social media accounts, I would shut them all down.
B: Ha ha! Really? I'd just share something embarrassing about them!

C SPEAK Work with another pair. Explain what you decided in Exercise B and why. Did you agree?

- Discuss community development projects
- Discuss responses to hypothetical situations

7.2 Make a change

- Talk about wishes and regrets
- Design and present a community project

S – inferring meaning
V – three-part phrasal verbs; compound nouns
G – *wish* and *if only*
P – two-stress phrasal verbs

READING

A SPEAK Work in pairs. Look at the infographic. What regrets do you think people might have in each of these categories?

B SCAN Read the comments. Match each regret to a category in the infographic. Were any of your ideas from Exercise A mentioned?

TOP FIVE

REGRETS IN LIFE

We all have regrets. That job we didn't take. That house we should have bought. However, according to a recent survey by Pulse Media, most people's biggest regrets are connected to – you guessed it – romance, with family coming in a close second. Here are some other interesting results of the survey.

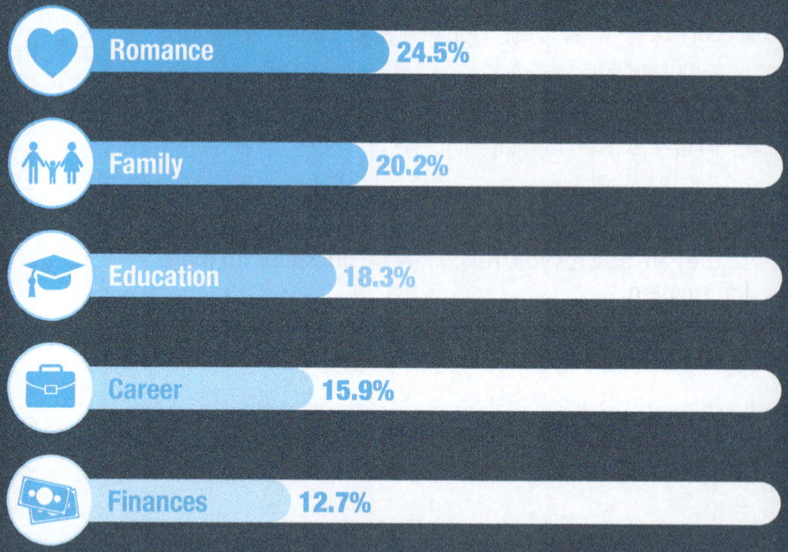

Hayley • 1 hr ago
[1]I wish I hadn't spent so much time worrying about what others thought of me when I was a child. It meant that I forgot to focus on the important issues. If only I'd spent more time studying. [2]I should have gone to a top college, but my grades just weren't good enough. I really feel like I missed out on a massive opportunity. Ex C Q1 Ex C Q2

Reply 5 0

Chris • 1 hr 30 min ago
I'm starting to regret my career choice. I chose a career in finance because I knew I could make a lot of money, but I wish I had chosen a career I enjoyed more. I spend all of Sunday night in a bad mood.

Reply 2 0

Nick • 1 hr 38 min ago
We've recently moved to another town because my dad thinks his career is more important than his family. My mom was happy to move but [3]I wish we still lived in our old town. [4]I wish people wouldn't think only of themselves. Ex C Q3

Reply 9 0

Sam • 1 hr 42 min ago
I really wanted to ask out a girl named Maria when I was 16! 🙂 I just used to blush and had no idea what to say to her! I was soooo painfully shy … I wish I had her number now!

Reply 4 0

Christina • 2 hrs ago
My sister and I haven't spoken for two years now. I miss her so much! I'd take back everything I said if I could. I wish she would just pick up the phone and call me. Ex C Q4

Reply 1 0

Kelly • 2 hrs 3 mins ago
The last summer of college was one of the happiest times of my life. We traveled so much back then. [5]I wish we could all go back to that beach in Thailand, but everyone's so busy now with work and family. Maybe I wouldn't eat the seafood this time, though! Ex C Q5

Reply 3 0

7.2 Make a change

LEAD-IN

Tell students something you regret about your education (e.g. *not working hard enough in school, choosing the wrong college*, etc) and encourage students to ask you follow-up questions for more information. Elicit that a feeling of sadness about something that you did or said in the past is called a *regret* and add this to the board. Then elicit a category for your regret (*education*) and add this to the board as well. Tell students this is one of the top five categories of regret. Then, put them into groups to guess the other four and which order they are ranked in. Monitor, helping with new vocabulary as necessary. Bring the class back together to share their ideas, encouraging students to briefly give examples of the kind of regrets people might have in each category if necessary. Try to agree on a top five list together, then ask students to open their books to check the list against the infographic.

READING

A If you haven't used the lead-in on the left, take the time to pre-teach the word *regret* by giving an example from your own life (real or made-up). Next, focus students' attention on the infographic and give them time to read the accompanying paragraph and statistics. Elicit one or two types of regret people might have in the most popular category, *romance*, then put students into pairs to think of more ideas. Monitor, helping with new vocabulary as appropriate. Bring the class back together, adding any useful emergent language to the board.

B Set a short time limit for students to scan the text before checking their answers with a partner. Tell them that one of the regrets doesn't fit a clear category. Give feedback as a class, encouraging students to highlight whether any of their ideas from Exercise A were mentioned. As Kelly's regret doesn't fit any of the given categories, elicit what an appropriate category might be (e.g. *travel, general regret*, etc).

Hayley – education; Chris – career; Nick – family and career; Sam – romance; Christina – family; Kelly – no match

TEACHING IDEA by David Seymour and Maria Popova

Speculation

Use this activity to review unreal conditionals.

In pairs, talk about your childhood and speculate about how things might have been different. For example:

If I had worked harder in school, I could have gotten a better job. If we had lived in the country instead of a big city, my parents wouldn't have worried about my safety so much.

In pairs, think about some recent events in the news. Discuss how they might have been different. For example:

If they had built the bridge properly, it wouldn't have fallen down in the earthquake. If the referee had been fair, Brazil would have won the soccer game.

GRAMMAR HUB

7.2 *wish* and *if only*

- We use *wish* + simple past to talk about things we would like to be different in the present or future, but are impossible or unlikely to change.

  I wish my brother lived closer to Chicago. (= This is unlikely to change – I'm just imagining.)

  I wish I could speak Japanese. (= This is unlikely to change soon – I'm just imagining.)
- We use *wish* + past perfect to talk about things we regret in the past.

  I wish I'd told Yuko how I felt before she moved back to Japan. (= but I didn't tell her)

  I feel sick! I wish I hadn't eaten so much at lunchtime! (= but I did eat too much)
- We use *wish* + object + *would* + base form to talk about things we want to happen or stop happening in the present, usually because they annoy us.

  I wish you'd stop talking with your mouth full – it's disgusting!

  I wish people wouldn't just throw their garbage in the street.
- We can use *if only* instead of *wish* in all of the structures above to sound more dramatic/ emphatic.

  If only I'd paid more attention in school!
- We can use *were* instead of *was* after *I/he/she/it* in the *if* clause.

  I wish I was/were a little bit taller. (= This is impossible – I'm just imagining.)

Be careful!

- When you want to make a wish about yourself, or you and other people, use *could* instead of *would*.

  I wish I could sit at home all day. NOT ~~*I wish I would sit at home all day.*~~

7.2 Make a change

C Write the following sentence on the board – *I chose a career in finance because I knew I could make a lot of money, but I wish I had chosen a career I enjoy more. I spend all of Sunday night in a bad mood.* Ask students why the writer spends Sunday in a bad mood (*they don't want to go to work on Monday*) and whether the sentence tells us this directly (*no, we guess it from other information in the sentence*). Tell students that guessing information from context like this is called 'inference', and explain that we can also use our general knowledge to do this. Next, give students time to answer the questions on their own before comparing their answers with a partner. Give feedback as a class, encouraging students to explain their reasoning.

D Put students into groups to discuss the question. Monitor, encouraging them to explain their reasoning and give examples. If appropriate, open the question up to class-wide discussion.

GRAMMAR

A Put students into pairs to look at the underlined sentences in the text and answer the questions. Give feedback as a class, asking a lot of CCQs to consolidate understanding (e.g. *Did Hayley go to a top college? Why not? Does Nick still live in his old town?* etc).

B–C Write the following sentence on the board – *I wish we were still friends.* Add *wish* + in another color above the sentence to illustrate the start of the structure and elicit which tense follows it (*simple past*). Complete the structure, then elicit one or two personal examples from the students. Follow the same process for the remaining structures, before giving students time to scan the comments again for more examples. Briefly give feedback to check answers, then direct students to the **Grammar Hub** (see below and TB78).

D Because sentence transformation exercises like this are fairly challenging, it's probably worth working through the first example as a class. Then, give students time to complete the remaining sentences alone before checking their answers in pairs. Give feedback as a class.

E Demonstrate the activity by completing one or two of the sentences stems with your own ideas, then put students into pairs to practice it themselves. Monitor, encouraging students to ask follow-up questions to keep their discussions going. Focus on accuracy of grammar at this point. Use the **Grammar Worksheet** on page W33 for extra practice.

SPEAKING

A Share one of your own wishes or regrets with the class based around one of the topics in the list. Then, give students time to write notes about their own ideas and experiences. Monitor, making it clear that they should only focus on experiences they are comfortable sharing with their classmates.

B Put students into pairs to discuss their wishes and regrets. Monitor, encouraging them to identify their biggest regret and why it is so important to them.

C Put students into groups to share their biggest regrets. Monitor, asking follow-up questions to keep their discussions going. Write a note about two or three of the most interesting regrets and, if students are willing to, ask them to share their experiences with the class. Add any useful emergent language to the board.

GRAMMAR HUB

7.2 *wish* and *if only*

A Complete the sentences with the correct form of the verb in parentheses. Use contractions where possible.

1. I've been dreaming about getting a new car. If only I ___had___ (*have*) enough money!
2. I sent an email to the wrong person today. I wish I ___hadn't made___ (*not make*) such a silly mistake.
3. You really should ___'ve bought___ (*buy*) that cheap laptop when you had the opportunity.
4. I wish you ___'d stop___ (*stop*) doing that – it's so annoying!
5. I love my job. If only I ___didn't have to___ (*not have to*) work weekends!
6. I wish I ___could___ (*can*) go with you tomorrow!
7. If only my grades ___had been___ (*be*) better. Then I would have gone to college, but it's too late now.
8. I wonder where Patrícia is now. I wish I ___'d asked___ (*ask*) her out all those years ago.

B Correct the mistakes in the sentences.

1. If only ~~I've~~ I'd spent more time studying when I was a student.
2. I wish I ~~didn't miss~~ hadn't missed out on that opportunity to teach at a summer camp last year.
3. I find it hard to meet people. If only ~~I'm not~~ I weren't/wasn't so painfully shy.
4. You're really hard to talk to today. I wish you ~~hadn't been~~ weren't in such a bad mood.
5. I wish I ~~would~~ could move back to where I grew up but I can't afford a house there.
6. I wish he ~~had~~ would stop thinking about himself.
7. I really wish we ~~had~~ hadn't moved here – it was a big mistake.
8. You shouldn't ~~tell~~ have told Mei Xing that you were leaving. Now she's upset.

➤ Go back to page 79.

C INFER MEANING Read the comments again and answer the questions. Use the information in the box to help you.

Inferring meaning

Writers do not always say directly what they mean. We usually have to use context and our general knowledge to infer meaning.

I chose a career in finance because I knew I could make a lot of money, but I wish I had chosen a career I enjoy more. I spend all of Sunday night in a bad mood.

Here we can infer that the writer spends Sunday night in a bad mood because he doesn't want to go to work the next day.

1 What does Hayley mean by 'the important issues'?
 a being popular
 (b) getting good grades
 c other people's opinions
2 What massive opportunity did Hayley miss out on?
 a having good friends
 (b) going to a top college
 c doing well at school
3 Why did Nick's family move?
 a His parents didn't like the old town.
 (b) His dad got a new job.
 c His mom wanted to move.
4 What happened between Christina and her sister?
 a They never got along.
 b Their parents preferred Christina.
 (c) They had an argument.
5 What didn't Kelly like about the trip?
 (a) She got food poisoning.
 b She was on her own.
 c She couldn't find her friends.

D SPEAK Work in groups. Do you think regrets can ever be beneficial? Why/Why not?

GRAMMAR
Wish and *if only*

A SPEAK Work in pairs. Read the comments again. Look at the underlined sentences and answer the questions.

1 Which sentence describes things that annoy us about other people or things? 4
2 Which sentences describe regrets about the past? 1; 2
3 Which sentences describe things we would like to be different in the present or future? 3; 5

B WORK IT OUT Complete the box with other examples from the comments.

wish* and *if only

We use *wish* + simple past to talk about how we would like the present to be different.

a *I wish we were still friends now.*

We use *wish* + past perfect to talk about things we regret in the past.

b *... but I wish I had chosen a career I enjoyed more.*

We use *wish* + object + *would* + base form to talk about something we want others to do or stop doing because it annoys us.

c *I wish she would just pick up the phone and call me.*

We can use *if only* instead of *wish* in all of these structures to sound more dramatic or emphatic.

d *If only I'd spent more time studying.*

C Go to the Grammar Hub on page 134.

D PRACTICE Rewrite the sentences using the words in bold.

1 It annoys me when people throw garbage on the street.
wish
I wish people wouldn't throw garbage on the street.
2 I regret moving to the country.
wish
I wish I hadn't moved to the country.
3 I don't want to work evenings and weekends.
If only
If only I didn't have to work evenings and weekends.
4 I forgot my passport and couldn't go on vacation.
If only
If only I hadn't forgotten my passport, I could have gone on vacation.
5 It annoys me when people are so rude online.
wish
I wish people wouldn't be / weren't so rude online.

E SPEAK Work in pairs. Complete the sentences with your own ideas. Tell your partner. Ask follow-up questions for more information.

I wish people wouldn't ... If only I'd bought ...
If I hadn't studied ... I wish I were ...

SPEAKING

A PREPARE Write notes about any wishes or regrets you have about the following areas:

career education family finances romance

B PLAN Work in pairs. Discuss your wishes and regrets from Exercise A. Which is your biggest regret?

C DISCUSS Work in groups. Explain your biggest regrets. What can you learn from them? How could you avoid making the same mistakes in the future?

LISTENING

A Read the article and answer the questions. Underline the parts of the text that gives you the answers.

1 What is the Freeconomy Community?

2 Why is Mark Boyle called 'the moneyless man'?

3 How did he pay for the farm in Ireland?

4 What system is used on the farm?

7.5 **B LISTEN FOR ORGANIZATION** Listen to an interview with someone who started their own Freeconomy Community. Put the topics in the order they are discussed.

__4__ starting networking events and workshops to share skills

__5__ holding community barbecues and street parties

__1__ starting a website to share goods and skills

__2__ finding a community site where people can meet

__3__ finding building materials and people to help

7.5 **C LISTEN FOR DETAIL** Listen again. Complete the sentences with no more than three words from the interview.

1 Callum's experience with one of his __neighbors__ inspired him to set up the Facebook group.

2 They only have a few users but everyone is pretty __active__.

3 They use an old __(abandoned) factory__ for their community building.

4 A __local restaurant__ gave them their old kitchen equipment to set up a café.

5 They run __(general) networking__ events twice a week for people to share their skills.

6 All the food in the café comes from the garden or __local farms__.

D SPEAK Work in groups. Discuss the questions.

1 How well do you know your neighbors?

2 What kind of community events are there in your area?

3 Would you like to be part of a moneyless community? Why/ Why not?

How We Live

returns for a second series

The popular documentary series *How We Live* returns this month, covering a diverse range of topics from ice fishing in Canada to surfing in Iran.

Episode one focuses on the Irish activist and writer Mark Boyle, best known for establishing the Freeconomy Community – an online network that encourages its members to share skills, tools and land for free. Boyle is commonly referred to as 'the moneyless man', a name he earned by living without money for almost two and a half years. Back in 2008, Boyle quit his job with an organic food company and set up home in a camper he got for free online. Generating electricity via a solar panel he bought for $360, Boyle spent the next few years growing his own food and volunteering on a local farm. In 2010, he published an account of his experience – *The Moneyless Man* – before returning to the monetary world in 2011.

Boyle uses proceeds from the book to purchase land for the Freeconomy Community, including the small farm in County Galway, Ireland, where he currently lives with his partner. The farm, which houses up to 30 volunteers rent free, is based around the idea of 'paying it forward', a system in which one member helps another with the understanding that they will go on to help someone else.

Episode one of How We Live *is available on August 31st.*

VOCABULARY

Three-part phrasal verbs

7.6 **A** Complete the sentences with the correct form of the phrasal verbs in the box. Use the definitions in parentheses to help you. Then listen and check.

come up with	come up against	cut down on
get around to	get along with	look up to

1 Well, obviously I __look up to__ (*respect and admire*) people like Mark Boyle. He's achieved amazing things.

2 Anyway, luckily, I __get along (really well) with__ (*have a good relationship with someone*) my neighbors and one of them is a professional decorator.

3 Anyway, it turned out he was looking for an accountant, so we __came up with__ (*think of*) a plan to help us both.

4 So, I set up the Facebook group to give people somewhere to share their skills or give away things they don't want anymore. It actually helps __cut down on__ (*reduce*) waste as well.

5 We had a lot of great ideas that we'd never __get around to__ (*to finally do something*) working on because we rarely met.

6 It's great because if you __come up against__ (*to have to deal with something difficult*) a problem, then you can usually find someone here to help.

B Go to the Vocabulary Hub on page 146.

LISTENING

A Give students time to answer the questions alone. See underlined answers in the text.

7.5 **B–D** Work through the exercises, allowing time for peer correction as necessary.

VOCABULARY

7.6 **A–B** Work through the first sentence as a class, then give students time to complete the others alone. Give feedback as a class. Now, direct students to the **Vocabulary Hub** (see TB121).

AUDIO SCRIPT

7.5

Listening, Exercise B
I = Interviewer C = Callum

I: Joining us next is activist and founder of the Free Life Project, Callum Castling. Callum, welcome to the show.
C: Thanks for inviting me.
I: So Callum, for some years now, you've been involved in a movement to set up a moneyless society.
C: That's correct.
I: So, how did you get started? What inspired you?
C: Well, obviously I look up to people like Mark Boyle. He's achieved amazing things. But it sort of all started in my son's bedroom.
I: Really?
C: Yeah, so my wife was pregnant with our first son and I needed to redecorate our spare bedroom. The thing is, I'm an accountant. I'm great with numbers, but not so good with anything practical. Anyway, luckily, I get along really well with my neighbors and one of them is a professional decorator. Anyway, it turned out he was looking for an accountant, so we came up with a plan to help us both. I started to do his accounts and he did some painting and decorating around the house. We've been friends ever since. (Ex C Q1)
I: So, is that what inspired your Facebook group?
C: Yeah, that's right. I just thought there must be a lot of people in the community that could help each other out. (Ex B) So, I set up the Facebook group to give people somewhere to share their skills or give away things they don't want anymore. It actually helps cut down on waste as well.
I: Right, so what kind of things do people get rid of?
C: Anything, really. Old bikes … couches … one guy even gave away his ex-girlfriend's stuff she had left at his house!
I: Really? So, has the group been popular?
(Ex C Q2) **C:** Well, yes and no. We only have about a thousand followers, but they are all pretty active.
I: So, why did you decide to move things offline?
C: Well, social media is great, but it can feel pretty impersonal at times. We had a lot of great ideas that we'd never get around to working on because we rarely met. (Ex B; Ex C Q3) Basically, we felt like a community with no home. So we scouted around the city, looking for a space to use and found an old abandoned factory. It was great but needed a lot of work.
I: How did you get the money to renovate it?
C: Well, the factory was owned by the council and once we explained what we were trying to do, they offered to let us use it until they were able to sell the land. Then we managed to renovate it for free.
I: For free?
(Ex B) **C:** Yep. We got all of the materials via our Facebook group. People volunteered their time and skills. It was amazingly easy really to get a lot of volunteer workers. We got building materials, plants, gardening equipment. (Ex C Q4) We even managed to get all of our tables and chairs and kitchen equipment from a local restaurant that was closing down. I couldn't believe it. People were just so generous.
I: And what do you do with the space?
(Ex B; Ex C Q5) **C:** It's become our community center, really. Twice a week, we have a general networking event. We provide drinks and snacks and anyone who is interested in sharing their skills or needs to find someone with a particular skill can come along. It's great because if you come up against a problem, then you can usually find someone here to help. People have started car-sharing systems, food banks to help the poor – all sorts of things really. Or you can just start something you're interested in – a language exchange, clubs, societies. You name it, people are starting it!
I: Sounds amazing!
C: People love it. Let's face it, it's more comfortable meeting someone face-to-face than just talking briefly on the phone or on a website. If something is really popular, many people are happy to run a workshop to teach people. This can be anything from basic bike maintenance to teaching people to find food in the countryside.
I: What else have you done?
C: We used the free kitchen equipment to set up a local café. And we've used the outdoor space for a kitchen garden, (Ex C Q6) so everything in the café comes from local farms or our own garden.
I: I must come for lunch sometime!
C: You should! The food is actually pretty good.
I: So, do you do any other interesting things?
C: One thing we always organize is regular parties. People like to come together to socialize with the people near them. (Ex B) We have two or three big street parties every year. You know, like a barbecue using the produce from the garden.
I: Well, it sounds like you're restoring a good old-fashioned sense of community.
C: I think we are. People move around so much these days, they rarely get to know their neighbors. Groups like ours bring people together and show them what can be achieved when they start to help each other out.
I: Thank you for coming in today, Callum. Hopefully, some of our listeners will take inspiration from your group and start their own community projects.

C–D If students completed the Vocabulary Hub exercises for homework, it might be worth briefly reviewing the meaning of the phrasal verbs in the box by eliciting example sentences for each. Otherwise, ask students to complete the questions alone before giving feedback as a class. Then, put students back into their pairs to discuss the questions. Monitor, encouraging students to ask follow-up questions to keep their discussions going. Use the **Vocabulary Worksheet** on page W34 for extra practice.

PRONUNCIATION

7.7 **A** Write the following sentence on the board, setting the phrasal verb in a different color – *They're looking at all options.* Elicit what part of speech *looking at* is (*a phrasal verb*) and which part is stressed (*looking*), circling the main stress to mirror the exercise. Tell students that some phrasal verbs actually have two stresses – a primary (or main) stress and a secondary stress. Explain that they will now focus on stress in three-part phrasal verbs and play the audio for them to complete the exercise. Give them time to check in pairs before giving feedback as a class. At this point, you could show students how this kind of stress is shown in a dictionary, by adding the phonemes for one of the phrasal verbs to the board and adding stress markers above and below the word.

7.8 **B** Play the audio for students to choose the correctly stressed sentences, then give them time to check their answers with a partner. Give feedback as a class, then practice the correct pronunciation of each sentence with the class, encouraging students to focus on their use of stress. To extend this section, elicit other multi-part phrasal verbs and build up a list on the board. Then, put students into pairs to write sentences with five of the phrasal verbs and practice reading them aloud.

VOCABULARY

Write the following sentence on the board – *My brother has a two-hour commute* – and ask if students can remember what part of speech *two-hour* is (*a compound adjective*). Now, explain that we can also form compound nouns in a similar way and give a few examples that students might be familiar with (e.g. *parking lot, team leader*, etc). Elicit more examples and add them to the board. Then, ask students to join the sentences alone, before checking their answers with a partner. Give feedback as a class, clarifying the meaning of any of the compound nouns that students are familiar with. If you have time, take the opportunity to do some vocabulary building by eliciting other compound nouns that take any of the words in bold from the exercise (e.g. *street market/ sweeper/food*, etc). Use the **Vocabulary Worksheet** on page W35 for extra practice.

SPEAKING HUB

A Tell students about one or two skills you have that you think might be useful to other people (e.g. *photography, gardening, sewing*, etc). Then, give them time to make a list of their own skills. Monitor, helping with new vocabulary as necessary.

B–C Tell students that they are going to come up with a plan for a new community project. Next, put them into groups to share the skills they thought of in Exercise A. Explain that the groups should choose one or more of these skills to combine into a single community project and encourage them to discuss the bullet points one by one. Remind them that they will need to present their ideas to the class so they should keep notes about what they discuss. With weaker classes, allow time for students to practice their presentations. Next, ask each group to present their project allowing time for follow-up questions from the class. Close this activity with a class vote on the most interesting community project.

METHODOLOGY HUB by Adrian Underhill

Primary and secondary stress

Longer words, especially when spoken in isolation, may have more than one stressed syllable (e.g. *popularity*), in which case one of the stresses is given more force than the other. The strongest is referred to as primary stress and the less strong as the secondary stress.

Both primary and secondary stress are in contrast to unstress. Secondary stress can be realized acoustically by duration and loudness and through clearer articulation. It merely has less energy than its neighboring primary stress. However, the pitch change quality of stress tends to occur as an attribute of primary stress only.

The following words are normally considered to have two stresses, a primary and secondary stress: *ˌinforˈmation, ˌcontroˈversial, ˌmotiˈvation.*

1. Try saying these words without any stressed syllable at all. What do you have to do in order to do that?
2. Now try to stress every syllable. Notice how you do this.
3. This time, put only one stress in each word. Put that stress on each syllable in turn, making sure you keep the other syllables unstressed. How does the word sound with only one stress?
4. Now stress the correct syllables, but *reverse your placement of primary and secondary stress*. Notice how this sounds. And now put the two stresses in the correct place.

TEACHING IDEA by David Seymour and Maria Popova

Compound nouns

Use this activity to review the compound nouns covered in this lesson.

Work in two teams and play tic-tac-toe. Take turns choosing a square. To win it you have to make a compound noun with the word in the square, e.g. *food – bank.*

food	volunteer	language
car	street	community
project	skill	local

street party – *We organized a street party to raise money for the area.*

project manager – *I think we need to find a new project manager!*

C Complete the questions with the correct form of the phrasal verbs in the box.

come up against	get along with	get around to
keep up with	look up to	run out of

1 What things do you regularly want to do but never __get around to__ doing?
2 Do you think it's important to __get along with__ your neighbors?
3 Do you have a hero that you __look up to__?
4 How do you __keep up with__ local news and community events?
5 If you __ran out of__ gas when driving, what would you do?
6 If you __come up against__ a difficult situation, who do you turn to for help?

D SPEAK Work in pairs. Discuss the questions in Exercise C.

PRONUNCIATION
Two-stress phrasal verbs

7.7 **A** Listen to the sentences. Which parts of the phrasal verbs are stressed? Circle the main stress. Underline the secondary stress.

1 We need to **come up with** a new way to use the space.
2 People create so much waste trying to **keep up with** the latest trends.
3 We **came up against** many challenges during the project.

7.8 **B** Listen to each sentence said in two different ways. Choose the sentence that is said with the correct stress on the phrasal verb (a or b).

1 Many old people don't have anyone to **take care of** them. (a) / b
2 We **teamed up with** the local government and worked on it together. a / (b)
3 It's a great way to **catch up with** friends. (a) / b

VOCABULARY
Compound nouns

Compound nouns

A compound noun is a single noun formed from two or more words. The most common type is formed by joining two nouns. For example, *community center, project leader, skill shortage*, etc.

Match the numbers (1–5) to the letters (a–e) to form compound nouns.

1 We need more **volunteer** … c
2 I want to improve my Spanish, so I've joined a **language** … a
3 We set up a **car-sharing** … e
4 We have opened a **food** … b
5 Next week we have organized a **street** … d

a **exchange** group.
b **bank** to distribute food to the poor.
c **workers** to help run the youth club.
d **party** in our neighborhood.
e **system** to help reduce pollution and congestion.

SPEAKING HUB

A PREPARE Create a list of skills you could use to help other people. For example, languages, accountancy, design, technology, etc.

B PLAN Work in groups. Discuss your individual skills and decide on a community project you could start together. Write notes about:

- who it will help
- how you will set it up and advertise it
- where it will be based
- what activities you will offer to engage people

C PRESENT Present your project to the class, explaining how it would help the community. Answer their follow-up questions.

Talk about wishes and regrets
Design and present a community project

Café Hub

7.3 A shared vision

A– *you know* S– talking on the telephone

An innovative solution

COMPREHENSION

A **Rank the following issues according to how big of a problem they are in your country.**

___ house prices ___ street crime
___ cost of living ___ corruption
___ job opportunities ___ access to health care

B **Work in pairs. Compare your lists from Exercise A.**

Glossary

freehold (n) the legal right to own a building or piece of land for an unlimited period of time

leasehold (n) the legal right to use a building or piece of land for a limited time (as agreed upon in a property contract)

C **Watch a news report about a housing project in London and answer the questions.**

1 How did the families address the issue of rising house prices?

2 Why is this a cheaper option for them?

3 What other benefits do the residents gain?

D **Watch the report again. Are these sentences true (T) or false (F)? Correct the false sentences.**

1 The project was part of a housing scheme offered by the local council. The families came up with the idea themselves. T / (F)

2 The houses have turned out to be approximately a fifth cheaper this way. (T) / F

3 The expert believes that properties which share facilities are a better use of land. (T) / F

4 Cressida says she likes how easy it is to socialize with other residents. (T) / F

5 Projects like this could help address housing issues because there is a lot of unused land in the capital. T / (F)
He says, 'finding suitable plots of land for sale in London is rare'.

E **Work in groups. Do you think community housing projects like this would be effective in your area? Why/Why not?**

AUTHENTIC ENGLISH

A **Work in pairs. Read the extract from the video. Why do you think the speaker says *you know*?**

So you can actually put what are, **you know**, fairly generous houses on quite a small plot of land.

B **Read the information in the box and check your answers to Exercise A.**

you know

In informal spoken English, we use *you know* for three main reasons:

a To show that what you are referring to is known or understood by the listener.
*Guess who I saw the other day? Juan! **You know**, the guy who used to work on the IT team.*

b To give yourself time to think about what to say next.
*Well, maybe it's time to, **you know**, move on with your life.*

c To emphasize what you're saying.
*It's just so different now, **you know**?*

C **Match the sentences (1–3) with the uses in the box (a–c).**

1 I was wondering if you'd like to, you know, go and see a movie or something. b

2 It's not easy being the only 50-year-old here, you know. c

3 What's the name of that movie – you know, the one with Emily Blunt in it? a

D **Work in pairs. Take turns finishing the sentences with your own ideas.**

1 What's the name of that guy in our class? You know, …

2 You know, you really should …

3 We're just going to go shopping and, you know, …

Living together

A Work in pairs. Discuss the questions.

1 Who is the first person you tell when you have big news? Why?
2 Would you ever tell someone something important over the phone or on Skype? Why/Why not?

B Watch the video and answer the questions.

1 Why do you think Amanda's mom mentions Mabel Sanderson at the beginning of the conversation?
2 Why doesn't Amanda's mom like the idea of a shared housing project?
3 What do you think Amanda is thinking when she says, 'you might just be right'?

SPEAKING SKILL

A Complete the box using the phrases below. Then watch the video again to check your answers.

Got to go. I'd better be going … I need to go
Is it a good time? is that you? I didn't catch that.
that brings me to what I was calling about.
What are you up to? What was that Yes, it's me
You're breaking up.

Talking on the telephone

Phone conversations generally follow a set routine. At the beginning of the conversation, we usually …

- confirm we're talking to the right person:
  Mom: Oh, Mandy, [1] *is that you?*
  Amanda: [2] *Yes, it's me*, Mom.
- find out what the person is doing:
  Amanda: [3] *What are you up to?*
- ask if they are free to talk:
  Amanda: [4] *Is it a good time?*

After exchanging greetings, we usually give a reason for calling:
Amanda: Actually, [5] *that brings me to what I was calling about.*

Having discussed the reason for calling, we try to bring the conversation to an end:
Amanda: [6] *I'd better be going …*
Amanda: So, [7] *I need to go*, Mom …
Amanda: [8] *Got to go.*

We also might need to let the other person know that we didn't hear what they said:
Mom: [9] *I didn't catch that.*
Mom: [10] *What was that*, darling?
Amanda: [11] *You're breaking up.*

B Work in pairs. You are going to role-play a telephone conversation.

Student A – Call your partner to discuss one of the topics from the list below.

Student B – Listen to your partner. Make helpful suggestions before trying to bring the conversation to an end.

Then, swap roles.

- discuss a problem at work
- ask for a restaurant recommendation
- try to sell a new product
- ask to borrow some money

SPEAKING HUB

A PREPARE Work in pairs. Brainstorm the advantages and disadvantages of shared housing.

B PLAN Role-play a telephone conversation. Student A – Plan how to convince your partner not to move into a shared housing project. Student B – Plan how to convince your partner that moving into a shared housing project is a good idea.

C SPEAK Role-play the telephone call.

A: *Yes, but if a lot of people are using the same facilities, they will break down sooner, so you might not be saving as much money as you think.*
B: *But houses are so expensive that we have to save money somehow.*

Give your opinion on a social initiative

➤ Turn to page 160 to learn how to write a formal letter of complaint.

7.3 A shared vision

An innovative solution

LEAD-IN

As a class, discuss the advantages and disadvantages of living alone. Then, put students into groups to discuss whether they would like to live alone or not. Bring the class back together to share their ideas.

COMPREHENSION

A–B Give students time to rank the items alone, before comparing their lists with a partner.

C ▶ Play the report for students to answer the questions. Give feedback as a class.

1 *They bought a plot of land together and built their own homes.*

2 *Because they share facilities (e.g. two washing machines between six properties), their houses can be slightly smaller than average.*

3 *The residents feel like they've created a community.*

D ▶ Give students time to read the sentences carefully, before playing the report again. Give feedback as a class.

E Put students into groups to discuss the question.

AUTHENTIC ENGLISH

A–B Put students into pairs to discuss the extract, then give them time to check their answers by reading the skills box.

The speaker is giving themselves time to think.

C Ask students to complete the exercise alone, before checking their answers with a partner. Then, give feedback as a class.

D Put students into pairs to practice using *you know*.

Living together

LEAD-IN

Write three pieces of news about yourself on the board – two false and one true. Try to make these interesting but believable to keep students engaged (e.g. *I'm going to have another baby; I'm quitting teaching*; etc). Tell students that they have to guess which is true by asking you a lot of questions.

A Put students into pairs to discuss the questions.

B ▶ Tell students they are now going to watch the next episode of the Café Hub series. Play the video for them to answer the questions, then give feedback as a class. You can find the **video script** for *Living together* on the Teacher's Resource Center.

1 *Probably because she wants Amanda to settle down and have children so she can have grandchildren like Mabel does.*

2 *She thinks that it sounds like she will be living like a student at her age.*

3 *Amanda is thinking that Harry might be the man for her.*

SPEAKING SKILL

A ▶ Give students time to complete the box alone, before playing the video again for them to check their answers.

B Put students into role play conversations.

SPEAKING HUB

A–C Put students into pairs to make lists. Then, give them time to plan what to say, before performing their role plays to the class.

▶ VIDEO SCRIPT

An innovative solution

C = Cressida P= Presenter L = Lily I = Interviewee

C: So, this is me – number four.

P: Cressida finally owns her dream home.

C: House prices in London are so crazy that I had to think of a different way of doing it.

Ex D Q1 **P:** And that's exactly what she did. She joined forces with five other families and together they came up with a more affordable solution. And here it is. Tucked away behind a row of Victorian houses on
Ex C Q1 this street in Stoke Newington. So the six families came together to buy this plot of land. They then commissioned an architect to design their homes.
Ex C Q2 While that might sound costly, it was actually cheaper than them buying individually. And that's mainly because the residents share facilities.

C: Certainly I couldn't have afforded to buy a house this size in this area. We've got two washing machines
Ex D Q2 rather than six. These have probably ended up being about 20% cheaper.

Ex D Q3 **I:** Because you're sharing facilities, the houses can be slightly smaller, and so it's just better land use. So you can actually put what are, you know, fairly generous houses on quite a small plot of land. So in that way the … the … the economics of it clearly work.

P: The families, who were all friends beforehand, formed a company which owns the freehold and common parts of the development. The individuals own the leaseholds to their property.

C: So yeah, so that's going to be where we grow the vegetables because that's the sunny quarter.

Ex C Q3 **P:** For Cressida and her neighbor Lily, there's more to this than just pure economics. They've created a community.

L: I've been here for three days and I've really enjoyed, you know, meeting a lot of people and sitting out here and then people come out and …

Ex D Q4 **C:** Cause you can do it if you're … if you want company you just park yourself at the table with a cup of tea and someone comes out.

L: … and then somebody else comes.

Ex D Q5 **P:** While finding suitable plots of land for sale in London is rare, this model could address some of the capital's housing issues.

I: People are constantly looking of ways of living, of ways of affording to live. You know, I mean that's the … that's the big pressure really, and I think if we can start to build things that do make better use of the land, and there is an economy of scale …

P: The project took almost five years to complete, but for the families living here, it was well worth the wait. Emilia Papadopoulos, BBC London News.

7 Writing

Write a formal letter of complaint

W hedging

A Work in pairs. Which of the following are issues in your neighborhood?

- graffiti
- trash
- crime
- noise pollution
- air pollution
- poor transportation systems
- lack of public spaces
- abandoned buildings

B Read the letter of complaint. What problem from Exercise A are mentioned? abandoned buildings; noise pollution

Dear Sir/Madam,

Ex B [1]I am writing to you with regard to the proposal to knock down the old clothing factory and construct a new library in our area. While I agree that our neighborhood would benefit enormously from such a wonderful facility, I'm afraid I do not agree with the proposal for a number of reasons.

[2]First, the clothing factory is a historical building and something we should be looking to preserve and restore, not demolish. Instead of demolishing the factory, I feel that proposals should look at converting it into the library instead. Simply destroying such a landmark and starting again is not something I expect many residents will find acceptable. Second, the current suggestion will create unacceptable levels of noise and take significantly longer than converting the factory. This is not something I feel residents will put up with and I have no option but to organize a campaign group against this. Ex B

[3]I feel that local residents should be consulted on this project and I would appreciate an open discussion on these plans. I look forward to hearing from you on this matter.

Kind regards,

John Hadland

C Match the paragraphs (1–3) to their function (a–c).

a describing the issues 2

b explaining your reason for writing 1

c requesting action 3

D Rewrite the sentences using the words in parentheses. Use the information in the box and the letter to help you.

Hedging

Hedges are used to soften an opinion, rather than simply saying 'I don't agree.' Instead of directly disagreeing, which might be seen as being rude, people usually write something such as *I'm sorry but I don't agree*. Hedging like this makes your opinion or suggestion less direct and less likely to cause offense.

1 I know we need a new road but I don't agree with the proposal. (While / afraid) While I agree we need a new road, I'm afraid I don't agree with the proposal

2 It is not acceptable to lose a local park. (sorry) I'm sorry, but it is not acceptable to lose a local park.

3 Most people won't be happy with the plan. (expect) I expect most people won't be happy with the plan.

4 I want your assistance on this matter. (appreciate) I would appreciate your assistance on this matter.

WRITING

A PREPARE You are going to write a letter of complaint about a proposal to build a new road through your local park. Write notes about potential issues with this proposal and possible alternatives.

B PLAN Organize your notes into a formal letter structure.

C WRITE Write your letter of complaint. Use your plan to help you.

D EDIT Work in pairs. Edit your partner's letter. Check:

- spelling and punctuation
- strength of analysis and recommendations
- use of hedging language

Refer students to this letter writing task.

Refer students to this checklist when editing their partner's work.

160 WRITING

LEAD-IN

Elicit one or two social issues (e.g. *graffiti*, *trash*, etc), then put students into groups to brainstorm more. Bring the class back together to share their ideas, adding useful vocabulary to the board.

WRITING

A Put students into pairs to discuss the issues. Bring the class back together to share the main points of their discussions.

B–C Give students time to quickly scan the letter to see if any of the issues they discussed are covered. Take this opportunity to clarify words or passages in the letter that students don't understand. Then, ask students to read the letter again to identify paragraph functions. Give them time to check their answers in pairs before giving feedback as a class.

D Read through the skills box as a class, eliciting situations in which it might be more polite to hedge. Then, give students time to rewrite the sentences, using expressions in the letter to help them. Allow time for peer correction before giving feedback as a class.

WRITING TASK

A Read the scenario as a class and elicit one or two potential issues with the proposal. Then, give students time to write notes alone.

B Ask students to organize their notes into a formal letter structure, using the model to help them. Monitor, encouraging them to focus on one or two ideas that they can expand upon.

C Tell students to write their letters. Monitor, helping with grammar and vocabulary as necessary. Remind them to use hedging language to soften their complaints but to remain clear and direct.

D Put students into pairs to edit each other's letters. Encourage students to give each other positive feedback. Students can then rewrite their letters either in class or for homework.

Unit 7 Review

VOCABULARY

A Choose the correct verbs to complete the sentences.

1 They plan to ***extend*** / ***construct*** the vacation resort by two square kilometers.
2 The local council are going to ***convert*** / ***relocate*** the hospital to a new site on the edge of town.
3 Almost all of the old factories in the city center have been ***restored*** / ***converted*** into apartments.
4 The old power station is going to be ***demolished*** / ***constructed*** to make way for a new shopping mall.
5 There are some beautiful old buildings in the city, but it would be expensive to ***restore*** / ***transform*** them.
6 After spending millions of dollars, the old docks have been ***transformed*** / ***extended*** into a vibrant area.
7 Plans to ***construct*** / ***relocate*** a new hospital have been put on hold due to financial constraints.

B Work in pairs. Discuss what changes you think should be made to your neighborhood and why.

C Match the numbers (1–8) with the letters (a–h) to form full sentences.

1 The city needs to come … d
2 New recycling bins have been installed in order to cut … h
3 The local government has teamed … a
4 While building the new road, the government ran … e
5 Facilities such as schools and hospitals can't keep … f
6 The country has spent a lot of money trying to catch … b
7 It's important to take care … c
8 I don't really get along … g

a up with local businesses to renovate the area.
b up with development in neighboring countries.
c of less fortunate people in society.
d up with a solution to the overcrowding.
e out of funding.
f up with the population growth in the area.
g with many of my neighbors.
h down on waste.

D Complete the compound nouns with the nouns in the box.

car food language street volunteer

1 A __street__ party was organized to celebrate the royal wedding.
2 Since the introduction of a __car__-sharing system, traffic levels have reduced almost by half.
3 For some people, access to a __food__ bank is vital in order to feed their families.
4 I've really improved my level of English since I joined a __language__ exchange.
5 After the floods, hundreds of __volunteer__ workers helped to clear up the area.

GRAMMAR

A Complete the first conditional sentences with the correct form of the verbs in the box.

call do finish reach sit work

1 If the city continues to grow, the population __will reach__ ten million inhabitants soon.
2 If you get lost, __call__ me.
3 What __will you do__ if it rains?
4 If they meet the deadline, the new stadium __will be finished__ by the start of the season.
5 If you arrive late, we __will be sitting__ on the beach.
6 You're not going to get promoted if you __don't work__ harder.

B Choose the correct options to complete the sentences.

1 I wish you ***'d hurried up*** / ***'d hurry up***. We're going to be late.
2 If only we ***left*** / ***'d left*** earlier! I was so annoyed that we missed the beginning of the concert.
3 There's so much more I want to see here in Rome. If only we ***'d had*** / ***had*** more time.
4 I wish you ***could have come*** / ***could come***. It was so much fun.
5 I wish it ***hadn't rained*** / ***wasn't raining***. I'm so wet!
6 I wish my roommate ***would do*** / ***would have done*** the dishes more often. He never does it!
7 I think we're lost. If only I ***listened*** / ***'d listened*** to the directions more carefully.
8 If only I ***'d had*** / ***had*** more money. I definitely won't be going on vacation this year.

C What might you say in these situations? Write sentences with unreal conditional structures.

1 You would like to get a taxi but you have no reception on your phone.
If I had reception on my phone, I would get a taxi.
2 The map on your phone isn't working so you got lost.
If the map on my phone was working, I/we wouldn't be / have gotten lost.
3 You would like to play soccer but your foot hurts.
If my foot didn't hurt, I would play soccer.
4 You should have started the essay sooner. You missed the deadline.
If I had started my essay sooner, I wouldn't have missed the deadline.
5 I stayed out in the sun too long yesterday and got sunburned.
If I hadn't stayed out in the sun for so long yesterday, I wouldn't have gotten sunburned.
6 Look at the weather in Lisbon this week! It's much better than last week when we were there.
If we had/we'd gone on vacation this week, we would have had much better weather.

D Work in pairs. Compare your ideas from Exercise C.

8 MYSTERY

The true mystery of the world is the visible, not the invisible.

Oscar Wilde

An ancient sequoia forest in Mendocino County, California.

OBJECTIVES

- speculate about past events
- summarize a cultural story
- write and perform a short scene
- speculate about the causes and consequences of a crime
- discuss how to test an idea
- write a complex essay

Work with a partner. Discuss the questions.

1 Read the quote. What do you think Wilde means? Do you agree with him? Why/Why not?

2 What crime novels or TV shows do you enjoy watching? Tell your partner about one of them.

3 What crimes are the biggest problem in your society? What do you think can be done to deal with them?

MYSTERY 85

Mystery (n) something that you are not able to understand, explain or get information about Collocations and idioms: *unexplained/unsolved* mystery, *solve a* mystery, *be cloaked/ shrouded in* mystery (*to be difficult to find out about or know the truth about*)

Wilde is suggesting that people frequently wonder about things they cannot see but accept the things around them without thinking too deeply about them. The real mysteries of life are how these things came to be.

Oscar Wilde (1854–1900) was an Irish author, playwright and poet. Some of his famous works include *The Importance of Being Earnest* and the novel *The Picture of Dorian Grey*, which this quote is taken from. Wilde was a very popular writer in his time and is remembered for his wit.

OBJECTIVES

Read the unit objectives to the class.

UNIT OPENER QUESTIONS

1 Read the quote as a class and put students into pairs to discuss it. Monitor, helping with new or unfamiliar vocabulary as necessary. Bring the class back together to share their ideas, adding any useful emergent language to the board. You could also take this opportunity to elicit any collocations with *mystery* that students know (e.g. *solve a mystery*, *an unexplained mystery*, etc) and add these in example sentences to the board.

2 If you enjoy crime novels or TV shows, briefly talk about your favorites. Then, put students into pairs to discuss their own favorites. Monitor, writing a note about any useful emergent language. Bring the class back together, nominating one or two students to talk about their favorites. Add any useful emergent vocabulary to the board.

3 Elicit examples of types of crime (e.g. *murder*, *theft*, *fraud*, etc) and build up a list on the board. Then, put students into groups to discuss the questions. Monitor, encouraging students to justify their answers with evidence and examples. Bring the class back together, encouraging students to question or comment of each other's ideas.

WORKSHEETS

Lesson 8.1 Myths and legends

Grammar: Past modals of deduction (W36)

Vocabulary: Word families (W37)

Lesson 8.2 Who did it?

Vocabulary: Easily confused verbs (W38)

Grammar: Order of adjectives (W39)

Vocabulary: Crime (W40)

- Speculate about past events
- Summarize a cultural story

S – decoding: similes and metaphors
V – word families
G – past modals of deduction
P – thought groups

READING

A Do you believe that ghosts, aliens or monsters exist? How certain are you on a scale of 1–5 (1 = I'm sure they don't exist, 5 = I'm sure they do exist)? Write notes.

B SPEAK Work in groups. Compare your answers from Exercise A. Explain your ideas, giving examples where appropriate.

HOW DO YOU EXPLAIN THAT?

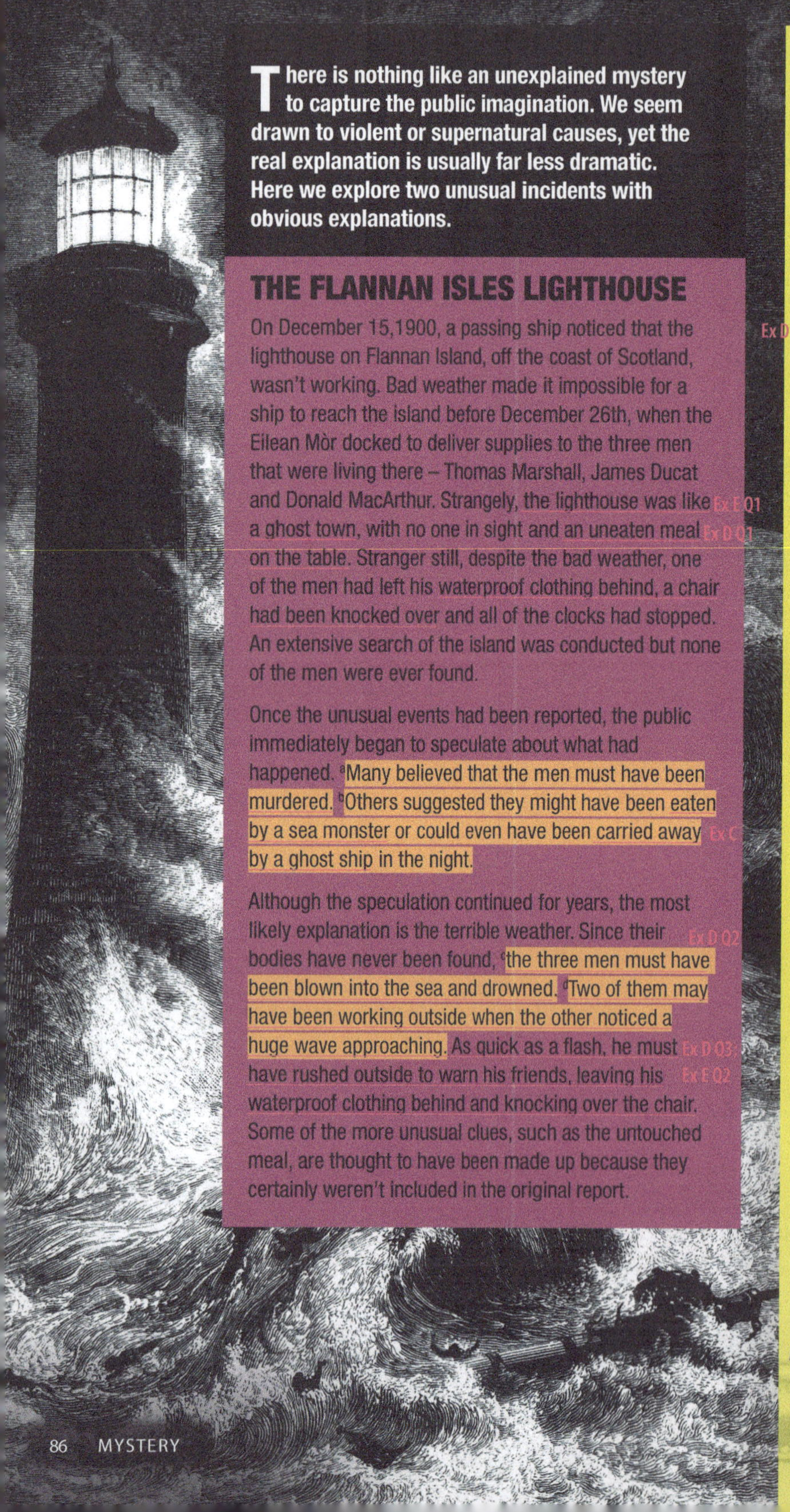

There is nothing like an unexplained mystery to capture the public imagination. We seem drawn to violent or supernatural causes, yet the real explanation is usually far less dramatic. Here we explore two unusual incidents with obvious explanations.

THE FLANNAN ISLES LIGHTHOUSE

On December 15,1900, a passing ship noticed that the lighthouse on Flannan Island, off the coast of Scotland, wasn't working. Bad weather made it impossible for a ship to reach the island before December 26th, when the Eilean Mòr docked to deliver supplies to the three men that were living there – Thomas Marshall, James Ducat and Donald MacArthur. Strangely, the lighthouse was like a ghost town, with no one in sight and an uneaten meal on the table. Stranger still, despite the bad weather, one of the men had left his waterproof clothing behind, a chair had been knocked over and all of the clocks had stopped. An extensive search of the island was conducted but none of the men were ever found.

Once the unusual events had been reported, the public immediately began to speculate about what had happened. Many believed that the men must have been murdered. Others suggested they might have been eaten by a sea monster or could even have been carried away by a ghost ship in the night.

Although the speculation continued for years, the most likely explanation is the terrible weather. Since their bodies have never been found, the three men must have been blown into the sea and drowned. Two of them may have been working outside when the other noticed a huge wave approaching. As quick as a flash, he must have rushed outside to warn his friends, leaving his waterproof clothing behind and knocking over the chair. Some of the more unusual clues, such as the untouched meal, are thought to have been made up because they certainly weren't included in the original report.

THE DYATLOV PASS INCIDENT

On February 2, 1959, nine hikers set out to climb Kholat Syakhl ('Mountain of the Dead') in Russia but never returned. Three weeks later, a search party found the group's badly damaged tent abandoned and half covered in snow. Footprints left by people who were either barefoot or wearing little on their feet led rescuers to the edge of a forest where they found five bodies, each with missing or ripped clothing. Although the hikers had sustained few external injuries, their skin had turned a strange shade of orange and investigators found high levels of radiation on their clothing. The other four bodies were found on May 4th, almost 100 meters away. Although better dressed than the first group, they had major injuries, including broken ribs and a fractured skull. Rescuers must have turned white as a sheet when they discovered that one of the female hikers was missing her tongue.

Theories of what had happened soon began to circulate. Some thought the group might have been murdered by the indigenous Mansi people. Others suggested they had been attacked by wild animals or even a yeti. However, the hikers can't have been murdered or attacked by animals because there were no signs of a fight. It is far more likely that the destruction of the tent and the second group's physical injuries were caused by an avalanche, while the missing tongue was probably eaten by a wild animal. The first group's lack of clothing can be explained by something called 'paradoxical undressing' – a phenomenon in which people in the final stages of hypothermia start to feel incredibly hot and take off their clothes in an attempt to cool down. Their orange skin and the radiation levels on their clothing are thought to have been caused by overexposure to the sun.

Glossary

avalanche (n) a large amount of snow and ice that suddenly falls down a mountain

8.1 Myths and legends

LEAD-IN

Show students a map of the area in the North Atlantic Ocean known as the 'Bermuda Triangle' (generally described as between the following three points – the coast of Florida, Bermuda and Puerto Rico). Explain that over the past hundred years, many planes and ships have disappeared in this area and ask students if they know what the area is generally called (*the Bermuda Triangle*). Next, put students into groups to speculate about what happened to the planes and ships that went missing in the area. Monitor, focusing on fluency of ideas, rather than the accuracy of their grammar (they will study modals of deduction later in this unit). Bring the class back together, nominating each group to share the best explanation they came up with. Add any useful emergent language to the board.

READING

A Use pictures to elicit the words *ghost*, *monster* and *alien*, adding them to the board. Elicit further examples of famous monsters (e.g. *the Yeti*, *Loch Ness monster*, etc) and any other well-known related terms (e.g. *Roswell*, *UFO*, etc) to consolidate understanding. Tell students that these are all examples of the *supernatural*, adding this word to the board. Next, give students time to write notes about the extent to which they believe in the supernatural. Monitor, helping with new vocabulary as necessary.

B Put students into groups to discuss their ideas. Monitor, encouraging students to justify their answers with evidence and examples. Bring the class back together to share their ideas. Stimulate class-wide discussion by encouraging students to question and comment on each other's ideas. Add any useful emergent language to the board.

C Give students a minute to scan the article, and identify the original explanations for the two mysteries. Ask students to briefly check their answers in pairs before giving feedback as a class.

The Flannan Isles Lighthouse – murder, a sea monster, a ghost ship; The Dyatlov Pass Incident – wild animals, a yeti

D Give students time to complete the exercise alone, before checking their answers with a partner. Give feedback as a class.

1 *An uneaten meal, waterproof clothing and a chair that had been knocked over.*

2 *They were swept out to sea during the storm and drowned.*

3 *One of the men probably knocked it over as he rushed to help his friends outside.*

4 *The first group was found several hundred meters away from their camp, at the edge of a forest. The second group was found nearly a hundred meters farther into the forest.*

5 *The first group had few external injuries; the second had several broken ribs, a fractured skull; one was missing a tongue.*

6 *It was eaten by a wild animal.*

E Write the following sentence on the board, setting the simile in a different color – *Tom may look small, but he's as brave as a lion.* Ask students whether this means Tom is actually a lion or is just a comparison (*just a comparison*). Tell students that comparisons like this that use *as* are called similes. Then, explain we can also use *like* before adding the following sentence to the board, setting the simile in a different color – *The show was so boring – it was like watching paint dry!* Again, consolidate understanding by asking CCQs (e.g. *Were they actually watching paint dry?*). Next, tell students that another creative way to make a comparison is a metaphor. Explain that this is a way to describe something as if it were something else, but doesn't use *as* or *like*. Then, add the following example to the board – *The snow was a white blanket.* Check understanding by asking CCQs (e.g. *Was the snow actually a blanket?*). Next, give students time to read the text again and answer the questions, encouraging them to underline the similes or metaphors that give them the answers. Then, put them into pairs to compare their answers before giving feedback as a class. Encourage students to tell you which similes or metaphors gave them the answers.

F Put students into groups to discuss the question. Monitor and help with any new vocabulary. In feedback, encourage students to share and expand on each other's ideas.

GRAMMAR HUB

8.1 Past modals of deduction

- We use *must have* + past participle to say that we are almost sure that something happened or was true.

  She's pale and her hands are shaking – she must have had a substantial shock. (= I'm sure she had a shock.)

  Being alone on a mountain all night must have been terrifying! (= I'm sure it was terrifying.)
- We use *can't have* + past participle to say that we are almost sure something didn't happen or wasn't true.

  It can't have been easy living in such an isolated village. (= I'm sure it wasn't easy.)
- We use *may/might/could have* + past participle to say that we think it's possible that something happened or was true.

  Héctor isn't here yet – he may/might/could have gotten stuck in traffic. (= It's possible he got stuck in traffic.)
- We use *may/might* + *not* + *have* + past participle to say that we think it's possible that something hasn't happened but we are not certain.

  I'll call Agnes because she may/might not have heard the news yet. (= It's possible she hasn't heard the news yet.)

Be careful!

- *Could have* means that something possibly happened in the past, but *couldn't have* means we are certain that something did not happen.

  You could have left your phone at the office. (= It is possible.)

  You couldn't have left your phone at the office, because you just called me. (= It's impossible.)

8.1 Myths and legends

GRAMMAR

A Draw students' attention to the highlighted sentences in the text, then put students into pairs to analyze them. Combine pairs to compare their answers, then give feedback as a class.

B–C Give students time to complete the rules alone before checking their answers with a partner. Give feedback as a class, providing further explanations of each structure as necessary and eliciting new examples to consolidate understanding. Then, direct students to the **Grammar Hub** (see below and TB86).

D Demonstrate the activity by talking through the first situation as a class. Encourage students to use past modals of deduction to speculate about what they think happened. Then, put students into pairs to discuss their own ideas. Monitor, asking several questions to help students make deductions (e.g. *Why would the children that brought in their own lunches be unaffected? Are you sure about that? Why? What else might have happened?* etc). Give feedback as a class, going through the situations one by one, then dealing with any common errors. Use the **Grammar Worksheet** on page W36 for extra practice.

Suggested answers

1 *The children must have gotten food poisoning from food at the school itself.*

2 *Somebody might have stolen her wallet on the train; she might have dropped her wallet on her way to work; she might have left her wallet at home.*

3 *The student can't have answered all of the questions; they might have found the exam too difficult and given up.*

SPEAKING

A–B Read the mystery as a class, pre-teaching the word *goblin* (*a creature in children's stories that looks like a small person and enjoys causing trouble*) and clarifying anything else students don't understand. Then, put them into groups to discuss what they think happened. Monitor, correcting mistakes with past modals as necessary and helping with any new vocabulary. Bring the class back together to share their explanations, but do not confirm or correct anything at this point. Now, direct students to the **Communication Hub** (see TB121) to read the explanation and discuss how it compared to their own.

GRAMMAR HUB

8.1 Past modals of deduction

A Choose the correct options to complete the sentences.

1 They're more than an hour late. They ***must have*** / *can't have* gotten lost.

2 Patrick ***can't have*** / *could have* gone to the opera. He hates classical music!

3 You passed! You *might have* / ***must have*** been so happy when you heard the results!

4 It *must have* / ***can't have*** been food poisoning. Nobody else who ate the fish got sick.

5 You ***can't have*** / *might not have* seen Marco in town. He's on vacation in Spain right now.

6 Sasha *couldn't have* / ***might not have*** heard the news yet, so let's call her just in case.

7 I *must have* / ***can't have*** left my bank card at the café – I used it just now to pay for the coffee.

8 He hasn't answered his phone for two days. I suppose he ***may have*** / *can't have* lost it.

9 I *can't have* / ***must have*** left my hat at the restaurant. That's the last place I had it.

10 It's not very likely because she's 103, but I suppose it ***can't have*** / *might have* been Grandma you saw at the grocery store.

B Complete the conversations with a modal verb and the correct form of the verbs in the box.

be do finish land make see

1 **A:** Here's that report you asked for.
B: You can't/couldn't have finished already! You only started it yesterday.

2 **A:** $20 for two cups of coffee!
B: That can't be right. The waiter must have made a mistake.

3 **A:** Did the children break the baby's toy?
B: They couldn't/can't have done it. They were at school all day.

4 **A:** Do you think Kobi's still on the plane?
B: Uh, he might/may/could have landed by now. It depends if there was a delay or not.

5 **A:** I can't imagine what Julie went through when she lost her father.
B: Yes, it must have been awful for her.

6 **A:** It's strange that Doug hasn't replied to my email.
B: He might/may not have seen it yet. He doesn't always check his email on the weekend.

➤ Go back to page 87.

C SCAN Scan *How do you explain that?* What explanations were originally given for each mystery?

D READ FOR DETAIL Read the stories again and answer the questions.

1 What had been left in the lighthouse?
2 What does the writer say happened to the men?
3 What does the writer think caused the chair to fall over?
4 Where were the two groups of bodies found?
5 What physical injuries had the hikers sustained?
6 What explanation is given for the missing tongue?

E DECODE: SIMILES AND METAPHORS Read the stories again. Answer the questions by identifying similes and metaphors in the text. Use the information in the box to help you.

Decoding: similes and metaphors

In articles describing dramatic events, writers frequently use descriptive language to make the story more engaging. Two common techniques used are:

a **Similes** – comparing one thing to another using *as* or *like*. *He may look small, but he's* ***as brave as a lion****.*

b **Metaphors** – describing something as if it were something else. *The snow* ***was a white blanket****. (= It wasn't actually a blanket; it just looked like one.)*

1 What was the lighthouse like when the ship arrived?
a like a small town (b) empty
2 How does the writer think the third man left the kitchen?
a slowly (b) quickly
3 How does the writer think the rescuers felt when they discovered the female hiker?
(a) frightened b angry

F SPEAK Work in groups. Why do you think people look for unusual explanations to mysteries, when there are frequently more obvious solutions?

GRAMMAR
Past modals of deduction

A Work in pairs. Look at the highlighted sentences in the article. Which sentence(s) mean …

1 it's almost certain that something happened or is true. a; c
2 it's possible that something happened or is true. b; d; e
3 it's impossible that something happened or is true. f

B WORK IT OUT Complete the structures in the box.

Past modals of deduction

We use modals of deduction to make guesses about what happened in the past.

a We use __must__ + *have* + past participle to say we're sure something happened because there's strong evidence.

b We use __may__ / __might__ / __could__ + *have* + past participle to say we think something is possible, but we aren't sure.

c We use __can't__ + *have* + past participle to say we're sure something didn't happen because there's strong evidence.

C Work in pairs. Go to the **Grammar Hub** on **page 136**.

D SPEAK Work in pairs. Read the situations (1–3) and discuss what you think happened using past modals of deduction.

1 Hundreds of children got sick at a school in New York. Children who brought in their own lunch were unaffected.
2 Tasmin took the train to work as normal and went to buy coffee from a café nearby. However, when she went to pay, she discovered her wallet was missing.
3 A math teacher was amazed when one of his students finished their exam in 20 minutes. The exam has 100 questions and usually takes an hour and a half.

SPEAKING

A DISCUSS Work in groups. Read *The Hopkinsville goblin case* and discuss what you think happened.

The Hopkinsville Goblin Case

In 1955, the Sutton family and their friend Billy Ray Taylor were relaxing on their porch. Suddenly, Billy Ray saw lights in the sky and shouted for everyone to come and take a look. They saw what they thought was an alien with glowing eyes, a large head, pointed ears and claws. The family and their friend grabbed their guns and started shooting. They heard their bullets hitting something metal, which they thought must have been the alien's spaceship.

B Go to the **Communication Hub** on **page 151** and compare your ideas from Exercise A with the likely solution.

LISTENING

A SPEAK Work in pairs. Look at the illustrations of three famous myths from around the world. What do you think happens in each story? Where do you think these stories are from?

B LISTEN FOR GIST Listen to an interview with an expert on myths and legends. Check your ideas from Exercise A.

8.1

C LISTEN FOR DETAIL Listen again. Choose the correct options (a, b or c) to complete the sentences.

8.1

1 According to Phillip Norris, myths and legends …
  a usually have the same origin.
  b are similar in neighboring countries.
  (c) have similar themes across cultures.

2 The tales of Sinbad the Sailor are given as an example of …
  (a) a hero myth.
  b a monster myth.
  c an urban legend.

3 Sinbad and his crew go to the castle on the island …
  a to look for food.
  (b) to escape from their attackers.
  c to shelter from the storm.

4 Anyone who looks directly at Medusa …
  a is bitten by the snakes in her hair.
  (b) is turned to stone.
  c is killed by Perseus.

5 The Yeti and Bigfoot are given as examples of …
  a stories inspired by wild animals.
  b ancient legends.
  (c) modern monster myths.

6 To call Hanako-San, you have to …
  a knock on the bathroom mirror three times.
  b say her name three times.
  (c) knock on the bathroom door three times and say her name.

7 According to Phillip Norris, myths like Hanako-San are …
  a unique to Japan.
  b surprisingly different across cultures.
  (c) popular with young children.

D SPEAK Work in groups. Why do you think myths and legends are still told today? Why do you think new ones are still created? Explain your reasoning.

1

2

VOCABULARY

Word families

A Complete the word families in the table. Use the information in the box to help you.

Word families

A word family is a group of words with the same root. Learning the associated words (e.g. the verb, noun, adjective and adverb) can help you to understand texts more easily and improve your accuracy when writing.

Verb	Noun	Adjective	Adverb
–	1 myth	mythical	–
2 believe	belief	3 believable	believably
–	4 hero	heroic	heroically
5 represent	representation	representative	representatively
–	6 tradition	traditional	7 traditionally
transform	8 transformation	transformational	–

8.1 Myths and legends

LISTENING

8.1 **A–B** Draw students' attention to the three illustrations, and explain that they show famous myths and legends from around the world. Next, put students into pairs to discuss the pictures. Monitor, encouraging them to describe the main characters in the scene, to identify any contextual clues and to discuss what they think is going on. Help with any new vocabulary as necessary. Bring the class back together to share their ideas, but don't confirm anything at this stage. Now, play the audio for students to check their answers. Give feedback as a class, nominating students to summarize while encouraging others to add details as appropriate. See the **Audio script** below and TB89.

1 *This is a myth from Japan known as Hanako-San – a spirit that appears in school bathrooms when children knock on the third stall door three times and ask, 'Are you there Hanako-San?'.*

2 *This is part of the third Sinbad the Sailor stories which originate from the Middle East. In this part of the story, Sinbad and his crew have been awoken by a huge one-eyed monster. It attacks them and although they try to run away, one is caught and eaten.*

3 *This is the story of Perseus and Medusa which is an ancient Greek myth. In the story, Perseus is sent to kill Medusa – a winged creature with poisonous snakes in her hair. Since anyone that looks at Medusa directly will turn to stone, Perseus uses his mirrored shield and eventually manages to chop off her head.*

8.1 **C** Before playing the track again, give students time to read through the questions and underline any key words that will help them choose the correct answers. Then, play the audio for students to complete the exercise before asking them to check their answers in pairs. Give feedback as a class, calling on individual students to answer the questions and explain what they remember from the interview.

D Put students into groups to discuss the questions. Monitor, encouraging students to justify their answers with examples. Bring the class back together to share their ideas. Add any useful emergent language to the board.

VOCABULARY

A Write the following sentence on the board, setting *imagine* in a different color – *It may be difficult to imagine, but the ancient Greeks really believed in monsters.* Below, draw the table in the Student's Book, with the parts of speech as headings for the four columns. Now, elicit what part of speech *imagine* is (*verb*) and add it to the table. Next, elicit other forms of this word, adding them to the table on the board (*imagination (n)*, *imaginary/imaginative/unimaginative (adj)*, etc). Ask students why being able to change the form of a word like this might be helpful (*it can help you understand texts more easily, improve your accuracy when writing*, etc). Now, give students time to complete the table alone before checking their answers in pairs. Give feedback as a class, filling in your table on the board.

AUDIO SCRIPT

8.1

Listening, Exercise B
I = Interviewer P = Phillip

I: Hello, and welcome to *Connections*. On this week's show, we're talking about the influence storytelling has on our culture. Why do so many countries have different variations of the same story? How do these stories grow and change? Here to help us answer these questions is Phillip Norris, author of *The myths that made us*, a new book about the history of storytelling. Phillip, welcome to the show.

P: Good morning. Thank you for inviting me.

I: Great that you can be here. Now, I'd always imagined that myths and legends were very specific to each culture. I thought they were essentially the mythical stories that people listened to before books. Is that not the case?

P: Well, in some ways it is. You're right that each culture has its own myths and legends that are specific to
Ex C Q1 them, but what we do have is common themes across all of them. These myths appear across places and societies that are thousands of miles apart, at a time when there would have been very little contact between these groups, so they can't have the same origins. However, there are striking similarities between these stories.

I: One story we all hear about in England when we are growing up is the legend of King Arthur and the Knights of the Round Table: a king of Britain who defended the country and led a group of knights against invaders. It's almost certainly not true and there are a lot of different versions with tales of his heroic deeds. Do other countries have such myths?

P: Very much so. This is something I would refer to as a 'hero myth'. I think this is common across all cultures. Some of the oldest books in many countries are essentially heroic tales – an individual fighting their way across lands on a mission to save someone or find something.

Ex C Q2 **I:** Do you have a particular favorite hero myth?

P: Yes. I love the tales of Sinbad the Sailor and his adventures at sea. In the original stories, Sinbad goes on seven voyages across the seas off East Africa and South Asia where he finds whales the size of islands, giant snakes and rivers filled with diamonds.

I: So, can you tell us a little more about one of the stories?

P: Of course. So the third voyage of Sinbad is probably one of the most exciting. As in many of the stories, Sinbad's ship is caught in a terrible storm and driven off course. They sail toward a small island but are attacked by a tribe of monkeys carrying spears.
Ex C Q3 Fearing for their lives, Sinbad and his crew swim to the island and rush to a castle they see at the top of a hill. Tired and hungry from their escape, the crew falls asleep on the floor of the castle but are awoken to find the ground shaking. In the doorway to their room, stands a giant over 20 meters tall. His eyes burn like fire, his teeth are long and sharp and his huge mouth has the lips of a camel. Sinbad and his crew try to run away but one of them is caught and eaten by the giant.

I: Wow! So how does Sinbad escape?

P: Well, you'll just have to read the story for yourself. I don't want to spoil the ending!

I: Fair enough. So it seems that dragons and other strange creatures appear across many cultures. Why do you think that is?

B Ask students to complete the sentences, referring back to the table if necessary. Allow time for them to check their answers in pairs before nominating individuals to share their answers with the class. Use the **Vocabulary Worksheet** on page W37 for extra practice.

PRONUNCIATION

8.2 A Give students time to quickly read the paragraph before playing the audio and so they can mark the pauses. Allow time for them to compare their ideas with a partner, then give feedback as a class. Highlight that the speaker has divided the paragraph into 'thought groups' and explain what this means (*a small group of words or phrase within a sentence that forms one unit of meaning*) and explain that the key words in each group are usually stressed.

8.3 B Give students time to predict where the pauses will be in the next part, marking them with a forward slash (/). Allow time for them to compare their ideas with a partner before playing the audio for students to check. Give feedback as a class.

C Put students into pairs to practice telling the story in Exercise B. Monitor, encouraging students to use pauses and stress to make their storytelling clearer and more dramatic.

SPEAKING HUB

A Draw students' attention to the three pictures and explain that they all show a famous myth or legend. Ask if students can name any of the myths and legends, adding any useful language/terms not covered in the wordpools to the board. Next, put students into pairs to speculate about the myth behind each picture. Monitor, helping with any new or unfamiliar vocabulary, but don't confirm any answers at this point.

B Tell students that they are now going to read about the three myths. Put them into groups of three (A, B and C) and direct them to the **Communication Hub** (see TB121).

C Put students back into groups and ask them to use their notes to summarize their myths. Monitor, helping with grammar and vocabulary as necessary.

D Put students into new pairs to discuss myths and legends from their own countries. Monitor, encouraging them to ask follow-up questions to learn as much as they can about each other's stories. Write down two or three of the most interesting myths and legend, then nominate students to share them with the class once they have finished their discussions. Add any useful emergent language to the board.

8.1 (continued)

P: Well, I think many of them were inspired by people finding the fossils of ancient creatures. Some are pure fantasy, though. Take the Greek myth of Medusa, who was a winged human with poisonous snakes in her hair. Ex C Q4 In the myth, anyone who looks at her face turns to stone. King Polydectes decides to send Perseus to kill Medusa. The hero Perseus is able to kill her by looking into a mirrored shield and chopping off her head. This myth also connects to other cultures as well though, such as the Berbers in Morocco. However, monster myths are not only present in ancient legends; Ex C Q5 we have many that still exist today. One that exists in many cultures is a variation of a giant human-like creature such as the Yeti in the Himalayas or Bigfoot in North America. Even today, we still create new stories that have striking similarities across cultures. We usually refer to these as urban myths or urban legends.

I: So are urban legends just modern tales about mythical creatures?

P: Many of them do involve monsters, but others focus on ghosts or murderers. One of the most popular stories in modern culture is of a person appearing in a mirror or bathroom. In Japan, this is known as Hanako-San, when the spirit of a young girl appears in school bathrooms.. Ex C Q6 People have to knock three times on the third stall door and ask, 'Are you there Hanako-San?' A small girl or a white hand appears from the stall. This is very similar to the Bloody Mary myth in America and many others around the world. Ex C Q7 It's largely a game for young children, for whom the stories are very believable, to test their bravery, and it's surprisingly similar across the world. As are various other tales about ghosts, murders and other strange events. I guess it just shows the way our ancestors interpreted the world around them differently.

I: Thank you for coming in today, this has been really interesting. For those of you interested in finding out more, Phillip's book, *The myths that made us*, is out this Friday.

TEACHING IDEA by David Seymour and Maria Popova

Similes

Use this activity to provide freer practice of similes.

In small groups, think of a short anecdote leading up to one of these similes. (Allocate one to each group, randomly chosen, without the other groups hearing. While they are working, write the similes on the board.) Read your anecdote to the class and see if they can guess which simile completes it.

The next day, he felt like death warmed up.

I felt like a fish out of water.

Oh well – like father, like son I suppose.

It was like getting blood out of a stone.

He was like a bull in a china shop.

TEACHING IDEA by David Seymour and Maria Popova

Like and as if

Use this activity to provide freer practice of similes.

Work in small groups. Use these prompts to write two sentences for each, one with *like* and one with *as if*, e.g. *He looks … – 1) He looks like someone I used to know. 2) He looks as if he hasn't slept for a week.*

You look … It feels … Your job sounds …

My head feels … Her apartment looked … Their baby looks …

This coffee tastes … It sounds … They seem …

The movie sounds … That man looks … The food tasted …

His hair looked … The town seemed … Kevin's car sounds …

B Complete the sentences with the correct form of the words in parentheses.

1 The minotaur is a ___mythical___ (*myth*) creature with the head of a bull and the body of a man.

2 The main character usually ___heroically___ (*hero*) saves a princess or someone else in distress.

3 Snakes are frequently used to ___represent___ (*represent*) danger.

4 ___Traditionally___ (*tradition*), stories were told and not written down so there are frequently variations of a legend.

5 Many stories frequently include the ___transformation___ (*transform*) of a person into some kind of monster.

PRONUNCIATION

Thought groups

8.2 **A** **Listen to the first part of a story from the interview. Mark any pauses with (/). Why do you think the speaker pauses at these points?**

To make the story easier to follow and more dramatic.

As in many of the stories,/Sinbad's ship is caught in a terrible storm/and driven off course./They sail toward a small island / but are attacked by a tribe of monkeys carrying spears./ Fearing for their lives,/Sinbad and his crew swim to the island/and rush to a castle they see at the top of a hill./

8.3 **B** **Read the next part of the story. Mark where you think the speaker will pause with (/). Then listen and check.**

Tired and hungry from their escape,/the crew falls asleep on the floor of the castle/but is awoken/to find the ground shaking./In the doorway to their room/stands a giant over 20/meters/tall./His eyes burn like fire,/his teeth are long and sharp,/and his huge mouth has the lips of a camel./Sinbad and his crew try to run away/but one of them is caught/and eaten/by the giant.

C **SPEAK** **Work in pairs. Practice telling the story from Exercise B. Remember to use pauses to make the story easier to follow.**

SPEAKING HUB

A **PREPARE** Work in pairs. Look at the pictures and use the words in the box to discuss what you think each myth might be about.

Greeks hidden horse war

fake lake monster Scotland

accident coat forest hitchhiker

B **PLAN** **Work in groups of three. Student A – Go to the Communication Hub on page 147. Student B – Go to the Communication Hub on page 149. Student C – Go to the Communication Hub on page 152.**

C **PRESENT** **Summarize the myth you have just read about to your group. Use your notes to help you.**

D **DISCUSS** **Work in pairs. Think about myths and legends in your own country. Tell your partner:**

- who the myth was about
- what the origins of the myth were
- what happened in the myth

Speculate about past events

Summarize a cultural story

8.2 Who did it?

- Write and perform a short scene
- Speculate about the causes and consequences of a crime

V – easily confused verbs; crime
S – following an argument
G – order of adjectives
P – adding information

READING

A PREDICT Work in pairs. You are going to read part of a story called *The curse of the black falcon*. Look at the picture and discuss the questions.

1 What do you think the Black Falcon is?
2 What do you think happens in the story?

B SKIM Read the story quickly and check your predictions from Exercise A.

C READ FOR MAIN IDEA Read the story again. Are these sentences true (T) or false (F)? Correct the false sentences.

1 Professor Bainbridge was excited about having a party. *T / F*
2 Professor Bainbridge was most excited by the value of the necklace. *T / F*
3 He only got to keep the necklace for a short time. *T / F*
4 Only members of the family knew the code for the safe. *T / F*
5 The safe was hidden in the desk. *T / F*
6 The burglar broke the window immediately. *T / F*
7 The burglar searched the room calmly at first. *T / F*
8 A sudden noise alerted the professor to the burglar's presence. *T / F*

The Curse of the BLACK FALCON

'So, how do I look?'

Professor Bainbridge smiled as he turned to face his daughter. She was wearing a beautiful blue dress that had once belonged to his mother. Although Alice had recently turned 20, to him she'd always be the little girl who was too scared to sleep with the lights off. 'Like a million dollars,' he said, returning her smile.

Tonight was supposed to be a celebration, but he'd never liked parties, especially when he was the focus. He sighed, put his glasses down and rubbed his eyes. Seeing his reaction, Alice touched her father's arm and asked, 'Daddy, what's wrong? Aren't you excited to show everyone what you found?'

All of this fuss over an old necklace. True, it was worth a lot of money to the right collector, but to him its historical value was far more important. He'd heard stories about the mysterious Black Falcon all his life and after years of research and hard work, he'd finally found it in a muddy French field. It was such a significant find that his family had insisted that they hold a party to celebrate. On Monday, the professor would deliver the necklace to the British Museum, but for the weekend it would stay locked away in the safe above his desk. Nobody outside of the family knew the combination to the safe, but it still made him nervous to have such a valuable object in his house. He looked up at the large rectangular painting above the desk, tried to straighten it and turned back to his daughter.

'I'll be happier when this weekend is over,' he said angrily. Recognizing that her father was nervous, Alice began to straighten his bow tie. 'You never know, you might have fun.' The professor was just about to reply when the doorbell rang. 'That'll be the Joneses!' Alice said excitedly. 'They're always early. Come on!' The professor sighed again and followed her out into the hallway.

For an hour, the study lay empty. The fire had died out and the only sound came from the antique gold clock on the desk and the thunderstorm outside. Suddenly, a figure dressed in black appeared at the window. Cautiously, they looked into the study. Satisfied that the room was empty, they raised a fist to the window. Yet, instead of breaking the glass immediately, they stopped. For two long minutes they waited, patiently watching the sky until suddenly, the moment came. A loud crash of thunder echoed through the sky and the figure calmly smashed the window, felt for the handle and climbed inside.

Slowly, they began opening drawers and pulling books off the shelves, but as the minutes ticked by, they became more and more desperate. Frustrated, the figure leaned against the desk and stared at the painting above it. Noticing it was hanging at a strange angle, the figure moved the painting to the side, revealing the strong metal safe behind. After a few minutes, the safe was open and inside lay the ultimate prize – the Black Falcon.

Just as the figure reached inside to grab the necklace, they heard the professor's voice ringing through the hallway outside. 'I'll just go and fetch my pipe … See you outside.' In their hurry to find somewhere to hide, the figure sent a small Chinese vase crashing to the ground. Terrified, the figure hid behind the open door, holding the necklace as the professor appeared on the other side. 'Tommy? Is that you?' he called, looking into the darkness. He listened for a reply but there was nothing but silence.

8.2 Who did it?

LEAD-IN

Find two or three interesting covers or pulp fiction detective stories or old detective movie posters and bring them to class. Make sure you also have a brief summary of each story since students will probably want to know what happens in them later on. Show students the first cover and elicit the genre (*crime*), which characters are shown and what they think happens in the story. Add any useful emergent language to the board, then briefly outline the story. Next, display the remaining posters and put students into groups to discuss them. Monitor, helping with new vocabulary as necessary. Bring the class back together to share their ideas, then briefly outline what actually happens in each story.

READING

A–B Draw students' attention to the title of the story and the illustration. Then, put them into pairs to discuss the questions. Monitor, helping with new vocabulary as necessary. Bring the class back together to share their ideas, but don't confirm anything at this point. Then, allow two to three minutes for students to scan the story and check their answers. Take the opportunity to clarify anything students don't understand at this point, teaching any key language and adding it to the board. However, avoid explaining *like a million dollars* because this is covered in Exercise D.

1 The Black Falcon is an old, valuable necklace.
2 A burglar breaks into Professor Bainbridge's study while he's downstairs hosting a party. The intruder searches the study for the necklace, eventually finding it in a safe behind a picture. Hearing the Professor returning, the intruder runs to hide behind the door.

C Ask students to read through the sentences, pre-teaching *burglar* (*someone who gets into buildings illegally and steals things*) and any other terms students don't understand. Then, give students time to read the story again and correct the sentences. Allow time for peer correction before giving feedback as a class. Encourage students to correct each other when necessary.

1 F (He's never liked parties and sighs as he puts his glasses down.)
2 F (He thinks the historical value of the necklace is far more important.)
3 T
4 T
5 F (The safe was hidden behind the painting above the fireplace.)
6 F (The burglar waited two minutes before breaking the window.)
7 T
8 T

GRAMMAR HUB

8.2 Order of adjectives

- When we use two or more adjectives before a noun, we usually put the adjectives in the following order:

Opinion	Size	Age	Shape	Color	Origin	Material
beautiful	huge	20th century	rectangular	blue	English	leather
great	long	ancient	round	green	Italian	silk
old-fashioned	tiny	up-to-date	square	white	Turkish	wooden

Monika bought a stunning old crystal vase. (= opinion → age → material)
We got some big heart-shaped gold balloons for the party. (= size → shape → color)
Rapini is a delicious green Italian vegetable. (= opinion → color → origin)

- Opinion adjectives (e.g. *unusual, disgusting*, etc) are always used before descriptive adjectives (e.g. *enormous, circular*, etc).

He was wearing a disgusting pink silk shirt. NOT ~~He was wearing a pink silk disgusting shirt.~~
They found a beautiful ancient golden crown. NOT ~~They found an ancient golden beautiful crown.~~

- We usually use *and* between two or more adjectives of the same type, especially with colors.

He showed me an old black and white photograph of his family.
I love Portugal's beautiful blue and white tiles.

Be careful!

- Although not grammatically incorrect, it's very unusual for a description to use more than three adjectives, so it's better to avoid this.
  She was sitting at a beautiful, long, modern, square table.

- Compound adjectives (e.g. *long-term, state-of-the-art*, etc) should also be used in this order.

She bought a great state-of-the art computer.

D Put students into pairs to discuss the questions. Monitor, encouraging students to support their ideas with sentences from the story. Give feedback as a class, encouraging students to refer back to the text when appropriate. It may also be worth eliciting what type of expression *like a million dollars* is (*a simile*) and whether there are any similar expressions in the students' own languages.

VOCABULARY

A Write the following sentences on the board – *I always listen to music on the train. / I always hear music on the train.* Ask students whether the sentences mean the same thing (*they don't*) and what the difference is (*'listen to' shows intention, the speaker has chosen to do this; 'hear' indicates that the speaker is not playing the music, it is being played nearby and they cannot avoid it*). Tell students that they are going to focus on other commonly confused sense verbs, then give them time to complete the sentences alone before scanning the text again to check their answers. Give feedback as a class.

B Give students time to complete the sentences alone before comparing their answers in pairs. Give feedback as a class. To consolidate understanding, encourage students to explain the differences between the pairs of verbs as they did in Exercise A.

C Put students into pairs to discuss the questions. Monitor, paying close attention to how accurately they use sense verbs and encouraging them to ask follow-up questions to keep the discussions going. Use the **Vocabulary Worksheet** on page W38 for extra practice.

GRAMMAR

A Write the following sentence on the board – *She was wearing a beautiful blue dress that had once belonged to his mother.* Ask students to identify the adjectives in the sentence (*beautiful, blue*), then give students time to underline any other sentences in the story in which two or more adjectives have been used to describe the same noun. Give them time to briefly check their answers in pairs before giving feedback as a class.

B–C Ask students to complete the rules alone, then give them time to compare their answers in pairs. In feedback, try to elicit the full order of adjectives from the class. Now, direct them to the **Grammar Hub** (see below and TB90).

D If students completed the Grammar Hub exercises for homework, it might be worth reviewing the grammar at this point by working through the first sentence together. Otherwise, give students time to complete the exercise alone before checking in pairs. Then, give feedback as a class.

E Put students into A/B pairs, then direct them to the **Communication Hub** (see TB121). Use the **Grammar Worksheet** on page W39 for extra practice.

SPEAKING

A Elicit how *The curse of the black falcon* ended (*the burglar was in the study and had found the Black Falcon. On their way out, they knocked over a vase and Professor Bainbridge heard the noise*). Tell students that they are now going to role-play the conclusion to that scene, then put them into pairs to discuss ideas. Monitor, asking several questions to help shape their ideas (e.g. *What happens next? Where is the professor at this point?* etc).

B Ask students to write their role plays, with one of them as the burglar and the other as the professor. Monitor, helping with grammar and vocabulary as necessary. Then, give students time to practice their scenes.

C Bring the class back together and call on pairs one by one to perform their scenes for the class. Once all pairs have performed, ask the class to vote for their favorite ending.

GRAMMAR HUB

8.2 Order of adjectives

A Add the adjectives in bold in the correct place in each sentence.

1. So, apparently, Saga used to have long ^blond^ hair. **blond**
2. What a ^beautiful^ silver bracelet that is! **beautiful**
3. The rupee is a small ^round^ Indian coin. **round**
4. We now have four delightful ^tiny^ puppies to take care of. **tiny**
5. There are some huge ancient ^bronze^ statues in the museum. **bronze**
6. She gently held the strange rectangular ^wooden^ box in her hand. **wooden**
7. If it's a stunning ^bright^ pink flower, it's probably a lotus. **bright**
8. 'What is this peculiar ^oval^ yellow fruit?' he wondered. **oval**
9. I have no idea what this odd-looking ^circular^ metal instrument was used for. **circular**
10. When I was younger, I had a ^ridiculous^ green and red jacket that I wore almost every day. **ridiculous**
11. My brother got a ^part-time^ new job at the hospital. **part-time**
12. They presented a comprehensive ^long-term^ plan. **long-term**

B Correct five mistakes with the order of adjectives in the extract.

There was silence, except for the regular ticking of the ~~Victorian tall~~ tall Victorian grandfather clock in the hallway. Noah and Emily stood at the bottom of the ~~wooden steep~~ steep wooden staircase, looking up into the darkness. Noah turned on his flashlight. Its strong bright beam lit up the wall. Hanging just above their heads was a painting – the ~~medieval priceless~~ priceless medieval portrait of Anne of Avalon which they had been searching for for so long.

As they stared at the picture, Emily felt something brush against her leg. 'What was that?' she said. Noah swung the flashlight around. By the large ancient stone fireplace was an old black and white cat, staring at them. Hanging from the cat's collar was a ~~rusty strange-looking small~~ small strange-looking rusty key. 'I wonder if that key opens the old metal box we found in the kitchen,' said Emily.

'I was just thinking the same thing,' Noah replied.

➤ Go back to page 91.

D INFER MEANING Work in pairs. Scan the story again and discuss the questions.

1 What does the professor mean when he says that Alice looks 'like a million dollars'? He means that she looks amazing.

2 Why does the figure in black wait before breaking the window? They wait to use the thunder to cover the noise they make breaking the window.

3 How does the burglar work out where the Black Falcon is? They notice that the painting above the fireplace is hanging at a strange angle.

VOCABULARY

Easily confused verbs

A Choose the correct options to complete the sentences. Then scan the story again to check your answers.

1 *Seeing / Watching* his reaction, Alice *felt / touched* her father's arm and asked …

2 For two long minutes they waited, patiently *watching / seeing* the sky until suddenly, …

3 … the figure calmly smashed the window, *touched / felt* for the handle and climbed inside.

4 … they *heard / listened* the professor's voice ringing through the hallway outside.

5 'Tommy? Is that you?' he called, *seeing / looking* into the darkness.

6 He *listened / heard* for a reply but there was nothing but silence.

B Complete the sentences with the correct form of the words in Exercise A.

1 Standing inside the room, he listened carefully to what they were saying outside.

2 He felt along the wall until he found the light switch.

3 He sat watching them to see what they would do.

4 Hearing the news, she rushed quickly to tell the others.

5 He looked in the direction of the safe and saw that the picture had been moved.

6 As he entered the room, he saw that the window had been smashed.

7 He carefully touched the necklace before picking it up.

8 Hearing a noise upstairs, she put down her broom and went to investigate.

C Work in pairs. Discuss the questions.

1 What's the most interesting piece of news you've heard this week?

2 Do you prefer to watch movies at the movie theater or stream them online? Why?

3 Do you think you could find your way around your home by touch alone?

4 Do you think listening to other people's conversations is a good way to learn English? Why/Why not?

5 What's the worst movie you've ever seen? Why was it so bad?

GRAMMAR

Order of adjectives

A Scan the story again. Underline sentences in which two or more adjectives are used to describe a noun.

B WORK IT OUT Choose the correct options to complete the rules. Use the sentences in Exercise A to help you.

Order of adjectives

When we use two or more adjectives to describe a noun, we usually put the adjectives in [1]*alphabetical order / a specific order*.

Opinion adjectives (e.g. *amazing, incredible*) are always used [2]*before / after* descriptive adjectives (e.g. *ancient, leather*).

C Go to the Grammar Hub on page 136.

D PRACTICE Rewrite the sentences using the adjectives in parentheses.

1 He drives a car. (*expensive / old*)
He drives an expensive old car.

2 They walked slowly through the woods. (*dark / quiet*)
They walked slowly through the quiet dark woods.

3 She opened the door. (*wooden / noisy*)
She opened the noisy wooden door.

4 She had a bag. (*leather / red*)
She had a red leather bag.

5 She was wearing shoes. (*Italian / beautiful*)
She was wearing beautiful Italian shoes.

6 In the living room there was a table. (*wooden / antique / stunning*)
In the living room there was a stunning antique wooden table.

7 The house was surrounded by trees. (*old / tall*)
The house was surrounded by tall old trees.

8 In the garden there was a statue. (*stone / ancient*)
In the garden there was an ancient stone statue.

E SPEAK Student A – Go to the Communication Hub on page 150. Student B – Go to the Communication Hub on page 153.

SPEAKING

A PREPARE You are going to write and perform the next scene from *The curse of the black falcon*. With a partner, discuss what might happen next. Does the burglar escape or are they caught by the professor? Write notes about the key events in your scene.

B PLAN Write a conversation with one of you as the burglar and the other as the professor. Practice acting it out.

C SPEAK Perform your scene for the class. Vote on which pair has the best ending.

VOCABULARY
Crime

A **Work in groups. Look at the pictures and discuss the questions.**

1 What do the pictures show? What's the connection between them?

2 Which do you think is more reliable? Why?

B **Complete the definitions with the correct form of the words in bold.**

1 There was a **burglary** here last night. The thieves took money, jewelry and electronic goods.

2 He tried to **bribe** the police with $5,000 to let him go.

3 I was a victim of **identity theft** when someone hacked into my computer and stole my bank details.

4 During the **robbery,** they threatened the sales clerk with a knife.

5 I was the victim of **fraud** when someone tricked me into giving them my bank details. They took $2,000.

6 I was **blackmailed** into helping the criminal gang to break into our offices.

a ___blackmail___ (v) to make someone give you money or do what you want by threatening to reveal compromising information about them

b ___burglary___ (n) when someone illegally enters a building and steals things

c ___fraud___ (n) the crime of obtaining money from someone by tricking them

d ___bribe___ (v) to give money or presents to someone so that they will help you

e ___robbery___ (n) the crime of taking money or property illegally by using threats or violence

f ___identity theft___ (n) the illegal use of somebody else's name and personal information to obtain goods, credit cards, etc.

C Go to the **Vocabulary Hub** on **page 146**.

D **SPEAK** Work in pairs. What do you think is the most effective way to catch the criminal in each example? Think about:

- CCTV
- digital footprints
- DNA
- eyewitnesses
- phone histories
- fingerprints

LISTENING

A **SPEAK** **Work in pairs. Tell your partner about something interesting, unusual or frightening that has happened to you. Then discuss the questions.**

1 How accurate do you think this memory is?

2 Think about other people there at the time. Would their memory of the event be the same?

8.4 **B** **LISTEN FOR ORGANIZATION** **Listen to a talk about memory and eyewitness testimony. Put the topics in the order they are discussed.**

_3_ using language to influence memory
_4_ creating false memories
_1_ how the human memory works
_5_ the impact on the real world
_2_ blocking out painful memories

8.5 **C** **LISTEN FOR CONCLUSIONS** **Work in pairs. Listen to the last part of the talk again. What conclusion does the speaker make about eyewitness testimonies?**

Given how easy it is to influence someone's memory of an event, we should rethink how eyewitness testimonies are used in the courtroom.

1

8.2 Who did it?

VOCABULARY

A Put students into groups to discuss the questions. Monitor, helping with any new or unfamiliar vocabulary. Bring the class back together to share their ideas, adding any useful emergent language to the board.

1 Picture 1 shows a DNA sample, picture 2 shows someone giving evidence in court. Connection: They're both forms of evidence.

B–C Give students time to complete the exercise alone before checking their answers with a partner. Give feedback as a class, providing further explanation or examples as necessary. Practice pronunciation of the target vocabulary (focusing on words students may struggle with such as *burglary*). With stronger groups, elicit any other connected vocabulary at this time (e.g. *burglar*, *rob*, etc). Then, direct students to the **Vocabulary Hub** (see page TB121).

D Put students into pairs to discuss the question using the vocabulary they have just learned. Monitor, writing a note about any useful emergent language. Open the discussion up to the class, encouraging students to explain their ideas. Again, add any useful emergent language to the board. Use the **Vocabulary Worksheet** on page W40 for extra practice.

LISTENING

A Think of something interesting, unusual or frightening that has happened to you, and share your story with the class. Put students into pairs to share their own stories, and discuss the questions. Monitor and ask follow-up questions to drive the conversations forward. Open up the discussions to the class if appropriate.

8.4 **B** Pre-teach *eyewitness* (*someone who saw something such as a crime or accident happen*), and elicit what they are usually expected to do (*give the police an account of the event*). Explain that this is called an *eyewitness testimony*, and ask students whether they think that these can be trusted and why. Next, give students time to read through the topics before playing the audio for them to complete the exercise. Then, put students into pairs to compare their answers before giving feedback as a class. This is a fairly challenging text, so it's worth taking this opportunity to clarify anything students don't understand. With weaker groups, you may want to listen again and pause to discuss the answers one by one. See the **Audio script** below and TB93.

8.5 **C** Put students into pairs, then play the audio for them to answer the question. Monitor, helping with any new or unfamiliar vocabulary as necessary. Give feedback as a class, encouraging students to give examples from the talk.

AUDIO SCRIPT

8.4

Listening, Exercise B
L = Lecturer

L: So, I want you all to think of an event from your childhood. Something that makes you smile every time you remember it. Got it? OK, now try to picture that event in your mind. Think about where you were, who you were with, what you could hear, what you could smell ... most importantly, think about how you felt. I bet you can remember everything pretty clearly, right? Well, I don't want to upset anyone, but when it comes to accurately recalling events, the human memory is pretty awful. [Ex B] We like to think that our memories are like recordings we can access and watch whenever we want. Yet in reality, [Ex D Q1] our memories change over time. Each time we recall an event, we rewrite the memory – adding details, updating things to match our current knowledge. Sometimes we combine two memories into one. Sometimes we even create memories. Sounds far-fetched, doesn't it? But actually, in study after study, a surprisingly high proportion of people have described memories of events that they cannot possibly have personally experienced.

'False memory syndrome' – the creation of entirely false memories – first came to the attention of the public in the late 1980s. [Ex B] At the time, many therapists believed that people who had experienced something terrible in their lives blocked out the memory of it, locking it deep in their minds and that the only way to access these 'repressed memories' was through therapy. Belief in this idea spread quickly, and many people who had gone into therapy looking for help with anxiety or depression were horrified to be told that they had blocked out the memory of a terrible experience years before. [Ex D Q2] However, during the 90s, the theory was heavily criticized and, in the years since, multiple studies have strongly suggested that the therapists were actually encouraging their patients to create false memories. But how is this possible? How can we encourage someone to remember something that never actually happened? To help us answer this, we need to look back at the work of the American cognitive psychologist, Elizabeth Loftus.

Loftus actually first started exploring the idea of false memories in the 1970s. She did this by showing people simulations of crimes and accidents, then asking them what they remembered. In a landmark study in 1974, Loftus showed a video of a simulated car crash and asked one group, 'How fast were the cars traveling when they hit each other?' She asked another group, 'How fast were the cars traveling when they smashed into each other?' [Ex B] Interestingly, when asked the question with the more dramatic verb, *smashed*, witnesses said the car was traveling faster. They were also more likely to say they saw broken glass flying through the air, even though this didn't actually happen. In other studies, researchers changed some of the details when discussing an accident and many of the participants added this information to their memory – they essentially rewrote what they remembered happening, simply because they were encouraged to by the interviewer. So, why is this important? [Ex D Q3] Well, studies like this clearly demonstrate that the way you ask questions or discuss an event can strongly influence someone's memory of it. Loftus and many others like her suspected that this went some way in explaining why so many people in the 1980s were suddenly remembering horrifying experiences from their childhood. [Ex D Q4] The therapists, whether intentionally or not, might actually have been encouraging patients to

8.4 **D** Read through the skills box as a class, clarifying each bullet point with further explanations and examples as necessary. Then, give students time to read the sentences carefully, before playing the audio again. Allow time for peer correction, then give feedback as a class. Highlight how each sentence builds on the next and paraphrases the main ideas from the talk, building toward the conclusion.

E–F Tell students that you are now going to test how accurate their memories are. Put them into A/B pairs and give them time to read their instructions. Then, direct both students to look at the picture on page 97. After 30 seconds, tell Student A to close their book and describe the image to Student B. Now, ask students to swap roles, directing both to the picture on page 109. Again, after 30 seconds, tell the new Student A to close their books and describe the image. When both students have described their pictures, allow time for them to discuss how accurate their eyewitness testimonies were.

PRONUNCIATION

8.6 **A–B** Tell students that they are going to listen to an extract from the lecture, then play the audio for them to answer the question. Give them time to briefly check their answers in pairs before giving feedback as a class. Then, put them back into pairs to identify the function of the phrase in bold. Give feedback as a class, highlighting that this is a good example of how you can use intonation to enhance meaning.

8.7 **C** Play the audio, pausing after each extract for students to listen and repeat, practicing accurate intonation on the phrases in bold.

SPEAKING HUB

A Pre-teach the words *victim* (*someone who has been harmed or effected by a crime*), *suspect* (*the person believed to have committed a crime*) and *alibi* (*an account of what someone was doing at the time of a crime*), then give students time to read the scenario and write notes about any important details.

B Put students into groups to solve the murder. Direct the groups to page 148 and ask them to read the alibis and answer the questions.

C Ask students to return to their groups and discuss which of the suspects they believe committed the crime and why. To add an extra level of challenge, tell groups they should try and reach a unanimous decision on who murdered Sofia. Monitor, encouraging students to use past modals of deduction to support their ideas (e.g. *It couldn't have been Linus, he was …,* etc). To close the activity, take a class vote to decide who the most likely suspect is, before revealing the answer.

The murder is most likely to have been committed by Linus Baldursson. He is described as 'quick-tempered' and was 'furious' that his father was planning to hand over the business to his sister. Although he claims he went to his room after the argument, he wasn't there when his father came to find him – just 10 mins before the body was found. All other suspects have an alibi that is confirmed by someone else in the group.

8.4 (continued)

Ex D Q4 rewrite their own memories. But could people be encouraged to create entirely new memories? In 1995, Loftus designed an experiment to test this very idea. In the study, participants were given a booklet containing four short stories about themselves, three of which were true and one which never actually happened. The false story described how when they were younger, they'd gotten lost in a shopping mall, cried and were eventually helped by an elderly woman. During the study, participants were asked to write down as much detail as they

Ex B could remember about each of the four stories. One in three remembered getting lost in the shopping mall, despite the fact that this never actually happened. In the 23 years since the shopping mall

Ex D Q5 experiment, multiple studies have supported the idea that, under the right conditions, it is possible to encourage people to create entirely false memories.

Ex B If this is true, then I'd argue that we need to seriously reconsider the use of eyewitness testimony in the courtroom. The information presented by a witness may have been influenced by the way in which they were questioned after the event. On top of that, lawyers could encourage witnesses to add or change details. Think about how many innocent people might have been wrongfully convicted of a crime they didn't commit on the strength of an entirely false memory. To most of us, our memories form the basis of our identity. They represent who we are and where we came from. But the research of Loftus and others like her shows that we cannot reliably distinguish between real and false memories, and in the courtroom, this could change the lives of innocent people forever. Thank you.

TEACHING IDEA by David Seymour and Maria Popova

Neighborhood watch

Use this activity to extend the theme of crime.

There has been an increase in crime in your neighborhood, especially violent crime and car crime. You are going to attend a meeting to decide what to do.

Prepare for the meeting in pairs. Discuss your ideas and write notes.

Pair A, you are:

The local representative – You represent the government's new 'get tough on crime' policy.

The local chief of police – You believe in zero tolerance toward criminals.

Pair B, you are:

A local youth worker – You want more money for community projects and you believe that prevention is better than punishment.

An ex-criminal – You are now working to help reformed criminals.

Pair C, you are:

The leader of the local tenants' association – You want a safer environment for the tenants.

A reporter from the local newspaper – You want to find out the views of all concerned.

Pairs A, B and C join to form groups of six. Role-play the meeting.

(If the class does not divide into groups of six, extra students can join pair C as reporters or local residents or act as chairperson to manage the meeting.)

2

🔊 8.4 **D FOLLOW AN ARGUMENT** **Listen to the full talk again. Complete the summary of each section with no more than three words from the talk. Use the information in the box to help you.**

Following an argument

In talks, speakers usually build to one clear conclusion. To reach this point, they use each section of the talk to develop their argument. To help you follow an argument, listen for when the speaker:

- asks a question, then answers it – this helps them highlight the main ideas
- uses pronoun referencing – this helps them refer back to the main ideas
- gives a definition – this allows them to use key vocabulary

1 Our memories are unreliable because we rewrite or add to them each time we ___recall an event___.

2 Although the idea of repressed memories was popular in the 1980s, studies since strongly indicate that patients were encouraged to create false memories ___by their therapists___.

3 The 1974 Loftus study showed that the way you ___ask questions___ or talk about an event can influence someone's memory of it.

4 To many, studies like this explained how patients in the 1980s might have been encouraged to ___rewrite___ their own childhood memories.

5 The 1995 Loftus study demonstrated that people can actually be convinced to create ___entirely false___ childhood memories.

E SPEAK **Work in pairs and follow these instructions:**

Student A – Turn to page 97. Look at the picture for 30 seconds. Close your book. Tell Student B as much that you can remember about the picture as possible.

Student B – Turn to page 97. Look at the picture and listen to your partner's description. How accurate is their memory?

F **Now change roles using the image on** page 109.

PRONUNCIATION

Adding information

🔊 8.6 **A** **Listen to an extract from the lecture. Is the phrase in bold said with a falling tone (↘), rising tone (↗) or fall-rising tone (↘↗)?** fall-rising tone

The information presented by a witness may have been influenced by the way in which they were questioned after the event. **On top of that**, lawyers could encourage witnesses to add or change details.

B **Work in pairs. What is the function of the phrase in Exercise A?**

a to change the topic

b to give an explanation

(c) to add information

🔊 8.7 **C** **Listen and repeat the sentences.**

1 Sounds ridiculous, doesn't it? **But actually**, the way we question someone can have a dramatic effect on how they describe what happened.

2 Juries are asked to pay close attention to eyewitness testimonies, but they are arguably not a reliable source. **Furthermore**, they can be affected by the stress and anxiety of, for instance, a violent robbery.

SPEAKING HUB

A PLAN **Read the situation and write notes about the victim, crime and any other important details.**

On Saturday, December 23, the billionaire oil tycoon Magnus Baldursson held a dinner party at his house to celebrate his retirement. At around 10:00 pm, his daughter's body was found at the bottom of the main staircase with a broken neck. She's thought to have been murdered.

B PREPARE **Work in groups. Turn to** page 148.

C DISCUSS **In your groups, discuss who you think killed Sophia and why.**

A: It must have been Albert. He said he is happy that Sofia's dead!

B: Yes, but he has an alibi. He was eating dinner in the kitchen.

○– Write and perform a short scene

○– Speculate about the causes and consequences of a crime

An urban legend

COMPREHENSION

A Work in groups. Which of the following do you think are true and which are urban legends?

They are all false/urban legends.

1 If you drop a penny from the top of a skyscraper it will kill anyone it lands on.

2 Sharks can detect a single drop of blood from the other end of a swimming pool.

3 Using your cell phone at a gas station could trigger an explosion.

Glossary

crane (n) a tall machine with a long arm used for lifting and moving heavy objects

dummy (n) a model of a person, typically used for displaying clothes in a store window

Portaloo™ (n) a temporary toilet inside a small building that can be easily moved from place to place

B Watch a segment from a TV show about urban legends and answer the questions.

1 Which urban legend is discussed in the video?

2 How does the presenter and his team test the legend?

3 What is the conclusion of the experiment?

C Watch again. Complete the sentences with no more than three words from the segment.

1 The team dropped the Portaloo™ from a height of thirty/30 meters onto a concrete surface.

2 The first test showed that doing nothing at all would result in serious injury.

3 The slow-motion video shows that the force of the impact travels upward through the body.

4 For the second test, the team makes the synthetic body-double 'jump' before impact.

5 The second test showed it isn't possible to jump upward quick enough to make a real difference to the speed that you're falling.

AUTHENTIC ENGLISH

A 00:47–01:12 Watch part of the video again. Do the reactions of the presenter and his colleague make the situation sound more or less serious than it is?

B Match the situations (1–5) with their understated descriptions (a–e). Use the information in the box to help you.

Understatement

An understatement is a sentence that makes a situation seem less important, serious, big, etc than it really is.

Two ways to make an understatement are by:

1 **modifying the noun**

*OK, so we have **a little** problem with the car – it's been stolen.*

*I'm afraid there's **a slight** issue with your card, sir. The payment has been declined.*

2 **rephrasing the sentence**

You've put me in a terrible position. → *This is not the best position to be in.*

I can't remember the last time I felt this bad! → *Well, I've definitely felt worse.*

1 You accidentally deleted an important document. e

2 You almost died in a car crash. b

3 Your house was robbed and everything was stolen. d

4 It's minus thirty degrees outside. a

5 You're so sick that you can't get out of bed. c

a 'It's a little bit cold outside.'

b 'Yeah, it was pretty scary I guess.'

c 'So, I'm not really feeling 100% to be honest.'

d 'OK, don't worry, but there's been a little incident at home.'

e 'Uh, there's a slight issue with the report.'

C Work in pairs. Take turns describing an extreme situation, then giving an understated description of it.

A: You broke your leg in a climbing accident!

B: Yes, it was kind of painful ...

Don't believe everything you hear

SAM MALCOLM AMANDA HARRY EMILY

A Work in pairs. Imagine that you are trapped in a room. What different methods might you use to try to escape?

B Watch the video and answer the questions.

1 Which of your ideas from Exercise A do Harry and Sam try?

2 Where are they getting their ideas from? From things they've seen in films/movies.

3 How do they eventually escape?
Amanda unlocks the door with a hairpin/bobby pin.

SPEAKING SKILL

A Work in pairs. Read the extract from the conversation and discuss the questions.

1 What is the function of the highlighted phrase?

2 Why is it appropriate in this situation?

3 What other phrases could you use?

Sam: What now?
Harry: OK. We'll just have to call someone and get them to open the door from the other side using the spare key. Does that sound like a plan?

B Watch the video again. Complete the box with examples from the conversation.

Maintaining a conversation

When we are working together to solve a problem, we frequently keep the discussion going by asking others what they think of our suggestions. To do this, we use phrases such as:

Does that sound like a plan?, What do you think about ...?, What do you reckon?, Shall we try that?, Are you all right with ...?.

C Read the situation below and brainstorm possible solutions.

You are driving through the countryside at night when suddenly your car breaks down. There's no cell phone signal and you didn't pass any houses or other buildings for miles before you broke down. There are no streetlights and very little moonlight.

D Work in groups. Discuss your ideas from Exercise C and try to agree on one solution. Use phrases from the box to maintain the conversation.

SPEAKING HUB

A PLAN Look back at the urban legends at the beginning of the lesson. Brainstorm different ways to effectively test each legend.

B PREPARE Choose your best suggestion for each test in Exercise A. Write notes about:

- what equipment you would need
- why this is an effective test
- how many times you would run the test and why
- any potential issues

C SPEAK Work in groups. Discuss your ideas from Exercise B and try to agree on one test for each urban legend.

Well, we can't really drop a coin from a skyscraper onto someone's head! I mean, I think that would hurt a little!

D PRESENT Present your ideas to the class and answer any questions.

Discuss how to test an idea

➤ Turn to page 161 to learn how to write a complex essay.

8.3 Fact or fiction?

An urban legend

LEAD-IN

Write the following on the board – *going out with wet hair, sitting on a cold floor, sleeping with the window open* and *leaving the air-conditioning on all night*. Elicit the connection (*these are all believed to be ways you can get sick*) and tell students that generally accepted theories or beliefs like these are examples of what's called *conventional wisdom*. Then put students into groups to discuss examples of conventional wisdom from their countries.

COMPREHENSION

A Put students into groups to discuss the three situations. Bring the class back together to share their ideas.

B ▶ Tell the students that you are going to watch part of a TV show about urban legends. Then play the video, encouraging students to write notes. Give feedback as a class.

1 *You can survive in a falling lift/elevator if you jump just before it hits the ground.*

2 *They put a dummy in a Portaloo™ and drop it from a crane to see the extent of a person's injuries if they don't jump before hitting the ground. They then install a system in the Portaloo that makes the dummy 'jump' before it hits the ground and run the test again.*

3 *The team concludes that there is no truth to the urban legend.*

C ▶ Play the video again for students to complete the exercise. Give feedback as a class.

AUTHENTIC ENGLISH

A ▶ 00:47–01:12 Play the video for students to answer the questions. Give feedback as a class.

The dummy's feet and ankles were both utterly destroyed in the fall. To describe this as 'not good' makes the situation sound far less serious than it really is. This is an example of an understatement.

B Read the skills box as a class, providing further examples if necessary. Then, ask students to complete the exercise alone before giving feedback as a class.

C Put students into pairs to practice making understatements.

Don't believe everything you hear

LEAD-IN

Tell students about a time when you had to work as part of a team to solve a problem or get out of a difficult situation. Then, put students into pairs to discuss their own experiences. Bring the class back together to share their anecdotes.

A Put students into pairs to discuss the question. Monitor, helping with new vocabulary as necessary. Bring the class back together to share their ideas.

B ▶ Tell students they are now going to watch the next episode of the Café Hub series. Give them time to quickly read the questions, before playing the video. Allow time for students to compare their ideas with a partner before whole-class feedback. You can find the **video script** for *Don't believe everything you hear* on the Teacher's Resource Center.

SPEAKING SKILL

A Put students into pairs to discuss the extract. Give feedback as a class.

1 *It invites Sam to comment on Harry's suggestion.*

2 *It's appropriate because they need to work together to find a way out of the room.*

3 *What do you think about …; Should we go with that then?; Does that sound like a good idea? etc.*

B ▶ Play the video again and for students to complete the skills box. Ask them to briefly compare their answers in pairs before giving feedback as a class.

C–D Give students time to read the situation and write notes about possible solutions. Then, put them into groups to discuss their ideas. Tell them they must agree on one solution. Bring the class back together to share their ideas.

SPEAKING HUB

A–B Give students time to list ideas and write notes.

C–D Put students into groups to discuss their tests. Then bring the class back together to share ideas.

▶ VIDEO SCRIPT

An urban legend

G = Greg Tm = Team member

G: So, you're at the top of an office block and you take the lift because you can't be bothered with the stairs. But something's wrong. You're going down, but far too fast. What do you do? You remember hearing someone say that if you jump at the last minute you can survive your perilous drop. But is it true? It's time to put the legend to the test with the help of a crane, a Portaloo [*This is going to be our willing lift drop volunteer*] and our body double. We're going to drop him from 30 meters up [Everyone all set?] to see what would happen if you did nothing at all. Three, two, one! Oh, yes! Ooh! Ooh, that looked painful. Oh, dear. That's not good.

(Ex B Q1; Ex B Q2; Ex C Q1 + 2)

Tm: That's not good.

Ex C Q3 **G:** That is one mangled foot. Looks like if you stand in a falling lift, the force of the impact goes straight through your feet and up through your body. We're going to need another dummy. So the legend says, 'If you jump at the last minute, you're gonna be fine.' Time to put it to the test. We've rigged up a spring-loaded platform we can use to make our synthetic stunt man jump just before he hits the ground. Three, two, one!

(Ex C Q4)

Tm: You've done it!

G: Ooh! Look at that, look. Let's get in. Look at the state of his feet. He's still a complete and utter …

Tm: As bad, as bad.

G: … broken man, isn't he? Even though our man jumped at the last minute, he was still traveling earthwards quicker than his jump was pushing him up. So if you do find yourself in a falling lift, you can try and jump, but it's going to make such a minor difference to the speed that you're falling. Plus you don't have a glass-bottomed lift so you're not going to know when to jump. There is no truth to that urban legend.

(Ex C Q5; Ex B Q3)

8 Writing

Write a complex essay

writing conclusions

A Read the essay prompt and answer the questions.

1 What claim is made in the prompt?

2 What does *this* refer to in the first question?

Many former criminals go on to reoffend following their release from prison. Is the prison system primarily to blame for this? Should more be done to support former criminals?

B Read the introduction and body of the essay. Choose the best summary (1 or 2) of the writer's position.

1 Support groups need to be established in local areas to help former criminals establish valuable roles in society.

2 The prison system needs to do more to provide criminals with the skills they need to succeed post release.

A large proportion of former criminals go on to reoffend when released from prison. This essay will explain that while the prison system certainly plays a role in this statistic, it is primarily the lack of employment opportunities on the outside that is to blame and, for this reason, support networks must be established to better integrate ex-convicts back into society.

One of the primary functions of the prison system is to reform criminals, not just punish them. To this end, most prisons offer training programs that provide inmates that are willing to learn with practical skills that should help them find employment post-release. However, many former criminals return to neighborhoods where opportunities are limited and they are forced to take low-paid jobs that don't reflect the skills they acquired while behind bars. Without a clear support network designed to help shape the careers of former criminals, many feel neglected by society. It is this lack of support that is the root of reoffending.

While most governments do offer guidance to former criminals, much more needs to be done to support sustainable reintegration into society. Support groups formed primarily of ex-convicts that have forged successful careers post-release should be founded in all major towns and cities. These groups should be given all of the funding and resources necessary to nurture the careers of former criminals, ensuring that they can play a valuable part in society.

C Work in pairs. Which is the best conclusion for the essay in Exercise B? Use the information in the box to help you.

Writing conclusions

Essays should finish with a simple conclusion summarizing the key arguments made in the body. Since no new ideas should be explored in the conclusion, it's easy to lose the interest of readers at this point. To avoid this, ensure your conclusions are short, simple and paraphrase your main ideas.

1

In conclusion, while most prisons offer training programs that provide inmates with valuable practical skills, many ex-convicts return to neighborhoods where opportunities are limited. All too frequently, they find themselves surrounded by others who have returned to a life of crime and cannot resist the urge to follow suit. By establishing support groups in major towns and cities, we would ensure that former criminals play a valuable part in society instead of turning back to a life of crime.

2

In conclusion, although the prison system should certainly shoulder some of the blame for the high volume of repeat offenders, it does provide inmates with the opportunity to acquire practical skills that are valuable to society. However, the existing networks available post-release do not offer former criminals the level of support they need in order to apply what they have learned. We need to establish well-resourced support networks throughout the country to help ex-convicts forge successful careers.

WRITING

A PREPARE Read the essay question below and brainstorm ideas.

Many ex-convicts struggle to adapt to life outside prison post-release. Is their attitude primarily to blame for this? Should more be done to help them adjust?

B PLAN Organize your ideas into paragraphs.

C WRITE Write your essay. Use your plan to help you.

D EDIT Work in pairs. Edit your partner's essay. Check:

- spelling and punctuation
- use of language
- strength of conclusion

WRITING 161

Answers

1 That many former criminals reoffend after being released from prison

2 The claim made in the first sentence

Answers

2 – the first conclusion introduces a new idea ('All too frequently, they find themselves surrounded by others who have returned to a life of crime and cannot resist the urge to follow suit.') and replicates chunks of text from the body rather than paraphrasing the ideas.

Refer students to this essay as a model for the writing task.

Refer students to this checklist when editing their partner's work.

LEAD-IN

Write the following sentence on the board – *Almost 1/3 of people who are sent to prison in the US will commit another crime.* Ask students to suggest whether or not they find this statistic surprising, and elicit one or two ways to address the issue. Then, put them into groups to discuss more ideas. Bring the class back together to share their ideas.

WRITING

A Give students time to read the essay prompt and answer the questions before briefly checking their answers with a partner. Give feedback as a class, eliciting the meaning of *reoffend* (*committing another crime after a first conviction*) and adding this term to the board.

B Give students time to read the body of the essay and choose the best summary. As it's a fairly challenging text, make sure they have enough to read carefully. Give feedback as a class, again clarifying anything students don't understand.

C Read the skills box as a class, giving further explanation if necessary. Then, give students time to complete the exercise alone before checking their answers with a partner. Give feedback as a class.

WRITING TASK

A–B Analyze the essay question as a class, then give students time to think of ideas in response. Monitor and help with any new vocabulary. Next, give them time to organize their notes into an essay plan using the essay they read earlier as a model.

C Tell students to write their essays. Monitor and provide support with structure and vocabulary when necessary.

D Put students into pairs to edit each other's essays. Encourage students to give each other positive feedback. Students can then rewrite their essays either in class or for homework.

Unit 8 Review

VOCABULARY

A Complete the text with the correct form of the words in bold.

The Kitsune is a [1] mythical Japanese creature.	**MYTH**
It has the ability to [2] transform from a fox into a human, but it does not look like a normal fox.	**TRANSFORM**
In [3] traditional stories, the Kitsune could fly, become invisible and produce fire and lightning. People had the	**TRADITION**
[4] belief that as the creature got older, it became stronger and more intelligent. Once it reached one hundred, the creature could take a form that	**BELIEVE**
[5] represented a human. It could also enter people's dreams and drive them mad. In many ways, the creature is similar to the	**REPRESENT**
[6] heroic characters in Pokémon, but the Kitsune was much more evil and considered a great trickster.	**HERO**

B Complete the sentences with the correct form of the words from the box.

feel hear listen look see touch watch

1 The fog was so thick we couldn't __see__ where we were going.
2 He hid behind the door, __listening__ as they argued about what to do.
3 They suddenly woke up. 'Did you __hear__ that noise?' she asked.
4 She reached out and gently __touched__ his hand.
5 They __watched__ in horror as the cars crashed into each other.
6 __Looking__ closely, he noticed that some of the things on his desk had been moved.
7 They could __feel__ the cold draft coming through the door.

C Choose the correct options (a, b or c) to complete the sentences.

1 At the courthouse last night, Mr. Taylor was ___ to 15 years in prison.
a committed b charged (c) sentenced
2 He admitted to using sensitive information to ___ the former star.
(a) blackmail b bribe c charge
3 Police have released footage of the armed ___ at the gas station.
(a) robbery b burglary c identity theft
4 Mr. Baxter says he ___ for five hours without a break.
a was charged b was arrested (c) was questioned
5 The men are accused of ___ multiple crimes in the area.
a witnessing (b) committing c investigating

D Work in pairs. Discuss the questions.

1 What do you think is the most common crime in your country?
2 What could be done to address crime in your city?
3 How can you protect yourself against identity theft?

GRAMMAR

A Rewrite the underlined sentences with *must* / *might* / *can't* + *have* + past participle.

1 They should be here by now. Maybe they got lost on the way.
They __might have gotten lost on the way__.
2 I'm sure it wasn't Erin you saw last night. She's in Madrid.
You __can't have seen Erin last night__.
3 I'm sure Max got the promotion. He was looking very happy earlier!
Max __must have gotten the promotion__.
4 I was cleaning up earlier. It's possible I threw the letter away by accident.
I __might have thrown the letter away by accident__.
5 I'm sure I didn't leave my phone at work. I had it on the train.
I __can't have left my phone at work__.
6 Oh, no! I'm sure you booked the wrong tickets by mistake!
You __must have booked the wrong tickets by mistake__.

B Work in pairs. Take turns reading the sentences below, then responding with a modal of deduction.

1 Where's Emily? She should be here by now.
2 Did you hear that weird noise this morning?
3 So I saw your best friend outside earlier.

C Choose the correct options to complete the sentences.

1 He collects *Japanese antique* / *antique Japanese* vases.
2 They found some *ancient gold* / *gold ancient* coins in the field.
3 We're staying in a *wonderful little* / *little wonderful* town on the coast.
4 The town is full of *amazing French* / *French amazing* architecture.
5 They've rented a *luxury huge* / *huge luxury* villa for their vacation.
6 It's a *beautiful 19th century* / *19th century beautiful* mirror.
7 The *valuable Russian gold* / *valuable gold Russian* egg sold for millions.
8 He wore a *new blue* / *blue new* shirt for their date.

A Vietnamese entrepreneur transports her products in Haiphong, Vietnam.

Business (n) the work of buying or selling products or services for money
Synonyms: commerce (n), trade (n)
Collocations and idioms: business *deal*, *generate* business, *go into* business, business *as usual* (*used to say something is continuing in the normal way*)

Ford is suggesting that it is important for businesses and individuals to invest their wealth into making improvements to society, rather than just accumulating more and more for themselves.

Henry Ford (1863–1947) was a very successful American businessman who founded the Ford Motor Company. He is famous for developing the first mass-produced automobile, transforming from a luxury item to one that was affordable for ordinary people. He also introduced many key business innovations including the assembly line in factories.

OBJECTIVES

- talk about the risks and benefits of apps
- make an effective complaint about a product or service
- conduct a survey about what influences our purchases
- design and present an ad campaign
- discuss investment opportunities
- write a proposal

Work with a partner. Discuss the questions.

1 Read the quote. What roles in society do you think businesses have other than making money?

2 Do you think the future belongs to big businesses or to start-up companies and entrepreneurs? Explain your reasoning.

3 When looking for a new job are you more attracted to a high salary or challenging work? Why?

BUSINESS 97

OBJECTIVES

Read the unit objectives to the class.

UNIT OPENER QUESTIONS

1 Read the quote as a class and ask what *capital* means in this context (*money*). Then, put students into pairs to discuss the question. Monitor, helping with new vocabulary as necessary. Bring the class back together, encouraging students to support their ideas with examples.

2 Focus students on the picture and the caption. Elicit the meaning of *entrepreneur* (*someone who starts their own business, especially when this involves risks*), and add the word and its definition to the board. Then, elicit examples of well-known entrepreneurs and what they are famous for. Next, read the question as a class, and elicit the difference between *big businesses* and *start-ups* (*small businesses that are just being set up*). Finally, put students back into pairs to discuss the question. Monitor, encouraging them to justify their opinions with reasons and examples. Bring the class back together to share their ideas.

3 Briefly explain to students why you became a teacher and whether it was the salary or the challenge that initially attracted you to the role. Then, put them into pairs to discuss their own job requirements. Monitor, helping with new vocabulary as necessary. Bring the class back together, adding any useful emergent language to the board.

WORKSHEETS

Lesson 9.1 Customers

Grammar: Adjective clauses (W41)

Vocabulary: Dependent prepositions: verbs (W42)

Lesson 9.2 Products

Vocabulary: Science (W43)

Grammar: Determiners and quantifiers (W44)

Vocabulary: Advertising (W45)

9.1 Customers

- Talk about the risks and benefits of apps
- Make an effective complaint about a product or service

G adjective clauses **P** pitch on non-essential adjective clauses
S fronting **V** dependent prepositions: verbs

READING

A SPEAK Work in groups. Would you trust a stranger to do the following? Why/Why not?

- drive you somewhere
- stay at your house
- recommend something
- give you advice
- rate your skills
- judge your interactions

B READ FOR MAIN IDEA Read *Who would you trust?* Complete the article with the headings below.

- affecting your career
- new technology, new economy
- the influence of the consumer
- the benefits of and need for reviews
- the future of ratings

Who would you trust?

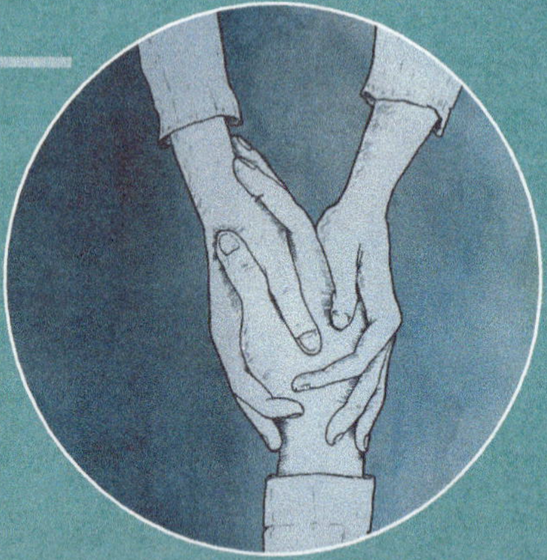

[1]Who are the people in your life that you place your trust in? What does someone have to do to earn your trust? In today's technology-driven world, it seems we are more willing than ever to trust the word of complete strangers.

By Leonard Jackson | July 16, 2018

a New technology, new economy

Trust has always played an essential role in the economy. [2]In the past, we placed our trust in our neighbors – people in our local community that had developed a good reputation for the products and services they offered. As major cities grew, we came to trust the reputation of companies and institutions. Individuals could start businesses, but it took time for them to establish a good reputation. Technology, and the way that it has enabled individuals to set up businesses and allowed others to rate them, has changed all of this. Just a few years ago, neither of the online services Uber or Airbnb existed, but both are now hugely popular. [3]Thanks to Uber, which lets people use an app to order a ride at a generally much lower rate than a normal taxi firm, we are all potential taxi drivers. And the website Airbnb, which lets you stay in other people's houses or apartments, means that a spare bedroom in your house is a money-making opportunity.

b The benefits of and need for reviews

Star-rating systems have been around for decades on Amazon and eBay, but mobile technology has made them much more accessible. Online shopping, which is clearly quicker and more efficient than regular shopping, doesn't allow us to physically try out the products. Ratings have helped to fill this gap. Consumers also tend to be good judges of how authentic a review is. For example, a product that doesn't have any negative reviews is likely to be viewed with some suspicion. Allowing customers to see both the good and bad in a product usually means they trust the reviews more – much more than something that constantly gets five stars.

c The influence of the consumer

Mobile technology has given people much more power to influence the reputation of a company. When Kylie Jenner sent a negative tweet about Snapchat, the company's value fell by over $1 billion in one day. [4]Of course, we don't all have the influence of famous celebrities, but companies now hire people whose job is to monitor mentions of their brands so they can provide instant customer support. Those companies that fail to react quickly run the risk of negative opinions and experiences going viral. In the past, complaining may have involved going into a store or writing a series of letters, but now good companies respond in minutes.

d Affecting your career

Our own online reputation can also have a significant effect on our real-world prospects. [5]Recruiters now regularly check out people's online profiles before interviewing or hiring them and the first thing they see are social media profiles. LinkedIn – the professional networking site – can have a huge influence on people's careers. In the past, employers posted job ads online hoping to attract the best talent; now they actively seek out prospective employees via endorsements on LinkedIn. Companies trust the accuracy of these online reviews of our experience and abilities even though they may have never met the people that wrote them.

e The future of ratings

So, how might our reputation be measured in the future? [6]Well, it's not difficult to imagine a world where our every interaction affects a social credit score. What we share or buy online, the content we 'like', even the people we connect with could all contribute to an overall rating that affects what we're able to do in the real world. Although this may sound like science fiction, a future in which we are rated on everything may not be that unrealistic.

LEAD-IN

Tell students about the last expensive item you bought and why you chose it (e.g. *customer reviews*, *relative cost*, *functionality*, etc). Next, put students into groups to discuss their own purchases and what influenced them. Monitor, encouraging them to ask follow-up questions to keep the conversation going. Bring the class back together to share their lists and try to agree on the top five. Add any useful emergent language to the board, covering any useful language from the text that you haven't pre-taught yet.

READING

A Put students into groups to discuss the question. Monitor, asking follow-up questions to keep the discussions going. Bring the class back together to share their ideas.

B Tell students you are going to read an article about trust. Read through the possible headings as a class, clarifying any new vocabulary. Then, give students time to complete the exercise alone, before checking their answers with a partner. Give feedback as a class, encouraging students to justify their answers with information from the text.

METHODOLOGY HUB by Jim Scrivener

Difficulties when reading a foreign language

What are your own main problems when trying to read a text in a language that you don't know very well? Maybe:

- I don't know enough vocabulary.
- I need the dictionary all the time.
- It's very slow – it takes a long time just to get through a few sentences.
- I usually get to the stage where I understand all the individual words, but the whole thing eludes me completely.
- Because it's slow, interest in the subject matter is soon lost.

Many learners approach reading texts expecting to read them thoroughly and to stop only when they have understood every word. Clearly, there is value in this as a way of improving their vocabulary and grammar, but, as with listening, this kind of approach does not necessarily make them better readers, because this plodding, word-by-word approach is not the way we usually read in real life. In order to make students better readers, we need first of all to raise their awareness that it's not always essential to understand every word and that practicing some different reading techniques in English may be very useful to them. And if their basic strategy is to read slowly and ponderously, then a good first strategy could be to help them learn to read fast; not worrying about understanding every word; not, possibly, even understanding most words, but still achieving a specific and useful goal.

TEACHING IDEA by David Seymour and Maria Popova

Bluff words

Use this activity to review adjective clauses in preparation for the grammar section.

In teams of three, find a word in the dictionary that you are sure nobody in class knows and write three definitions, two false and one correct, e.g. *bluff.*

1 *A bluff is a soft stick that you use for hitting a drum.*

2 *Bluff is a color which is mid-way between blue and grey.*

3 *To bluff is to make someone believe something that is untrue.*

Take turns reading your definitions. The other teams have to choose one of your definitions. If they choose one of your false definitions, your team wins a point. If they choose the correct one, they win a point.

(Variation: Choose words from the list below. Your selection should include things, people and places. Finish the activity by writing up more words and asking for imaginative definitions from the whole class.)

blacksmith, caretaker, flea, fluff, harvest, hinge, hive, hook, idler, kennel, kiln, kipper, kite, lobster, maggot, maze, miser, outcast, ox, padlock, pantry, paw, plowman, potty, ragamuffin, sawmill, sewer, skip, socket, spinster, stroller, swap, thorn, thug, tickle, toddler, trap, twig, undertaker, venue, whip, wig, wrench, yawn

GRAMMAR HUB

9.1 Adjective clauses

Types of adjective clause

- We use essential adjective clauses to identify exactly which person or thing we are talking about.

  The woman who sits next to me at work is studying for an MA in her free time.
- We use non-essential adjective clauses to give extra, non-essential information about a person or thing. We use commas to separate this clause from the rest of the sentence.

  The band, whose debut album was released in 1991, has sold over 32 million records in the US alone.
  (= We don't need to know when their debut album was released – this is just extra information.)

Relative pronouns

- All adjective clauses begin with a relative pronoun. We use *who* for people, *which* for things, *where* for places, *when* for times and *whose* for possession.

  Apparently, the store where I bought my computer closed down recently.

  Sam, whose mom owns a business, wants to open his own store.

- In essential adjective clauses:

  a we can use *that* instead of *who* or *which.*
  We're really looking for someone who/that has experience teaching children.

  b we can omit *who, that* and *which* when they are the object of the adjective clause.
  The employee (that) we spoke to wasn't very helpful.

  c we can never omit *where* or *whose.*
  My parents have just sold the house where I grew up.
  NOT ~~My parents have just sold the house I grew up.~~

- In non-essential adjective clauses:

  a we cannot use *that* instead of *who* or *which.*
  My sister, who recently graduated from Harvard, just got a new job. NOT ~~My sister, that recently graduated from Harvard, just got a new job.~~

  b we cannot omit the relative pronoun.
  Michael Jackson, who died in 2009, was known as the 'King of Pop'. NOT ~~Michael Jackson, died in 2009, was known as the 'King of Pop'.~~

C Ask students to complete the exercise alone, before checking their answers with a partner. Give feedback as a class.

D Put students into groups to discuss the questions. Monitor, encouraging students to justify their answers with examples. Bring the class back together, opening up each question for further discussion. Add any useful emergent language to the board.

GRAMMAR

A Write the following question on the board – *Who are the people in your life that you place your trust in?* Ask students to identify the adjective clause (*that you place your trust in*) and underline it on the board. Next, ask students to identify the relative pronoun (*that*), either rewriting it in a different color in your sentence or drawing a box around it. Now, draw students' attention to the remaining highlighted sentences in the article, and give them time to underline the adjective clauses in each. Ask them to briefly check their answers in pairs before giving feedback as a class.

B Refer back to the sentence that you wrote on the board, and elicit whether it is an essential or non-essential adjective clause (*essential*) and how you can tell (*the information given in the adjective clause is essential to the meaning of the sentence*). Now, put students into pairs to discuss the other adjective clauses from Exercise A. Give feedback as a class.

C–D Give students time to complete the rules alone, before comparing their answers with a partner. Give feedback as a class, then direct students to the **Grammar Hub** (see below and TB98).

E Read the second line of the review as a class, and elicit one or two ideas of how to improve it using adjective clauses to give more information. Then, put students into groups to rework the rest. Bring the class back together to share their ideas, working through the review line by line to build an improved version on the board. Use the **Grammar Worksheet** on page W41 for extra practice.

Suggested answer

This is the best app that I've ever downloaded! It has a lot of useful features including a meal tracker, which allows you to record the food you eat every day. I also really like the recipes, which are all delicious and easy to make. Another good feature is the fitness section, where you can plan new exercise routines. There's also a community space where you can share content with other users. I was actually sent a recipe by an old friend who I haven't spoken to for years! Anyway, I'd definitely recommend this app for anyone that's trying to be healthier.

PRONUNCIATION

A (9.1) Explain that you have focused a lot so far on intonation (i.e. the way your voice goes up and down when you speak), but now you are going to focus on pitch (i.e. how high or low a sound is), using your voice to demonstrate the difference. Next, read the rubric as a class, eliciting the difference between *step up* (*said at a higher pitch*) and *step down* (*said at a lower pitch*). Then, play the audio for students to identify the pitch change. Give feedback as a class, eliciting why the clause might be said at a lower pitch (*the information is additional and not as important*).

B (9.2) Play the audio, pausing between each sentence so students can copy the changes in pitch.

SPEAKING

A–C Give students time to make a list of apps that they use, then put them into pairs to discuss them. Then, ask them to rank the apps before bringing the class back together to share their ideas.

GRAMMAR HUB

9.1 Adjective clauses

A Choose the correct options to complete the sentences.

1. Last summer, I visited my cousin, *who* / *whose* lives in a nice apartment in New York. (who)
2. There's the new store *–* / *where* I was telling you about. (–)
3. The recruiter *who* / *which* helped is my cousin, Léo. (who)
4. The woman *whose* / *who* house we stayed in had listed it on Airbnb. (whose)
5. It's usually late at night *where* / *when* I feel hungriest. (when)
6. My car, *that* / *which* I've had since May, uses a lot of gas. (which)
7. Thanks, Fiona. The recommendation *–* / *who* you gave me was a great idea. (–)
8. The house *which* / *in which* I grew up is now a hotel. (in which)

B Combine the sentences using an adjective clause. Omit the relative pronoun where possible.

1. San Francisco is where the company was founded. It is also home to TechCorp.
   San Francisco, which is where the company was founded, is also home to TechCorp
2. I used to work in a call center. It's just gone out of business.
   The call center where I used to work has just gone out of business.
3. Mark Allen created the app in his bedroom. He is now worth $20 billion.
   Mark Allen, who created the app in his bedroom, is now worth $20 billion
4. Sadly it was no longer under warranty. This means I can't get my money back.
   Sadly it was no longer under warranty, which means I can't get my money back
5. The app allows users to order food 24 hours a day. It has received mixed reviews.
   The app, which allows users to order food 24 hours a day, has received mixed reviews
6. I sit next to a woman at work who has a degree in customer service management.
   The woman (that) I sit next to at work has a degree in customer service management

C Are these sentences correct or incorrect? Rewrite the incorrect sentences.

1. My company, ~~that~~ which is based in New York, has offices all over the world.
2. The slight problem ~~that~~ which you told me about, can't easily be fixed.
3. ✓ The movies that are playing at that movie theater are never very good.
4. My coffee maker, which I paid a lot for, makes terrible coffee!
5. ✓ Where's the complaint form the customer filled out?
6. The customer who/that called about the problem is still on the phone.
7. The woman, whose tablet I was borrowing, just told me to keep it!
8. The store that/which I got bad service from which isn't getting my business anymore!

➤ Go back to page 99.

C READ FOR DETAIL Read again. Complete the sentences with no more than two words from the article.

1. New technology has allowed customers to ___rate___ new businesses.
2. A rating system can reduce the ___gap___ between customers and sellers.
3. People are unlikely to trust a product with no ___negative reviews___.
4. Customers can now ___influence___ what a company does.
5. Businesses employ people to monitor ___mentions___ of their company online so that they can deal with issues quickly.
6. Our own personal online ___reputation___ could affect our future job prospects.
7. Companies look for ___prospective employees___ using networking sites like LinkedIn.
8. The writer believes that in the future we may use a ___social credit score___ based on how we interact online.

D SPEAK Work in groups. Discuss the questions.

1. Do you usually check online reviews before buying or doing something? Why/Why not?
2. Have you ever complained about a product or service via social media?
3. What can you do to protect or improve your online reputation?

GRAMMAR

Adjective clauses

A Look at the highlighted sentences in the article. Underline the adjective clauses in each.

B SPEAK Work in pairs. Are the clauses you underlined in Exercise A essential or non-essential? How do you know?

C WORK IT OUT Match the sentences (1–6) from Exercise A to the rules (a–f).

Adjective clauses

In essential adjective clauses:

- we can use *that* instead of *who* or *which* a ___2___
- we can omit the relative pronoun when it's the object of the adjective clause b ___5___

In non-essential adjective clauses:

- we use commas to separate the clause from the rest of the sentence c ___3___

In both types of adjective clause:

- we use *where* to talk about places d ___6___ and *whose* to talk about possession e ___4___ – neither of which can be omitted
- we use prepositions at the beginning of a clause in formal English and at the end in informal English f ___1___

D Go to the **Grammar Hub** on **page 138**.

E SPEAK Work in groups. Try to improve the following review using adjective clauses like the one in the example.

Apps Games Reviews

★★★★☆

Meal Maker
is a great app!

ClaireP | 2 days ago

This is the best app *that I've ever downloaded!* It has a lot of useful features including a meal tracker. I also like the recipes. Another good feature is the fitness section. There's also a community space. I was actually sent a recipe by an old friend! Anyway, I'd definitely recommend this app.

PRONUNCIATION

Pitch on non-essential adjective clauses

9.1 **A** Listen to this extract from a radio show about apps. Does the speaker's pitch step up or down on the non-essential adjective clause? Down

Trello, which I use to stay organized at work, is the most useful app on my phone.

9.2 **B** Listen and repeat the sentences.

1. MyFitnessPal, which records daily food and exercise, is a good app for helping you lose weight.
2. Spotify, which allows you to stream music offline, is something I use every day.
3. Mint, which links all your bank cards, is a great app for keeping track of your finances.

SPEAKING

A PLAN Make a list of apps that you use regularly on your phone or tablet.

B PRESENT Work in pairs. Compare your lists from Exercise A. Explain any apps that your partner doesn't know or use.

A: I've heard of most of these, but what's Strava?
B: Uh, It's a fitness app that tracks how far you run.

C DISCUSS Work in pairs. Rank the apps in Exercise B from most to least useful. Then discuss any risks involved with each and how they might be improved.

LISTENING

A SPEAK Complete *Are you a good complainer?* Compare your answers with a partner. Give reasons for your approach.

B Go to the Communication Hub on page 153 to find out what type of complainer you are.

9.3 **C LISTEN FOR GIST** Listen to a customer make a complaint about something they ordered online. Answer the questions.

1 What does the customer want to complain about?
2 What two solutions does the customer service representative offer?
3 Is the customer happy with these solutions? Why/Why not?
4 Why can't the customer service representative resolve the issue now?

9.3 **D LISTEN FOR FRONTING** Listen again. Choose the correct options (a, b or c) to complete the sentences. Use the information in the box to help you.

Fronting

In informal spoken English, speakers sometimes move part of a clause from its normal position to the beginning of a sentence.

How you thought you'd get away with it, I'll never know.

Never have I been so disappointed.

This non-standard word order is called fronting and is used for emphasis or dramatic effect.

1 The customer had to wait for ___ to speak to a customer service representative.
   a two minutes
   b five minutes
   (c) 40 minutes
2 The customer doesn't think the delivery should have been left ___
   (a) in the backyard.
   b under the patio table.
   c in the children's playhouse.
3 The customer expects the company to ___
   (a) issue a full refund for the damaged books.
   b offer a discount on his next purchase.
   c replace the most damaged books.
4 The customer paid ___ for the books.
   a $10
   (b) $150
   c $100
5 The customer thinks ___ is ridiculous.
   a the customer service representative
   b the company's terms of service
   (c) the company's refunds and exchange policy

E SPEAK In some cultures, people prefer not to complain directly. How common is it to complain in your culture? How do you think people react to bad service or faulty products?

Are you a good complainer?

In some countries, complaining could almost be a national sport. In others, people rarely complain about anything. To find out what type of complainer you are, decide what you would do in the following situations.

1 You order some books from a well-known online retailer, but when they arrive most of them are damaged.
   a Say nothing and keep the books. It's still possible to read them; they just don't look very nice.
   b Share the story on social media, swearing to never use the company again.
   c Contact the company directly and ask for a refund or a replacement.

2 You order a cup of coffee at a well-known chain, but when it arrives it's the wrong drink.
   a Drink it anyway. It might not be what you ordered, but it's still delicious.
   b Post a comment publicly shaming the company on their social media page.
   c Politely point out the mistake to staff and ask for a new drink.

3 You accidentally sit in the first class section of train and are caught by the ticket inspector.
   a Pay the fine. You made a mistake, so you should face the consequences.
   b Refuse to pay and post a video of the argument that follows on social media.
   c Accept responsibility, but send an email to the train company suggesting they use clearer signs in first class.

4 You order a tuna sandwich from Andy's Café, but ask them to remove the cucumber because you don't like it. When you take your first bite, you realize they haven't done what you asked.
   a Remove the cucumber yourself and eat the sandwich anyway.
   b Share a picture of the sandwich online with the hashtag '#avoidandyscafe'
   c Politely explain the issue to staff and ask for a new sandwich.

5 You oversleep on a business trip and miss an early morning flight. The airline company won't let you on the next flight without a new ticket.
   a Buy a new ticket. It's your fault that you missed the flight.
   b Post a video of your argument with the airline company on social media.
   c Accept responsibility, but email the airline company suggesting they offer more support to customers in your situation.

LISTENING

A–B Give students time to complete the quiz alone. Then, put them into pairs to compare their answers before directing them to the **Communication Hub** (see TB121) to see their results. Bring the class back together, asking a few students whether they agree with their results or not.

9.3 **C** Play the audio, encouraging students to write notes as they listen. Put students into pairs to compare their answers before giving feedback as a class.

1 *Some of the books he received were damaged.*
2 *$10 off his next purchase; replacing the most damaged books.*
3 *No; he finds the offer of $10 off insulting, and he doesn't understand why he should be expected to keep books that were damaged.*
4 *Her manager has to authorize refunds or exchanges over $100.*

9.3 **D** Read through the skills box as a class, giving further explanations or examples as necessary. Then, give students time to read the questions and options before playing the audio again. Put them into pairs to compare their answers before giving feedback as a class.

E Put students into groups to discuss the questions. Monitor, encouraging them to give examples to support their ideas. Bring the class back together to share their ideas.

AUDIO SCRIPT

9.3

Listening, Exercise C
R = Recorded message   A = Amy   C = Customer

R: Thank you for holding, we appreciate your call. A customer service operator will be with you in approximately two minutes.
A: Good morning, Top Books, Amy speaking. Sorry to keep you waiting.
Ex D Q1 **C:** Finally! I've been on hold for 40 minutes! Aren't you supposed to answer within five minutes?
A: That is our goal sir, yes, but we've been experiencing an unusually high number of calls today. Again, I apologize for the delay, sir. How can I help you today?
C: I'm calling to complain about the condition of the books I received.
A: Oh, I'm sorry to hear that. What seems to be the problem?
Ex C Q1 **C:** Well, whoever delivered them left the box out in our backyard. We were away that weekend and it was raining pretty heavily so some of the books got damaged.
A: I see. OK. Could I just take your name and order number?
C: Of course. It's Harry Jenkins and the order number is 077-ADEP-9261.
A: Thank you. OK, here we are. Right, so it says here that the books were delivered on the 12th and that your safe place is the backyard. Is that right?
C: Well … yes, but it obviously isn't safe from the rain!
A: I appreciate that, sir, although according to our terms of service, all deliveries are left in a safe place specified by the customer.
C: I understand that, but at no point did I consent to the books being left somewhere they could get damaged! It shows a complete lack of common
Ex D Q2 sense. Underneath the patio table, that's where they should have been left. Or even in the children's playhouse. At least then they would have been protected from the elements! I'm sorry, but it simply isn't good enough. It's just terrible customer service!
A: I'm very sorry you feel that way, sir. How would you like us to address the issue?
Ex D Q3 **C:** A full refund, that's what I expect.
A: Well, while I am sympathetic to your situation, the books were delivered in accordance with our terms of service.
C: I understand that, but I really must insist on a full refund.
A: I'm afraid that since we have adhered to your delivery
Ex C Q2 instructions, the most I'd be able to offer is $10 off your next purchase.
Ex D Q4 **C:** Are you joking? Those books cost me $150! More to the point, why would I want to buy anything from you again when my first purchase has been such a disaster? If you can't offer a refund, I'd like all of the books picked up and replaced.
A: I see … And, are all of the books damaged?
C: To a certain extent, yes, although some are much worse than others.
A: Well, maybe we could explore some other options?
Ex C Q2 How about replacing the most damaged books?
Ex C Q3 **C:** Absolutely not! Why should I have to pay for damaged books? If your delivery driver had used a little common sense, we wouldn't be in this situation in the first place.
A: Well, as I mentioned earlier, we have followed …
C: Look, I don't want to argue about this anymore! If you don't replace all of the books, I'll take my complaint higher. And I'll be posting about the poor service on social media; I can assure you of that!
A: I'm sure that won't be necessary, sir. I'll register your complaint in our system and someone will be in touch within 24 hours to discuss what happens next.
C: 24 hours? Why can't this be dealt with right now? What is the point of speaking to you if you can't help me?
A: I can only apologize for any inconvenience caused.
Ex C Q4 I'm afraid I'm not authorized to deal with refunds or exchanges over $100 without the approval of my manager. It's company policy.
Ex D Q5 **C:** It's ridiculous, that's what it is! You need to make some serious changes to your organization!
A: Thank you for your feedback, sir. I'll raise your concerns to my manager after this call.
C: Yes, you do that!
A: Now, could I get the names of the books you'd like to return?
C: Certainly. There are three books on marketing and one on … anger management.
A: Sorry, did you say, 'anger management'?
C: Yes, that's right.
A: Uh, I'm just going to put you on hold a minute if that's OK?
C: No, it isn't OK. I demand to …

VOCABULARY

9.4 **A** Write the following sentence on the board – *How do you intend to deal ______ this issue?* Elicit the missing word (*with*), adding it to the sentence in a different color. Next, ask students if any other preposition could be used in this blank (*no*) and whether they can remember what you call prepositions that are usually joined to another word like this (*dependent prepositions*). Tell students that you are going to focus on verbs with dependent prepositions, and elicit any other examples you think students will already know (e.g. *listen to*, *agree with*, *believe in*, etc). Then, give students time to complete the sentences alone before playing the audio for them to check. Give feedback as a class, consolidating understanding by eliciting new examples for each dependent preposition and adding them to the board.

B Read through the first sentence as a class and elicit whether the dependent preposition is correct (*it is*). Then, ask students to complete the exercise alone before comparing their answers with a partner. Give feedback as a class. Use the **Vocabulary Worksheet** on page W42 for extra practice.

SPEAKING HUB

A Write the following headings on the board – *Making a complaint* and *Responding to a complaint*. Then, elicit one or two phrases to add to each column (e.g. *I'm calling to complain about …*, *I'm very sorry to hear that …*, etc). Then, put students into pairs to list any other phrases they can think of. Monitor, helping with grammar and vocabulary as necessary. Bring the class back together, building up the lists on the board.

B–C Tell students that they are going to role-play a complaints phone call. Then, put them into A/B pairs, asking the As to follow the instructions in the box and directing the Bs to the **Communication Hub** (see TB121). Monitor, helping with staging of the phone call as necessary. Then, ask students to change roles, directing the As to the **Communication Hub** (see TB121). Write a note about any useful emergent vocabulary.

D Put students back into pairs to assess their complaints, then bring the class back together to explain how successful they were.

TEACHING IDEA by David Seymour and Maria Popova

For crying out loud

Use this activity to extend the theme of complaints.

In small groups, tell each other about a real complaint you have made. Did you express your misgivings in a polite but assertive way? Was your complaint properly dealt with? Choose the most interesting complaint and write a script for it to read out to the class.

TEACHING IDEA by David Seymour and Maria Popova

Letters of complaint

Use this activity to extend the theme of complaints.

Look at the following information about poor products or services.

Car $999 (used)	**Vacation $600**
Noisy brakes	Filthy hotel
Leaking sunroof	No swimming pool
Faulty indicator	Construction work
Backfiring	12-hour delay
Jacket $200	**EFL School**
Tear in armpit	30 students/class
Buttons missing	Wrong level
Lining missing	Rude staff
Stain	Cold classroom

In pairs, choose one of them and write a letter of complaint. Swap letters with another pair and write a reply, e.g. *In your brochure you said the hotel had a swimming pool.*

METHODOLOGY HUB by Jim Scrivener

Running a role play: some guidelines

Choose the most interesting complaint and write a script for it.

- Make sure the students understand the idea of the role play. Do they know what's going to happen? Do they know what is required of them? Are they comfortable doing that or not?
- Make sure the context or situation is clear.
- Do they understand the information on their own card? Allow reading/dictionary/thinking time (during which you go around and help if necessary).
- Give them time to prepare their ideas before they start – maybe encourage note writing – but when the activity starts, encourage them to improvise rather than rely on prepared speeches and notes. The preparation work they have done will inform their role play, but could simply get in the way if they over-rely on it. It may help to take away the cards when the role play starts.
- At the end of the role play, make sure that you give some feedback on how well (or not) the students completed the activity. Remember to comment on the language used as well as the appropriacy of what was said. Students will need to feel that they have achieved something.

VOCABULARY

Dependent prepositions: verbs

Dependent prepositions: verbs

Some verbs and prepositions are commonly used together. These are called dependent prepositions and they are followed by either a noun or *-ing*.
For example:
How do you intend to deal with this issue? NOT ~~*How do you intend to deal about this issue?*~~

9.4 **A** Complete the extracts from the phone call with the prepositions in the box. Then listen and check.

about (x2) for (x2) on to (x2) with

1 Thank you ___for___ holding; we appreciate your call.
2 I'm calling to complain ___about___ the condition of the books I received.
3 I understand that, but at no point did I consent ___to___ the books being left somewhere they could get damaged!
4 I understand that, but I really must insist ___on___ a full refund.
5 I'm afraid that since we have adhered ___to___ your delivery instructions, the most I'd be able to offer is $10 off your next purchase.
6 Look, I don't want to argue ___about___ this anymore!
7 24 hours? Why can't this be dealt ___with___ right now?
8 I can only apologize ___for___ any inconvenience caused.

B Are these sentences correct or incorrect? Rewrite the incorrect sentences.

✓ 1 Cheap Flights would like to apologize for any inconvenience caused by this delay.
2 You should have complained ~~at~~ about having to wait so long to be served.
✓ 3 I'm sick of being passed between different people – I just want someone to deal with this issue!
4 I realize you've adhered ~~in~~ to company policy, but I'm still not satisfied.
5 Gary, can you help me? There's a customer downstairs who keeps insisting ~~at~~ on speaking to the manager.
6 Look, we've been arguing ~~on~~ about this for the past 45 minutes. Either issue a refund or let me speak to your manager.
7 When you completed the purchase online, you consented ~~with~~ to our terms and conditions.
✓ 8 Let me take this opportunity to thank all of you for giving us your feedback today.

SPEAKING HUB

A PLAN Work in pairs. Think of phrases you could use to complain about a product and how you could respond to these complaints.

B SPEAK Student A – Imagine you are a customer service representative. Use the stages below to help you resolve your partner's complaint. Student B – Imagine you are a customer. Go to the Communication Hub on page 149.

1 Find out how you can help the customer.
2 Find out if the product is broken.
3 Ask if something else could be causing the fault, e.g. the internet provider.
4 Check if the product is still under warranty.
5 Suggest sending someone out to repair the product.
6 Tell the customer that exchanges are not part of the company policy.
7 Tell the customer you will refer the complaint to your supervisor.

C REPEAT Change roles. Student A – Go to the Communication Hub on page 150.
Student B – Use the stages in Exercise B to help you resolve your partner's complaint.

D DISCUSS Who had the most successful complaint? Tell the class and give reasons.

– Talk about the risks and benefits of apps
– Make an effective complaint about a product or service

- Conduct a survey about what influences our purchases
- Design and present an ad campaign

V – science; advertising
P – connected speech: determiners and quantifiers
G – determiners and quantifiers
S – topic sentences

VOCABULARY

Science

A Read *The book club*. Complete the definitions with the words in bold.

1 ___analysis___ (n) a process of studying or examining something in order to understand or explain it

2 ___researchers___ (n) people who study something carefully to discover new information about it

3 ___theory___ (n) one or more ideas that explain how or why something happens

4 ___evidence___ (n) facts or signs that make you believe something is true

5 ___data___ (n) facts or information used for making calculations or decisions

B Complete the sentences with words from Exercise A.

1 The company has collected ___data___ from over 20,000 people worldwide.

2 ___Researchers___ claim the results indicate a clear link between stress and high blood pressure.

3 I'm sorry, but there simply isn't enough ___evidence___ to support that claim.

4 ___Analysis___ of the data showed a link between the consumption of fish and improved memory.

5 One ___theory___ is that consumers don't actually question the claims made in advertising.

The Book Club

Episode 402: Science fact or fiction?

According to **researchers** from the McCallun Institute, over 80% of Americans still believe that Vitamin C cures the common cold, despite the fact that there is little to no **evidence** to support this **theory**. In her new book, *Science fact or fiction?*, Professor Dawn Jackson uses her **analysis** of hundreds of consumer studies to argue that believing in health myths may actually affect the products we buy. She goes on to claim that companies take advantage of this fact in their marketing campaigns. But are Jackson's observations really supported by the research **data**? Michael Evans spoke to her earlier this week to find out.

LISTENING

A SPEAK Work in pairs. Do you think the following sentences are facts (F) or myths (M)? Explain your reasoning.

1 We should drink eight glasses of water a day. ___
2 Eggs are bad for your heart. ___
3 Yogurt is good for digestion. ___
4 Eat less food when you have a fever. ___
5 Eating cheese can give you nightmares. ___
6 Natural sugar is better for us than processed sugar. ___

9.5 **B LISTEN FOR MAIN IDEA** Listen to a radio interview about health myths. According to the scientist, which three of the claims in Exercise A are myths? 1; 6; 3 depends on the type of yogurt

Glossary

dehydration (n) a dangerous lack of water in the body

9.5 **C LISTEN FOR DETAIL** Listen again. Complete the sentences with no more than three words or a number from the podcast.

1 According to the professor, the ___bottled water industry___ benefits from the commonly held belief that we need to drink eight glasses of water a day.

2 There's no evidence that increasing your intake of ___vitamin C___ will help the body fight infections such as the common cold.

3 The professor argues that we can only be confident of a health claim if there is a large body of ___scientific evidence___ to support it.

4 Probiotics, also known as '___friendly___ bacteria', are generally thought to be beneficial to the digestive system.

5 Companies need to be careful about ___the wording___ used in advertising as they cannot legally make claims that aren't supported by evidence.

6 While ___free sugars___ are associated with a number of negative health effects, the professor says we don't need to worry about how much fruit we consume.

D SPEAK Work in pairs. Why do you think so many companies focus on health? How do companies try to promote unhealthy products?

LEAD-IN

Tell the students you have a cold and elicit how to deal with the symptoms. If no one suggests it, ask whether they think vitamin C will help.

VOCABULARY

A Give students time to complete the definitions alone, before checking their answers in pairs. Give feedback as a class.

B Ask students to complete the sentences alone before checking their answers in pairs. Then, give feedback as a class. Use the **Vocabulary Worksheet** on page W43 for extra practice.

LISTENING

9.5 **A–B** Put students into pairs to discuss the claims. Then, play the audio for them to check their ideas.

9.5 **C** Play the recording for students to complete the exercise alone, before checking their answers in pairs. Give feedback as a class.

D Put students into pairs to discuss the questions.

AUDIO SCRIPT

9.5

Listening, Exercise B
P = Presenter D = Dawn

P: I'm here today with Professor Dawn Jackson, from BLB University, who has just written a book, *Science fact or fiction?* which focuses on common health myths related to the food industry. So Professor Jackson, can you give us an example of one of the myths you discuss in the book?

Ex B **D:** Well, possibly one of the most common myths is that we need to drink two liters of water every day.

P: Is that a myth? I definitely remember hearing that we should try to drink at least eight glasses of water a day to stay hydrated.

D: Well, yes, that's the claim but there isn't really any evidence to support it. We get plenty of water through food. Even drinks like coffee, which some people believe dehydrate you, are actually a good source of water. The bottom line is – trust your body. It will tell you when you're dehydrated.

P: So, where has this myth come from?

Ex C Q1 **D:** Well, I don't know the exact origins, but it's certainly useful for the bottled water industry, isn't it? They make billions of dollars a year.

P: Yes, it's a huge industry these days, isn't it? When I was a kid, no one drank bottled water.

D: Yes, the industry has grown rapidly with flavored water, vitamin drinks and even water that claims to be some kind of energy drink! All sorts of varieties.

P: Surely, the added vitamins and minerals help?

D: No, not really. This is another huge myth created by creative advertising. A large number of people think taking vitamin C is a good way of fighting a cold, but there is no evidence that this is the case. Actually, once you have a cold, it will do very little to help you fight it. Vitamin C is good for you, and low levels may mean you get more colds, but increasing your intake once you have an infection won't help fight it in the slightest. (Ex C Q2)

P: So what should people do? How can they tell whether a claim is true or not?

D: Well, it really comes down to thinking critically about the things you read. Don't just take claims made in advertising at face value. If you're interested in a product, especially a health product, do a little research into the claim. Is there any scientific evidence to support it? Have there been multiple large-scale studies that consistently give the same results? Only then can you be confident that a claim is based on real evidence. (Ex C Q3)

P: So we need to do a little homework?

D: Exactly!

P: OK, so we asked our listeners to send in their questions and one topic that kept coming up is yogurts. They're good for digestion, aren't they?

Ex B **D:** Well, depending on the type of yogurt – yes. Most yogurt sold in the US is described as 'live yogurt' because it contains living bacteria. The proper name for this type of bacteria is probiotics, but you've probably heard them described as 'friendly bacteria'. This is because they're widely thought to help your digestive system. (Ex C Q4)

P: But wasn't a large yogurt company – I won't say who – actually taken to court over false claims linking yogurt to digestion?

D: Yes, that's true, but that was largely due to the wording they used in their ads. You just can't say something is 'scientifically proven' if you don't have enough evidence to support your claim. In fact, in Europe, companies actually have to get the approval of the European Food Safety Authority – the EFSA – before they're allowed to make health claims in their ads. In the US, they need approval by the Food and Drug Administration - the FDA. Applications are frequently rejected by the EFSA or FDA because the company simply doesn't have enough evidence to support their claim. (Ex C Q5)

P: So I guess companies have to word their ads pretty carefully?

D: That's right. You can say things like 'may help to aid digestion', but you can't say 'clinically proven to help aid digestion' unless you back this up with evidence.

P: OK, so another hot topic for our listeners is sugar. Is it really that bad for you?

D: I'm afraid so, yes. Overconsumption of 'free sugars' – those that have been added to things like sodas or chocolate – can lead to weight gain, which ultimately is linked to things like heart disease, cancer and diabetes. They're obviously really bad for your teeth, too. (Ex C Q6)

P: But doesn't fruit contain a lot of sugar?

D: Uh, it does, but it also contains fiber which actually slows down the rate at which the body absorbs sugar. You'd have to eat *a lot* of fruit to get the same amount of sugar as you'd get from, say, a soda.

P: So I'm OK to keep drinking a smoothie every morning then?

Ex B **D:** Actually, no. When you blend fruit into a smoothie, the natural sugars are released – meaning you consume more sugar than you would by just eating a piece of fruit.

P: Really? But I always think of them as being healthy!

D: Haha! Just another example of creative advertising I'm afraid.

GRAMMAR

A–C Put students into pairs to discuss sentences, before giving feedback as a class. Then, ask them to complete the rules alone. Check their answers as a class, before directing them to the **Grammar Hub** (see below). Use the **Grammar Worksheet** on page W44 for extra practice.

PRONUNCIATION

9.6 **A** Play the audio for students to answer the questions. Ask them to check in pairs before giving feedback as a class.

9.7 **B** Give students time to make predictions, before playing the audio. Give feedback as a class.

SPEAKING

A Direct students' attention to the model survey, and elicit how to change one or two of the sentences to focus on technology. Next, put them into pairs to choose a topic and adapt the survey accordingly.

B Give students ten minutes to interview as many of their classmates as possible, and write down their answers.

C–D Put students back into their original pairs to analyze their findings. Next, call on pairs to present their results to the class, encouraging them to highlight anything that they were particularly surprised about or confused by.

GRAMMAR HUB

9.2 Determiners and quantifiers

few, much, many, a little, etc

- We use *(too) many, few, a few, several, a large number of* and *hundreds/thousands of* with countable nouns.

  Not many people can afford to buy designer clothes.
  There are hundreds of bargains to choose from.
- We use *(too) much, a little, little, a great deal of* and *a large amount of* with uncountable nouns.

  We spend a great deal of money on things we don't need!
- We can use *a lot of, lots of, plenty of, enough, some* and *any* with both countable and uncountable nouns.

  Plenty of successful people never went to college.
  Did I put enough milk in your coffee?

all, each, every

- We use *all, all the, all of the* with plural nouns to talk about every person or thing in a group.

  All participants were asked to complete an online survey about their phobias.
- We use *each* and *every* with singular nouns to talk about all of the people or things in a group when considered separately.

  Each competitor was given a medal for taking part.

both, either, neither

- We use *both* with plural nouns to talk about two people or things. *Both* or *both of* can be used before a determiner (e.g. *the, my, those*, etc), but we always use *both of* before pronouns (e.g. *her, their, its*, etc).

  Both restaurants offer a range of vegetarian options.
- We use *either* (*… or*) with singular nouns to talk about one of two people or things when it's not important which, or to mean *both*.

  Which color do you prefer? I'm happy with either.
- We use *neither* (*… nor*) with singular nouns to mean *not either* of two people or things.

  Neither side played very well in the last game.
- We use *either of / neither of* with plural pronouns or plural nouns with determiners.

  Neither of them could decide which car to buy.

no, none, any

- We use *no* or *none* in positive sentences and *any* in negative sentences to refer to zero quantity.

  It seems there are no tickets left for tonight's show.

9.2 Determiners and quantifiers

A Choose the correct options to complete the sentences.

1. I know *a little* / *a few* brands in this store. [a few]
2. There isn't *much* / *many* information on this label. [much]
3. *A large amount* / *A large number* of products were recalled. [A large number]
4. *Neither* / *Both* the seller and the buyer are concerned about prices. [Both]
5. *Either* / *Neither* you exchange it or issue a refund! [Either]
6. *A few* / *A little* of the customers complained. [A few]
7. Sadly, there are *none* / *no* left. [none]
8. *All* / *Each* products must be returned with a receipt. [All]

B Choose the correct option (a, b or c) to complete the sentences.

1. Contrary to popular belief, ___ people make purchases based on online reviews.
   a much b neither (c) few
2. It's important that you include at least ___ vegetables in your diet if you want to stay healthy.
   a few b both (c) a few
3. ___ food bloggers have become very important because they can influence food trends.
   (a) Plenty of b Much c Every
4. ___ food companies make health claims about their products to encourage consumers to buy them.
   (a) Both b Neither c Either
5. Drinking a large ___ of coffee does not actually dehydrate you.
   (a) amount b plenty c number
6. Drinking ___ coffee may help to improve your concentration, but don't drink too much.
   (a) a little b little c plenty
7. ___ product was successful because they were considered to be too unhealthy.
   a Both (b) Neither c Either
8. ___ of the products turned out to be healthy as they claimed to be.
   a No (b) None c Any

➤ Go back to page 103.

GRAMMAR
Determiners and quantifiers

A Work in pairs. Read the sentences. Which of the determiners or quantifiers in bold describe 100%, a large amount, a medium to small amount or 0%?

1 There's **little** evidence to support many of the health claims made about yogurt. a medium to small amount
2 You need **plenty of** fruits and vegetables in your diet. a large amount
3 It's not true that we need to drink **several** glasses of water a day. a medium to small amount
4 There is **no** evidence to support that claim. 0%
5 **All** companies have to be careful with the wording of their ads. 100%
6 **Neither** ad was particularly accurate. 0%
7 **Every** claim must be supported by evidence. 100%
8 There isn't really **any** evidence to support that claim. 0%
9 **None** of those claims are based on real data. 0%

B WORK IT OUT Choose the correct options to complete the rules.

Determiners and quantifiers

few, much, many, a little, etc

- We use *many, few, a few, several, a large number of* with [1]*countable / uncountable / countable and uncountable* nouns.
- We use *much, a little, little, a great deal of, a large amount of* with [2]*countable / uncountable / countable and uncountable* nouns.
- We use *a lot of, lots of, plenty of, some* and *any* with [3]*countable / uncountable / countable and uncountable* nouns.

all, each and *every*

- We use *all* with [4]*singular / plural* nouns.
- We use *each* and *every* with [5]*singular / plural* nouns.

both, either and *neither*

- We use *both* with [6]*singular / plural* nouns.
- We use *either* and *neither* with [7]*singular / plural* nouns.

no, none and *any*

- We use *no* + noun in [8]*positive / negative* sentences and *any* + noun in [9]*positive / negative* sentences.
- We use *none* in short answers, in [10]*positive / negative* sentences, or with *of* + pronoun / countable or uncountable nouns.

C Go to the **Grammar Hub** on **page 138**.

PRONUNCIATION
Connected speech: determiners and quantifiers

9.6 **A** Listen to the extracts from the radio show. Is there a pause between the words in bold? Is the pronunciation of *of* strong or weak? No pause; weak *of*

1 We get **plenty of water** through food.
2 You'd have to eat **a lot of** fruit to get the same amount of sugar as you'd get from, say, a soda.

9.7 **B** Draw (‿) to show the connected speech in the determiners and quantifiers below. Then listen and check.

1 A large number‿of people pay attention to claims in advertising.
2 A‿lot‿of people are influenced by product reviews.
3 Plenty‿of respondents don't pay attention to the wording of an ad.
4 A‿few‿of the people interviewed said that price wasn't a factor when choosing clothes.
5 Hundreds‿of people buy products because of celebrity endorsements.

SPEAKING

A PLAN Work in pairs. You are going to conduct a survey on factors that influence people's shopping habits. Adapt the sample questions to fit one of the topics in the box.

clothes food vacations technology

1 Do you regularly eat out in restaurants? Yes/No

2 Which factors are the most important when choosing a restaurant?

	not significant						significant
price	1	2	3	4	5	6	7
location	1	2	3	4	5	6	7
décor	1	2	3	4	5	6	7
type of food	1	2	3	4	5	6	7

3 Restaurant reviews have an influence on my choice of restaurant.

strongly agree | agree | neutral | disagree | strongly disagree

4 Which ONE of these has the most influence when you write your own review of a restaurant?

value for money service quality of the food

B SPEAK Ask your questions from Exercise A to as many people as possible in ten minutes. Write down their answers.

C DISCUSS Work in pairs. Analyze your answers from Exercise B.

Our results show that the most important thing when eating out is the quality of the food ...

D PRESENT Present your findings to the class.

OPRAH WINFREY

- founder of The Oprah Winfrey Network (OWN)
- grew up in extreme poverty
- net worth = $2.9 billion

JEFF BEZOS

- co-founder of Amazon
- quit a well-paid job on Wall Street to develop Amazon
- net worth = $157.4 billion

ZHOU QUNFEI

- founder of Lens Technology
- left school at 16 to work in a factory
- net worth = $5.4 billion

READING

A SPEAK Work in groups. Look at the infographic and discuss the questions.

1 Can you think of any other famous entrepreneurs? What products or services did they create?

2 What qualities do you think make a good entrepreneur?

3 Would you like to start your own business? Why/Why not?

B READ FOR GIST Read *The path to success* and choose the best sub-heading (1–3).

1 Setting up a new fashion label can be difficult, especially with minimal advertising.

2 How the courage to follow a childhood dream led to an international success story.

3 How celebrities can help promote your values.

C TOPIC SENTENCES Read the article again. Match the topic sentences (1–5) to the blanks (a–e). Use the information in the box to help you.

Topic sentences

Topic sentences express the main idea of a paragraph. They are usually found at the beginning of a paragraph and are frequently supported by further related information or examples. Identifying topic sentences can help you get a quick overall understanding of a text without having to read in detail.

1 The brand has since become known for its colorful floral prints, which are inspired by Nicola's happy childhood memories of the summer in the English countryside.

2 The story of many successful entrepreneurs is the stuff of Hollywood – rags-to-riches tales of people who overcame great challenges in order to succeed.

3 In an age where so many of us seem content to remain in well-paid, but ultimately dissatisfying jobs, it's refreshing to see someone have the courage to make a dramatic lifestyle change.

4 Yet like many of us, Nicola felt that something was missing and decided to do something about it.

5 In the past decade, Beautiful Soul has used a variety of techniques to raise brand awareness.

THE PATH TO SUCCESS

a ____ Oprah Winfrey was born into extreme poverty, yet recently became the world's first black female billionaire. Bill Gates and Mark Zuckerburg both dropped out of college, but went on to create two of the most influential companies in modern history. Starting out on the wrong foot seems to be the inspiration many entrepreneurs need to create an empire, and Nicola Woods is no exception. For 11 years, Nicola built a successful career in the fast-paced world of corporate insurance. She wore designer clothing, drove sports cars and went on dream vacations.

b ____ Looking for inspiration, she took a six-month sabbatical to travel around the world. Sitting among the cherry blossom in a park in central Tokyo, Nicola's thoughts turned to her childhood dream of working in the fashion industry. Realizing that she needed a radical change of lifestyle, Nicola enrolled in college and earned a BA in Fashion, Design and Technology. She then went on to launch the luxury womenswear **brand**, Beautiful Soul, in 2008.

READING

A Focus students' attention on the infographic, and elicit what it shows (*information about three famous entrepreneurs*). Next, put them into groups to discuss the questions. Monitor, asking follow-up questions to keep the discussions going. Bring the class back together to share their ideas, encouraging further discussion as appropriate. Add any useful emergent language to the board.

B Tell students they are going to read an article about a successful entrepreneur, and go through the potential subheadings as a class. Then, give students time to read the article alone and choose the best subheading. Make sure you give students plenty of time to read this text as it's fairly challenging. Monitor, helping with new and unfamiliar vocabulary as necessary. Allow time for students to compare their answers in pairs before giving feedback as a class. Take this opportunity to go through anything students don't understand, ensuring you cover the terms in the glossary. Add any useful emergent language to the board.

C Ask students to read the first paragraph of *The path to success*, before summarizing the key information with a partner (*entrepreneurs usually have a difficult path to success*). Next, ask which of the sentences best matches the meaning of the paragraph (*2*), and explain that sentences that describe the main idea of a paragraph like this are called 'topic sentences'. Tell students that these are usually found at the beginning of a paragraph and are usually supported with further information and examples. Ask students why it might be useful to identify topic sentences (*they can help you get a quick overall understanding of each paragraph without having to read in detail*). Then give them time to complete the rest of the exercise alone. Ask students to compare their answers with a partner before giving feedback as a class. Encourage them to explain what clues in the text they used to find the answers.

METHODOLOGY HUB by Christine Nuttall

Organizing sequences of sentences

Sequences of sentences are generally organized into paragraphs. These are sometimes just a way of breaking up a long text visually; but there is usually some unity of thought, and frequently (not always) this is given focus in a topic sentence (one that sums up the main idea of the paragraph).

Recognizing the organization of a paragraph means identifying the topic, the main point, the minor or supporting points and so on. It also involves recognizing that, for example, the first sentence makes an assertion, the second and third support it with examples, the fourth modifies it by a reservation and so on.

Clearly this builds on other skills, particularly the skill of recognizing functional value. In fact, the two are interdependent: you need to identify the value of each sentence in order to plot the structure of the paragraph. Equally, if you recognize the paragraph structure, this will help you assign the value of each sentence.

Many paragraphs conform to patterns which can be found in a wide variety of text types. For instance, the paragraph may be organized according to the sequence of events described or according to logical progression from general to specific or from specific to general. Other commonly occurring structures are *problem–solution; evidence–hypothesis; classification–examples; cause–result* and so on. Some patterns are particularly frequent in certain types of text. For example, *assertion – substantiation* (examples, explication, etc) is a common pattern in textbooks. (The present paragraph is of this pattern).

TEACHING IDEA by David Seymour and Maria Popova

Inventors

Use this activity to extend the theme of entrepreneurs.

In pairs, invent an object – the stranger, the better – which you think will be useful to people. Make some sketches and write a brief description to explain it, e.g. *This is a pedal-powered computer that will give you exercise while you work.*

Team up with another pair. Each pair takes turns playing the role of bank managers. Try to persuade the bank managers to lend you the money to produce your invention.

TEACHING IDEA by David Seymour and Maria Popova

Hard sell

Use this activity to extend the theme of entrepreneurs.

In pairs, think of arguments to persuade people to buy these objects, e.g. empty soda can – *You could use this as a vase, a snowball, a dirty comb, one sock, a used teabag, a broken plate, cold fish and chips, a clock with no hands, a house with no roof, a bucket with a hole, a piece of string*

D Give students time to read the questions carefully before reading the text a final time. Monitor, encouraging them to underline the parts of the text that give them the answers. Put students into pairs to compare their ideas, then give feedback as a class.

1 *She was dissatisfied with her job and went looking for inspiration.*
2 *She quit her job and enrolled in college and earned a BA in Fashion, Design and Technology.*
3 *The brand is built on sustainability and the regenerating British manufacturing and textile industries.*
4 *They use materials that are organic, locally sourced and fair trade and operate a zero-waste policy, using leftover fabric from one season in the creation of the next.*
5 *The brand's international profile has been raised by high-profile celebrities.*
6 *Its involvement in the London, Milan and Paris fashion weeks brought it to the attention of the media.*
7 *Private fittings allow Nicola to connect with her customers face-to-face and better understand her target market.*
8 *The writer thinks she should be congratulated for her strength of character.*

E Write the question in the center of a spider diagram and elicit the meaning of *career satisfaction* (*the feeling that you have when you enjoy your work*). Elicit one or two ideas, adding them to your spider diagram, before putting students into groups to think of more ideas. Monitor, encouraging students to support their ideas with reasons and examples. Bring the class back together to share their ideas, building up your spider diagram on the board.

VOCABULARY

A Draw students' attention to the first word in bold, asking students to suggest what it means before finding the matching definition together (*5*). Then, ask students to complete the remaining definitions alone before giving feedback as a class. Consolidate understanding by giving further explanations as necessary, and elicit new example sentences for each word. You could also take this opportunity to do some word building by eliciting other forms of the words in this set (e.g. *advertisement, trending, consumerism*, etc).

B–C Give students time to complete the sentences alone, before checking their answers with a partner. Give feedback as a class, then put students into pairs to discuss the questions. Monitor, encouraging students to ask follow-up questions to keep their conversations going. Open some of the more interesting questions for class-wide discussion if appropriate, adding any useful emergent language to the board. Use the **Vocabulary Worksheet** on page W45 for extra practice.

SPEAKING HUB

A Ask students to suggest what makes a successful advertising campaign (e.g. *appeals to the emotions, catchy jingle or slogan, celebrity endorsements*, etc). Now, put them into groups, and tell them they are going to design their own campaign. Then, direct them to the **Communication Hub** (see TB121). Monitor, asking a lot of questions to help students shape their ideas.

B Ask each group to present their advertising campaigns and allow time for follow-up questions from the class. To close the activity, take a class vote to decide which campaign was the best.

METHODOLOGY HUB by Jim Scrivener

Learner training

For me, learner training means 'raising student awareness about how they are learning and, as a result, helping them to find more effective ways of working, so that they can continue working efficiently and usefully, even when away from their teacher and the classroom'. More simply, it means 'working on teaching learning as well as teaching English'.

Learner training, therefore, includes:

- work on study skills, e.g. use of dictionaries, reference material, workbooks, notebooks, filed material
- student examination of the process of learning and reflection on what is happening, e.g. of teaching strategies you use (and the reasons why you use them).

In both cases, it seems important to include these as strands throughout a course.

Three ideas to start learner training

1 Integrate study-skills work

Include study-skills work as an integrated feature of your lessons, e.g. when working on vocabulary, include a short exercise that involves efficiently looking up information in a dictionary. Similarly, when the students have found some new words to learn, you could make them aware of the variety of ways of recording vocabulary in their notebooks.

2 Let them into the secret

Teachers sometimes prefer the 'surprise' approach to teaching methodology; usually, students don't really know why they followed a particular procedure or did a particular activity. Teachers frequently assume that their own reasoning will be transparently obvious to their students, but it rarely is. So it can be very useful to tell students before a lesson what's going to happen and why. At the end of the lesson, you can review not only the content but also the way that it was studied. For example, after a listening skills lesson, talk through the procedure with the students: Why did I set a task first? Was it necessary to understand every word? What did we do next? What helped you learn? What didn't help?

In this way, they will also be learning a methodology that they can repeat for their own use when they listen to audio recordings at home or in a language laboratory.

3 Discuss process as well as content and procedure

The content of your lessons is the English language. The 'procedures' are your methodology (which, as I suggested above, is worth talking about with students). The third area is 'process'. By this, I mean the lesson as viewed from the learner's point of view. You're doing certain things as a teacher, but what is going on for each individual student?

It can be very valuable to set aside time in class simply to discuss the subject of 'learning on this course' in order to recall what's happening and reflect on it. This 'process review' will allow you and the learners to clarify what is happening.

D READ FOR DETAIL Read the article again and answer the questions. Underline the parts of the text that give you the answers.

1 Why did Nicola take six months off work to go traveling?
2 What lifestyle change did Nicola make when she returned from Japan?
3 Which two values is the brand built upon?
4 How do these values influence their use of materials?
5 Who has helped to raise the brand's international profile?
6 What has brought the company to the attention of the media?
7 What do the private fittings allow Nicola to do?
8 What does the writer think Nicola should be congratulated for?

E SPEAK Work in groups. Nicola had a successful career in corporate insurance that made her wealthy, yet she was still dissatisfied. What do you think are the most important factors in career satisfaction?

c 1 Her clothes are proudly feminine and offer a modern interpretation of classic British designs. However, maybe as interesting as the designs themselves are the values that lie behind them. There is an industry-wide **trend** toward clothing that does not damage the environment and Nicola is excited to lead the charge. The brand is committed to sustainability and the regeneration of the British manufacturing and textiles industries. Ex D Q3 Materials are organic, locally sourced and fair trade, proving to the **consumer** that luxury clothing can still be produced ethically. Ex D Q4 The company also operates a zero-waste policy, using leftover fabric from one season in the creation of the next.

d 5 Rather than expensive **ad campaigns**, the fashion label has largely relied on word of mouth, driven to a large extent by the support of **high-profile** celebrities. Pippa Middleton, Taylor Swift Ex D Q5 and Katy Perry are among those to publicly **endorse** the brand, helping to raise its international profile. Beautiful Soul has also attracted vast media attention through its involvement in the London, Ex D Q6 Milan and Paris fashion weeks and is now stocked at high-end boutiques around the world. However, Nicola is also eager to connect with her customers face-to-face, so the brand has recently begun offering private fittings at their studio in Portobello, West London. The hope is that **marketing strategies** like these, as well as studio open days, will allow Nicola to better understand her **target market** and adapt accordingly. Ex D Q7

e 3 Nicola Woods may not have been born into poverty, nor did she drop out of college before becoming successful. Yet like all entrepreneurs, she too had to show great strength of character to get where Ex D Q8 she is today.

Glossary

fair trade (n) a system that ensures the original producer receives a fair price for their goods
sabbatical (n) a period of time when someone (usually a college professor) is allowed to stop working in order to travel or study
sustainability (n) the use of methods that cause little to no damage to the environment and can therefore continue for a long period of time

VOCABULARY
Advertising

A Scan the article again. Complete the definitions with the words in bold.

1 ad campaign (n) a series of advertisements that share a single idea or theme
2 marketing strategy (n) a plan of how to encourage people to buy a product or service
3 consumer (n) someone who buys or uses goods and services
4 endorse (v) to express support for someone or something, especially in public
5 brand (n) a product or group of products that has its own name and is made by one company
6 target market (n) the group of people that a product or service is directed toward
7 high-profile (adj) frequently seen in public, mentioned in newspapers or appearing on television
8 trend (n) a gradual development or change in a situation

B Complete the sentences with the correct form of the words in Exercise A.

1 Which recent TV ad campaigns do you think have been most effective? Why?
2 Do you think high-profile celebrities should be involved in advertising? Why/Why not?
3 Are you more likely to buy a product if it's endorsed by a celebrity? Why/Why not?
4 Who do you think is the target market for the following products – energy drinks, electric cars, video game consoles, high-end sports equipment? Why?
5 Which brands do you associate with luxury and quality? Why?
6 How can consumers influence the way products or services are advertised?
7 Which marketing strategies would discourage you from buying a product or service? Why?
8 Do you follow the latest fashion trends? Why/Why not?

C SPEAK Work in pairs. Ask and answer the questions in Exercise B.

SPEAKING HUB

A PLAN Work in groups. Go to the **Communication Hub** on **page 153**.

B PRESENT Present your campaign to the class and answer their follow-up questions.

Conduct a survey about what influences our purchases

Design and present an ad campaign

9.3 Raising capital

A – illustrating your argument S – reformulating and paraphrasing

Crowdfunding

Glossary

film **(n) (British)** = movie **(n) (American)**

COMPREHENSION

A **Work in pairs. What do you think is the best way to raise money for a new business or project? Why?**

Glossary

commission (n) a payment made to someone that is directly related to the amount they sell of something

donor (n) someone who gives money or goods to an organization that needs help

B **Watch a news report about getting investment for new projects. Answer the questions.**

1 How did the director raise money for his film?

2 How does this system work?

3 Why do people donate money like this?

C 00:00–01:42 **Watch the first part of the report again. Are these sentences true (T) or false (F)? Correct the false sentences.**

1 The director produced a video about the project as part of his Kickstarter campaign. T / F

2 To date, the campaign has raised over two thousand dollars more than its original goal. T / F

3 Some donors are given the opportunity to appear in the films they support. T / F

4 Kickstarter only makes money if a project is successful. T / F

D 01:43–02:37 **Watch the second part of the report again. Choose the best options to complete the sentences.**

1 Kickstarter CEO, Yancey Strickler, says most ideas *wouldn't be profitable* / *aren't interesting* enough to gain traditional investment.

2 Michael Moore has *successfully funded projects on* / *publicly endorsed* Kickstarter.

3 Moore states that he *would be happy to invest* / *has previously invested* in film projects via Kickstarter.

4 A major issue of crowdfunding is that many projects *are never finished* / *cost more than estimated*.

AUTHENTIC ENGLISH

A **Work in pairs. Read the extract from the report. What is the speaker's main argument? How does he illustrate it?**

99% of ideas will never be a good fit for investment because they're not going to make a lot of money. But if instead the notion is, 'What do we want to see exist? What do we think would be cool and interesting? What would we want to see?', there's a lot more things that become possible.

B **Match the arguments (1–3) with the questions that could be used to illustrate them (a–c). Use the information in the box to help you.**

Illustrating your argument

In natural spoken English, we frequently ask rhetorical questions to emphasize or support our arguments:

We have to ask ourselves, 'What do we want to highlight about our project? How can people benefit from supporting us?'

1 Almost two thirds of the people surveyed still believe Vitamin C cures the common cold.

2 The results of the survey indicate that unemployment is still on the rise.

3 Over the past year, we've seen a 60% increase in profits.

a The obvious question is, 'What influenced such a positive performance?'

b Which begs the question, 'What steps can be taken to get people back into work?'

c This raises the question, 'How can we better inform the public?'

C **Work in pairs. Take turns making sentences about the topics below, then illustrating your ideas with a question.**

- sports
- health
- employment

A: Arsenal has admitted that they need a better striker to compete at the highest level.

B: The only question is, 'How much are they willing to pay for one?'

Starting positions

SAM MALCOLM AMANDA HARRY EMILY

A Work in pairs. Think of the steps that are involved in starting a new business. What order do they have to be done in?

B Watch the video. Choose the best summary (1 or 2).

1 Inspired by Sam's advice, Emily decides to take a traditional route to funding her new business venture.

2 Despite Sam's advice, Emily decides to take a more modern approach to funding her new business venture.

SPEAKING SKILL

A Watch the video again. Answer the questions.

1 What is the function of the phrases *I just meant …, What I meant to say was …* and *What I meant is …?*

2 What is the function of *essentially* and *basically?*

B Read the information in the box and check your answers to Exercise A.

Reformulating and paraphrasing

Sometimes in conversation we need to explain something in a different way to help the listener understand. This is called reformulating.

To do this, we use phrases such as: *I just mean (that) …, What I'm trying to say is …, What I meant to say was …, In other words …, What I mean is (that) …, That's to say …*

Sometimes the listener doesn't understand because we've used a word or phrase that they're unfamiliar with. Rather than give a long explanation, we usually focus on the essential details. This is called paraphrasing.

To do this, we use phrases such as: *(So) essentially/basically …*

C Choose a topic that you know a lot about (e.g. a particular subject, sport, etc) and brainstorm a list of interesting, technical terms associated with it.

D Work in pairs. Tell each other about the topic you chose in Exercise A, using technical language. Reformulate or paraphrase when necessary.

SPEAKING HUB

A PREPARE Look at the following ideas that people are hoping to crowdfund. Brainstorm the strengths and weaknesses of each.

- Idea A: a chip that is inserted in your brain to allow you to access the internet with your mind. Will allow users to access the internet instantly without using a device. Will be very expensive.
- Idea B: wireless electricity. No more power cables in the home or across the country. There are concerns about electromagnetic radiation damaging people's health.
- Idea C: a tablet that turns a container of ocean water into drinking water. Will help stop water shortages. Production process of tablets creates toxic pollution.

B SPEAK Work in groups. You have $50,000 to invest in crowdfunding projects. Discuss each of the projects in Exercise A and decide how much, if anything, to invest in them.

We should be asking, 'Which idea is tackling the most important issue of the day?' And it seems to me that renewable energy is the most important.

C REFLECT As a class, discuss which ideas got the most/least funding and why.

Discuss investment opportunities

➤ Turn to page 162 to learn how to write a proposal.

Crowdfunding

LEAD-IN

Tell students you have an idea for a business, and elicit ways to get funding for it. Build up a list of useful language on the board.

COMPREHENSION

A Put students into pairs to discuss the question. Bring the class back together to share their ideas.

B ▶ Play the video for students to answer the questions.

1 *He used the crowdfunding platform, Kickstarter.*
2 *Creators make a page explaining exactly what their project is (sometimes via a pitch video), how much money they are trying to raise and what kind of rewards backers will receive.*
3 *Because 'it feels good to donate money to an artistic project'; they get rewards like T-shirts, DVDs, content-related merchandise, etc; and they get to contribute to projects they want to get made.*

C ▶ 00:00–01:42 Give students time to read through the sentences carefully, before playing the first part of the report again. Give feedback as a class.

D ▶ 01:43–02:37 Play the second part of the report again for students to complete the sentences. Give feedback as a class.

AUTHENTIC ENGLISH

A Put students into pairs to discuss the extract.

We can make more interesting content if we think less about how much money a project will make and more about what we'd like to see. The speaker uses questions to illustrate their argument.

B–C Give students time to complete the exercise alone, before giving feedback as a class. Then, put students into pairs to practice illustrating their own arguments.

Starting positions

LEAD-IN

Tell students about a small business that you think would be successful in your area and why. Then, put students into groups to discuss their own ideas.

A Put students into pairs to discuss the question. Bring the class back together to share their ideas.

B ▶ Play the video for students to complete the exercise alone, then give feedback as a class. You can find the **video script** for *Starting positions* on the Teacher's Resource Center.

SPEAKING SKILL

A–B ▶ Play the video again for students to answer the questions. Then, give them time to read the skills box to check their answers.

1 *To help the speaker explain something in a different way.*
2 *To help the speaker paraphrase something.*

C–D Give students time to prepare, then put them into pairs to discuss their chosen subjects.

SPEAKING HUB

A–C Give students time to write notes alone, before putting them into groups to discuss them. Bring the class back together to share their ideas.

▶ VIDEO SCRIPT

Crowdfunding

P = Presenter Pa = Paul A = Andrew Semans
Y = Yancey Strickler M = Michael Moore N = Nancy

P: Director Andrew Semans with his cast at the world premiere of *Nancy, Please*.

Pa: I said, 'hey', Nancy.

Ex B Q1; Ex B Q2; Ex C Q1 **P:** This black comedy is just one of a dozen films at Tribeca financed through crowdfunding. Here's how it works – Andrew Semans went online to the funding platform Kickstarter and created a page detailing his film. Part of the pitch included an explanatory, self-made video.

A: Er, I'm here to talk to you today about a very exciting project that I'm working on, it's my very …

Ex C Q2 **P:** Individual donors, drawn from Kickstarter's online users, responded. He raised more than $10,000.

A: Crowdfunding was, er, essential to executing the project and executing it in the way we wanted to. If … if we hadn't done this and if we … if it hadn't been successful, er, I don't know if we'd have a film at all.

P: What is it that people actually get out of donating?

Ex C Q3 **A:** Er, I think people want to donate to projects like ours just because it … it feels good to donate money to an artistic project.

P: In addition to the satisfaction of giving, donors can get rewards. T-shirts, DVDs, content-related merchandise, perhaps the opportunity of appearing as an extra in a film. It's from this building in New York's Lower East Side that Kickstarter, the world's top online crowdfunding platform, has its headquarters. So far, the workers here have seen almost $60 million raised for films. Ex B Q3; Ex C Q4 The company gets by through a 5% commission on donations. In the Kickstarter world, donors are giving to filmmakers not to make a financial investment, but because they want to see a project come into being.

Ex D Q1 **Y:** 99% of ideas will never be a good fit for investment because they're not going to make a lot of money. But if instead the notion is just, 'What do we want to see exist? What do we think would be cool and interesting? What would we want to see?', there's a lot more things that become possible.

Pa: Why don't you just end it?

N: Why are you dragging it out like this? Why …

Ex D Q2 **P:** *Nancy, Please* is just one of 5,000 films that have successfully raised funds via Kickstarter. Right now, crowdfunding is basking in the glory of some big name endorsements, including the support of film director, Michael Moore.

Ex D Q3 **M:** Absolutely, it's really helped a lot of people, and I've participated in it. I mean I'll go on Kickstarter whatever and I'll … I'll contribute to movies that sound like they should be made.

Ex D Q4 **P:** There are some problems with crowdfunding platforms – there's little oversight, filmmakers may fail to deliver the final project or use the donations for a different purpose. But in the world of independent film, where every penny counts, crowdfunding has become a much valued and expected component of the money-raising process. Tom Brooke, BBC News, New York.

9 Writing — Write a proposal

W– using discourse markers in formal writing

A Read the proposal task below and answer the questions that follow.

Ex A Q1 Your hotel has been getting low ratings from users on a popular travel website. Your boss has asked you to look at the reviews and to write a proposal for changes that can be made to the hotel. You should include information about the Ex A Q2 weaknesses reviewers have mentioned and suggest improvements.

1 What is the current problem?
2 What recommendations do you need to make?

Proposal for improvements to the hotel

Introduction

The purpose of this proposal is to examine weaknesses identified in the hotel's online reviews and to suggest ways to address them.

Hotel weaknesses

Analysis of the reviews has revealed that most customers feel the hotel décor is dated and in much need of modernization. In fact, many feel the old-fashioned look of the hotel makes it feel unclean. Furthermore, consumers usually leave poor reviews of the food in the hotel restaurant. The menu is considered to be too limited, and the service during breakfast too slow. Consequently, fewer and fewer guests are eating in the hotel itself.

Hotel improvements

Modernizing the look of the hotel would be hugely beneficial since there seems to be little doubt that we are attracting fewer customers as a result of the outdated décor. The hotel should be given a simple, fresh and clean look that is more in keeping with our competitors. The restaurant should be a way for the hotel to maximize profits, but due to the limited menu and poor service, people are choosing to eat elsewhere. Therefore, updating the menu and hiring more service staff is essential.

Recommendations

Implementation of the ideas outlined above would result in an increased level of customer satisfaction and more positive online reviews. Improving the restaurant would also encourage more guests to dine in, increasing overall profitability.

B Read the proposal. According to the writer, what are the main weaknesses of the hotel? What solutions do they recommend?

C Underline four formal discourse markers in the text. Use the information in the box to help you.

Using discourse markers in formal writing

In formal writing, we use a range of discourse markers to connect ideas. These include adding ideas (e.g. *additionally*), talking about effects and results (e.g. *subsequently*) and giving examples (e.g. *for instance*).

D Complete the sentences using discourse markers from Exercise C.

1 The hotel has had little investment in recent years. Consequently, the volume of reservations has fallen.
2 As a result of the limited menu, customers are leaving negative reviews online.
3 A lot of our customers said they received poor service. Furthermore, many complained our staff was rude.
4 The new menu simply isn't popular. Therefore, we should reinstate the old one.

WRITING

A PREPARE Work in pairs. Read the proposal task below. Brainstorm issues a coffee chain might experience and how to address them.

You work for a large, successful coffee chain. However, lately your customer service department has been receiving increasingly negative reviews on social media. You have been asked to write a proposal highlighting the main issues and how to address them.

B PLAN Organize your ideas into appropriate sections.

C WRITE Write your proposal. Use your plan to help you.

D EDIT Work in pairs. Edit your partner's proposal. Check:

- spelling and punctuation
- strength of analysis and recommendations
- use of formal discourse markers

162 WRITING

Answers

Main weaknesses: old-fashioned décor, which also makes the hotel look unclean; poor reviews of the hotel food; limited menu; slow service during breakfast

Solutions: invest in modernizing the décor to give the hotel a fresh and clean look; updating the menu and hiring more staff in the restaurant

Answers

1 Low ratings for your hotel on a travel website

2 Improvements to be made based on the current weaknesses

Refer students to this proposal as a model for the writing task.

Refer students to this checklist when editing their partner's work.

LEAD-IN

Tell students about a terrible hotel experience you've had (real or made-up). Explain where you stayed, what the main issues were and whether you did anything about them. Then, put students into pairs to discuss their own experiences.

WRITING

A Give students time to read the proposal question and complete the exercise alone. Give feedback as a class.

B Give students time to skim the proposal to identify the hotel's weaknesses and proposed solutions. Give feedback as a class.

C–D Read the skills box as a class, giving further explanation and examples as necessary. Then, give students time to underline examples in the proposal. Next, ask students to complete the exercise alone, before giving feedback as a class.

WRITING TASK

A–B Read the proposal question as a class, and elicit one or two issues a coffee chain might experience and how to deal with them. Add the ideas to the board, ensuring a clear link between the issue and the proposed solution. Then, put students into pairs to discuss more issues and solutions. Next, give students time to organize their ideas into a proposal structure. Monitor, encouraging students to think of titles for section headings and the best way to present their ideas.

C Tell students to write their proposals. Monitor and provide support with structure and vocabulary when necessary.

D Put students into pairs to edit each other's proposals. Encourage students to give each other positive feedback. Students can then rewrite their proposals either in class or for homework.

Unit 9 Review

VOCABULARY

A Match the numbers (1–8) to the letters (a–h) to form full sentences.

1 I am responsible … e
2 Our brand is associated … a
3 All of our products are made … c
4 I'm sick … h
5 It is important for businesses to show that they care … f
6 When the dress arrived, I was really dissatisfied … b
7 The success of a company is dependent … d
8 I'm interested … g

a with luxury and success.
b with it. It looked nothing like the pictures.
c from locally sourced materials.
d on many factors.
e for a team of 20 people at work.
f about the people who work for them.
g in the idea of moving to a new house but my husband wants to stay where we are.
h of people on social media showing off about their lives.

B Complete the text with the words in the box.

analysis data evidence researchers theory

The pursuit of happiness

For decades, the simplest way to address unhappiness has been to go shopping. But does retail therapy actually work? Can we buy our way to happiness?

To test the [1] ___theory___, a group of [2] ___researchers___ from the Institute for Social Sciences interviewed thousands of shoppers before and after a spending spree. [3] ___Analysis___ of the [4] ___data___ seemed to indicate that retail therapy does make us happier immediately after the purchase. However, as yet, there is no [5] ___evidence___ to suggest that shopping can buy you long-term happiness. The key to this, it seems, remains a mystery!

C Work in groups. Discuss the questions.

1 Why do you think people frequently continue to believe something, despite a large amount of scientific evidence against it?
2 What kind of research do you think governments should fund? Why?

D Choose the correct options (a, b or c) to complete the sentences.

1 To work in fashion, it's important to keep up with ___ and influencers.
a brands (b) trends c campaigns
2 We are trying to ___ young males from a professional background.
(a) target b advertise c campaign
3 ___ social media stars are paid a lot of money to advertise particular brands.
a Consumers (b) High-profile c Trend
4 We hired six athletes to ___ our new health-food range.
a campaign b target (c) endorse
5 Our company is going to try to raise our ___ awareness by sponsoring national sporting events.
a campaign b advertise (c) brand
6 ___ frequently buy products that represent a certain lifestyle.
(a) Consumers b Brands c High profile

E Work in pairs. Discuss the questions.

1 Which brands are you most loyal to? Why?
2 How can consumers influence the products and services they use?
3 Which products do you think are marketed at your age range? Why?

GRAMMAR

A Rewrite the sentences as one sentence using an adjective clause. Leave out the relative pronoun where possible.

1 Have you read the book? The one I lent you.
Have ___you read the book (which/that) I lent you___?
2 There was some leftover pizza in the fridge. Where is it?
Where's ___the leftover pizza that was in the fridge___?
3 That's the boy. His brother has joined our soccer team.
That's ___the boy whose brother has joined our soccer team___.
4 I bought a new cell phone. It's really good.
The ___new cell phone (which/that) I bought is really good___.
5 Here's the beach. My family had our first vacation here.
This is ___the beach where my family had our first vacation___.

B Are these sentences correct or incorrect? Rewrite the incorrect sentences.

✓1 I think every city should have bike lanes.
2 It was a great game of tennis. ~~Either~~ Both players played amazingly.
3 ~~Any~~ None of you can leave until the exam is finished.
✓4 Every person is influenced by advertising to at least some degree.
5 Not many people came. Just ~~few~~ a few friends from college.
✓6 We haven't received any positive reviews for over a week.
7 I'm happy with ~~neither~~ either restaurant since both look nice.
8 Did you do ~~many~~ much / any / a lot of sightseeing on vacation?

10 MEDIA

> Ignorance, the root and stem of all evil.
>
> Plato

A Japanese commuter on the Yamanote Rail Line in Tokyo, Japan.

Media (n) radio, television, newspapers, the internet and magazines, considered as a group
Collocations and idioms: *social* media, *mass* media, media *interest*, media *baron/tycoon (someone who controls a large number or newspapers, TV companies, magazines, etc and as such is able to influence public opinion)*

Plato is suggesting that bad or 'evil' thoughts and actions grow from a basic lack of education or understanding.

Plato (428 BCE–348 BCE) was an ancient Greek philosopher who was the student of Socrates, teacher of Aristotle and the founder of the Academy in Athens, the first university to be opened in the West. The majority of his writing has survived to the present day, and his ideas are still hugely influential on Western thought.

OBJECTIVES

- give opinions on recent news stories
- intervene appropriately in a discussion
- report a conversation
- plan and create a viral marketing ad
- give your opinion on streaming services
- write a persuasive essay

Work with a partner. Discuss the questions.

1 Read the quote. Do you think the internet makes us more or less ignorant? Why?
2 Should the media respect the privacy of famous people? Why/Why not?
3 What media sources do you read on a regular basis? Why do you read those ones?

MEDIA 109

OBJECTIVES

Read the unit objectives to the class.

UNIT OPENER QUESTIONS

1 Read the quote as a class and elicit the meaning of *ignorance* (*lack of knowledge about a situation or subject*), *root* (*the cause of something*) and *stem* (*the central part of something from which things can grow*). Next, put students into pairs to discuss the questions. Bring the class back together to share their ideas.

2 Ask students what aspects of celebrities' lives should be reported on, giving examples that are increasingly intrusive on their private lives (e.g. *upcoming movies*, *personal relationships*, *love lives*, etc). Now, put students into pairs to discuss the privacy of celebrities. Bring the class back together to share their ideas.

3 Tell students which media sources you read regularly and why, then add these to a spider diagram on the board. Elicit other popular sources (e.g. *newspapers*, *news websites*, *Facebook*, etc), building up a spider diagram on the board. Next, put students into pairs to discuss their favorites. Bring the class back together to share their ideas.

WORKSHEETS

Lesson 10.1 Reporting the news

Grammar: Reported speech (W46)

Vocabulary: Traditional media (W47)

Lesson 10.2 Digital media

Grammar: Reporting verbs (W48)

Vocabulary: Social media (W49)

Vocabulary: Adjective + noun collocations (W50)

10.1 Reporting the news

- Give opinions on recent news stories
- Intervene appropriately in a discussion

G reported speech S listening for repair and elaboration V traditional media P avoiding interruption

READING

A SPEAK **Work in pairs. Discuss the questions below.**

1 When was the last time you bought a magazine or newspaper?

2 Why do you think people now get more of their news online than in the traditional media?

10.1 **B Listen to a press conference with the editor of a lifestyle magazine called *Healthy Me*. Answer the questions.**

1 What is the announcement about?

a a new print and digital magazine coming out

(b) a print magazine becoming digital-only

c an online magazine releasing a print version

2 What trend inspired the new business model?

(a) the increased popularity of digital content in general

b the increased popularity of the magazine

c the increased popularity of health-based apps

3 According to the speaker, what type of print media will be affected by digital?

(a) lifestyle magazines

b fiction

c reference books

C READ FOR MAIN IDEA **Read *The death of print?* and choose the best summary of the writer's opinion (1–3).**

1 The shift toward digital content is the beginning of the end for print products.

2 Sales of print products may actually be improved by the shift toward digital content.

(3) Despite the shift toward digital content, there is still a market for print products.

D READ FOR DETAIL **Read the article again and answer the questions. Underline the parts of the text that give you the answers.**

1 What two things prompted LMI Media to make their magazine digital-only? declining print sales; increased popularity of digital content

2 What method do online publications use to try to generate income? introducing paywalls

3 How do the public feel about this? that online content should be free

4 What type of magazine is thriving? magazines with specialized content

5 What type of magazine does the author think will struggle? lifestyle magazines

6 What types of print media are still successful? printed fiction; reference books; local newspapers

E SPEAK **Work in groups. Discuss the questions.**

1 Do you prefer print or digital media? Why?

2 What type of magazines, if any, do you think will survive in the future?

3 Do you think all online content should be free? Why/Why not?

GRAMMAR

Reported speech

A Scan the article again. Underline the reported speech that matches the following extracts from the press conference.

1 'We've gone from a distribution of just over 500,000 copies a month to under 100,000.'

2 'In fact, yesterday saw the total number of registered users reach over one million.'

3 'Will other publications from LMI Media make the same transition?'

4 'I'm sure all magazine publishers will start to re-evaluate their options over the next five to ten years.'

5 'What does this trend mean for print media in general?'

6 'However, for lifestyle magazines like ours, which are predominantly directed toward a younger audience, it simply doesn't make any financial sense to produce print media any longer.'

The DEATH of PRINT?

Lucy Morgan | 04/29/2019

As *Healthy Me* becomes the latest high-profile magazine to abandon print, Lucy Morgan makes the case against the digital revolution.

LMI Media has recently announced that January's issue of the lifestyle magazine *Healthy Me* will be the final print edition, making it the latest in a long line of publications to go digital-only. Yet is this really the right approach or do print magazines simply need to adapt to the changing marketplace?

LEAD-IN

Ask students whether they prefer physical or digital media and why. Add any useful emergent language to the board.

READING

10.1 **A–E** Work through the exercises, allowing time for peer correction and encouraging students to justify their answers with examples from the texts.

AUDIO SCRIPT

10.1

Reading, Exercise B

S = Sally P1 = Press 1 P2 = Press 2 P3 = Press 3

Ex B Q1 **S:** Good morning. It is with a heavy heart that I announce the discontinuation of *Healthy Me* as a print publication. From our January issue onward, the magazine will be exclusively available in a digital format on all portable devices. I will now take questions from the press.

P1: James Patterson, *CBNR*. What motivated the shift away from print?

S: Well, sales have been falling for five years now. We've gone from a distribution of just over 500,000 copies a month to under 100,000. During the same period, downloads of the *Healthy Me* app have increased by almost 300%. In fact, yesterday
Ex B Q2 saw the total number of registered users reach over one million. It's just clear from the numbers that the majority of our readers prefer to consume content online.

P2: Emily Davis, the *Evening Inquirer*. Will other publications from LMI Media make the same transition?

S: Uh, no, not yet anyway. However, I'm sure all magazine publishers will start to re-evaluate their options over the next five to ten years.

P3: Martin Webb, *CityTimes.com*. What does this trend mean for print media in general?

S: Well, I think that really depends on the type of publication. For example, despite the increased popularity of e-readers, people still seem to love physical copies of fiction titles. Students still seem to prefer printed textbooks over digital. However, for lifestyle magazines, like ours, which are predominantly
Ex B Q3 directed toward a younger audience, it simply doesn't make financial sense to produce print media any longer. Fewer young people are buying physical media, and we have to recognize this if we're to continue publishing our magazine. Thank you.

GRAMMAR HUB

10.1 Reported speech

- When we report what someone said, we usually change the main verb by moving it back one tense into the past.

Direct speech	Reported speech
simple present 'I'm completely exhausted.'	simple past She said (that) she was completely exhausted.
present progressive 'We're trying to find a solution.'	past progressive They said (that) they were trying to find a solution.
simple past 'Online hits went up.'	past perfect He said (that) online hits had gone up.
past progressive 'We were finding it hard.'	past perfect progressive She said (that) they had been finding it hard.
present perfect 'I've made a decision.'	past perfect He said he'd made a decision.
present perfect progressive 'I've been working.'	past perfect progressive She said (that) she had been working.
will/can/may 'I'll let you know tomorrow.' 'I can double-check for you.' 'You may need to book early.'	*would/could/might* He said (that) he'd let me know the next day. She said (that) she could double-check for me. She said (that) we might need to book early.

- We don't need to change the tense in reported speech:
  - **a** when the direct speech is in the past perfect (simple or progressive).
    'We had wanted to move for some time.' → He said they had wanted to move for some time.
  - **b** with the modal verbs *could, should, would, might* and *need*.
    'You might be able to get some money back.' → He said that we might be able to get some money back.
    'You don't need to worry.' → She said that I don't need to worry.
  - **c** when the information is still true or relevant, or the reporting verb is in the present tense.
    'My sister lives in Japan.' → She told me that her sister lives in Japan. (= It's still true that her sister lives there.)
- We usually do need to change time references, pronouns, etc.
  'See you tomorrow.' → She told me that she would see me the next day.

Reported questions

- When we report questions, the tense of the main verb changes but we don't use the auxiliary verb *do*. We also use the same word order as a positive sentence.
  'Where did you grow up?' → She asked me where I had grown up.
  NOT ~~*She asked me where did I grow up.*~~
- When we report yes/no questions we use *if* or *whether*.
  'Did you enjoy it?' → She asked me if I had enjoyed it.
  'Does she usually finish at 4 pm?' → He asked me whether she usually finishes at 4 pm.

10.1 Reporting the news

GRAMMAR

A Write the first direct quote on the board and ask the class where it is taken from (*the press conference*) and who said it (*the editor, Sally Ronson*). Elicit that this is an example of *direct speech* and write it as a heading on the board. Ask students to suggest how this sentence would be reported before finding the answer in the text and adding this alongside the example on the board. Then, add the heading *reported speech* above it. Now, give students time to complete the exercise alone before checking their answers in pairs. Give feedback as a class.

B–C Ask students to complete the rules alone before comparing their answers in pairs. Give feedback as a class, providing further explanations for each bullet point as necessary and eliciting new example sentences to add to the board. Then, direct students to the **Grammar Hub** (see below and TB110).

D Tell students they are going to interview each other about their reading habits, and elicit a couple of example questions that could be used. Next, put them into pairs to interview each other using the prompts. Monitor, encouraging students to write notes about their partner's answers and to ask follow-up questions to get more information.

E Put students into groups to report the main points from their interviews, reminding them to use reported speech. Monitor, encouraging students to identify any similarities and trends. Focus on the accuracy of students' grammar at this point. Bring the class back together to share the main similarities and trends they identified. Use the **Grammar Worksheet** on page W46 for extra practice.

SPEAKING

A–B Tell students about a recent news story you read that you think they will be interested in. Explain the main events and report anything that was said by the key figures involved. Now, give students time to write notes about stories that they have read. Monitor, ask questions to ensure they've made detailed enough notes to summarize the story in the next stage. Next, put students into pairs to discuss their news stories. Monitor, encouraging students to ask follow-up questions for more information and to give their opinions. If you have time (or if there is a big news story that everyone is interested in), bring the class back together to focus on one news story. Add any useful emergent language to the board.

GRAMMAR HUB

10.1 Reported speech

A Complete the second sentence so it has a similar meaning to the first.

1 'I've been working here for almost six months.'
Francis said that she 'd/had been working at the company for almost six months.

2 'I'm going to be a little late for the meeting.'
Andy says he 's/is going to be a little late for the meeting.

3 'Can I have a quick word with you, please, Mr. Jenkins?'
Susie asked me if she could have a quick word with me.

4 'I'd been hoping you'd have found a solution by now.'
Their boss said he 'd/had been hoping we would have found a solution by then.

5 'What time did you get home from work yesterday, Sofia?'
He asked me what time I 'd/had gotten home from work the day before.

6 'I think I know someone who might be able to fix this.'
Thais said she thought she knew someone who might be able to fix the problem.

7 'I'll call you around seven o'clock.'
Lars told me that he 'd/would call me around seven o'clock.

8 'We were driving around for a long time before we found a place to park.'
Mom said they 'd/had been driving / were driving around for a long time before they found a place to park.

B Rewrite the sentences and questions in reported speech. Add any information necessary.

1 'I'm not interested in hearing your excuses.'
Olga told me (that) she wasn't interested in hearing my excuses.

2 'In the end, the event was a big success.'
Juan said that, in the end, the event had been / was a big success.

3 'Do you want to meet for coffee after work?'
She asked me if I wanted to meet for a coffee after work.

4 'I've decided I am going to move to a new house soon.'
Jonas said he had decided he was going to move to a new house soon.

5 'What are you planning to do about your noisy neighbors?'
Daryl asked me what I was planning to do about my noisy neighbors.

6 'Can you play somewhere else? I'm trying to work!'
Mom asked the kids if they could play somewhere else as/because/since she was trying to work.

7 'Hi Mateo! I was looking for you yesterday.'
Renata told me that she had been looking for me the day before / the previous day.

8 'I've been working on a secret project.'
He said he had been working on a secret project.

➤ Go back to page 111.

B WORK IT OUT Complete the rules in the box. Use the examples in Exercise A to help you.

Reported speech

- When we report what someone said, we usually change the verb by moving it back one tense into the past.
  - present progressive → past progressive
  - simple past / present perfect → [1] ___past perfect___
  - *will* → [2] ___*would*___
  - *can* → *could*
- We usually need to change time and place references.
  - *yesterday* → [3] ___*the previous day*___
  - *here* → *there*
- It isn't necessary to change the tense when:
  - the information is still true or relevant now.
  - the reporting verb is in the [4] ___present___ tense.
- When we report questions, we don't use the auxiliary verb [5] ___*do*___.
- With *yes/no* questions we use *if* or [6] ___*whether*___.

C Go to the **Grammar Hub** on **page 140**.

D SPEAK Work in pairs. Use the prompts below to interview your partner about their print and digital reading habits. Write notes about their answers.

- How often / read magazines?
- Which magazines?
- Print or digital? Why?
- Which / online magazines?

E DISCUSS Work in groups. Report your findings from Exercise D. What similarities or trends can you identify?

SPEAKING

A PLAN Think about an interesting news story you read recently. Write notes about:

- the main ideas / key events
- things that people said

B SPEAK Work in pairs. Explain your news stories and give your opinions on them.

In a press conference yesterday morning, an emotional
Sally Ronson, editor-in-chief of *Healthy Me*, stated that a
combination of declining sales over the past five years and Ex D Q1
the increased popularity of digital content had motivated the
change. She told reporters that the publication had gone
from a distribution of just over 500,000 copies a month to 1
under 100,000 – a huge number of readers to lose in such a
short period of time. However, the magazine is still popular.
Since 2014, downloads of the *Healthy Me* app have increased
by 300%. In fact, Ronson said that the previous day had seen 2
the total number of registered users reach over one million.
The issue for publications like this is how to turn this interest
into sales. One method is to introduce paywalls – a feature
in an app or website that stops people who have not paid Ex D Q2
a subscription from accessing some or all of the content.
However, the general perception of the public seems to be that
online content should be free and, as a result, few are willing to Ex D Q3
pay to access their favorite publications.

When asked whether other publications from LMI Media 3
would make the same transition, Ronson said no. Yet it's clear
that she believes the future of magazine publishing is digital.
In fact, she said she was sure that all magazine publishers 4
would start to re-evaluate their options over the next five to ten
years. However, I'm not sure this is true. Magazines with highly
specialized content, such as the *Spectator*, *The Economist* Ex D Q4
and *Prospect* have all seen significant growth. However, I do
agree with Ronson when she says that for lifestyle magazines
like hers, which are predominantly directed toward a younger Ex D Q5; 6
audience, it simply doesn't make any financial sense to
produce print media any longer. Not surprisingly, people aren't
willing to pay for 'empty' news about barely famous people
or to read articles about serious content produced by barely
credible journalists.

The press also asked Ronson what this digital trend 5
meant for print media in general and she very rightly
pointed out that this depends entirely on the type
of publication. Print media is thriving in many areas.
E-book sales are now falling while the sales of printed
fiction are actually increasing. E-books also never really Ex D Q6
had any serious impact on the sales of reference books.
Furthermore, local papers with content focused on
a small region still tend to be popular.

Magazines and newspapers will no doubt have to evolve and those that do so innovatively will prosper. Those that focus on celebrity gossip and news found more easily on the internet will almost certainly disappear, but specialist magazines and local news are likely to continue to thrive.

LISTENING

A SPEAK Work in pairs. Look at the news headlines and discuss which you think are from real news stories and which are fake. They are all fake except '40,000 people watch game designer do nothing for 10 hours on Christmas Eve'.

B PREDICT Work in groups. How big is the problem of fake news? What can be done to help people deal with fake news?

10.2 **C LISTEN FOR GIST** Listen to an interview with a journalist about fake news. Do they mention any of your ideas from Exercise B?

10.2 **D LISTEN FOR DETAIL** Listen again. Complete the sentences with no more than three words from the interview.

1 Some fake news is for fun but many articles want you to believe the content is ___genuine___ news.
2 The internet, specifically ___social media___, has changed the way we consume media.
3 Internet advertising comes from ___search engines___ understanding the things you read and look at.
4 People have less ___faith___ in sources like CNN or the BBC than they used to.
5 People rarely ___check the facts___ behind the stories they read.
6 Teaching students ___to think critically___ would help them better identify fake news.

10.2 **E LISTEN FOR REPAIR AND ELABORATION** Listen again. Are these sentences true (T) or false (F)? Correct the false sentences. Use the information in the box to help you.

> **Listening for repair and elaboration**
>
> In presentations and interviews, speakers sometimes make mistakes and need to correct themselves. When making a repair like this, we frequently use phrases such as:
>
> *Let me rephrase that …, Sorry, what I meant to say was …*
>
> At other points, the speaker may feel that their point has been misunderstood and try to give more detail or explain something in a different way. When elaborating like this, we frequently use phrases such as:
>
> *What I mean is …, In other words …, To be more precise …*

According to the speaker …

1 it's easier to publish fake news online. (T) / F
2 ~~opinion has no place in real~~ personal opinion always comes into journalism. T / (F)
3 there is no agreement on the extent of the damage climate change will cause. (T) / F
4 ~~the government is~~ owners of these sites are ultimately responsible for content published online. T / (F)
5 ~~75%~~ 79% of students can't spot fake news. T / (F)

F SPEAK Work in groups. Discuss the questions.

1 Have you ever been tricked by fake news?
2 Whose responsibility is it to deal with fake news?
3 Do you think it should be illegal to publish fake news stories? Why/Why not?

LISTENING

A Draw students' attention to the news headlines, then put them into pairs to discuss which are real and which are fake. Monitor, encouraging students to explain their reasoning, but don't confirm answers at this stage. Bring the class back together, discussing each headline in turn. Encourage students to give clear reasons for their answers, then reveal the answers headline by headline.

B Ask students what we call news stories like these that aren't true or based on real events (*fake news*) and add this term to the board. Ask why they think stories like this are created (e.g. *to confuse, or deceive people into believing them*, etc), then put students into groups to discuss the questions. Monitor, encouraging them to support their ideas with examples and reasons. Bring the class back together to share their ideas, adding any useful emergent language to the board.

10.2 **C** Tell students you are going to listen to an interview about fake news, then play the audio for them to see if any of their ideas from the previous exercise are discussed. Give feedback as a class, taking this opportunity to clarify anything in the text students don't understand. See the **Audio script** below and TB113.

10.2 **D** Use CCQs to check that students understand the activity (e.g. *How many words can you use in each blank? Can you change the form?* etc), then give students time to read through the sentences and predict how to complete them. Then, play the audio again, before asking them to check their answers in pairs. Give feedback as a class.

10.2 **E** Tell students to move on to Exercise F, then correct yourself by saying, *Sorry, what I meant to say was let's look at Exercise E.* Tell students that correcting a mistake like this is called *repair* and elicit other phrases you can use, adding them to the board. Next, ask students what they do when someone doesn't understand what they are saying, suggesting the concept of elaboration if it isn't mentioned. Elicit one or two phrases you can use to help you clarify what you've said (e.g. *What I mean is …, In other words*, etc), and add these to the board for reference. Then, give students time to read the sentences before playing the audio again. Ask them to compare their answers with a partner, before giving feedback as a class.

F Put students into groups to discuss the questions. Monitor, encouraging further discussion by asking follow-up questions (e.g. *What do you think the punishment should be for sites that publish fake news?* etc). If you have time, bring the class back together to either share one or two of their experiences with fake news or discuss questions two or three in more detail.

Extra activity
To extend the theme of this lesson, ask students to research their own news stories, writing down three headlines – two fake and one real. Encourage them to try and find interesting or funny headlines and to familiarize themselves with the stories behind them so they can answer questions in class. Next lesson, nominate students to read their headlines and encourage the class to ask them follow-up questions to help them guess which story is real and which are fake.

AUDIO SCRIPT

10.2

Listening, Exercise C
P = Presenter E = Emily

P: Fake news is a phrase and a concept that didn't even really exist a few years ago, but today it's one of the biggest buzzwords in the media. To discuss why fake news has become so prevalent and what, if anything, can be done about it, I have journalist Emily Woolf with me here today. So, Emily, what exactly is fake news?

E: Essentially, it is news that is not true. Some of it is clearly written as a joke and is simply there to amuse people, but a lot of it is written in a way so as to trick the reader. [Ex D Q1] The writer wants you to believe that it is genuine news.

P: So, how new is the concept of fake news?

E: Well, it's not new at all, really. There has always been fake news, but in the past it was less common, largely because there was no money to be made from it. All of a newspaper's income was made from advertising and no company wanted to advertise alongside fake news articles because it wasn't good for their reputation. You may have found an occasional fake story in a tabloid because they didn't always have such high standards, but you certainly wouldn't have found any in the high-end newspapers.

P: So, what's changed?

[Ex D Q2] **E:** In a word, the internet. The internet and social media have been massive game changers. It's so much easier for people to share stories and they don't always check that they're true before they do so.

P: But surely, advertisers still want to be associated with good quality content?

E: To a certain extent, yes, but [Ex D Q3] advertising on the internet is based on search engines knowing what you like to look at and then showing you ads that you want to click on, so the association with the content has been lost a little, I think. These days, advertisements and headlines appear together on your news feed and are tailored to your personal tastes or behaviors online, usually showing you more of the same thing. The problem is it can be difficult to tell what the source of a headline is, so it may look similar to genuine news providers, and when you click through, it's very difficult to tell if the website is genuine or not.

P: That's true. I frequently click on links to websites just based on the headline and the websites look very professional once you get there.

E: They are, and it can be difficult to tell if the news is fake or real. We're no longer so sure which sources to trust. [Ex E Q1] Traditionally, print newspapers have been held to a much higher standard. In other words, unlike bloggers and people writing on social media, large newspapers can't just lie or make things up. [Ex D Q4] I think we used to have more faith in sources like CNN, but now people don't know who to trust. In the past, we could be fairly certain information from those sources was real. We could also tell fairly easily which articles were factual and which ones contained opinions that could be biased or subjective.

P: So, you think some traditional media outlets could be biased or subjective?

VOCABULARY

A Tell students that you are going to focus on vocabulary related to traditional media and read the first sentence as a class. Elicit the meaning of *editor*, and identify the matching definition (c). Now, ask students to work alone to complete the remaining definitions, before checking their answers in pairs. Give feedback as a class, providing further explanations as necessary and eliciting new example sentences. This might also be a good opportunity to do some vocabulary building, by eliciting other forms, synonyms, antonyms, etc of the words in the set (e.g. *editorial*, *objective*, *bias*, etc).

B–C Pre-teach the word *sensationalist* (*a way of writing or talking about events that makes them seem as exciting or shocking as possible*), adding it to the board and eliciting one or two examples of sensationalist headlines. Next, give students time to complete the sentences alone before checking their answers in pairs. Briefly give feedback as a class, before putting students back into pairs to discuss the questions. Monitor, encouraging students to justify their ideas with evidence and examples. If you have time, bring the class back together to discuss one or two of the questions in more detail. Add any useful emergent language to the board. Use the **Vocabulary Worksheet** on page W47 for extra practice.

PRONUNCIATION

10.3 **A** Ask one of the students an open question, ensuring it's something that requires a fairly extensive answer. Allow them to say one or two sentences before interrupting to ask them a question or comment. Let them respond, then return to what they were saying before interrupting them again. Ask them if this is annoying, then elicit how you can avoid being interrupted. If students don't mention it, explain that you can also avoid interruption using intonation and that the speaker in the interview did this fairly effectively. Now, play the audio for students to identify the intonation pattern they used and why. Give them time to compare their ideas in pairs before giving feedback as a class. Because this is a fairly subtle pronunciation point, it's probably worth reading the extract aloud slowly, accentuating the rise-fall-rise intonation. If necessary, explain that it's a more subtle variation of the intonation we use when reading a list (i.e. rise, rise, rise, fall).

10.4 **B** Give students time to predict where the rise-fall-rise intonation will be used, before playing the audio for them to check. Then, play the recording again, pausing after each sentence for students to copy the intonation. Again, it might be worth reading these aloud slowly yourself, accentuating the intonation pattern.

SPEAKING HUB

A Tell students that they are going to have a group discussion about the media and give them time to write down their opinions on each question. Monitor, helping with any new or unfamiliar vocabulary as necessary.

B Now, give students time to think about other potential viewpoints and how they might diplomatically respond to them.

C Put students into groups to discuss their ideas. Monitor, encouraging them to justify their answers with examples and to use a rise-fall-rise intonation where appropriate to avoid interruption. Encourage students to respond to each other's ideas with diplomacy and tact – especially when they disagree. If you have time, bring the class back together to discuss one or two of the questions in more detail, adding any useful emergent language to the board.

10.2 (continued)

Ex E Q2 **E:** Yes. Definitely! Let me rephrase that, personal opinion always comes into journalism so there will inevitably be articles that reflect the views of the writer. In the past, it was much clearer that these were simply opinions. Now, some 'opinions' are presented as 'facts'.

P: This is obviously a huge problem.

E: It is. The problem is that people tend to believe a lot of the things they read. Despite the ease of searching

Ex D Q5 on the internet, people don't tend to check the facts in a story on various other sites or from different sources. They are especially likely to believe stories about serious issues.

P: So if someone writes an article, for example, claiming that climate change is a myth, people will usually believe it.

E: Unfortunately, yes. That's a good example actually. Pretty much all scientists agree that climate change is real and there's a lot of evidence to support it. To be

Ex E Q3 more precise, the only real debate is how quickly it is happening and how bad the effects will be. It's very worrying, and dangerous, that several people might read one article and go away with the conclusion that it isn't happening.

P: So, what can be done about fake news? Who should be responsible for controlling it?

E: Governments need to take a much stronger stance. Anyone writing news should be held accountable to the same standards as a journalist. Editors of newspapers were always held responsible for the content of the newspaper whereas website owners aren't necessarily. In other words, the owners of these

Ex E Q4 sites need to be held responsible for the content of their site.

P: The problem there, is that people read websites from all around the world and there might not be the same rules in one country as another.

E: That's true. One other thing that would be useful is

Ex D Q6 encouraging people, students especially, to think critically. Who wrote the text? What is the source? Why was it written? I know some schools are now training students to spot fake news and I think that could really

Ex E Q5 help. In a recent study 75% of students, excuse me 79%, were unable to accurately identify fake news stories.

P: Wow! That's shocking. Critical thinking is clearly a skill people need to learn at a young age. OK, let's see how easy it is to spot fake news. Here are some headlines. Are they real or fake?

VOCABULARY
Traditional media

A Complete the definitions with the words in bold.

1 The **editor** lost his job after the paper was accused of publishing fake news.

2 The **headline** was misleading because it said they had found a long-term cure.

3 **Tabloid** newspapers are mainly full of photos and celebrity gossip.

4 The press **coverage** of the royal wedding lasted all day.

5 The newspaper was accused of being **biased** in favor of the president.

6 The journalist refused to reveal the **source** of their story.

7 Her views are highly **subjective** and rarely based on hard evidence.

8 The **broadsheet** newspapers all included an in-depth analysis of the situation.

a tabloid (n) a small newspaper with a lot of pictures and short articles, frequently about famous people

b coverage (n) the way news is reported on television or radio or in the newspapers

c editor (n) a person who is in charge of a newspaper or magazine

d source (n) where information comes from

e subjective (adj) based on your own feelings and beliefs, not facts

f broadsheet (n) a large newspaper generally considered to be more serious than smaller newspapers

g biased (adj) preferring one person, thing, or idea to another in a way that is unfair

h headline (n) the title of a newspaper story that is printed in large letters

B Complete the questions with the correct form of the words in Exercise A.

1 Is it OK for journalists to write articles that are subjective or should they be objective?

2 Do you prefer to read serious broadsheet newspapers or less serious tabloid papers?

3 Should an editor take responsibility for all stories in their paper?

4 Sensationalist headlines are written to encourage people to buy papers and click on articles online. Should they be banned?

5 Should press coverage of people's lives be controlled to allow more privacy?

6 Why should we pay attention to the source of a newspaper article?

7 Newspapers are frequently biased toward certain political parties. Should this be banned?

C SPEAK Work in pairs. Discuss the questions in Exercise B. Explain your reasoning.

PRONUNCIATION
Avoiding interruption

10.3 **A Listen to this extract from the interview. What intonation is used on the highlighted words – falling (↘) or rise-fall-rise (↗)? Why?** rise-fall-rise indicates the speaker hasn't finished, fall indicates they have.

I think we used to have more faith in sources like CNN, but ↗ now people don't know who to trust. ↘

10.4 **B Underline the word(s) you think will have a rise-fall-rise tone. Then listen and check.**

1 Governments need to take much stronger action against companies that circulate fake news stories; it's just not OK to misinform the public.

2 In other words, unlike bloggers and people writing on social media, large newspapers can't just lie or make things up.

SPEAKING HUB

A PLAN Read the questions. Write notes about your opinions on the following questions:

1 Do large media organizations have too much influence?

2 Do you think the government should be involved in making sure the media isn't biased?

3 What are the advantages and disadvantages of people getting news from the internet?

4 Whose responsibility is it to fact-check content that is produced online?

5 Do you think less fake news would exist if the individual writers were held responsible for the content they produced?

6 Do you think journalists and the media should be allowed to say they can't reveal their sources?

B PREPARE Think about other possible viewpoints and how you would respond to them.

C SPEAK Work in groups. Take turns answering the questions while politely waiting for an opportunity to ask a follow-up question to explore different points of view.

- Give opinions on recent news stories
- Intervene appropriately in a discussion

10.2 Digital media

- Report a conversation
- Plan and create a viral marketing ad

S – substitution
G – reporting verbs
V – social media; adjective + noun collocations
P – using intonation to attract and keep interest

READING

A SPEAK Work in groups. Discuss the questions.

1 How do you know that an article you are reading comes from a credible source?

2 How can your own bias affect what you read and how you interpret it?

B PREDICT Work in pairs. Read the headlines from three different news stories and look at the pictures. What do you think each story is about?

C SKIM Skim the news stories and check your predictions from Exercise B.

D SUBSTITUTION Read again. What do the words in bold refer to? Use the information in the box to help you.

Substitution

To avoid repetition, writers frequently replace phrases, clauses or ideas with other words. This is called substitution. Common substitutes are:

- *one, ones, some*
  There are many reasons to doubt the statement, but ***one*** *of the most important is that the timings just don't add up.*
  (*one* = a reason to doubt the statement)
- *do*
  While Mr. Evans didn't have access to the property, the investigation has revealed that his partner ***did****.*
  (*did* = have access to the property)
- *either/neither*
  I've never seen him before in my life. ***Neither*** *has my husband.*
  (*neither* = not seen him before)

1 '… but apparently Mr. Rodriguez **did**.' confuse the animal for a bear

2 '**Some** even work all night…' programmers at FTP Systems

3 '… yet **neither** have been named as part of the investigation.' two current employees of BIOS Technologies that the police are eager to talk to

4 '… **one** being how the chocolate could have possibly survived for over 3,000 years.' thing we don't know about the chocolate discovery

5 'Believe me, **so do I**.' have a lot of questions

E SPEAK Work in groups. Do you think any of the stories are true? Why/Why not? None of the stories are true, although the Egyptian story is loosely based on the recent discovery of the world's oldest cheese, which was found in a 3,200-year-old tomb near Cairo.

GRAMMAR

Reporting verbs

A Read the news stories again. Match the highlighted sentences (1–5) to the direct speech (a–e).

a 'No, I'm sorry. I cannot discuss an on-going investigation.' 3

b 'We simply need to run a lot of tests. Until then, this is nothing more than a fun news item.' 5

c 'I'm sorry the police were called out unnecessarily.' 1

d 'That's correct. The animal was delivered home safely.' 2

e 'Earlier today my team discovered two additional bars nearby – both in a similar state.' 4

Terrified New Yorker sees 'bear'

CALLS 911

Brooklyn Heights, New York –

Brooklyn Heights resident Anthony Rodriguez was terrified to see a bear rummaging through the trash cans outside his apartment early yesterday morning. Rodriguez called the NYPD and officers were soon at the scene. Fortunately for attending officers Liam Henderson and Alyssa Romano, the 'bear' turned out to be a hungry but harmless domestic dog. 'We arrived at approximately 6:30 am to find a large brown dog checking trash cans on the street for leftover food,' Officer Romano told reporters. She added, 'I have no idea how anyone could confuse the animal for a bear, but apparently Mr. Rodriguez did.' [Ex D Q1] [1]Rodriguez later apologized for wasting police time. The story has prompted a number of animal rights groups to raise concerns over the dog's welfare. [2]In response, a spokesperson for the police department confirmed that the animal had been safely returned to its owners.

TECH CRIMINAL CAUGHT HANGING AROUND

An employee of IT giant FTP Systems was arrested last night following a failed burglary attempt at the company's head office.

Neil Aitken broke into the London office shortly after midnight in order to steal sensitive computer data. Having downloaded over five terabytes of confidential information to his personal laptop, Mr. Aitken got stuck in the elevator on the 54th floor and was forced to use the alarm to call for help. 'I wasn't surprised to hear the alarm,' said Geoff Payton, the maintenance worker on duty that night. 'A lot of programmers work late and some even work all night. [Ex D Q2] But Mr. Aitken kept asking me not to call the police, which seemed suspicious, so I called the authorities.' When Mr. Aitken was finally rescued from the elevator over two hours later, he was promptly arrested and will stand trial for burglary next month. [3]Although investigators have refused to comment on their current progress, it is widely believed that Mr. Aitken had intended to sell the stolen data to FTP Systems' biggest competitor, BIOS Technologies. Our sources have also suggested that [Ex D Q3] the police are eager to talk to two current employees of BIOS Technologies, about their dealings with Mr. Aitken, yet neither has been named as part of the investigation.

LEAD-IN

Before the lesson, prepare some small strips of paper (big enough for students to write one or two words on), ensuring you have enough for three per student. In class, draw students' attention to the lesson title, and elicit one or two words connected to it (e.g. *blog*, *social media*, etc). Now, give each student three strips of paper (or one each if you have a big class), and ask them to write one word or a phrase connected to digital media on each slip. When students have finished, collect the strips of paper in a hat or small bag. Now, put students into teams. Tell them that you are going to give one member from each team a minute to describe as many of the words in the hat as possible without using the word itself. Demonstrate the activity yourself, then nominate a student to the start the game. Tell them to put anything their group guesses correctly to one side, not back in the hat and to discard anything that has already been described. Award one point for every word their team guesses correctly, then move on to the next team. If any of the teams run out of strips before the time is up, add the previously guessed words back to the hat. To extend the game, you can use the same words for other rounds, by changing the rules (e.g. *you can only use three words in your description*, *you must mime the words*, etc).

READING

A Tell students that you read an article published by a famous sporting goods company, saying that their new sneakers apparently make you run faster. Ask students whether they think this is true and why not. If they don't mention it, ask whether you can trust a story about a product written by the company that made it using this to review the concept of *bias*. Explain that a source that can be believed or trusted can be described as *credible* adding this term to the board.

To consolidate understanding, elicit two or three examples of sources that students consider to be credible and why. Now, put students into groups to discuss the questions. Monitor, encouraging students to support their ideas with reasons and examples. Bring the class back together to share their ideas, building up a checklist to help students identify a credible source on the board (e.g. *check who wrote the article and what their credentials are*, *check how up-to-date the information is*, etc).

B–C Draw students' attention to the headlines and the accompanying pictures, then put them into groups to discuss them. Monitor, helping with new vocabulary as necessary, but don't confirm anything at this point. Next, give students time to quickly skim each story to check their ideas. Bring the class back together, nominating pairs to summarize each story and encouraging peer correction as necessary.

D Write the following sentence on the board – *There are many reasons to doubt the statement, but one of the most important reasons to doubt the statement is that the timings just don't add up.* Ask students how you could make the sentence more succinct, crossing out *of the most important reasons to doubt the statement* in the sentence on the board and writing *one* in a different color. Explain that replacing phrases, clauses or ideas like this is called *substitution*, and elicit why writers might do it (e.g. *to make their writing more succinct*, *to avoid repetition*, etc). Then, read through the other examples in the skills box as a class, eliciting further examples of each bullet to consolidate understanding. Now, give students time to complete the exercise alone before comparing their answers with a partner. Give feedback as a class.

E Put students into groups to discuss the question. Monitor, encouraging them to explain their reasoning. Bring the class back together to share their ideas before revealing the answer.

METHODOLOGY HUB by Jim Scrivener

Learning about grammar

- Don't try and sit down with a grammar book and learn it; better to integrate your learning with your teaching. If you are going to teach the past perfect tomorrow, then sit down and research it tonight. Read and write notes. Make friends with the item.
- Slowly build up your grammar knowledge in this way, lesson by lesson, item by item.
- Make good use of the notes in Teacher's Books that accompany all major textbooks. There are usually a lot of helpful hints about the lesson's grammar. But don't rely only on this information. You must get and use your own grammar references as well.
- I frequently find that I need to refer to two or three different sources to really get my head around an item of grammar. It's interesting that grammatical description isn't fixed and set in stone. Different books can take very different angles on things, usually classifying in different ways and giving different names. You need to gather and sort all this out in your head and decide what is most useful and helpful from your perspective.
- After researching and getting comfortable with a new grammar item, let it settle in your head and then think coolly and calmly as to what small part of that you can deal with in a single lesson.
- Some new native-speaker teachers get 'grammar drunk' when they start teaching. Having previously known little about their own language, they do their research and then find it so exciting that they go into class wanting to tell their students about all that they have learned. Remember, you need to know as much as you can about grammar. But your students cannot absorb it all in one day. Good research should not lead to a 40-minute lecture on 'Everything I know about the present perfect'.

  Other useful resource books include:
- Traditional grammar, written mainly for academics or native speakers, can be a little overwhelming for the teacher.
- Pedagogic grammar books are written specifically for teachers. These usually include helpful notes about typical errors and student problems.
- Usage books are guides on how the language is used. They refer to grammatical points but also include information on vocabulary and pronunciation issues, style, idioms and so on. The items may be organized alphabetically or according to meanings or functions rather than by grammatical class.
- Student grammar books and workbooks usually present bite-sized (or one-page-sized) nuggets of grammatical information alongside exercises to practice those points. Students usually like working through these, exercise by exercise, at home. They are also a useful resource for teachers because of their clear, straightforward and short explanations, usually with usable teaching examples and contexts.

GRAMMAR

A Ask students to complete the exercise alone, before briefly checking their answers with a partner. Give feedback as a class.

B–C Give students time to complete the rules alone, before checking their answers with a partner. Then, give feedback as a class, consolidating understanding by eliciting new example sentences for each structure. Now, direct students to the **Grammar Hub** (see below).

D If students completed the Grammar Hub exercises for homework, it might be worth reviewing the grammar at this point by working through the first sentence together. Otherwise, give students time to complete the exercise alone before checking in pairs. Then, give feedback as a class. To extend this activity, ask students to write three funny or interesting sentences in direct speech, then give them to a partner to report. Use the **Grammar Worksheet** on page W48 for extra practice.

SPEAKING

A Tell students that you are going to play a game and read the rubric as a class. Ask ICQs if necessary to confirm students understand what they need to do (e.g. *Do you answer all questions honestly? How many lies do you need to tell?* etc). Then, give students time for them to plan what they will say for each question. Remind them to create believable lies so that their partner will find it difficult to guess. Monitor, helping with grammar and vocabulary as necessary.

B–C Put students into pairs to play the game. Monitor, encouraging them to ask follow-up questions to probe for more information. When they've finished, combine pairs into groups to discuss what they found out. Remind them to use reporting verbs to explain what their partner said, reading the example to clarify how to do this if necessary. Monitor, asking students to reveal their lies to the group at the end of each discussion.

GRAMMAR HUB

10.2 Reporting verbs

- As well as *say* or *tell*, we can also use other reporting verbs (e.g. *threaten, promise, warn*, etc) to help summarize the meaning of what was said, to describe the speaker's attitude, or to indicate our stance.

  'I'm sorry I'm late.' → She apologized for being late.
- Reporting verbs are followed by a range of different structures:

  a *argue, claim, confirm, decide, recommend, state, suggest*, etc + (*that*) + clause.

  He claimed that he was innocent.
  The police stated that they have made an arrest.

  b *assure, inform, promise, remind*, etc + object + (*that*) + clause.

  Sarah assured me that she would pay me back.
  She promised him that it would never happen again.

  c *decide, promise, refuse, threaten*, etc + the infinitive.

  She refused to tell me why I had been unsuccessful.
  Neighbors threated to call the police.

  d *advise, ask, convince, encourage, persuade, remind, warn*, etc + object + the infinitive.

  My wife encouraged me to apply for the position.

  e *accuse (sb) of, admit, apologize (to sb) for, blame (sb) for, confess to, insist on, recommend, regret, report, suggest*, etc + verb + *-ing*.

  She insisted on paying for the meal.
- Some reporting verbs, such as *persuade, warn, tell* and *ask*, can be followed by a negative infinitive.

  They persuaded her not to say anything at the press conference.

10.2 Reporting verbs

A Complete the news story with the reporting verbs in the box.

apologized assured blamed confirmed decided insisted refused stated

XPS TO CLOSE ITS LONDON OFFICE AFTER 50 YEARS

In an announcement yesterday afternoon, Michael Winters, CEO of XPS, [1] confirmed rumors that the company would be closing its London offices after almost half a century in the capital. After talking about how important the site had been to the company, Winters [2] insisted on reminding reporters that XPS was still one of the most profitable businesses in its sector. He said that the board had only [3] decided to do it because there was no alternative, and [4] blamed the economy for falling sales. Winters [5] apologized to the staff for causing them anxiety about the future but he [6] assured them that they would be offered jobs in different locations. He [7] refused to comment on whether more offices were going to be closed and [8] stated that he would give further information when it was available.

B Are these sentences correct or incorrect? Rewrite the incorrect sentences.

✓ 1 A confidential source revealed that the company had lost $10 billion.

2 The police refused ^to^ comment on an open investigation.

3 She threatened ~~calling~~ to call the police if they didn't leave immediately.

✓ 4 His lawyers advised him not to publish the story until after the hearing.

5 They assured ^him^ that his name wouldn't be mentioned in the article.

✓ 6 Under pressure, she admitted fabricating the entire story.

7 The company accused Ms. Hartmann ~~with~~ of leaking information to the press.

8 In court, Mr. Petrov confessed to willingly ~~mislead~~ misleading the public.

➤ Go back to page 115.

EGYPTIAN DISCOVERY MAY CHANGE THE HISTORY OF CHOCOLATE

Human civilization has a long history with chocolate. As far back as 1900 BCE, the Mayans of Central America prepared a bitter, frothy drink with crushed cocoa beans, cornmeal and chili peppers. The Aztecs used cocoa beans as currency and drank chocolate at royal feasts.

However, it wasn't until 1847 that Fry & Sons produced the first bar of chocolate as we know it. At least, that's what historians thought until a ground-breaking discovery made 10 km north of Cairo last month.

A team of archeologists digging outside the tomb of a wealthy Egyptian official from the 13th century were amazed to find what appeared to be several ancient chocolate bars buried in the sand. 'We discovered four bars in total, each wrapped in white fabric,' explained lead researcher Arnaud Laurent. 'Each bar appears to be divided into five sections, maybe to make them easier to eat.' [4]Laurent later informed local journalists that his team had found two more bars in a similar condition.

Although images of all six chocolate bars have been widely shared online, not everyone is convinced of their authenticity. In an article published in the Journal of Archaeological Studies, [5]Professor Richard Hamilton advised historians not to take the discovery seriously until further research has been conducted. 'It's certainly an interesting discovery,' writes Professor Hamilton, 'but there are still a lot of things we don't know – one being how the chocolate could have possibly survived for over 3,000 years.' Ex D Q4 In a response on Twitter posted late last night, Laurent wrote, 'Everyone has a lot of questions. Believe me, so do I.' Ex D Q5

B WORK IT OUT Complete the rules with verbs from Exercise A.

Reporting verbs

We can use reporting verbs to explain the way in which something was said. Reporting verbs are followed by a range of different structures:

a *argue,* [1] *confirm* *, state, suggest* + (*that*) + clause
b *assure,* [2] *inform* *, tell, warn* + object + (*that*)
c *agree, demand, offer,* [3] *refuse* *, threaten* + infinitive
d [4] *advise* *, encourage, persuade, remind, warn, convince* + object + infinitive
e *admit,* [5] *apologize* *, deny, insist, suggest* + (preposition) + verb + *-ing*

C Go to the **Grammar Hub** on **page 140**.

D PRACTICE Rewrite the quotes in reported speech using the verbs in the box.

apologize blame encourage refuse threaten

1 'We won't leave until our demands are met.'
The protestors refused to leave until their demands were met.
2 'We will fire any employee who is one minute late.'
The company threatened to fire any employee who was one minute late.
3 'We want to say we're sorry to the 100 people who got food poisoning last week.'
The restaurant apologized to the 100 people who had gotten food poisoning the previous week.
4 'Can anyone who saw anything please contact us?'
The police encouraged anyone who had seen anything to come forward/contact them.
5 'The service is slow because of the internet provider.'
The TV company blamed the internet provider for the slow service.

SPEAKING

A PLAN You are going to discuss the following questions with a partner. You must tell the truth in response to three of the questions and lie in response to the other. Write notes about what you want to say.

1 Have you ever blamed someone else for something that you did?
2 Have you ever cheated on a test?
3 What's your biggest regret?
4 Have you ever been persuaded to do something stupid?

B SPEAK Work in pairs. Discuss the questions in Exercise A. Remember to tell one lie.

C DISCUSS Work with another pair. Report your partner's answers from Exercise B and explain which one you think was a lie and why.

Luis denied ever cheating on a test, but that can't be true!

VOCABULARY
Social media

A Work in pairs. Look at the pictures (1–3). What do they have in common? Have you done any of these things?

B Complete the definitions with the correct form of the words in bold in *#nomakeupselfie*.

1 When something goes ___viral___ it becomes very popular and spreads quickly, especially on the internet.

2 A ___campaign___ is a series of organized activities designed to achieve a particular social, commercial or political result.

3 When something is ___trending___, it is frequently being mentioned or discussed on the internet, particularly on social media platforms.

4 To ___reach___ people with a message or program means they see or hear it.

5 A ___follower___ is someone who chooses to receive updates and messages from another person on a social media platform.

6 A ___hashtag___ is a symbol used on social media to describe the general subject of a post.

7 An ___influencer___ is someone who changes the way people behave, especially through social media.

#nomakeupselfie

The no make-up selfie **campaign** was developed to raise awareness of cancer research in the UK. The **hashtag** nomakeupselfie started **trending** on various social media websites asking women to post a selfie with no make-up and to donate money to Cancer Research UK. The campaign quickly spread across the internet especially when celebrities such as Lady Gaga, Alicia Keys and Heidi Klum also shared selfies with their **followers** on Instagram. This, along with other social media **influencers** following suit, helped the campaign to **reach** a much wider audience. The trend went **viral** and donations reached $8 million in six days.

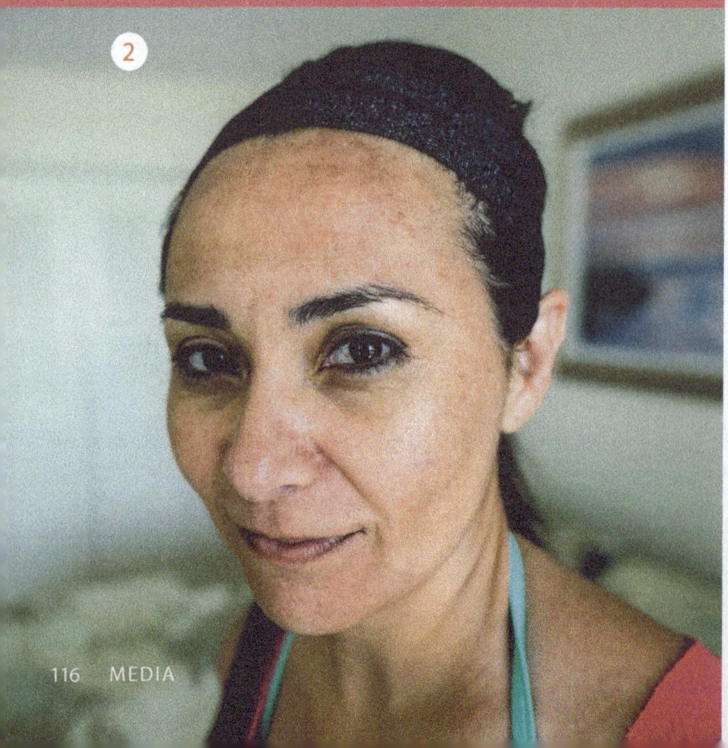

2

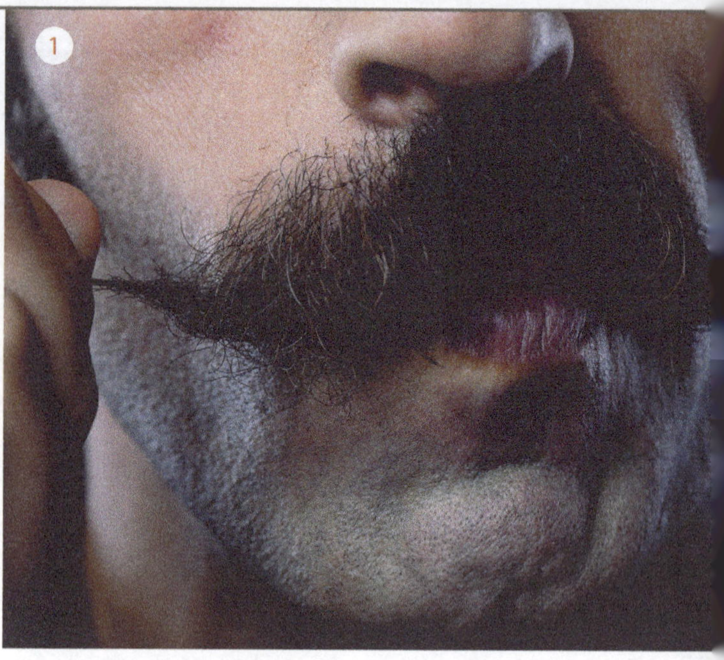

1

C Go to the **Vocabulary Hub** on page **146**.

D SPEAK Work in groups. Discuss the questions.

1 Who do you follow on social media? Why?

2 Which hashtags have you seen trending lately?

3 What do you think makes a campaign go viral?

LISTENING

10.5 **A LISTEN FOR ORGANIZATION** Listen to a talk on viral marketing campaigns. Put the topics in the order they're discussed.

_2_ the research behind viral success

_4_ create content which affects people's emotions

_1_ successful charity campaigns that went viral

_3_ understand the people you are hoping to reach

_5_ social media influencers can help raise awareness

_6_ build relationships with donors to ensure long-term success

10.5 **B LISTEN FOR DETAIL** Listen again. Complete the sentences with no more than three words or a number from the talk.

1 The Ice Bucket Challenge had ___2/two billion___ mentions online and 15 million videos were watched ___10/ten billion___ times online.

2 People will react similarly when they see an ___act of kindness___.

3 The speaker suggests using Pinterest in a campaign directed toward younger ___women___.

4 Videos go viral when they affect people's ___emotions___.

5 Frequent ___long-term donations___ are integral to a charity's continued success.

6 A ___competitive challenge___ is a great way to get people involved because it affects people's emotions and is fun.

C SPEAK Work in pairs. Do you think viral campaigns are an effective way to raise awareness of an issue? Why/Why not?

VOCABULARY

A Put students into pairs to discuss the questions, then bring the class back together to share their ideas.

The pictures are all of successful charity campaigns (1 – Movember, 2 – #nomakeupselfie and 3 – The Ice-Bucket Challenge).

B–C Give students time to complete the exercise alone, before checking with a partner. Give feedback as a class. Then, direct students to the **Vocabulary Hub** (see TB121).

D Put students into groups to discuss the question. Use the **Vocabulary Worksheet** on page W49 for extra practice.

LISTENING

10.5 **A** Play the recording for students to complete the exercise alone, then give feedback as a class.

10.5 **B** Give students time to read through the sentences and predict which word(s) might fit each blank. Next, play the audio so students can complete the exercise, then allow time for peer correction. Give feedback as a class.

C Put students into pairs to discuss the question. Monitor, encouraging them to support their opinions with reasons and examples.

AUDIO SCRIPT

10.5

Listening, Exercise A
P = Presenter

Ex A **P:** No doubt many of you have seen videos and posts that have gone viral, such as the mannequin challenge, the running man challenge or silly challenges like recreating the 'Harlem Shake' video. When these things start trending, or get a popular hashtag, they can really take off. Some organizations have been smart enough to realize that this meme concept can be used to help charities.

Many of you have no doubt also heard of Movember and the Ice Bucket Challenge, both of which started off small, but grew to capture the world's attention. The Movember event was conceived in Australia by two friends – Travis Garone and Luke Slattery – who were joking about reviving old trends. Inspired by a friend's mother who was fundraising for breast cancer, they decided to use the idea for a good cause – to raise money for prostate cancer and other men's health issues. In its first year, the event made no money and only had 30 participants. By 2014, it had exploded and garnered 1.2 million mentions on social media, with participants in over 20 countries. Movember gradually built success over a sustained period of time, but the Ice Bucket Challenge took off much more quickly and, arguably, had a larger overall reach. In 2014, Facebook, Twitter and Instagram were flooded with people challenging each other to throw a bucket of ice water over their head to raise awareness of ALS – a disease that affects nerve cells in the brain. Ex B Q1 The campaign got over two billion online mentions that year and in the first three months, 15 million videos of willing victims were shared on Facebook. These were viewed 10 billion times by 440 million people in countries all over the globe, which in turn led to a significant increase in donations to charity groups like the ALS Foundation. For example, in 2013 ALS's best week saw them raise $25,000, yet after the campaign it raised $2.4 million dollars in one week.

So, what made these campaigns go viral? Ex A Well, research from Sander van der Linden, a psychology professor from the University of Cambridge, tells us that Ex B Q2 watching an act of kindness performed by a peer makes people want to behave in a similar manner. These effective campaigns also help us to better understand the condition these people are suffering from. They encourage people to act and inspire positive reactions from people.

So, how can we use this research to influence the content we create? Ex A In order to create good viral content, you need to understand your target audience. In other words, you need to know who you are trying to reach and how. Campaigns only go viral if they speak to people on a personal level, so you need to create an image that represents the demographic, that is the age and gender of the people you want to reach. Ex B Q3 For example, if you want to target women aged between 18–24, then it's probably a good idea to try and incorporate Pinterest into your campaign since the majority of the platform's users fit this demographic. Second, you need to create content that has high levels of engagement. Most social media platforms rank content using incredibly complex algorithms. If you don't create engaging content, it will receive a low ranking and is far less likely to be shared as a result. Ex B Q4 Short videos typically go viral if they are shocking, memorable or funny because viral marketing is about emotions. People will share content that makes them react emotionally and this is the key to rapid growth. Using a hook that makes people happy or makes them laugh will make the content go viral.

So, once you have a good campaign together, how do you spread the word? Ex A One efficient way to promote your campaign is to use social media influencers. Social media influencers have the ability to give brands a reach they wouldn't normally get. We've all seen, and been jealous of, people paid to travel the world and share their experiences online. Most of these are social media influencers who are usually paid to promote brands.

Ex A Capturing contact information is also vital because, although it is fairly easy to create a viral success, it is phenomenally difficult to maintain this success long-term. Ex B Q5 Charities, for example, need long-term regular donations, rather than just one great year. Finding a way to encourage people to give you their email address will allow you to build a relationship long-term and gain regular payments from them. One way to get people to hand over their email address is to offer something for free. The word 'free' is a great way to get people engaged and is one of the best hooks you can utilize. I'm sure a lot of you are here today because the talk is free and we have free coffee!

Ex B Q6 Finally, some kind of competitive challenge is always fun. This challenge could be fun or silly, but ideally a combination of both, since this tends to be what engages people the most. It also needs to create an emotional reaction to the charity being supported. In just a few seconds, you have taken people on an emotional rollercoaster and gone viral.

VOCABULARY

Write the following sentence on the board – *Using celebrities is a great way to increase public______ of an issue.* Elicit what part of speech fits the blank (*a noun*) and what it might be, eliciting *awareness* if it isn't mentioned and adding it to the sentence. Ask students what we call words that are commonly used together like this (*collocations*) and elicit what part of speech both words are (*adjective + noun*) adding this structure in a different color above the sentence on the board. Elicit any other examples you think students might know (e.g. *strong coffee*, *old age*, *heavy traffic*, etc). Then, give students time to complete the exercise alone, before checking their answers in pairs. Give feedback as a class. Use the **Vocabulary Worksheet** on page W50 for extra practice.

PRONUNCIATION

10.6 **A** Ask students to suggest ways that people make a talk interesting to the audience. When someone mentions the way the speaker talks, encourage them to suggest ways people make their voices more engaging (e.g. *speeding up*, *slowing down*, *varying intonation*, etc), adding these to the board. Then, play the audio for students to identify the most enthusiastic speaker before briefly checking their answers with a partner. Give feedback as a class, asking students which of the techniques on your list the enthusiastic speaker used.

Speaker 2 uses stress and a rise-fall intonation on the words 'exploded', 'million' and 'twenty' to make their delivery more dynamic.

10.7 **B–C** Give students time to predict the stress and intonation on the three sentences before playing the audio for them to check their answers. Give feedback as a class, before playing the track again, pausing between each sentence for students to copy the pronunciation.

SPEAKING HUB

A Tell students about a charity or cause that is important to you and elicit from the class what issues matter to them. Explain that they are going to work in groups to create a viral marketing campaign, and put them into groups of four to plan their campaign. Encourage them to think about the advice given in the talk they listened to, as well as answer the questions to help them prepare. Monitor and help with any new or unfamiliar vocabulary as necessary.

B Tell students to film their viral campaigns using their cell phones. If students are not allowed to have cell phones in class, then this task can be set for homework or performed live.

C Call on each group to show their ads to the class. Encourage them to share their answers to the questions in Exercise A and allow time for others to ask follow-up questions. At the end, take a class vote on which video is the most likely to go viral.

Extra activity

Ask students to research successful charity ads and write notes about what they think made them so impactful. Next lesson, play the videos in class and analyze them as a group, highlighting any emotive language, use of intonation to attract and keep interest etc.

METHODOLOGY HUB by Scott Thornbury

Priming

Priming describes the process by which, through repeated encounters, a word gathers particular associations. These associations may be with other words, as is the case with collocations. For example, the word *encounter* is primed to occur with adjectives like *chance*, *first* and *close*: *a chance encounter with an applied linguist*. Or words may be primed to occur in association with particular meanings (called semantic associations). Thus, the verb *to encounter* is frequently associated with problems and difficulties, as in *Krashen's theory encountered widespread rejection*. Or words may be primed to occur in particular grammatical patterns and not in others (this is sometimes called colligation). For example, the noun *encounter* is twice as likely to occur in indefinite contexts (*an encounter*; *encounters*) than in definite ones (*this encounter*; *her encounter*). And, when it occurs in definite contexts, it almost never occurs with the definite article *the*. This contrasts with the word *meeting*, a word of similar meaning to *encounter*, which occurs twice as often in definite contexts as it does in indefinite ones, and mostly with the article *the* (*The meeting went on and on*). The primings of *meeting* and *encounter* are almost mirror images of each other, which is frequently the case with synonyms. They tend to divide up their shared semantic territory.

Recent research into how the brain works (neurobiology) helps explain how priming happens. The brain extracts recurring patterns from the input it receives. These patterns are strengthened through repeated encounters and 'chunked' into larger units before being stored in long-term memory.

The theory of lexical priming, first elaborated by Michael Hoey, suggests that learning a language is essentially learning the primings of its words. This includes its grammar, which itself is the accumulated effect of the primings of function words, like *is*, *do*, *by* and *that*. This theory, in turn, supports a lexical approach to teaching. According to this approach, learners need massive exposure to input, and guidance in extracting patterns from it.

VOCABULARY
Adjective + noun collocations

Adjective + noun collocations

Some adjectives and nouns are commonly used together. For example, we say *negative attitude* NOT ~~negative belief~~.

Match the numbers (1–6) with the letters (a–f) to form adjective + noun collocations.

1 The number of **online** … b
2 There has been a **positive** … e
3 One **key** … d
4 Hashtags are a great way to raise **public** … a
5 Using Twitter allows us to reach a **wider** … c
6 The company has made a **substantial** … f

a **awareness** of a new campaign.
b **comments** posted is a good measure of success.
c **audience** than through other social media platforms.
d **factor** was the use of social media influencers.
e **reaction** both online and in print media.
f **donation** to the campaign.

PRONUNCIATION
Using intonation to attract and keep interest

10.6 **A** Listen to the sentence below being said in two different ways. Check (✓) the one that sounds more engaging.

By 2014, it had exploded and garnered 1.2 million mentions on social media, with participants in over twenty countries.

☐ Speaker 1 ☑ Speaker 2

B Underline the words you think will be stressed and draw arrows to show where you think the intonation will rise.

1 It's important to show that they aren't alone, that they do have someone to turn to.
2 Just one small donation from you could change the lives of these children forever.
3 It's time we put a stop to this unnecessary suffering. It's time we took a stand.

10.7 **C** Listen and check your answers to Exercise B.

SPEAKING HUB

A PLAN Work in groups of four. You are going to create a viral marketing campaign for a charity or to raise awareness of an issue (e.g. mental health, homelessness, etc). To help you plan, discuss the questions below.

1 Which charity are you going to raise awareness of and try to get regular donations for?
2 How are you going to get more online mentions for your chosen charity?
3 What key factors will hook your audience into the video?
4 Who is going to be your target audience?
5 How are you going to get higher engagement and create viral content?

B PREPARE Film your viral ad.

C PRESENT Play your viral ad to the class. Take a class vote for the ad most likely to go viral.

3

- Report a conversation
- Plan and create a viral marketing ad

The rise of streaming

COMPREHENSION

A Work in groups. Discuss the questions.

1. Do you prefer streaming movies on platforms like Netflix and Amazon Prime or going to the movie theater?
2. Overall, do you think streaming services have had a positive or negative effect on the movie industry?
3. How do you think movie theaters could adapt to survive the rise of 'on demand' content?

Glossary

influx (n) the arrival of a large amount of people or things at the same time

metric (n) a system or standard for measuring things

B Watch a news report about the rise of video streaming services. Choose the best summary (1 or 2).

1. Streaming services like Netflix have provided a platform for films that might not otherwise have been made.
2. (circled) Streaming services like Netflix are now forcing people in the film and TV industry to rethink their approach.

C Watch the report again and answer the questions.

1. According to the presenter, what is usually essential to the success of large film franchises?
2. According to the first interviewee, what won't audiences be able to stream online?
3. Which two examples does the presenter give of cinemas diversifying their business?
4. According to the independent producer, why are many people leaving the film industry to work in TV?

D Work in pairs. Read the extract from the report. What do you think might explain lower ticket sales but higher overall attendance?

Box office sales are no longer the sole metric of success. In fact, so far this year, box office receipts are down, whilst cinema admissions are up. Suggested answer: Although fewer people are going to the cinema/movie theater to watch films/movies, more overall are going to cinemas/movie theaters for other events (e.g. live conversations, meet-up groups, etc).

Glossary

cinema **(n) (British)** = movie theater **(n) (American)**

mum **(n) (British)** = mom **(n) (American)**

AUTHENTIC ENGLISH

A Work in pairs. Read the extract from the report. Why do you think the speaker uses *from … to*? What does this emphasize?

As a result of this revolution, cinemas are changing. They're diversifying to become hubs for community events, **from** live conversation **to** meeting places for new mums.

B Read the information in the box and check your answer to Exercise A.

from … to

In natural spoken English, *from … to* is generally used when talking about the highest and lowest points in a range:

Subscription packages cost anywhere ***from*** *$22* ***to*** *$65 a month.*

However, it can also be used to make arguments sound more persuasive by giving two very different examples that show how big the range of something is.

These days, we can stream everything ***from*** *the latest blockbuster movies* ***to*** *children's cartoons.*

Although this structure usually follows the main claim or argument, it can also be used to introduce it:

From *the atmosphere* ***to*** *the size of the screen, a movie theater offers a great deal that streaming services simply cannot match.*

C Work in pairs. Take turns completing the sentence prompts with *from … to* and your own ideas.

1. My hometown has a lot to offer, …
2. … , there are many clear benefits of social media.
3. There are a lot of people who could play me in a movie, …
4. There's a lot we can do to tackle climate change, …
5. … , there are a lot of advantages to being self-employed.
6. There are multiple reasons to go vegetarian, …

My hometown has a lot to offer, from world-class theater to excellent burgers and fries.

Some big news

A Work in pairs. To what extent would the following factors affect your decision to take a new job?

- length of the commute
- salary
- working hours
- vacation time, benefits and perks

B Watch the video and answer the questions.

1 What are the advantages of Amanda's new job?
2 Why do you think she is reluctant to take it?

SPEAKING SKILL

A Match the extracts (1–3) to their meanings (a–c).

1 Well, that's certainly not near here. c
2 And I know that I certainly wouldn't be disappointed if you decided not to go. a
3 I guess I just need to be given a good reason to stay by someone, really. b

a I don't want you to go.
b Give me a reason to stay.
c It's really far away.

B Work in pairs. Are Harry and Amanda being vague or direct? Why?

C Read the information in the box and check your answers to Exercise A.

> **Circumlocution**
>
> Using more words than is necessary when fewer would do is called circumlocution. This is something we do to be vague or evasive, usually because we are embarrassed, uncomfortable or simply want to avoid saying something. Circumlocution is typically signaled by phrases such as: *I guess what I'm trying to say is …, I just kind of want you to know that …, I suppose what I mean is …*

D Work in pairs. Take turns breaking the bad news below to each other using circumlocution.

- All the money has been stolen out of their bank account.
- You have spilled coffee on their brand-new white carpet.
- You had said that they could have the day off tomorrow, but now you need them to come in to work.
- You have forgotten to send the important letter that they asked you to mail.
- They are going on vacation tomorrow, but the airline they are flying with has gone out of business.

SPEAKING HUB

A PREPARE Work in pairs. Brainstorm the advantages and disadvantages of video streaming services.

B PLAN Work in two groups. You are going to debate the following:

Video streaming services have had a negative impact on the movie and television industry.

Group A – You agree with the idea above.

Group B – You disagree with the idea above.

Plan your arguments. Think about how to support your position, as well as what the other group might say.

C SPEAK Hold your debate.

Give your opinion on streaming services

➤ Turn to page 163 to learn how to write a persuasive essay.

The rise of streaming

LEAD-IN

Write the following sentence on the board – *Watching movies at the movie theater is much better than watching them at home.* Then, put students into A/B pairs, asking the As to argue in favor of the statement and Bs to argue against it. Bring the class back together to share their ideas.

COMPREHENSION

A–B ▶ Put students into groups to discuss the questions. Then, play the news report for students to choose the best summary. Give feedback as a class.

C ▶ Play the report again for students to answer the questions. Ask them to briefly check in pairs, before giving feedback as a class.

1 *Their international appeal (particularly in countries such as China).*
2 *The biggest superhero films/movies.*
3 *Hosting live conversation events and serving as a meeting place for new mums/moms.*
4 *They find traditional filmmaking exhausting and see that television is now doing many of the things they enjoyed about film/movies.*

D Put students into pairs to discuss the questions.

AUTHENTIC ENGLISH

A–B Put students into pairs to read the extract. Then, give them time to read the information in the box to check their answers.

From … to is used when talking about the highest and lowest points in a range. It can also be used to help make arguments sound more persuasive by giving two very different examples that show the extent of the range.

C Complete the first prompt with your own example to model the exercise. Then, put students into pairs to complete the sentences with their own ideas.

Some big news

LEAD-IN

Tell students about the last time you had an awkward conversation with someone (ideally something funny or embarrassing as students are more likely to respond to this). Now, put students into pairs to share their own experiences.

A Put students into pairs to discuss the question.

B ▶ Play the episode for students to answer the questions. Ask them to briefly check their answers in pairs, before giving feedback as a class. You can find the **video script** for *Some big news* on the Teacher's Resource Center.

1 *It's an opportunity for Amanda to move into documentary film making; the pay is good and there are some great perks; many of her friends are in New York.*
2 *Amanda seems to be hoping that there is a chance of a romantic relationship with Harry.*

SPEAKING SKILL

A–C Give students time to complete the exercise alone, before comparing their answers with a partner. Briefly give feedback as a class, before putting students back into pairs to discuss the question. Monitor, but don't confirm answers at this point. Then, give students time to read the box to check their answers.

They are being vague because although they really want to tell each other how they feel, they are too shy, or perhaps not confident that they both feel the same way.

D Put students into pairs to practice the speaking skill.

SPEAKING HUB

A–C Put students into pairs to discuss ideas. Next, put them into groups to plan for their side of the debate. Finally, hold the debate.

▶ VIDEO SCRIPT

The rise of streaming
P = Presenter I1 = Interviewee 1 I2 = Interviewee 2 I3 = Interviewee 3

P: Streaming services from the likes of Amazon and Apple first revolutionized TV. Now movies are getting the same treatment. And it's changing the economics of the industry. Franchises, such as the latest Marvel film, *Ant Man and the Wasp*, have
Ex C Q1 dominated the list of top-grossing films in the last few years. They appeal to international, and particularly Chinese audiences, who, in precarious times, are often vital to make productions viable.

I1: The rise of the golden age of TV and the
Ex C Q2 franchization of film are connected. We all have almost all the kinds of content that you want to see, except for the biggest, er, superhero films. You'll be able to see everything else at home if that's what you prefer. But for those of us who love theaters, it, it might be a bit sad.

P: Front row please, mate. As a result of this revolution, cinemas are changing. They're diversifying to
Ex C Q3 become hubs for community events, from live conversation to meeting places for new mums. Box office sales are no longer the sole metric of success. In fact, so far this year, box office receipts are down, whilst cinema admissions are up. And the *Electric* here in Birmingham, founded in 1909 and the oldest working cinema in the country, is at the forefront of this very modern trend.

I2: I think if the smaller cinemas want to compete, they need to continue to, er, reinvent themselves and come up with new ideas. It gives people a reason to leave their living rooms and head back into the cinema again.

P: In the age of the smartphone, competition is unprecedented. One former boss of BBC films who is now an independent producer, can see power shifting towards smaller television screens.

I3: A lot of talented producers are probably feeling that film is less worth their while, I think they get to the point where it's exhausting and it often doesn't work, and, erm, they're seeing that many
Ex C Q4 of the things that they enjoy about film are happening in television and they want to be a part of that. And they can build a business on the back of that.

P: An extraordinary influx of money from technology companies, for whom cinemas are a distraction, is changing film forever. In the movie business, the big picture is getting smaller. Amol Rajan, BBC News.

10 Writing

Write a persuasive essay

W concession

A Read the essay question below and answer the questions that follow.

> Some think social media has a negative impact on individuals and society as a whole. Others argue the effects have largely been positive. Discuss both views and give your opinion.

1 What two points of view do you need to discuss?
Positive and negative impacts of social media

2 What else do you need to do?
Give your own opinion

B Work in pairs. What positive and negative effects do you think the writer might discuss?

C Read the essay. Were any of your ideas from Exercise B mentioned?

> Social media has had a huge impact on people's lives, and in recent years, many have argued that this effect has been detrimental to both individuals and society as a whole. Although there are undeniably many negative effects of social media, I believe that its impact on society has been predominantly beneficial.
>
> It must be acknowledged that social media brings with it a number of negative consequences. Arguably, as we spend more and more of our time online, we're engaging far less in the real world. As a result, as much as some people may feel they have a great deal of support from their online community, they are potentially losing touch with valuable support networks around them. Furthermore, because of the anonymous nature of online communities, interaction is frequently very confrontational, or worse – guided by people whose only agenda seems to be to cause conflict or to promote controversial views.
>
> Nevertheless, despite these potential issues, the advantages of social media are apparent in many aspects of our lives. First, it has enabled people to stay in touch with a wider group of friends, which they might otherwise have lost contact with. Additionally, these platforms provide a simple way to connect and share content with people around the world that have common interests – something that, while possible before social media, was certainly far more difficult.
>
> Overall, although social media can lead to conflict and the breakdown of face-to-face communication with those around us, it has also made many bonds stronger.

Refer students to this essay as a model for the writing task.

D Scan the essay again. Underline the words and phrases used to make concessions. Use the information in the box to help you.

> **Concession**
>
> In writing, concession means admitting that part or all of an opposing viewpoint is valid. Doing so not only shows you have a well-rounded view of the topic, but can also be used to further develop your own argument.
>
> ***While*** *it's true that social media can make some people feel isolated, the majority of us feel better connected in this day and age.*

E Rewrite the sentences using the words in bold.

1 Social media allows for more open discussion. It frequently leads to conflict.
While ... may While social media may allow for more open discussion, it frequently leads to conflict.

2 Social media divides some people. It brings many more together.
Although ... may Although social media may divide some people, it brings many more together.

3 It's clear that many people enjoy using social media. It makes others feel isolated.
Many ... but Many people enjoy using social media, but it makes others feel isolated.

4 I don't like the idea of policing social media. It's an important next step.
Nevertheless I don't like the idea of policing social media. Nevertheless, it's an important next step.

5 I don't like social media personally. I can understand its appeal.
As much as As much as I don't like social media personally, I can understand its appeal.

WRITING

A PREPARE Read the essay question below and brainstorm your ideas.

> Today, many people prefer to socialize online rather than in person. Some people feel this is a positive development while others argue it has had a negative impact on our relationships. Discuss both views and give your opinion.

B PLAN Organize your notes from Exercise A into an appropriate essay structure.

C WRITE Write your essay. Use your plan to help you.

D EDIT Work in pairs. Edit your partner's essay. Check:

- spelling and punctuation
- strength of arguments
- use of concession phrases

Refer students to this checklist when editing their partner's work.

WRITING 163

LEAD-IN

Tell students about any social media platforms that you use regularly and what you like and dislike about them. Then, put students into groups to talk about their own social media habits. Bring the class back together to share the main points from their discussions.

WRITING

A Give students time to read the essay question and answer the questions. Give feedback as a class.

B–C Elicit one or two positive and negative effects from the class, before putting them into pairs to discuss more. Briefly bring the class back together to share their ideas, before giving them time to read the essay.

D Read the skills box as a class, giving further explanation and examples as necessary. Then ask students to complete the exercise alone, before giving feedback as a class.

E Work through the first example as a class, then ask students to rewrite the remaining sentences on their own using the words in bold. Allow time for peer correction, before giving feedback as a class.

WRITING TASK

A–B Give students time to read the essay question thoroughly and think of ideas for both sides of the argument. Next, ask them to organize their ideas into a plan for their essay. Monitor and give feedback as necessary.

C Tell students to write their essays. Monitor and provide support with structure and vocabulary when necessary. Remind them to support their arguments with reasons and/or examples, use concession to help provide a well-rounded view of the topic and to refer to the model for help with structure.

D Put students into pairs to edit each other's essays. Encourage students to give each other positive feedback. Students can then rewrite their essays either in class or for homework.

VOCABULARY

A Complete the text with the correct form of the words in the box.

bias broadsheet coverage editor headline tabloid

What your newspaper says about you

The newspaper a person reads says a lot about who they are. In the US and many other countries, 1 ___tabloid___ newspapers are traditionally smaller in size and their stories are shorter. The 2 ___headlines___ are usually more shocking and many of the stories focus on people and celebrities. 3 ___Broadsheets___, on the other hand, are usually larger in size and much of the 4 ___coverage___ in these newspapers focuses on serious stories rather than celebrity gossip. In both cases, the paper's 5 ___editor___ decides what gets published and can have a huge influence on their readers. Many newspapers in the US tend to be 6 ___biased___ toward one of the two main political parties and people will usually not buy a paper that supports the other party.

B Complete the infographic with the correct form of the words in the box.

campaign follower hashtag influencer meme reach trend viral

The power of Social Media

Katy Perry, Justin Bieber and Barack Obama all have over **100 million** 1 ___followers___ on Twitter.

2 ___Hashtags___ are used **125 million** times a day on Twitter.

PewDiePie is, without a doubt, one of the **biggest** 3 ___influencers___ on social media, with over **60 million** subscribers to his YouTube channel.

When a music video goes 4 ___viral___ it can 5 ___reach___ **billions** of people. 'Despacito' has had over **5 billion** views.

A short 6 ___meme___ is much more likely to be **successful** than a long one.

A social media marketing 7 ___campaign___ is a cheap and quick way to reach **millions** of people.

'Stranger Things' was the **highest** 8 ___trending___ search for a TV show on Google in 2017.

C Choose the correct options to complete the sentences.

1 Celebrity endorsement is a great way to raise public *awareness* / *understanding* of a campaign.
2 Going viral was a *key* / *main* factor in the charity's success.
3 The charity has received a lot of positive online *posts* / *comments* recently.
4 Overall, we've had a pretty *positive* / *affirmative* reaction from the public.
5 The actress made a *consequential* / *substantial* donation to charity.
6 In order to reach a *wider* / *deeper* audience, you need a good hashtag.
7 We need to carry out a *thorough* / *deep* investigation into why this campaign failed.
8 I don't understand why there was such a *negative* / *poor* reaction to our ad.

GRAMMAR

A Rewrite the sentences in reported speech.

1 'I've been working every night this week.'
Nicki said ___she'd been working every night this week___.
2 'I'm going to be about ten minutes late.'
Jonas says ___he's going to be about ten minutes late___.
3 'Have you always wanted to go to college?'
He asked ___if/whether I'd always wanted to go to college___.
4 'We were trying to find somewhere to park.'
She said ___they'd been trying to find somewhere to park___.
5 'I'll let you know when I'm finished.'
Marco said ___he'd let me know when he had finished___.
6 'I'd wanted to tell her for months.'
Alex said ___he'd wanted to tell her for months___.
7 'I will need some help with my project.'
Pablo says ___he'll need some help with his project___.
8 'Where can I find a good seafood restaurant?'
Sofia asked ___where she could find a good seafood restaurant___.

B Are these sentences correct or incorrect? Rewrite the incorrect sentences.

1 Piotr agreed ~~coming~~ to come to the meeting.
✓ 2 She refused to apologize for being late.
3 Maria offered ~~working~~ to work this weekend.
4 They insisted on ~~to pay~~ paying for dinner.
✓ 5 He congratulated her on passing the exam.
6 She reminded me ~~sending~~ to send the email.
7 They invited us ~~having~~ to have dinner with them.
✓ 8 They advised me to get there fifteen minutes early.

Vocabulary and Communication Hub

Contents

1.1 Feelings

A Label the pictures (1–8) with the adjectives in the box.

awkward devastated disgusted frustrated furious overwhelmed relieved stunned

1 furious

2 awkward

3 disgusted

4 overwhelmed

5 frustrated

6 devastated

7 stunned

8 relieved

B Choose the correct options (a, b or c) to complete the sentences.

1 I was so ___ I had to leave the room. I didn't want a serious argument.
  (a) furious b stunned c relieved

2 I was ___ when I lost my ring. My grandma had given it to me when I was little.
  a disgusted b relieved (c) devastated

3 I was ___ by the lack of help. How could people just watch and do nothing?
  a furious b overwhelmed (c) disgusted

4 To be honest I felt a little ___. We hadn't parted on good terms.
  (a) awkward b relieved c frustrated

5 I'm so ___ we didn't miss our flight! I don't know what we would have done if we had.
  a furious b stunned (c) relieved

6 I think my grandpa gets pretty ___ that he can't do everything for himself anymore.
  a furious b overwhelmed (c) frustrated

➤ Go back to page 3.

1.2 Personality adjectives

A **Match the personality adjectives (1–8) with the definitions (a–h).**

1 I loved his talk. He was so **passionate** about what he was saying. d
2 You're always so **optimistic**. I wish I could be more positive like you. f
3 Don't be so **pessimistic**. It might not be so bad. a
4 She's really **ambitious**. She wants to own her own company in two years. h
5 Try not to be so **sensitive**. I'm sure he didn't mean to upset you. b
6 He's really **naïve**. He'll believe anything you tell him. c
7 She was **determined** to finish the race, even though she was injured. g
8 You need to be really **flexible** to work here. They are always changing our jobs. e

a thinking that the worst thing will happen in every situation
b likely to become upset quickly
c lacking experience in life and too ready to trust or believe in others
d showing or expressing strong beliefs, interest or enthusiasm
e able to make changes or deal with a situation that is changing
f being hopeful about the future and expecting that good things will happen
g not willing to let anything prevent you from doing what you have decided to do
h wanting to be successful, rich, famous, etc

B **Complete the job ads with adjectives from Exercise A. Use each adjective only once.**

Salesperson

We are looking for a new salesperson to join our team. We need hard-working people who can reach our high targets. You should be [1] ambitious, with big plans for your career. We work long hours, including weekends, so you will need to be [2] flexible about when you work. Some of our products are challenging to sell so you will need to remain positive and not develop a [3] pessimistic attitude.

CHARITY WORKER

Is someone being [4] naïve and unrealistic when they think they can change the world? We don't think so! We welcome [5] optimistic people who believe that we really can make a difference and that even small things can have a huge impact. We are looking to hire someone who can be [6] sensitive toward people's needs and who is [7] determined to help make other people's lives better. If you are [8] passionate about making the world a better place, then this could be the job for you!

➤ Go back to page 9.

2.1 Health and fitness

Complete the sentences with the words and phrases in the box.

level of fitness	life expectancy	mental health	physical	processed foods	reduce the risk	slow the aging process

1 To remain healthy, adults should do at least 150 minutes of moderate physical activity, like bike riding, every week.
2 The average life expectancy for women is typically two or three years longer than for men.
3 Some processed foods contain high levels of salt, fat and sugar.
4 Eating a balanced diet and exercising regularly may help slow the aging process.
5 A healthy diet and regular exercise can both significantly reduce the risk of of high blood pressure.
6 Improving your level of fitness can help to fight various heart-related diseases.
7 Surprisingly, exercise can also be good for your mental health because it reduces levels of stress and anxiety.

➤ Go back to page 14.

Vocabulary Hub

3.1 Descriptive verbs

Complete the sentences (1–8) with the verbs in the box.

crackling creaked growling rumbled screeched slamming smashed whirring

1 It was pouring rain and thunder __rumbled__ in the distance.

2 The tires __screeched__ as she tried to stop the car in time.

3 The floorboards __creaked__ under his weight as he tried to tiptoe down the stairs.

4 They sat around the __crackling__ fire, wondering what to do next.

➤ Go back to page 29.

5 He stormed out of the room, __slamming__ the door behind him.

6 Shining his flashlight through the chain link fence, Todd was greeted by an angry __growling__ dog.

7 The figure __smashed__ the window and reached inside.

8 The fan was __whirring__ in the corner of the room.

4.2 Intensifiers

Choose the correct options (a, b or c) to complete the sentences.

1 The risks of this kind of technology are ___ greater than any potential benefit.
 a intensely b utterly (c) considerably

2 All of the medical professionals that we spoke to said that the idea robots could perform complex surgery was ___ ridiculous.
 a disastrously b extremely (c) utterly

3 To be honest, the results were ___ unexpected. I thought we'd need to run several more tests.
 a considerably (b) totally c painfully

4 Seeing a computer program that I designed beat a human competitor is ___ satisfying.
 (a) intensely b totally c disastrously

5 If we don't put the proper safety measures in place, the results could be ___ bad.
 (a) disastrously b utterly c intensely

6 I am ___ sorry to announce that Maria Sanchez will be retiring from the field of robotics.
 a utterly b totally (c) extremely

➤ Go back to page 45.

5.2 Prefixes

Choose the correct prefix to complete the sentences.

1 Levels of pollution were so high they needed to ***decontaminate*** / ***uncontaminate*** the river.
2 They were ***disqualified*** / ***unqualified*** from the race for cheating.
3 In order to improve travel times, they decided to ***upgrade*** / ***downgrade*** the subway system.
4 The solution was ***unpossible*** / ***impossible*** to put into place.
5 The company ***misled*** / ***disled*** the community about the development.
6 People don't use the train because they feel it is ***overpriced*** / ***underpriced***.
7 The cost of building new road networks was significantly ***underestimated*** / ***overestimated***.
8 The excellent infrastructure has allowed the city to ***overperform*** / ***outperform*** many similarly sized cities.

➤ Go back to page 55.

6.1 Education

Complete the sentences with words from the box.

campus	elementary schools	entrance exam	graduate	high schools	lectures	scholarship	seminar	vocational

1 The __entrance exam__ for All Souls College at Oxford University has been called the world's hardest test. It is impossible to study for because there are no right or wrong answers and the questions are very abstract. The prize is a seven-year __scholarship__!

2 The Open University is designed for distance-learning students. Those who attend can watch __lectures__ online and write notes. They can also join in smaller online __seminar__ groups, where they can discuss ideas.

3 In American __high schools__, students take a traditional academic path. However, in college they can choose a __vocational__ path that leads to professions such as an electrician or beautician.

4 In China, there is a __campus__ of the University of Nottingham. Some of the buildings are identical to the ones on the UK site. Students here __graduate__ with a University of Nottingham degree.

5 Some five to eleven-year-olds in Bangladesh study in __elementary schools__ on boats due to frequent flooding in the country.

➤ Go back to page 64.

7.2 Three-part phrasal verbs

A **Match the words in bold to the definitions.**

1 I can't **keep up with** all of the technological changes.
2 I think people need to **stand up for** the things they believe in.
3 We seem to **run out of** money every month. We can only just afford our rent!
4 We **teamed up with** a local company to design the gallery.
5 The event lets me **catch up with** old friends.
6 The shelter **takes care of** homeless people in the city.

a to not have any more of something
b to work together
c to continue to learn about something or find out about something
d to find out someone's news
e to look after someone or something
f to defend someone or something that is being criticized or attacked

B **Complete the sentences with the correct form of the phrasal verbs in Exercise A.**

1 We wanted to __stand up for__ the rights of young people in the community.
2 The plans keep changing so frequently that it's hard to __keep up with__ what is happening.
3 We have __teamed up with__ local cafés to provide free food for the homeless.
4 Giving people a more beautiful environment encourages them to __take care of__ it.
5 A street party is a great way to __catch up with__ neighbors you haven't seen in a while.
6 Our project __ran out of__ government funding, so we crowdsourced the rest of the money needed.

➤ Go back to page 80.

8.2 Crime

Complete the sentences with the correct form of the words in the box.

arrest catch charge commit innocent investigate punishment question sentence witness

1 The police __questioned__ him for two hours and then __charged__ him with identity theft.
2 She claimed to be __innocent__ but three separate __witnesses__ identified her as being responsible for the crime.
3 He was __caught__ with people's credit card details on his computer and was __arrested__ for credit card fraud. After they __investigated__ further, he was taken to court, where the judge __sentenced__ him to six years in prison.
4 Some people argue that imprisonment isn't the best __punishment__ for someone who __commits__ a crime, because many go on to reoffend when released.

➤ Go back to page 92.

10.2 Social media

Match the words in bold (1–5) to the definitions (a–f).

1 I was trying to do some online research, but I kept on getting distracted by all the **clickbait** stories. c
2 You will need to go further back in that **thread** to find the message about the changes to the schedule. d
3 I used to enjoy social media until a **troll** started writing horrible comments on my posts. e
4 I think everyone has seen that **meme** of the president dancing – it's hilarious. f
5 Why don't you **DM** me so we can discuss this some more? b
6 I think that message goes against **netiquette** – it's really aggressive. a

a the polite way of expressing yourself or communicating with other people when you are using the internet
b to send a direct message to someone on the microblogging service Twitter
c a link on a website that is designed to catch people's attention and encourage them to read on
d a series of email messages or messages on a forum about a particular subject
e someone who writes negative and hostile comments on a website in order to provoke people
f an image, video or piece of text that spreads very quickly on the internet, typically one which people create different funny versions of

➤ Go back to page 116.

8.1 Student A

Read the story and write notes to help you summarize it for your group.

TROJAN HORSE

The Trojan horse was a huge hollow wooden horse made by the Greeks during the Trojan War. The Greeks had pretended to give up in the war but had secretly sailed to the island of Tenedos. They had left one soldier, Sinon, to persuade the Trojans that the horse was an offering from the Greek gods. Laocoön and Cassandra, who were both important people in the city of Troy, warned against taking the horse into the city, but the Trojans accepted it anyway. In the middle of the night, Greek soldiers, who were hidden inside, emerged from the horse and let the rest of the Greek army into the city. The Greeks then captured and destroyed the city of Troy.

➤ Go back to page 89.

5.2

A PLAN You're going to select three candidates to join the Mars One mission. Read the profiles and write notes on who you would like to select and why.

ADRIAN JENKINS

Leadership Has led teams of dozens of men in dangerous situations.
Personality traits Very determined and strong-minded. Always believes he is right. Not willing to listen to others.
Certifications An MBA.
Unique skills Worked as paramedic. Is an expert in emergency situations.

LINA WANG

Leadership No leadership experience.
Personality traits Quickly forms strong relationships with others. A very creative problem-solver.
Certifications Currently completing a PhD in Physics.
Unique Skills Is recognized as one of the most talented scientists in the world for her age. Three products she has designed have won international awards.

ANA RAMOS

Leadership Has led small teams of marine biologists.
Personality traits Excellent attention to detail. Very organized and well prepared.
Certifications A PhD in Marine Biology.
Unique Skills Experience at spending time in small spaces. Has been on many long research trips to isolated places.

NICOS ALEXOPOULOS

Leadership Has led teams of surgeons for over ten years.
Personality traits Hard-working, with a never-give-up attitude. A perfectionist.
Certifications Certified doctor.
Unique Skills Has worked in many hospitals including many years with Doctors Without Borders in very difficult environments.

VIKTOR POPOV

Leadership No leadership experience.
Personality traits Prefers to spend time on his own. Finds relationships with others difficult.
Certifications Engineering degree.
Unique Skills An experienced explorer. Has done survival training in the jungle and the desert.

GRACE ADEBAYO

Leadership Leads team of volunteers to help build schools and medical facilities in rural areas.
Personality traits Kind, caring and open-minded.
Certifications A degree in Agriculture.
Unique Skills Experienced at growing food in difficult climates.

B DISCUSS Work in groups. Compare your choices in Exercise A. Agree on two candidates to join the Mars One mission.

➤ Go back to page 57.

8.2 Speaking Hub, Exercise B

Read the profiles and answer the questions for each suspect. Underline the part of the text that gives you the answers.

1 Where were they at the time of the murder?
2 Why might they have committed the murder?
3 What is their alibi and does anyone else confirm it?

MAGNUS BALDURSSON

- Swedish billionaire oil tycoon
- Mild-mannered, yet a ruthless businessman
- Hates family secrets getting out and works hard to ensure nothing is made public Q2

ALIBI

'What an awful night! I told Sofia that she would be taking over the business when I retire and my son, Linus, was furious. He started shouting about how much debt Sofia was in – apparently she owed over a million dollars to some pretty bad people. Anyway, that's when Sofia ran out in tears. Linus said he was going to his room, but when I went to speak to him at about 9:50 pm, he wasn't there. I went downstairs to the study and found my son-in-law in there. He was furious about something. I was just about to sit down when we heard Sofia's scream.' Q1; 3

LINUS BALDURSSON

- Magnus Baldursson's eldest child
- Quick-tempered and loud, but generally fun to be around Q2
- Bankrupt after several bad business deals

ALIBI

'Yeah, I told my father about Sofia's debts – he deserved to know. Anyway, after the three of us argued, I went up to my room to think. I came down as soon as I heard the scream. That's when I found my sister's body.' Q1; 3

JAMES RUTHERFORD

- Has been married to Sofia for nine years
- Caring and dependable, but prone to fits of jealousy Q2
- Frequently argues with his wife, but has never been violent

ALIBI

'I went to find my wife and saw her talking to Max on the stairs. It must have been just before 10:00 pm. He had his arm around her! I was so angry that I had to get away, so I went straight to the study to calm down! Magnus had just come in when we heard the scream.' Q1; 3

MAX FISHER

- Internationally recognized movie star who went to school with Sofia and Linus
- Sociable, always fun at a party
- Has loved Sofia his entire life and has always been jealous of her husband Q2

ALIBI

'I found Sofia crying on the stairs at around 9:45 pm. I gave her my jacket and we talked for about ten minutes. Then she went upstairs to redo her make-up and said she'd be back down in a minute. I was feeling hungry, so I went to the kitchen to get a snack and found Bletchley eating his dinner. That's when I heard that awful scream.' Q1; 3

ALBERT BLETCHLEY

- Has served as the family butler for 36 years
- Hard-working, loyal and well-dressed
- Would do anything to protect the family Q2

ALIBI

'Frankly, I'm glad Sofia's dead. She was always horrible to me and I never liked her. But it wasn't me who killed her. Ask Mr. Fisher. He was with me in the kitchen when it happened.' Q1; 3

➤ Go back to page 93.

1.2 Student A

Read the text and write notes about:

- who the person is and why they're famous
- any challenges they faced and how they overcame them
- any other interesting/relevant information

Emily Blunt

Emily Blunt was born in London in 1983. As a young girl, she felt confident and had a lot to say but unfortunately, she struggled because of a stutter. The stutter made it very difficult for Emily to say anything and between the ages of 12 and 13, she was badly bullied by other children. Strangely, whenever she spoke in a different accent or a funny voice, she lost the stutter and was able to communicate. Spotting her talent for different voices and for making people laugh, one of her teachers encouraged her to take part in the school play. But how could someone who struggled to speak stand up in front of the whole school and perform? Emily did the play in one of her funny voices and caught the acting bug. She has since gone on to win a BAFTA and a Golden Globe for her acting and has starred in many successful movies such as *Sicario*, *The Girl on the Train* and *A Quiet Place*.

Glossary

stutter (n) to have difficulty saying something because you can't stop yourself from repeating the first sound of some words several times

➤ Go back to page 7.

8.1 Student B

Read the story and write notes to help you summarize it for your group.

The Loch Ness Monster

There are carvings from almost 1,500 years ago showing a huge monster in a Scottish lake and written reports from the 7th century describing the same creature. However, there were very few other reported sightings until 1933, when a doctor, Colonel Robert Wilson, took the famous photo of the supposed Loch Ness monster and sent it to a local newspaper in Inverness. They in turn then reported a sighting of an enormous creature in one of Scotland's largest lakes. However, in 1994, a man named Ian Wetherell confessed he had helped his father create the 'monster' using plastic and a toy submarine. His father had then given the photo to Wilson to submit to the papers because he thought people were more likely to believe a doctor. Despite the fact that people now know that the photo was a fake, there are still regular reports of sightings of the Loch Ness monster every year.

➤ Go back to page 89.

9.1 Student B

Read the situation below and role-play a conversation with your partner.

You have bought a new cell phone. It keeps turning off whenever you try to connect to wi-fi. The phone also crashes whenever you try to install a new operating system. The product is still under warranty. You don't want it repaired because you have read online that these faults are common. You would like it replaced with a different type of phone.

➤ Go back to page 101.

Communication Hub

3.1

A PREPARE Work in pairs. Use the pictures (a–g) to tell a story.

B PLAN Join another pair. Together work out the details of your story. Use narrative tenses to help describe the sequence of events.

➤ Go back to page 27.

8.2 Student A

Use adjectives to describe the objects in the picture to your partner. Are there any similarities between your pictures?

There's a large old-fashioned camera in the top left-hand corner.

➤ Go back to page 91.

9.1 Student A

Read the situation below and role-play a conversation with your partner.

You have bought a new TV and it hasn't been working properly. Many of the functions don't work and other functions work really slowly. It's not the internet provider because your laptop and phone work fine. The product is still under warranty. You don't want it repaired because you have read online that these faults are common. You would like it replaced with a different model TV.

➤ Go back to page 101.

6.2 Student A

A Complete the text with *a, an, the* or – (no article).

[1] The Maasai of Kenya and Tanzania have several age traditions that lead into [2] – manhood. Boys between [3] the ages of 12 and 25 are taught to become [4] – new warriors of [5] the tribe. [6] The night before [7] the ceremony, they sleep outside in [8] a / the forest, and at [9] – sunrise they come back for singing and dancing. They drink [10] a special drink, while also eating large amounts of [11] – meat. For [12] the next ten years they stay at [13] a camp to learn to be warriors. After [14] the final ceremony takes place, they become [15] – senior warriors and can get married.

B You are going to explain the ceremony in Exercise A to your partner. Write notes to help you.

➤ Go back to page 67.

8.1

Answer
It can't have been aliens since there were no signs of anything landing nearby. The family provided a sketch of one of the aliens which showed it must have been a large bird, probably a great horned owl. The sounds of bullets hitting metal must have been the surrounding farm buildings being hit.

➤ Go back to page 87.

5.1

A Work in pairs. Read the scenario and predict the cause and effect relationships between the pictures (1–10).

A chemical was sprayed to kill the mosquitoes.

In the early 1950s, an outbreak of malaria threatened the survival of the Dayak people of Borneo. Not knowing how to control the spread of the disease, the islanders turned to the outside world for help.

B Work with another pair. Compare you ideas from Exercise A.

➤ Go back to page 51.

6.2 Student B

A Complete the text with *a, an, the* or – (no article).

The *fiesta de quince años* celebrates [1] _a_ girl's 15th birthday and is popular throughout [2] _–_ Latin America. In Argentina, Peru and some other countries, the girl traditionally arrives at the party with her father, wearing [3] _an_ elaborate dress. [4] _The_ pair then dance alone, before inviting [5] _–_ friends and family to join them. After this, the evening typically alternates between [6] _a_ three-course meal and more formal dances, before the father gives a speech and presents his daughter with [7] _a_ large cake. This stage of the evening usually involves [8] _a_ ritual in which female friends and family pull [9] _–_ ribbons from a bunch. Each of [10] _the_ ribbons has a lucky object attached to it, except for one which is attached to a ring. Whoever gets [11] _the_ ring is said to be the next person to get married.
In Cuba, the final dance involves dancing with 14 different people and blowing out [12] _a_ candle and collecting a rose after each dance. With each candle the girl gets [13] _a_ wish and then [14] _the_ flowers are given as [15] _a_ gift to her mother.

B You are going to explain the ceremony in Exercise A to your partner. Write notes to help you.

➤ Go back to page 67.

8.1 Student C

Read the story and write notes to help you summarize it for your group.

The Vanishing Hitchhiker

One night, a group of friends were driving to a dance when they spotted a young woman hitchhiking. The group decided to give the woman a ride and asked her to come to the party with them. She was obviously cold, so one of the group gave her a coat. They eventually got to the party and after a night of dancing, they drove the woman home. The next day, one of the friends remembered they had forgotten to ask for his coat back, so he drove to the woman's house. However, when he knocked on the door he was told by the couple that lived there that the woman had been killed in a car accident years before. Scared, the man drove back to the corner where he and his friends had met the woman the night before. There, hanging on a road sign, was his coat.

➤ Go back to page 89.

1.2 Student B

Read the text and write notes about:

- who the person is and why they're famous
- any challenges they faced and how they overcame them
- any other interesting/relevant information

Jean-Dominique Bauby

Jean-Dominique Bauby was born in France in 1952. He was an actor and author. He also edited the famous fashion magazine *Elle*. In December 1995, at the age of just 43, he suffered a massive stroke. When he finally woke up, he discovered he had been asleep for 20 days. Most of his body had been paralyzed by the stroke and he had lost his speech. Despite his physical problems, he started writing the book *The Diving Bell and the Butterfly*. He did this by blinking his left eye while someone was reading the alphabet very slowly. He wrote and edited the book completely in his head while dictating one letter at a time. Unfortunately, two days after the book was published, he died. The book went on to be made into a movie, which was nominated for four Oscars and won two Golden Globe Awards.

Glossary

stroke (n) a sudden change in the blood supply to the brain

➤ Go back to page 7.

9.1

Are you a
good complainer? *quiz results*

Mostly A's You don't like making a fuss, especially over things that just aren't very important. You'd rather put up with the mistake and get on with your day than get into an argument. You're also more than happy to face the consequences of your mistakes and wouldn't dream of blaming anyone else.

Mostly B's You're tired of big companies getting away with terrible customer service and see social media as the perfect place to fight for your rights. It's important to you that you get what you paid for and you're more than happy to publicly complain if you don't. After all, if you don't stand up to these companies, who will?

Mostly C's You don't see complaining as a way to get revenge. You understand that everyone makes mistakes, but expect a quick resolution when they affect you. You're more than willing to face the consequences of your own mistakes, but want to make sure steps are taken to help others avoid making the same mistakes in the future.

➤ Go back to page 100.

8.2 Student B

Use adjectives to describe the objects in the picture to your partner. Are there any similarities between your pictures?

There's a modern black camera in the bottom left-hand corner.

➤ Go back to page 91.

9.2

A Choose one of the products below to design an ad campaign around.

1 an electric sports car that is one of the most eco-friendly on the market
2 a sports brand directed toward wealthy young and successful people
3 a range of health-food products that are low in calories but nutritionally balanced
4 a fitness app that tracks all your activities and sets you new physical challenges

B Design an ad campaign around the product you chose in Exercise A. Use the following questions to help you:

1 How are you going to raise awareness of your product?
2 What high-profile celebrities would you get to endorse your product?
3 What trends are you going to link your product to?
4 What features will make customers fall in love with your product brand?
5 What is unique about your product compared to other products on the market?

➤ Go back to page 105.

Feelings

A Complete the sentences with adjectives to describe feelings.

1. Samira was **d** _ _ _ _ _ _ _ _ _ when the family dog died last year.
2. They were **s** _ _ _ _ _ _ by a last-minute winner in what had been a tight game.
3. I have to admit, I'm **i** _ _ _ _ _ _ _ _ by what I've seen so far.
4. To be honest, I was just **t** _ _ _ _ _ _ _ to see her again after all this time.
5. I was **h** _ _ _ _ _ _ _ _ to hear about the accident in the town center.
6. Maria was **f** _ _ _ _ _ _ when I told her that I'd crashed the car.
7. I can't tell you how **r** _ _ _ _ _ _ _ I am that my exams are over.
8. Commuters are getting increasingly **f** _ _ _ _ _ _ _ _ with all of the delays.

B Work in pairs. Discuss the questions.

1. What do you find overwhelming about your work or studies?
2. When you feel tense, what do you do to relax?
3. What are you disgusted by?
4. When was the last time you were in an awkward situation?
5. When was the last time you were truly furious about something?
6. What kind of situations make you feel really frustrated?

1.1 Grammar

Question forms

A Use the prompts to write questions, adding other words if necessary.

1 Could / tell / which country / born

____?

2 What / industry / you / work

____?

3 Is / anything / not enjoy / job

____?

4 Who / biggest impact / life

____?

5 How / describe / yourself

____?

6 Would / mind / tell me / biggest regret

____?

7 Have / met / famous person

____?

8 What / would / say / weaknesses

____?

B Imagine you are a famous person. Write answers as them to the questions in Exercise A. Now work with a partner to ask and answer the questions. Can you guess each other's secret identities?

1 ____

2 ____

3 ____

4 ____

5 ____

6 ____

7 ____

8 ____

Tense review

A Complete the article with the correct form of the verbs in parentheses.

Six ways to overcome big challenges

1 Learn from the success of others. Talk to people who [1]______________ (*experience*) the same problem and find out what they [2]______________ (*do*) to overcome it.

2 Reflect on past achievements. Think about what you [3]______________ (*do*) that [4]______________ (*be*) so successful.

3 Keep your goals in mind. Think about what you [5]______________ (*try*) to achieve and why.

4 Stop and think. People [6]______________ (*make*) bad decisions when they are angry or upset. Wait until you [7]______________ (*calm down*) before deciding what to do next.

5 Make sure you know exactly what you need. You don't want to look back and regret the fact that when the time came to deliver, you [8]______________ (*not do*) enough preparation beforehand.

6 Reflect on challenges that you have faced. Think about a time when something went wrong and ask yourself what you [9]______________ (*do*) differently.

B Work in groups. Rank the advice in the article from best (1) to worst (6).

C In your group, add four more pieces of advice to the list. Change the ranking as necessary.

D Present your list from Exercise C to the class. Explain your reasoning.

Personality adjectives

A Complete the article with the adjectives in the box. There are three words you do not need.

ambitious arrogant determined down-to-earth easy-going flexible naïve open-minded optimistic passionate pessimistic self-centered sensitive stubborn witty

Roommates

Max Sturmburg's new sitcom about a group of Dallas, Texas roommates starts tonight. Here's a brief intro to each of the characters …

John is a dreamer. He is very [1] ____________ and believes everything his friends tell him but he is [2] ____________ and never judges anyone. He is the most [3] ____________ of the group, so he is always the one they go to with their problems.

Clara is the [4] ____________ one, who always puts her work life first. She is very [5] ____________ and never gives up on a problem. Her friends like her because she is so [6] ____________, she sees the best in everyone and everything.

Ibrahim is the [7] ____________ one who is never stressed about anything except for soccer, which he is really [8] ____________ about. He's really practical and sensible – just an all-around [9] ____________ kind of guy, I guess.

Maria works with John at the gallery. Everyone thinks she is a little [10] ____________ because she always bring the conversation around to the subject of herself! She can also be really [11] ____________ and frequently points out why her ideas are so much better. So why does everyone spend time with her? She is the [12] ____________ one, who makes everybody laugh.

B Work in pairs. Decide if the adjectives in the box in Exercise A are positive, negative or could be both.

C Work in groups. Discuss the questions.

1 What are the most important qualities in a friend, a colleague or a classmate?

2 Do you know anyone like the characters in the sitcom?

Noun suffixes

A Complete the paragraph with the noun forms of the adjectives in parentheses.

I have always felt that the key to [1]____________ (*happy*) is having good friends around you. My best friend is Jenny and she has a big [2]____________ (*influential*) on my life. Jenny is a great artist, and I am always amazed by her [3]____________ (*creative*). Her latest exhibit was on the theme of [4]____________ (*silent*), and it got really good reviews. She takes [5]____________ (*critical*) well too though; I never see her getting upset when a bad review comes in. If I could take on one of Jenny's characteristics, I think I would pick her [6]____________ (*mature*). I can be a little too silly sometimes and I frequently make mistakes, but she always acts with [7]____________ (*cautious*) and makes sensible decisions. And her best characteristic? It has to be her [8]____________ (*kind*).

B Complete the table with the noun forms of the adjectives in the box.

confident ~~determined~~ fit flexible independent optimistic secure

-ion	-ity	-ence	-ness	-ism
determination				

C Work in pairs. Which of the qualities in Exercises A and B do you think are the most important for happiness? Why?

Health and fitness

A Complete the article with the words in the box.

aging anxiety cholesterol depression fitness life mental obesity processed

A healthier life!

In today's busy world, it is important that we take good care of ourselves. But that doesn't mean making big changes! We asked three people to share two things they do to help reduce their stress levels:

'Number one: drink a lot of water! Not only does it keep you healthy, but it can also slow the [1] ______________ process and maybe even increase your [2] ______________ expectancy. Number two: exercise. It doesn't have to be at the gym; even walking for 15–30 minutes a day can help improve your general level of [3] ______________.'

Jack, Personal Trainer.

'I suffer from [4] ______________, so I try to avoid caffeine since it can make you feel more on edge and apparently can lead to [5] ______________. I also make sure I take time to sit and breathe. Meditation is great for my [6] ______________ health.'

Lena, Marketing Assistant.

'For me, the most important thing is to keep my diet balanced. When I eat badly, I have no energy. Also, too much fat or sugar can cause [7] ______________ and high [8] ______________. I guess the most important thing I do is avoid [9] ______________ foods. I cook fresh whenever I can, and I love trying new things from the organic market.'

Henry, Café Owner.

B Work in pairs. Which of the tips in Exercise A do you agree with? Which do you disagree with? Why?

C Work in groups. Make a list of four more health tips to add to the article.

1 ______________________________

2 ______________________________

3 ______________________________

4 ______________________________

D Present your tips from Exercise C to the class. Explain your reasoning.

Present perfect and present perfect progressive

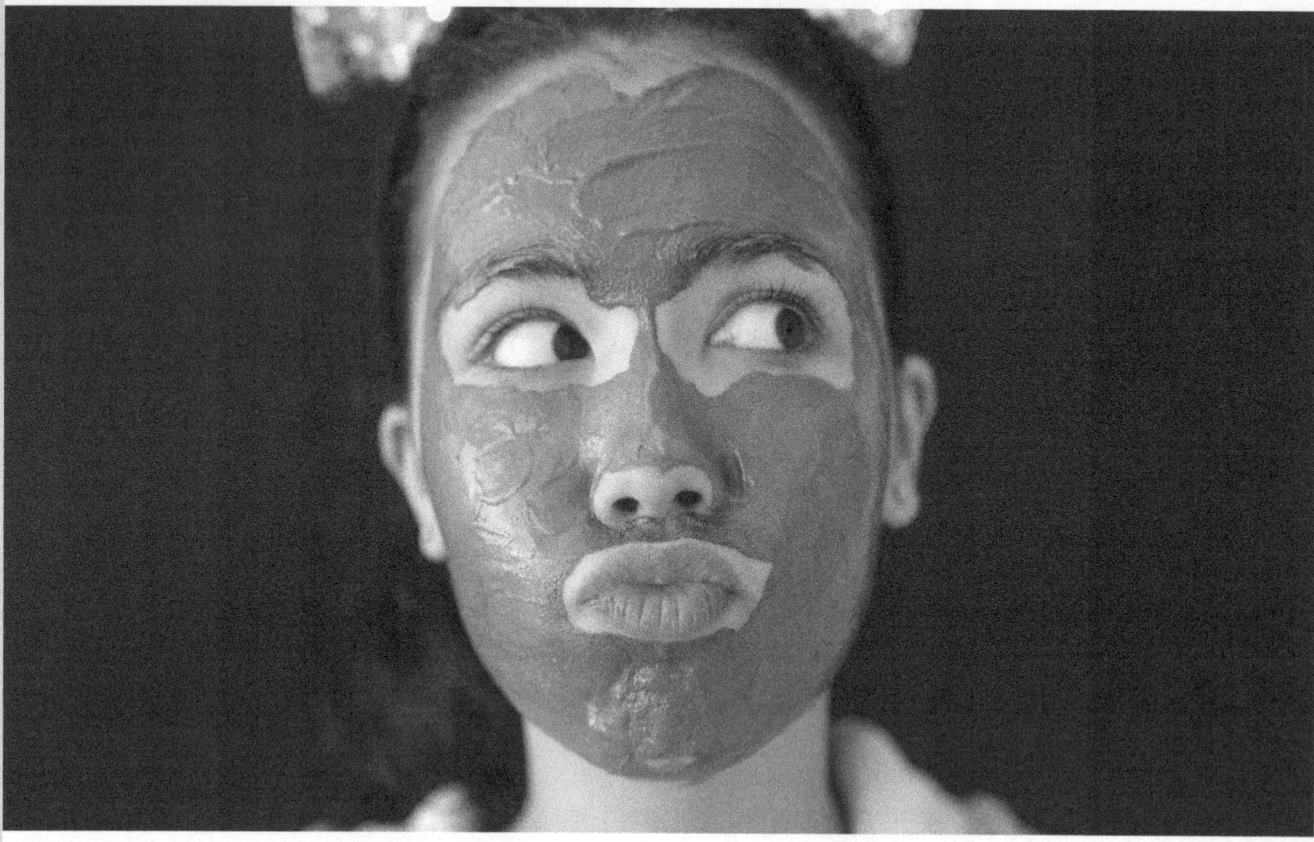

A **Complete the sentences with the present perfect or present perfect progressive form of the verbs in the box.**

be	email	clean	give up	rain	stay	try out	work

1 I ____________________ her about it several times, but she hasn't replied.

2 I ____________________ at a friend's house while my house is being renovated.

3 I ____________________ on this report all morning and I still haven't finished it!

4 Why ____________________ the bathroom? You said you'd do it today.

5 Sara ____________________ to this spa twice before – she loves it here.

6 It ____________________ all day, so I haven't been out of the house.

7 I was going to make spaghetti bolognese for dinner but John says he ____________________ red meat.

8 Hugo ____________________ this new raw food diet, but I don't think he'll stick to it.

B **Work in groups. Discuss the questions. Ask follow-up questions to get more information.**

1 How long have you known your closest friends?

2 What lifestyle changes have you made recently?

3 Which movies have you seen more than five times? Why?

4 What hobbies or interests have you had for a long time?

5 What have you been listening to recently?

used to, would, get used to, be used to

A Correct the mistakes in the sentences.

1 I would live in Seattle when I was a child.
2 I don't think I'll ever get use to the weather in this country.
3 I not used to living on my own yet, but I'm sure it'll get easier.
4 Mira was used to be blonde, but she's dyed her hair purple now.
5 Sun, sea and sand! I could be used to this.
6 Did you used to have a computer when you were young?
7 Jamie still hasn't used to wearing his glasses yet.
8 Apparently, Sami is used to play soccer professionally.

B Work in pairs. Discuss the questions using *used to, would, get used to* or *be used to*. Ask follow-up questions for more information.

1 What kind of TV shows did you watch when you were a child?
2 Where did you usually go on vacation when you were younger?
3 Have you ever given up a sport or a hobby? Why?
4 What would someone moving to your country have to get used to?
5 What's something that you found difficult at first but is normal for you now?

Adverbs of stance

A Match the statements (1–8) with the correct response (a–h).

1 It was a hard project, but I eventually got it all finished.
2 Do you remember Mr. Greene? What's he doing now?
3 What did you say to her? She's really upset.
4 I am so excited about the event next week!
5 Thank you so much for dinner, Jane. It was great.
6 Did you enjoy the play last night?
7 You got us lost!
8 Getting this new computer system has made our department far more efficient.

a Nothing, I was **merely** trying to explain the situation.
b **Naturally**! You always get your work done on time.
c Yes, it was **simply** delicious!
d **Admittedly**, I have the map, but you aren't listening to my directions.
e **Apparently**, he retired last year.
f It was, **undoubtedly**, the right decision.
g **Frankly**, I thought it was terrible. A real waste of money.
h **Sadly**, I can't go. It sounds like a lot of fun.

B Work in pairs. Write a role play that includes at least three of the pairs of sentences from Exercise B.

C Perform your role play for the class.

2.2 Vocabulary

Adverb + adjective collocations

A Choose the correct adverbs to complete the sentences.

1 I am ***deeply*** / ***utterly*** / ***bitterly*** concerned about the influence of social media.

2 It is ***deeply*** / ***highly*** / ***utterly*** unlikely that I will change my job this year.

3 The last movie I watched was ***utterly*** / ***ridiculously*** / ***highly*** ridiculous.

4 I was ***highly*** / ***deeply*** / ***bitterly*** disappointed with my last exam result.

5 It's ***ridiculously*** / ***bitterly*** / ***highly*** difficult for people my age to buy a house.

B Now talk to your classmates. Try to find someone who agrees with each statement. Write their name in the box and ask a follow-up question to get more information.

Question	Name	Answer
1		
2		
3		
4		
5		

Narrative tenses

A Choose the correct options to complete the story.

Lost at sea

One November, a group of Mexican fishermen [1]***headed / were heading*** out into the Pacific on a deep-sea fishing trip, when disaster struck. They [2]***had been planning / planned*** to visit a familiar spot, but a storm [3]***knocked / had knocked*** them off course, and they [4]***were pushed / had pushed*** into still waters. They were stranded on the ship without a radio and no one [5]***brought / had brought*** a cell phone. When they [6]***did not return / were not returning*** home, their families [7]***had assumed / assumed*** they [8]***were drowning / had drowned***. The ship [9]***only carried / was only carrying*** enough food and water for two weeks, but surprisingly, they [10]***survived / were surviving*** for ten months. They [11]***were being rescued / were rescued*** when another fishing ship [12]***was passing / had passed*** through and tried to make contact with them. The men were sunburned and [13]***had lost / lost*** a lot of weight, but other than that, they were in good health. After their supplies [14]***had run out / had been running out***, they survived by eating fish and sea birds they [15]***had caught / were catching*** and drinking rain water.

B You are going to tell a dramatic survival story. Use the prompts below to help you write notes.

- Who are the main characters?
- Where is the story set?
- What happens to put the characters in danger?
- How do they survive?

C Work in groups. Tell your stories using your notes from Exercise B. Try to make your stories as dramatic as possible and ask follow-up questions for more information.

3.1 Vocabulary

Descriptive verbs

A Label the pictures (1–6) with the verbs in the box.

crackle crunch growl hiss smash trickle

1 ______________

2 ______________

3 ______________

4 ______________

5 ______________

6 ______________

B Complete the sentences with the correct form of the verbs in the box.

groan rumble screech slam snap

1 The tires ______________ as the car swung around the corner.

2 My stomach ______________ for the last hour and all I could think about was food.

3 I was pushing so hard as I wrote that I ______________ my pencil.

4 The bridge was ______________ under the children's weight as they jumped up and down.

5 He ______________ his hand down on the desk and told us to get out of his office.

C Work in pairs. Write five sentences with verbs from Exercises A and B.

D Work with another pair. Mime your sentences and try to guess the verbs.

Alternatives to *if* in conditionals

A Rewrite the sentences using the words in bold.

1 If the train leaves on time, we should be there at 9 pm.
provided that
We should ______________________________.

2 If we don't leave now, we'll miss the start of the movie.
unless
We'll miss ______________________________.

3 Promise me you'll call the minute you land in New York.
as soon as
Promise me ______________________________.

4 If they aren't provoked, most bears won't attack you.
unless
Most bears ______________________________.

5 If I'm happy, my parents don't really care what I do.
as long as
My parents ______________________________.

6 You might get lost, so you should definitely take your phone.
in case
You should ______________________________.

B Work in pairs. Take turns completing the prompts below with a conditional structure and your own ideas.

1 We'll never get there on time …
2 You should take …
3 Why don't you buy some more …
4 Promise to call me …
5 I'll help you …
6 In New York, you should …

Phrasal verbs to describe problems

A Complete the questions with the correct form of the phrasal verbs in the box.

deal with	go through	put up with	sort out	stay calm	talk over	weigh out	work out

1. Is there anything you would rather ________________ than change?
2. When something goes wrong, do you tend to panic or do you find it easy to ________________?
3. Do you know anyone who ________________ a difficult time at work? What is the problem?
4. When you make a decision, how do you ________________ your various options?
5. Do you know anyone who is good at ________________ other people's problems but not their own?
6. Do you agree that you can usually ________________ a solution if you think about a problem for long enough?
7. When you have a problem, do you prefer to ________________ it ________________ with friends or family? Why?
8. Why do you think some people are better at ________________ their problems than others?

B Work in pairs. Ask and answer the questions in Exercise A. Explain your reasoning.

Dependent prepositions: adjectives

A Choose the correct prepositions to complete the sentences.

1 Sometimes I am envious ***for* / *of* / *with*** people who don't need to work.
2 The media should be more sensitive ***toward* / *for* / *at*** people's feelings.
3 I always get really anxious ***at* / *with* / *about*** giving presentations at work.
4 I try to stay aware ***to* / *of* / *with*** what's happening in the news.
5 I am sick ***of* / *to* / *from*** looking at other people's vacation photos online.
6 I never feel ashamed ***of* / *about* / *at*** the mistakes I have made.

B Rewrite the sentences in Exercise A so they are true for you.

1 ______________________________
2 ______________________________
3 ______________________________
4 ______________________________
5 ______________________________
6 ______________________________

C Work in pairs. Discuss your sentences. Ask follow-up questions for more information.

I always get really anxious about meeting new people.

Oh, really? Why's that?

I don't know really. I just never know what to say.

4.1 Grammar

Future forms

A Complete the sentences with the correct future form of the verbs in parentheses.

1 He's still not here? OK, I ________________ (*give*) him a call now and see where he is.

2 I'm off tomorrow, so I probably ________________ (*see*) you until next week.

3 I ________________ (*apply*) to a few different colleges and see what happens.

4 We ________________ (*get*) on the train – there are way too many people waiting.

5 Apparently, the store ________________ (*close*) early on Sundays, so we should hurry up.

6 I ________________ (*see*) her tonight actually. We're going to that new Japanese restaurant.

7 What ________________ you ________________ (*do*) after you graduate?

8 I ________________ (*go*) and pick her up if you want.

B Work in pairs. Write six predictions about your partner's future using appropriate tenses.

You will have five children – three boys and two girls.

1 ________________________________

2 ________________________________

3 ________________________________

4 ________________________________

5 ________________________________

6 ________________________________

C Work in pairs. Share your predictions from Exercise B, saying how likely you think each is to come true.

You're going to the movies with your sister tonight.

Actually, I am seeing my sister tonight, but we're going out for dinner not to the movies.

Noun + preposition collocations

A Choose the correct prepositions to complete the sentences.

ErikatheBrave

So, big news! I've decided to go back to college!! I'm starting a course [1]***of / in*** hotel management next week. So busy, but so excited!!!!

Like | Reply | 7:49 pm

Max B

Yay! Congratulations [2]***on / in*** getting in. We are so proud. Love you! Mom and Dad xx

Mike Davies

I hope you won't be too busy to be able to make time [3]***for / with*** your friends! Remember: all work and no play …

ErikatheBrave Ha ha, I don't think there is much risk [4]***in / of*** that happening – I couldn't live without seeing you guys!

Amy K

Oh wow!! That is so exciting!! Think of all the cool places [5]***on / in*** the world you will be able to work. Any possibility [6]***of / on*** taking me with you when you go? #bestfriendsforever

B Work in groups. Take turns completing the prompts with the correct preposition and your own ideas. Ask follow-up questions for more information.

1 I have always wanted to take a course …

2 I need to make more time …

3 In my future, there is a possibility …

4 My favorite place …

5 I'm worried about the risk …

Nouns and verbs with the same spelling

Student A

A Complete each pair with the correct noun and verb forms of the words in the box. There are three words you do not need to use.

balance	benefit	challenge	control	influence	produce

1 **a** I sometimes find it difficult __________ my temper.

b I have no __________ over what happens at work.

2 **a** It is important to keep a good work-life __________.

b I try to __________ the time I spend online with other activities.

3 **a** Organic __________ is better for your health.

b Companies should be charged for any waste they __________.

B Work in pairs. Discuss whether you agree with the sentences in Exercise A. Explain your reasoning.

Student B

A Complete each pair with the correct noun and verb forms of the words in the box. There are three words you do not need to use.

balance	benefit	challenge	control	influence	produce

1 **a** Governments should offer __________ to help people with low incomes.

b It always __________ people to study outside of class.

2 **a** Celebrities have too much __________ over young people today.

b My parents have always tried to __________ my choice of career.

3 **a** Running a marathon is a __________ I'd like to take on one day.

b Every year, I __________ myself to try something new.

B Work in pairs. Discuss whether you agree with the sentences in Exercise A. Explain your reasoning.

Future perfect, future progressive and future perfect progressive

A Correct the mistakes in the sentences.

1 This time next month, I am sitting on a beach!
2 In November, I will have working here for 15 years.
3 My teacher will have been retired before I finish this assignment!
4 By the end of this decade, most people will be drive electric cars.
5 If it's still around in 2029, people have been using Facebook for 25 years.
6 I think we'll have been discovering a cure for most forms of cancer by the end of the century.
7 Next September, you and I will have been being friends for 25 years.
8 At this rate, I'll still have been living with my parents when I'm 40!

B Work in groups. Discuss the questions. Ask follow-up questions for more information.

1 What will you be doing this time next week?
2 Is there anything you hope to achieve before your next birthday?
3 Where do you think you'll be living in ten years?
4 What do you think will have changed in our world 100 years from now?
5 What you think you'll have achieved by the time you turn 80?

4.2 Vocabulary

Intensifiers

A Complete the sentences with the adverbs in the box.

disastrously entirely extremely incredibly painfully significantly utterly widely

1 Our camping trip went ______________ wrong when Tim accidentally set fire to our tent!

2 It is ______________ believed that you can see the Great Wall of China from space, but that isn't true.

3 The weather forecast warned of ______________ high winds later tonight.

4 Cell phone prices can be ______________ cheaper online than in store.

5 When Josie finished the marathon, she was ______________ exhausted.

6 I find the sound of my own voice ______________ annoying.

7 Dev's answers in the test were almost ______________ wrong. He only scored 3/20.

8 I was ______________ aware that everyone was watching me walk out onto the stage.

B Work in pairs. Discuss the questions.

1 Are you firmly committed to any charities or causes?

2 Is there anything you are especially good at cooking?

3 Which was the last city that you were greatly impressed by?

4 Would you agree that cell phones have made life considerably easier?

5 What do you find intensely annoying?

The passive voice

A Complete the sentences with the correct passive voice form of the verbs in parentheses.

1. Annoyingly, the Trevi Fountain ________________ (*repair*) when I visited Rome.
2. An announcement about the royal baby ________________ (*made*) at 3 pm tomorrow.
3. A quarter of coral reefs around the world ________________ (*consider*) damaged beyond repair.
4. The post ________________ (*share*) over 20,000 times on Facebook already.
5. We were devastated to find that our house ________________ (*break into*) while we were away.
6. This letter ________________ (*deliver*) by hand yesterday.
7. Currently, research ________________ (*carry out*) into new solutions for energy.
8. All staff members ________________ (*notify*) by the end of the week.

B Write passive voice questions using the prompts below.

1. Where / TV / invent

   ____?

2. Who / Harry Potter / write / by

   ____?

3. How many / people / kill / sharks / every year

   ____?

4. What / discovered / Alexander Fleming / 1928

   ____?

5. Which / two languages / speak / Canada

   ____?

C Work in groups. Answer the questions in Exercise B.

5.1 Vocabulary

Green vocabulary

Student A

A Complete half of the crossword with the clues below.

3 Across: ______________ in the attic helps to keep the heat in. (10)

5 Across: We have replaced our radiators with underfloor ______________. (7)

8 Across: ______________ lightbulbs use much less electricity than normal ones. (6, 9)

9 Down: Maya collects rainwater in a ______________ then uses it in her garden. (4, 6)

10 Across: You can turn sunlight into energy by having ______________ installed. (5, 6)

B Work in pairs. Give each other clues to help you complete the crossword.

What's three across?

It is something you put in the walls, ceiling and floor to keep your house warm.

Student B

A Complete half of the crossword with the clues below.

1 Down: ______________ produce energy from wind power. (4, 8)

2 Down: We put all our food waste on the ______________ in the garden. (7, 4)

4 Down: You control the temperature in a home with the ______________. (10)

6 Down: Windows with ______________ can help to make your home quieter. (6, 7)

7 Down: A ______________ will tell you how much energy you are using. (5, 5)

B Work in pairs. Give each other clues to help you complete the crossword.

What's one down?

It is something that turns wind into electricity.

Causative *have* and *get*

A Complete the sentences with the causative *have* or *get* form of the verbs in the box.

clean cut install redecorate service take whiten write

1 We ____________ new windows ____________ next week.

2 Merve ____________ her car ____________ every year.

3 Where did you ____________ your hair ____________? It looks amazing!

4 Politicians usually ____________ their speeches ____________ for them.

5 Carmen ____________ the kitchen ____________ twice since they bought the house.

6 I would love ____________ my apartment ____________ for me, but I can't afford it.

7 Josh used to ____________ his teeth ____________ when we first met.

8 You need ____________ your passport photos ____________ soon.

B Work in pairs. Discuss which of the activities (1–6) you usually do yourself and which you pay to have done and why.

1 Washing the car

2 Decorating the house

3 Washing windows

4 Laundry

5 Cleaning the house

6 Fixing your car

I always have my car washed at the same place.

Oh really, I usually wash mine at home, it is much cheaper and it can be fun!

Describing areas of a city

A Complete the blog post with the words in the box.

commercial housing industrial residential rural slums suburbs urban

New home, new start

@SayakaN

Tue April 20, 2019 09:21

So, here it is! My first blog post from my new home, Istanbul. I've been here for a month now, so I thought you might like to know a little about where I will be living for the next few years. My new place is away from the city center in the [1]______________, in an area called Kartal on the Anatolian side of the city. Apparently, it used to be a [2]______________ area, just trees and fields, but Istanbul's [3]______________ area seems to grow bigger every day as new buildings appear. Luckily the [4]______________ around here is fairly cheap – that's one advantage of not being close to the city center.

The offices where I work are in the main [5]______________ zone. It is an area called Levent, and all the major banks have their buildings there. I like it, but the commute is a nightmare because I have to travel through the [6]______________ zone, and there's a lot of pollution from the factories. Nearby, you can also see a lot of [7]______________, with makeshift houses that are falling apart. But, like I said, the city is changing and these are being replaced with new [8]______________ areas, full of brand new houses and apartments everywhere. I hope you enjoy the pictures!

B Work in pairs. Discuss the questions.

1 Would you prefer to live in an urban area or a rural area? Why?

2 Are there any industrial areas near where you live? Which industries are based there?

3 Do you think there is enough housing where you live? How could the existing residential areas be improved?

5.2 Vocabulary

Prefixes

A **Complete the sentences with the correct form of the words in parentheses.**

1 something you find completely ____________ (*possible*) to do
2 something you'd like to buy that is ____________ (*affordable*)
3 a job where people are typically ____________ (*paid*)
4 a movie you have ____________ (*watch*) three times or more
5 something you think is ____________ (*moral*)
6 an ____________ (*logical*) fear you suffer from
7 something you love that is ____________ (*popular*)
8 a crime that shouldn't be ____________ (*legal*)
9 something ____________ (*ordinary*) you have done

B **Write responses to the prompts in Exercise A.**

C **Work in pairs. Discuss what you wrote in Exercise B and why.**

5.2 Grammar

-ing and infinitive forms

A **Match the beginnings of the sentences (1–6) with the correct ending (a–f). Then, complete the sentences with the correct form of the verbs in the box.**

announce do go see take tell

1	Do you feel like	**a**	____________ time off work to study overseas.
2	I'll always remember	**b**	____________ this weekend?
3	I will never regret	**c**	____________ their engagement.
4	My roommate forgot	**d**	____________ her for the first time.
5	Michel and Elena couldn't wait	**e**	____________ to the movies tonight?
6	What do you want	**f**	____________ me you called.

B **Work in pairs. Take turns finishing the prompts below with your own ideas. Ask follow-up questions for more information.**

1 Next week, I want to finish …
2 I have recently decided …
3 I always forget …
4 I wish I had stopped …
5 I'll never forget …
6 I've always regretted …

6.1 Grammar

Obligation, prohibition and permission

A Match the sentences to the option (a or b) that has the same meaning.

1 Students **are obliged to** buy their own copy of the textbook.

a Students must buy a copy of the book.

b Students can buy a copy of the book if they wish.

2 Students **should** do two or three hours of homework per week.

a Students need to do two or three hours of homework.

b It is recommended that students do two or three hours of homework.

3 Cell phones **cannot** be used in the classroom.

a Cell phones are never allowed in the classroom.

b Cell phones can be used on some occasions.

4 Students **are not supposed to** talk during lectures.

a Students should talk during lectures.

b Students shouldn't talk during lectures.

5 Smoking **is not allowed** on the school grounds.

a No one can smoke on the school grounds.

b Some people can smoke on school grounds.

6 Visitors **are required to** sign in at the front desk.

a Visitors may have to sign in.

b All visitors must sign in.

B Work in groups. Use the modals of obligation, prohibition and permission to write a list of new rules for your language school. Try to use a variety of structures.

C Present your rules to the class. Vote on which, if any, to start following.

Education

A Choose the correct options to complete the sentences.

1 In some countries, education is only ***boarding*** / ***compulsory*** until the age of ten.

2 The most famous ***state*** / ***private*** school in the US, costs over $30,000 per year.

3 These days, almost 10% of American adults go on to earn a master's degree after they ***graduate*** / ***scholarship***.

4 There is a ***vocational*** / ***seminar*** school in India dedicated to preparing students for a career in snake charming.

5 Students who study at ***high*** / ***boarding*** schools usually have classes on the weekend.

6 Children in Finland start ***high*** / ***elementary*** school at seven years old, one of the latest in the world.

7 Famous UK universities Oxford and Cambridge have ***entrance*** / ***campus*** exams that are thought to be among the hardest in the world.

8 A ***seminar*** / ***lecture*** is a class in college where small groups of students discuss topics with a professor.

B Work in pairs. Discuss the questions.

1 Did you go to a good high school?

2 What would you say are the advantages and disadvantages of a state school education?

3 What do students in your country need to do to get into a good college?

4 What changes would you make to the education system in your country?

Articles

A Complete the email with *a/an*, *the* or –.

To: lazicledazicle@email.com
From: DaisyB@mail.co.us
Subject: How are things?

Hey Gina,

How's life in [1] ________ Texas? I'm so sad you couldn't make it to my birthday party last night ☹. It was [2] ________ best party ever! [3] ________ everyone we know was there – about 35 people in total. [4] ________ theme was 'glamour', like [5] ________ awards ceremony, and [6] ________ girls all wore beautiful dresses. [7] ________ everybody agreed mine was stunning – check out [8] ________ photos I've attached! The party was held in [9] ________ old warehouse in town. I know it sounds grim, but [10] ________ warehouse gets rented out for parties all the time. We had sushi, which was amazing! My parents arranged for [11] ________ head chef from Oishi to come and make it. But OMG, you won't believe this! When I asked my dad if we could have [12] ________ live band, I never dreamed he would get Tiara Tantrums! Anyway, write back when you can.

Daisy

B Write notes about the best, worst or strangest party you have ever been to. Use the questions to help you.

- Whose party was it?
- Where was it held?
- Who was there?
- Why was it so good/bad/strange?

C Work in groups. Discuss your experiences using your notes from Exercise B. Ask follow-up questions for more information.

Compound adjectives

A **Complete the sentences with the compound adjectives from the box.**

365-meter-high	coming-of-age	high-risk	old-fashioned
part-time	six-bedroom	up-to-date	well-known

1 I never do ____________ activities like bungee-jumping and rock climbing.

2 The most ____________ celebrity from my country is Javier Bardem.

3 My mother's cell is so ____________ that you can only use it for calls and messages.

4 If I won the lottery, I'd build a ____________ house on a tropical island.

5 I use social media to stay ____________ with the latest fashion trends.

6 The tallest structure in my country is the ____________ Skelton Mast.

7 I enjoy watching ____________ movies like *The Fault in Our Stars*.

8 When I was younger, I had a ____________ job in a pet store.

B **Rewrite the sentences in Exercise A so they are true for you.**

1 ______________________________

2 ______________________________

3 ______________________________

4 ______________________________

5 ______________________________

6 ______________________________

7 ______________________________

8 ______________________________

C **Work in pairs. Discuss your sentences from Exercise B.**

Phrases with *make* and *do*

A Complete the questions below with the correct form of *make* or *do*.

1 What was the last favor you ______________ for someone?

2 How long do you think you could ______________ without your cell phone?

3 What do you think ______________ more harm to the environment – plastic or carbon emissions?

4 What's the best way to ______________ a good impression in an interview?

5 When things go wrong, do you get upset or do you try to ______________ the best of the situation?

6 Should all public places ______________ allowances for children or are there places their parents shouldn't take them?

7 Do you think that the world will ever ______________ away with cash?

8 Have you ever considered quitting your job and trying to ______________ a living by starting your own business?

B Match the questions from Exercise A to answers a–h.

a In my opinion, the best way is to have a few good questions to ask them!

b Actually, I've always wanted to sell my paintings, but I'm not sure I could make enough money.

c I think it's very possible. I don't even remember the last time I went to an ATM.

d It has to be plastic. Our oceans are full of it.

e I couldn't. I feel really isolated if I don't have it with me.

f Most places, yes. But sometimes it would be nice to have a meal or a flight in peace.

g I'm fairly optimistic, so I usually just try and find a solution.

h Actually, I took care of my brother's dog for him last week.

C Work in pairs. Discuss the questions in Exercise A.

First conditional with different future forms

A **Are these sentences correct or incorrect? Rewrite the incorrect sentences.**

1. If you're coming to the party, bring some people with you.
2. Text me if you get here early.
3. What are you going to do if she won't call you back?
4. To be honest, I'm going to be amazed if we've finished by 6 pm.
5. We will going to the movie theater if you want to join us.
6. Nicky will call me if she's running late.
7. Unless the train's late, we're arriving before 8 pm.
8. What will you have done if it rains?

B **Work in pairs. Take turns completing the prompts below with your own ideas. Ask follow-up questions for more information.**

1. If you're going to visit my city, you …
2. If I win the lottery, I …
3. If you're feeling sad, you …
4. If you have time, you …
5. Take a flashlight if …

Verbs to describe change

A Complete the article with the correct form of the verbs in the box.

construct convert demolish extend relocate restore transform

Council plans big changes to town center

By Michael Chang

Sept. 6, 2019, 11:55 | Updated: Sept. 6, 2019, 12:20

Big changes were announced regarding the improvements to the town center at a Town Hall meeting yesterday. The local council is planning to [1] ______________ the area – turning it from a gray, concrete square into somewhere that people will want to start visiting again.
One of the proposals was to [2] ______________ the old shoe factory into a community center. In addition, work will begin next week to [3] ______________ the old office building next to the square in order to [4] ______________ the existing open area. Grass and trees will be planted, and there are plans to [5] ______________ the old bandstand to its former glory. The existing bus stop [6] ______________ to the end of Main Street, where local company Zone Builds [7] ______________ a new shopping complex. We can't wait to see how it all looks when the project is completed next year.

B What changes have you seen in your hometown? Write notes below about:

- housing
- shopping
- things to do

C Work in pairs. Use the vocabulary from Exercise A and your notes to talk about the changes in your hometown with your partner.

7.1 Grammar

Unreal conditionals

A Complete the questions with the correct form of the verbs in parentheses.

1 What __________ (*do*) differently in your life if __________ (*start*) again?

2 How __________ your life __________ (*be*) different if you __________ (*not study*) English?

3 If you __________ (*won*) free flights for a year, where __________ (*visit*)?

4 If you __________ (*design*) a house, what interesting rooms __________ (*include*)?

5 What __________ (*do*) if a UFO __________ (*land*) on our planet?

6 How __________ the world __________ (*be*) different if the internet __________ (*not invent*)?

7 If you __________ (*go back*) in time and change one thing, what __________ (*do*)?

8 If you __________ (*only keep*) three of your possessions, which __________ (*choose*)?

B Use the questions in Exercise A to interview as many people as you can in the class. Ask follow-up questions for more information. Write down any interesting answers.

C Work in groups. Discuss what you found out in Exercise B.

7.2 Grammar

Wish and *if only*

A Choose the correct options to complete the sentences.

1 Do you ever wish the internet ***hadn't*** / ***wasn't*** been invented?

2 I wish the teacher ***would*** / ***will*** give us more time for the assignment.

3 Do you ever wish you ***could be*** / ***would be*** someone else for a day?

4 I wish I ***can*** / ***could*** be more like Amal, she's so confident.

5 If only we ***wouldn't*** / ***didn't*** have to work today, we could go to the beach instead.

6 More animals could be saved if only people ***would use*** / ***were using*** less plastic.

B Work in groups. Discuss the questions. Ask follow-up questions for more information.

1 What do you wish you had done when you were younger?

2 Do you wish you had paid more attention in school?

3 What's the one thing you wish people would stop doing? Why?

4 What do you wish you had done more of last year?

5 Where do you wish you had grown up?

Three-part phrasal verbs

A Match sentences (1–6) with their endings (a–f), using the three-part phrasal verbs to help you.

1 I drink coffee when I **run**
2 Companies encourage staff to **team**
3 It is important for people to **stand**
4 My job is very busy, so I sometimes **catch**
5 I haven't started the report yet, but I'll **get**
6 We need to **come**

a **up with** some ideas for our new campaign.
b **up with** each other and share ideas.
c **around to** it tomorrow.
d **out of** energy. It helps me recharge.
e **up with** work over the weekend.
f **up for** their beliefs.

B Complete the questions with the correct form of the phrasal verbs in the box.

come up against cut down on get along with keep up with look up to take care of

1 When you were younger, did you have to ________________ your younger siblings?
2 Are there any celebrities you particularly ________________ or respect?
3 What do you do when you ________________ a problem?
4 Do you think it is becoming more common for people to ________________ the amount of meat they eat?
5 Who do you ________________ best in your family? What do you do together?
6 How do you ________________ the latest news from your country?

C Work in pairs. Discuss the questions in Exercise B.

Compound nouns

A Rewrite the questions using the compound nouns in the box to replace the phrases in bold.

a car-sharing system	food banks	language exchange	street party	volunteer workers

1 Do you know any **people who help out with a charity**?

____

2 Does your company offer **an incentive for people who travel to work together**?

____

3 Have you ever taken part in a **program that encourages people to help each other learn a language**?

____

4 Do you have any **places you can donate canned meals, etc to people who need them** in your town?

____

5 Have you ever been to a **celebration on the road where you live**?

____

B Work in pairs. Discuss the questions in Exercise A. Write down your partner's answers below.

1 ______________________________

2 ______________________________

3 ______________________________

4 ______________________________

5 ______________________________

C Work in new pairs. Report what you found out in Exercise B.

Past modals of deduction

A Rewrite the underlined sentences with *must* / *might* / *can't* + past participle.

1 Meghan is in Tokyo right now, so I'm sure it wasn't her you saw.

It ______________________________.

2 Maybe someone handed your wallet in at the front desk. You should ask.

Someone ______________________________.

3 Don't worry, I'm sure they got stuck in traffic or something.

They ______________________________.

4 Oh, no! Where are my keys? Maybe I dropped them on the way here.

I ______________________________.

5 There's no way you've finished the report already. You only started an hour ago!

You ______________________________.

6 Fourteen hours? I'm sure you were tired after such a long flight.

You ______________________________.

B Work in groups. Read the lateral thinking puzzles (1–3) and discuss the possible answers.

1 Someone fell out of a 40-story building. There was no crash mat or net, but they survived. How?

2 There was a carton of six eggs. Six people divided the eggs equally between them, but there was still one egg in the box. How?

3 A woman walked up to a counter and hands another woman a book. The woman behind the counter charged her $2.50. The first woman paid and then left without the book. Why?

Word families

A **Complete the sentences with the correct form of the word in parentheses.**

1 My favorite stories come from Greek ______________ (*myth*).

2 My dream was always to ______________ (*represent*) my country in basketball.

3 I didn't enjoy the movie very much. I just didn't find it very ______________ (*believe*).

4 The passenger ______________ (*hero*) jumped onto the tracks to rescue the young boy.

5 They completely ______________ (*transform*) the plot for the movie – I barely recognized it as the same story!

6 Our town has a party every year where people dress up in ______________ (*tradition*) clothes.

B **Write six true sentences about yourself using the words from Exercise A in any form.**

1 ______________________________

2 ______________________________

3 ______________________________

4 ______________________________

5 ______________________________

6 ______________________________

C **Work in pairs. Take turns sharing your sentences. For each sentence, ask a follow-up question that uses a different form of the word.**

Harrison Ford is one of my heroes.

Really? Why do you think he's heroic?

8.2 Vocabulary

Easily confused verbs

A Complete the sentences with the correct forms of the verb pairs in the box.

feel/touch   listen/hear   see/watch

1 Sometimes when I ______________ to songs on the radio, I find it difficult ______________ all of the words.

2 Have you ______________ the acrobats performing in the town square? They're amazing! I spent my lunch hour ______________ them.

3 I think I have broken my arm. When I ______________ it, it ______________ really painful.

4 She said she ______________ what I was saying, but I don't think she was really ______________.

5 My skin ______________ itchy ever since I ______________ that plant.

6 While you ______________ the fireworks last night, I ______________ a new play at the theater.

B Work in groups. Take turns finishing the sentences below. Ask each other follow-up questions for more information.

1 The best song I've heard recently was …

2 One TV show I always watch is …

3 When I feel happy, I …

4 The radio station I listen to …

5 I would love to see …

6 The strangest item I have touched is …

Order of adjectives

A Rewrite the sentences with the adjectives in parentheses.

1 My mother just gave me her collection of jewelry. (*antique / silver*)

____

2 Can you pass me that vase? (*green / tall*)

____

3 The painting was bought by a lawyer. (*wealthy / Italian*)

____

4 They're building a recreation center near my house. (*state-of-the-art / huge*)

____

5 She was wearing an evening dress. (*unusual / silk*)

____

6 Apparently, he has a plan for the company. (*long-term / new*)

____

7 Saga drives a Porsche 911. (*beautiful / old / green*)

____

8 That T-shirt needs to be thrown away! (*disgusting / stained / old*)

____

B Work in pairs. Take turns adding more and more adjectives to the sentences below.

1 He rode a horse.

2 It's on the table.

3 Can I have a cup?

4 I work in an office.

He rode a *beautiful* horse.

He rode a beautiful, *white* horse.

He rode a beautiful, white, *French* horse.

Crime

A **Complete the sentences with the correct form of the words in the box. There are three words you do not need to use.**

accuse	blackmail	bribe	catch	commit	identity theft
investigate	punishment	question	robbery	sentence	

1 Police say they are ____________ a possible link between the two men.

2 He was ____________ to ten years in prison for his role in the cover-up.

3 Miss Gibbons used the information to ____________ her former employer.

4 Choosing a strong password can help protect you from ____________.

5 After eight hours of ____________, he was released without charge.

6 The 16-year-old was ____________ trying to break in shortly after midnight.

7 CCTV footage shows the gang leaving the bank shortly after the ____________.

8 Mr. Taylor offered police a $75,000 ____________ to drop the charges against him.

B **Work in pairs. Discuss the questions.**

1 Do you think there is such a thing as a victimless crime? Why/Why not?

2 What do you do to protect yourself from identity theft?

3 Do you think the punishment always fits the crime? Why/Why not?

4 Do you think it's ever OK to break the law? Why/Why not?

5 What kind of crime do you think will increase in the future? Why?

6 Do you believe your country is a safe place to live? Why?

American Language Hub Level 4 Teacher's Book.

Adjective clauses

A **Rewrite the sentences using an appropriate adjective clause.**

1 I lived in that house for 12 years. Now, it's being knocked down.

The house ______________________________.

2 Have you seen that woman again? The one we saw yesterday.

Have ______________________________?

3 The sculpture is being displayed at the National Gallery. It is worth $4.5 million.

The sculpture, ______________________________.

4 The plane was delayed by over over three hours. It was supposed to land at 5 pm.

The plane, ______________________________.

5 The singer is getting married next year. Her album is currently at number one in the charts.

The singer, ______________________________.

6 That cat is in the yard again! The one with the blue collar.

That cat ______________________________!

7 Vegans often eat tofu for protein. Vegans don't consume animal products.

Vegans, ______________________________.

8 A man was arrested for the robbery. He was well-known in the area.

The man, ______________________________.

B **Work in pairs. Interview each other about the following topics. Write notes.**

- job/work
- hobbies and interests
- work

C **Write five sentences about your partner in Exercise B using adjective clauses.**

Dependent prepositions: verbs

A Complete the spider diagram with the verbs in the box.

adhere apologize complain deal object rely thank worry

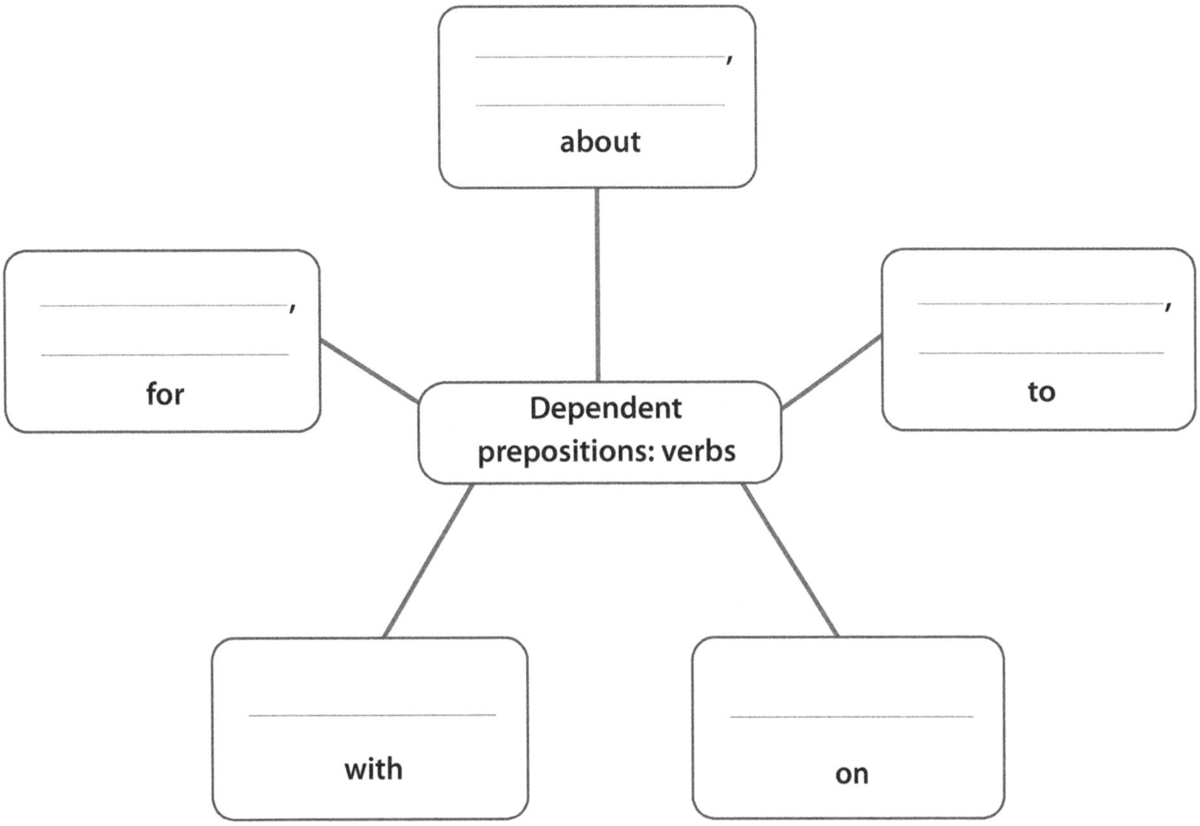

B Work in pairs. Take turns completing the following sentences with an appropriate preposition and your own ideas. Ask follow-up questions for more information when appropriate.

- When I was younger, my parents would always complain …
- Personally, I think people rely too much …
- I once had to apologize …
- I've always found it difficult to deal …
- I strongly object …
- I never got the chance to thank …

Science

A Complete the article with the words in the box.

analysis   data   evidence   researchers   theory

*By **Lara Pelham***

Tue, April 20, 2019, 8:55 EST

Possibly one of the biggest issues of getting older is the loss of mobility. Past the age of 60, you start to lose muscle at an alarming rate, which has a huge impact on your ability to get around. However, [1]_____________ at Seismic, a wearable technology company based in the US, have designed a 'super suit' that may very well solve the problem.

The suit contains 'electric muscles', which are designed to behave in the same way as the human body. These are activated by tiny sensors which track the body's movements and are powered by motors, batteries and control boards incorporated into pods on the wearer's back. The [2]_____________ is that making the technology so discrete will encourage more people to wear it.

While the 'super suit' was designed with older people in mind, there's increasing [3]_____________ to suggest that wearable technology may have far wider benefits. [4]_____________ of products to assist people that have suffered a stroke is already underway and [5]_____________ is being collected on potential safety and industrial applications. Whatever the future holds, it's clear that wearable technology is set to play an increasingly important role in our lives over the next few decades.

B Work in groups. Discuss the questions.

1. Do you think wearable technology will ever become the norm? Why/Why not?
2. Do you own any wearable technology?
3. What applications of wearable technology do you think we will see in the future?

Determiners and quantifiers

A Choose the correct options to complete the sentences.

1. ***Neither*** / ***Either*** my brother nor I eat meat or dairy products.
2. A large ***amount*** / ***number*** of processed food contains coloring and preservatives.
3. A lot of people sign up for gyms, but ***little*** / ***few*** end up going regularly.
4. ***All of the*** / ***Every*** work must be finished by July 10th at the latest.
5. Artur goes swimming ***every*** / ***all*** Thursday after work.
6. I'm trying to save ***a little*** / ***little*** every month to buy a new car.
7. ***Plenty of*** / ***Most of*** grocery stores have a gluten-free food section.
8. My aunt and uncle ***all*** / ***both*** work in the health industry.

B Work in pairs. Take turns completing the sentences with your own ideas.

1. I try to … plenty of …
2. It is important to have a little …
3. Both my closest friend and I …
4. All the people I know …
5. Neither of my … are …

Advertising

A Complete the definitions with advertising vocabulary.

1 c __ __ __ __ __ __ __ **(n)** person who buys or uses goods and services

2 b __ __ __ __ **(n)** product or group of products that has its own name

3 h __ __ __ **-p** __ __ __ __ __ __ __ **(adj)** frequently seen in public, mentioned in newspapers or appearing on television

4 a __ **c** __ __ __ __ __ __ __ **(n)** a series of advertisements that share a single idea or theme

5 t __ __ __ __ __ **m** __ __ __ __ __ **(n)** the group of people that a product or service is directed toward

6 t __ __ __ __ **(n)** a gradual development or change in a situation

7 e __ __ __ __ __ __ **(v)** to express support for someone or something, especially in public

8 m __ __ __ __ __ __ __ __ **s** __ __ __ __ __ __ __ **(n)** a plan of how to encourage people to buy a product or service

B Work in pairs. Discuss the questions.

1 What is the most memorable advertisement you have ever seen?

2 Do you keep up to date with fashion and technology trends?

3 What are your favorite brands? Are there any you don't like?

4 How important are consumer reviews to you?

5 Do you think you are more likely to buy a product if it's endorsed by a celebrity? Why/Why not?

6 What kind of products do you think you are part of the target market for? Why?

Reported speech

A Read the news article. Rewrite the sentences in bold in reported speech.

Man arrested for breaking into own home

By Michael Chang

Sept. 28, 2019, 9:27 | Updated: Sept. 28, 2019, 9:33

A 75-year-old man was arrested in New York last night for breaking into his own house. [1]**'I was walking home from the store,'** said Mr. Smith, [2]**'and I suddenly realized I'd left my keys at home.'** Noticing his bathroom window was open, Smith climbed a tree in the front yard to gain access to the property.

Unfortunately, his neighbor saw him climbing through the window and called the police. [3]**'You can never be too careful!'** said Mrs. Whitshaw. [4]**'Three of my friends have been burglarized recently,'** she added.

When the police finally arrived on the scene, an embarrassed Mr. Smith managed to explain what had happened. [5]**'He's lucky he didn't break his neck!'** said Police Chief Meadows. [6]**'But it's very impressive for a man of his age.'**

1 Mr. Smith said that … ______.

2 He explained that … ______.

3 Mrs. Whitshaw claims that … ______.

4 And added that … ______.

5 Police Chief Meadows said that Mr. Smith … ______.

6 But went on to say … ______.

B Work in pairs. Ask and answer the questions below. Write notes about your partner's answers.

1 Have you read any interesting books recently?

2 Where is the most unusual place you have been on vacation?

3 What were you doing at 8 pm last night?

4 Are you currently following any news stories?

C Work in new pairs. Report your partner's answers from Exercise B. Ask follow-up questions for more information.

10.1 Vocabulary

Traditional media

A Complete the sentences with the correct form of the words in the box.

biased	broadsheet	coverage	editor	headlines	source	subjective	tabloid

1 An opinion piece is, by definition, highly ____________ since it gives the writer's point of view.

2 ____________ seem to be obsessed with celebrity gossip and shocking news stories.

3 In the US, ____________ are generally considered to be the most trustworthy source of information.

4 My father-in-law just seems to look at the ____________ instead of reading the whole article.

5 Many of the newspapers in my country are ____________ toward specific political parties.

6 There was extensive ____________ of the wedding in all of the papers.

7 It's important that journalists get information from multiple ____________.

8 The newspaper published a letter from the ____________ in response to the accusations.

B You are going to give a short presentation. Think of a famous journalist or newspaper from your country. Write notes about the following:

- the name of the journalist/newspaper
- why they are / it is famous
- any other interesting information

C Work in groups. Take turns giving your presentations. Ask follow-up questions for more information.

Reporting verbs

A Are these sentences correct or incorrect? Rewrite the incorrect sentences.

1 Mr. Welch claimed that he had been treated unfairly during his time at the company.
2 Police reminded that anything he said might be used as evidence against him.
3 She refused to tell what I had done wrong and slammed the door in my face!
4 My parents encouraged me to apply for a position in the graduate training program.
5 The company apologized for mislead the public over claims made in their advertising.
6 Miss Jansen's lawyer warned her to say anything to the press before the trial was over.
7 He promised to call me back as soon he got home from work.
8 Neighbors threatened calling the police if the noise continued.

B Complete the questions with the correct form of the verbs in the box.

accuse agree confess convince encourage

1 When was the last time you ____________ someone to do something for you?
2 Have you ever ____________ someone of something they didn't do?
3 Who ____________ you to apply for your current job/course?
4 Have you ever ____________ to do something that you later regretted?
5 When was the last time you ____________ to doing something wrong?

C Work in groups. Discuss the questions in Exercise B.

Social media

A Complete the sentences in the table with social media vocabulary.

Find someone who …	Name	Information
regularly uses **h** __ __ __ __ __ __ __ to make their posts easy to find.		
has more than 100 **f** __ __ __ __ __ __ __ __ on their social media accounts.		
can name a famous social media **i** __ __ __ __ __ __ __ __ __.		
has ever shared a **m** __ __ __.		
can think of a video that has gone **v** __ __ __ __.		
can name a **t** __ __ __ __ __ __ __ story from today.		
has ever taken part in a social media **c** __ __ __ __ __ __ __ __ (e.g. The Ice Bucket Challenge).		

B Think about how to phrase the statements in Exercise A as questions. Then walk around and talk to your classmates to find people who the statements are true for. Ask follow-up questions to learn more information.

10.2 Vocabulary

Adjective + noun collocations

A Choose the correct options to complete the questions.

1 Do you make ***high*** / ***regular*** / ***key*** donations to any charities?

2 What can charities do to reach a ***wider*** / ***deeper*** / ***higher*** audience online?

3 What is ***target*** / ***popular*** / ***viral*** content? Can you think of an example?

4 What are the ***main*** / ***key*** / ***big*** factors in a successful charity campaign?

5 Which recent charity campaigns have had ***deep*** / ***strong*** / ***high*** levels of engagement from the public?

6 Have you ever bought a product because it received a lot of ***web*** / ***online*** / ***internet*** mentions?

B Work in pairs. Discuss the questions in Exercise A. Write notes on your partner's answers below.

1 ______________________________

2 ______________________________

3 ______________________________

4 ______________________________

5 ______________________________

6 ______________________________

C Work in new pairs. Report what you found out in Exercise B.

Answer key

1.1 Vocabulary

A

1 devastated 2 stunned 3 impressed
4 thrilled 5 horrified 6 furious
7 relieved 8 frustrated

1.1 Grammar

A

1 Could you tell me which country you were born in
2 What industry do you work in
3 Is there anything you don't enjoy about your job
4 Who has had the biggest impact on your life
5 How would you describe yourself
6 Would you mind telling me about your biggest regret
7 Have you (ever) met a famous person
8 What would you say are your weaknesses

1.2 Grammar

A

1 have experienced 2 did
3 did 4 was
5 are trying 6 make
7 have calmed down 8 hadn't done
9 could have done

1.2 Vocabulary

A

1 naïve 2 open-minded
3 sensitive 4 ambitious
5 determined 6 optimistic
7 easy-going 8 passionate
9 down-to-earth 10 self-centered
11 arrogant 12 witty

B

Suggested answers
Positive: ambitious; determined; down-to-earth; easy-going; flexible; open-minded; optimistic; passionate; witty
Negative: arrogant; naïve; pessimistic; self-centered; stubborn
Both: sensitive

1.2 Vocabulary

A

1 happiness 2 influence 3 creativity
4 silence 5 criticism 6 maturity
7 caution 8 kindness

B

***-ity*:** flexibility; security
***-ence*:** confidence; independence
***-ness*:** fitness
***-ism*:** optimism

2.1 Vocabulary

A

1 aging 2 life 3 fitness
4 anxiety 5 depression 6 mental
7 obesity 8 cholesterol 9 processed

2.1 Grammar

A

1 've emailed 2 've been staying
3 've been working 4 haven't you cleaned
5 's been 6 's been raining
7 's given up 8 's been trying out

2.2 Grammar

A

1 I **used to** ~~would~~ live in Seattle when I was a child.
2 I don't think I'll ever get use**d** to the weather in this country.
3 **I'm** not used to living on my own yet, but I'm sure it'll get easier.
4 Mira ~~was~~ **used** to be blonde, but she's dyed her hair purple now.
5 Sun, sea and sand! I could ~~be~~ **get** used to this.
6 Did you use~~d~~ to have a computer when you were young?
7 Jamie still hasn't **gotten** used to wearing his glasses yet.
8 Apparently, Sami ~~is~~ used to play soccer professionally.

2.2 Vocabulary

A

2 e 3 a 4 h 5 c 6 g 7 d 8 f

2.2 Vocabulary

A

1 deeply 2 highly 3 utterly
4 bitterly 5 ridiculously

3.1 Grammar

A

1 were heading 2 had been planning
3 knocked 4 were pushed
5 had brought 6 did not return
7 assumed 8 had drowned
9 was only carrying 10 survived
11 were rescued 12 was passing
13 had lost 14 had run out
15 had caught

3.1 Vocabulary

A

1 trickle 2 hiss 3 crunch
4 smash 5 growl 6 crackle

B

1 screeched 2 had been rumbling
3 snapped 4 groaned
5 slammed

3.2 Grammar

A

1 be there at 9 pm, provided that the train leaves on time
2 the start of the movie unless we leave now
3 me as soon as you land in New York, you'll call.
4 won't attack you unless they're provoked
5 don't really care what I do as long as I'm happy
6 definitely take your phone in case you get lost

3.2 Vocabulary

A

1 put up with 2 stay calm
3 is going through 4 weigh out
5 sorting out 6 work out
7 talk; over 8 dealing with

3.2 Vocabulary

A

1 of 2 toward 3 about
4 of 5 of 6 of

4.1 Grammar

A

1 'll give 2 won't see
3 'm going to apply 4 aren't going to get
5 closes 6 'm seeing
7 are; going to do 8 'll go

4.1 Vocabulary

A

1 in 2 on 3 for 4 of 5 in 6 of

4.1 Vocabulary

Student A

A

1a to control 1b control
2a balance 2b balance
3a produce 3b produce

Student B

A

1a benefits 1b benefits
2a influence 2b influence
3a challenge 3b challenge

4.2 Grammar

A

1 This time next month, I **will be** ~~am~~ sitting on a beach!
2 In November, I will have **been** working here for 15 years.
3 My teacher will have ~~been~~ retired before I finish this assignment!
4 By the end of this decade, most people will be **driving** ~~drive~~ electric cars.
5 If it's still around in 2029, people **will** have been using Facebook for 25 years.
6 I think we'll have **discovered** ~~been discovering~~ a cure for most forms of cancer by the end of the century.
7 Next September, you and I will have been ~~being~~ friends for 25 years.
8 At this rate, I'll still **be** ~~have been~~ living with my parents when I'm 40!

4.2 Vocabulary

A

1 disastrously 2 widely 3 extremely
4 significantly 5 utterly 6 incredibly
7 entirely 8 painfully

5.1 Grammar

A

1 was being repaired 2 will be made
3 are considered 4 has been shared
5 had been broken into 6 was delivered
7 is being carried out 8 will be notified

B

1 Where was TV invented
2 Who was Harry Potter written by
3 How many people are killed by sharks every year
4 What was discovered by Alexander Fleming in 1928
5 Which two languages are spoken in Canada

C

1 Scotland 2 J.K. Rowling 3 98
4 Penicillin 5 French and English

5.1 Vocabulary

Student A

A

3 insulation 5 heating
8 energy-efficient 9 rain barrel
10 solar panels

Student B

A

1 wind turbines 2 compost heap
4 thermostat 6 double glazing
7 smart meter

5.1 Grammar

A

1 are having/getting; installed
2 has/gets; serviced
3 get; cut
4 have; written
5 has had; redecorated
6 to have; cleaned
7 have/get; whitened
8 to get; taken

5.2 Vocabulary

A

1 suburbs 2 rural 3 urban
4 housing 5 commercial 6 industrial
7 slums 8 residential

5.2 Vocabulary

A

1 impossible 2 unaffordable
3 overpaid/underpaid 4 rewatched
5 immoral 6 illogical
7 unpopular 8 illegal
9 extraordinary

5.2 Grammar

A

1 e; going 2 d; seeing 3 a; taking
4 f; to tell 5 c; to announce 6 b; to do

6.1 Grammar

A

1 a 2 b 3 a 4 b 5 a 6 b

6.1 Vocabulary

A

1 compulsory 2 private
3 graduate 4 vocational
5 boarding 6 elementary
7 entrance 8 seminar

6.2 Grammar

A

1 – 2 the 3 –
4 The 5 an 6 the
7 – 8 the 9 an
10 the 11 the 12 a

6.2 Vocabulary

A

1 high-risk 2 well-known
3 old-fashioned 4 six-bedroom
5 up-to-date 6 365-meter-high
7 coming-of-age 8 part-time

6.2 Vocabulary

A

1 did 2 do 3 is doing / does
4 make 5 make 6 make
7 do 8 make

B

1 h 2 e 3 d 4 a 5 g 6 f
7 c 8 b

7.1 Grammar

A

1 Correct
2 Correct
3 What are you going to do if she **doesn't** ~~won't~~ call you back?
4 To be honest, **I'll** ~~I'm going to~~ be amazed if we've finished by 6 pm.
5 We **are** ~~will~~ going to the movie theater if you want to join us.
6 Correct
7 Unless the train's late, **we'll arrive** ~~we're arriving~~ before 8 pm.
8 What will you **do** ~~have done~~ if it rains?

7.1 Vocabulary

A

1 transform
2 convert
3 demolish
4 extend
5 restore
6 is being relocated / will be relocated
7 is constructing / will be constructing / will construct

7.1 Grammar

A

1 would you do; you could start
2 would; be; hadn't studied
3 won; would you visit
4 could design; would you include
5 would you do; landed
6 would; be; hadn't been invented
7 could go back; would you do
8 could only keep; would you choose

7.2 Grammar

A

1 hadn't 2 would 3 could be
4 could 5 didn't 6 would use

7.2 Vocabulary

A

1 d 2 b 3 f 4 e 5 c 6 a

B

1 take care of 2 look up to
3 come up against 4 cut down on
5 get along with 6 keep up with

7.2 Vocabulary

A

1 Do you know any volunteer workers?
2 Does your company offer a car-sharing system?
3 Have you ever taken part in a language exchange?
4 Do you have any food banks in your town?
5 Have you ever been to a street party?

8.1 Grammar

A

1 can't have been Meghan you saw
2 might have handed your wallet in at the front desk
3 must have gotten stuck in traffic or something
4 might have dropped them on the way here
5 can't have finished the report already
6 must have been tired after such a long flight

B

1 They fell out of the first-floor window.
2 One of the people took the box as well as the egg.
3 The counter was in a library, and the money was a fine.

8.1 Vocabulary

A

1 mythology 2 represent 3 believable
4 heroically 5 transformed
6 traditional

8.2 Vocabulary

A

1 listen; to hear 2 seen; watching
3 touch; feels 4 heard; listening
5 has felt / has been feeling; touched
6 were watching; saw

8.2 Grammar

A

1 My mother just gave me her collection of antique silver jewelry.
2 Can you pass me that tall green vase?
3 The painting was bought by a wealthy Italian lawyer.
4 They're building a huge state-of-the-art recreation center near my house.
5 She was wearing an unusual silk evening dress.
6 Apparently, he has a new long-term plan for the company.
7 Saga drives a beautiful, old, green Porsche 911.
8 The disgusting, old, stained T-shirt needs to be thrown away!

8.2 Vocabulary

A

1 investigating 2 sentenced
3 blackmail 4 identity theft
5 questioning 6 caught
7 robbery 8 bribe

9.1 Grammar

A

1 (that) I lived in/(where) I lived for 12 years is being knocked down
2 you seen the woman (that/who) we saw yesterday again
3 which is worth $4.5 million, is being displayed at the National Gallery
4 which was supposed to land at 5 pm, was delayed by over three hours
5 whose album is currently at number one in the charts, is getting married next year
6 with the blue collar is in the yard again
7 who don't consume animal products, often eat tofu for protein
8 who is well-known in the area, was arrested for the robbery

9.1 Vocabulary

A

complain; worry **about**
apologize; thank **for**
rely **on**
adhere; object **to**
deal **with**

9.2 Vocabulary

A

1 researchers 2 theory 3 evidence
4 Analysis 5 data

9.2 Grammar

A

1 Neither 2 amount 3 few
4 All of the 5 every 6 a little
7 Plenty of 8 both

9.2 Vocabulary

A

1 consumer 2 brand
3 high-profile 4 ad campaign
5 target market 6 trend
7 endorse 8 marketing strategy

10.1 Grammar

A

1 he had been walking home from the store
2 he suddenly realized / he had suddenly realized that he'd left his keys at home
3 you can never be too careful
4 three of her friends had been burglarized recently
5 was lucky he hadn't broken his neck
6 it was very impressive for a man of his / Mr. Smith's age

10.1 Vocabulary

A

1 subjective 2 Tabloids 3 broadsheets
4 headlines 5 biased 6 coverage
7 sources 8 editor

10.2 Grammar

A

1 Correct
2 Police reminded **him** that anything he said might be used as evidence against him.
3 She refused to tell **me** what I had done wrong and slammed the door in my face!
4 Correct
5 The company apologized for mislead**ing** the public over claims made in their advertising.
6 Miss Jansen's lawyer warned her **not** to say anything to the press before the trial was over.
7 Correct
8 Neighbors threatened **to call** ~~calling~~ the police if the noise continued.

B

1 convinced 2 accused 3 encouraged
4 agreed 5 confessed

10.2 Vocabulary

A

1 hashtags 2 followers 3 influencer
4 meme 5 viral 6 trending
7 campaign

10.2 Vocabulary

A

1 regular 2 wider 3 viral
4 key 5 high 6 online